P9-DHN-344

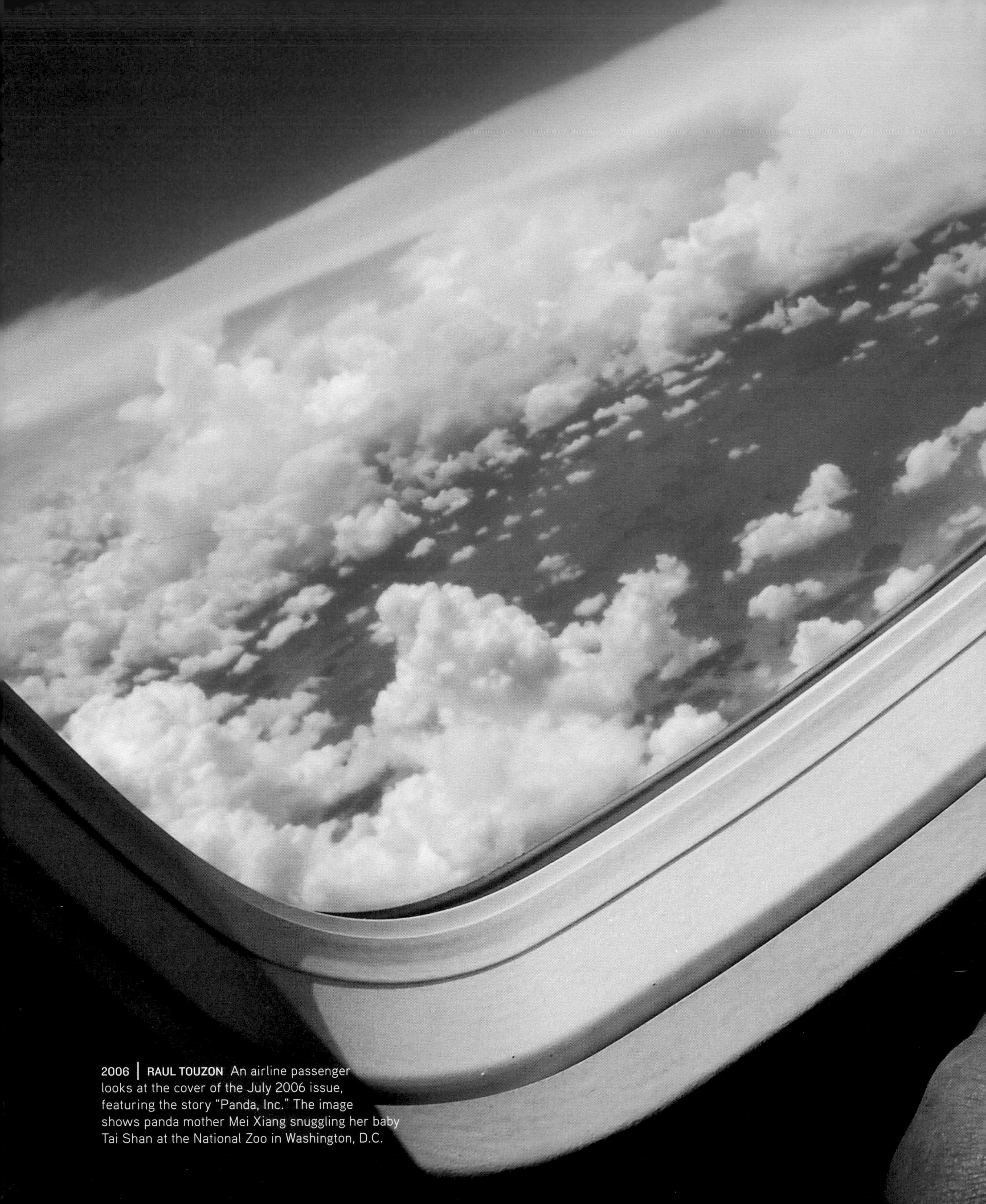

2006 | **RAUL TOUZON** An airline passenger looks at the cover of the July 2006 issue, featuring the story "Panda, Inc." The image shows panda mother Mei Xiang snuggling her baby Tai Shan at the National Zoo in Washington, D.C.

NATIONAL GEOGRAPHIC THE COVERS

MARK COLLINS JENKINS

WASHINGTON, D.C.

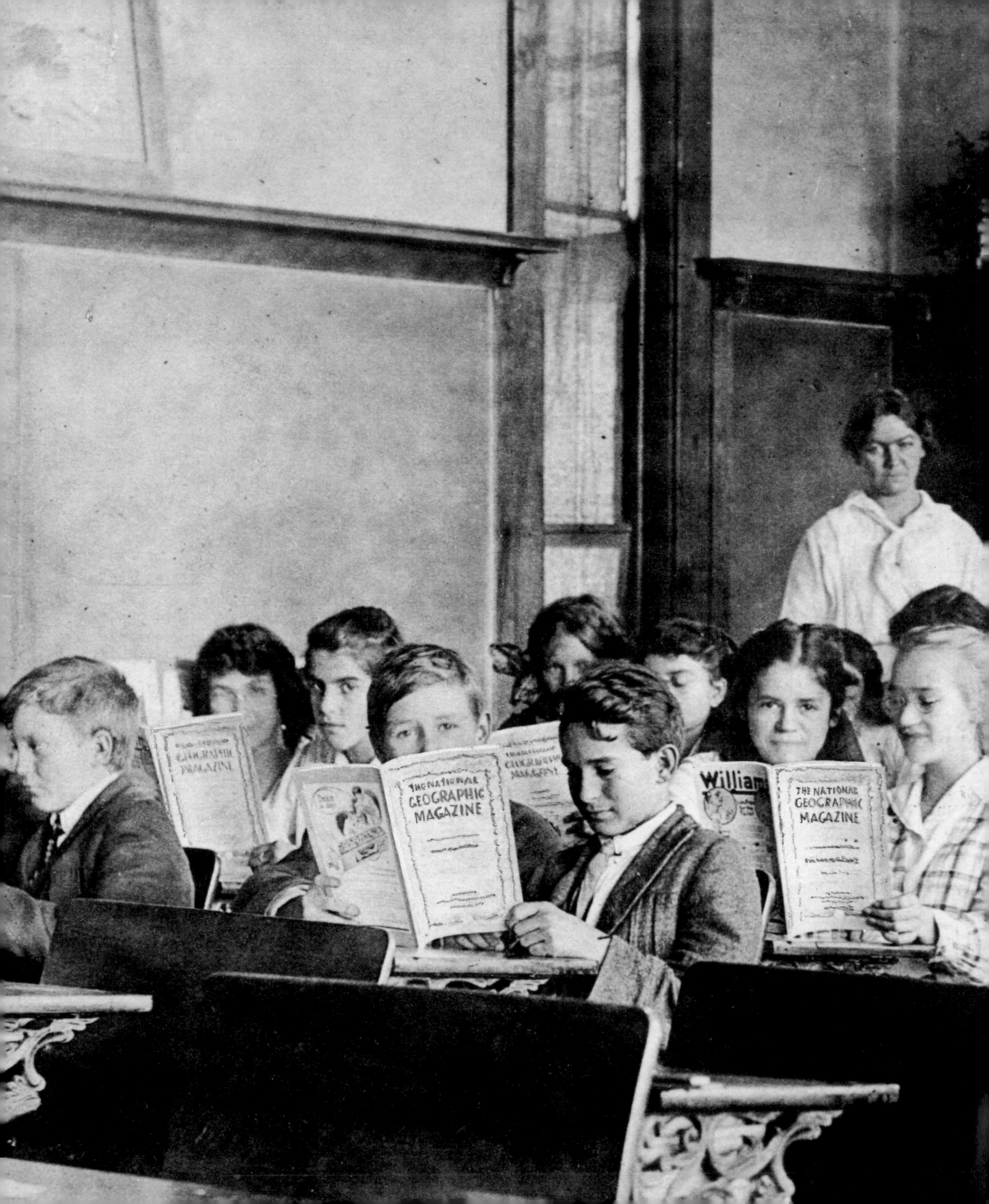
GEOGRAPHIC MAGAZINE
THE NATIONAL GEOGRAPHIC MAGAZINE
THE NATIONAL GEOGRAPHIC MAGAZINE

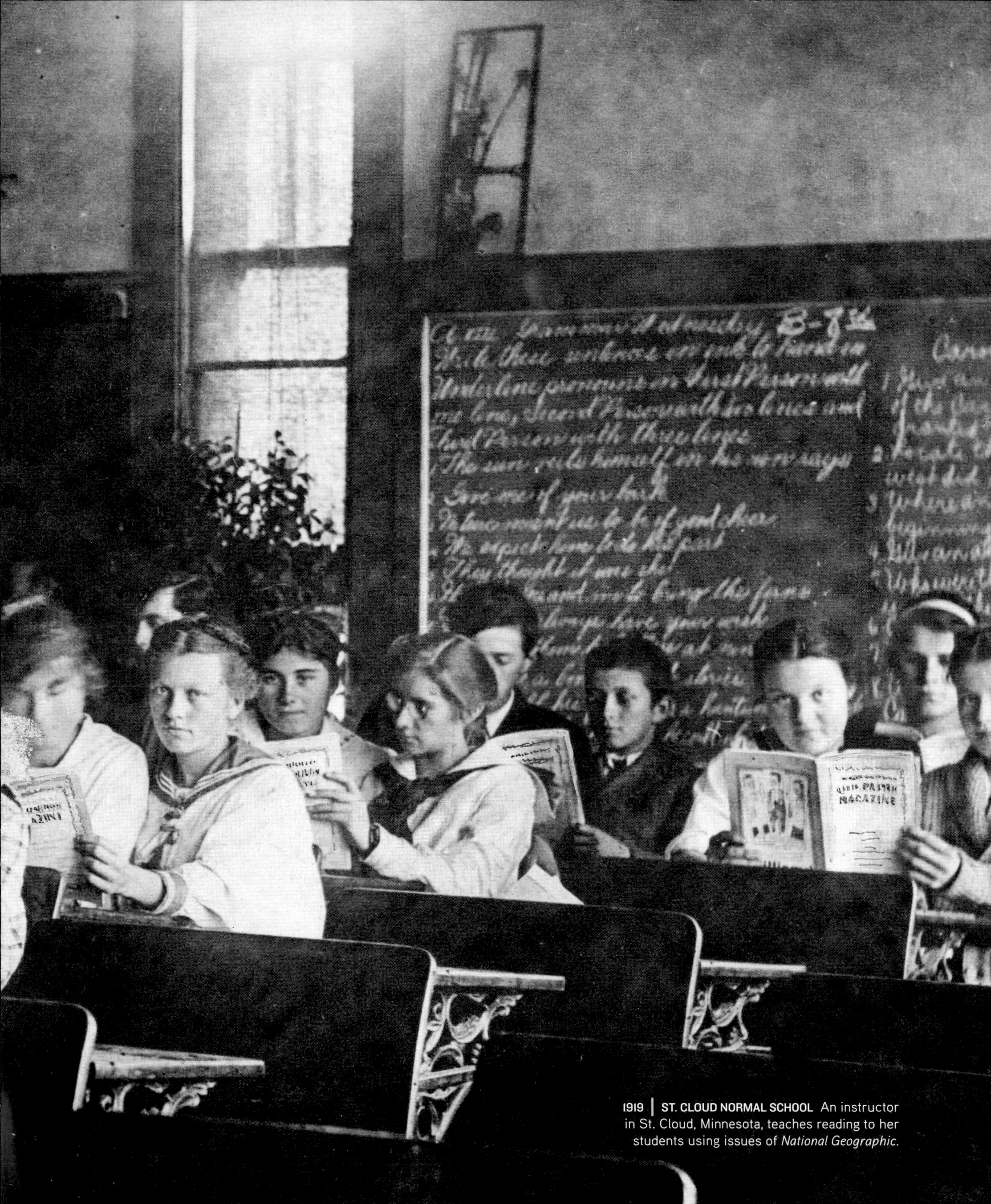

1919 | **ST. CLOUD NORMAL SCHOOL** An instructor in St. Cloud, Minnesota, teaches reading to her students using issues of *National Geographic*.

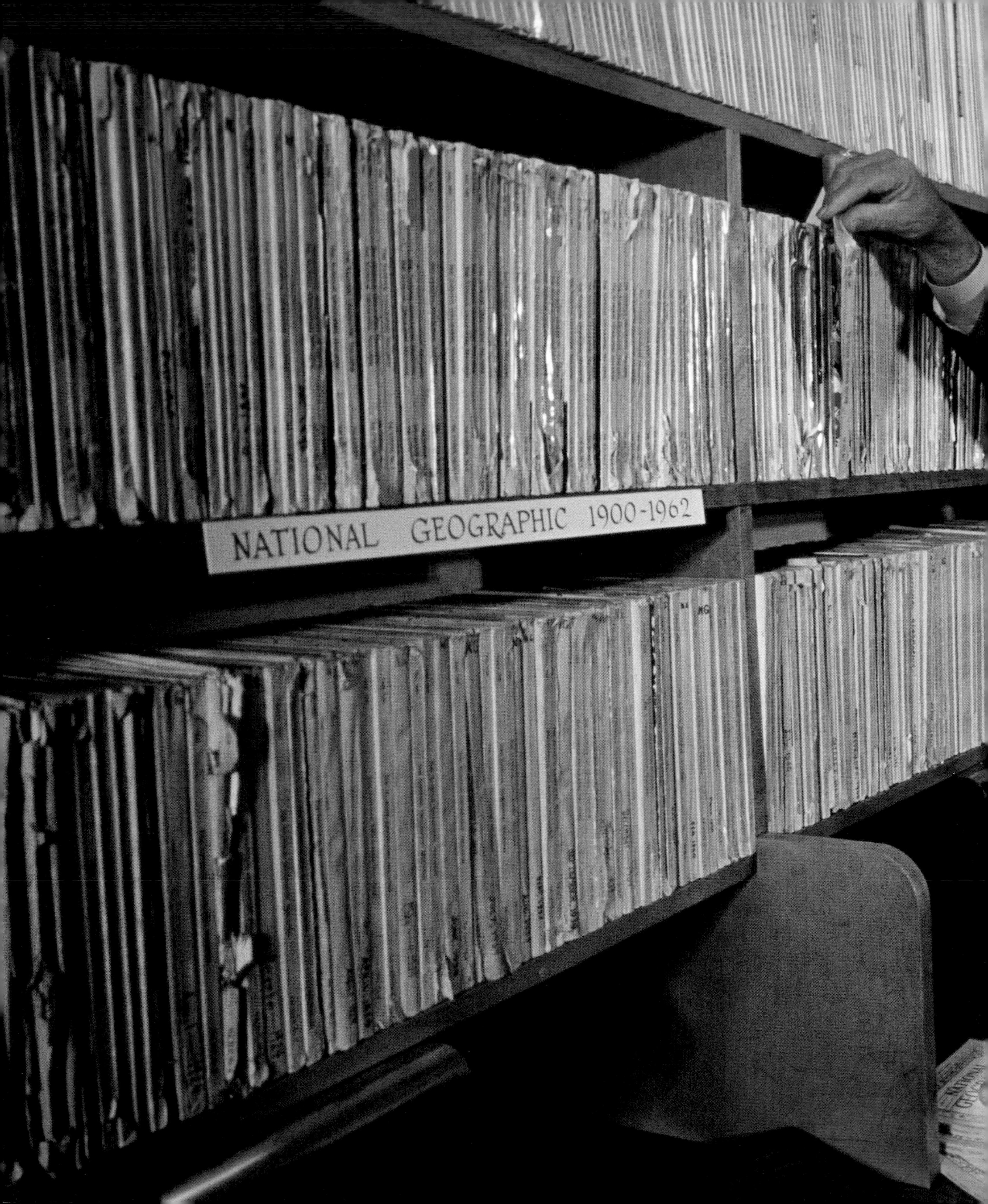
NATIONAL GEOGRAPHIC 1900-1962

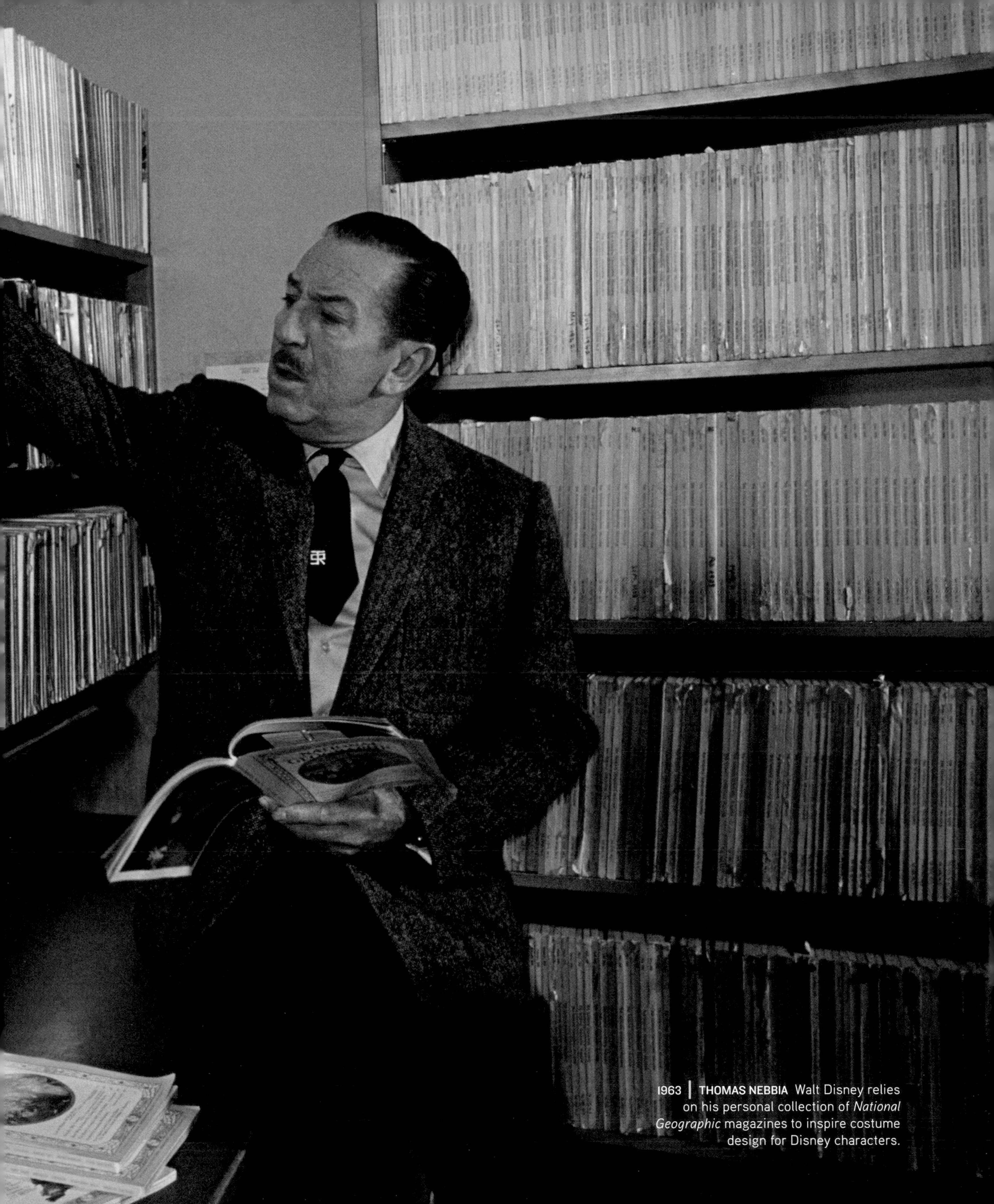

1963 | **THOMAS NEBBIA** Walt Disney relies on his personal collection of *National Geographic* magazines to inspire costume design for Disney characters.

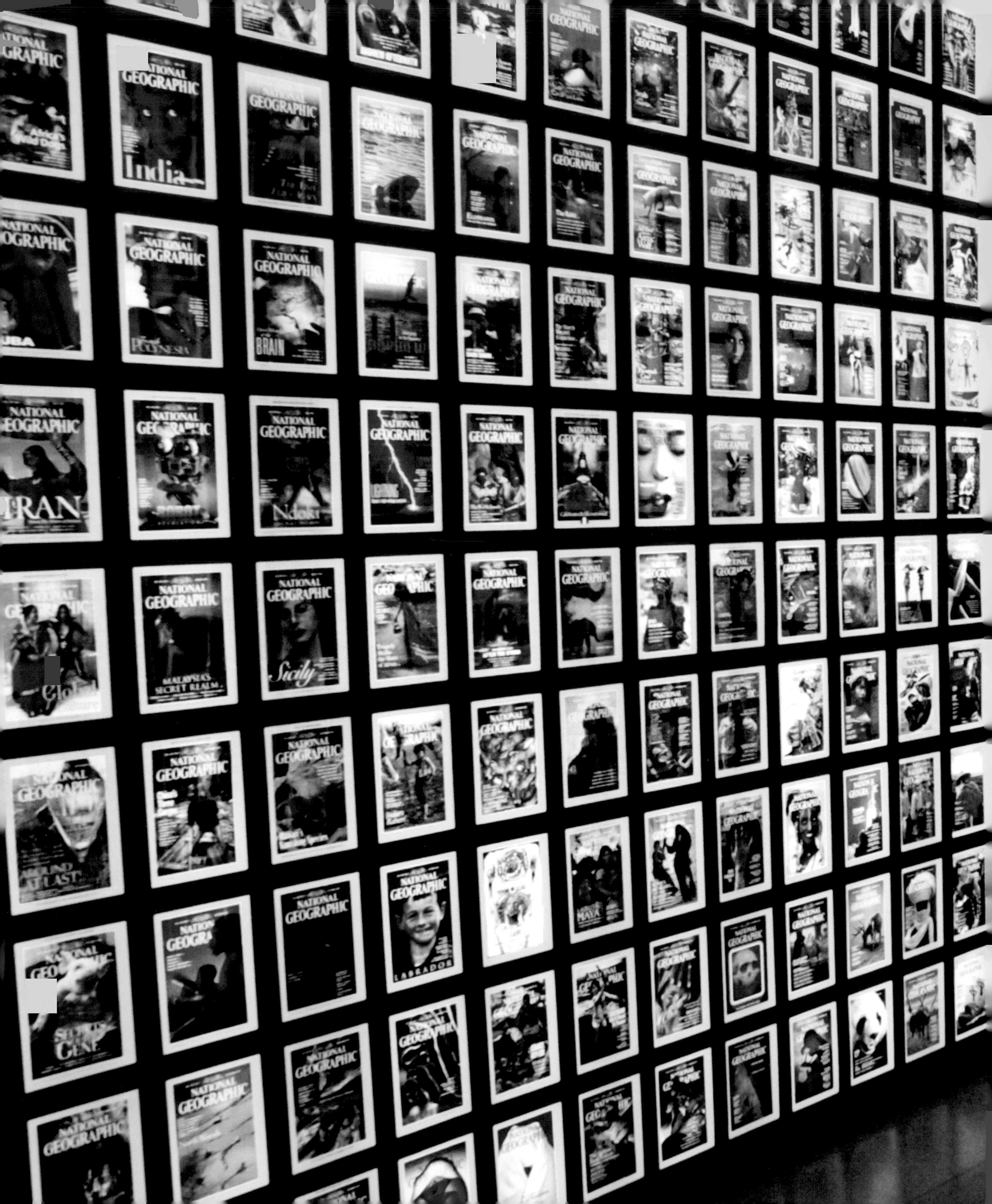

NATIONAL GEOGRAPHIC
India
IRAN
BRAIN
Sicily
MALAYSIA'S SECRET REALM
LABRADOR
MAYA

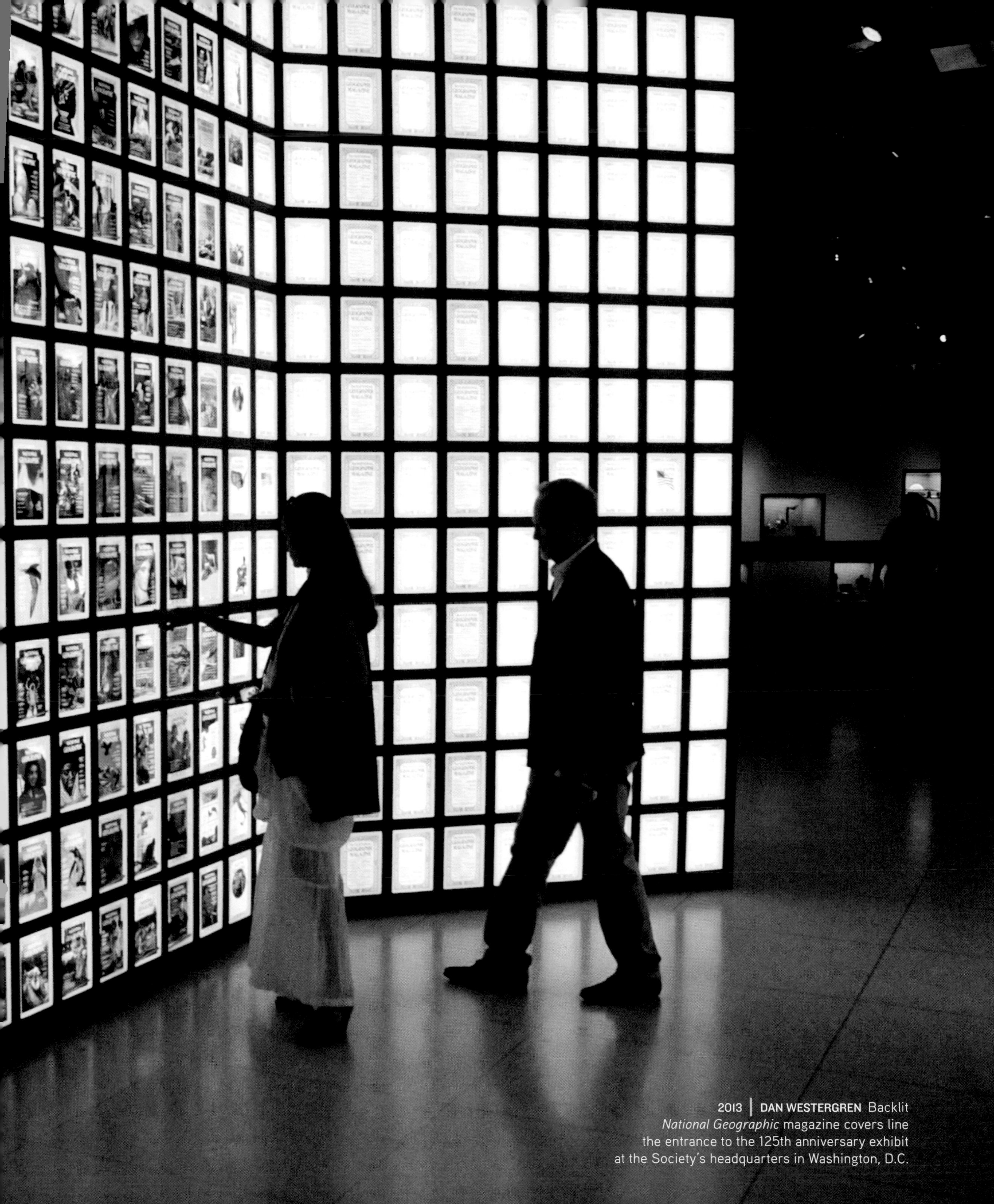

2013 | **DAN WESTERGREN** Backlit *National Geographic* magazine covers line the entrance to the 125th anniversary exhibit at the Society's headquarters in Washington, D.C.

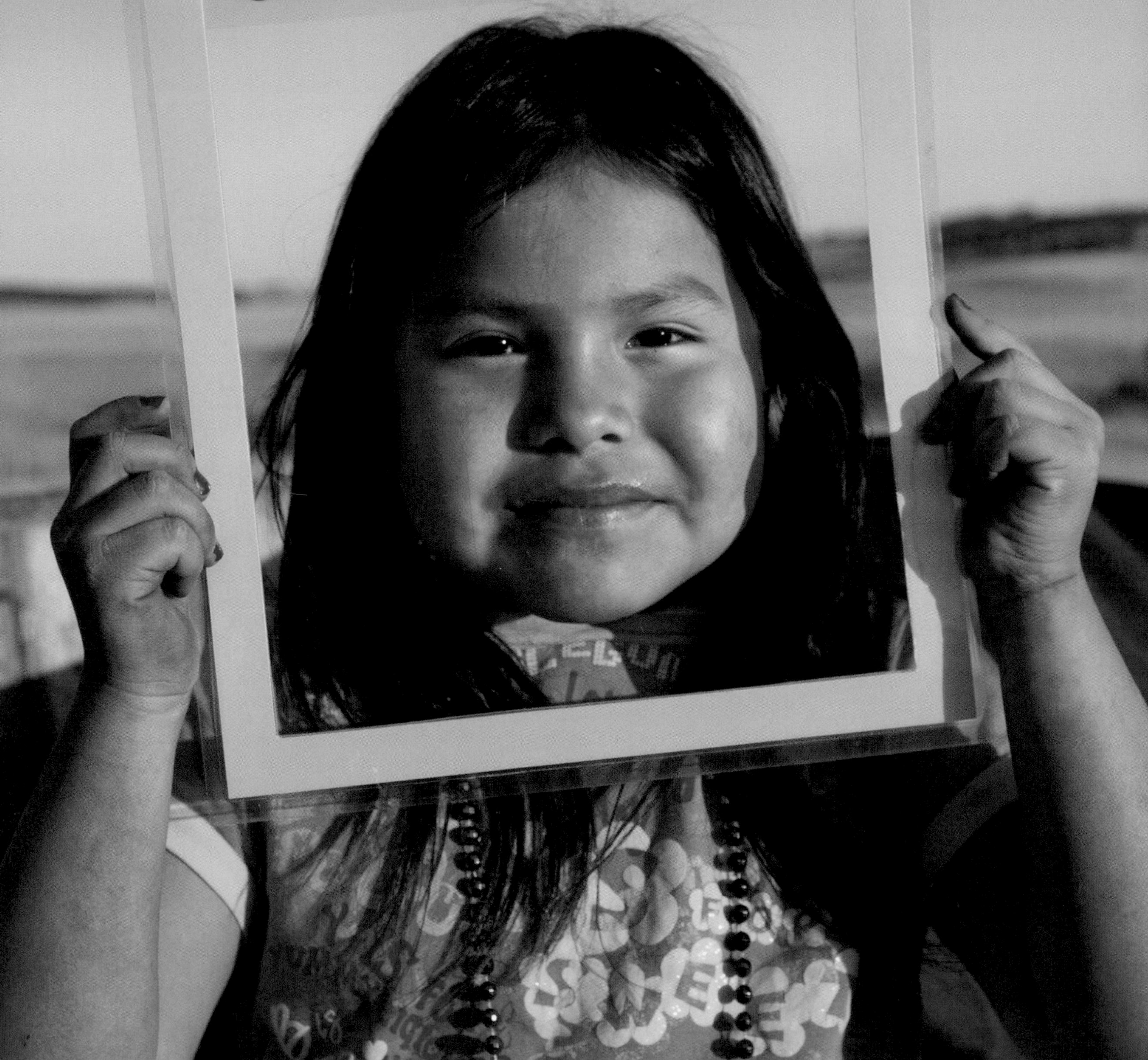
NGM.COM AUGUST 2012
NATIONAL GEOGRAPHIC

[CONTENTS]

◀ 2012 | AARON HUEY While covering the Oglala living on the Pine Ridge Indian Reservation in South Dakota, photographer Aaron Huey created a mock yellow border on a piece of acetate for some informal photos. He wanted to bring a sense of inclusion to those not featured in the story—such as this girl, Wanahca Rowland.

WATCH "BLACKBEARD" ON NG CHANNEL, SUNDAY, MARCH 12, 8 P.M. ET/9 P.M. PT

NATIONALGEOGRAPHIC.COM/MAGAZINE MARCH 2006

NATIONAL GEOGRAPHIC

The Greatest Journey Ever Told

THE TRAIL OF OUR DNA

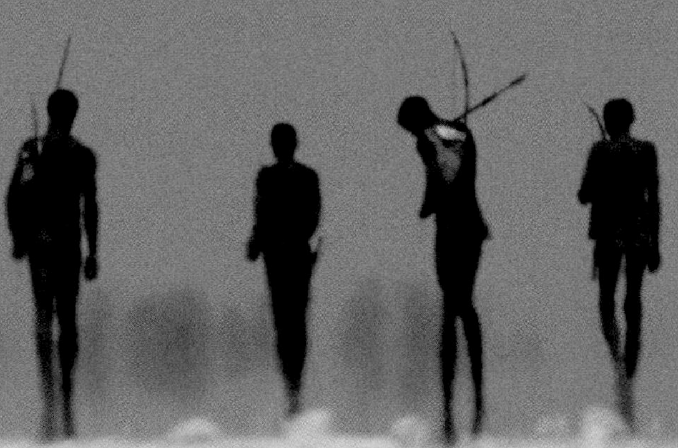

MARCH 2006 | CHRIS JOHNS Bushmen cross a shimmering salt pan in Namibia.

[PUSHING THE LIMITS]

BY CHRIS JOHNS
Former Editor in Chief, National Geographic

THE COVER OF *NATIONAL GEOGRAPHIC* is an invitation. Come look, it says. See what wonder the world contains. Experience it. Embrace it. The cover, you see, is the gateway to our magazine and to a wider world.

In this book you can see the arc of *National Geographic* covers from the very first issue we produced in 1888 (a drab 98-page scientific publication in an austere brown wrapper relieved only by black type) through our tentative steps to a consistently visual presentation, beginning in July 1959 with the single image of an American flag, to full-page images in the 1960s to today's high-impact photographs and illustrations.

Making that monthly choice of what to put on the cover was the most humbling thing I did as Editor in Chief. I'd make a decision, think I succeeded, then watch it fizzle. Sometimes the opposite would happen; the cover would exceed expectations and be a winner.

What makes a winning cover, aside from the obvious requisite of a stunning image? "Irresistible" is the word I reach for in trying to explain what I want. In particular, the cover matters most on the newsstand, where the magazine first started appearing in 1998. A good cover has to grab you in less than five seconds. Subject is paramount. We know from experience that ancient civilizations—if it's a fresh, new look—are usually a winner, as are covers on space. On the other hand—and surprisingly so, because our natural history photography is unsurpassed—animals don't do well, with the exception of pets. It's about seeing an image of an animal you can connect with. I challenge you to look at the "Animal Minds" story with the appealing border collie shot by photographer Vince Musi and not want to grab that issue—March 2008, by the way—and find out just what that collie is thinking.

CHRIS JOHNS served as Editor in Chief of *National Geographic* magazine for nine years before being named Chief Content Officer of National Geographic in April 2014. He was the ninth editor of the magazine since its founding in 1888. Johns became a *National Geographic* contract photographer in 1985 and joined the magazine staff in 1995. As a photographer, he produced more than 20 articles for *National Geographic,* eight of which were cover stories. His defining images are of Africa and its wildlife. He has taken readers down the Zambezi River, examined the Bushmen's ongoing struggle for cultural survival, and provided important documentation of Africa's endangered wildlife. He was named one of the world's 25 most important photographers by *American Photo* magazine in 2003.

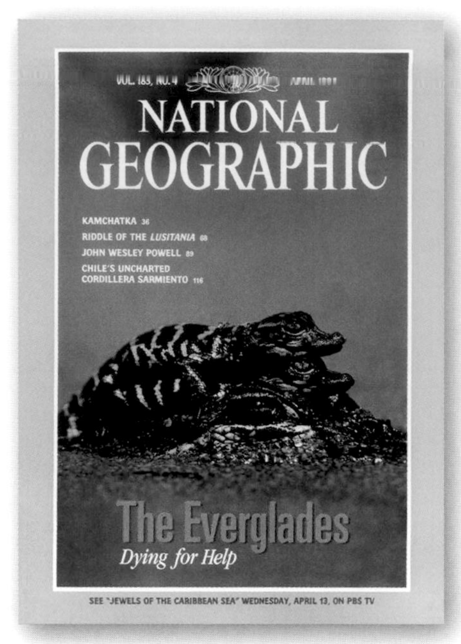

APRIL 1994 | CHRIS JOHNS

▲ **CATCHING A RIDE** Swimming through duckweed in the Everglades, an alligator carries her vulnerable young on top of her head. Though luck helped, patience and persistence played a larger role in capturing this image, allowing Johns to take advantage of the opportunity when it presented itself.

Portraits are another less than optimal choice for a cover, but again the exception belies the rule. The most stupendous example of a portrait (which we've run three times on the cover) is the Afghan Girl, Sharbat Gula, with her haunting sea green eyes. The same young girl, in fact, whose eyes stare out from the cover of this book. Which goes to show that like most things in life, just when you've got it figured out, the game changes.

Authenticity is another credo. It's a lie that you can't tell a book by its cover—or, in this case, a magazine—and journalism is not a lie. A cover has to be truthful to who we are. We could put a celebrity on the cover, but it wouldn't sell. It would be a betrayal of our values and of who we are.

Some photographers will tell you they don't give the cover a second thought, but when I was a photographer for this magazine I thought of the cover every day on assignment. Why wouldn't I want the story I was working on to have as much reach and exposure as possible?

So let me tell you about the cover photograph of the Bushmen that opens this introduction, an image that took me ten years to make.

I was deeply moved by David Lean's films and loved the scene in *Lawrence of Arabia,* where Ali, played by Omar Sharif, approaches Lawrence on a camel. At first we see nothing more than the shimmering haze of the desert's long horizon, then a tiny black speck that grows bigger, until finally the mirage materializes into a man. I kept that image in my head, tried to duplicate the idea, and failed time after time.

Then I went to Namibia and one day gave a lift to a group of Bushmen who wanted to go out hunting. As I watched them walk on the white soda flats, I could see the faint beginnings of my dream image coming together. I lay down on the salt pan and started firing off frames. The heat was searing; sweat poured down my face. The light bounced up from the pan; heat rose from the ground in shimmering waves; the atmosphere elongated the legs of the Bushmen as they walked. Men, landscape, light—all aligned in one magic frame. Then, the image was gone, like a mirage itself. Except that I had captured it on film.

Over the years we've had covers with holograms (December 1988), covers with painstakingly created reconstructions of early humankind (October 2008), and covers that illustrate a concept a photograph is unable to show (April 2013). No doubt, the cover of *National Geographic* will continue to evolve in ways we can't imagine. Ours is a constant search for improvement. The cover may change. Our values, passion for excellence, and engagement will not. ■

"GREAT MIGRATIONS" PREMIERES SUNDAY, NOVEMBER 7 AT 8 P.M. ON NAT GEO CHANNEL

NGM.COM NOVEMBER 2010

NATIONAL GEOGRAPHIC

MYSTERIES OF Great Migrations

What Guides Them Into the Unknown?

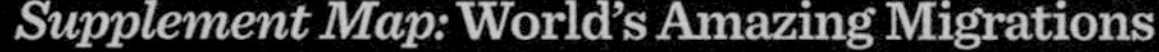

Supplement Map: World's Amazing Migrations

NOVEMBER 2010 | CHRIS JOHNS Sunset illumines wildebeests in Zambia's Liuwa Plains National Park.

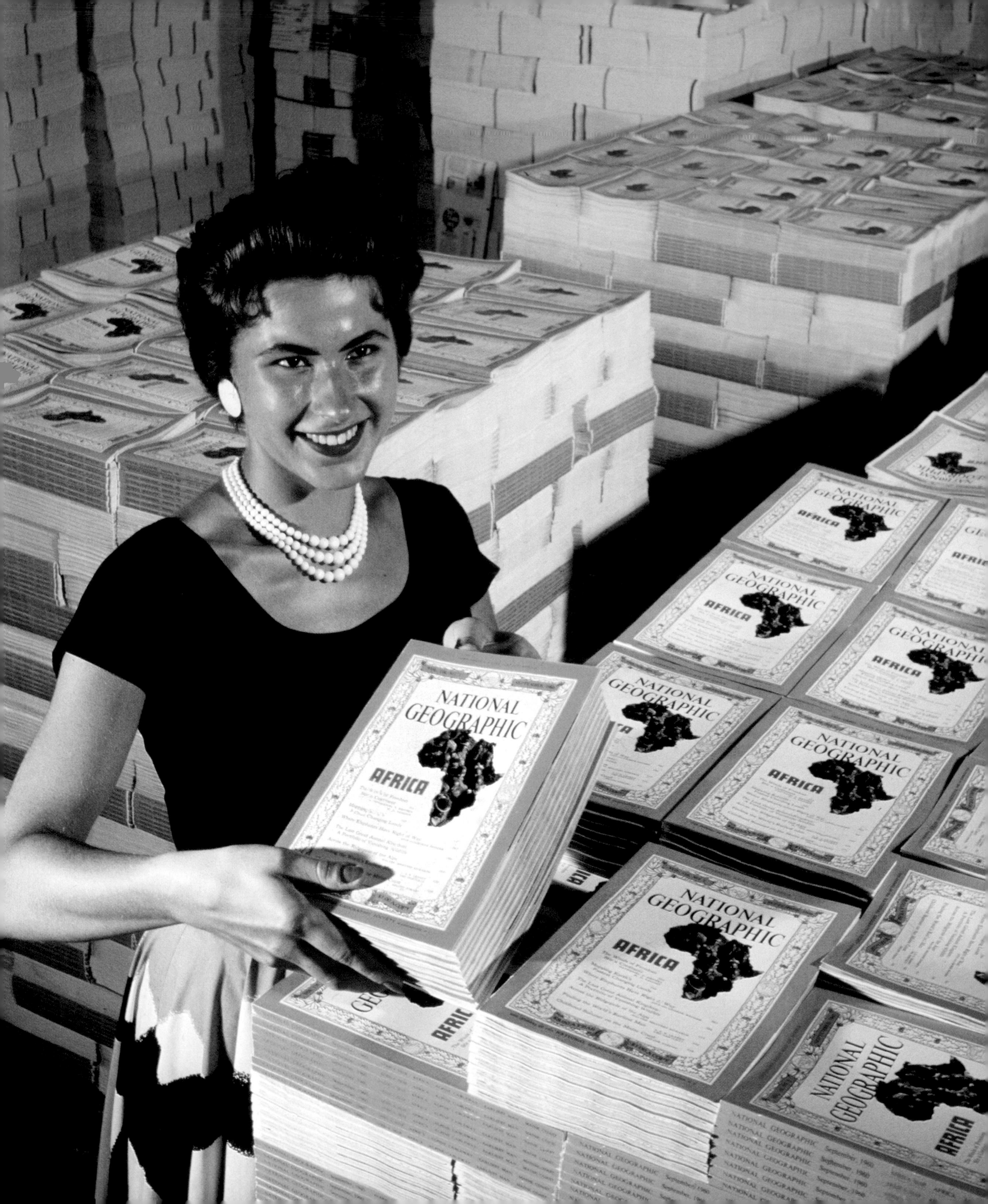
NATIONAL GEOGRAPHIC
AFRICA

COVER TO COVER

"After a few understated, almost unreadable cover formats, the Victorian oak-and-laurel-leaf border evolved and became a fixture for almost 70 years."

—Wilbur E. Garrett, from "Within the Yellow Border,"
National Geographic, *September 1988*

BEFORE THE summer of 1959, *National Geographic* editors never lost a night's sleep worrying about the cover. Month after month, only its table of contents had ever varied. The rest of the design—the border of oak leaves and acorns, the crown of laurel—had scarcely altered in five decades.

That changed in September 1959 with the appearance of the first cover photograph (not counting a few American flags): a picture of a U.S. Navy fighter jet. October then featured an attractive woman studying sea urchins. November's cover depicted the Golden Gate Bridge, December's a geisha.

Then the letters began arriving. "Gentlemen," wrote one correspondent, "The addition of a colored picture on the cover . . . is completely unnecessary and destroys the impression of dignity and timelessness that have heretofore been associated with the magazine."

Another reader implored: "We most sincerely—and hopefully—urge that you please discontinue having pictures on our beloved magazine's cover. It is so comforting to have something that hasn't changed—please."

Then there's the apocryphal story of the irate Englishman who wrote:

FACTS & FIGURES

- **1888** Year the National Geographic Society was founded
- **33** Number of founders—including explorers—who formed the Society in Washington, D.C.
- **1970** Year the vertical yellow rectangle was registered as a Society trademark
- **20** Number of logos in use in the 1990s
- **1999** Last year the crown of laurels appeared on the cover

◀ **STACKING UP** By September 1960—the date of this issue on Africa—*National Geographic* was being sent to nearly three million members worldwide.

COVER BACKGROUND COLORS

1888–PRESENT
From 1888 to 1909, the background colors changed from terra-cotta to brownish red to beige. After 1910, the space enclosed by what became the yellow border gradually lightened before giving way entirely to illustrations.

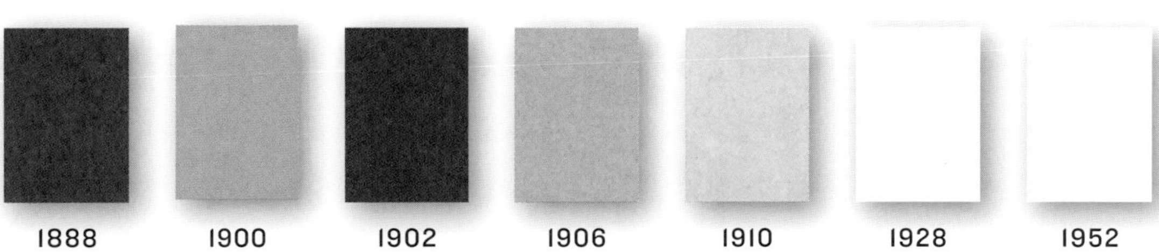

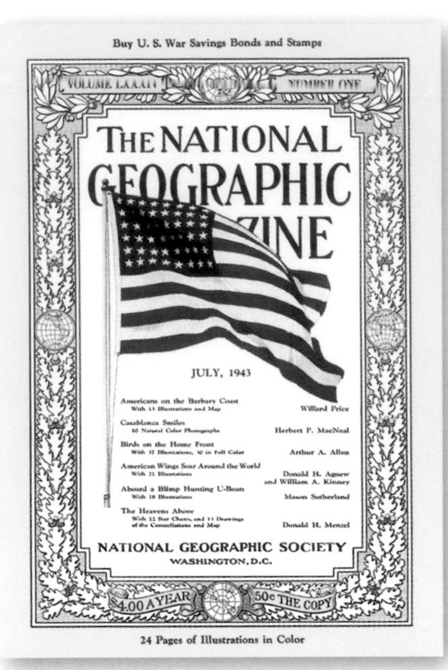

JULY 1943 | B. ANTHONY STEWART

▲ **FIRST PHOTOGRAPH** Responding to a Treasury Department appeal that all major magazines print a flag on their June or early July 1943 covers, *National Geographic* publishes the first photograph—as opposed to the artwork which appeared a year earlier (see opposite page)—ever to appear on its cover. This image of the billowing U.S. flag was made by staff photographer B. Anthony Stewart, giving him pride of place in the long line of distinguished photographers who would follow.

"If the Lord had intended a picture on the cover of *National Geographic*, he would have put one there in the first place!"

There were many letters of complaint written throughout 1959 and 1960. *National Geographic* readers felt strongly about their cover. Although some members applauded the changes (Change "isn't blasphemy," one declared), more people inveighed against them, even the trivial ones: replacing Roman numerals with Arabic ones for the volume and number, dropping the word *Magazine* from the title, even dropping *The* from *The National Geographic.* Others targeted the yellow border ("a most unbecoming color in a library").

But the addition of a cover illustration created a monthly variable with the power to attract or repel readers at a glance, hence those sleepless nights for the editor responsible for choosing one.

That much loved oak-leaf design first appeared on the February 1910 *Geographic.* Preceding it had been five cover formats, beginning in 1888 with a terra-cotta one, suitable for a sober professional publication, the journal of the newly formed National Geographic Society, founded to promote the "increase and diffusion of geographic knowledge." Eleven years passed before the appearance of an editor who instinctively understood the importance of cover appeal. Gilbert H. Grosvenor—first of three editors bearing that surname—was the protégé (and eventually son-in-law) of the Society's second president, Alexander Graham Bell. Grosvenor spent his first decade at the magazine's helm discarding one cover design after another on a quest to find something that better epitomized the gravitas he wanted to confer upon the *Geographic.* In 1909, he found it in a design executed by Robert Weir Crouch, an artist who worked with a Buffalo, New York, engraving firm.

It was the oak-leaf-bordered cover.

Inspired by floral motifs prominent in the decorative arts of his day, Crouch's oak leaves and acorns came to symbolize the origins and sturdy growth of the Society. Stretching above the oak he placed a garland of laurel leaves and berries, which traditionally *Continued on page 23*

NAMEPLATE EVOLUTION

TRIMMING DOWN
On the cover of December 1959—after 71 years and 801 previous issues—*The National Geographic Magazine* becomes *The National Geographic.* In March 1960 it is further shortened to simply *National Geographic.*

The NATIONAL GEOGRAPHIC MAGAZINE	THE NATIONAL GEOGRAPHIC MAGAZINE	THE NATIONAL GEOGRAPHIC MAGAZINE
1904–1910	1910–1959	1959–1959

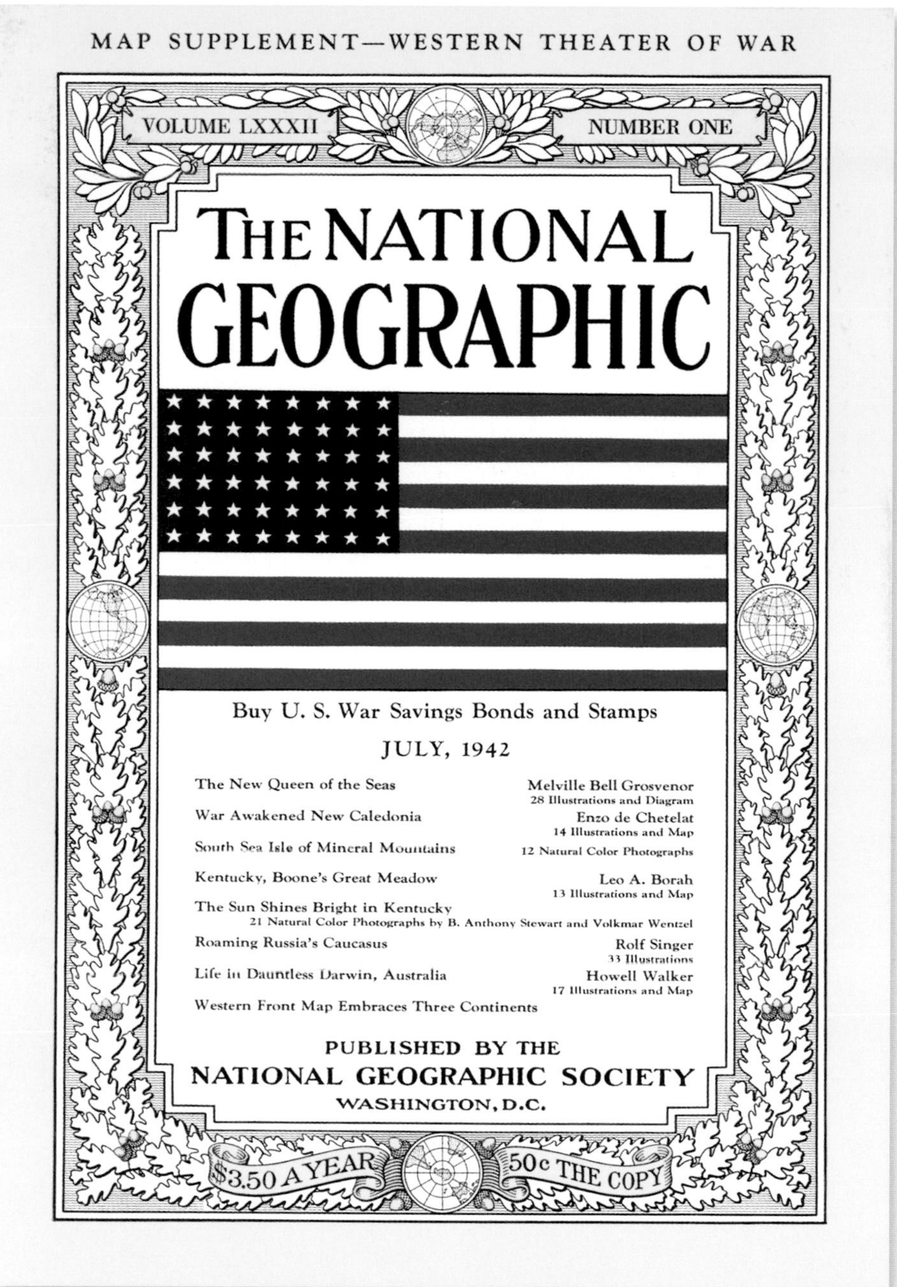

MAP SUPPLEMENT—WESTERN THEATER OF WAR

VOLUME LXXXII | NUMBER ONE

THE NATIONAL GEOGRAPHIC

Buy U. S. War Savings Bonds and Stamps

JULY, 1942

The New Queen of the Seas — Melville Bell Grosvenor, 28 Illustrations and Diagram
War Awakened New Caledonia — Enzo de Chetelat, 14 Illustrations and Map
South Sea Isle of Mineral Mountains — 12 Natural Color Photographs
Kentucky, Boone's Great Meadow — Leo A. Borah, 13 Illustrations and Map
The Sun Shines Bright in Kentucky — 21 Natural Color Photographs by B. Anthony Stewart and Volkmar Wentzel
Roaming Russia's Caucasus — Rolf Singer, 33 Illustrations
Life in Dauntless Darwin, Australia — Howell Walker, 17 Illustrations and Map
Western Front Map Embraces Three Continents

PUBLISHED BY THE
NATIONAL GEOGRAPHIC SOCIETY
WASHINGTON, D.C.

$3.50 A YEAR | 50c THE COPY

JULY 1942 | U.S. GOVERNMENT

▲ **STARS AND STRIPES** In 1942, the U.S. Treasury Department asks all of the nation's major magazines to print a U.S. flag and "Buy United States War Savings Bonds and Stamps" on the cover of their July issues. *National Geographic* complies and publishes the first cover illustration in its history.

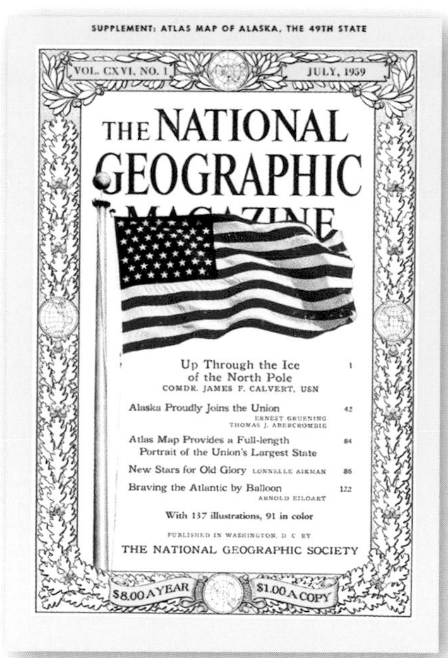

SUPPLEMENT: ATLAS MAP OF ALASKA, THE 49TH STATE

VOL. CXVI, NO. 1 | JULY, 1959

THE NATIONAL GEOGRAPHIC MAGAZINE

Up Through the Ice of the North Pole — COMDR. JAMES F. CALVERT, USN — 1
Alaska Proudly Joins the Union — ERNEST GRUENING, THOMAS J. ABERCROMBIE — 42
Atlas Map Provides a Full-length Portrait of the Union's Largest State — 84
New Stars for Old Glory — LONNELLE AIKMAN — 86
Braving the Atlantic by Balloon — ARNOLD ELOART — 122

With 137 illustrations, 91 in color

PUBLISHED IN WASHINGTON, D. C. BY
THE NATIONAL GEOGRAPHIC SOCIETY

$8.00 A YEAR | $1.00 A COPY

JULY 1959 | B. ANTHONY STEWART

▲ **49 STARS** Because the July 1959 issue contains several articles on Alaska, which that January had been admitted into the republic as the 49th state, the new 49-star Old Glory appears on its cover. Thanks to the flags published during World War II, this was a careful way of inaugurating the new decision to put pictures permanently on the magazine's cover. The 49-star flag was already obsolete, however: Hawaii would be admitted as the 50th state only several weeks later, on August 21, 1959.

THE NATIONAL GEOGRAPHIC

1959–1960

NATIONAL GEOGRAPHIC

1960–2000

NATIONAL GEOGRAPHIC

2000–PRESENT

THE MAGAZINE'S CHANGING FACE

Numerous discarded cover designs littered *National Geographic*'s history until the basic oak-leaf-and-laurel format emerged in 1910. Although it held sway for half a century, illustrations—which first appeared in 1959—would eventually dominate the cover. Though horizontal photographs were often cropped to fit the vertical space, at least one photographer taped a piece of transparent acetate embossed with nameplate and cartouche to a camera's viewfinder screen.

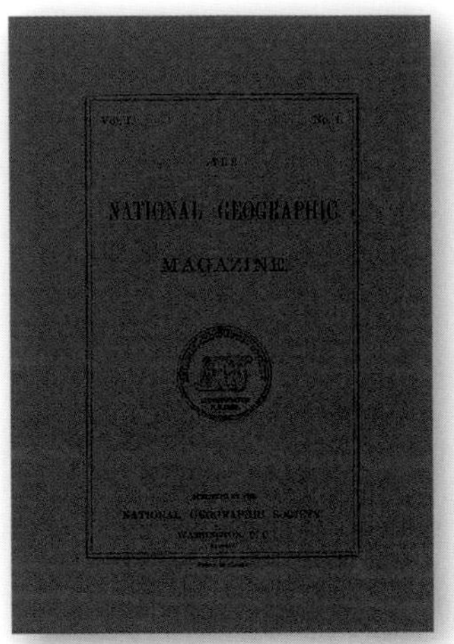

OCTOBER 1888
The first cover format (1888–1895) features plain terra-cotta-colored wrappers.

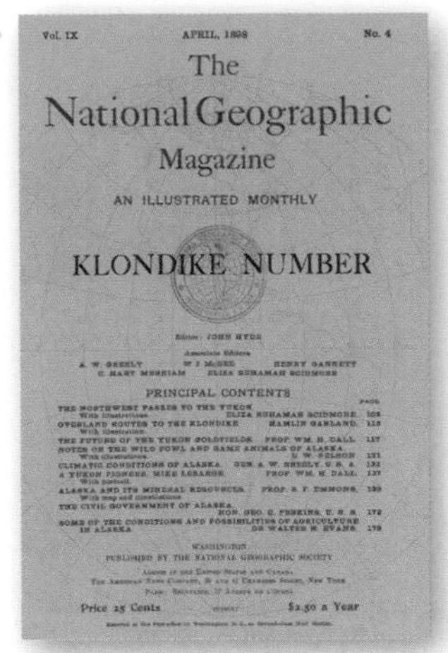

APRIL 1898
The second cover format (1896–99) features a map of the Western Hemisphere.

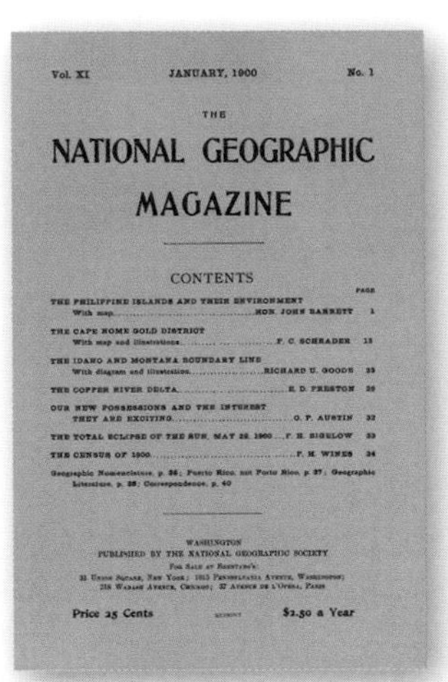

JANUARY 1900
The third cover format (1900) is printed in one color as a cost-cutting measure.

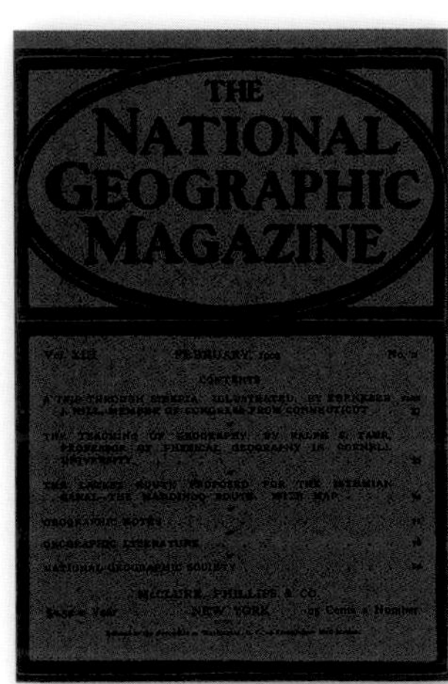

FEBRUARY 1902
The fourth cover format (1901–03) changes color and adds some stylistic detailing.

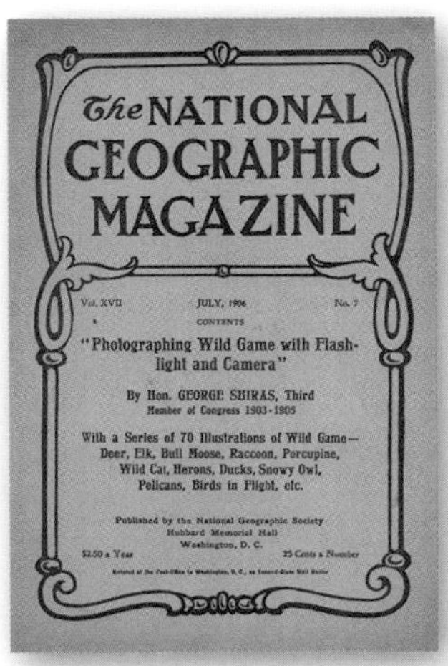

JULY 1906
The fifth cover format (1904–1910) adds an art deco frame to the table of contents.

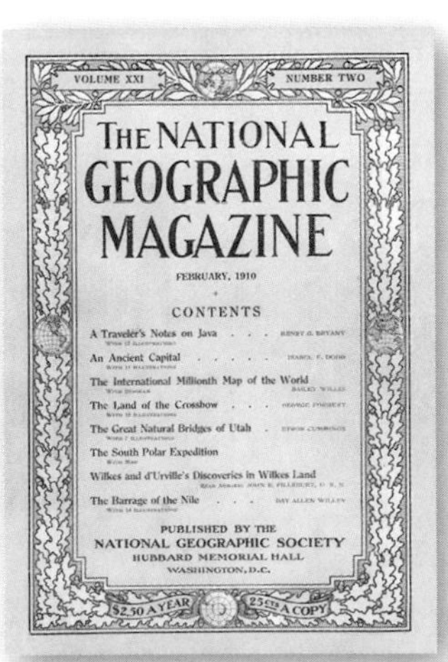

FEBRUARY 1910
The sixth cover format, introduced with this issue, is the basis of all future ones.

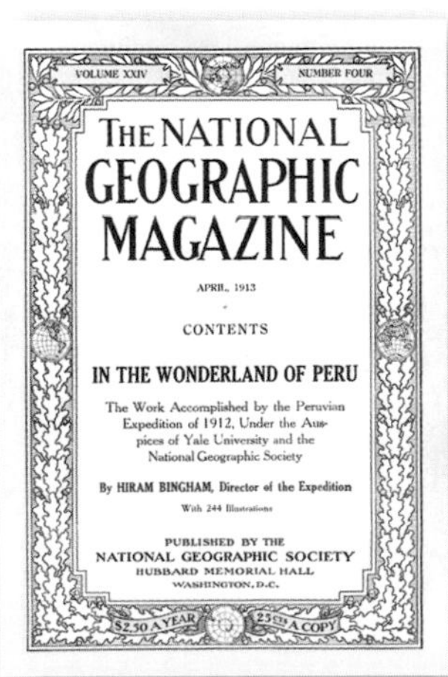

APRIL 1913
The buff color is replaced by a yellow border and white interior panel.

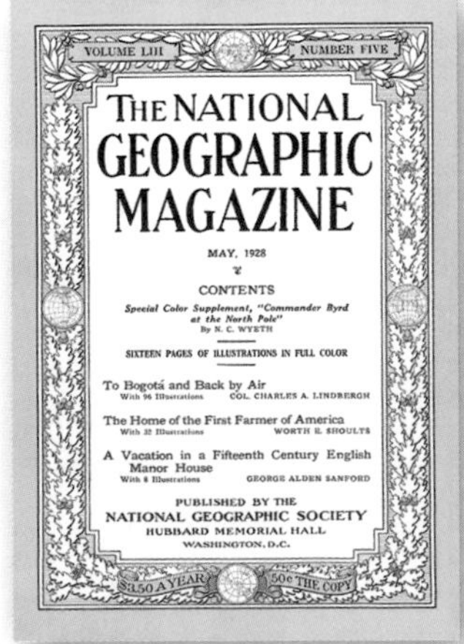

MAY 1928
The oak leaves become thicker.

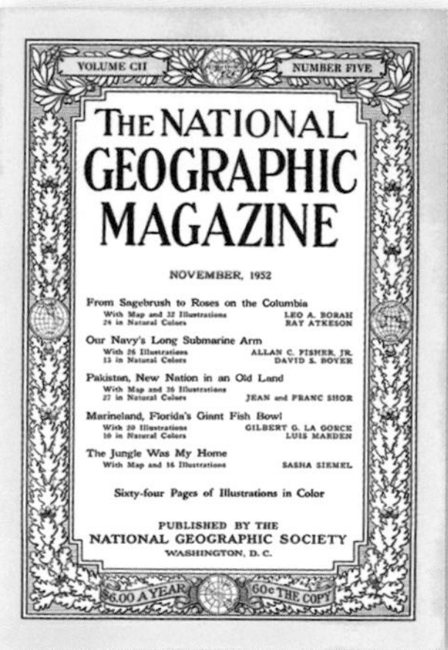

NOVEMBER 1952
Over the years the border color has varied between yellow and gold.

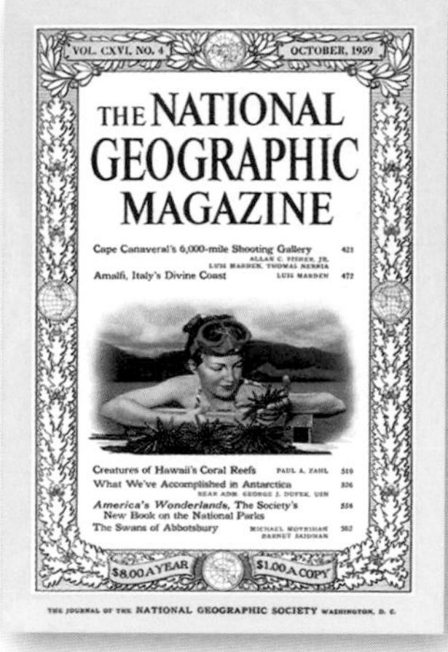

OCTOBER 1959
The first human appears on the cover: Eda Zahl was the wife of staff naturalist Paul Zahl.

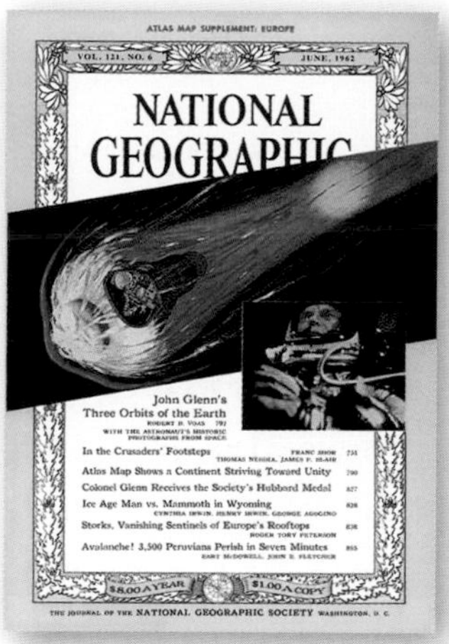

JUNE 1962
Illustrations are already eclipsing the old design.

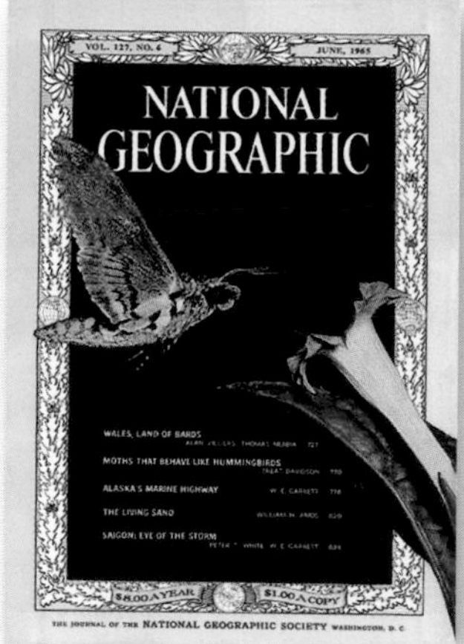

JUNE 1965
The old design continues to fade behind the prominent illustrations.

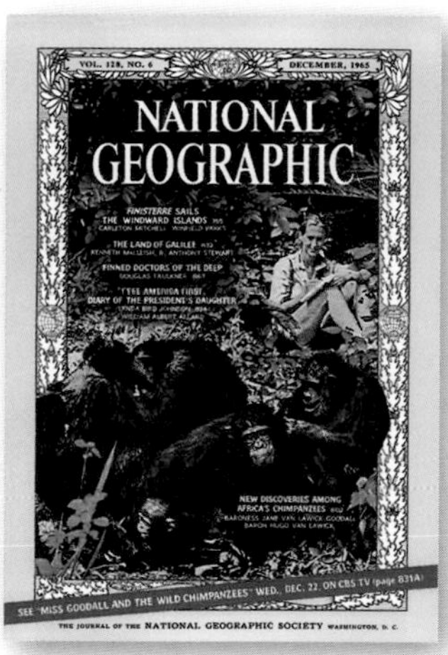

DECEMBER 1965
The first red stripe—announcing National Geographic Television Specials—appears.

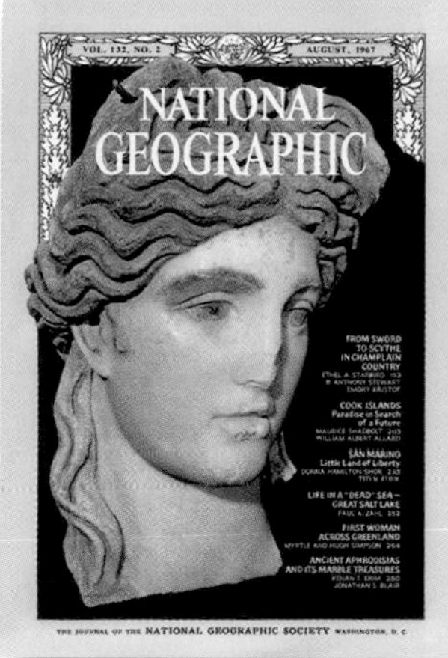

AUGUST 1967
The pruning of oak leaves commences.

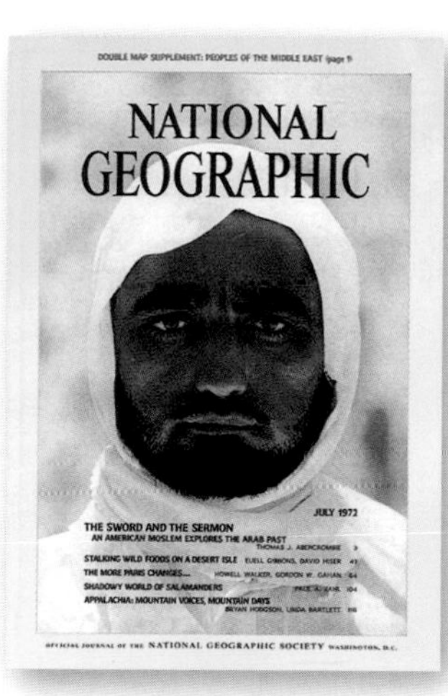

JULY 1972
This is the first—and, for many years, the only—issue entirely bereft of vegetation.

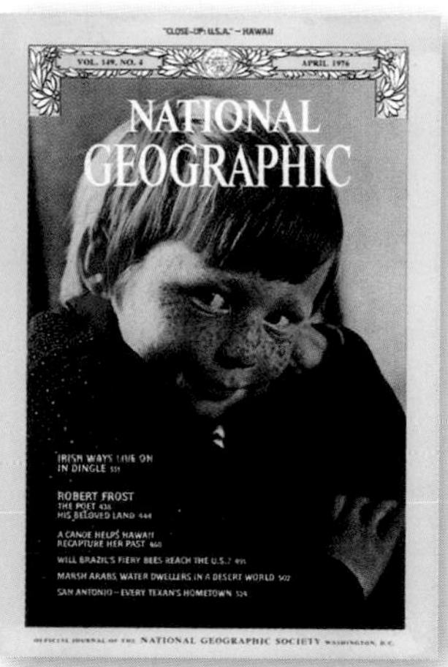

APRIL 1976
The oak leaves are getting shorter, again.

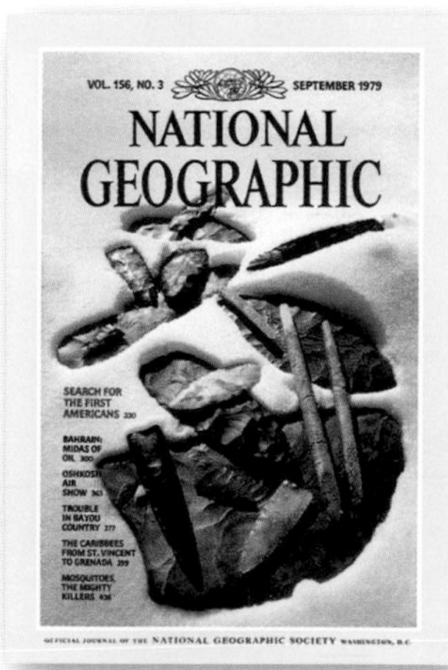

SEPTEMBER 1979
The oak leaves finally disappear, leaving only the laurel cartouche at top.

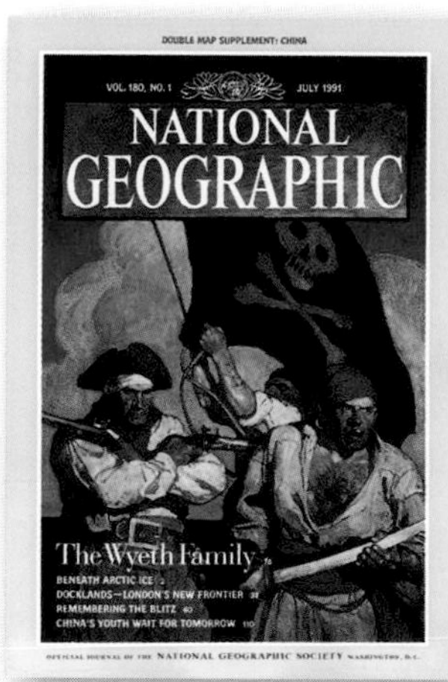

JULY 1991
Paintings often vie with photographs for the cover honors.

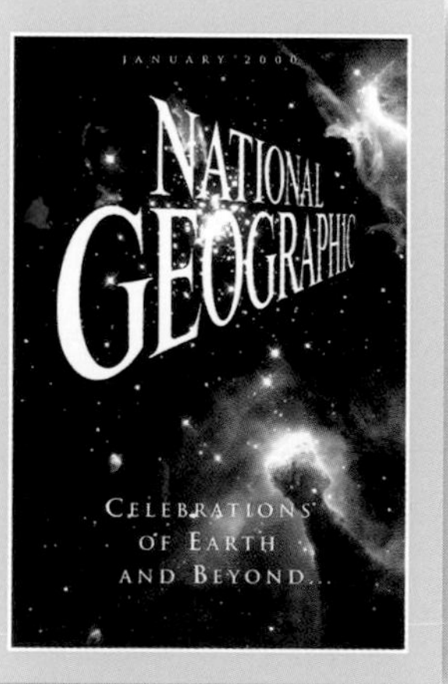

JANUARY 2000
A cover celebrating the millennium coincides with the disappearance of the cartouche.

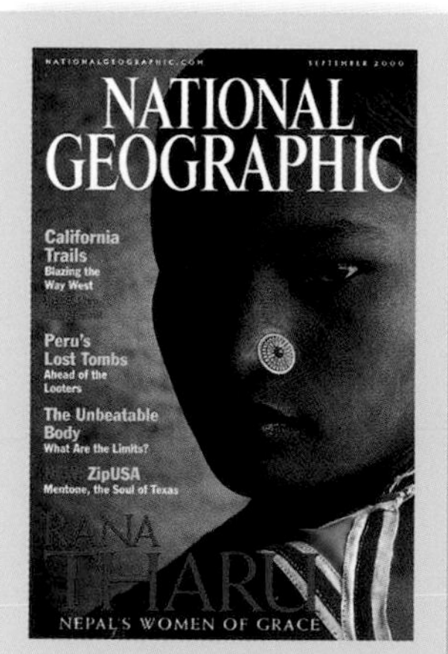

SEPTEMBER 2000
A new font for the masthead might go unnoticed by many readers.

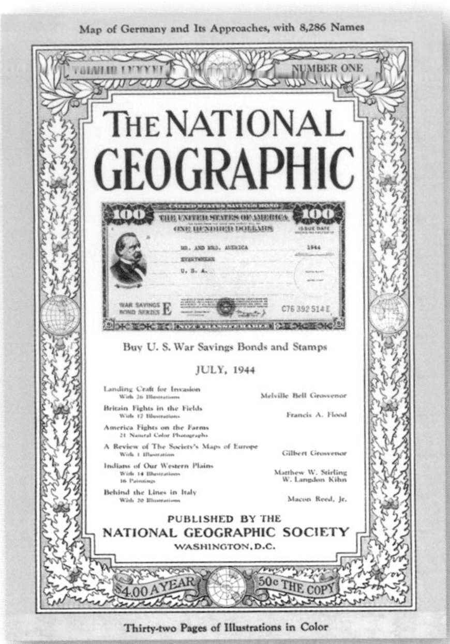
Map of Germany and Its Approaches, with 8,286 Names

NUMBER ONE

THE NATIONAL GEOGRAPHIC

Buy U. S. War Savings Bonds and Stamps

JULY, 1944

Landing Craft for Invasion With 26 Illustrations	Melville Bell Grosvenor
Britain Fights in the Fields With 12 Illustrations	Francis A. Flood
America Fights on the Farms 21 Natural Color Photographs	
A Review of The Society's Maps of Europe With 1 Illustration	Gilbert Grosvenor
Indians of Our Western Plains With 14 Illustrations 16 Paintings	Matthew W. Stirling W. Langdon Kihn
Behind the Lines in Italy With 20 Illustrations	Macon Reed, Jr.

PUBLISHED BY THE
NATIONAL GEOGRAPHIC SOCIETY
WASHINGTON, D.C.

$4.00 A YEAR 50¢ THE COPY

Thirty-two Pages of Illustrations in Color

JULY 1944 | U.S. TREASURY

▲ **PITCHING IN** It's the summer of 1944, and once again the *Geographic* responds to the Treasury Department's campaign to boost the sale of war bonds by promoting them on popular magazine covers. The image provided for this drive features a photograph of a $100 war bond in the name of "Mr. and Mrs. America" from "Everywhere, U.S.A." Participating magazines were asked to print the image on the covers of issues available between June 10 and July 1.

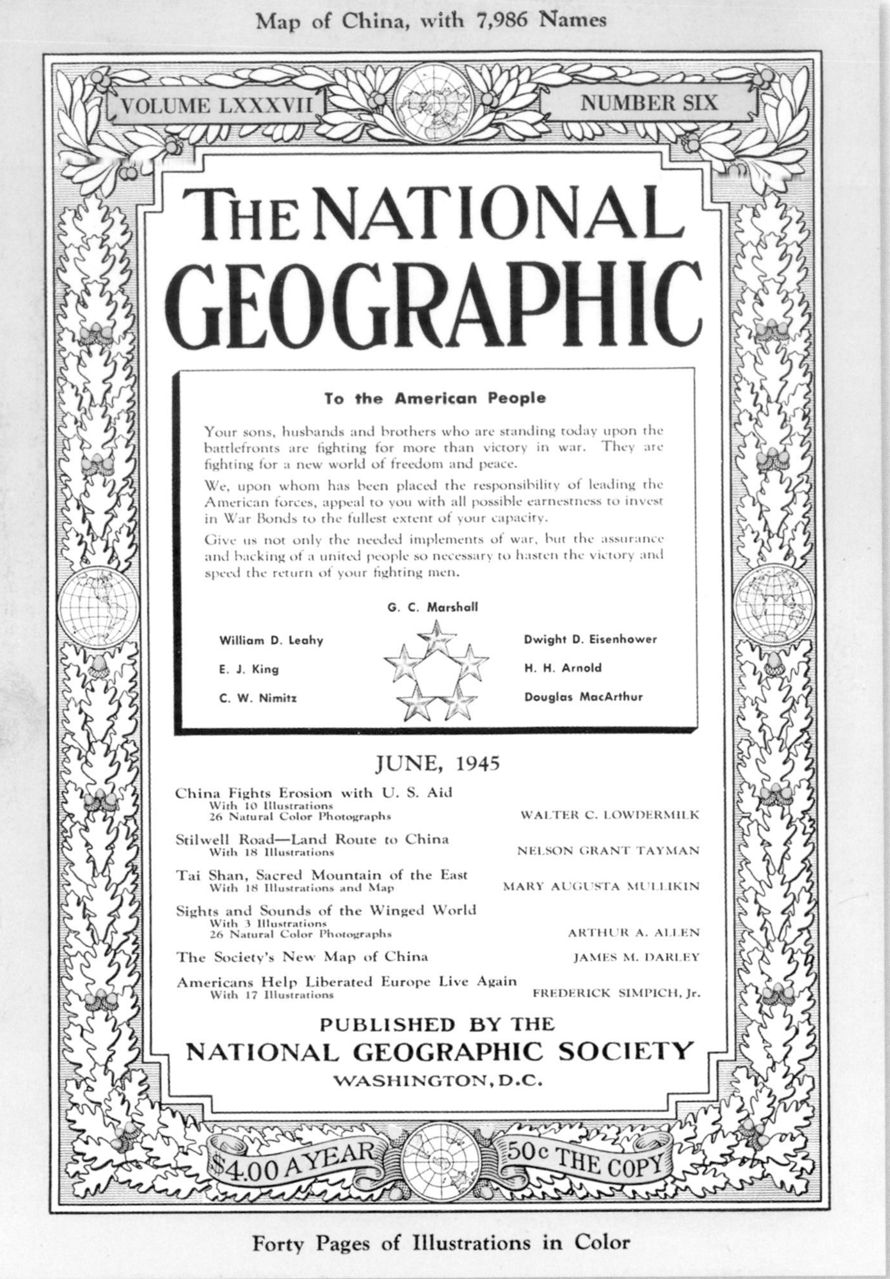
Map of China, with 7,986 Names

VOLUME LXXXVII — NUMBER SIX

THE NATIONAL GEOGRAPHIC

To the American People

Your sons, husbands and brothers who are standing today upon the battlefronts are fighting for more than victory in war. They are fighting for a new world of freedom and peace.

We, upon whom has been placed the responsibility of leading the American forces, appeal to you with all possible earnestness to invest in War Bonds to the fullest extent of your capacity.

Give us not only the needed implements of war, but the assurance and backing of a united people so necessary to hasten the victory and speed the return of your fighting men.

G. C. Marshall

William D. Leahy — Dwight D. Eisenhower
E. J. King — H. H. Arnold
C. W. Nimitz — Douglas MacArthur

JUNE, 1945

China Fights Erosion with U. S. Aid With 10 Illustrations 26 Natural Color Photographs	WALTER C. LOWDERMILK
Stilwell Road—Land Route to China With 18 Illustrations	NELSON GRANT TAYMAN
Tai Shan, Sacred Mountain of the East With 18 Illustrations and Map	MARY AUGUSTA MULLIKIN
Sights and Sounds of the Winged World With 3 Illustrations 26 Natural Color Photographs	ARTHUR A. ALLEN
The Society's New Map of China	JAMES M. DARLEY
Americans Help Liberated Europe Live Again With 17 Illustrations	FREDERICK SIMPICH, Jr.

PUBLISHED BY THE
NATIONAL GEOGRAPHIC SOCIETY
WASHINGTON, D.C.

$4.00 A YEAR 50¢ THE COPY

Forty Pages of Illustrations in Color

JUNE 1945 | U.S. GOVERNMENT

▲ **AN OPEN PLEA** One final time the *Geographic* participated in the Treasury Department's magazine cover promotion plan—featuring a box containing a message from the commanders of the armed services: Generals Marshall, Eisenhower, MacArthur, and Arnold; and Admirals Leahy, King, and Nimitz.

THE BORDER EVOLUTION

THE OAK-LEAF BORDER
Before the 1970s, when they were finally pruned away, the oak leaves on the cover waxed and waned. Here are samples from four different years.

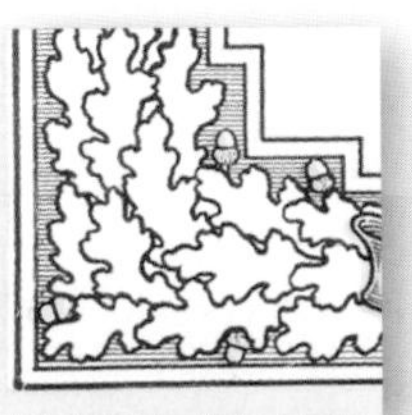
1913

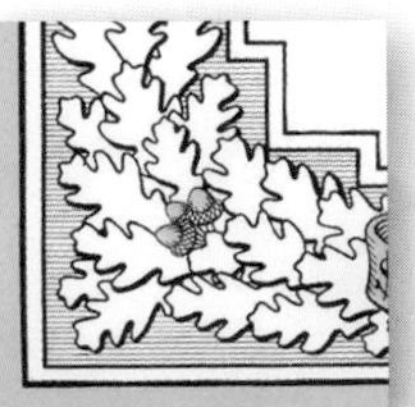
1928

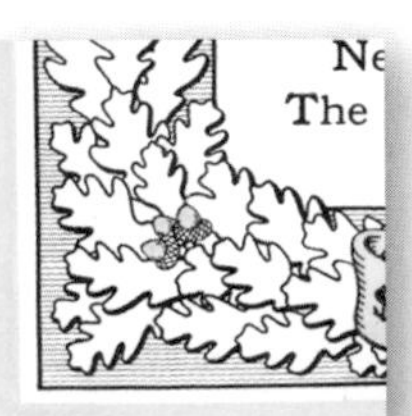

1959

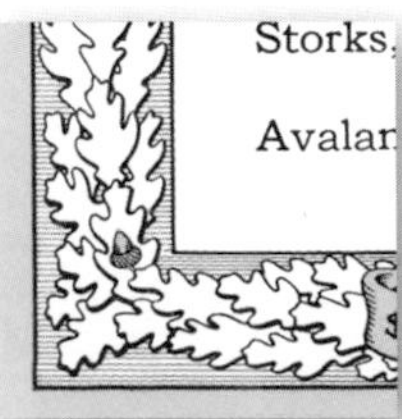

1962

crowned achievements in the arts and sciences. Inset at the design's cardinal points he placed the Earth's four hemispheres—Eastern, Western, Northern, and Southern—suggesting that the table of contents was bounded, in Bell's phrase, by the "world and all that is in it."

With only minor modifications, this cover design would endure for nearly half a century. While magazines like the *Saturday Evening Post, Time, Life,* and the *New Yorker* all featured distinctive cover illustrations, *National Geographic* carried on with just a table of contents set in an oak-leaf frame, its trim size—made for easy binding and shelving—still that of academic journals. Only during World War II did the magazine, at government request, print a few flags and war-bond solicitations above those contents.

Many members clearly cherished the design, calling it "our cover" when they wrote their scolding letters in 1959–1960. Ironically, Editor Melville Bell Grosvenor—Grosvenor II—originally intended the cover pictures to *help* members quickly find any given issue: The one with the Golden Gate Bridge features the article on California. But design considerations were never far from his mind. "I was particularly pleased to hear that you liked our new cover," he wrote a friend in 1960, because "a good deal of courage and painstaking research went into it." Still he preferred the pictures to remain small so as to preserve something of the cover's traditional character.

Now that pictures had escaped the contents and gained the cover, they quickly took over all of the real estate. At the same time, designers favoring a modern look wanted those oak leaves gone. That was an excruciatingly slow business. Gilbert M. Grosvenor—Grosvenor III—editor between 1970 and 1980, agonized over every oak leaf he pruned. When the July 1972 issue appeared without any foliage whatsoever, he braced himself for a deluge of criticism. But much of the fire must have gone out of the old guard. He recalls receiving only one admonishing letter—from his aunt. Yet the leaves were back on the very next issue, and it took the rest of the decade to eliminate them.

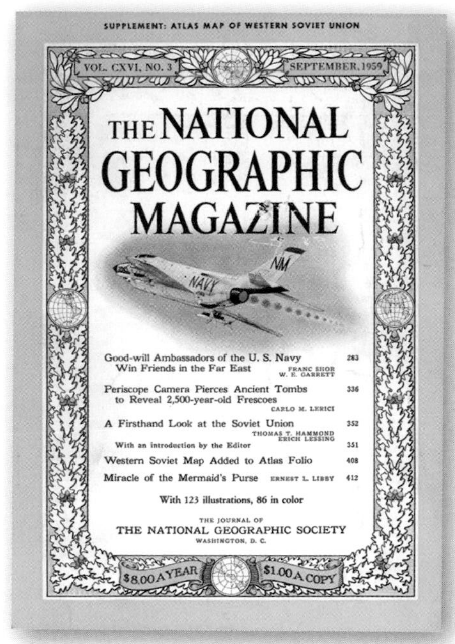
SUPPLEMENT: ATLAS MAP OF WESTERN SOVIET UNION

VOL. CXVI, NO. 3 | SEPTEMBER, 1959

THE NATIONAL GEOGRAPHIC MAGAZINE

Good-will Ambassadors of the U. S. Navy Win Friends in the Far East — FRANC SHOR, W. E. GARRETT — 283

Periscope Camera Pierces Ancient Tombs to Reveal 2,500-year-old Frescoes — CARLO M. LERICI — 336

A Firsthand Look at the Soviet Union — THOMAS T. HAMMOND — 352

With an introduction by the Editor — ERICH LESSING — 351

Western Soviet Map Added to Atlas Folio — 408

Miracle of the Mermaid's Purse — ERNEST L. LIBBY — 412

With 123 illustrations, 86 in color

THE JOURNAL OF THE NATIONAL GEOGRAPHIC SOCIETY, WASHINGTON, D. C.

$8.00 A YEAR | $1.00 A COPY

SEPTEMBER 1959 | WILBUR E. GARRETT

▲ **IN FLIGHT** "Mach diamonds"—shock waves produced during supersonic flight—stream out of a U.S. Navy McDonnell F3H Demon jet fighter. This picture was the first image to appear on the cover that was not of a war-bond solicitation or a billowing U.S. flag. The pilot of the plane was Editor Melville Grosvenor's son, naval aviator Alex Grosvenor. Photographer Wilbur E. (Bill) Garrett made the picture while seated in a jet flying in echelon.

THE HEMISPHERES

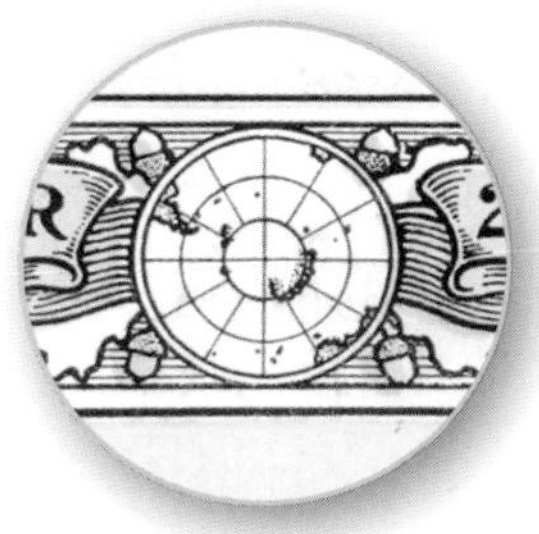

1910–1928
Antarctica is still a great white blank.

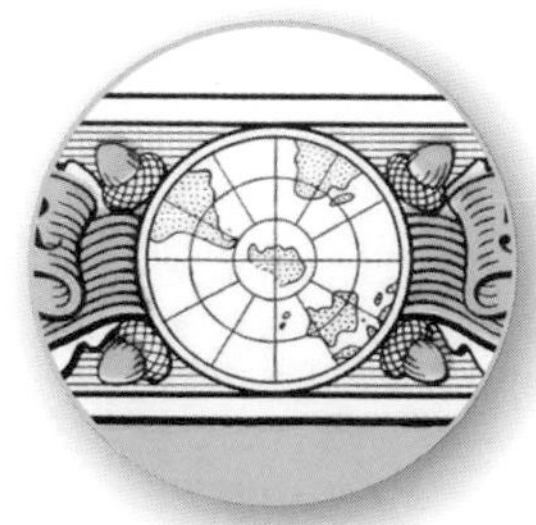

1928–1961
Antarctica appears better delineated.

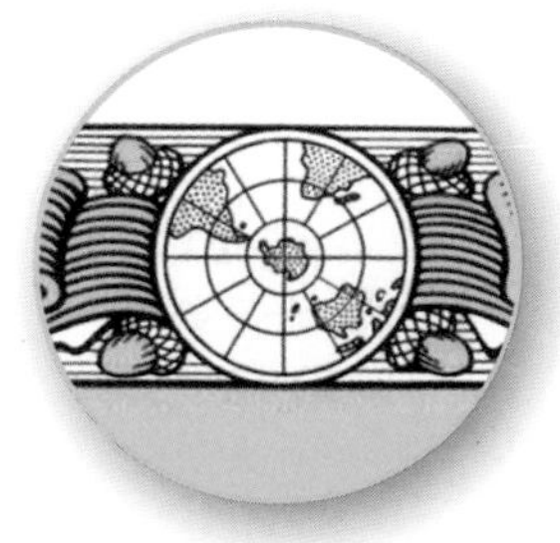

1961–1966
Increased stippling makes Antarctica stand out.

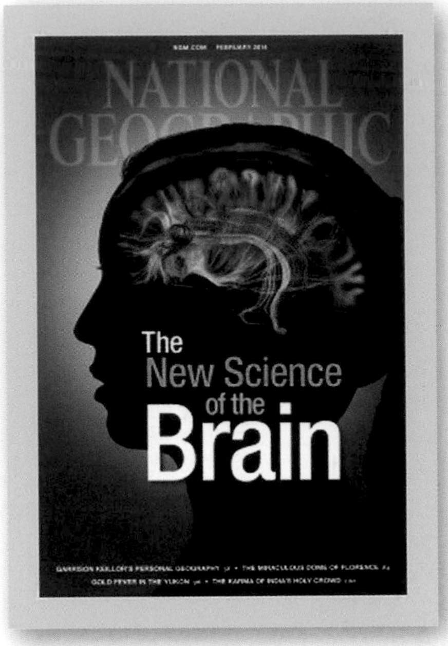

FEBRUARY 2014 | VAN WEDEEN AND L. L. WALD

▲ **INTERNAL EXPLORATION** Magnetic resonance imaging with colorized fiber shows the connections between different regions of the brain.

The rest of the story is best told in the following pages because it is such a richly visual one. You can see the evolution of style and imagery as the cover moves away from that dignified original toward today's clean, bold appearance.

Before 1998, when the worldwide growth of local-language editions of *National Geographic* was gaining momentum and the U.S. edition was released for sale on newsstands, the great majority of cover images began as one of thousands of 35mm frames being considered for a given issue. After a severe winnowing process, they simply "bubbled up" to the top toward the end of the editorial process, one of three or four potential covers dummied up for the editor to choose from.

The editor always monitored reader survey responses. He read letters and suggestions, which by the 1980s swelled mostly in response to particular images—February 1985's child mummy from Greenland, for instance, shocked many readers. But at a time when the magazine was available only to Society members, editors like Bill Garrett (1980–1990) saw the *Geographic*'s rising membership as the key endorsement of his cover choices. He might put three holograms there, which some readers found puzzling. He might digitally shift the Pyramids—which he did in February 1982—and be criticized for it in the *New York Times*. But then he might pick the "Afghan Girl" to top the June 1985 issue. If he lost sleep over the others, he didn't lose it over that one.

After 1998, however, everything changed. Increasing reliance on newsstand sales has meant that the cover stakes have never been higher. It's the "five second" rule mentioned by Johns in his foreword to this book. Five seconds to catch your eye. Five seconds to intrigue your interest. But that translates into many more hours spent conceiving and planning *National Geographic* covers that might have maximum impact. In today's media-saturated world it's hard to gauge the reading public's mood. Yet every month when decision time rolls around again, the Editor in Chief studies the various cover alternatives, takes a deep breath—and chooses one. ■

THE YELLOW BORDERS

SHADES OF YELLOW Due to the shifting preference of editors, the exact shade of the yellow border has changed many times. Here are some samples from different years.

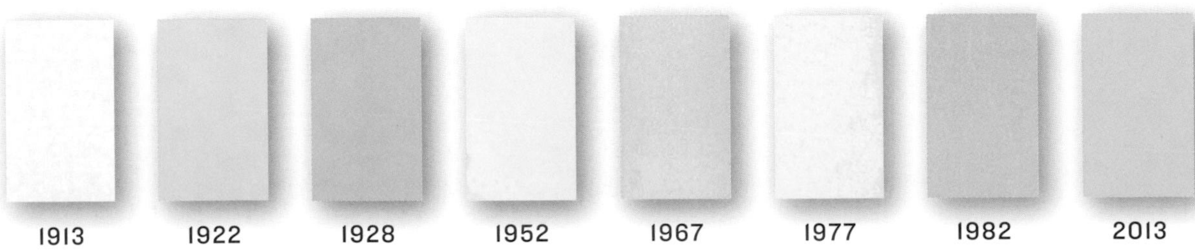

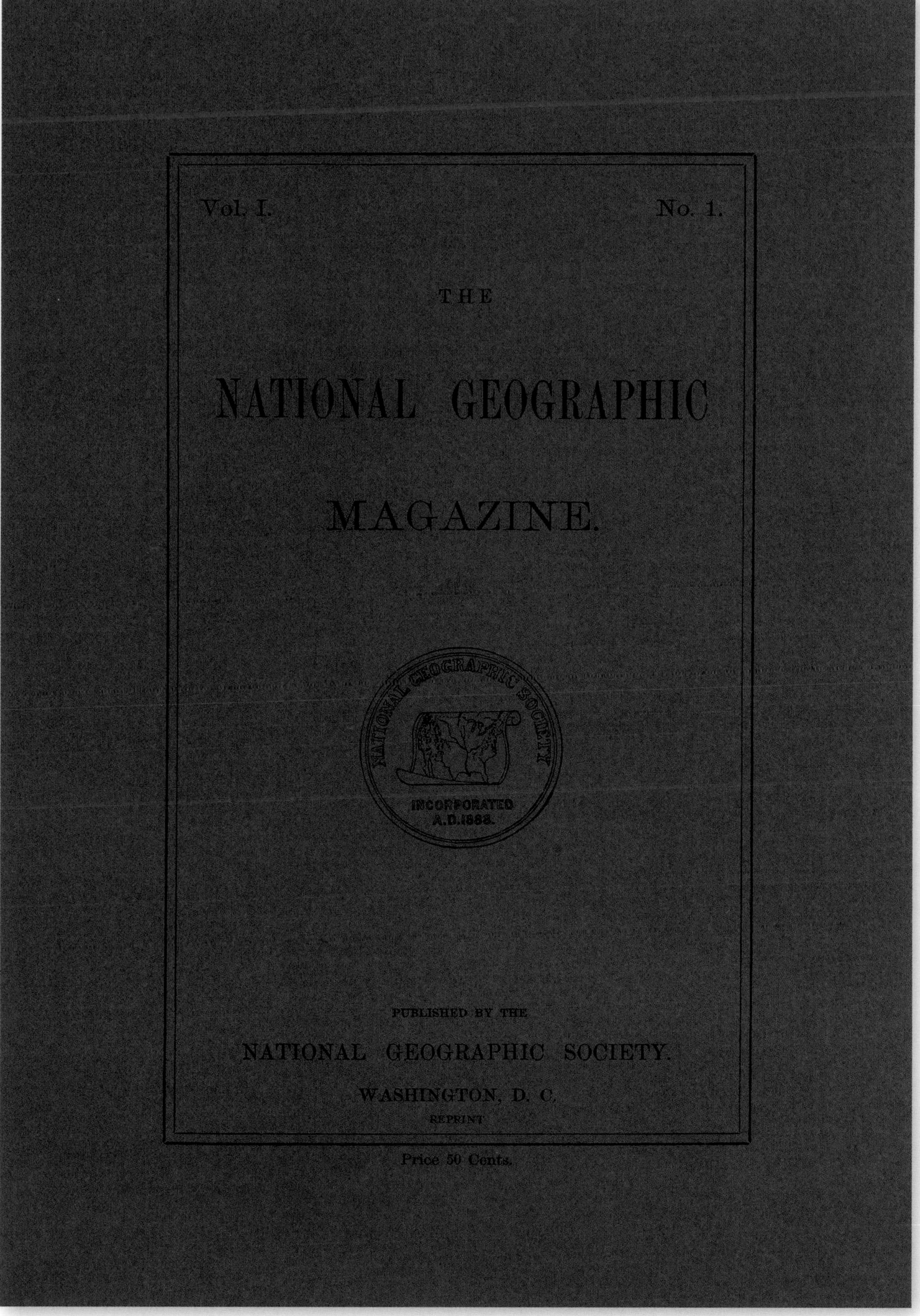
Vol. I.
No. 1.
THE
NATIONAL GEOGRAPHIC
MAGAZINE.
NATIONAL GEOGRAPHIC SOCIETY
INCORPORATED A.D. 1888.
PUBLISHED BY THE
NATIONAL GEOGRAPHIC SOCIETY.
WASHINGTON, D. C.
REPRINT
Price 50 Cents.

OCTOBER 1888 | **NGS** Volume I, number 1 features the Society's first seal, a map of the United States.

[BY THE NUMBERS]

LET'S "SPICE UP THE LEAD WITH A FEW STATISTICS," former *National Geographic* editor Ted Vosburgh urged a staff writer in the late 1960s. That passion for precision had given the magazine an unsurpassed reputation for accuracy long before his dictum. Here, in an homage to the tradition that bequeathed the world the phrase "according to National Geographic . . . ," we offer up a few statistics of our own.

THE MAGAZINE

60,000,000

Number of *National Geographic* readers worldwide

80 Number of countries in which *National Geographic* is distributed

1,465

Number of covers *National Geographic* magazine published October 1888 to January 2015

165

Number of members who received the first issue of *National Geographic*

669

Total number of illustrated covers of *National Geographic*, through January 2015

THREE

Number of covers that have been designed without a yellow border since 1959

13 Number of cover stories featuring U.S. national parks

TEN Number of Editors in Chief who have run the magazine in its lifetime

11.5 MILLION

Number of physical items (photographic prints, slides, art) housed in National Geographic's image archive

11,000+

Scientific research, conservation, and exploration projects funded by the Society

$178,900

Paid for one of the most famous cover photos, the Afghan Girl, at the Christie's auction in December 2012

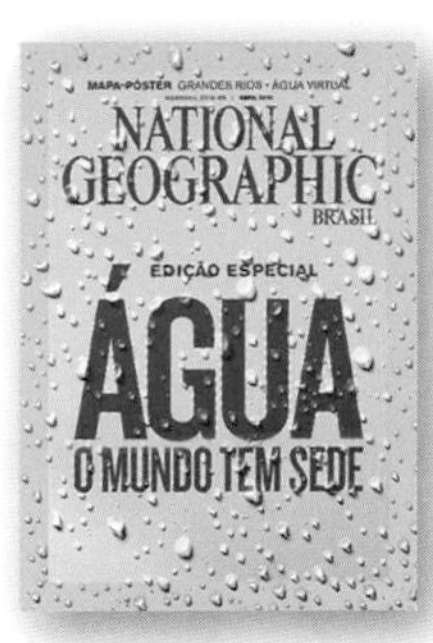

BRAZIL

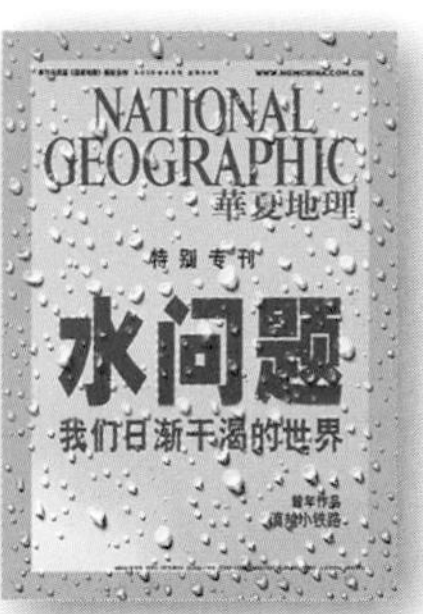

CHINA

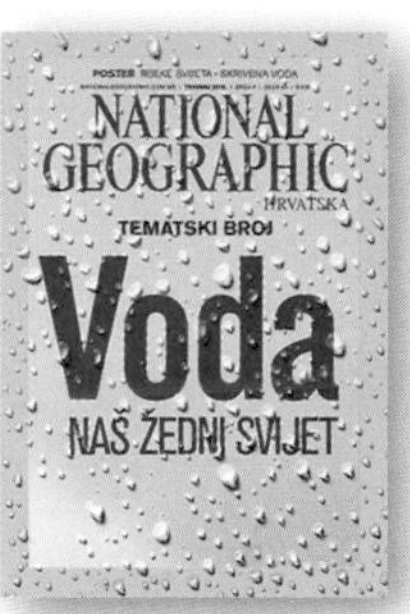

CROATIA

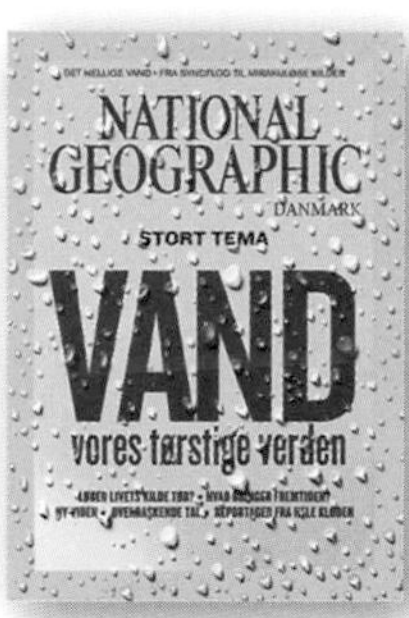

DENMARK

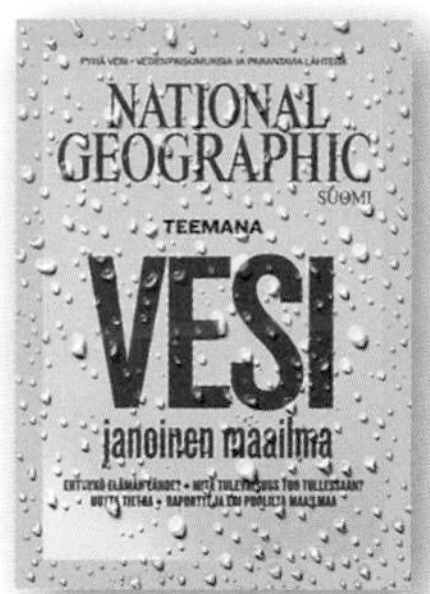

FINLAND

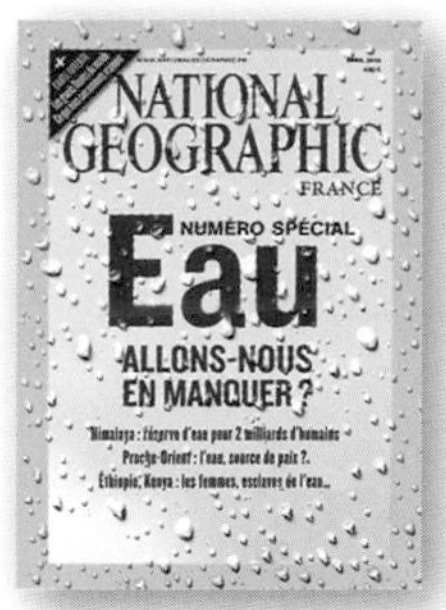

FRANCE

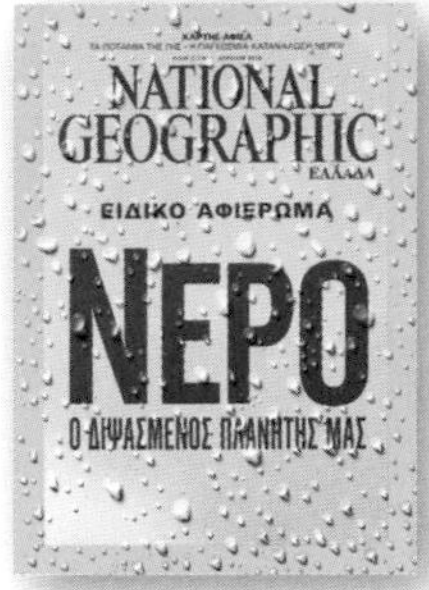

GREECE

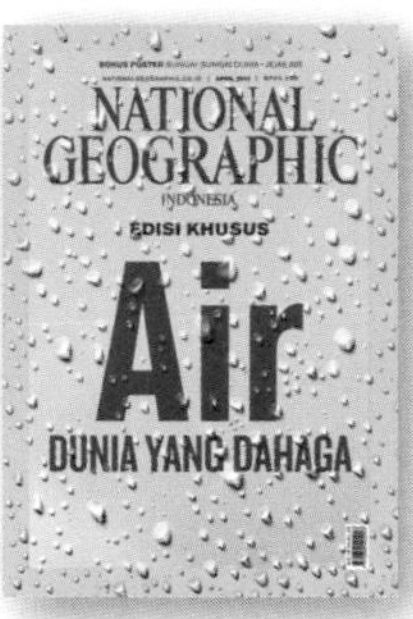

INDONESIA

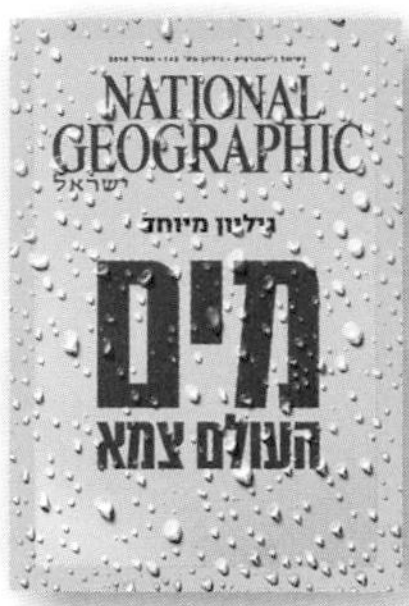

ISRAEL

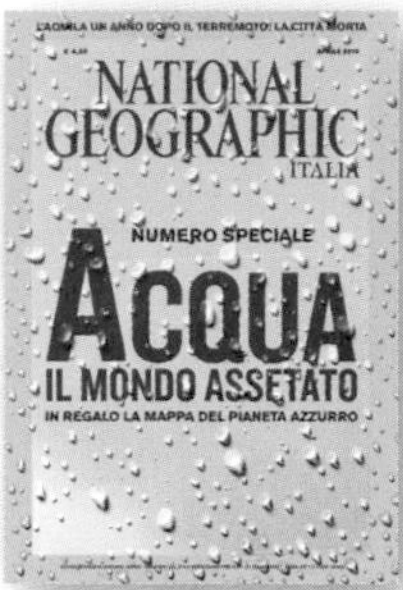

ITALY

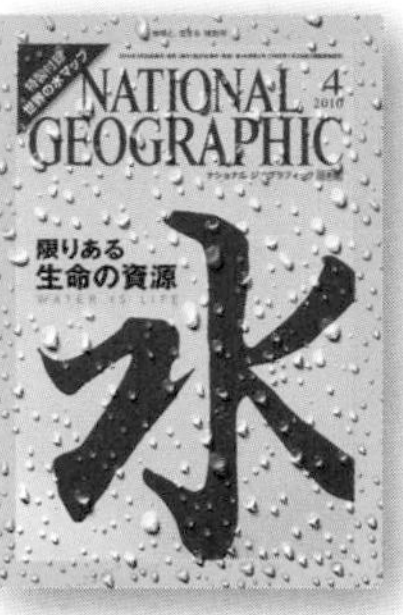

JAPAN

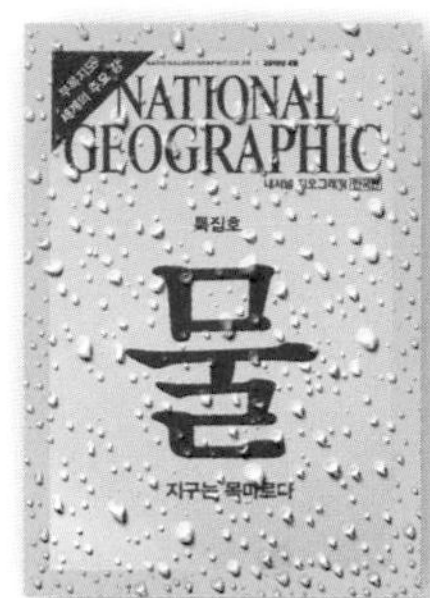

KOREA

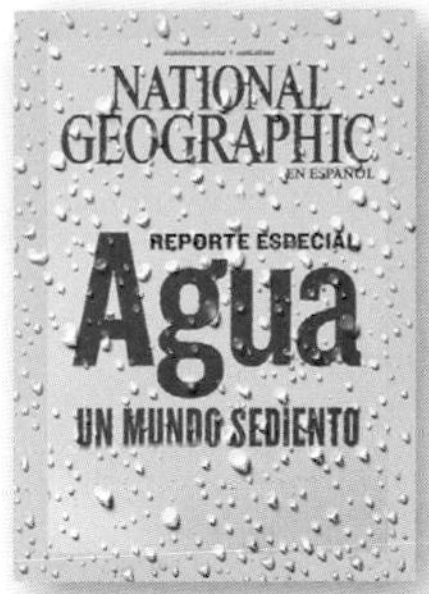

LATIN AMERICA

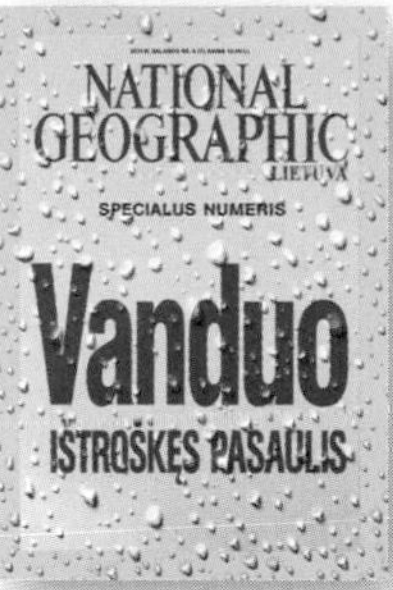

LITHUANIA

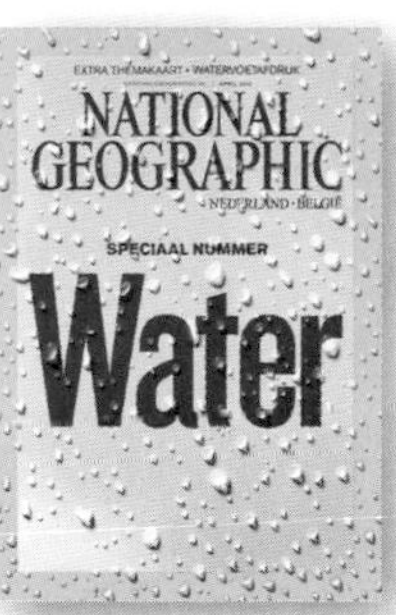

NETHERLANDS

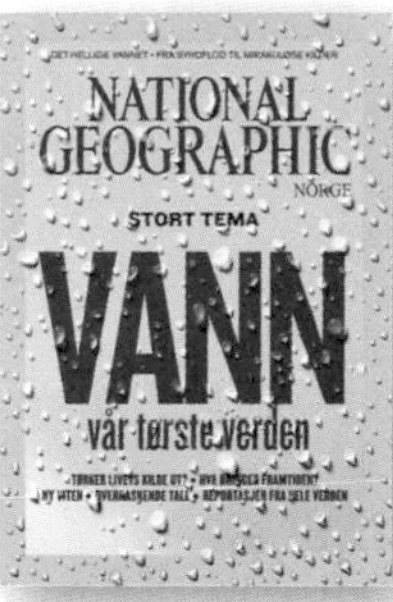

NORWAY

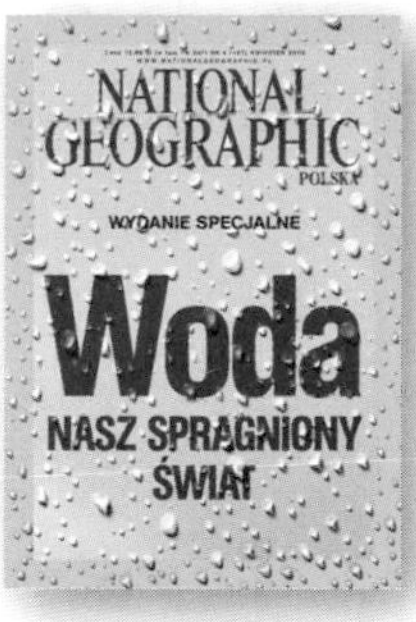

POLAND

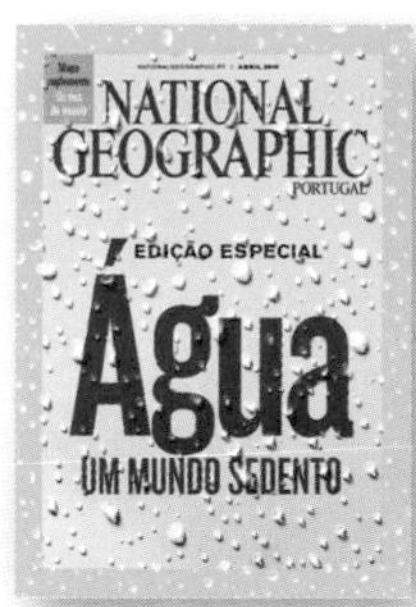

PORTUGAL

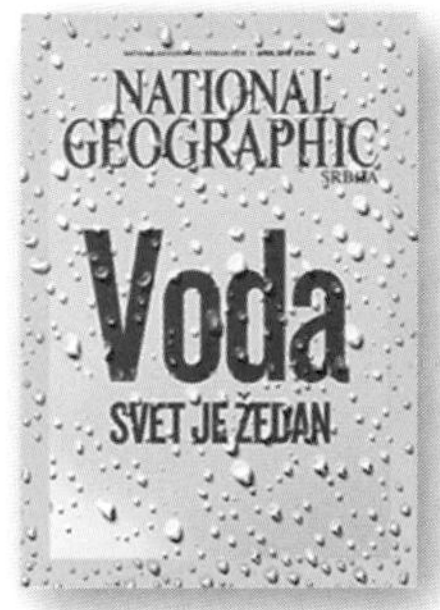

SERBIA

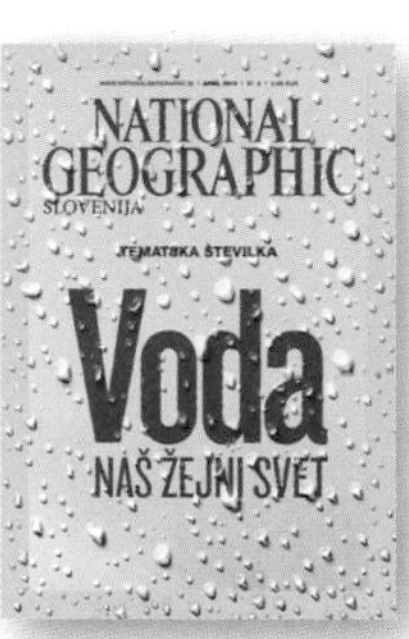

SLOVENIA

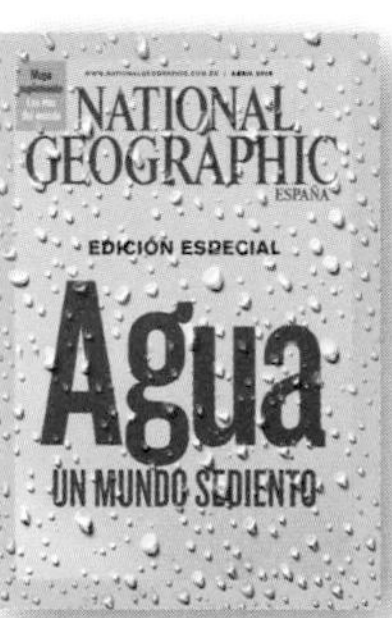

SPAIN

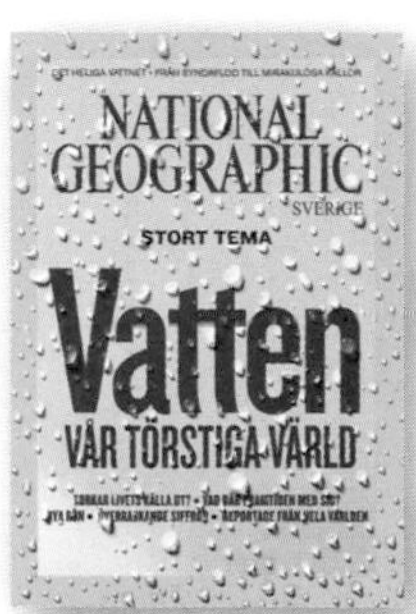

SWEDEN

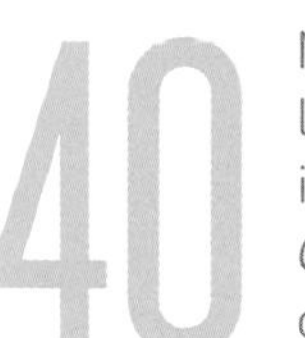

Number of local language editions in which *National Geographic* is distributed

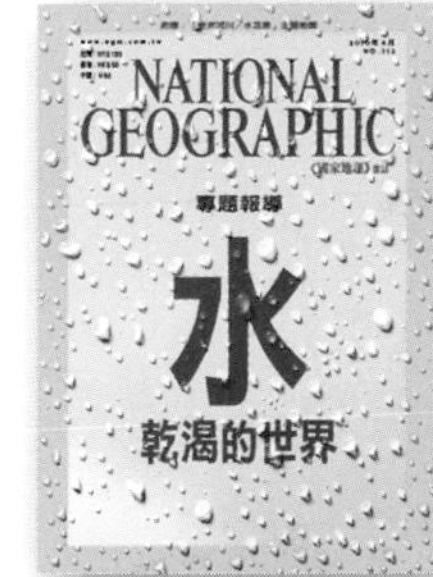

TAIWAN

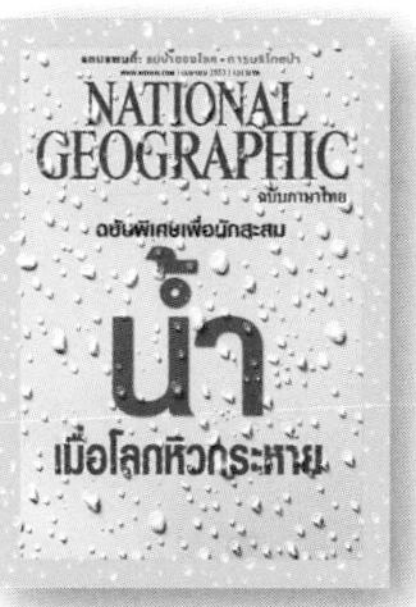

THAILAND

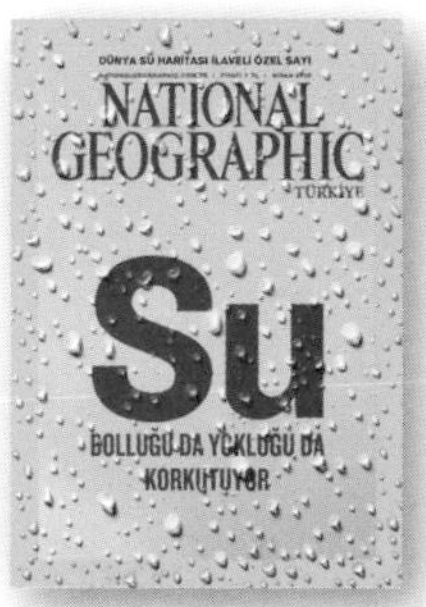

TURKEY

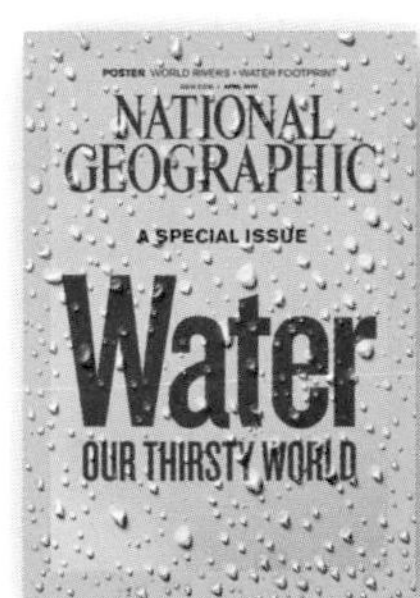

UNITED STATES

Besides the covers pictured, language editions also include:

ARABIC
AZERBAIJAN
BULGARIA
CZECH REP.
ESTONIA
GEORGIA
GERMANY
HUNGARY
INDIA
IRAN
LATVIA
ROMANIA
RUSSIA
UKRAINE

ANCIENT FASCINATION

Discoveries from ancient Egypt have enthralled *National Geographic* readers for many years.

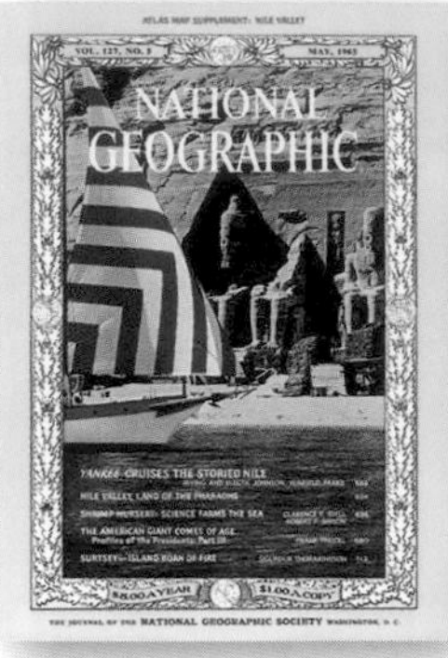

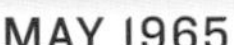

MAY 1965

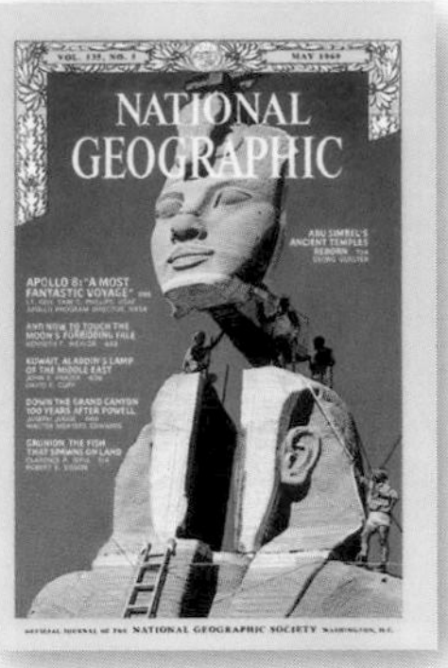

MAY 1969

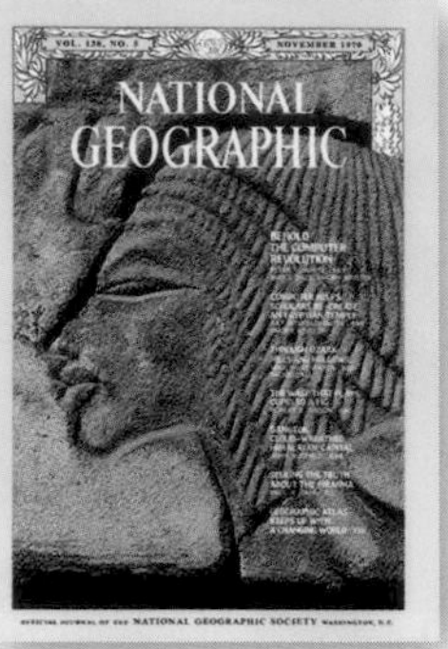

NOVEMBER 1970

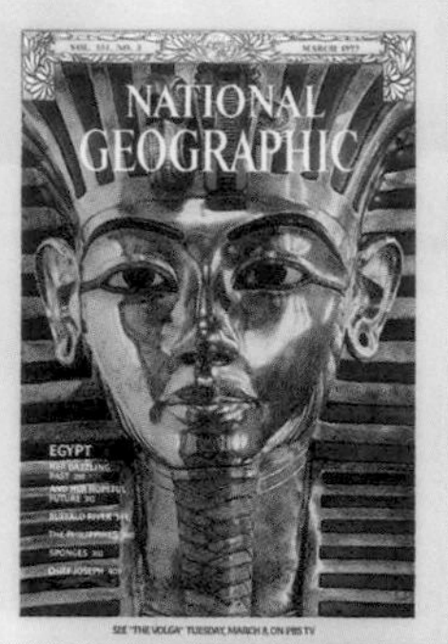

MARCH 1977

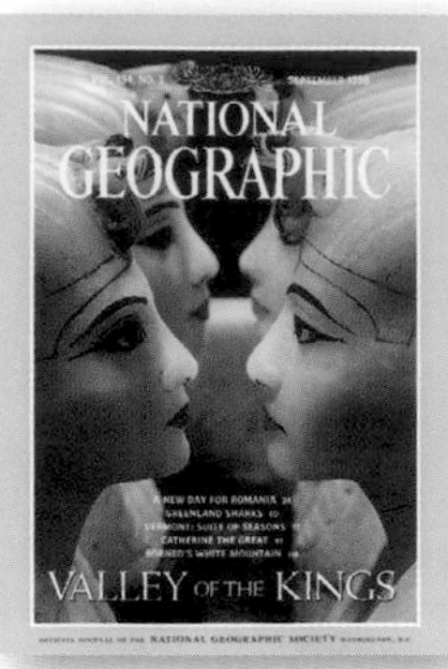

SEPTEMBER 1998

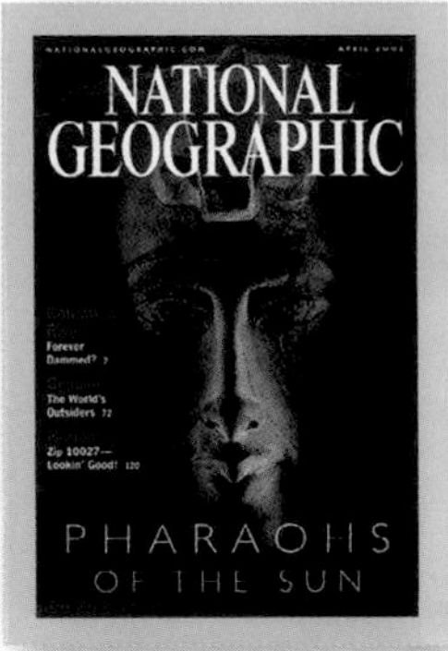

APRIL 2001

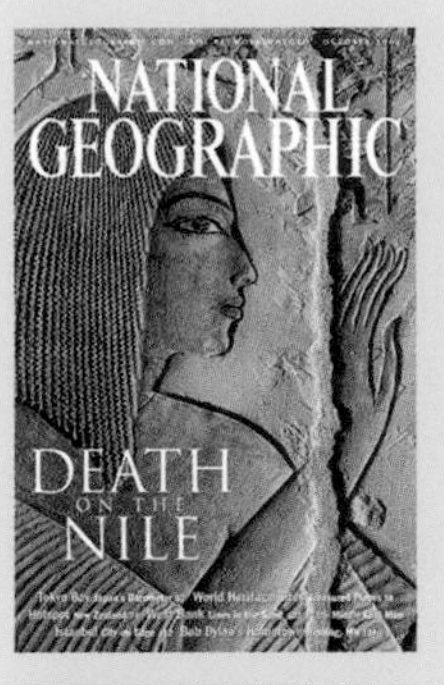

OCTOBER 2002

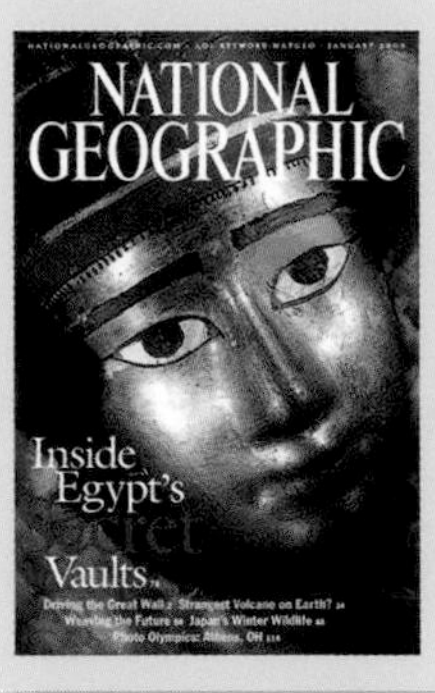

JANUARY 2003

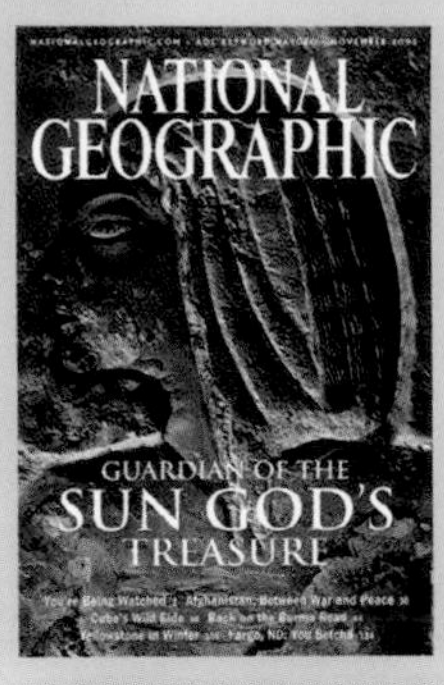

NOVEMBER 2003

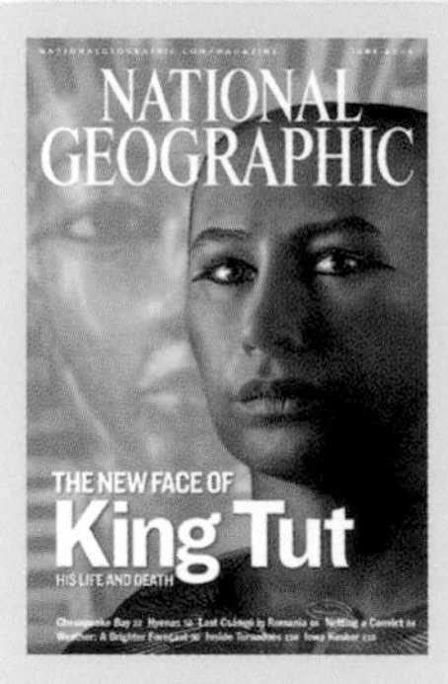

JUNE 2005

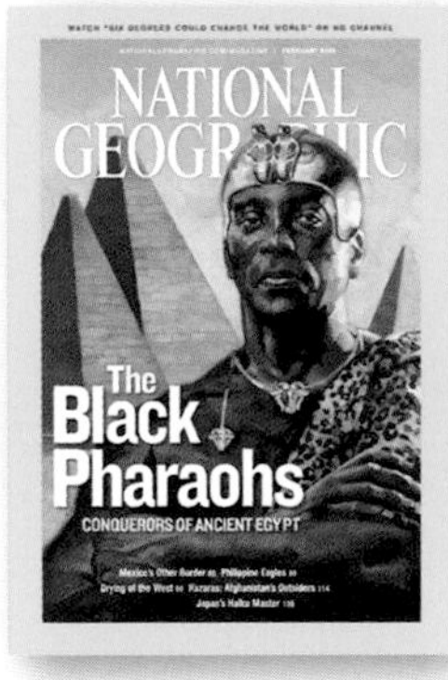

FEBRUARY 2008

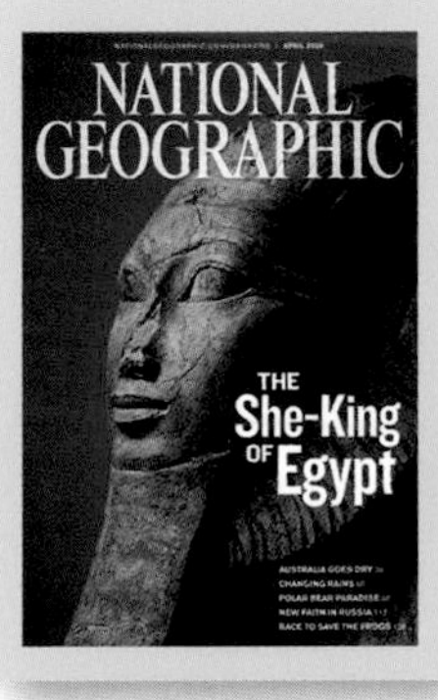

APRIL 2009

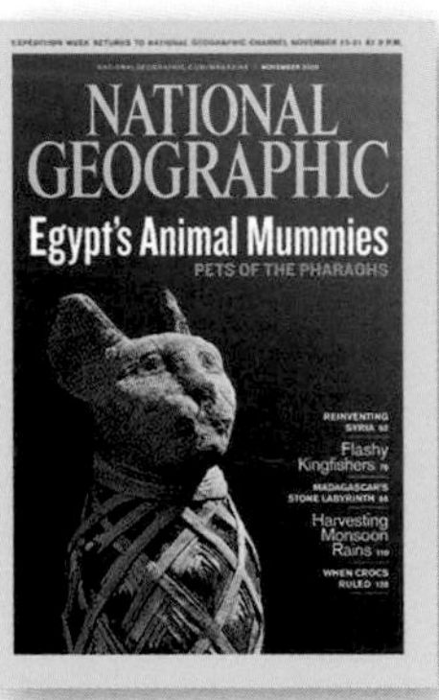

NOVEMBER 2009

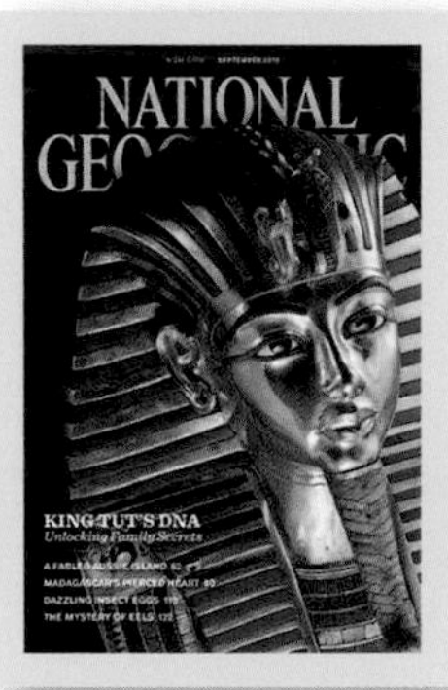

SEPTEMBER 2010

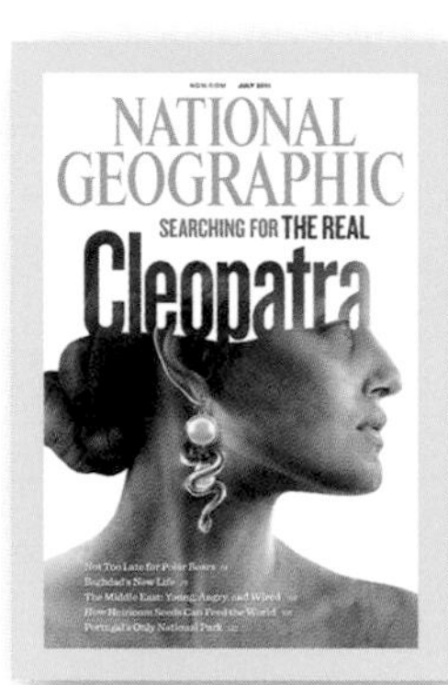

JULY 2011

Number of Egypt cover stories by decade, 1960-2014

Increased funding for Egyptian archaeology in the 2000s led to an increase in Egyptian cover stories.

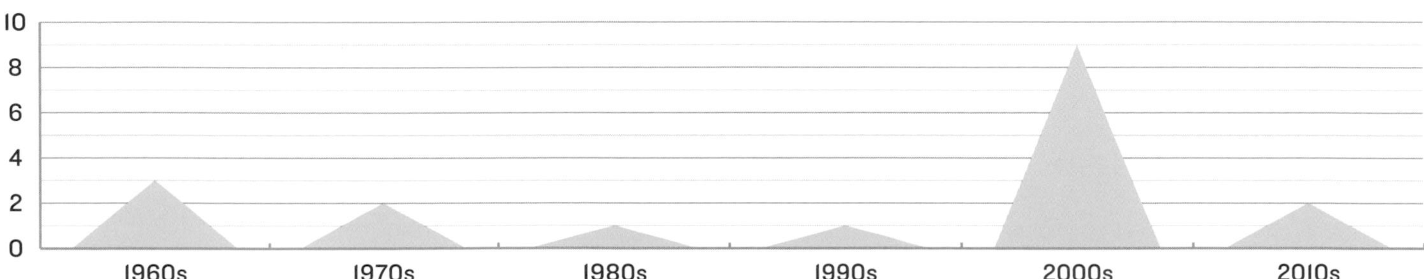

BABY FACES

Photographs of children provide a different perspective on cultures all over the world.

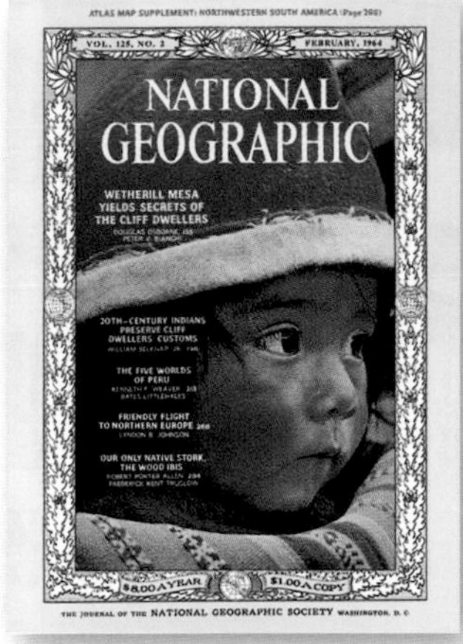

FEBRUARY 1964

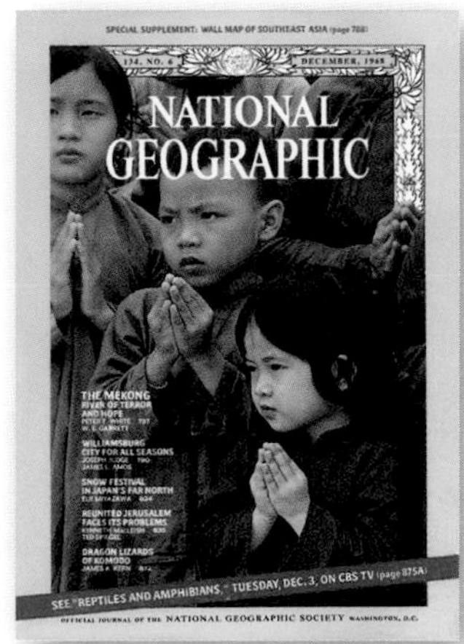

DECEMBER 1968

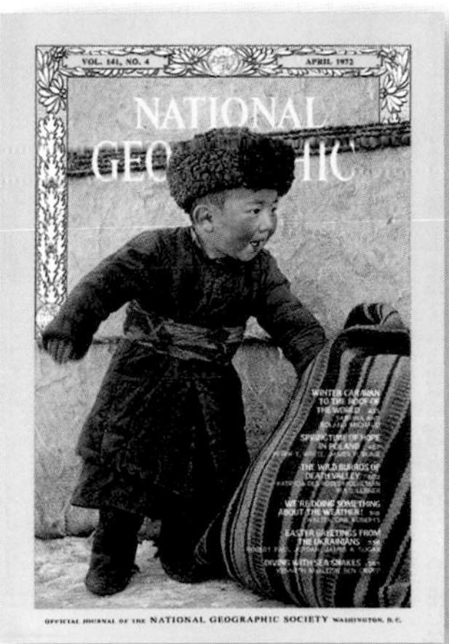

APRIL 1972

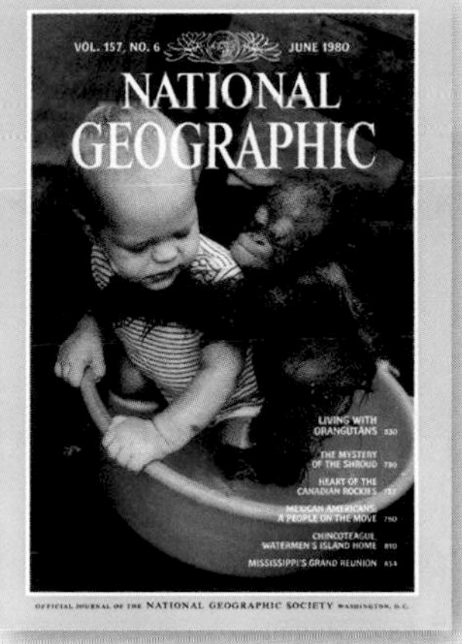

JUNE 1980

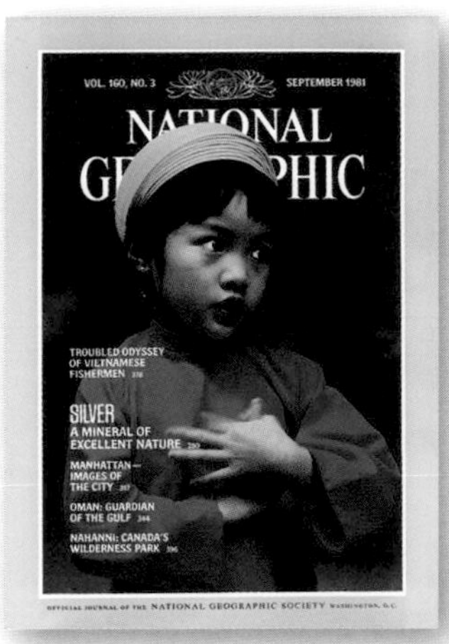

SEPTEMBER 1981

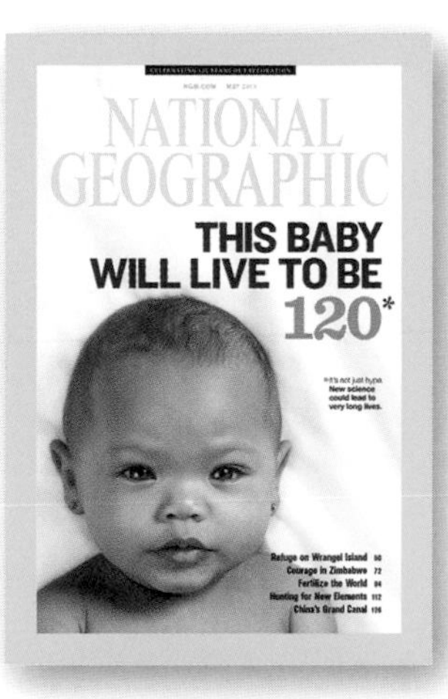

MAY 2013

COVERS WITH BITE

Readers love stories they can sink their teeth into.

Sharks of all species, shapes, and sizes have appeared on the cover five times since 1960.

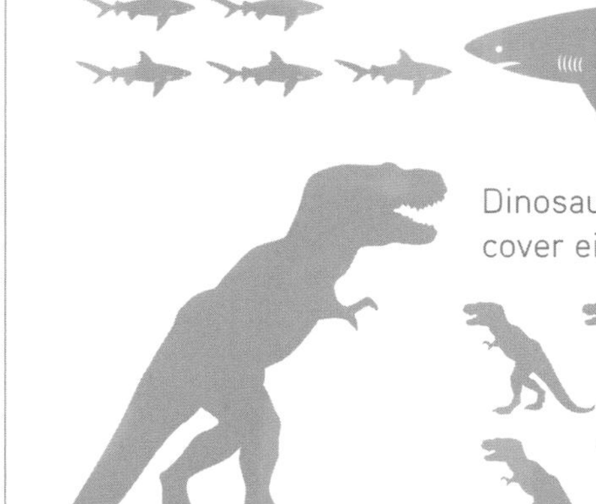

Dinosaurs have appeared on the cover eight times since 1960.

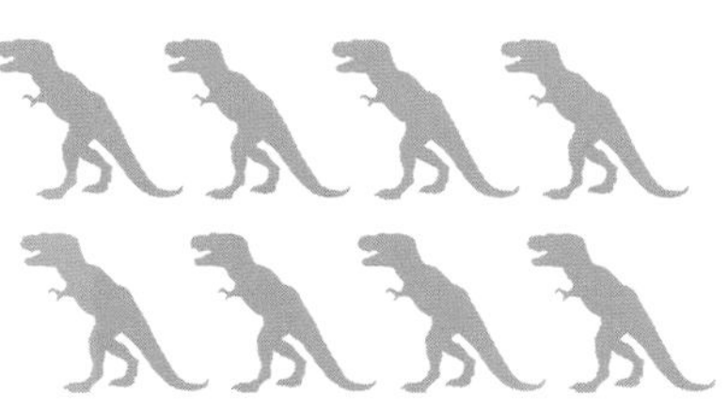

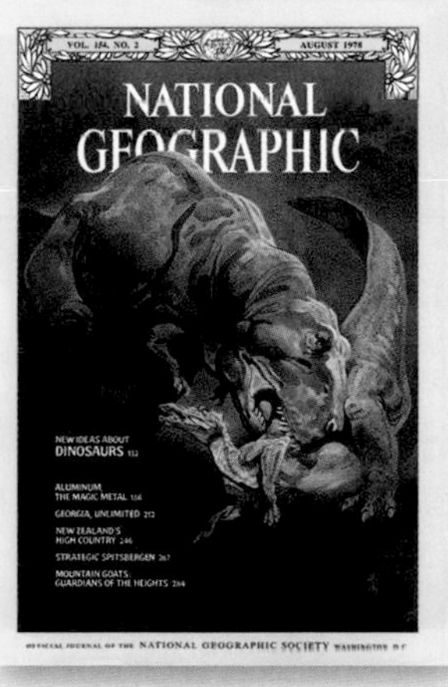

AUGUST 1978

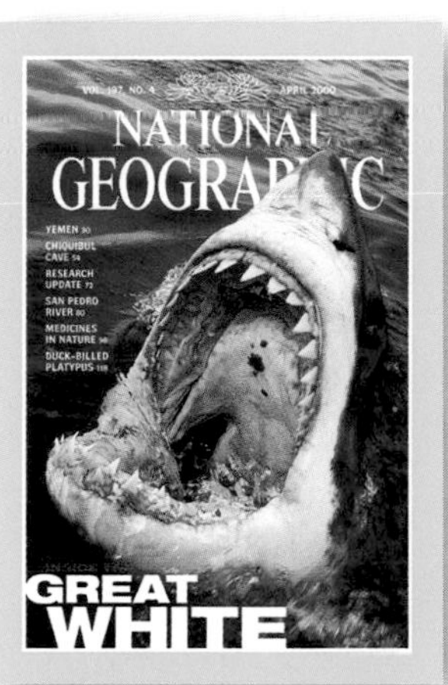

APRIL 2000

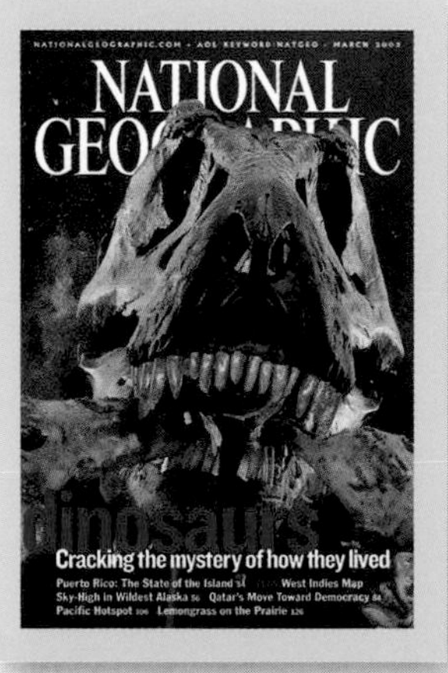

MARCH 2003

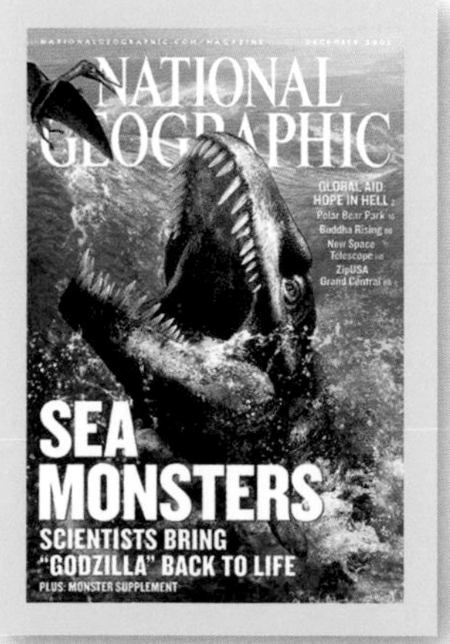

DECEMBER 2005

A MOTHER'S LOVE

Animal mothers and their young have appeared frequently on the cover.

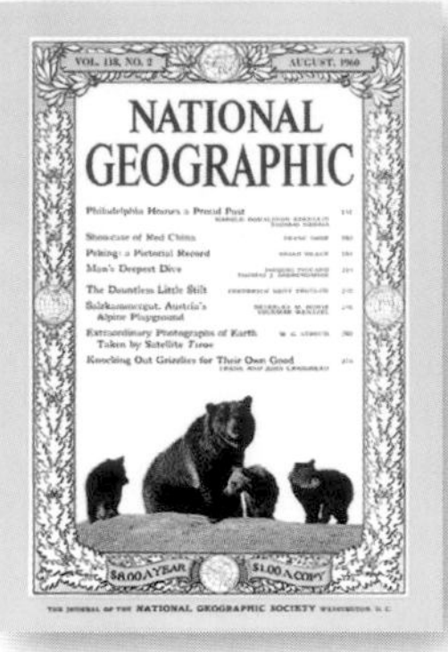

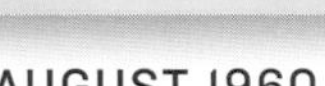

AUGUST 1960

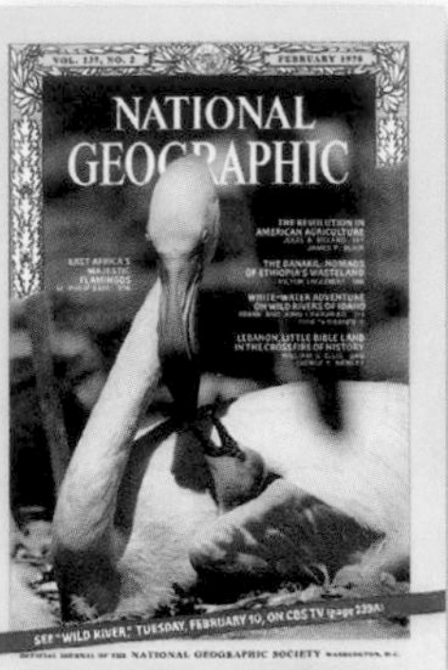

FEBRUARY 1970

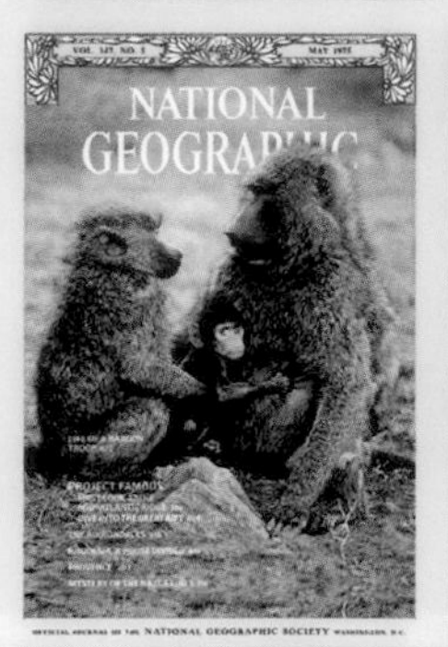

MAY 1975

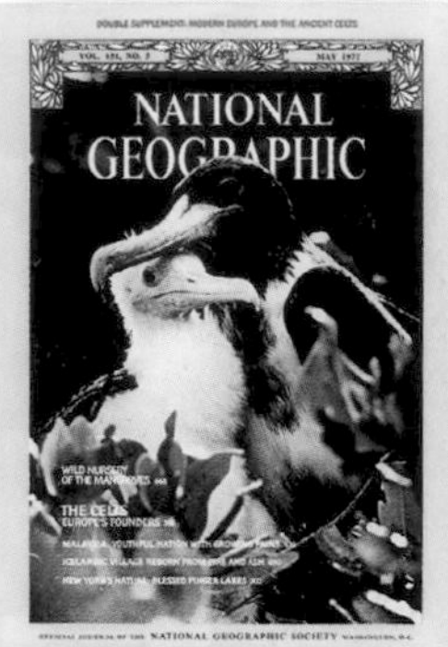

MAY 1977

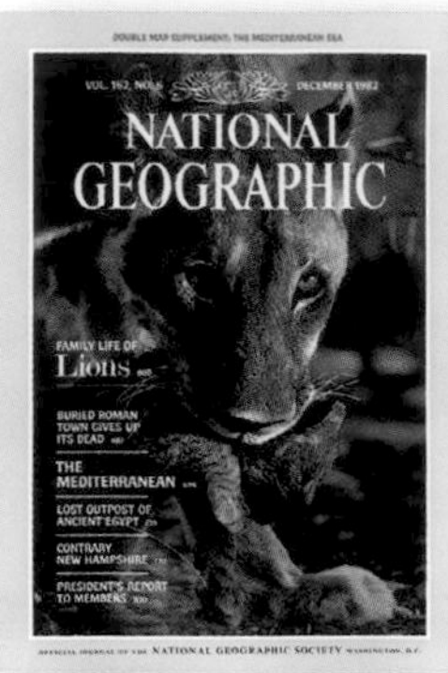

DECEMBER 1982

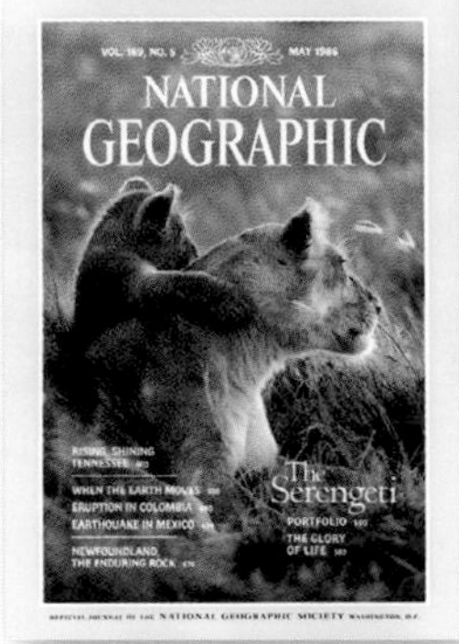

MAY 1986

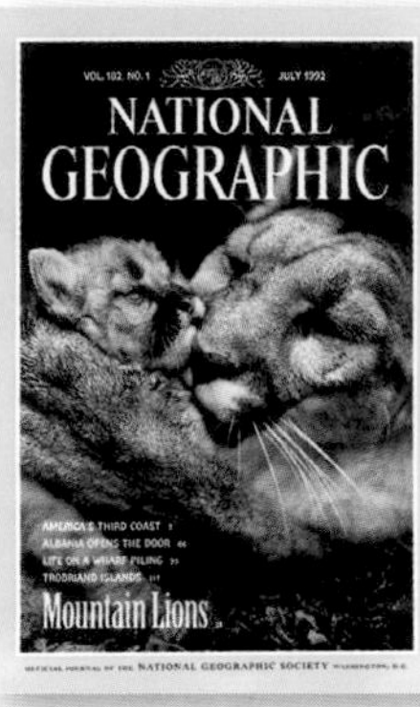

JULY 1992

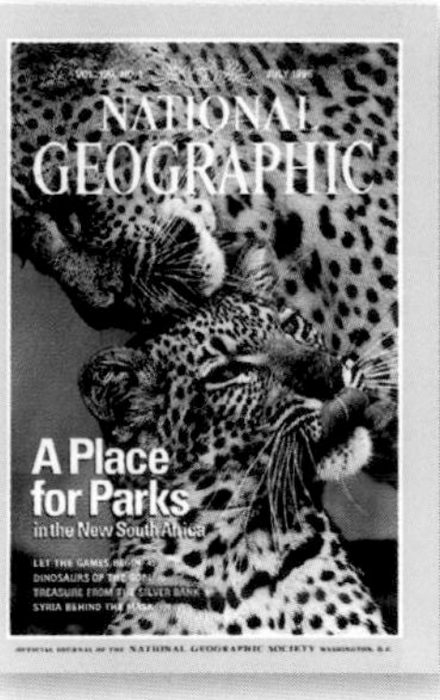

JULY 1996

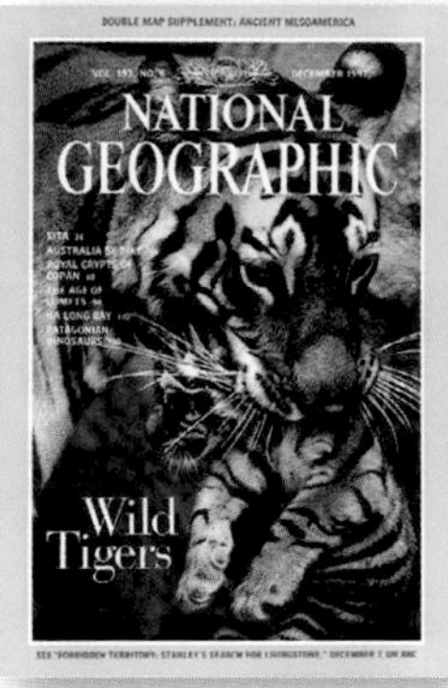

DECEMBER 1997

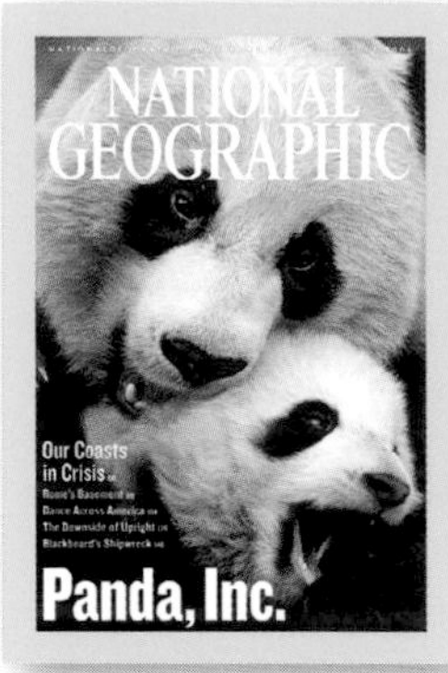

JULY 2006

READY TO RUMBLE!

Battling bears, sparring stallions, and jousting joeys

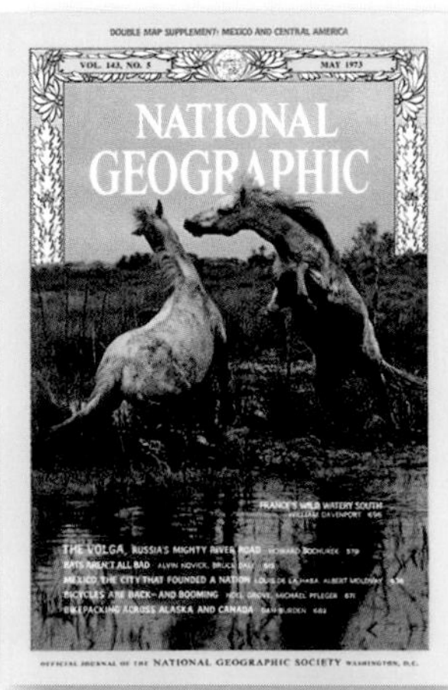

MAY 1973

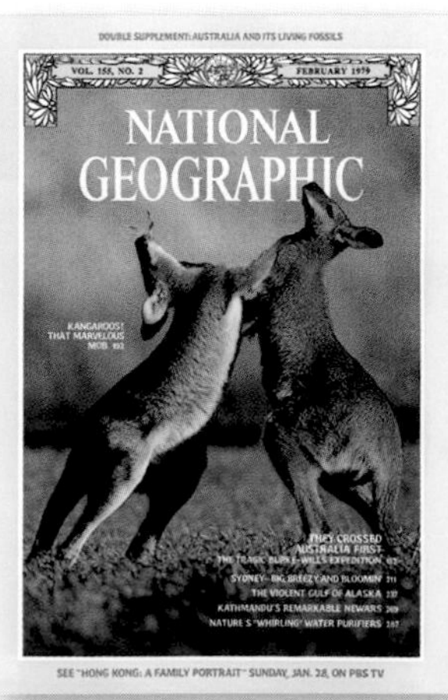

FEBRUARY 1979

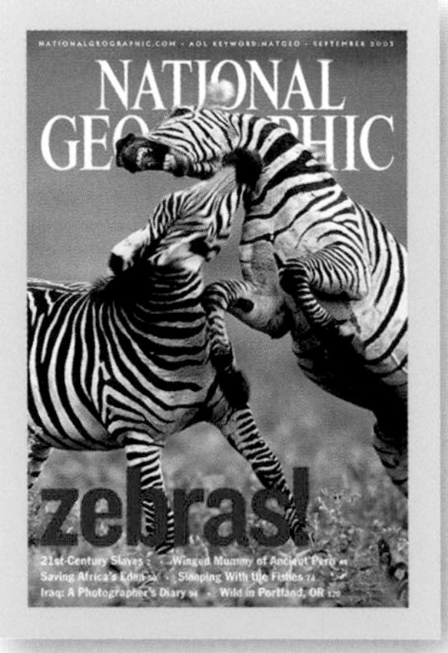

SEPTEMBER 2003

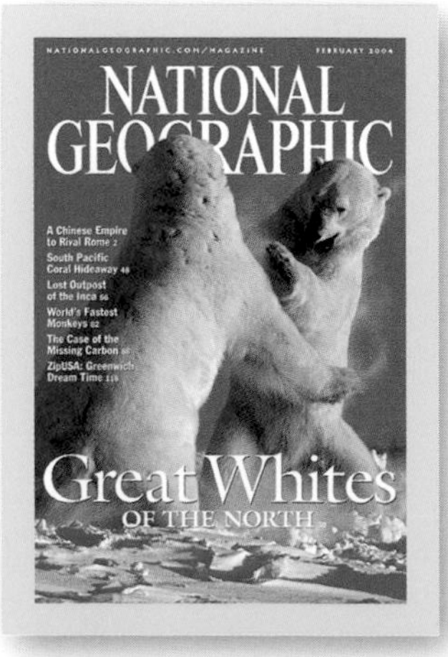

FEBRUARY 2004

THE WILD THINGS

Lions and tigers and bears—plus snakes, birds, elephants, fish, insects, and mollusks—sized by frequency of appearance on the covers

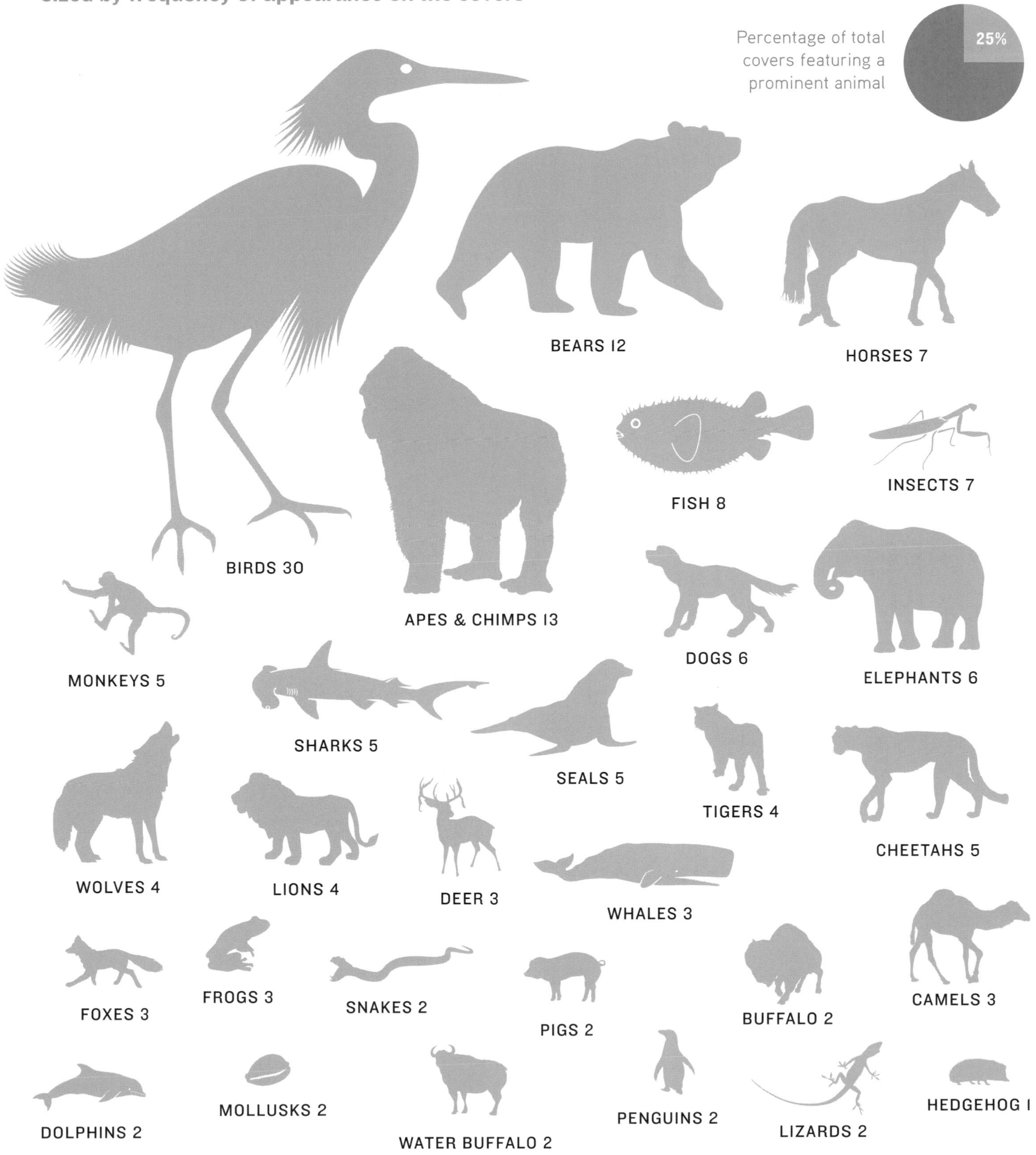

Percentage of total covers featuring a prominent animal

25%

BIRDS 30

BEARS 12

HORSES 7

APES & CHIMPS 13

FISH 8

INSECTS 7

MONKEYS 5

DOGS 6

ELEPHANTS 6

SHARKS 5

SEALS 5

TIGERS 4

CHEETAHS 5

WOLVES 4

LIONS 4

DEER 3

WHALES 3

FOXES 3

FROGS 3

SNAKES 2

PIGS 2

BUFFALO 2

CAMELS 3

DOLPHINS 2

MOLLUSKS 2

WATER BUFFALO 2

PENGUINS 2

LIZARDS 2

HEDGEHOG 1

THE MOST BEAUTIFUL GIRL IN THE WORLD

Captivating images of women with fascinating smiles drew in readers.

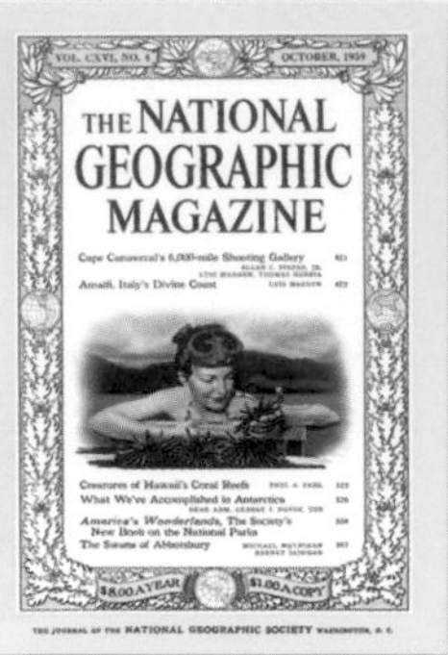

OCTOBER 1959

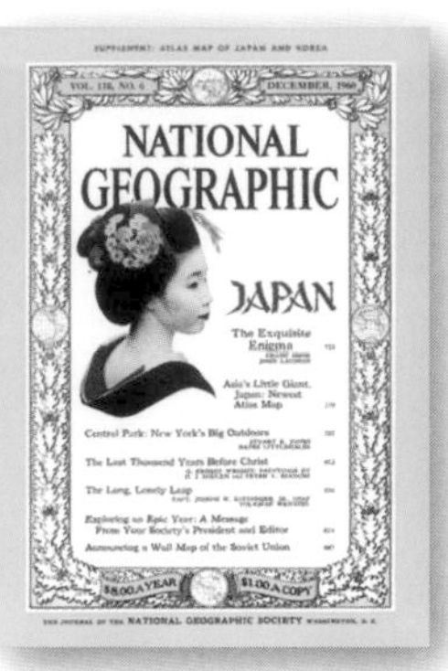

DECEMBER 1960

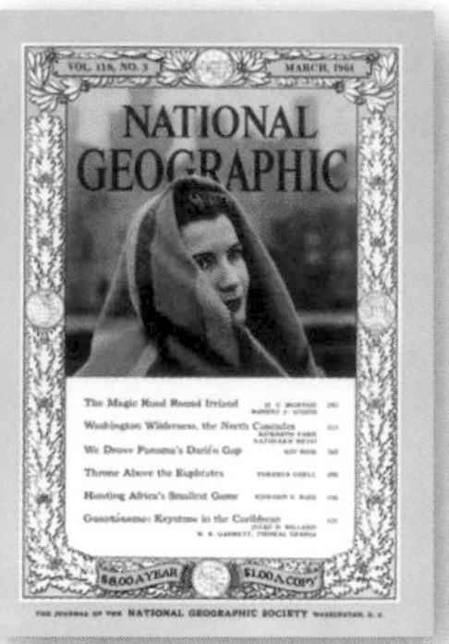

MARCH 1961

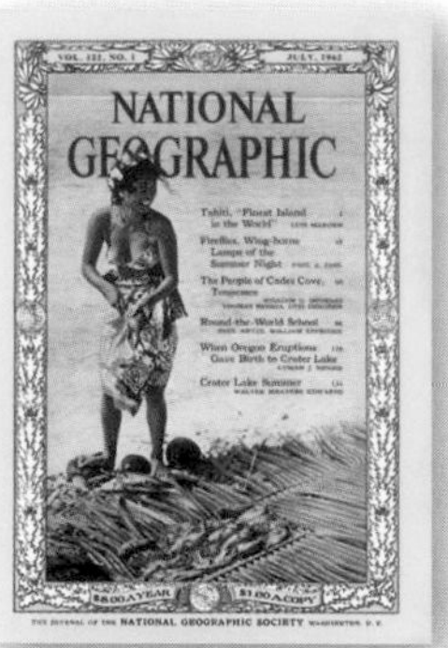

JULY 1962

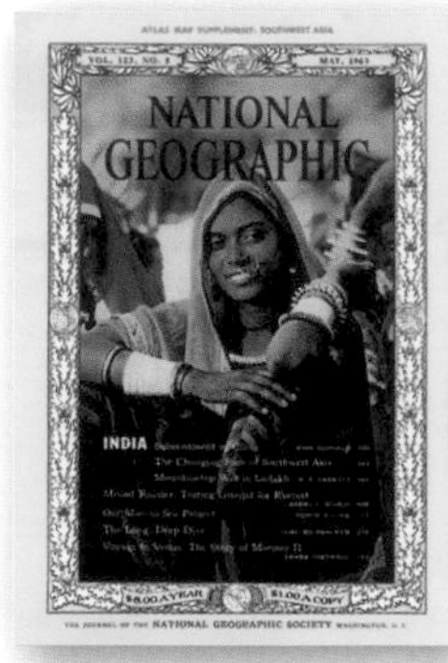

MAY 1963

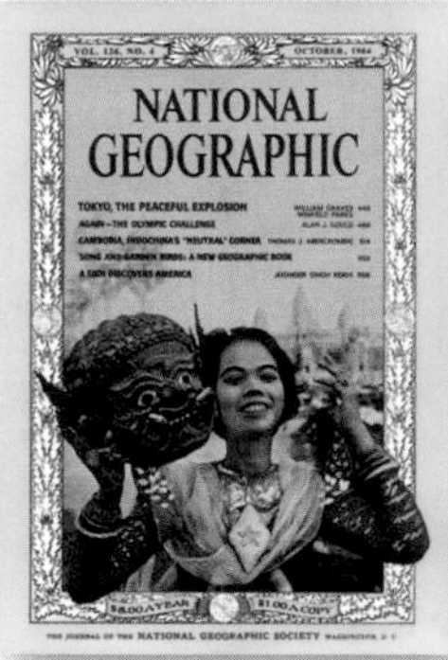

OCTOBER 1964

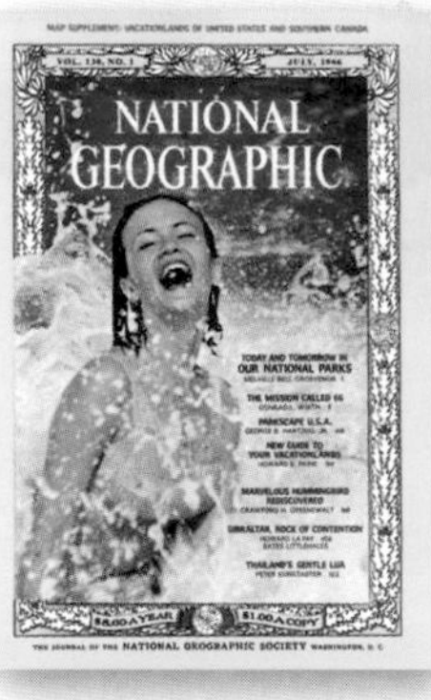

JULY 1966

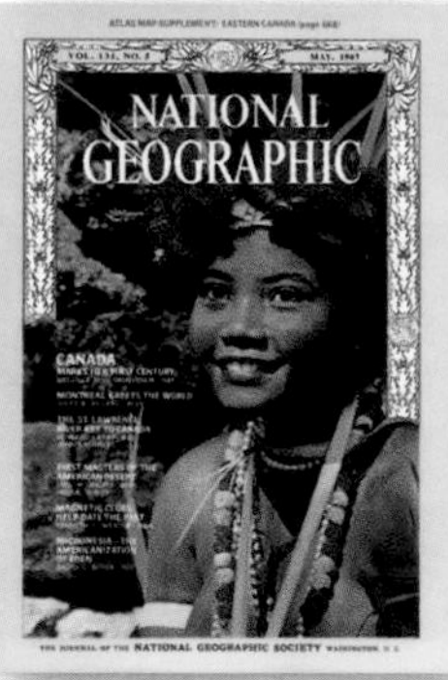

MAY 1967

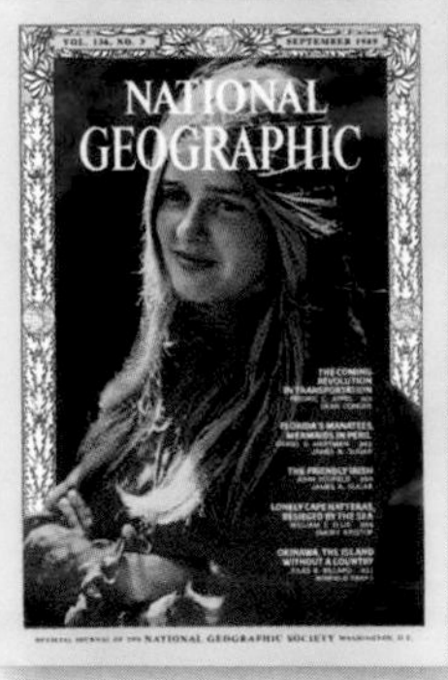

SEPTEMBER 1969

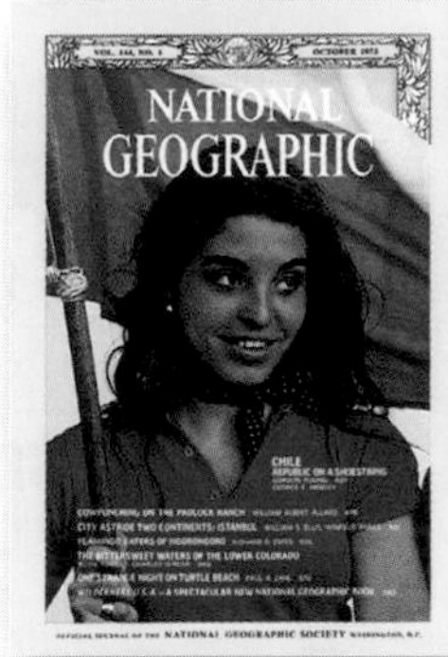

OCTOBER 1973

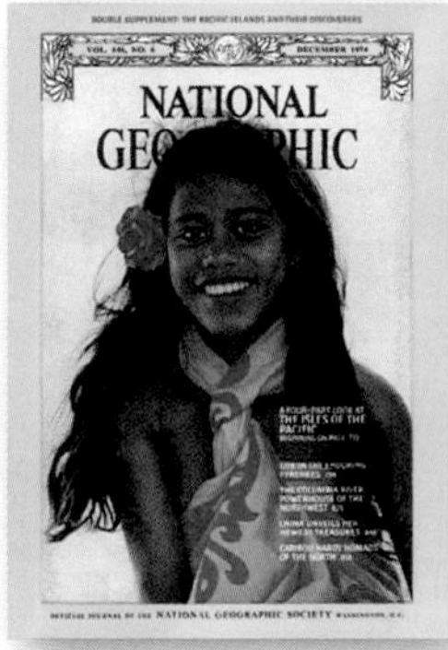

DECEMBER 1974

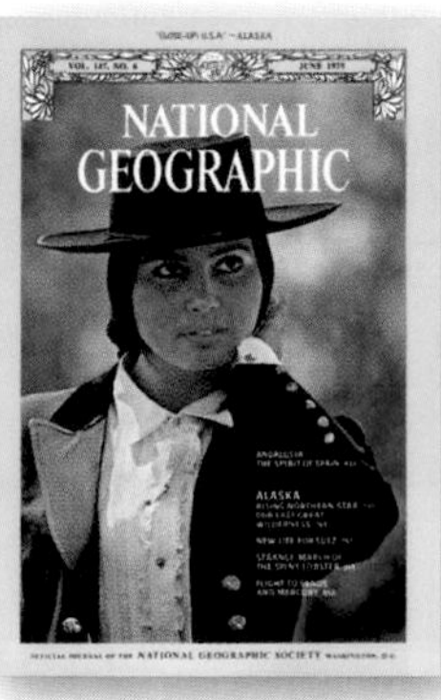

JUNE 1975

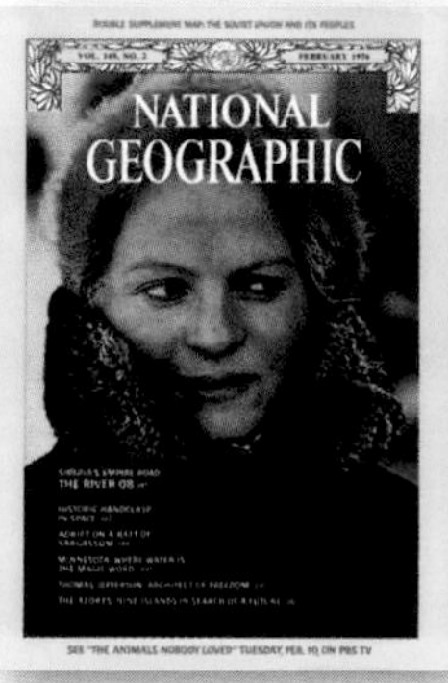

FEBRUARY 1976

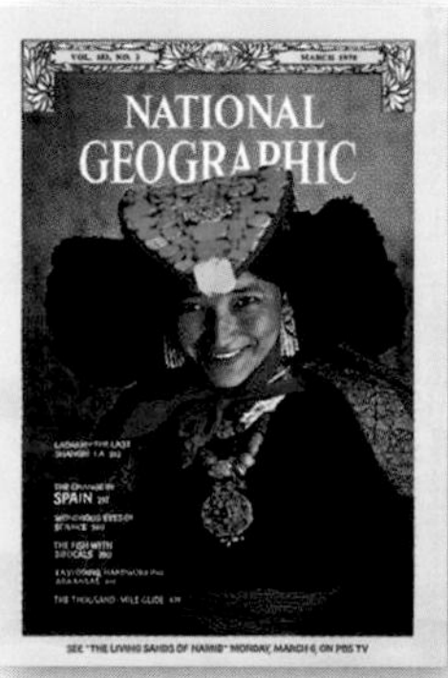

MARCH 1978

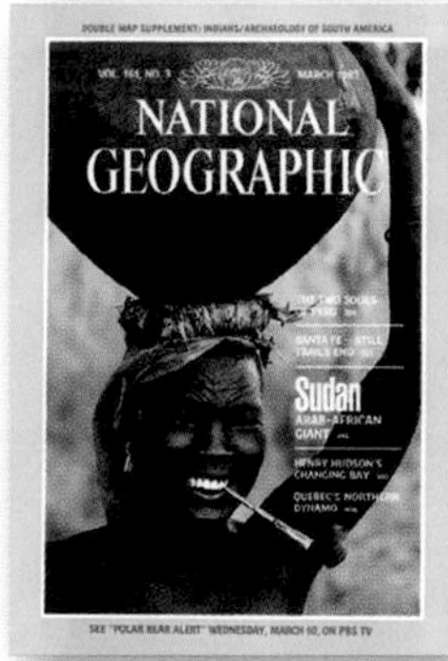

MARCH 1982

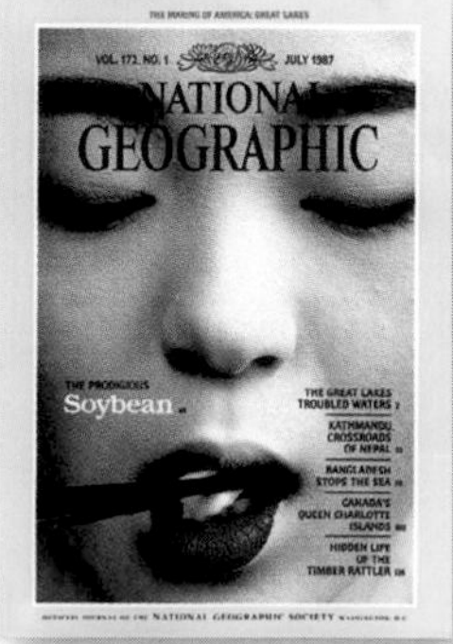

JULY 1987

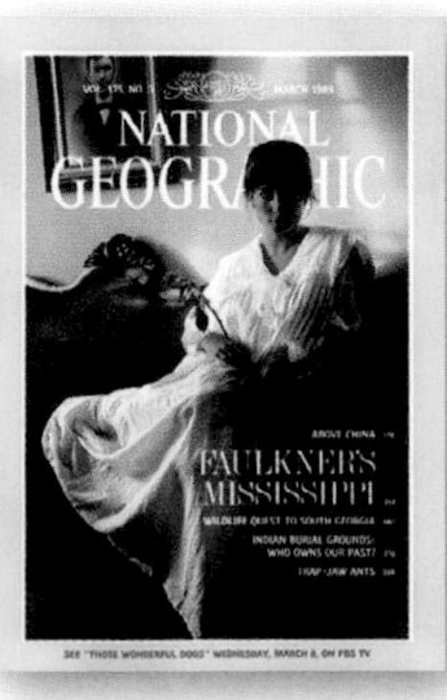

MARCH 1989

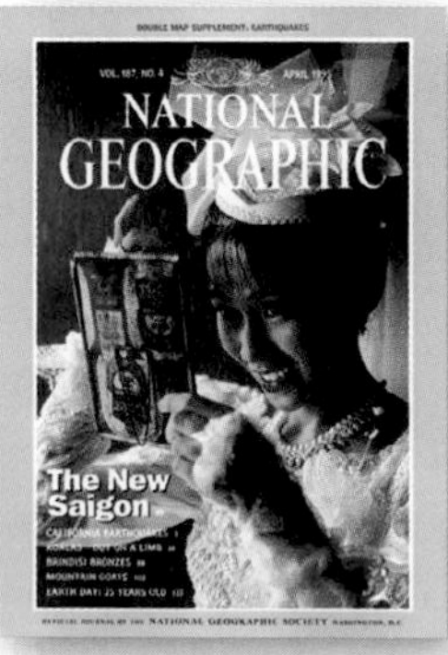

APRIL 1995

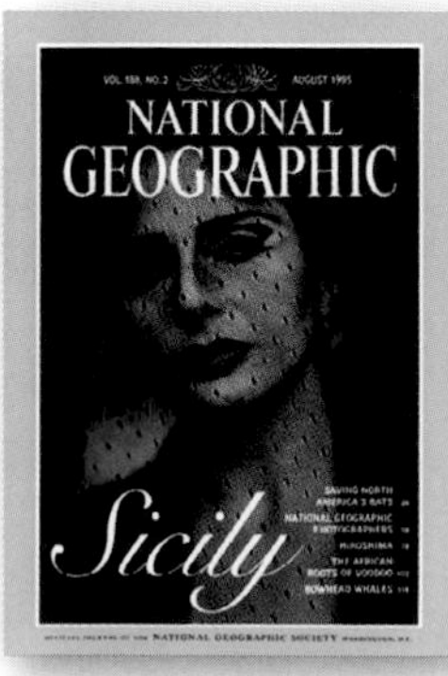

AUGUST 1995

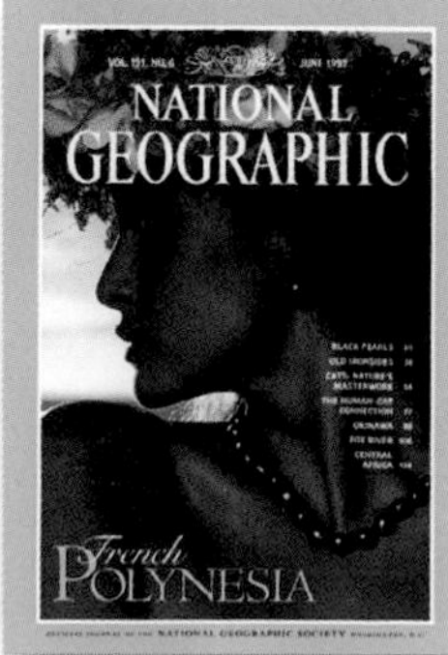

JUNE 1997

COPYCATS

Imitation: both flattering and funny

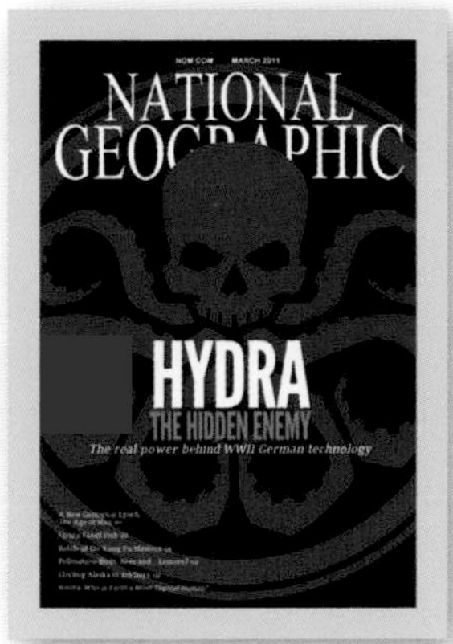

MARVEL COMICS

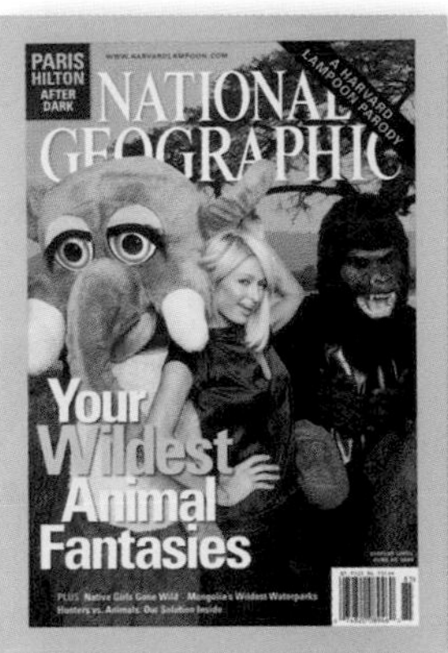

HARVARD LAMPOON

KIM GRIFFITHS–MEDIAVENGERS

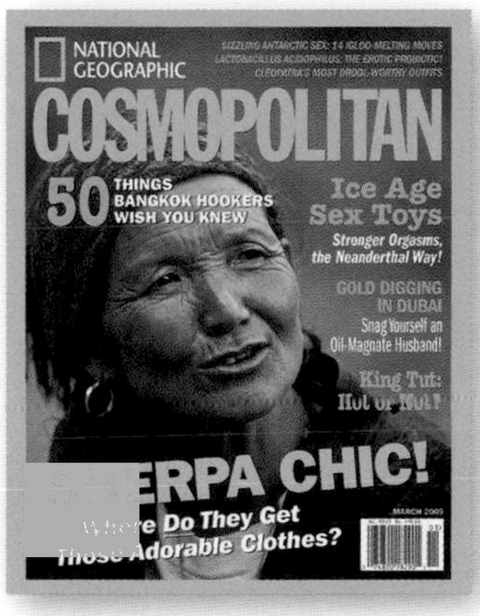

COSMOPOLITAN

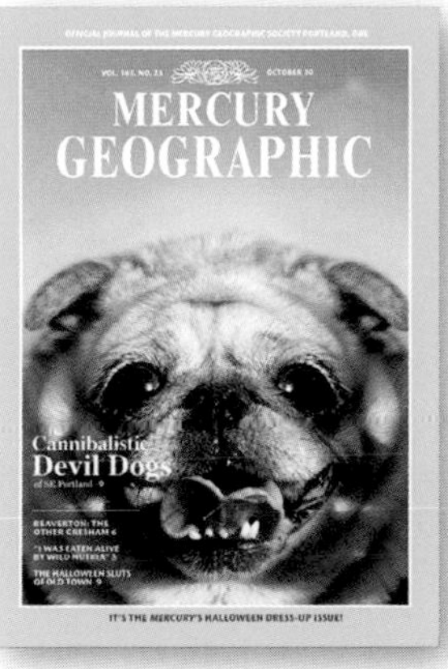

THE *PORTLAND MERCURY*

ANDREW HEARST FOR *VANITY FAIR*, 2009

MUMMIES

Wrapped in mystery

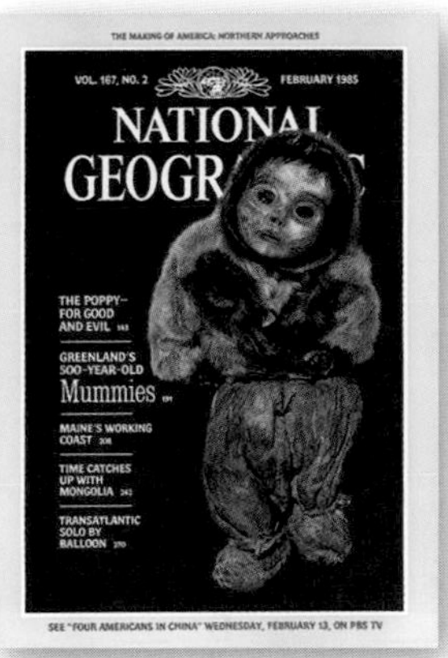

FEBRUARY 1985

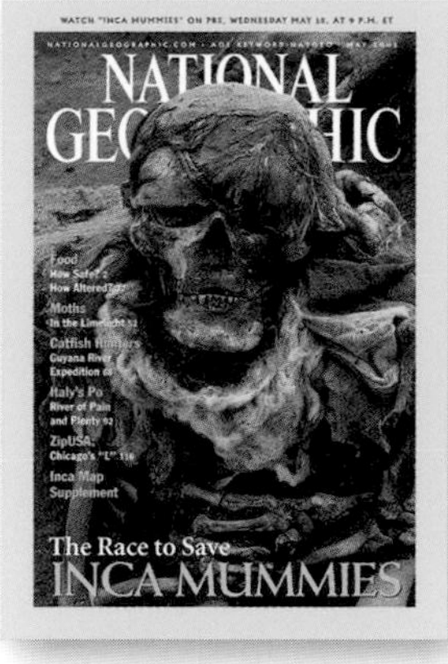

MAY 2002

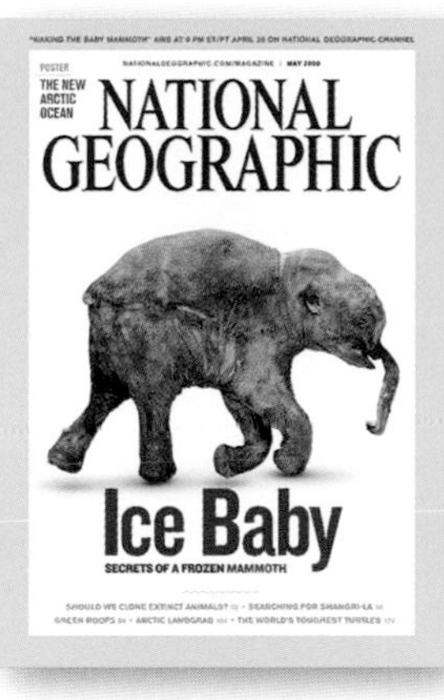

MAY 2009

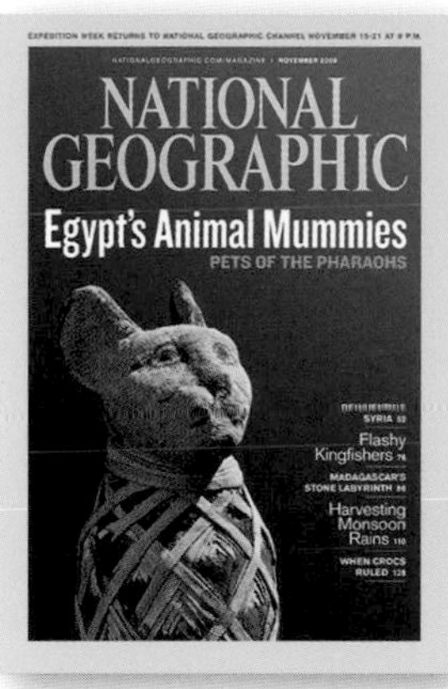

NOVEMBER 2009

FORENSIC RECONSTRUCTIONS

Looking into the faces of the past

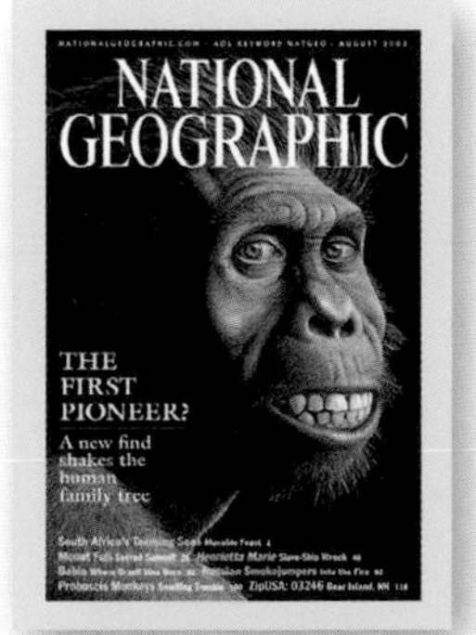

AUGUST 2002

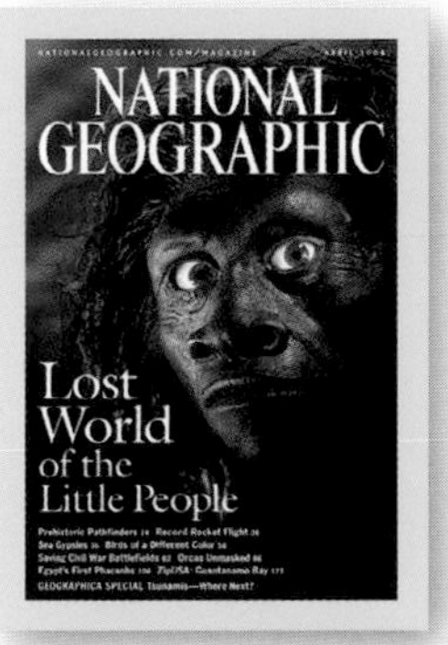

APRIL 2005

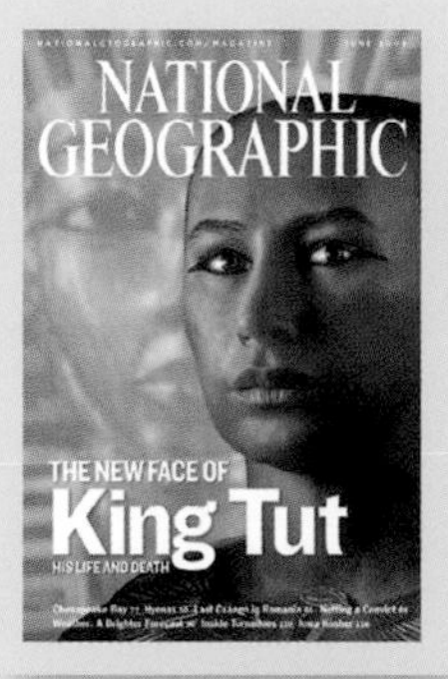

JUNE 2005

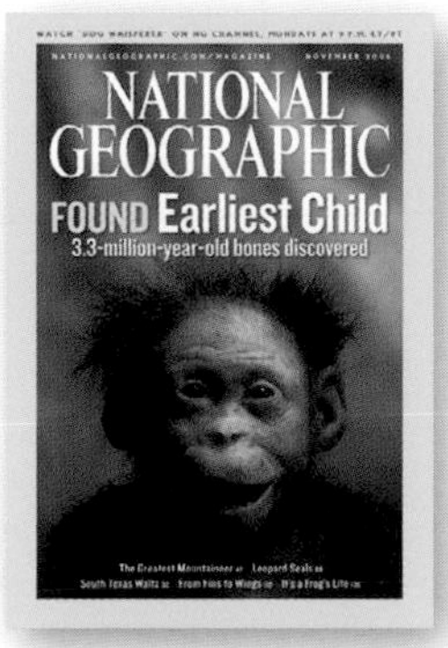

NOVEMBER 2006

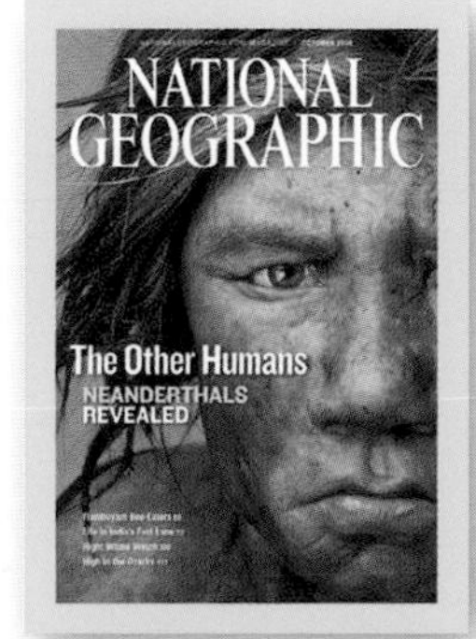

OCTOBER 2008

COVERING THE WORLD

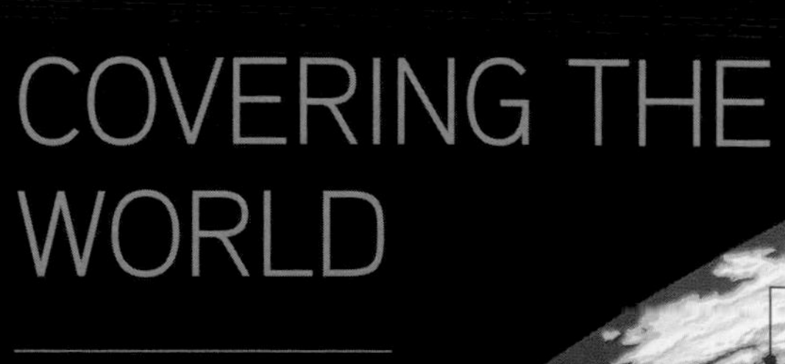

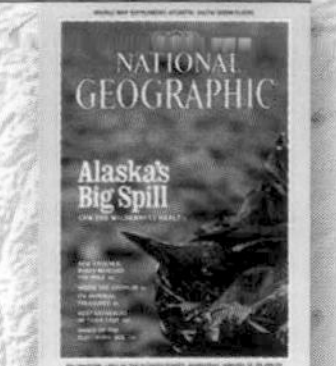

JANUARY 1990

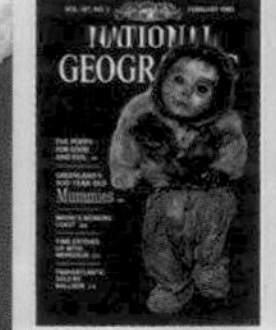

FEBRUARY 1985

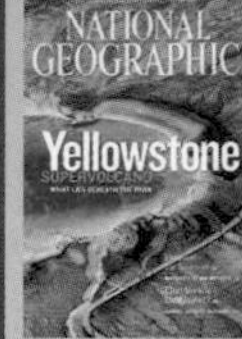

AUGUST 2009

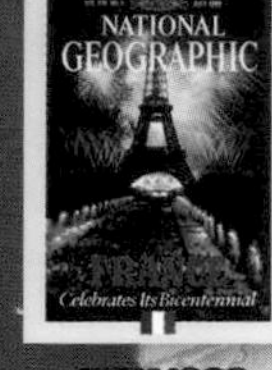

JULY 1989

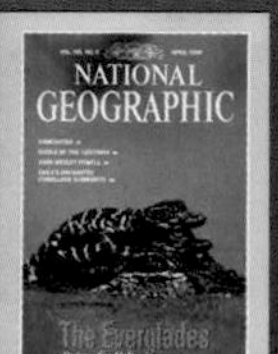

DECEMBER 1985

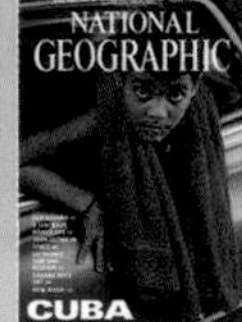

APRIL 1994

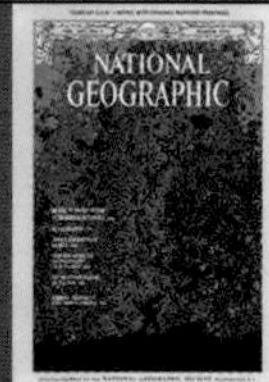

MARCH 1975

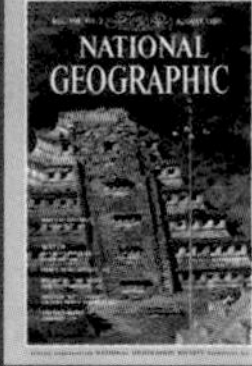

AUGUST 1980

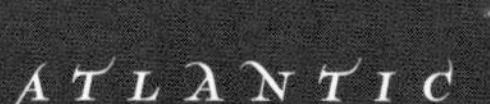

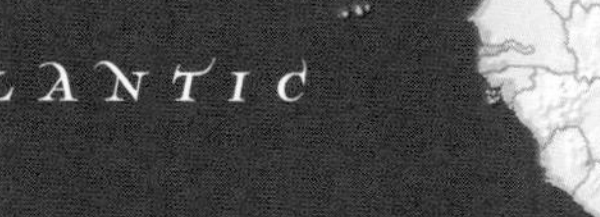

JUNE 1999

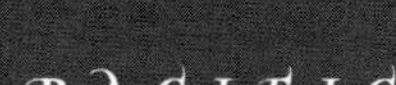

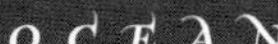

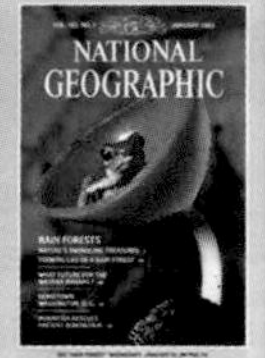

JANUARY 1983

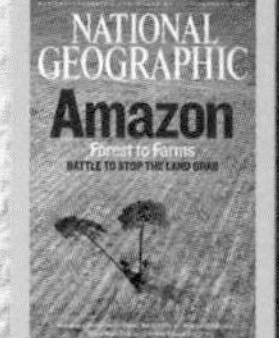

JANUARY 2007

OCTOBER 1983

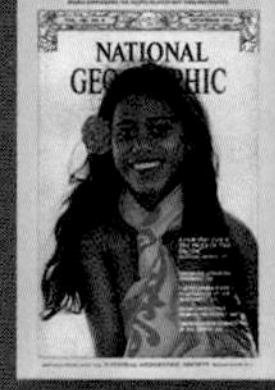

DECEMBER 1974

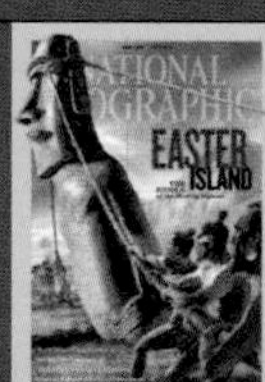

JULY 2012

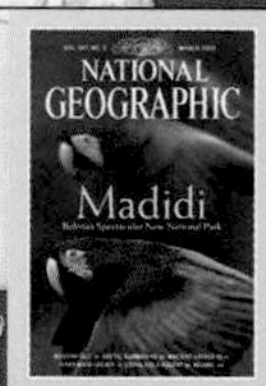

MARCH 2000

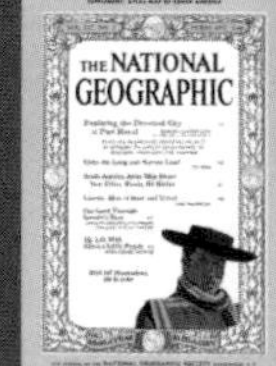

FEBRUARY 1960

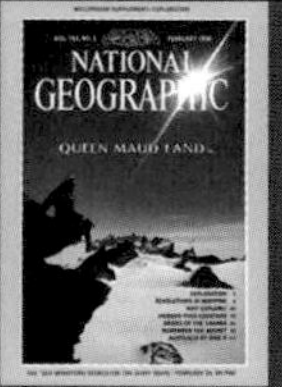

FEBRUARY 1998

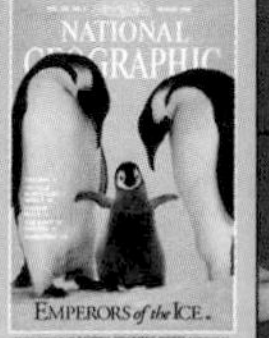

MARCH 1996

National Geographic cover images have been shot on every continent, across the oceans, and even in space. While it would be impossible to plot every single cover on one map, this shows the wide range of the photography.

OCEAN

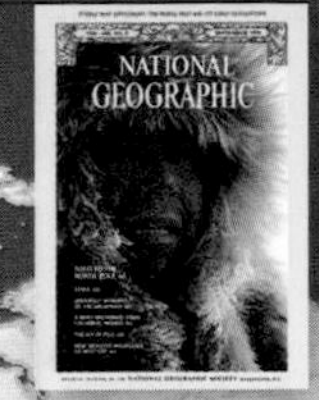

SEPTEMBER 1978

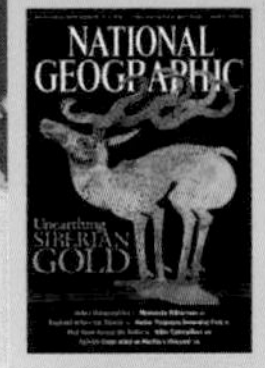

JUNE 2003

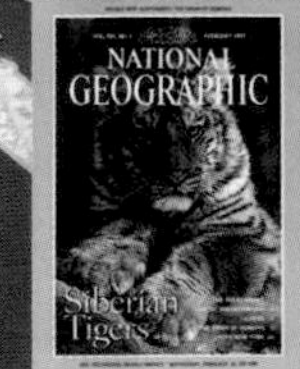

FEBRUARY 1997

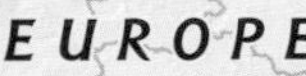

ASIA

JUNE 1985

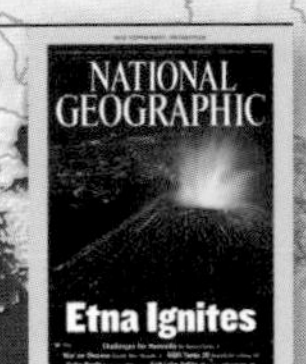

FEBRUARY 2002

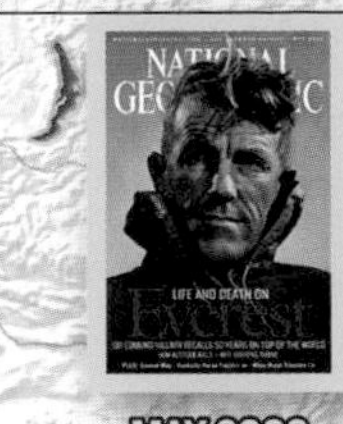

MAY 2003

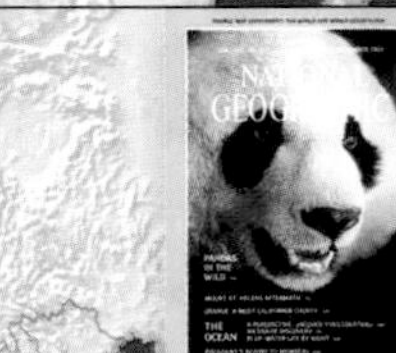
DECEMBER 1981

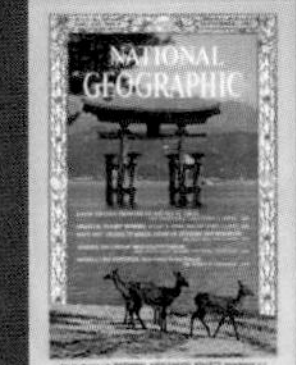

SEPTEMBER 1967

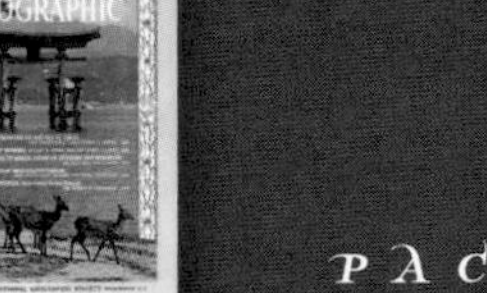

MARCH 1977

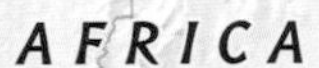

OCEAN

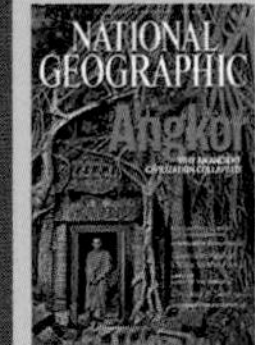

JULY 2009

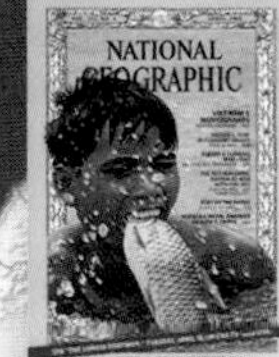

APRIL 1968

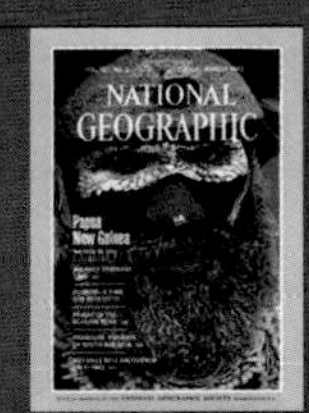

AUGUST 1982

FEBRUARY 1969

INDIAN OCEAN

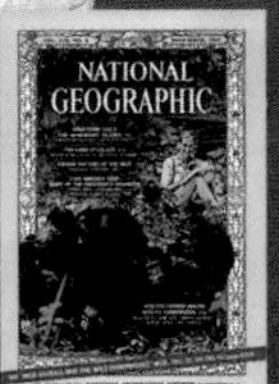

DECEMBER 1965

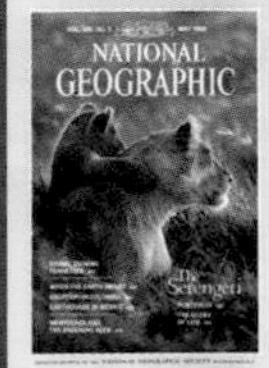

MAY 1986

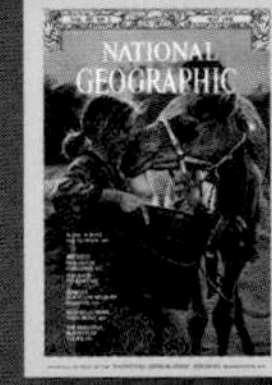

MAY 1978

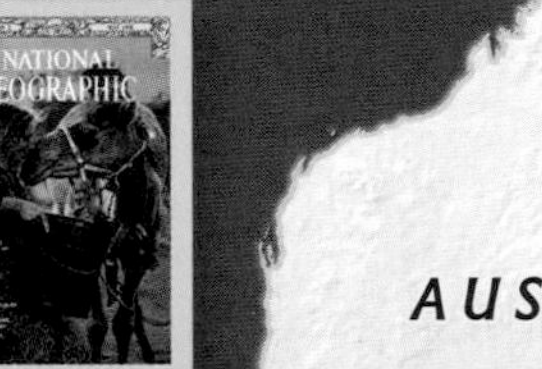

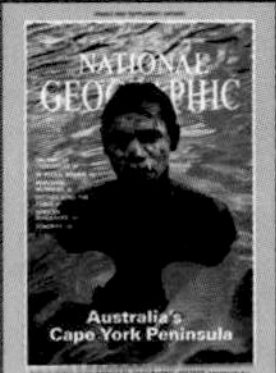

JUNE 1996

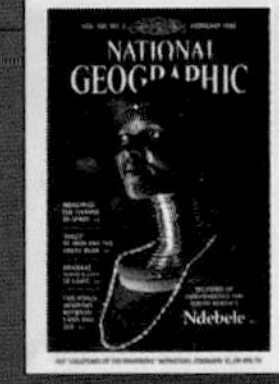

FEBRUARY 1986

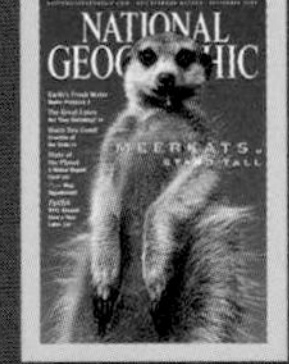

SEPTEMBER 2002

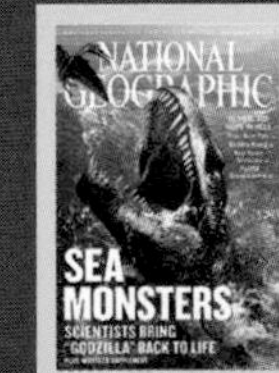

DECEMBER 2005

ANTARCTICA

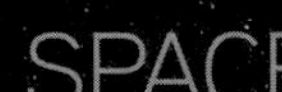

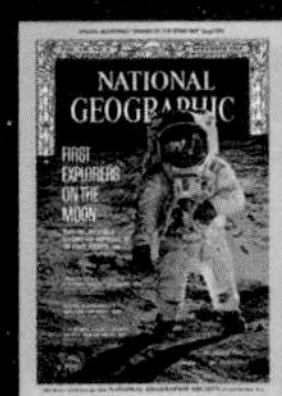

DECEMBER 1969

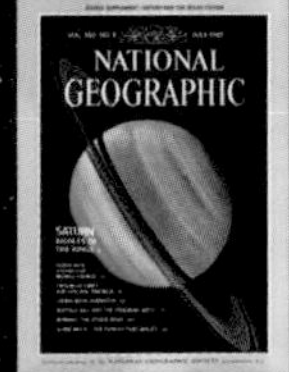

JULY 1981

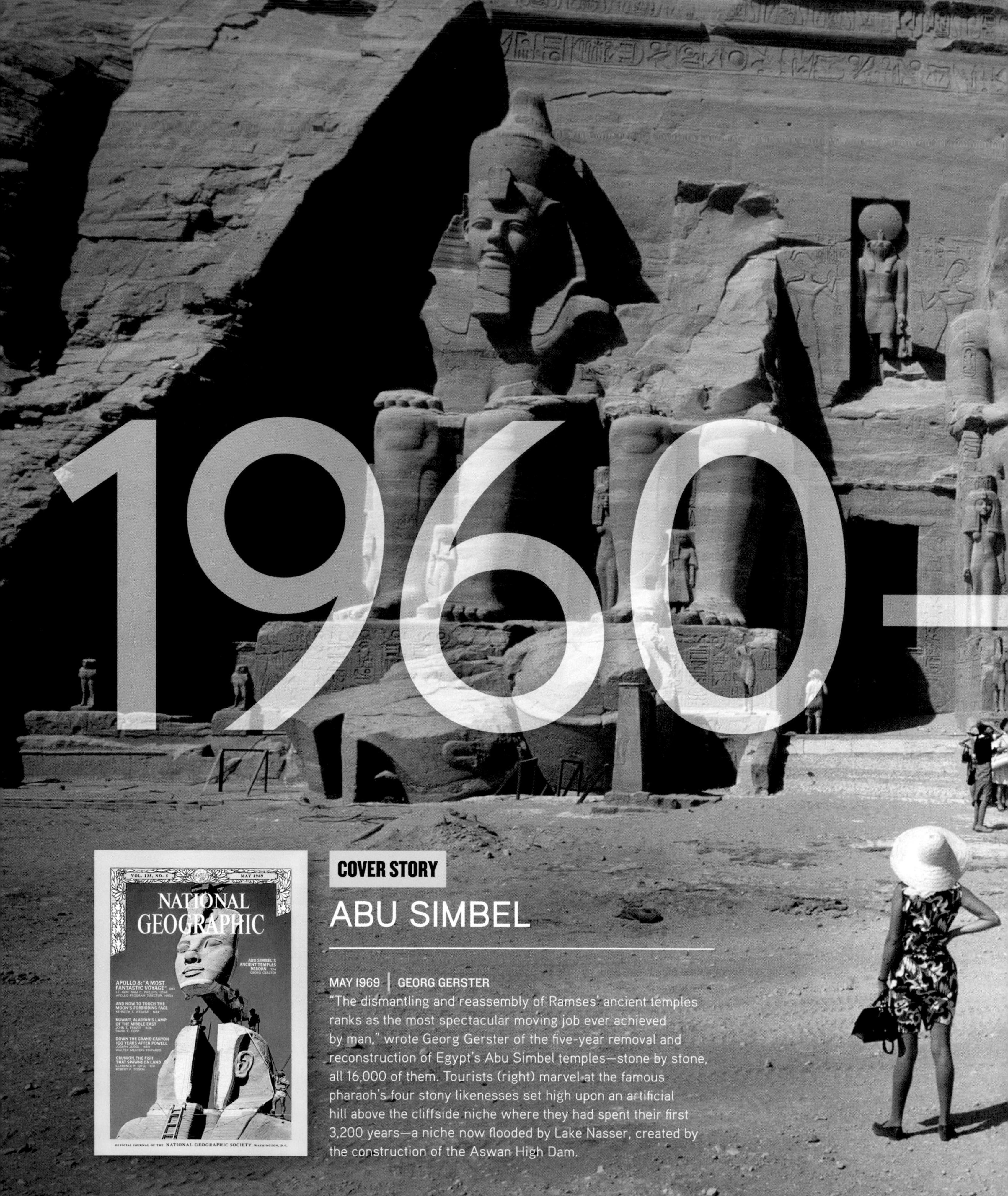

1960–

COVER STORY

ABU SIMBEL

MAY 1969 | GEORG GERSTER

"The dismantling and reassembly of Ramses' ancient temples ranks as the most spectacular moving job ever achieved by man," wrote Georg Gerster of the five-year removal and reconstruction of Egypt's Abu Simbel temples—stone by stone, all 16,000 of them. Tourists (right) marvel at the famous pharaoh's four stony likenesses set high upon an artificial hill above the cliffside niche where they had spent their first 3,200 years—a niche now flooded by Lake Nasser, created by the construction of the Aswan High Dam.

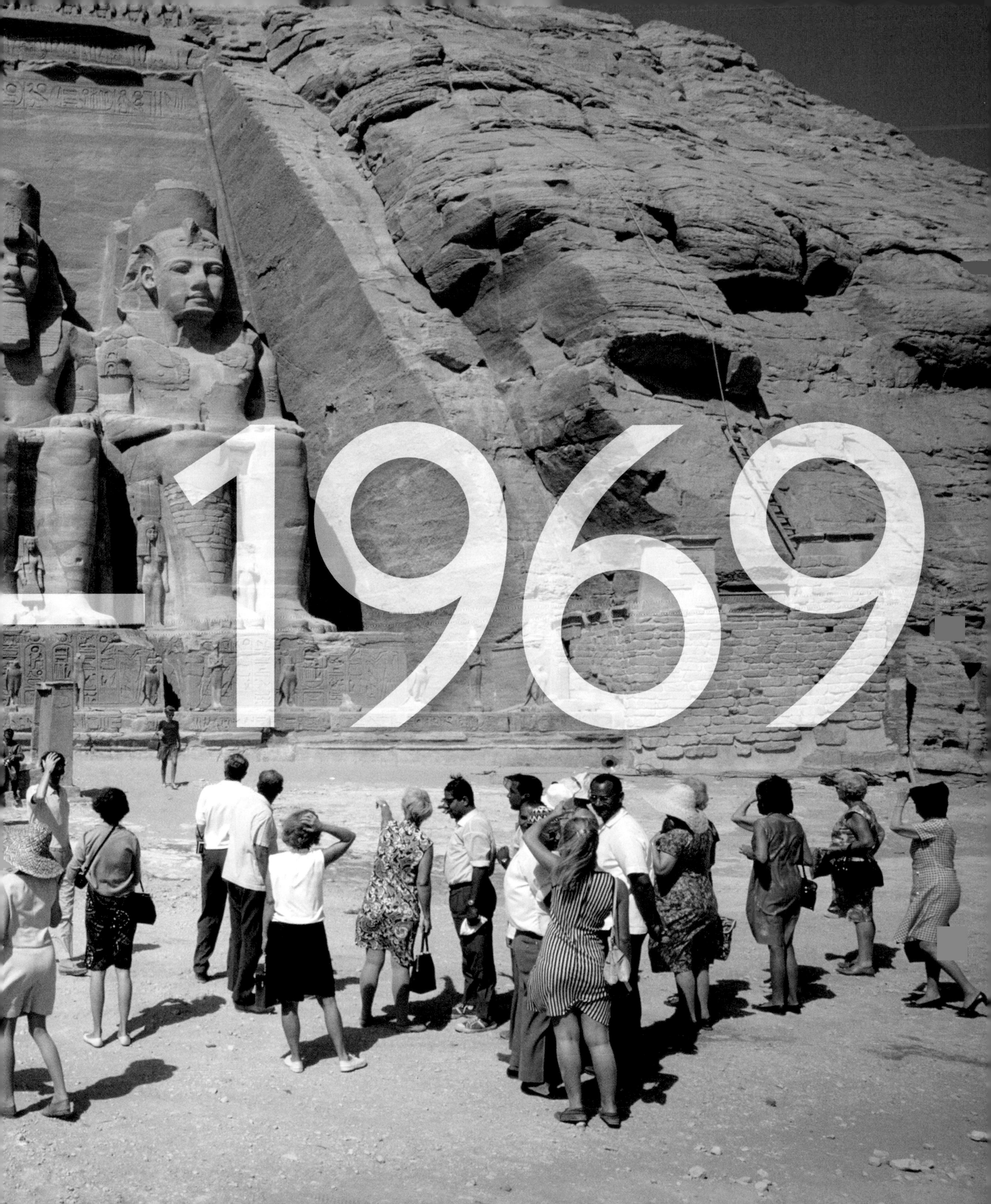
1969

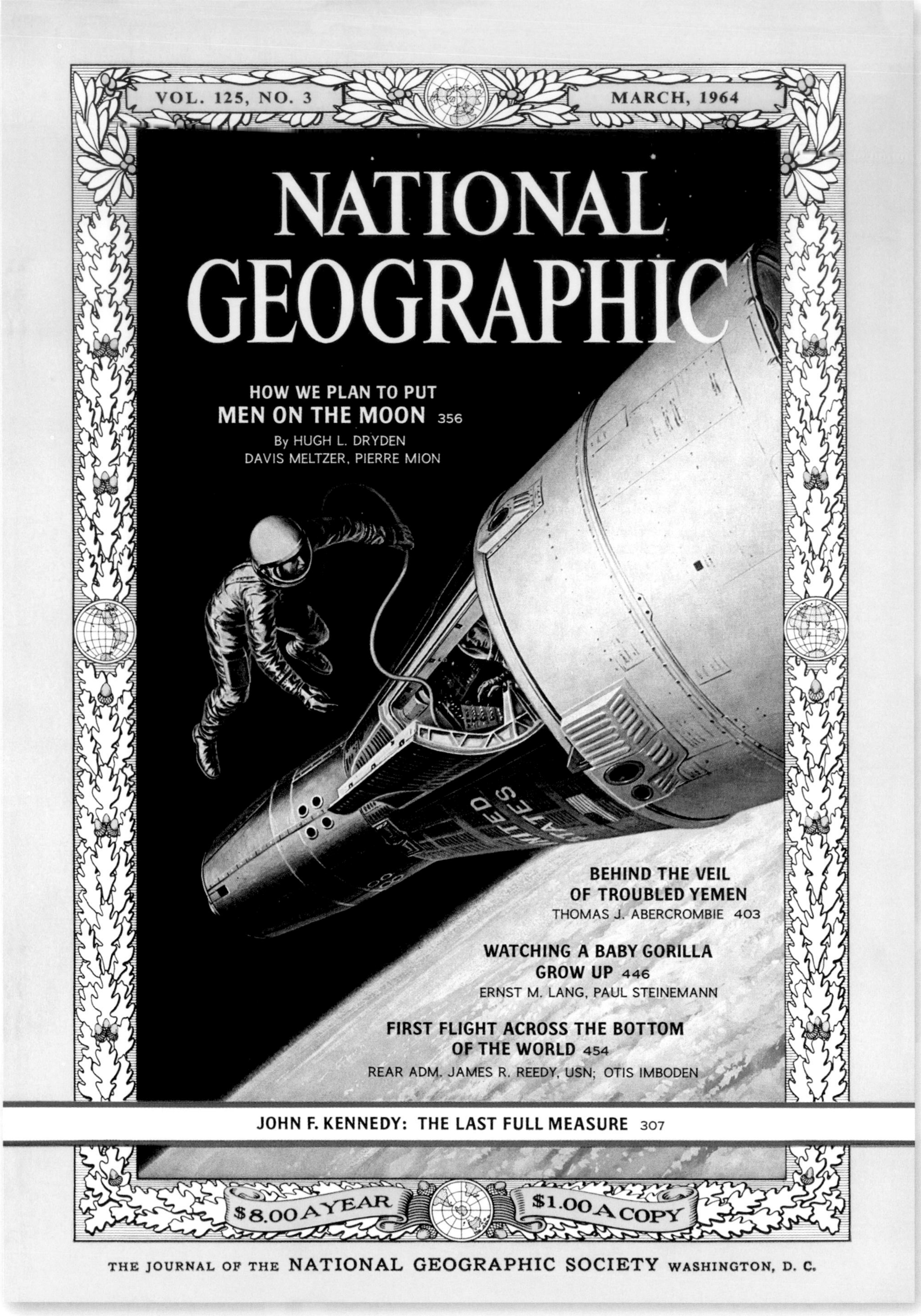

VOL. 125, NO. 3

MARCH, 1964

NATIONAL GEOGRAPHIC

HOW WE PLAN TO PUT
MEN ON THE MOON 356
By HUGH L. DRYDEN
DAVIS MELTZER, PIERRE MION

BEHIND THE VEIL OF TROUBLED YEMEN
THOMAS J. ABERCROMBIE 403

WATCHING A BABY GORILLA GROW UP 446
ERNST M. LANG, PAUL STEINEMANN

FIRST FLIGHT ACROSS THE BOTTOM OF THE WORLD 454
REAR ADM. JAMES R. REEDY, USN; OTIS IMBODEN

JOHN F. KENNEDY: THE LAST FULL MEASURE 307

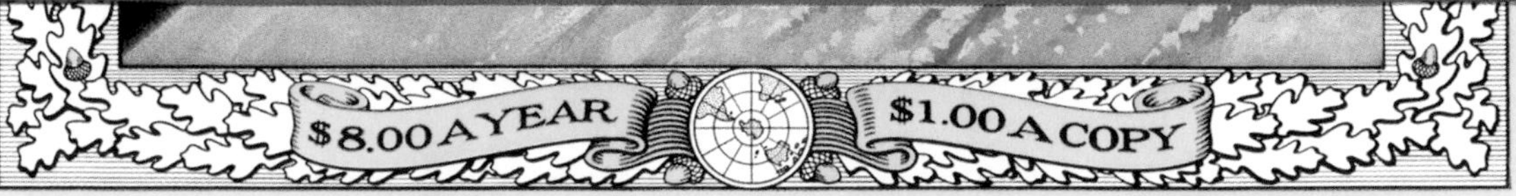

$8.00 A YEAR

$1.00 A COPY

THE JOURNAL OF THE NATIONAL GEOGRAPHIC SOCIETY WASHINGTON, D. C.

MARCH 1964 | DAVIS MELTZER A tethered Gemini astronaut ventures into space, one stage in the reach for the moon.

THE WORLD IN THE 1960S

"His life was such—the radiance he shed—that if we live to be a hundred, we will remember how he graced this earth, and how he left it."

—Melville Bell Grosvenor, from "John F. Kennedy: The Last Full Measure"

HE VOWED TO HIS FELLOW AMERICANS that he would put a man on the moon before the end of the decade. Yet when people, glued to their televisions, watched that boot touch the lunar surface, a flame was flickering on John F. Kennedy's grave.

Triumph and tragedy marked the polarizing 1960s. It was an era of aspiration—the Peace Corps, Martin Luther King, Jr.'s "I Have a Dream" speech, the Civil Rights Act, and the Great Society as well as the space program—but also one of disillusionment. It saw the Berlin Wall go up in 1961 and Soviet tanks crush the Prague Spring in 1968, the same year that Robert F. Kennedy and Dr. King were assassinated. It witnessed the decolonization of Africa as 32 countries gained their independence, most of them facing an uncertain future. It gave rise to the 1967 Six Day War, which remade the map of the Middle East. And it nearly turned the Cold War radioactive during the 13 days in 1962 called the Cuban missile crisis.

Growing American involvement in Vietnam, however, proved to be the most divisive issue of the decade. What started with a handful of advisers had by 1965 become a full-scale U.S. military engagement. Public support decreased as body counts increased. By the time Richard Nixon reached the White House it had cost 30,000 American lives.

FACTS & FIGURES THE 1960s

- **27** covers in Asia
- **25** covers in the United States
- **14** covers in Europe
- **11** covers in Africa
- **7** covers in Australasia and Oceania
- **6** covers in South America
- **6** covers underwater
- **4** covers in space

AROUND THE WORLD

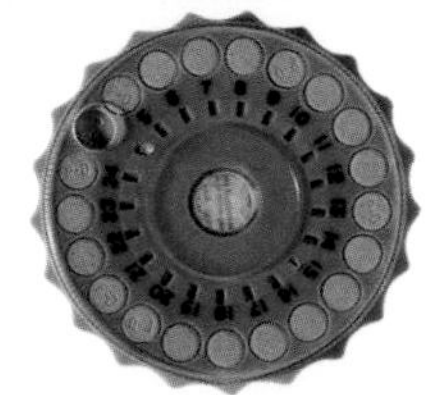

THE PILL 1960
After many decades, an oral contraceptive is approved for use in the United States.

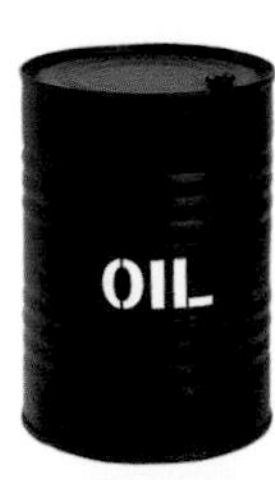

OPEC 1960
The Organization of Petroleum Exporting Countries is created in Baghdad by Iraq, Kuwait, Iran, Saudi Arabia, and Venezuela.

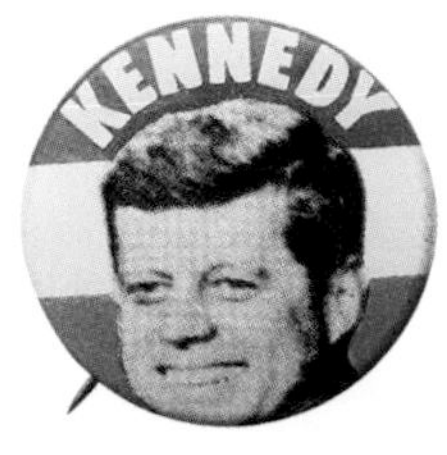

JFK 1960
At 43, John F. Kennedy becomes the youngest person ever elected President, and the first Roman Catholic.

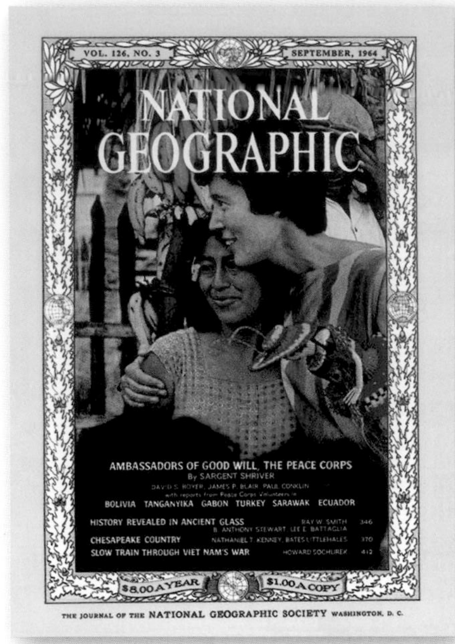

SEPTEMBER 1964 | DAVID S. BOYER

▲ **MISSION'S END** Peace Corps volunteer Rhoda Brooks parts from the Ecuadorian villagers she served for two years.

The growing discord was exacerbated by the "generation gap." By the mid-1960s fully half of Americans were under the age of 25. These baby boomers had not been seared by the Great Depression and World War II. They grew up watching television—not only *The Flintstones* and *The Jetsons* but also news footage of civil rights struggles, urban riots, and student protests as well as of Vietnam. Often their opinions differed from those of their parents.

Thus was born the "counterculture," which rejected the crew cuts and gray flannel suits, the beehives and pillbox hats of an older generation in favor of Afros, sideburns, miniskirts, and tie-dye. America's youth turned on, tuned in, dropped out, and dodged the draft. Hippies wore flowers in their hair. The Beatles, the Rolling Stones, Bob Dylan, and Jimi Hendrix drowned out Sinatra, bebop, and doo-wop. Psychedelic drugs permeated the 1967 Summer of Love in San Francisco, the 1969 Woodstock Festival in upstate New York, the movies, the art scene, the music scene, the meditation scene, the "free love" scene—it was simply the Swinging Sixties.

Precious little of America's counterculture could be found in the pages of *National Geographic.* You went to *Life* magazine, then in its heyday, for spot news and photographs that mirrored the turbulent times. You opened the *Geographic* to escape. There were indeed many valuable articles in those pages—profiles of faraway countries, reports on archaeological projects, pictures of exotic animals and plants, adventures in undersea exploration, even peeks behind the Iron Curtain or tantalizing glimpses of Red China—but aside from Vietnam coverage, politically the magazine played it safe. It remained patriotic and a tad pious: Presidents Kennedy, Johnson, and Nixon had all appeared in it, as had every branch of the armed forces; December often featured an article on the Holy Land. Moreover, its older editors, suspicious of the nascent environmental movement, preferred popular fare such as national parks and birds. The Society's membership—overwhelmingly white and

AROUND THE WORLD

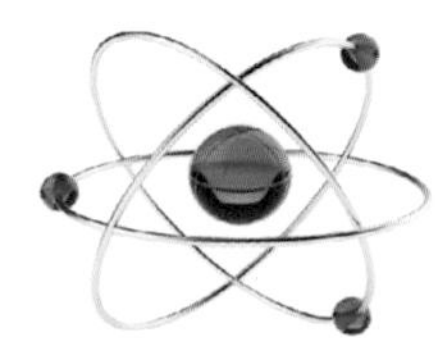

GIMME SHELTER 1961
A nationwide network of fallout shelters capable of holding millions of people is planned.

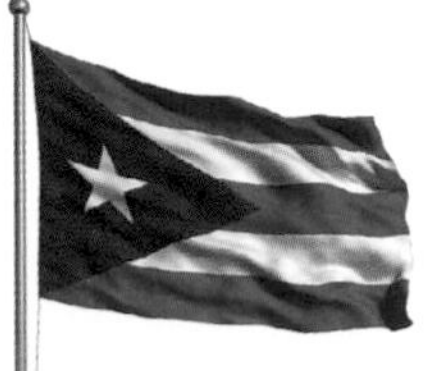

CUBA 1962
The 1962 Cuban missile crisis brings the world to the brink of nuclear war.

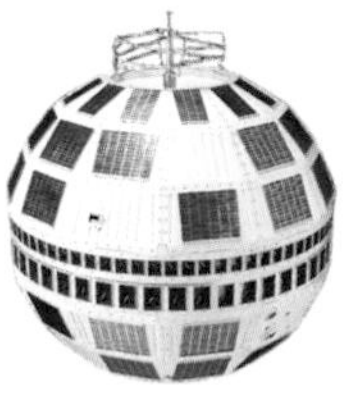

TELSTAR 1962
Telstar becomes the first communications satellite to relay telephone calls and television pictures.

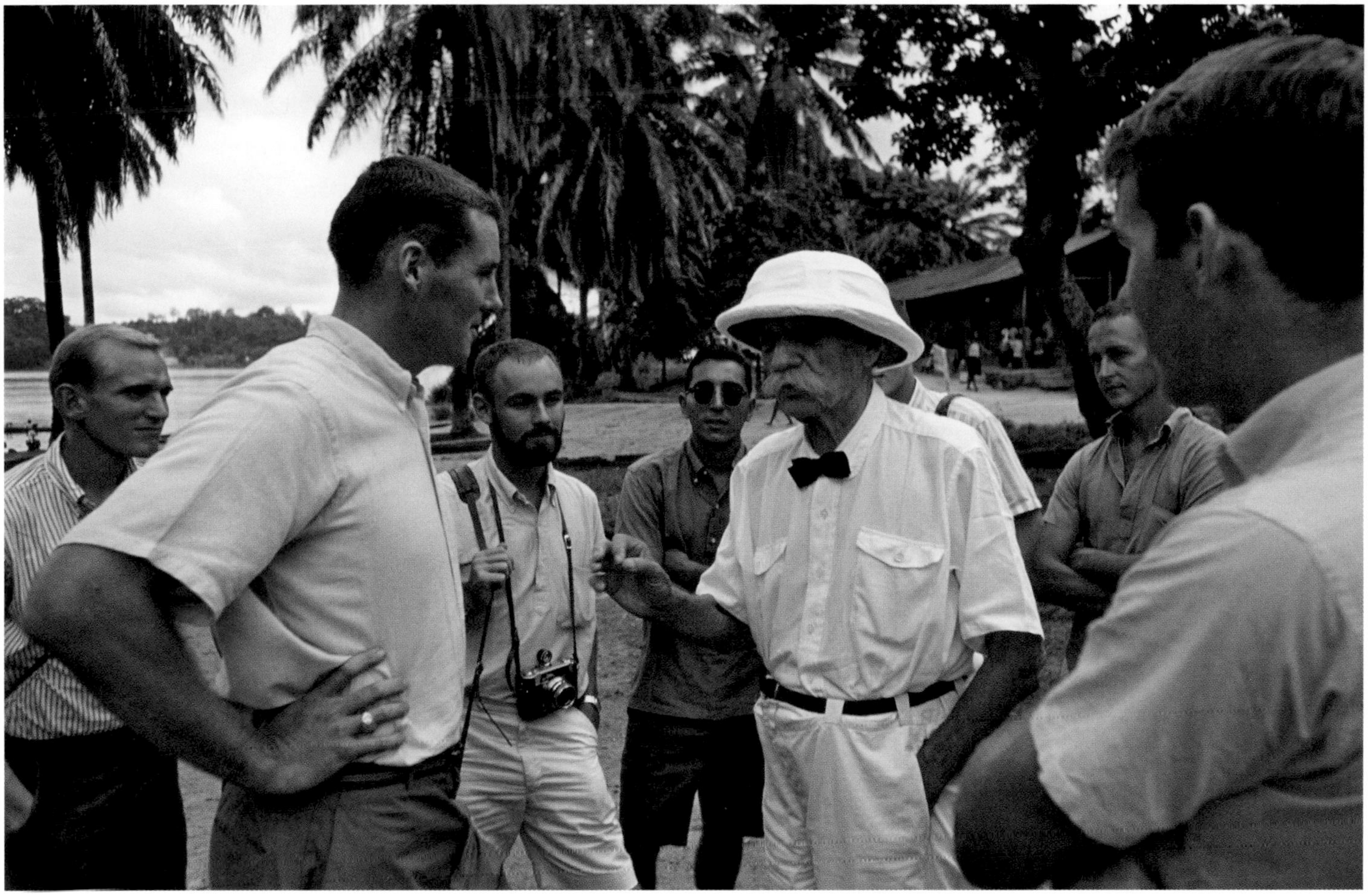

1963 | JAMES P. BLAIR Peace Corps volunteers visit Dr. Albert Schweitzer at his jungle hospital in Gabon.

affluent—lay on the older side of the generation gap. Those conventionally minded readers liked what they saw in their monthly magazine; membership tripled in the 1960s and renewal rates remained sky-high.

The *Geographic* remained aspirational as well as inspirational; it gravitated toward triumph, not tragedy. It may have begun the decade with a cover photograph of a rice farmer in war-torn Laos, but it ended it with an image of a man on the moon. ■

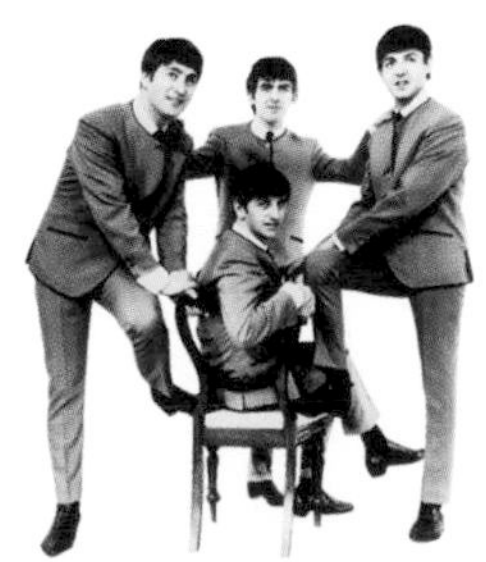

BEATLEMANIA 1964
The Fab Four spearhead the British Invasion of America's rock-and-roll music scene.

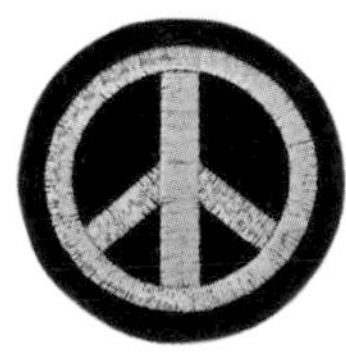

PEACE SIGN 1967
By the Summer of Love, it's everywhere, a decade after it originated in England.

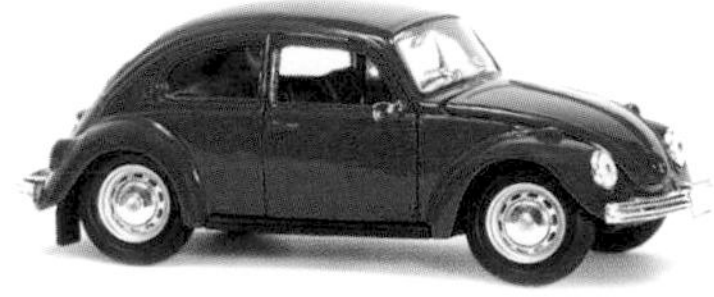

VW BUG 1968
The Love Bug confirms that the Volkswagen Beetle is among America's favorite cars.

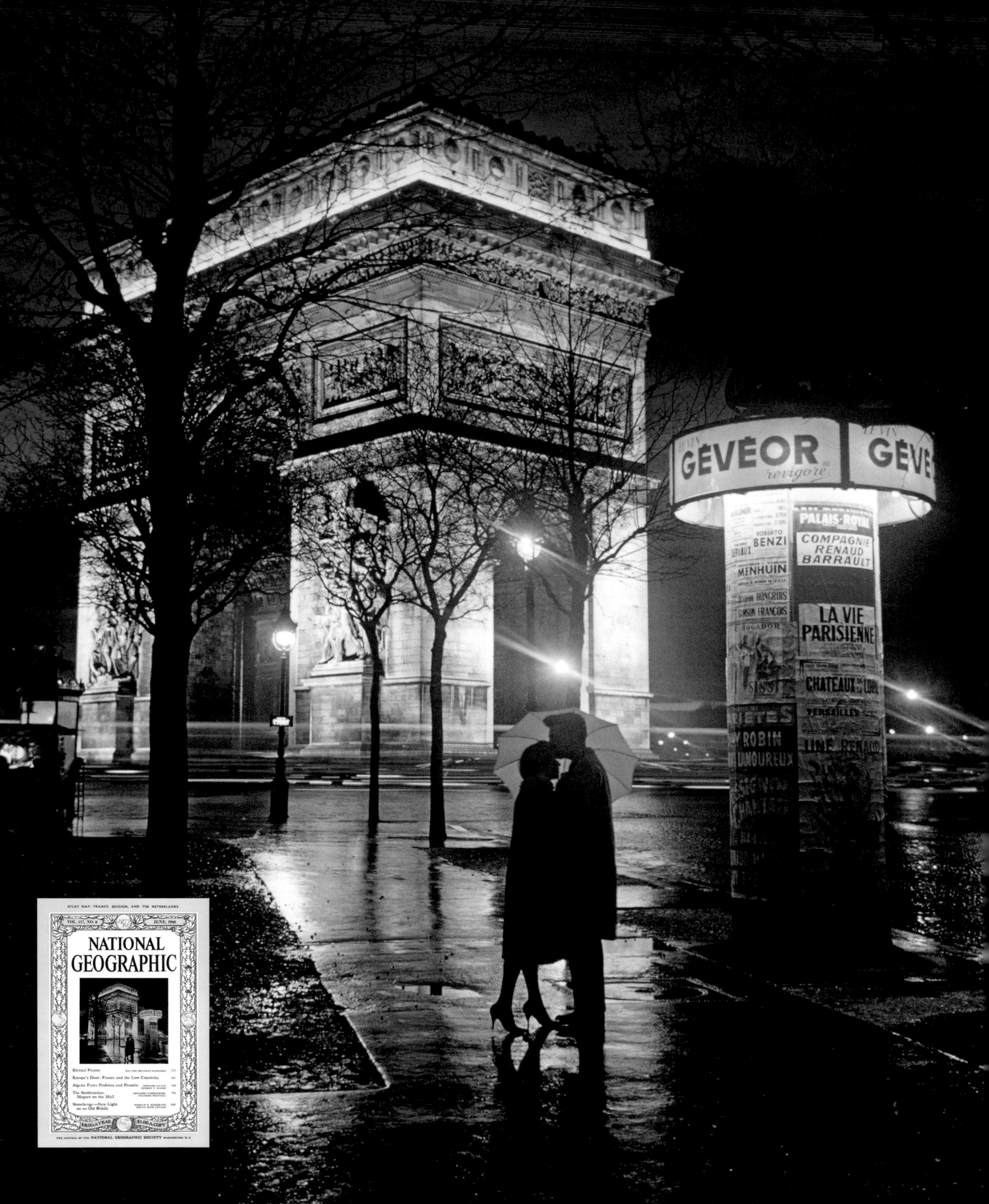

GÉVÉOR
revigore
PALAIS-ROYAL
COMPAGNIE
RENAUD
BARRAULT
ROBERTO
BENZI
MENHUIN
LA VIE
PARISIENNE
VERSAILLES
ROBIN
ATLAS MAP: FRANCE, BELGIUM, AND THE NETHERLANDS
VOL. 117, NO. 6
JUNE, 1960
NATIONAL
GEOGRAPHIC
Eternal France
Europe's Door: France and the Low Countries
Algeria Faces Problem and Promise
The Smithsonian,
Magnet on the Mall
Stonehenge—New Light
on an Old Riddle
$8.00 A YEAR
$1.00 A COPY
THE JOURNAL OF THE NATIONAL GEOGRAPHIC SOCIETY WASHINGTON, D.C.

LOVE'S *TRIOMPHE*

LOVE CONQUERS ALL, THE picture suggests in its artfully arranged way: The couple embracing on the rain-slick Paris sidewalk, the conveniently close advertising kiosk, the yellow umbrella, even the streaks of passing taillights (two-horsepower Citroëns, one likes to think), betraying a tripod-mounted camera making a time exposure—all these elements take center stage, while in the background looms the floodlit Arc de Triomphe, enduring symbol of *la gloire,* the glory of France, its sculptured friezes recalling the victories of the French Revolution and Napoleonic Wars.

Staff photographer Tom Nebbia's image evokes the popular perception of Paris being the City of Love as well as of Light. When it appeared on the cover of the June 1960 *Geographic,* announcing an article on "Eternal France" written by his colleague Walter Edwards, it suggested that *l'amour,* at least, had triumphed over the nation's recent reversals.

Its former glory had indeed been badly tarnished. Recently France had lost another war and also a colony in Indochina. It was humiliated during the 1956 Suez Crisis. And it was presently fighting an insurrection in Algeria, a struggle that would kill upward of a million people—a third war that it was destined to lose.

Yet love endured. We'd always have Paris. And even if that quintessentially French art, gastronomy, was reeling before the onslaught of fast food—well, "drive-in restaurants" might sell cheeseburgers, but as Edwards observed, "one may still wash them down with champagne."

"'An article on all of France?' But it is impossible! We have more than 300 different kinds of cheese alone!"

—painter Jean Lurcat,
as quoted by Walter Edwards in "Eternal France"

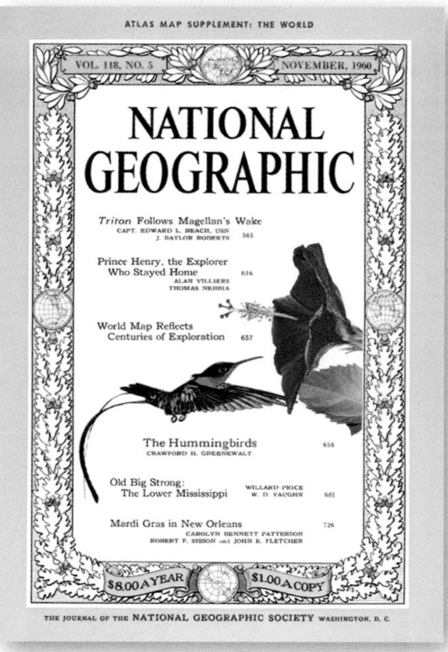
ATLAS MAP SUPPLEMENT: THE WORLD

VOL. 118, NO. 5 — NOVEMBER, 1960

NATIONAL GEOGRAPHIC

Triton Follows Magellan's Wake — CAPT. EDWARD L. BEACH, USN; J. BAYLOR ROBERTS — 585

Prince Henry, the Explorer Who Stayed Home — ALAN VILLIERS; THOMAS NEBBIA — 616

World Map Reflects Centuries of Exploration — 657

The Hummingbirds — CRAWFORD H. GREENEWALT — 658

Old Big Strong: The Lower Mississippi — WILLARD PRICE; W. D. VAUGHN — 681

Mardi Gras in New Orleans — CAROLYN BENNETT PATTERSON; ROBERT F. SISSON and JOHN E. FLETCHER — 726

$8.00 A YEAR — $1.00 A COPY

THE JOURNAL OF THE NATIONAL GEOGRAPHIC SOCIETY WASHINGTON, D. C.

NOVEMBER | CRAWFORD H. GREENEWALT

▲ **SWEET NECTAR** This Jamaican hummingbird sampling hibiscus nectar is one of numerous avian portraits made by businessman Crawford Greenewalt, whose passion was photographing "hummers."

"*The French, with uncharacteristic lack of imagination, say* oiseau-mouche, *or fly-sized bird. The Spanish and Portuguese do a bit better with, respectively,* pica flor—*peck the flower—and* beija flor—*kiss the flower.*"

—Crawford H. Greenewalt
from "The Hummingbirds"

◀ **JUNE** | **THOMAS NEBBIA** The City of Light is also the City of Love the world over.

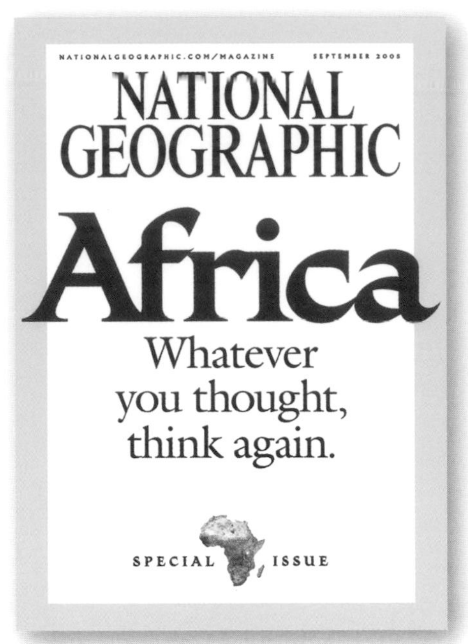

SEPTEMBER 2005 | WORLDSAT INTERNATIONAL, INC.

AFRICA'S WARNING TO THE WORLD ▶

FREEDOM. POTENTIAL. POSSIBILITY. The September 1960 *National Geographic*—with four articles profiling Africa from Cairo to Cape Town and from Dakar to Mombasa—teems with such hopeful words. Nineteen newly independent nations graced its supplement map; more nations would join that roster in the coming years. Even if, as this issue patronizingly put it, Europeans and Americans would soon "teach her the skills she must have for survival."

Only the prospects for African wildlife looked dim. East Africa was seen as the last great game refuge on the continent, but there was no mention whatsoever of two countries appearing on the map: Gabon and Bechuanaland—today's Botswana.

Exactly 45 years later, when the September 2005 Special Issue on Africa was released, those two nations harbored some of the last pristine wilderness areas on a continent otherwise straining under the burden of the human footprint. Here was an Africa whose dreams were dashed long ago—by political malfeasance, widespread corruption, poverty, disease, war, and genocide. Here was a continent whose environmental degradation—widespread soil erosion, illegal logging, eradication of wildlife by poachers and bush-meat hunters—was strongly linked to those conflicts and humanitarian disasters.

Africa's struggle to balance human needs with the preservation of the environment was the issue's message. Yet there were also hopeful signs that Africans themselves were learning to cope with their problems, promoting local land-use reforms that promised a more sustainable approach to managing their natural resources—a lesson the rest of the world might heed.

2005 ▸▸▸▸ FAST FORWARD

AFRICAN NATIONS Forty-five years later, featuring only a small satellite image of Africa, emphasizing its natural features, the September 2005 issue is a dramatic break in the magazine's sequence of illustrated covers. Editor Chris Johns thought that no single photograph could sum up the continent. "Africa isn't just a place, it's a million places," he said.

◀ SEPTEMBER 1960 | W. D. VAUGHN, PETER TURNER Africa's cultural diversity on display

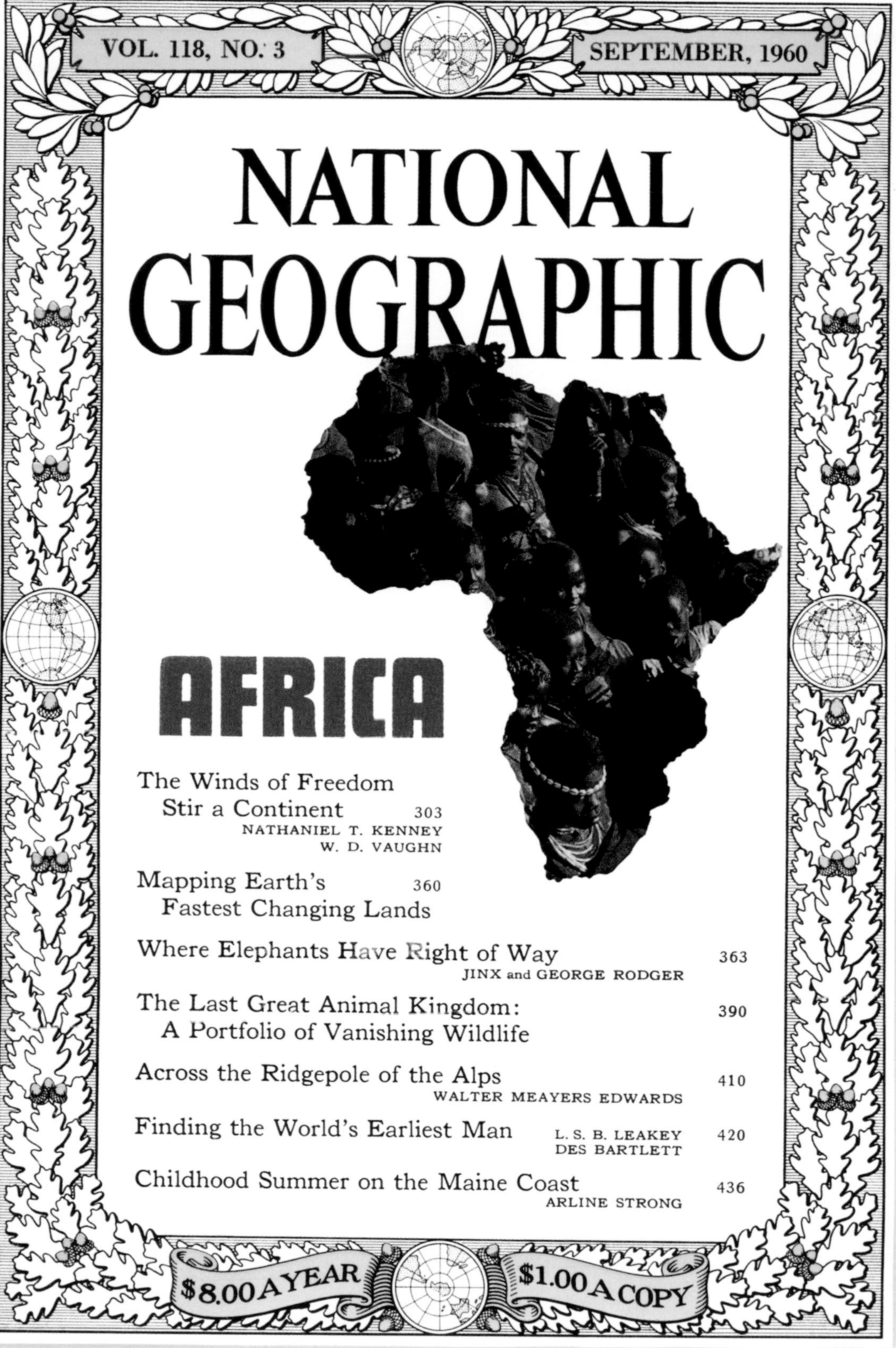

SEPTEMBER | GEORGE RODGER Women of Karamoja, Uganda, are crowned with cowrie shells.

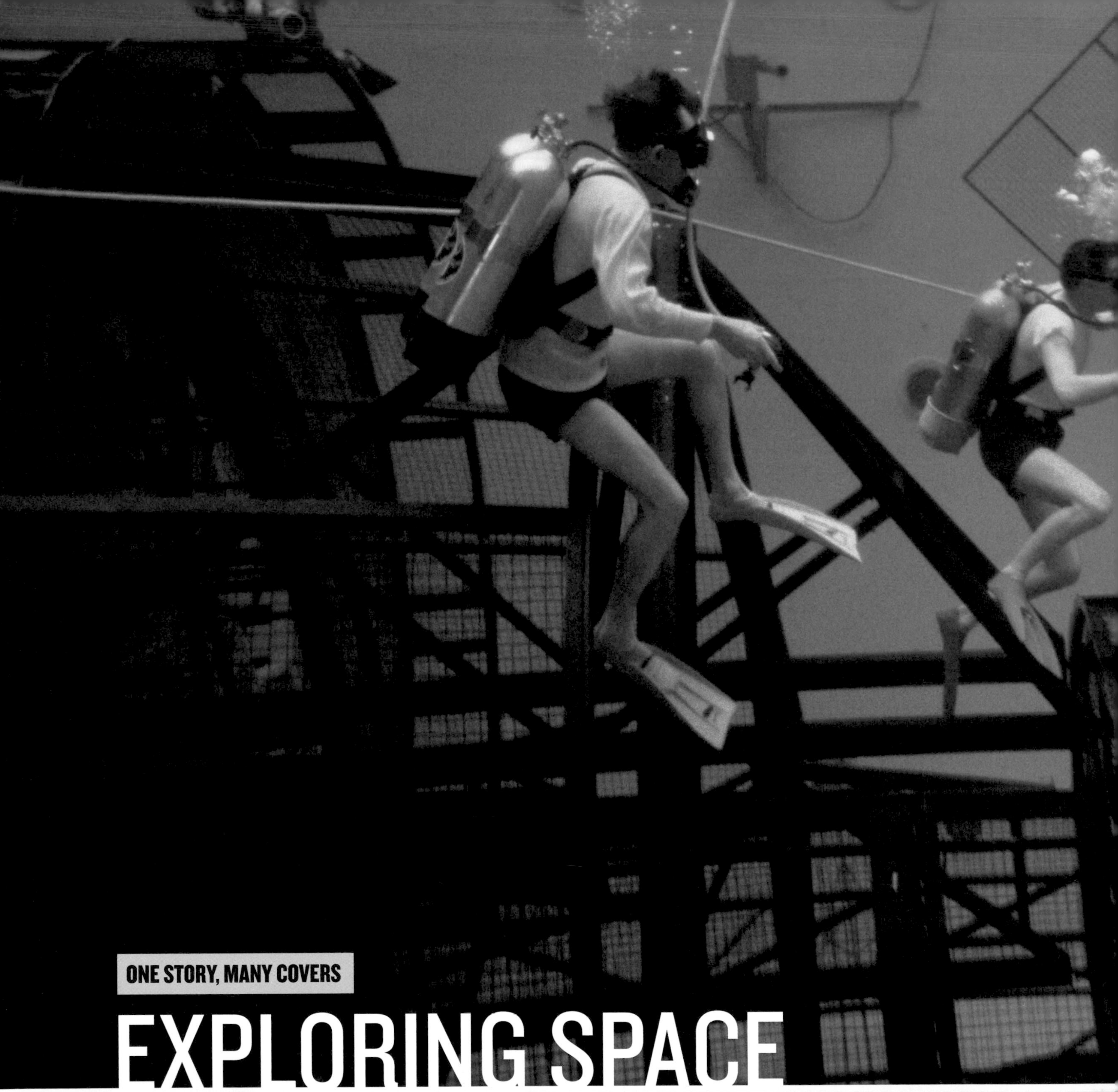

ONE STORY, MANY COVERS

EXPLORING SPACE

▲ JUNE 1973 | EMORY KRISTOF
Astronauts training for Skylab practice space walk maneuvers underwater—a good simulation of the weightlessness they will encounter in space.

FROM THE HEADY DAYS of Projects Mercury and Apollo to the exciting discoveries of far-flung solar systems, every step in humanity's most awe-inspiring adventure has been charted on the covers of the *Geographic*. Some depict spacecraft, others astronauts walking on the moon. Some show solar flares, others the red sands of Mars (and one of those in 3-D). Some gaze back at the face of our own planet, still others on the stupendous rings of Saturn or the birth of stars or distant galaxies—altogether 30 covers so far

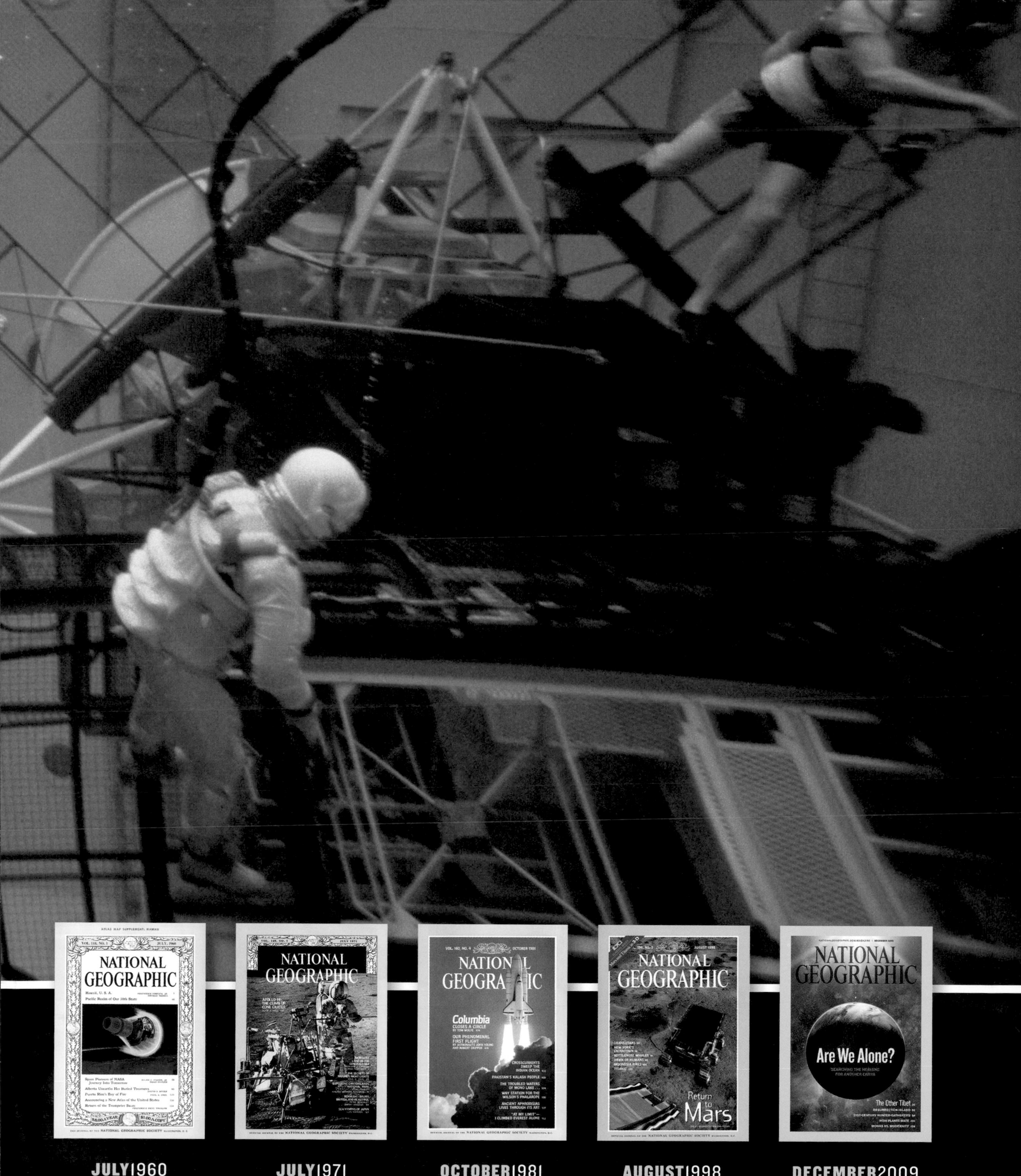

NATIONAL GEOGRAPHIC
JULY 1960
NATIONAL GEOGRAPHIC
JULY 1971
NATIONAL GEOGRAPHIC
Columbia
OCTOBER 1981
NATIONAL GEOGRAPHIC
Return to Mars
AUGUST 1998
NATIONAL GEOGRAPHIC
Are We Alone?
The Other Tibet
DECEMBER 2009

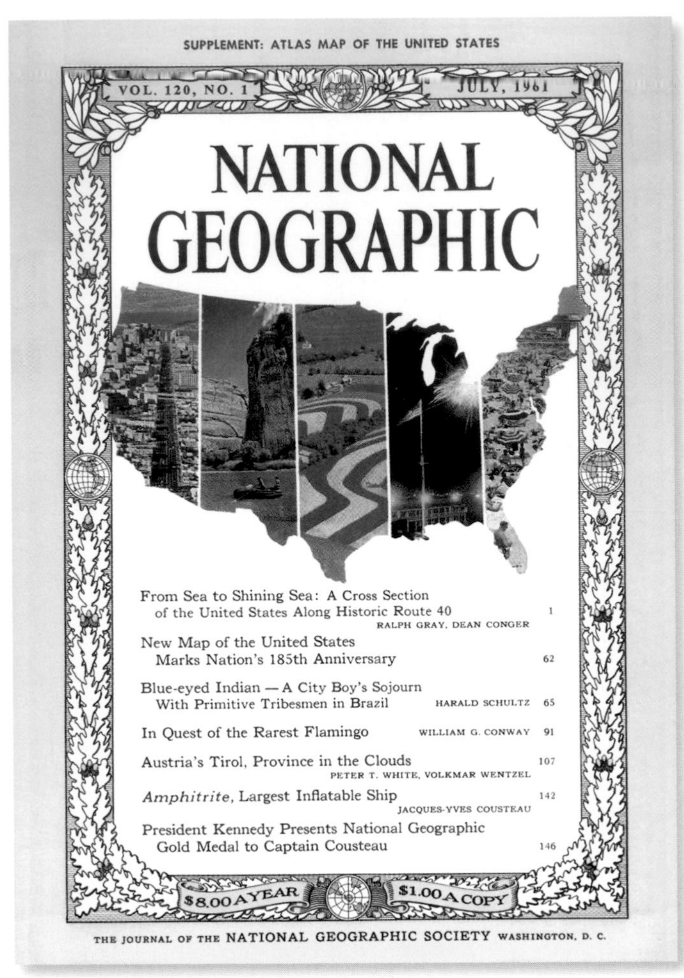

JULY | DEAN CONGER, B. ANTHONY STEWART, VOLKMAR WENTZEL

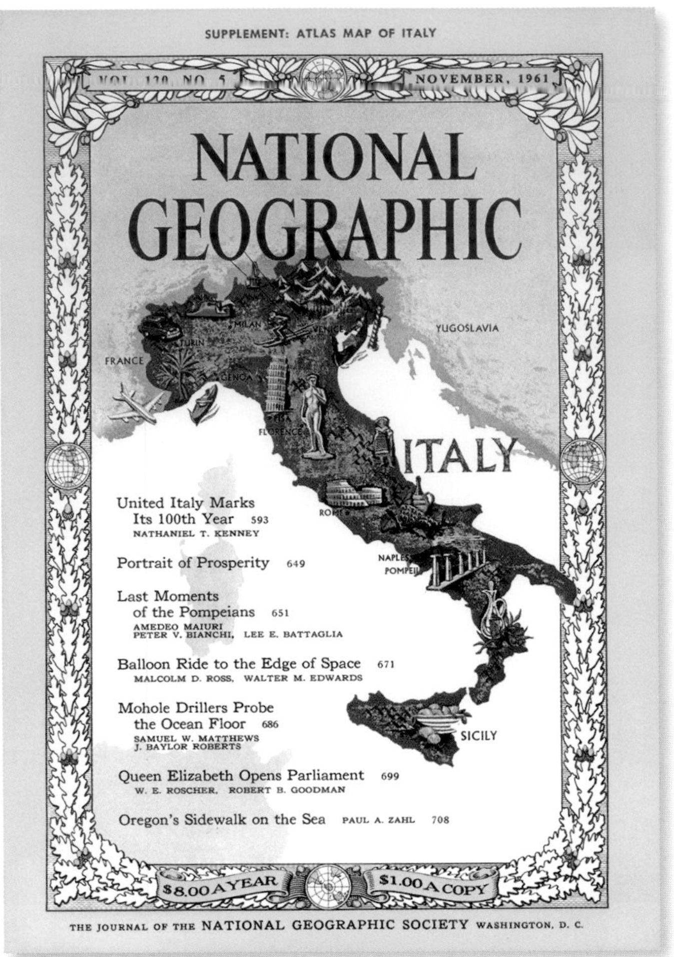

NOVEMBER | WILLIAM PALMSTROM, JOSEPH E. BARRETT

▲ **FROM SEA TO SHINING SEA** Historic Route 40, at the dawn of the interstate age, did indeed run a leisurely course "from sea to shining sea"—from Atlantic City, New Jersey, to San Francisco—traversing every kind of landscape pictured on the July cover. Author Ralph Gray and his family journeyed by station wagon from the crowded eastern seaboard, across the fertile farmlands of the Midwest, through the spectacular Rocky Mountains, to the Pacific coast, visiting curious places along the way.

▲ **ITALIAN ATTRACTIONS** "Italy swings like a Christmas stocking from the mantel of Europe," states the original caption to this cover—which to some eyes appears more like the place mat at your local Italian restaurant, festooned with every tourist attraction from the Colosseum to the Leaning Tower of Pisa.

> *"On the way we checked the tower in Pisa. It is still leaning. The people would not have it otherwise, for who would come to see an ordinary straight tower?"*
>
> —Nat Kenney
>
> *from "United Italy Marks Its 100th Year"*

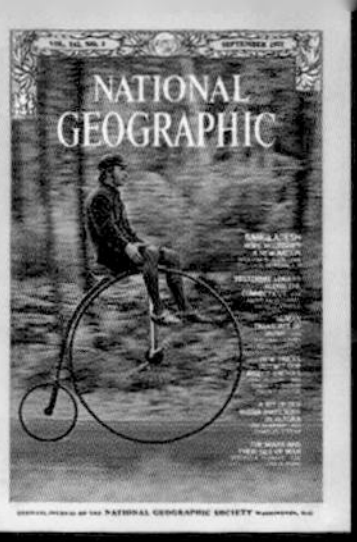

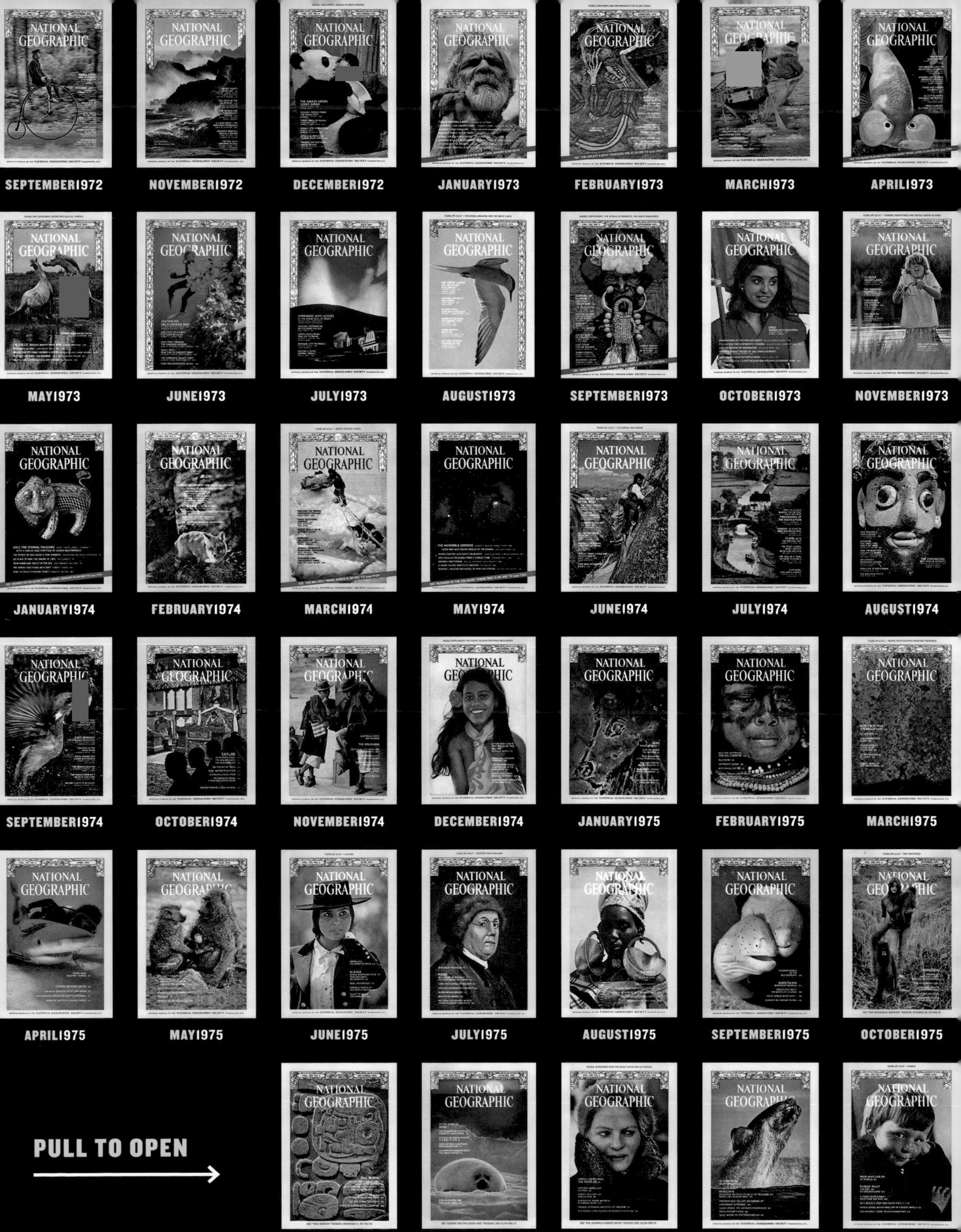

SEPTEMBER1972

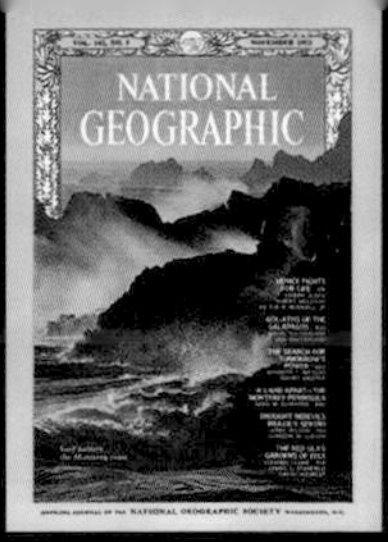

NOVEMBER1972

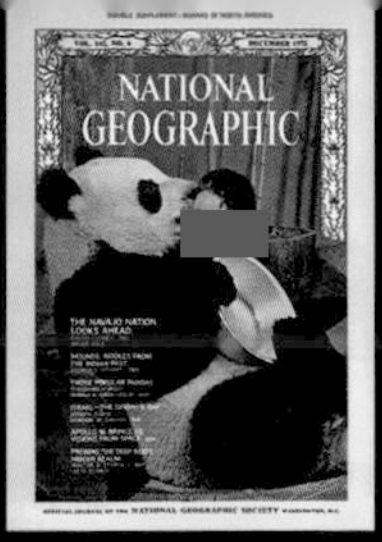

DECEMBER1972

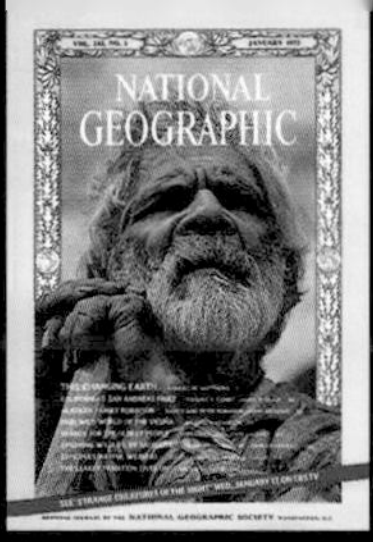

JANUARY1973

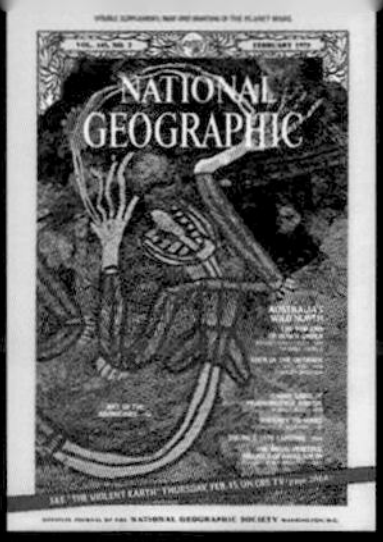

FEBRUARY1973

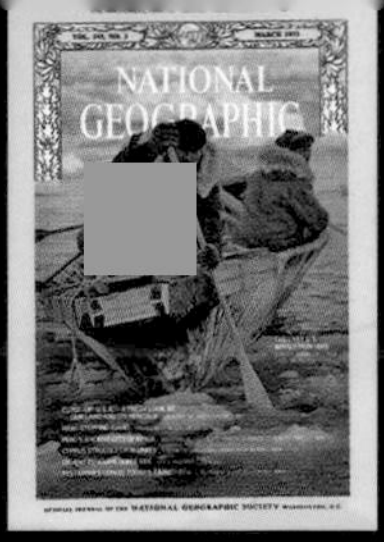

MARCH1973

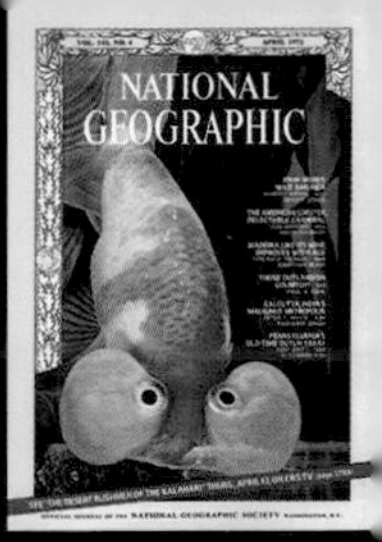

APRIL1973

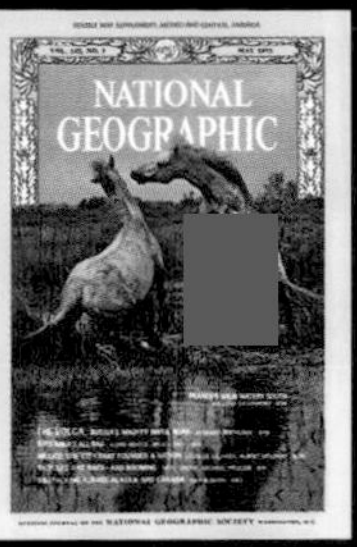

MAY1973

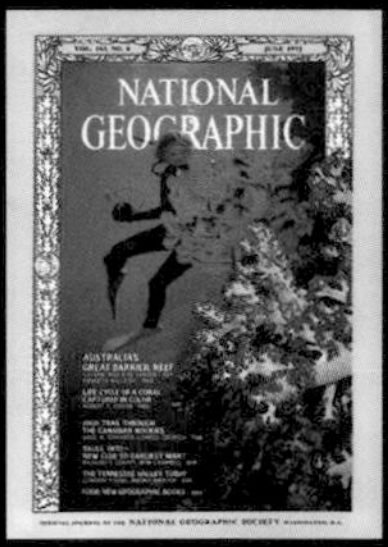

JUNE1973

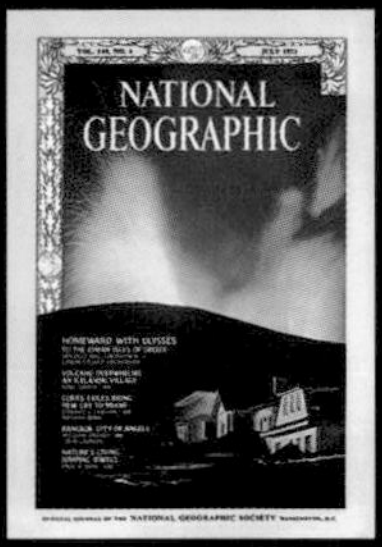

JULY1973

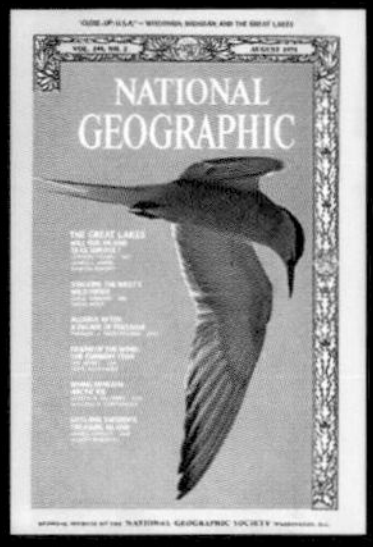

AUGUST1973

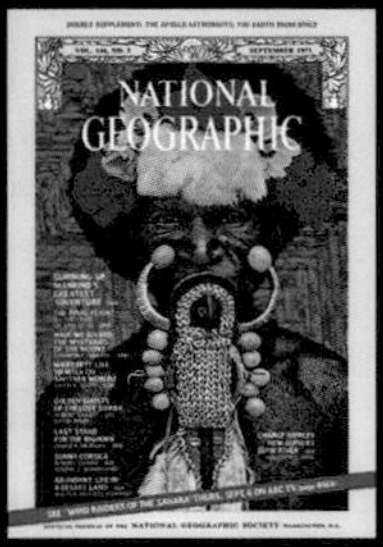

SEPTEMBER1973

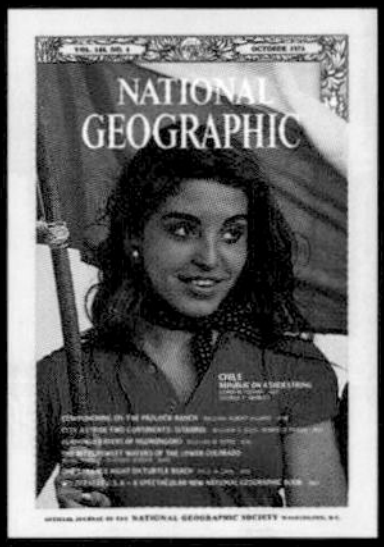

OCTOBER1973

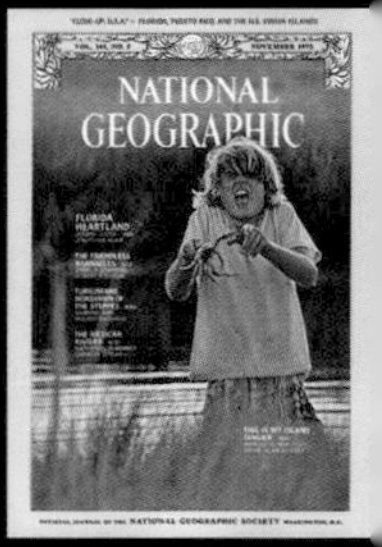

NOVEMBER1973

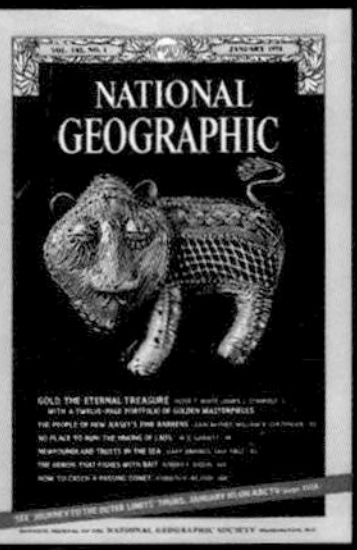

JANUARY1974

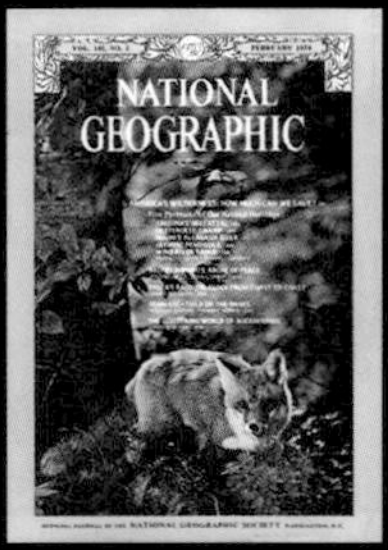

FEBRUARY1974

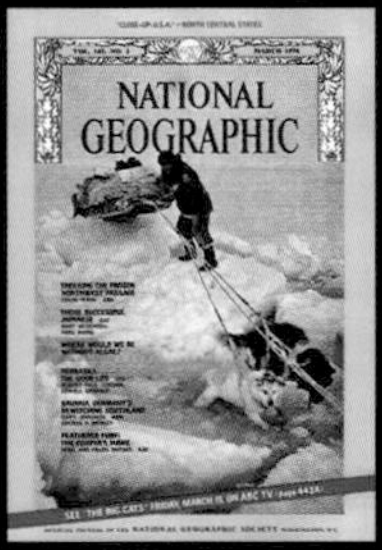

MARCH1974

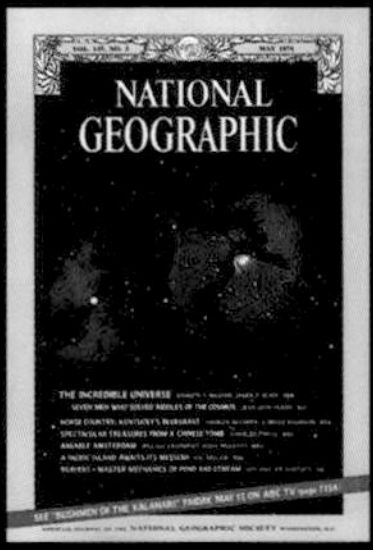

MAY1974

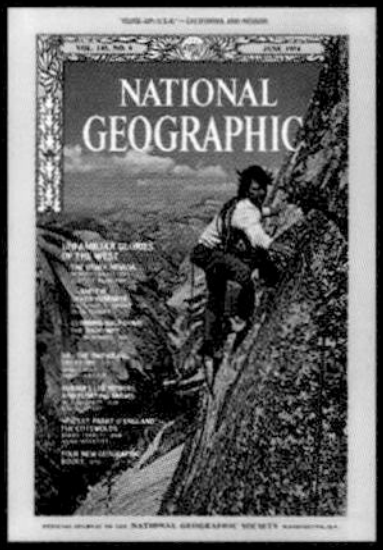

JUNE1974

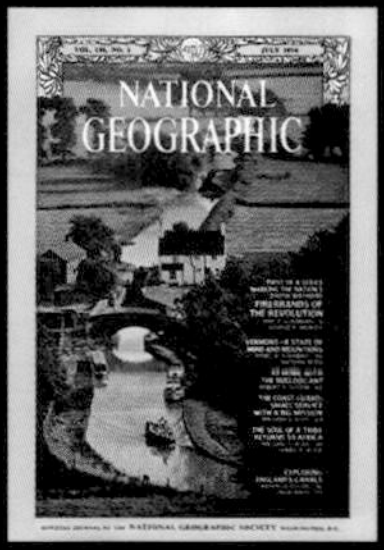

JULY1974

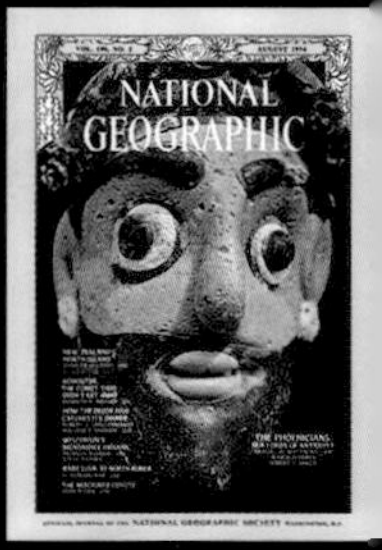

AUGUST1974

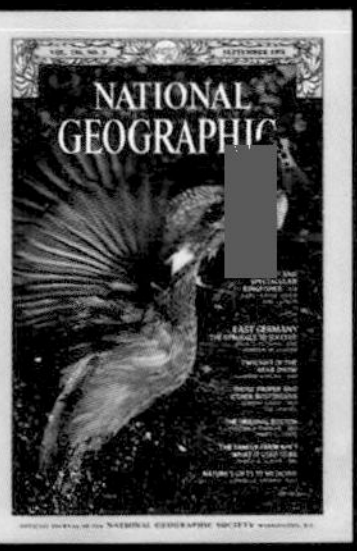

SEPTEMBER1974

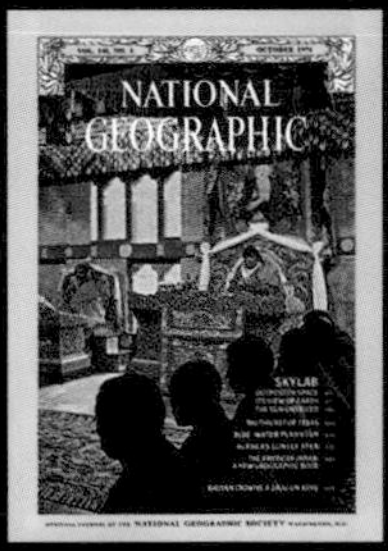

OCTOBER1974

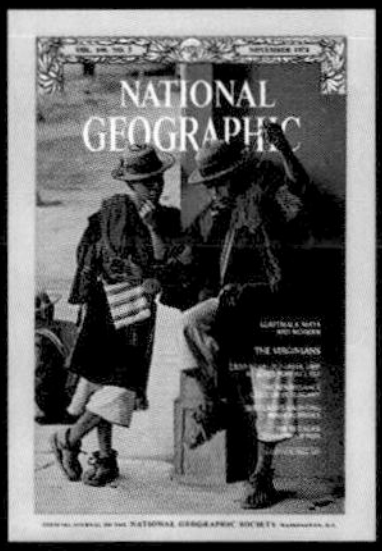

NOVEMBER1974

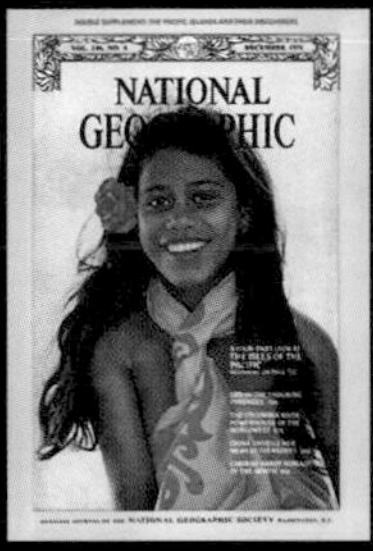

DECEMBER1974

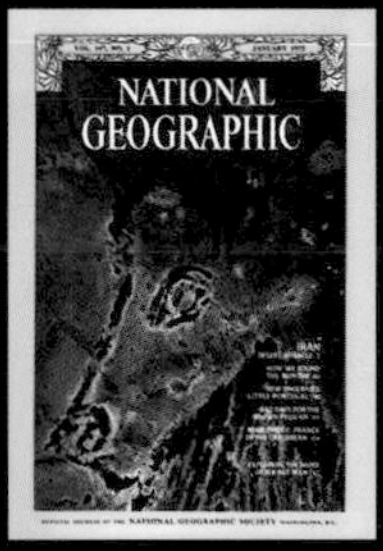

JANUARY1975

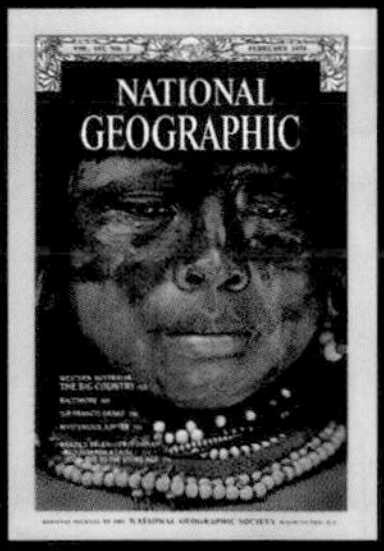

FEBRUARY1975

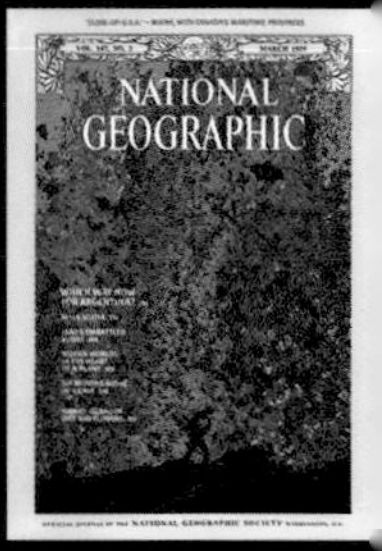

MARCH1975

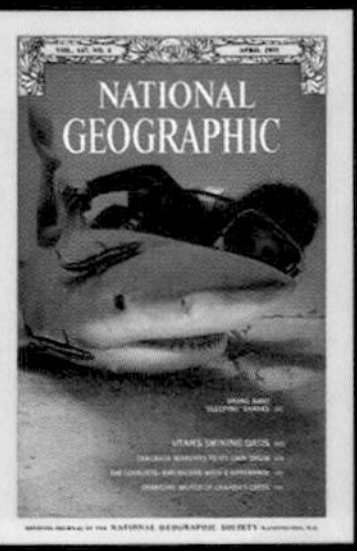

APRIL1975

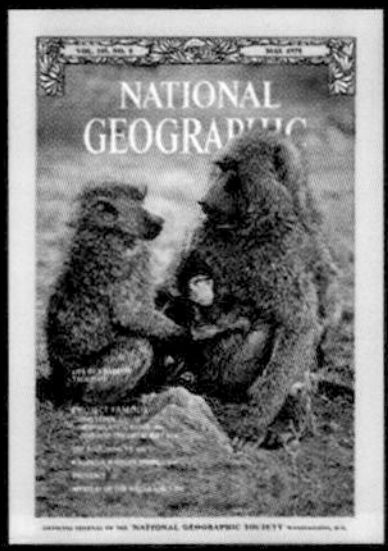

MAY1975

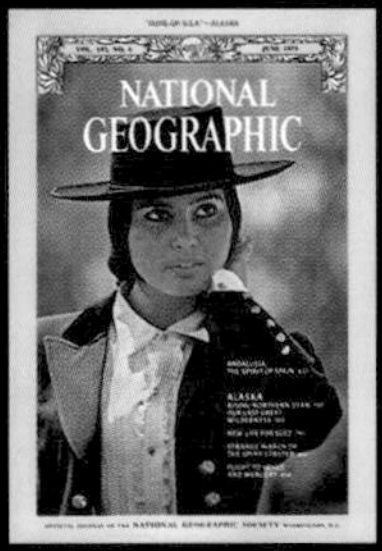

JUNE1975

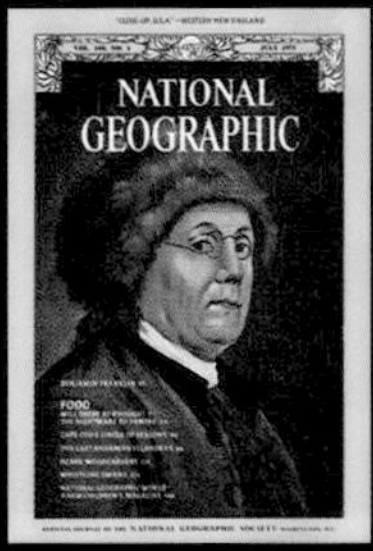

JULY1975

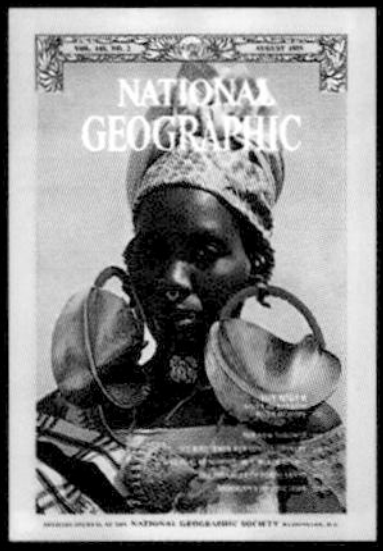

AUGUST1975

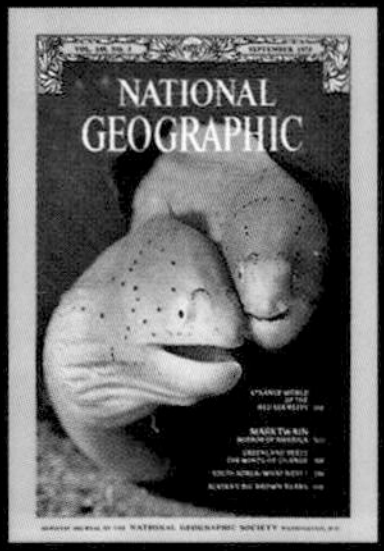

SEPTEMBER1975

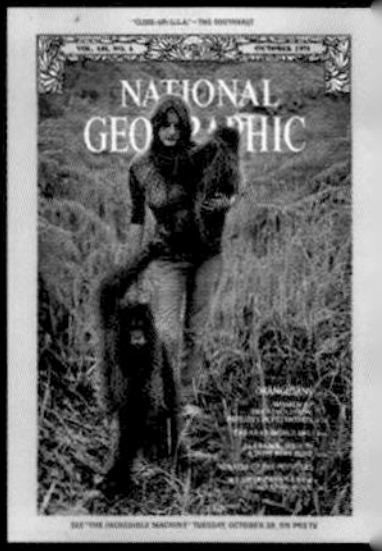

OCTOBER1975

PULL TO OPEN →

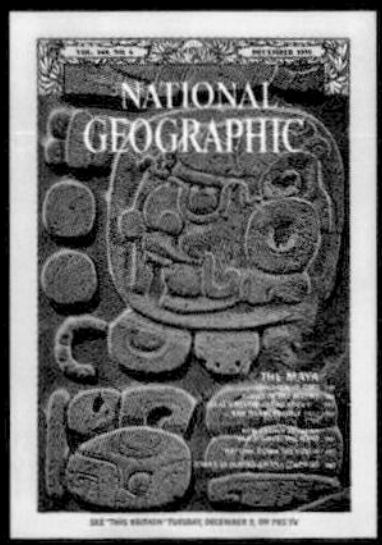

DECEMBER1975

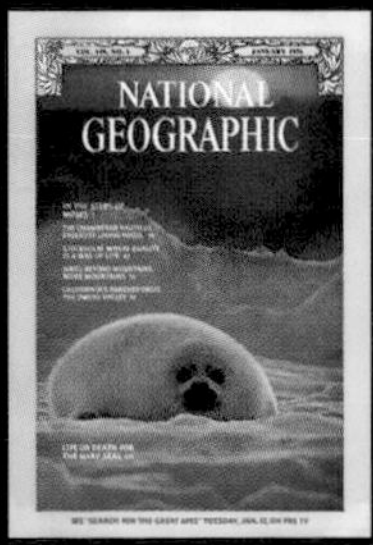

JANUARY1976

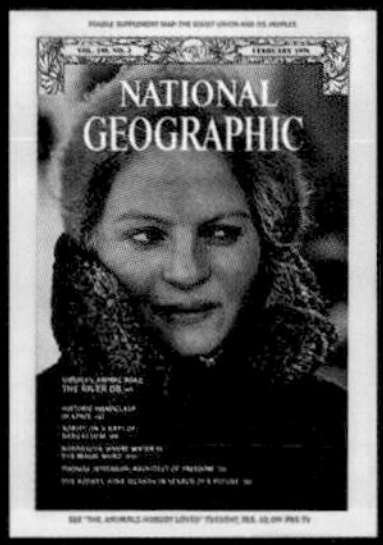

FEBRUARY1976

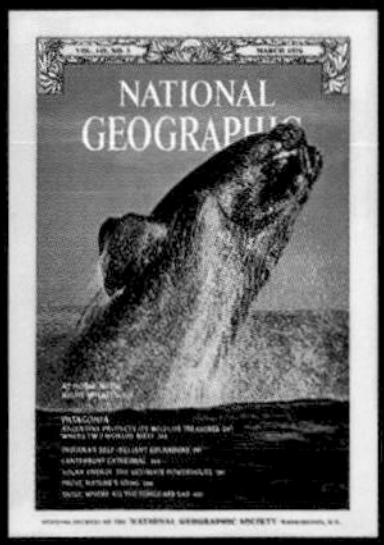

MARCH1976

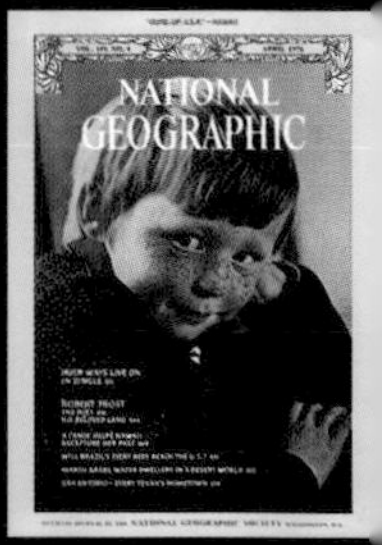

APRIL1976

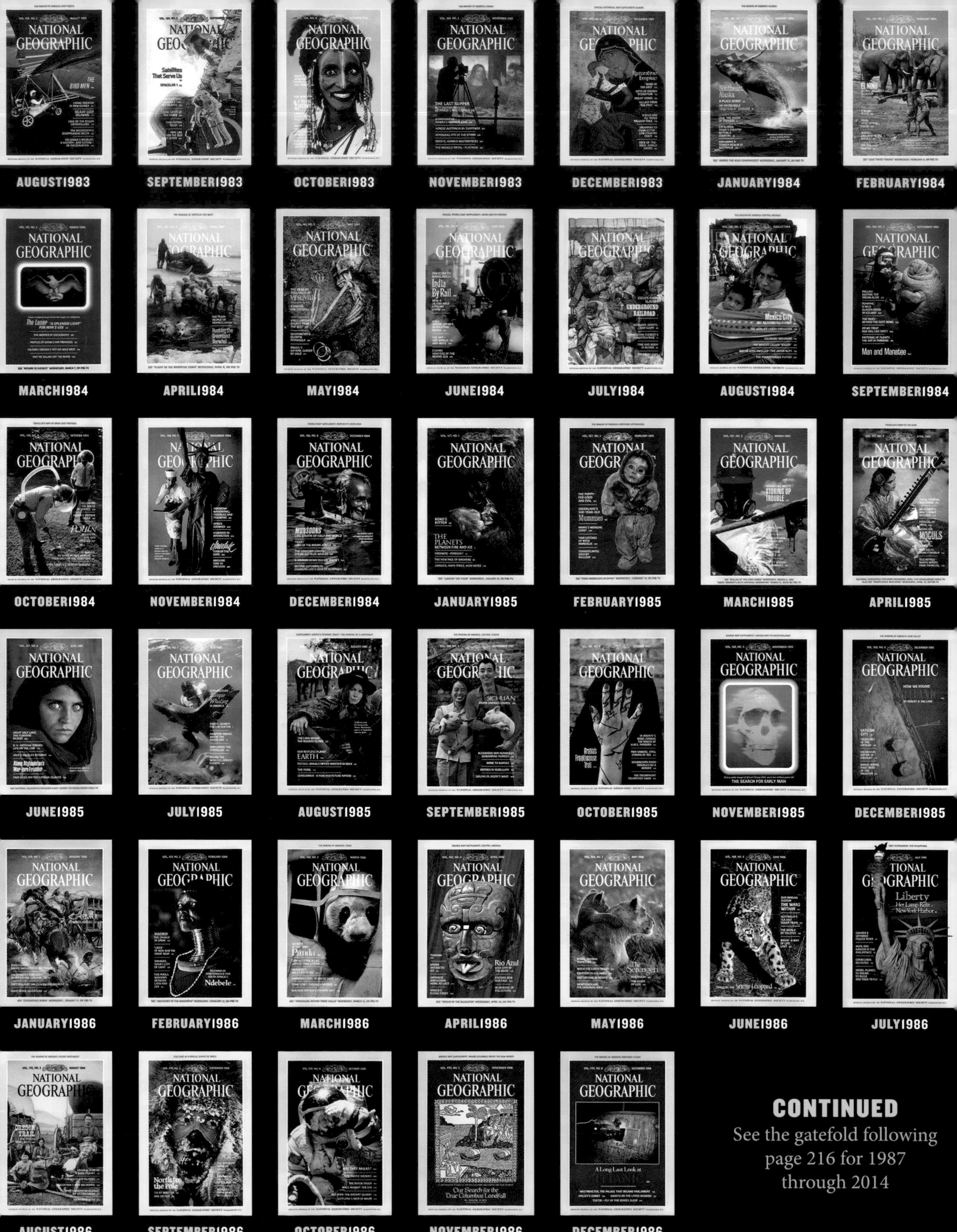

CONTINUED

See the gatefold following page 216 for 1987 through 2014

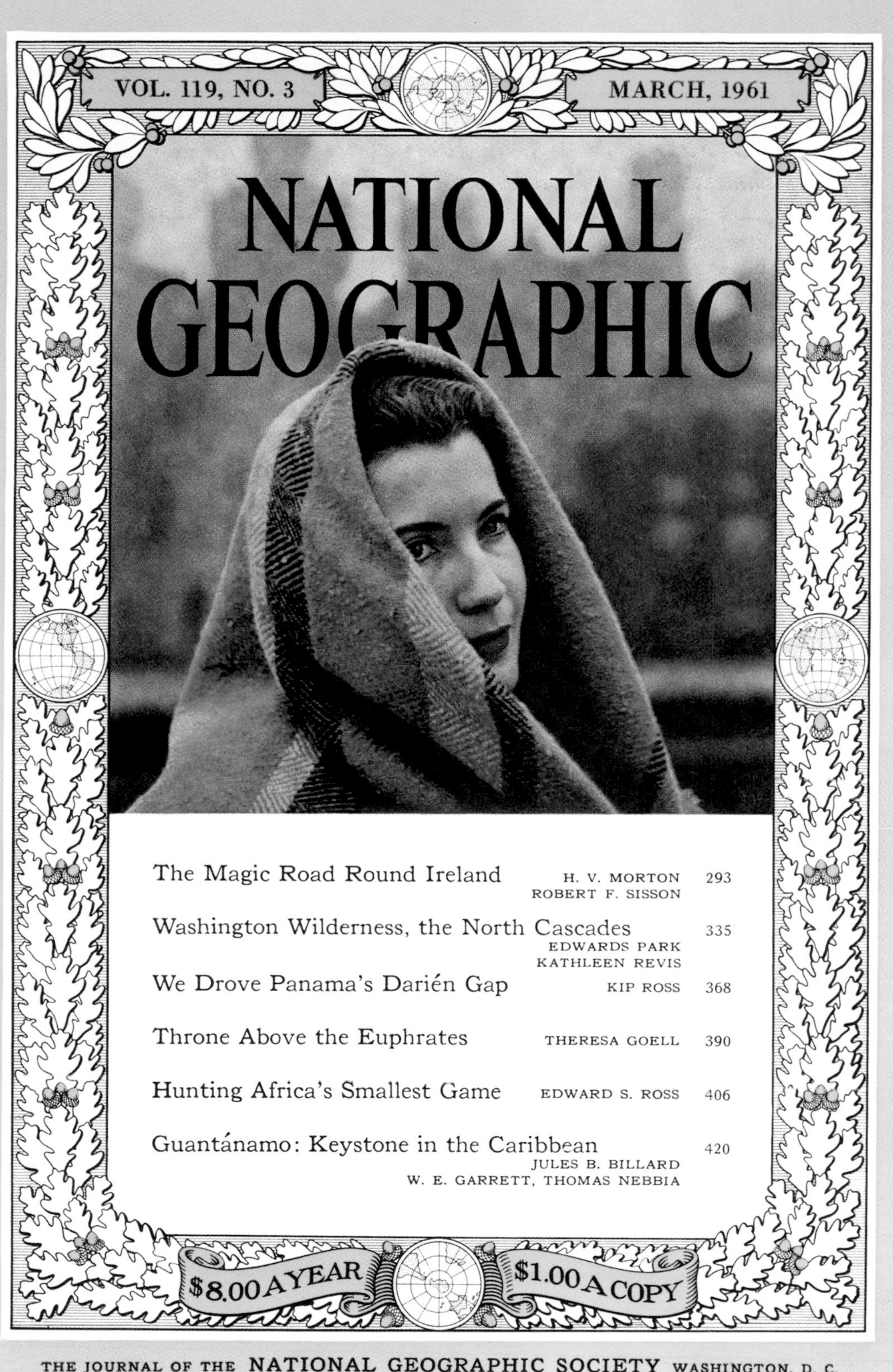

VOL. 119, NO. 3 MARCH, 1961

NATIONAL GEOGRAPHIC

The Magic Road Round Ireland	H. V. MORTON ROBERT F. SISSON	293
Washington Wilderness, the North Cascades	EDWARDS PARK KATHLEEN REVIS	335
We Drove Panama's Darién Gap	KIP ROSS	368
Throne Above the Euphrates	THERESA GOELL	390
Hunting Africa's Smallest Game	EDWARD S. ROSS	406
Guantánamo: Keystone in the Caribbean	JULES B. BILLARD W. E. GARRETT, THOMAS NEBBIA	420

$8.00 A YEAR $1.00 A COPY

THE JOURNAL OF THE NATIONAL GEOGRAPHIC SOCIETY WASHINGTON, D. C.

MARCH | DAVID DOUGLAS DUNCAN

KODACHROME COLLEEN This portrait of a woman wrapped in a handwoven shawl represents the era's color film at its saturated best. She was photographed while visiting Ashford Castle in County Mayo, recognizable to millions of moviegoers as one location for the 1952 hit *The Quiet Man* starring John Wayne and Maureen O'Hara.

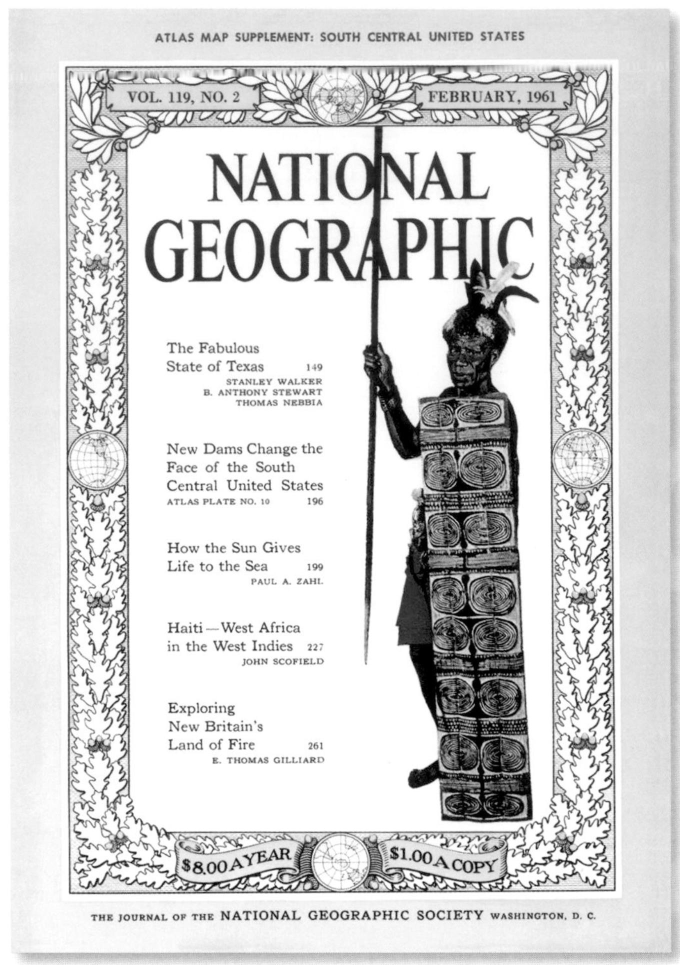

FEBRUARY | E. THOMAS GILLIARD

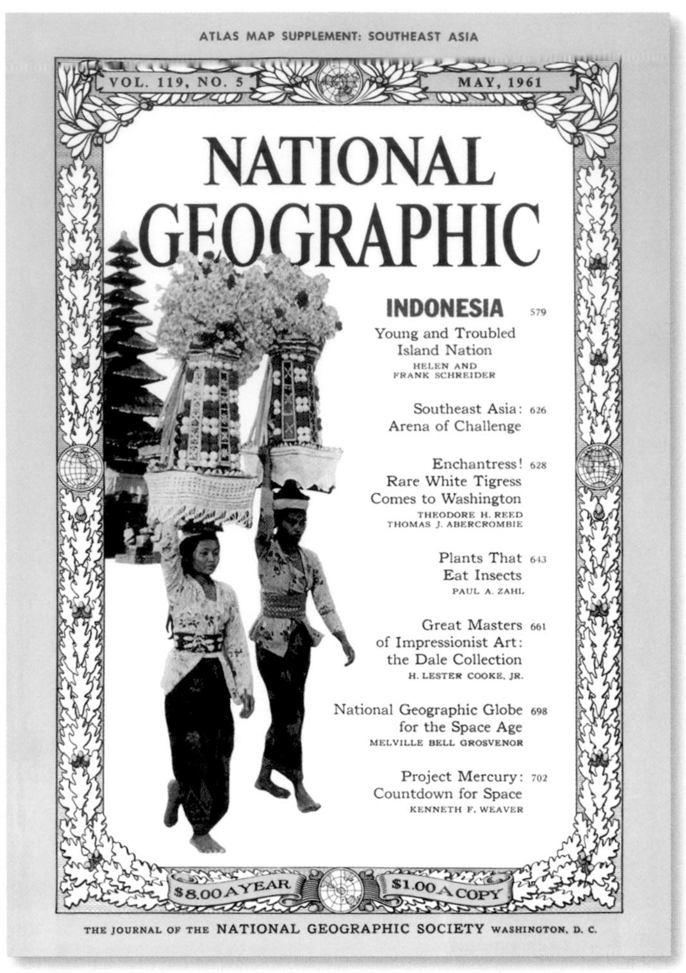

MAY | HELEN AND FRANK SCHREIDER

▲ **STANDING PROUD** Though he hefts a palm-wood spear, this Arawe hunter was the least formidable obstacle that ornithologist Tom Gilliard encountered while leading the first expedition to reach the mountainous interior of New Britain, an island in the Bismarck Archipelago.

"I now understood all too clearly why earlier surveys had failed to collect the avifauna of New Britain. Simply getting to these savage heights had been an appalling chore."

—E. Thomas Gilliard

from "Exploring New Britain's Land of Fire"

▲ **SWEET OFFERINGS** In a typical tableau of Bali, girls carry towers of fruit and flowers, temple offerings that are sometimes four feet high. Embarking in 1959, Helen and Frank Schreider spent 13 months—driving an amphibious jeep and accompanied by a German shepherd named Dinah—traversing the island arc of turbulent Indonesia, dodging both guerrillas and policemen while producing two articles for the *Geographic* and a book, *The Drums of Tonkin* (1963).

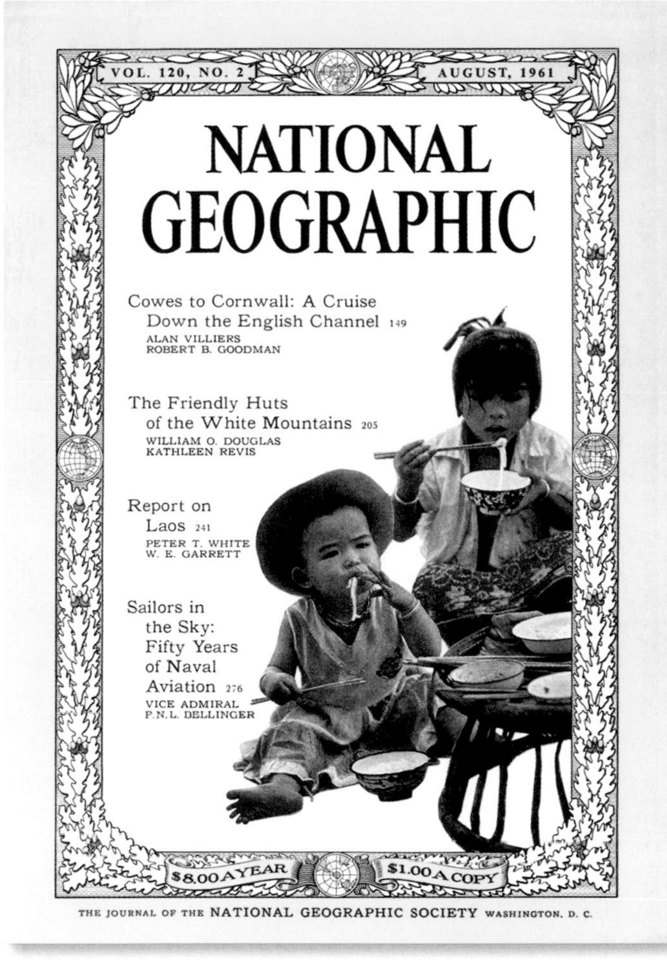

VOL. 120, NO. 2 AUGUST, 1961

NATIONAL GEOGRAPHIC

Cowes to Cornwall: A Cruise Down the English Channel 149
ALAN VILLIERS
ROBERT B. GOODMAN

The Friendly Huts of the White Mountains 205
WILLIAM O. DOUGLAS
KATHLEEN REVIS

Report on Laos 241
PETER T. WHITE
W. E. GARRETT

Sailors in the Sky: Fifty Years of Naval Aviation 276
VICE ADMIRAL F.N.L. BELLINGER

$8.00 A YEAR $1.00 A COPY

THE JOURNAL OF THE NATIONAL GEOGRAPHIC SOCIETY WASHINGTON, D. C.

AUGUST | WILBUR E. GARRETT

ATLAS MAP SUPPLEMENT: MEXICO AND CENTRAL AMERICA

VOL. 120, NO. 4 OCTOBER, 1961

NATIONAL GEOGRAPHIC

South Viet Nam Fights the Red Tide 445
PETER T. WHITE, W. E. GARRETT

Mexico in Motion 490
BART McDOWELL, KIP ROSS

New Atlas Map Focuses on Lands to the South 539

Into the Well of Sacrifice
I: Return to the Sacred Cenote 540
EUSEBIO DÁVALOS HURTADO
II: Treasure Hunt in the Deep Past 550
BATES LITTLEHALES

National Parks and Bird Books Reissued 562

Exploring 1,750,000 Years Into Man's Past 564
L. S. B. LEAKEY
ROBERT F. SISSON

Clock for the Ages: Potassium-Argon 590
GARNISS H. CURTIS

$8.00 A YEAR $1.00 A COPY

THE JOURNAL OF THE NATIONAL GEOGRAPHIC SOCIETY WASHINGTON, D. C.

OCTOBER | KIP ROSS

▲ **CIVIL WAR** Although the picture was taken in northern Laos, the children devouring their rice noodles from a roadside stand are actually Chinese. Not only was Laos being devastated by a civil war between royalist troops and a Communist insurgency, but also several Chinese nationalist divisions had been lurking in the kingdom's northern jungles for the past 12 years, living largely off the clandestine opium trade, having been chased out of their own country by Mao Zedong's victorious Red Army back in 1949.

▲ ***ABUNDANCIA*** With her colorful blouse embroidered with designs inspired by the plants of sun-splashed Chiapas and her lacquered gourd brimming with calla lilies, this girl embodies a popular image of Mexico. She and her fellow countrymen were enjoying a rising tide of prosperity, thanks largely to her nation's increasing industrial output.

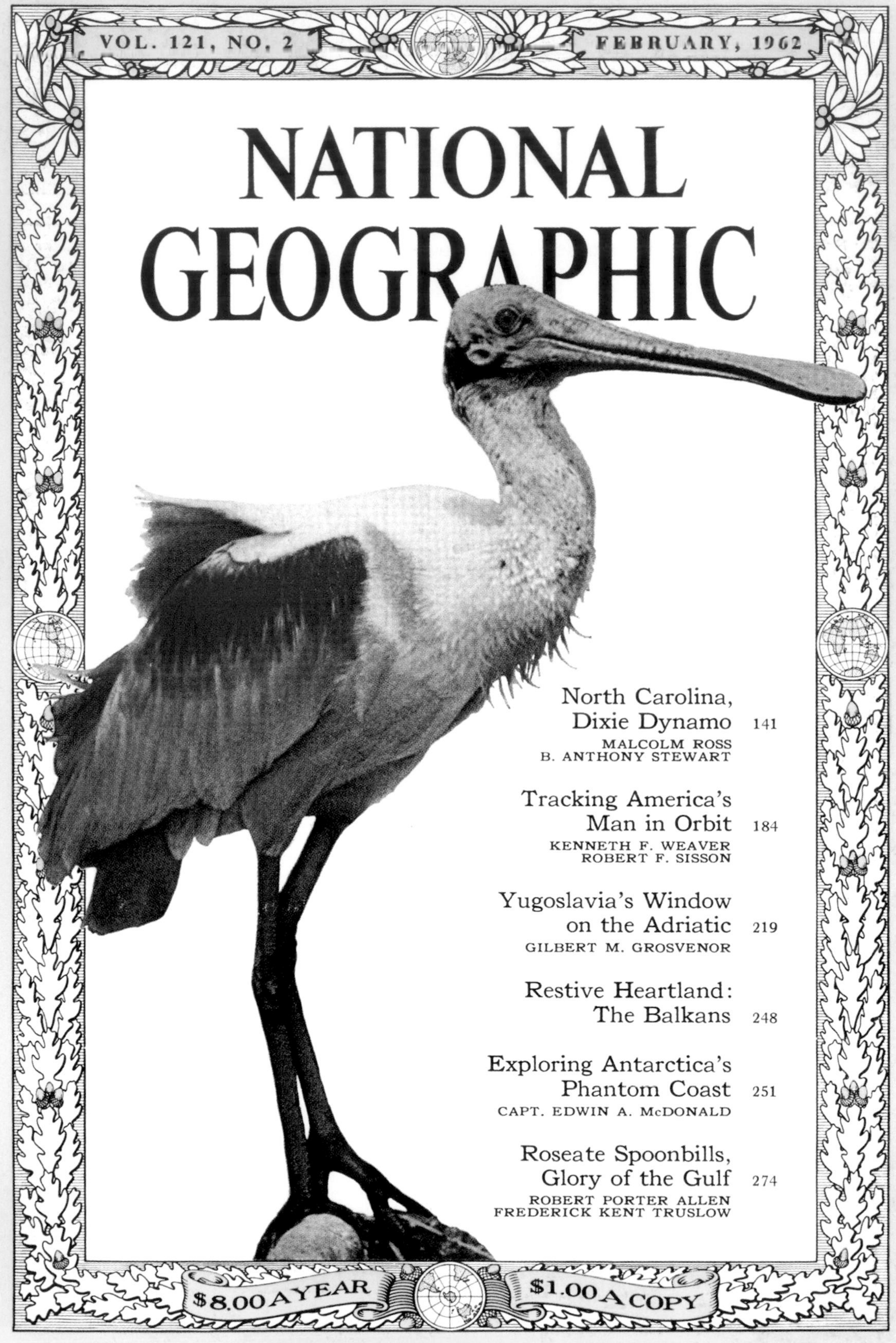

FEBRUARY | FREDERICK KENT TRUSLOW A 400mm lens brought this bird into sharp focus.

ON THE REBOUND

The regal bird looming over the cover of the February 1962 *National Geographic* was once a common sight along the shores of the Gulf of Mexico. Although still plentiful in the bays and marshes of South America, the roseate spoonbill *(Platalea ajaja)* had by the early 20th century all but vanished from the coasts of Florida, Louisiana, and Texas—thanks to the depredations of plume hunters.

Here and there, however, it was beginning to return, and the *Geographic* article detailing its reappearance featured illustrations made by Frederick Kent Truslow, a refugee from a corporate boardroom who relatively late in life found solace in photographing birds—and found it, happily enough, just as cameras and faster color films had advanced to the point where superb bird photography was at last attainable.

By 1958 Truslow's remarkable pictures were appearing in the *Geographic,* and two years later—on the strength of his photographs and the magazine's reputation—the National Audubon Society permitted him to visit an otherwise restricted sanctuary in Galveston Bay, Texas, where a colony of spoonbills bred.

Because here they nested in low bushes rather than in dense mangroves, Truslow had an unrivaled advantage for documenting the birds' behavior. Although it could be a stifling 138 degrees in his blind, he succeeded in capturing what no professional ornithologist had yet seen: every stage in the nesting and rearing of young. After being published in *National Geographic,* his pictures also contributed to a greater appreciation of the roseate spoonbill, which is still struggling to make a comeback along the northern shores of the Gulf.

Today excellent bird photography is common. In those days it was exceptional, and Truslow's results—he published a dozen stories in the magazine—were often unprecedented.

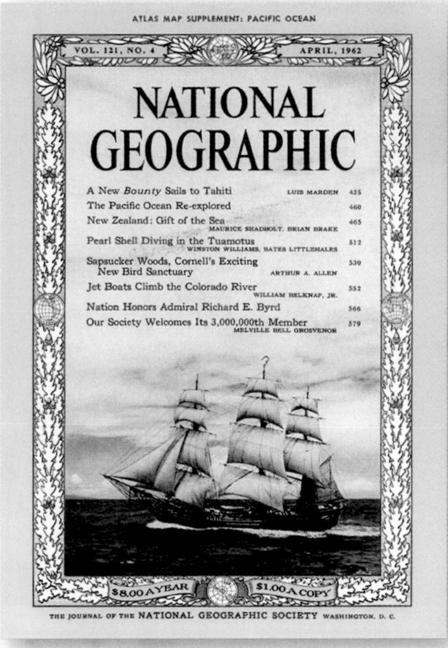

ATLAS MAP SUPPLEMENT: PACIFIC OCEAN

VOL. 121, NO. 4 — APRIL, 1962

NATIONAL GEOGRAPHIC

A New *Bounty* Sails to Tahiti — LUIS MARDEN 435
The Pacific Ocean Re-explored 460
New Zealand: Gift of the Sea — MAURICE SHADBOLT, BRIAN BRAKE 465
Pearl Shell Diving in the Tuamotus — WINSTON WILLIAMS, BATES LITTLEHALES 512
Sapsucker Woods, Cornell's Exciting New Bird Sanctuary — ARTHUR A. ALLEN 530
Jet Boats Climb the Colorado River — WILLIAM BELKNAP, JR. 552
Nation Honors Admiral Richard E. Byrd 566
Our Society Welcomes Its 3,000,000th Member — MELVILLE BELL GROSVENOR 579

$8.00 A YEAR — $1.00 A COPY

THE JOURNAL OF THE NATIONAL GEOGRAPHIC SOCIETY WASHINGTON, D. C.

APRIL | LUIS MARDEN

▲ ***BOUNTY II*** Sails bellying, a square-rigger sets course for Tahiti during the filming of MGM's *Mutiny on the Bounty.* Photographer Luis Marden—who also served as third mate aboard this replica of the storied *Bounty*—was reliving the great days of Pacific exploration when all voyagers arrived in the South Seas by ship. The vessel, however, was doomed: It sank off North Carolina in 2012, a victim of Hurricane Sandy.

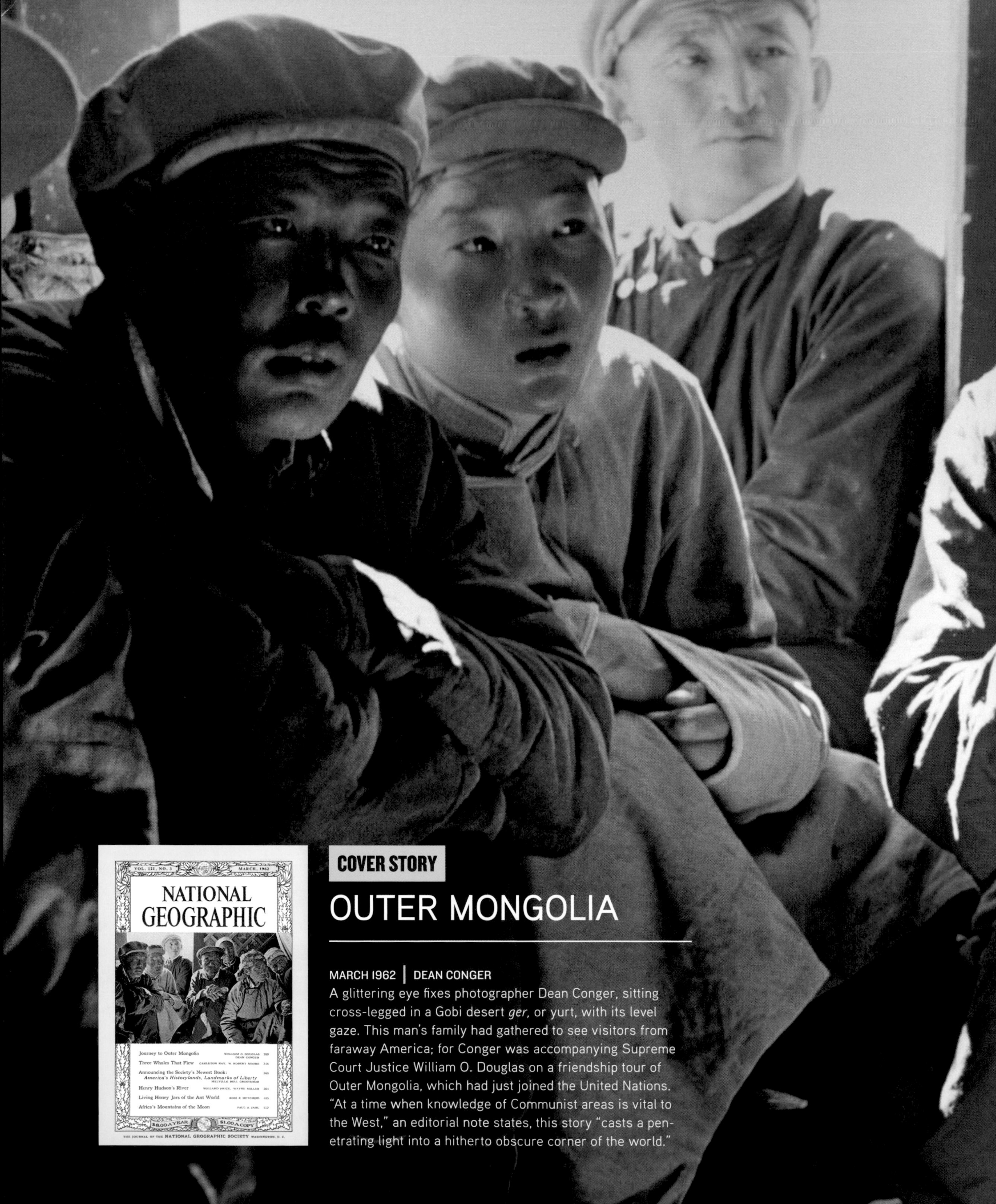

COVER STORY

OUTER MONGOLIA

MARCH 1962 | DEAN CONGER

A glittering eye fixes photographer Dean Conger, sitting cross-legged in a Gobi desert *ger,* or yurt, with its level gaze. This man's family had gathered to see visitors from faraway America; for Conger was accompanying Supreme Court Justice William O. Douglas on a friendship tour of Outer Mongolia, which had just joined the United Nations. "At a time when knowledge of Communist areas is vital to the West," an editorial note states, this story "casts a penetrating light into a hitherto obscure corner of the world."

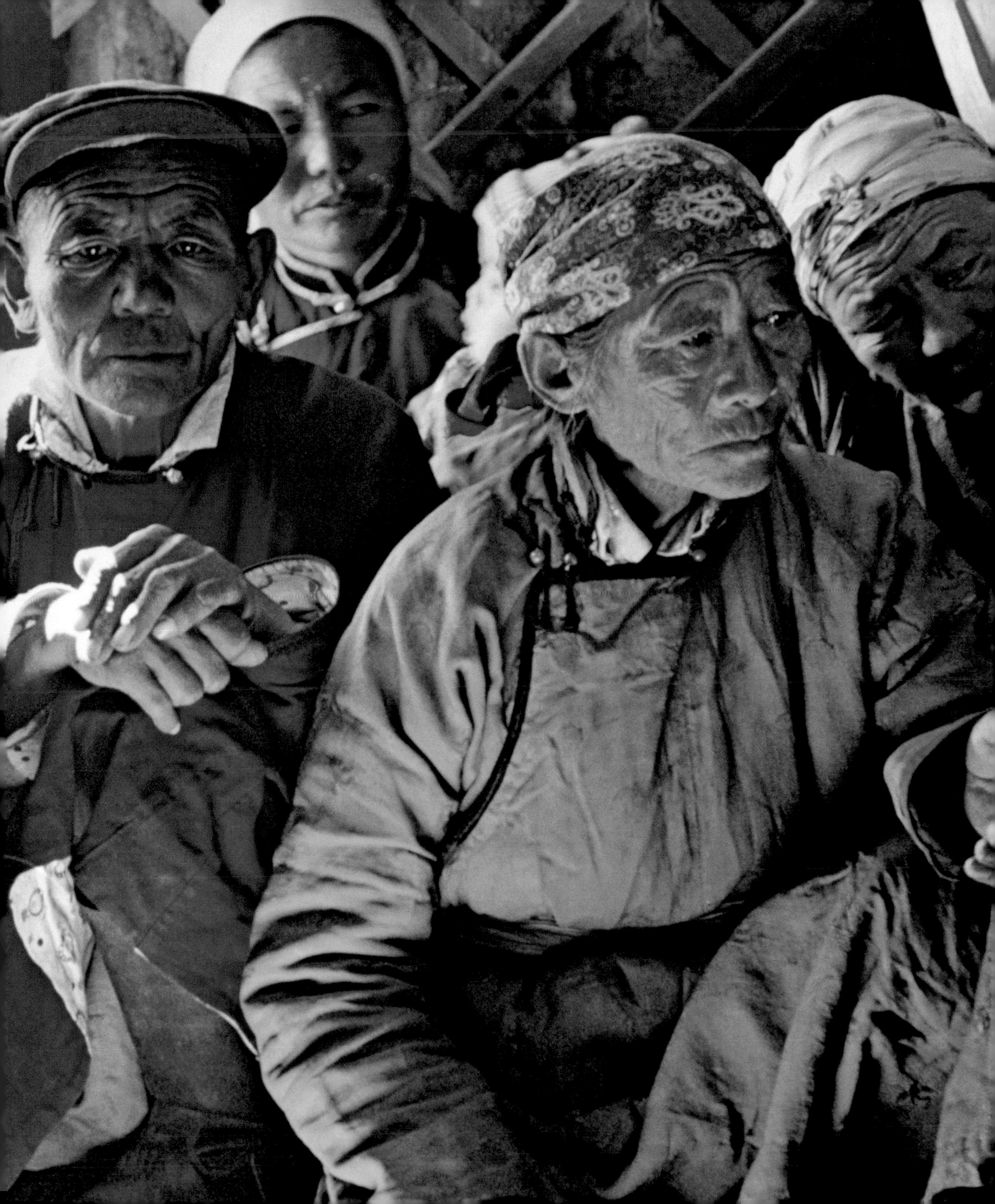

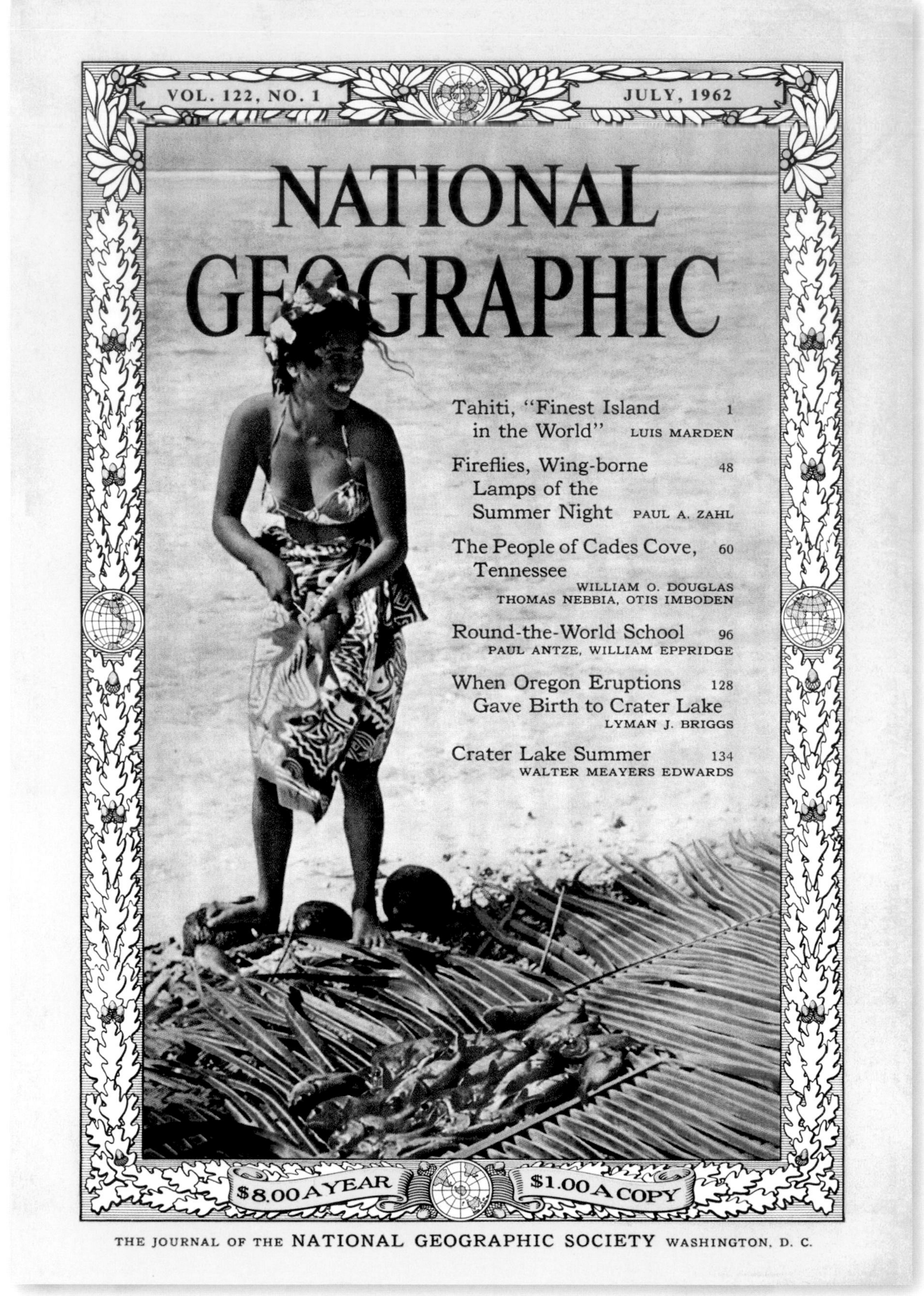

JULY | LUIS MARDEN

TAHITIAN DREAMS "Everything is fun, an excuse for laughter," wrote Luis Marden of Tahiti, and this gardenia-crowned girl laughs even when cleaning squirrelfish. In the pre–jumbo jet era, the island remained an idyllic place—"always there, somewhere beyond the horizon, far away and approachable only by sea, the golden dream of everyman."

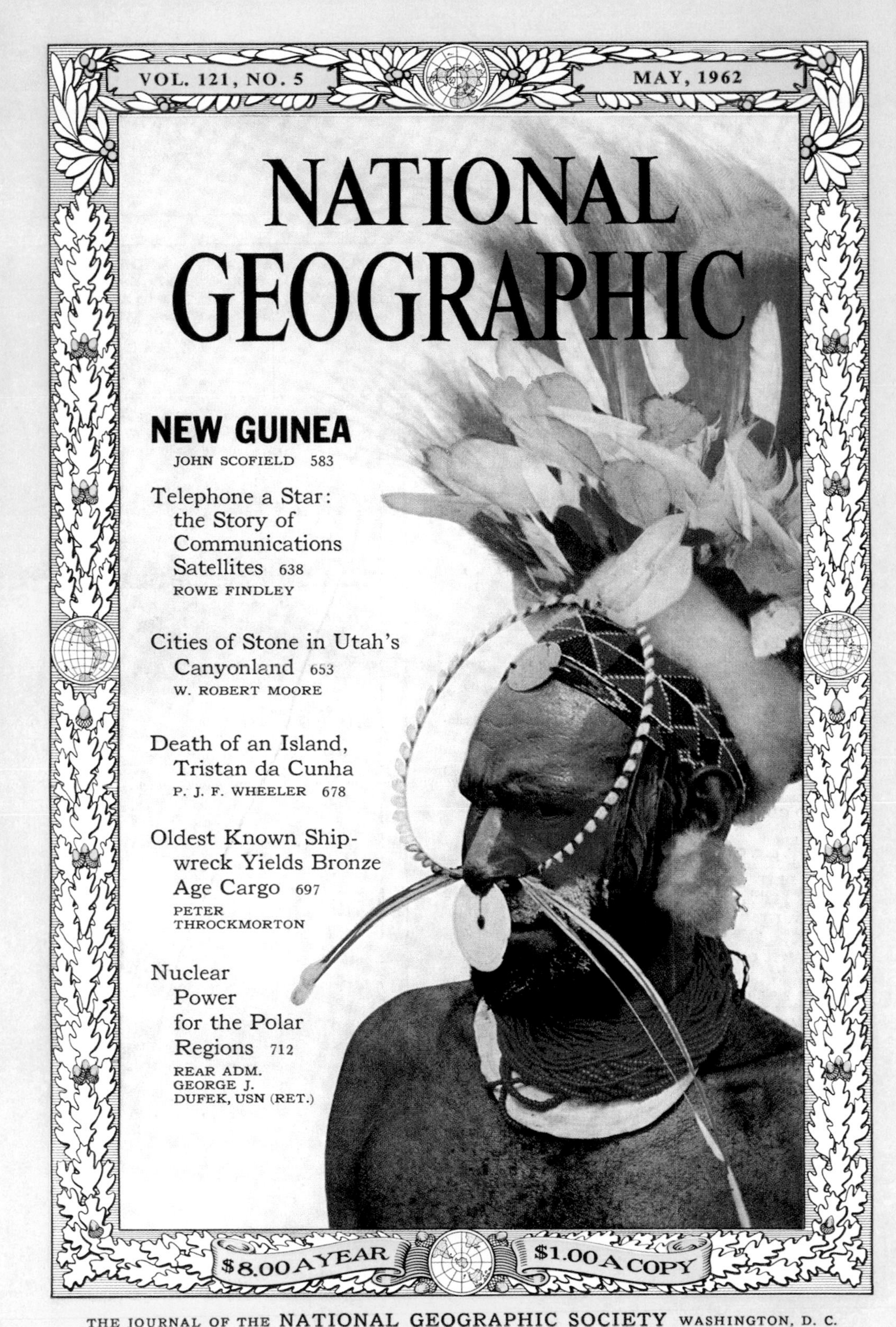

VOL. 121, NO. 5 MAY, 1962

NATIONAL GEOGRAPHIC

NEW GUINEA
JOHN SCOFIELD 583

Telephone a Star: the Story of Communications Satellites 638
ROWE FINDLEY

Cities of Stone in Utah's Canyonland 653
W. ROBERT MOORE

Death of an Island, Tristan da Cunha
P. J. F. WHEELER 678

Oldest Known Shipwreck Yields Bronze Age Cargo 697
PETER THROCKMORTON

Nuclear Power for the Polar Regions 712
REAR ADM. GEORGE J. DUFEK, USN (RET.)

$8.00 A YEAR $1.00 A COPY

THE JOURNAL OF THE NATIONAL GEOGRAPHIC SOCIETY WASHINGTON, D. C.

MAY | JOHN SCOFIELD

SING-SING This Papua New Guinea chief—sporting plumes from cockatoos, parrots, and birds of paradise—was photographed in September 1961 as he strolled around the Mount Hagen Sing-Sing, the largest tribal gathering ever to take place in the South Pacific at that time. Perhaps 50,000 to 70,000 festive Papuans mixed with a handful of Europeans.

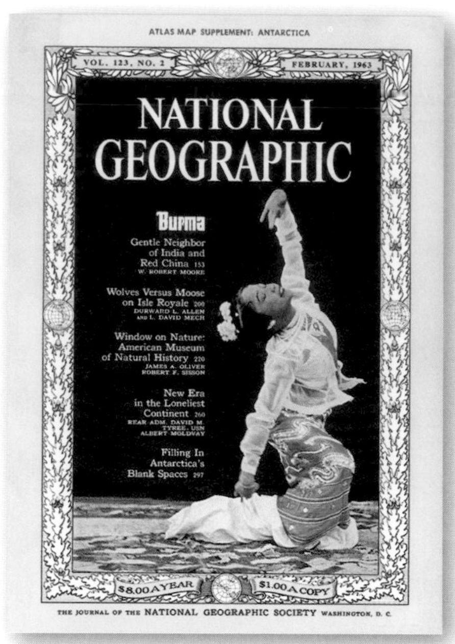

FEBRUARY | W. ROBERT MOORE

▲ **ELEGANT GESTURE** Wearing an antique court costume, a dancer in Mandalay, Burma, concludes a classical performance.

> *"Spicing my peanuts with the sour-peppery zithees [plums], I watch swirling dancers whose litheness seemed beyond the capacity of human joints, and heard jokes with double meanings as flexible as the dancers' movements."*
>
> —W. Robert Moore
>
> *from "Burma: Gentle Neighbor of India and Red China"*

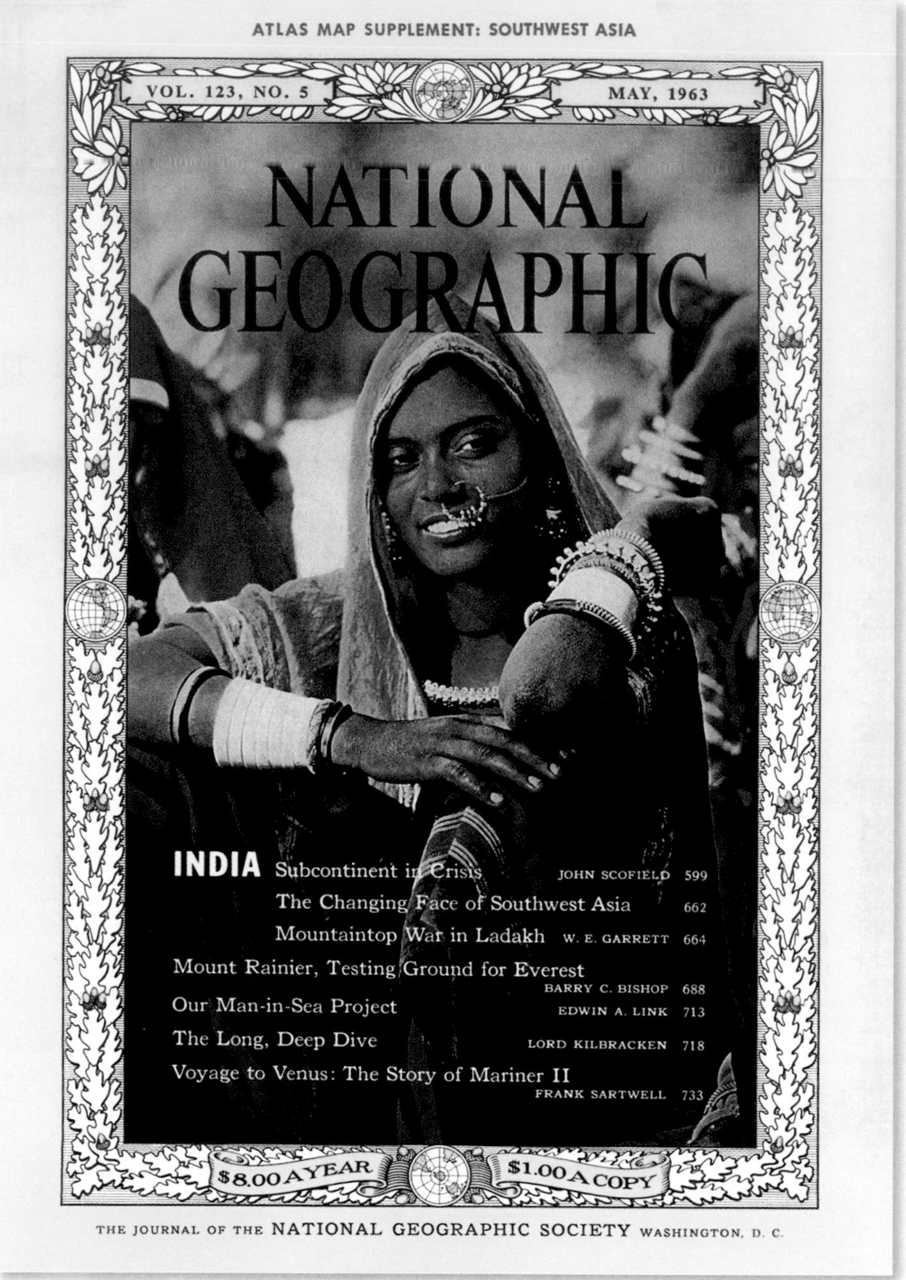

MAY | JOHN SCOFIELD

▲ **DRESSED FOR THE FAIR** Nose ring anchored to her ear by a finely worked chain, a woman enjoys the festivities at the Pushkar Camel Fair, held annually in Rajasthan for at least 1,500 years. Perhaps a hundred thousand people—with their herds of camels, horses, and cattle—mingle on the dusty plains when the moon is full in autumn. Turbaned and sandaled herdsmen haggle over livestock while women congregate at stalls buying and selling fabrics, bracelets, bangles, or other gold and silver ornaments.

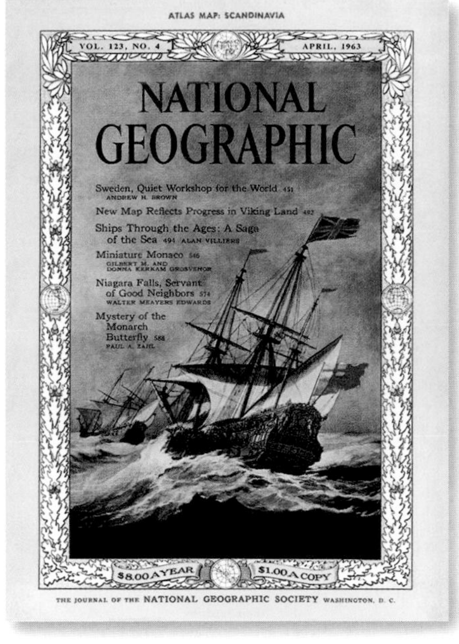

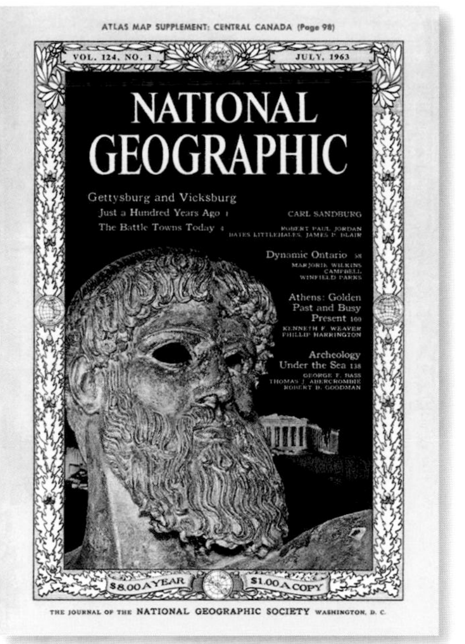

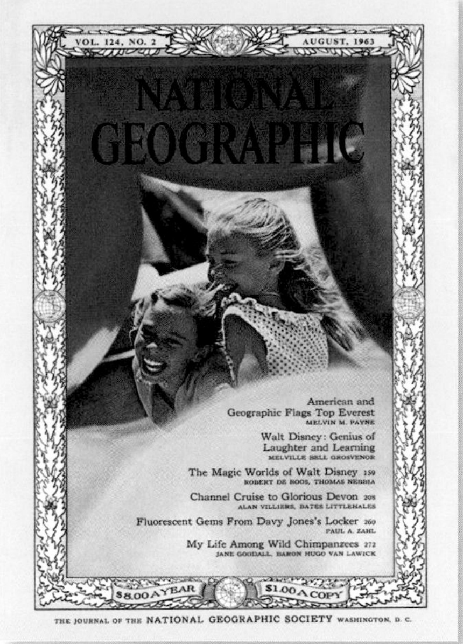

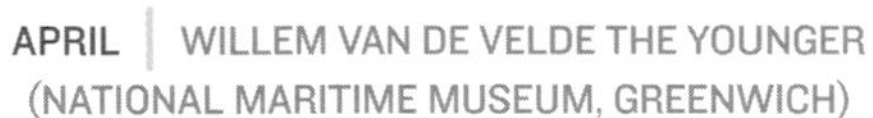

APRIL | WILLEM VAN DE VELDE THE YOUNGER (NATIONAL MARITIME MUSEUM, GREENWICH)

JULY | PHILLIP HARRINGTON, JEAN AND FRANC SHOR

AUGUST | THOMAS NEBBIA

THE PUSHKAR CAMEL FAIR

Despite border conflicts with China and Pakistan, postcolonial India still pivoted around its immemorial festivals. Yet those, too, had their starker side, as *National Geographic*'s John Scofield discovered while mingling with the throngs at the Pushkar Camel Fair:

> On the path that led from the fairground to the sacred lake, the figure of a man lay sprawled. Knots of laughing women, wearing red and orange saris that made them look like huge bobbing tulips, swept unceasingly by, not even pausing in their chatter as they picked their way around the motionless form. The man lay on his side in the dust with one arm flung out, the fingers still resting on a brass water jug. He was dead. I never learned what had happened. No one seemed to know or care. In the end, I moved on, like the others.
>
> *—From "India: Subcontinent in Crisis," John Scofield*

▲ **MAGIC KINGDOM** A fast shutter speed captures the delight reflected in these girls' faces as they bounce about in air-cushioned Flying Saucers, one of the many rides they enjoyed during their visit to Disneyland. Tom Nebbia was granted the rare opportunity not only to photograph Walt Disney himself but also to document all of the behind-the-scenes activities of his world-renowned entertainment company.

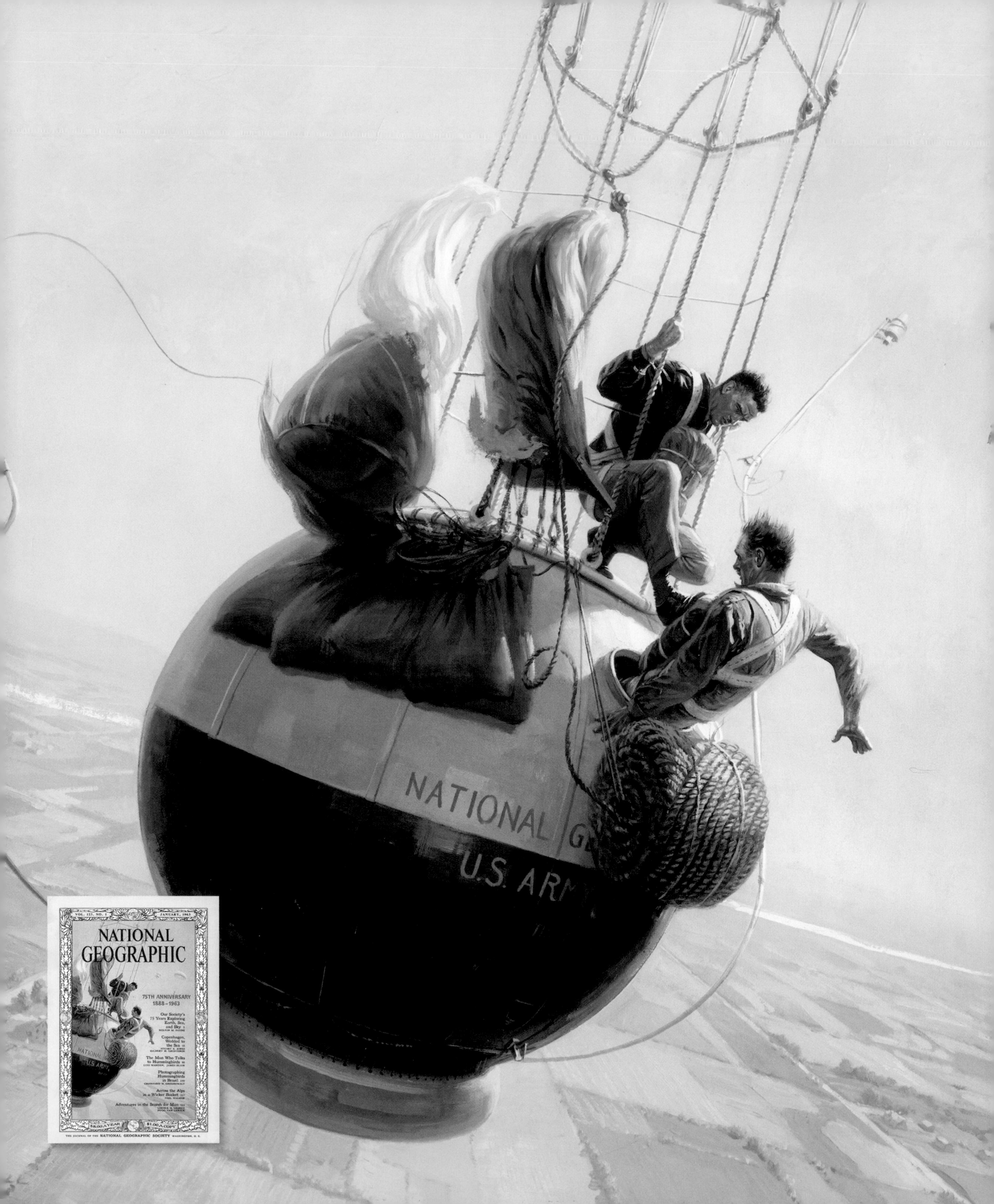
NATIONAL GE
U.S. ARM
VOL. 123, NO. 1
JANUARY, 1963
NATIONAL GEOGRAPHIC
75TH ANNIVERSARY
1888–1963
Our Society's 75 Years Exploring Earth, Sea, and Sky
Copenhagen, Wedded to the Sea
The Man Who Talks to Hummingbirds
Photographing Hummingbirds in Brazil
Across the Alps in a Wicker Basket
Adventures in the Search for Man
$8.00 A YEAR
$1.00 A COPY
NATIONAL GEOGRAPHIC SOCIETY

75TH ANNIVERSARY OF THE SOCIETY

AT A TIME WHEN space capsules were flying across the magazine's cover, why did the *Geographic*'s editors choose to honor the Society's 75 years of exploring land, sea, and sky with a specially commisioned depiction of a near disaster that had occurred three decades earlier? Because Tom Lovell's painting commemorated an important moment in the upward thrust toward space.

On July 28, 1934, a hydrogen balloon as tall as a 26-story building was launched from a pad in South Dakota, carrying inside a hermetically sealed gondola—*The Explorer*—the three aeronauts of the National Geographic–U.S. Army Air Corps Stratosphere Project. Maj. William Kepner, Capt. Orvil Anderson, and Capt. Albert Stevens—the genius behind the launch—hoped to ascend to a record-setting 75,000 feet. But as they passed 60,000 feet the balloon ripped; and as they plummeted downward, it exploded.

Two of the aeronauts managed to climb out of the gondola. The third, Captain Stevens, was stuck in the porthole. Thanks to Kepner's well-placed kick—the moment illustrated here—Stevens was freed, and the two men followed Anderson in parachuting to safety only seconds before *Explorer* smashed into a Nebraska cornfield.

The following year Stevens and Anderson returned to the stratosphere in *Explorer II*, which topped out at 72,395 feet, setting a record unbroken for 21 years while also pioneering new ways of protecting humans—including pressurized cabins and heat suits—as they approached the edge of the atmosphere. These Society-sponsored balloon launches blazed the way for the manned space program.

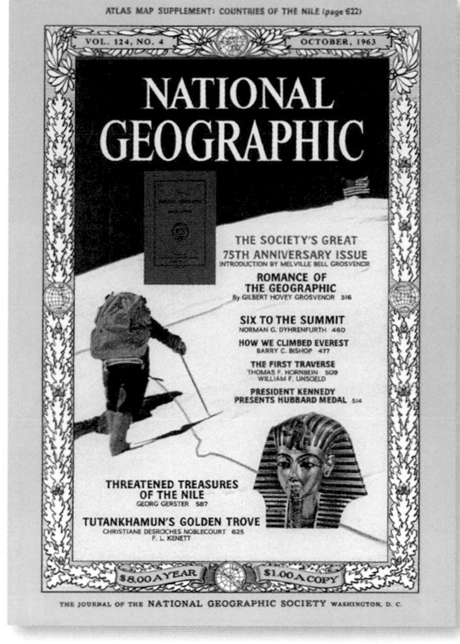

OCTOBER | BARRY BISHOP, GEORGE RAINBIRD, LTD.

▲ **75TH MAGAZINE ANNIVERSARY** Everest's icy slopes, King Tut's funeral mask, and the first cover mark the publication's 75th year. Barry Bishop, the mountaineer who took the main picture on this cover collage as a member of a 1963 climbing expedition, epitomized the courage of National Geographic explorers. He not only lost all ten toes to frostbite but also nearly lost his life when forced to spend a night in the open on those same slopes.

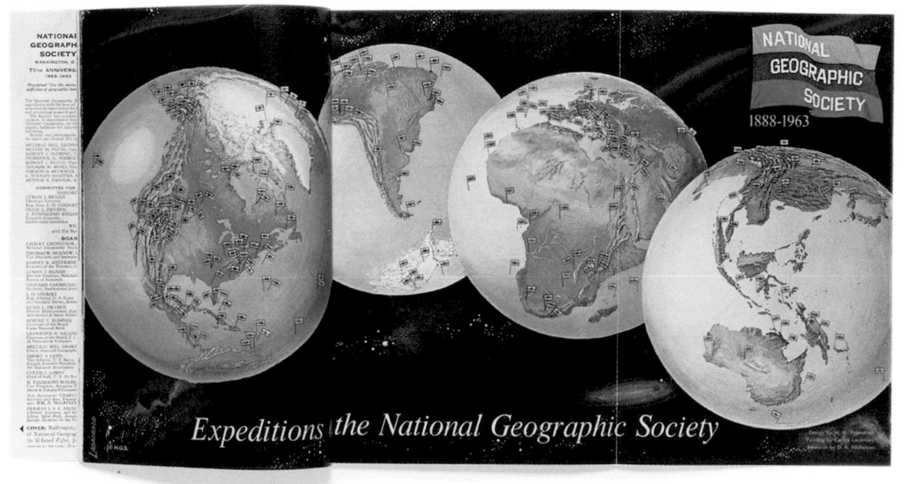

▶ **JANUARY 1963** | **CARLOS LACÁMARA** Map showing the global reach of the Society's expeditions

◀ **JANUARY 1963** | **TOM LOVELL** In a cover marking the 75th anniversary of the Society, Capt. Albert Stevens is freed from *Explorer*'s gondola.

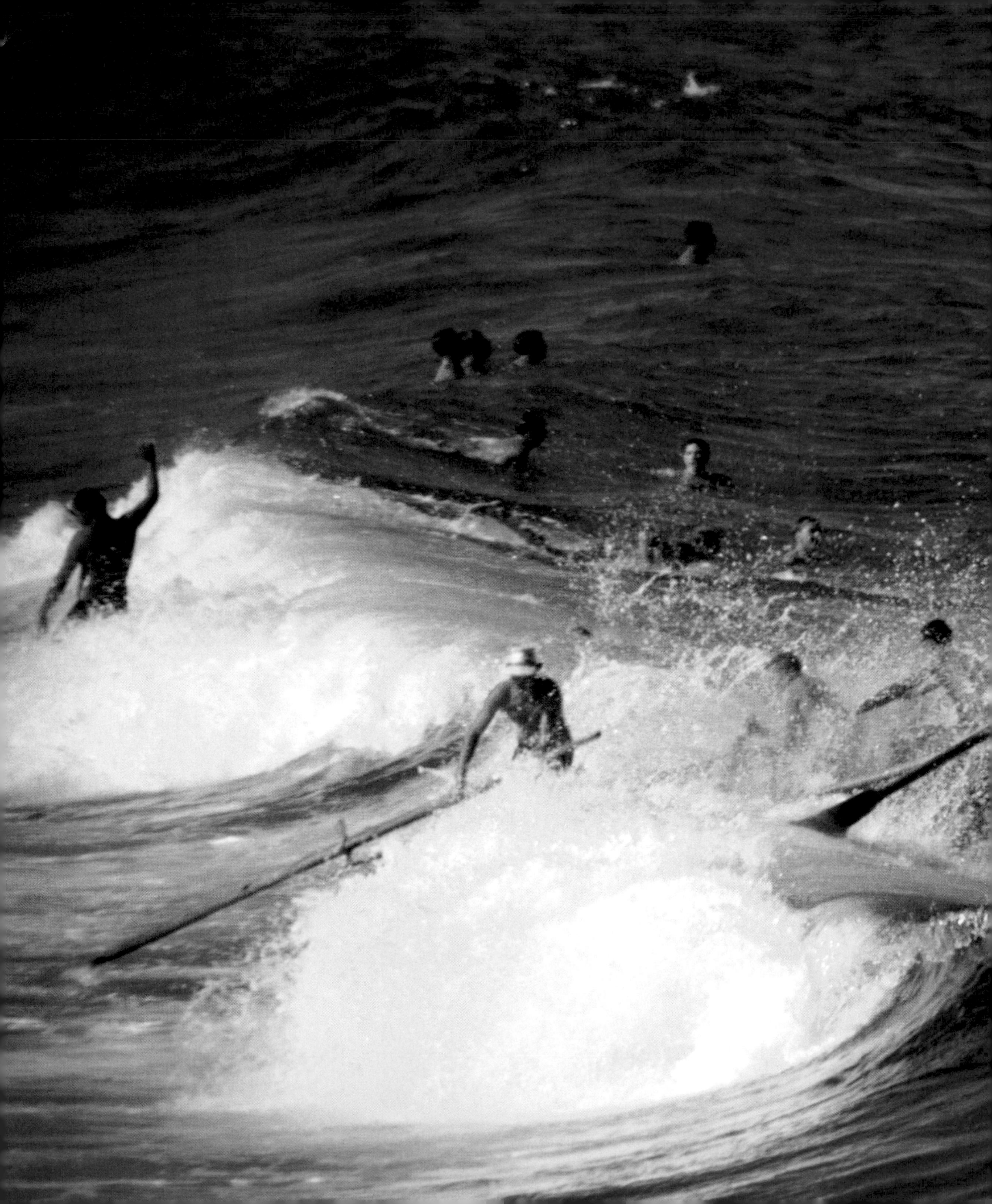

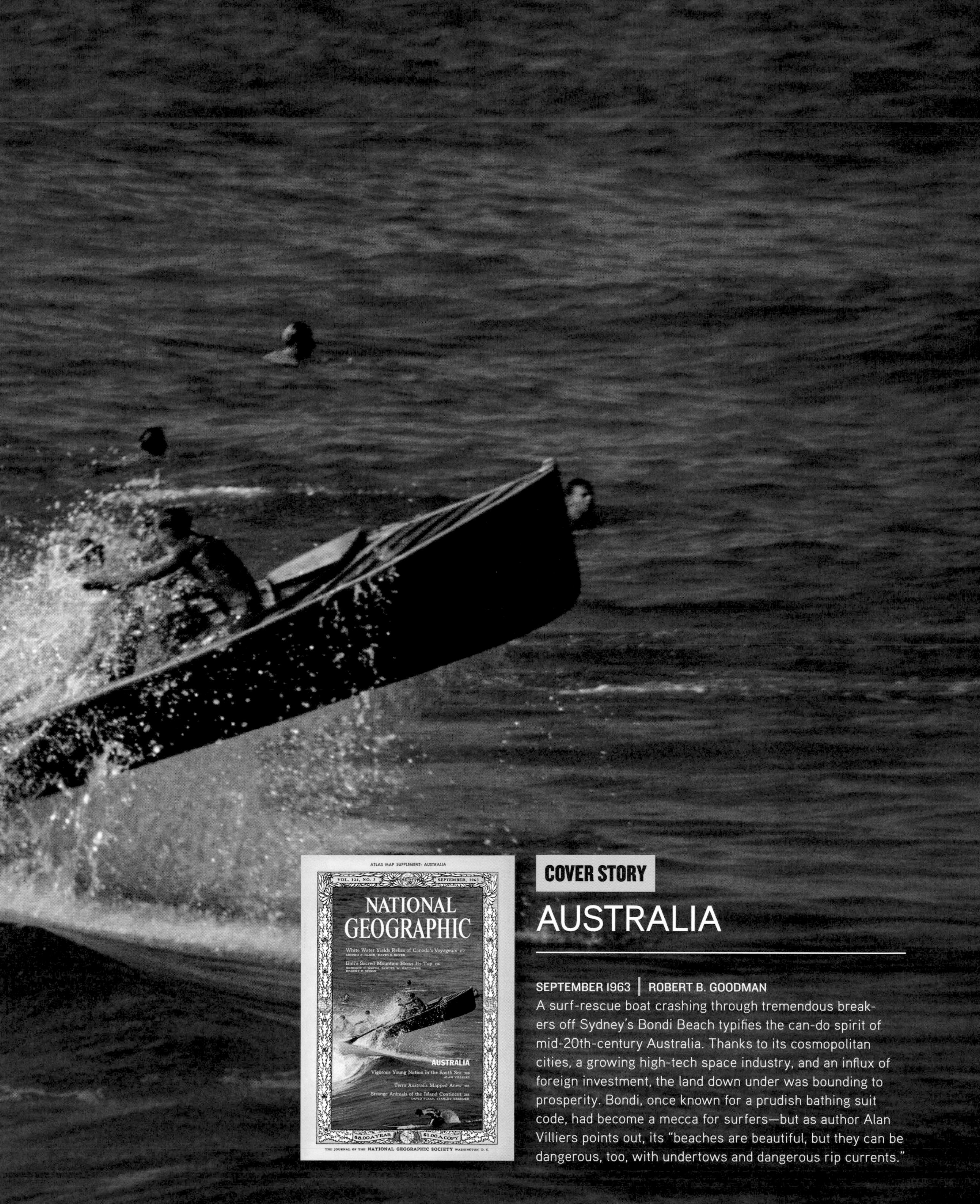

COVER STORY

AUSTRALIA

SEPTEMBER 1963 | ROBERT B. GOODMAN

A surf-rescue boat crashing through tremendous breakers off Sydney's Bondi Beach typifies the can-do spirit of mid-20th-century Australia. Thanks to its cosmopolitan cities, a growing high-tech space industry, and an influx of foreign investment, the land down under was bounding to prosperity. Bondi, once known for a prudish bathing suit code, had become a mecca for surfers—but as author Alan Villiers points out, its "beaches are beautiful, but they can be dangerous, too, with undertows and dangerous rip currents."

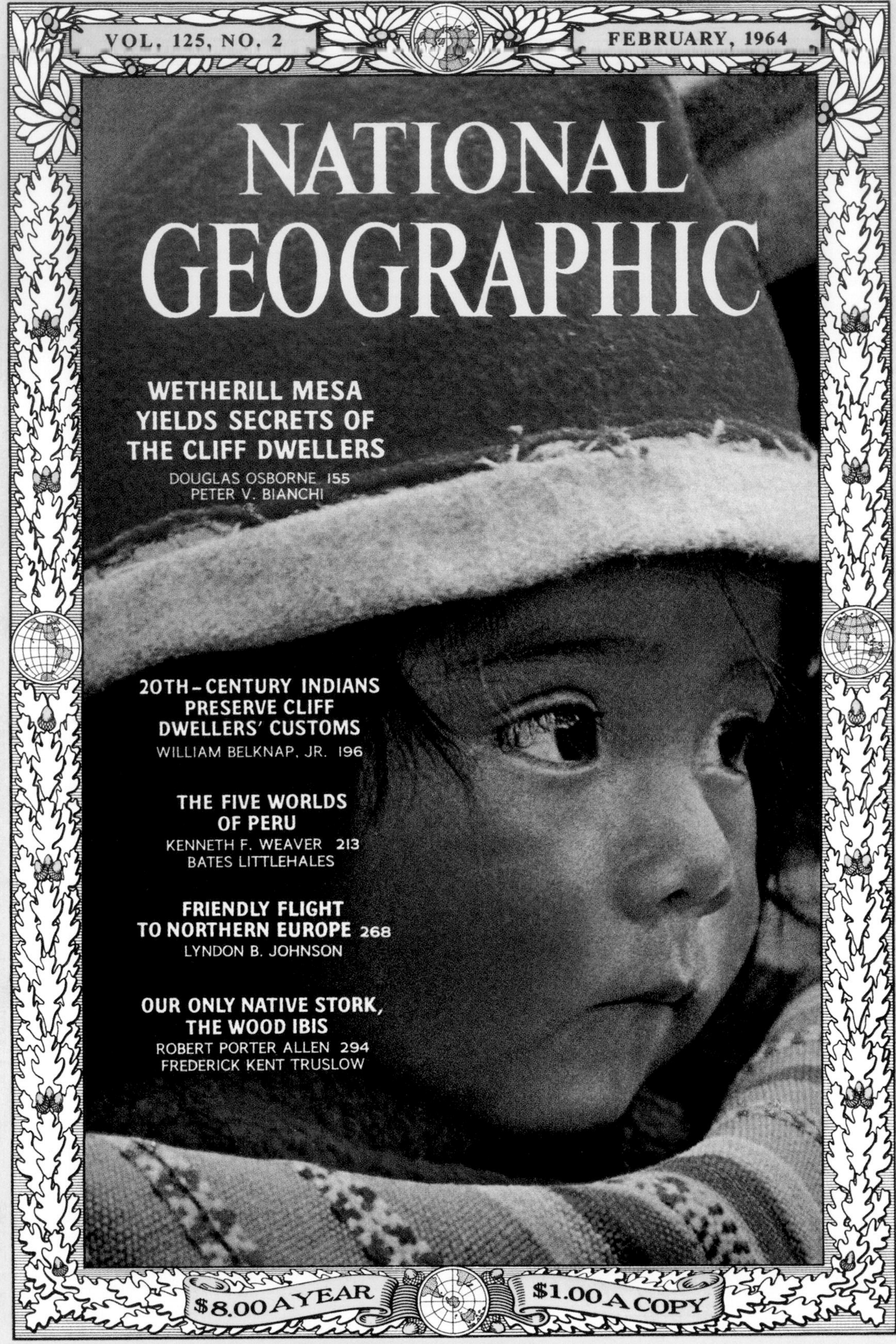

FEBRUARY | **BATES LITTLEHALES** A child carried on its mother's back eyes an Andean world.

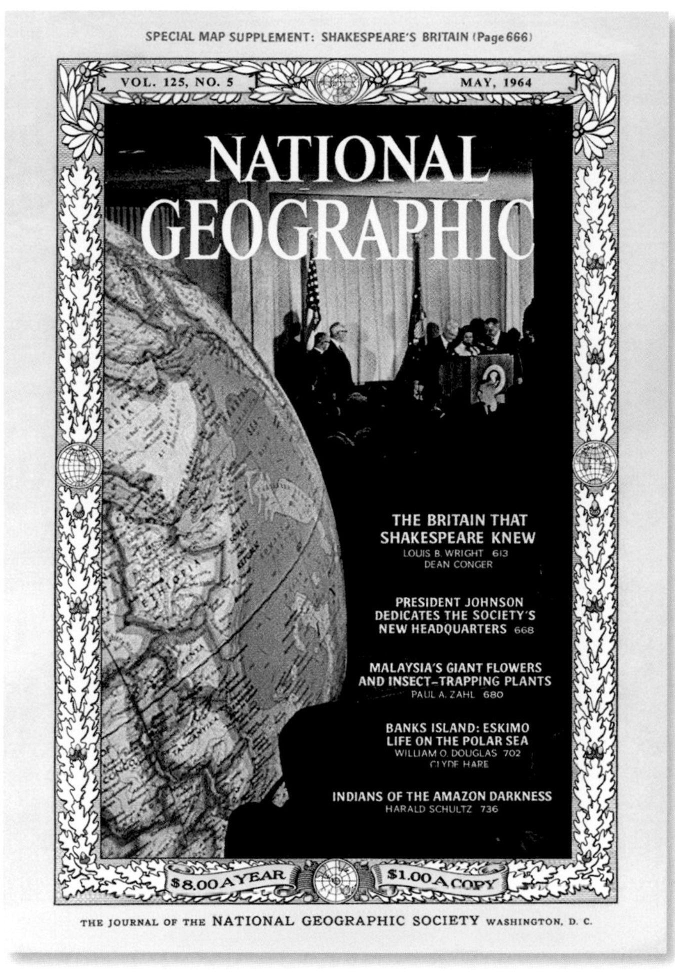

SPECIAL MAP SUPPLEMENT: SHAKESPEARE'S BRITAIN (Page 666)

VOL. 125, NO. 5 MAY, 1964

NATIONAL GEOGRAPHIC

THE BRITAIN THAT SHAKESPEARE KNEW
LOUIS B. WRIGHT 613
DEAN CONGER

PRESIDENT JOHNSON DEDICATES THE SOCIETY'S NEW HEADQUARTERS 668

MALAYSIA'S GIANT FLOWERS AND INSECT-TRAPPING PLANTS
PAUL A. ZAHL 680

BANKS ISLAND: ESKIMO LIFE ON THE POLAR SEA
WILLIAM O. DOUGLAS 702
CLYDE HARE

INDIANS OF THE AMAZON DARKNESS
HARALD SCHULTZ 736

$8.00 A YEAR $1.00 A COPY

THE JOURNAL OF THE NATIONAL GEOGRAPHIC SOCIETY WASHINGTON, D. C.

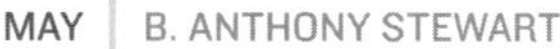

MAY | B. ANTHONY STEWART

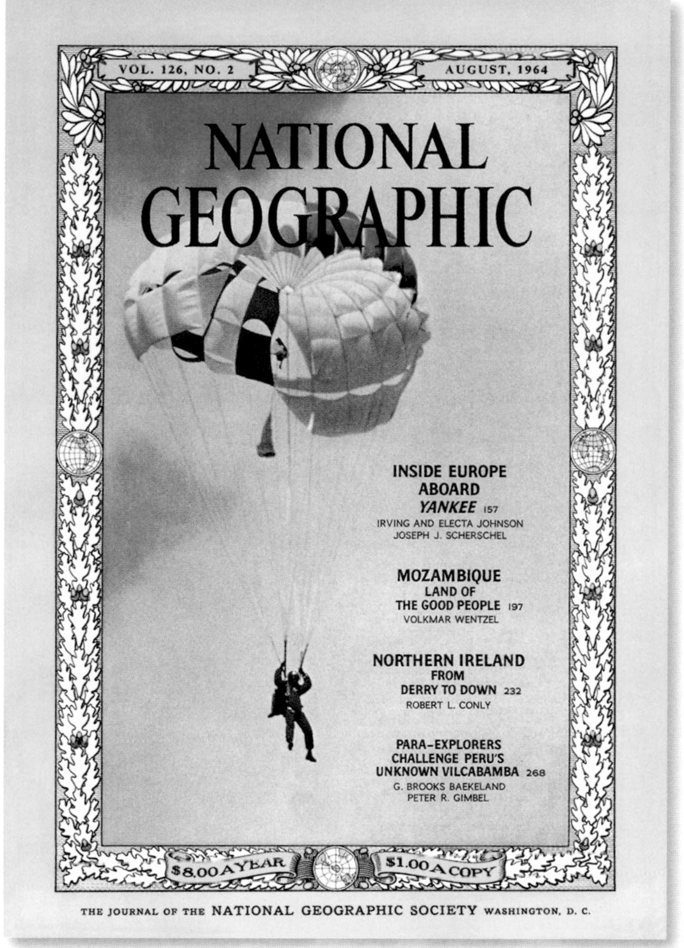

VOL. 126, NO. 2 AUGUST, 1964

NATIONAL GEOGRAPHIC

INSIDE EUROPE ABOARD *YANKEE* 157
IRVING AND ELECTA JOHNSON
JOSEPH J. SCHERSCHEL

MOZAMBIQUE LAND OF THE GOOD PEOPLE 197
VOLKMAR WENTZEL

NORTHERN IRELAND FROM DERRY TO DOWN 232
ROBERT L. CONLY

PARA-EXPLORERS CHALLENGE PERU'S UNKNOWN VILCABAMBA 268
G. BROOKS BAEKELAND
PETER R. GIMBEL

$8.00 A YEAR $1.00 A COPY

THE JOURNAL OF THE NATIONAL GEOGRAPHIC SOCIETY WASHINGTON, D. C.

AUGUST | PETER R. GIMBEL

▲ **AS THE WORLD TURNS** Hardly had President Lyndon B. Johnson stepped away from the microphone on that January day in 1964 when he dedicated the Society's soaring new headquarters building—having declared, "Today, in this house of exploration, let us invite exploration, by all nations for all nations"—when the world began to spin. His wife, Lady Bird Johnson, had pressed the button setting in motion a giant globe—11 feet from Pole to Pole, 34.5 feet around its Equator, and weighing 1,100 pounds—that for over two decades attracted guests to the exhibit space still called Explorers Hall.

▲ **PERUVIAN PLUMMET** A special high-altitude parachute allows a member of a four-man expedition to drop through thin mountain air and land on a 10,500-foot-high shelf in the Peruvian Andes. No attempt to explore by foot the remote Cordillera Vilcabamba, rumored to hold lost Inca cities, had yet succeeded. But Peter Gimbel and his companions spent three months slogging 150 miles across its treacherous terrain on foot and by canoe before rafting back to civilization—the first men known to have traversed the range.

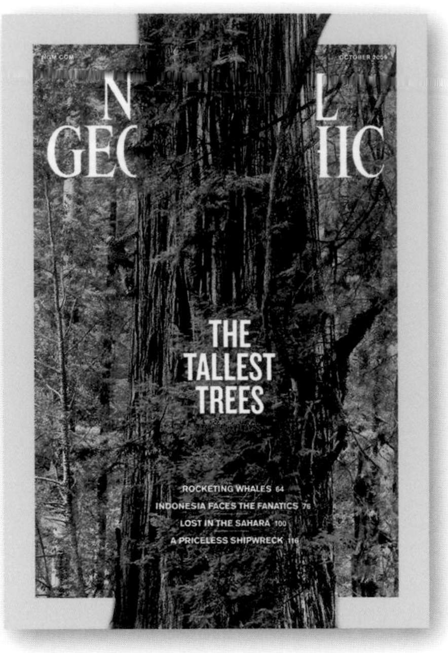

OCTOBER 2009 | MICHAEL NICHOLS

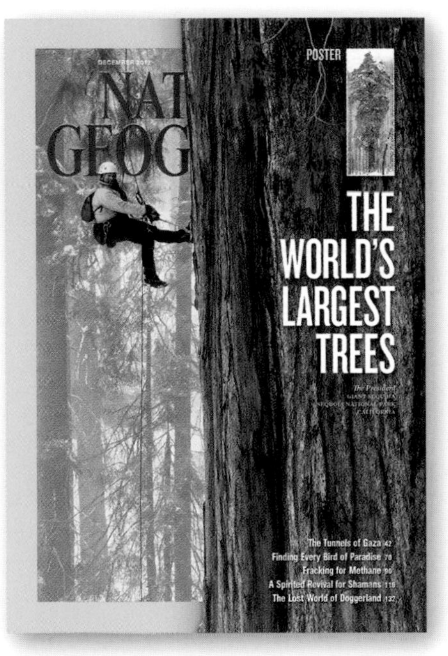

DECEMBER 2012 | MICHAEL NICHOLS

2009 ▸▸▸▸ FAST FORWARD

MONUMENTAL TREES Forty-five years elapsed before another giant tree graced the cover. Nichols says of his October 2009 redwood and December 2012 sequoia covers that they are "postage stamps compared to big maps," depicting only fractions of the large foldout images included in each issue.

GIANT TREES ▸

RANGING THE REDWOOD FORESTS of California in 1960, *Geographic* staff naturalist Paul Zahl discovered, in a grove of splendid trees soaring above a creek bend, what was then believed to be the tallest tree in the world. Editor Melville Bell Grosvenor was so impressed by the giant that he wanted a photograph of himself taken standing near its base.

"He stood on a gravel bar of the creek and I went well downstream so I could get him tiny in the foreground with the tree rising above him. This was just a record photograph of him in front of the tree to show scale," staff photographer George Mobley remembered. So he was appalled when this "boring picture" appeared on the July 1964 cover—making it, in his opinion, the worst cover in the magazine's history.

Nearly half a century later, when Michael "Nick" Nichols became the first to successfully photograph a redwood from base to crown, he chose a 300-foot tree at least 1,500 years old—and again humans were used to provide scale. The feat took months of planning, three weeks to execute, and was accomplished by rigging a camera on a rope-and-pulley system suspended between nearby trees, Nichols releasing the shutter remotely via laptop. The best 84 images were stitched together for an extraordinary arboreal portrait.

Even more heroic efforts were undertaken when Nichols photographed the President, a giant sequoia some 3,200 years old. More rope tricks with cameras, more humans to give scale, and three weeks laboring under blizzard conditions resulted in a composite of 126 images. Said Nichols, "I wanted to honor the tree."

> "*These trees belong to the silences and millenniums. They seem, indeed, to be forms of immortality, standing there among the transitory shapes of time.*"
>
> —Edwin Markham
>
> *from "Finding the Mt. Everest of All Living Things"*

ATLAS MAP SUPPLEMENT: NEW YORK CITY

VOL. 126, NO. 1

NATIONAL GEOGRAPHIC

JULY, 1964

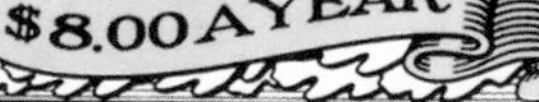

$1.

JULY | GEORGE F. MOBLEY Towering? Yes, but taller redwoods have since been found.

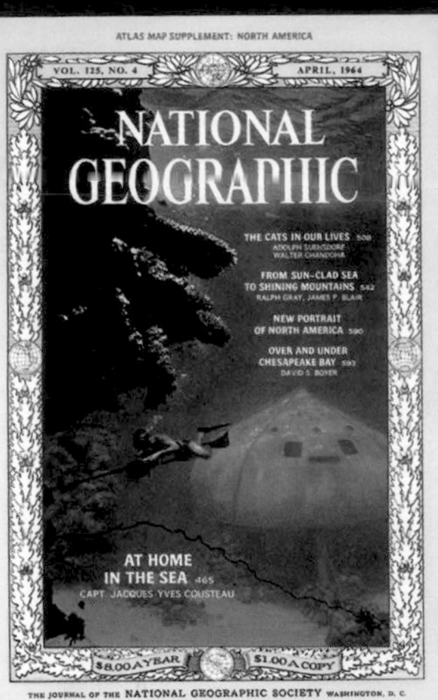

COVER STORY

JACQUES-YVES COUSTEAU

APRIL 1964 | ROBERT B. GOODMAN

To live and work on the seafloor—Jacques-Yves Cousteau put that dream to the test when in 1963 he erected a submarine village on a coral reef in the Red Sea. The onion-shaped dome—hanger for a "diving saucer"—is part of a complex that also included a "starfish house" where five men lived for a month 36 feet below the surface. Divers swam about armed with long shark billies. But the worst assaults came from ravenous little crustaceans that resembled fleas—"as vicious for their size as fearsome piranhas," Cousteau reported.

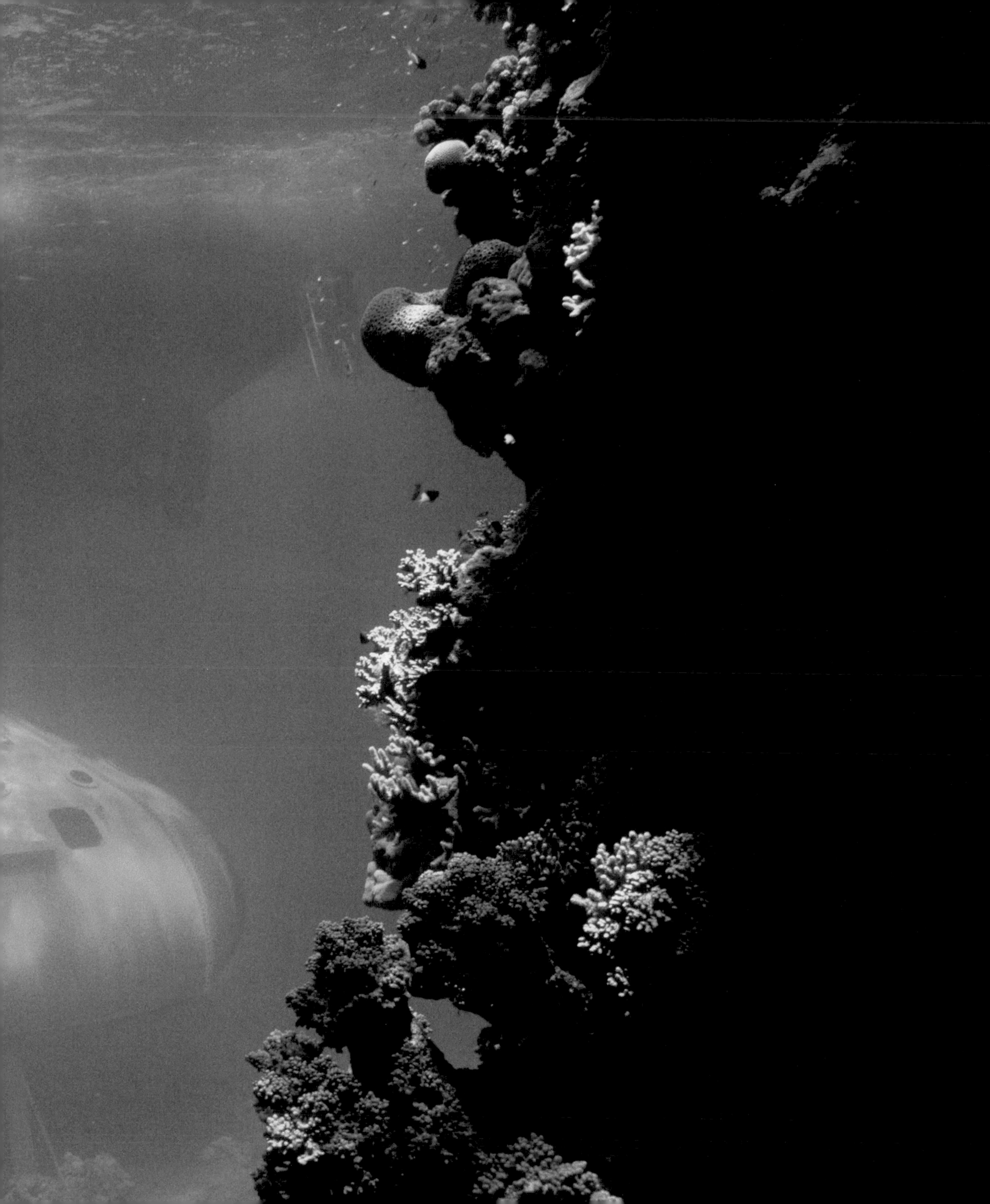

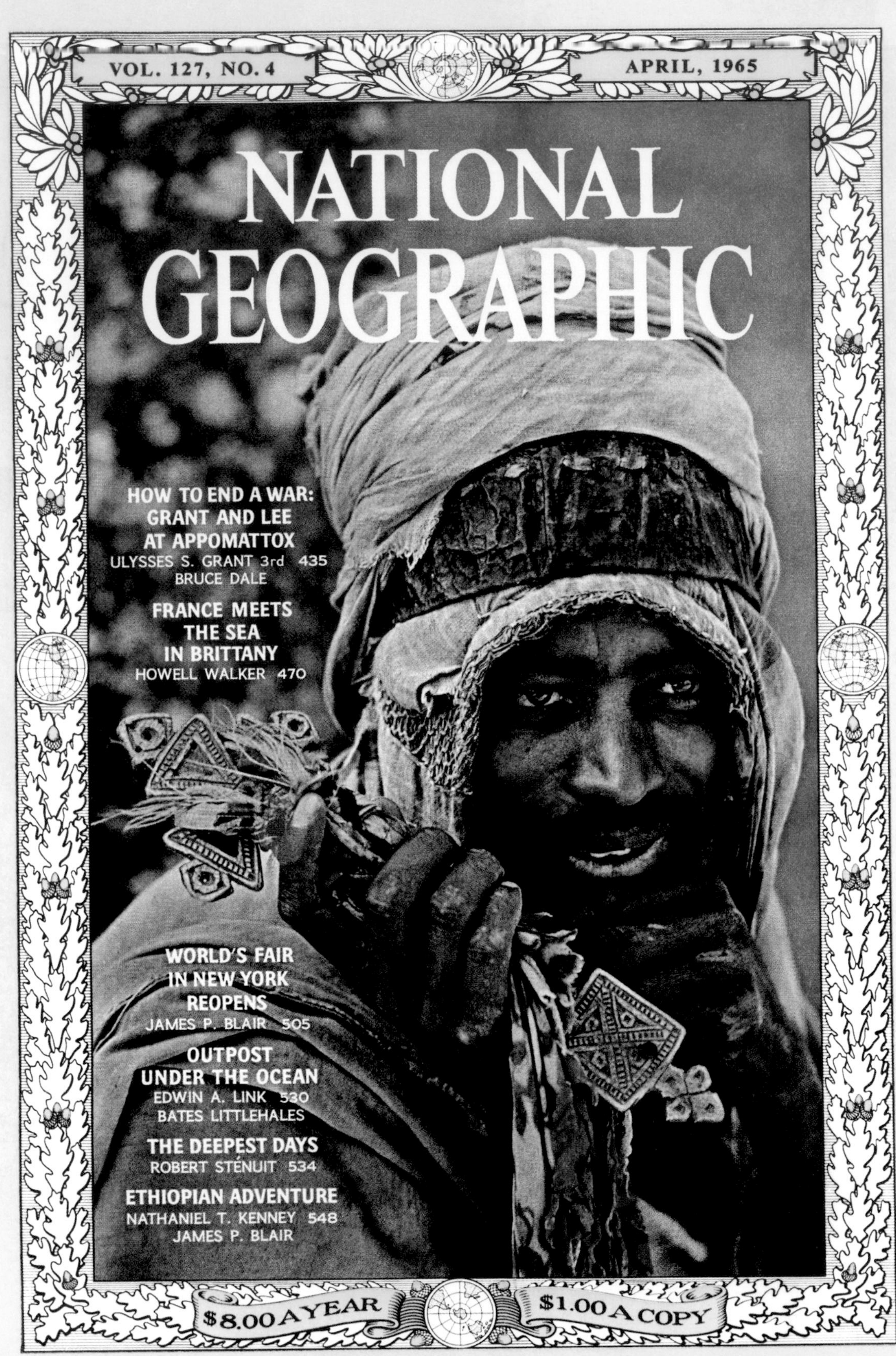

APRIL | **JAMES P. BLAIR** An Ethiopian monk at Debro Damo cherishes his Coptic cross.

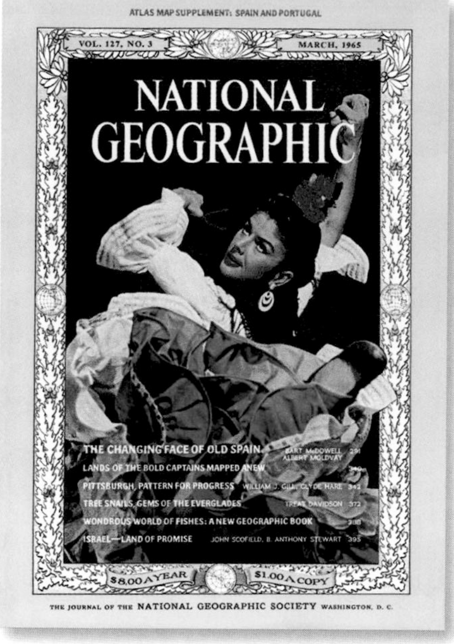

MARCH | ALBERT MOLDVAY

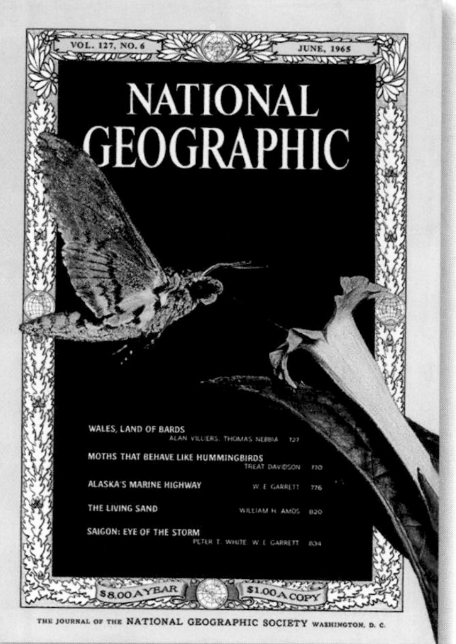

JUNE | TREAT DAVIDSON

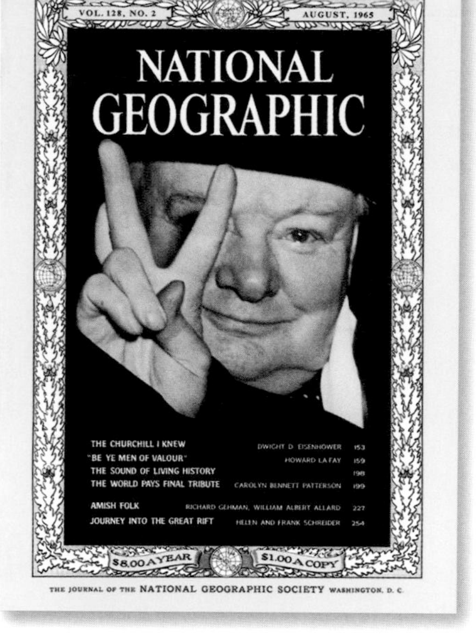

AUGUST | HARRIS & EWING

ETHIOPIAN SHANGRI-LA

To *Geographic* staff writer Nat Kenney, Ethiopia was the "Tibet of Africa," a land of soaring mountains little removed from the time of Solomon and Sheba. After spending three months in a Land Rover with Kenney, staff photographer Jim Blair was inclined to agree, especially upon arriving at a sheer-sided mesa called Debro Damo, crowned by a sixth-century Christian monastery.

It was a realm off-limits to all females, whether human or goat; and the only way up there was to climb a leather cable hand-over-hand. The middle-aged Kenney demurred; the 33-year-old Blair ascended, first having his cameras hoisted up ("always an incentive" to follow).

He found himself in a medieval setting, an Ethiopian Shangri-la, where dreamy-eyed monks lived in an almost tangible sense of "absolute peace," he later recalled. He remembered thinking at the time he made the portrait at left that here was a place "about as exotic as any I had ever dreamed of."

ON THE RECORD Jim Blair was a member of the *Geographic* team flown to London in January 1965 to photograph the state funeral of Sir Winston Churchill. Included with their pictures in the August issue was a phonograph record featuring sound bites from Churchill's speeches—the first time a record was bound into a mass-circulation magazine.

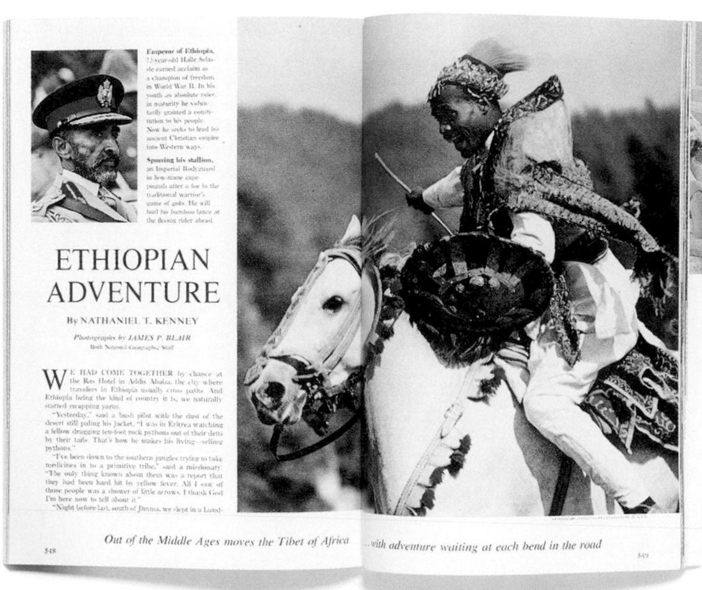
ETHIOPIAN ADVENTURE

By NATHANIEL T. KENNEY

Out of the Middle Ages moves the Tibet of Africa ... with adventure waiting at each bend in the road

APRIL 1965 | **JAMES P. BLAIR** Mounted bodyguards in lion-mane capes honor Ethiopian emperor Haile Selassie.

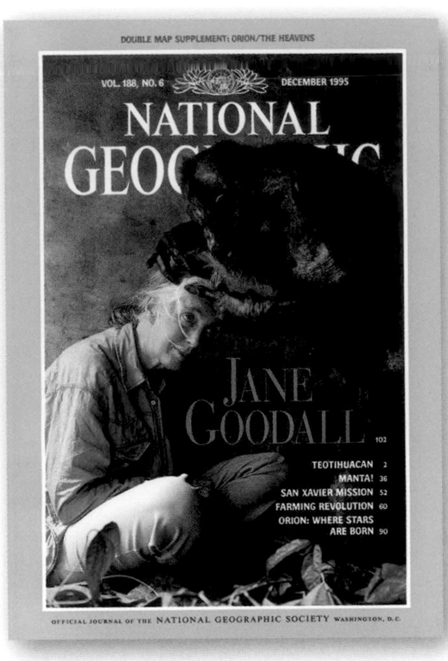

DECEMBER 1995 | MICHAEL NICHOLS

JANE GOODALL ▶

PORTRAIT OF GOODALL, PART ONE: On the December 1965 cover, the researcher sits among the chimpanzees, notebook in hand, watching as Mr. McGregor and Leakey, Flo and Figan, Flint and Fifi groom one another. Turn the cover of December 1965 and find inside the magazine a famous set of photographs depicting Goodall playfully interacting with the chimps, photographs made by her husband, Dutch nobleman Baron Hugo van Lawick—which only increases the charm of this African idyll for millions of *Geographic* readers the world over.

In truth, she finds posing for such pictures to be annoying, for it interferes with her work. After all, she has made astonishing observations about our closest cousins, discovering that not only are they toolmakers, too, but that they also need a rich and varied social life.

Portrait of Goodall, Part Two: Three decades later, she has ventured into a filthy cage hardly opened in decades—closed for so long that its door had rusted shut. Lurking in the recesses of this dingy cell in Congo's Brazzaville Zoo is an emaciated chimpanzee named Grégoire, and he has endured this solitary confinement since 1944. Photographer Michael "Nick" Nichols follows Goodall, not without trepidation, for chimps are stronger than humans, and deprived of socialization can be severely disturbed, even psychotic. So Grégoire's increasingly agitated movements are worrisome.

Yet Goodall first calms, then soothes the captive. Nichols's shot of the moment Grégoire tentatively reaches to groom her in return—a touch denied him for half a century—will make the cover of the December 1995 *Geographic*.

1995 ▶▶▶▶ FAST FORWARD

THIRTY YEARS LATER To Michael "Nick" Nichols, this portrait of Goodall redeeming the captive summed up the thrust of her life and work. Happily enough, the gentle Grégoire was eventually moved to the Jane Goodall Institute's Tchimpounga Sanctuary in Congo, where he lived out his days—dying in 2008 at about 66—in contentment among fellow chimps.

> *"I knew I had to use the knowledge the chimps gave me in the fight to save them."*
>
> —Jane Goodall
>
> *from "Jane Goodall: Crusading for Chimps and Humans"*

▶ DECEMBER 1965 | HUGO VAN LAWICK
Van Lawick and Goodall were married from 1964 to 1974.

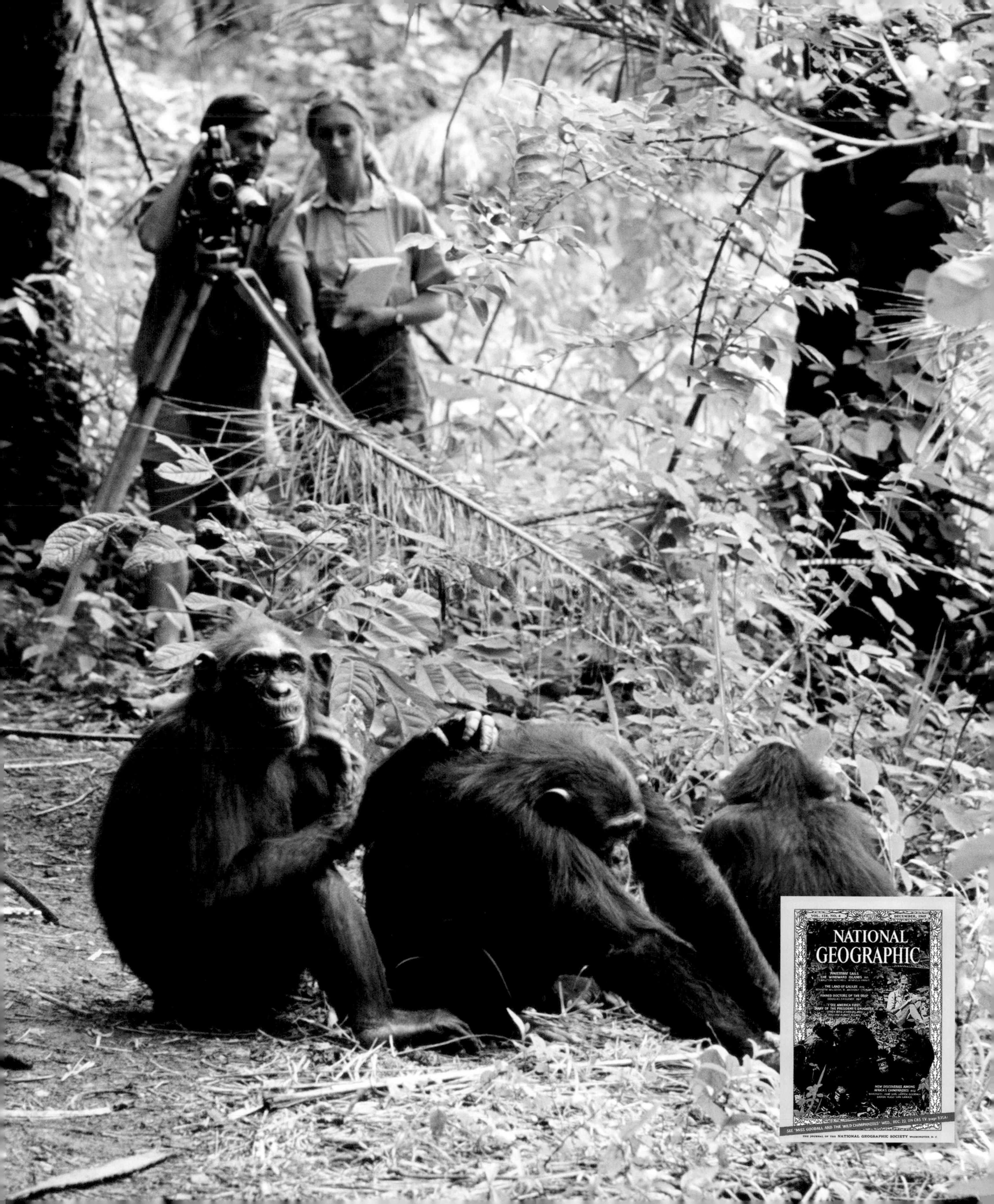
VOL. 128, NO. 6
DECEMBER, 1965
NATIONAL GEOGRAPHIC
FINISTERRE SAILS THE WINDWARD ISLANDS
THE LAND OF GALILEE
FINNED DOCTORS OF THE DEEP
"I SEE AMERICA FIRST": DIARY OF THE PRESIDENT'S DAUGHTER
NEW DISCOVERIES AMONG AFRICA'S CHIMPANZEES
SEE "MISS GOODALL AND THE WILD CHIMPANZEES" WED., DEC. 22, ON CBS TV (page 831A)
THE JOURNAL OF THE NATIONAL GEOGRAPHIC SOCIETY WASHINGTON, D. C.

ONE STORY, MANY COVERS

COVERING VIETNAM

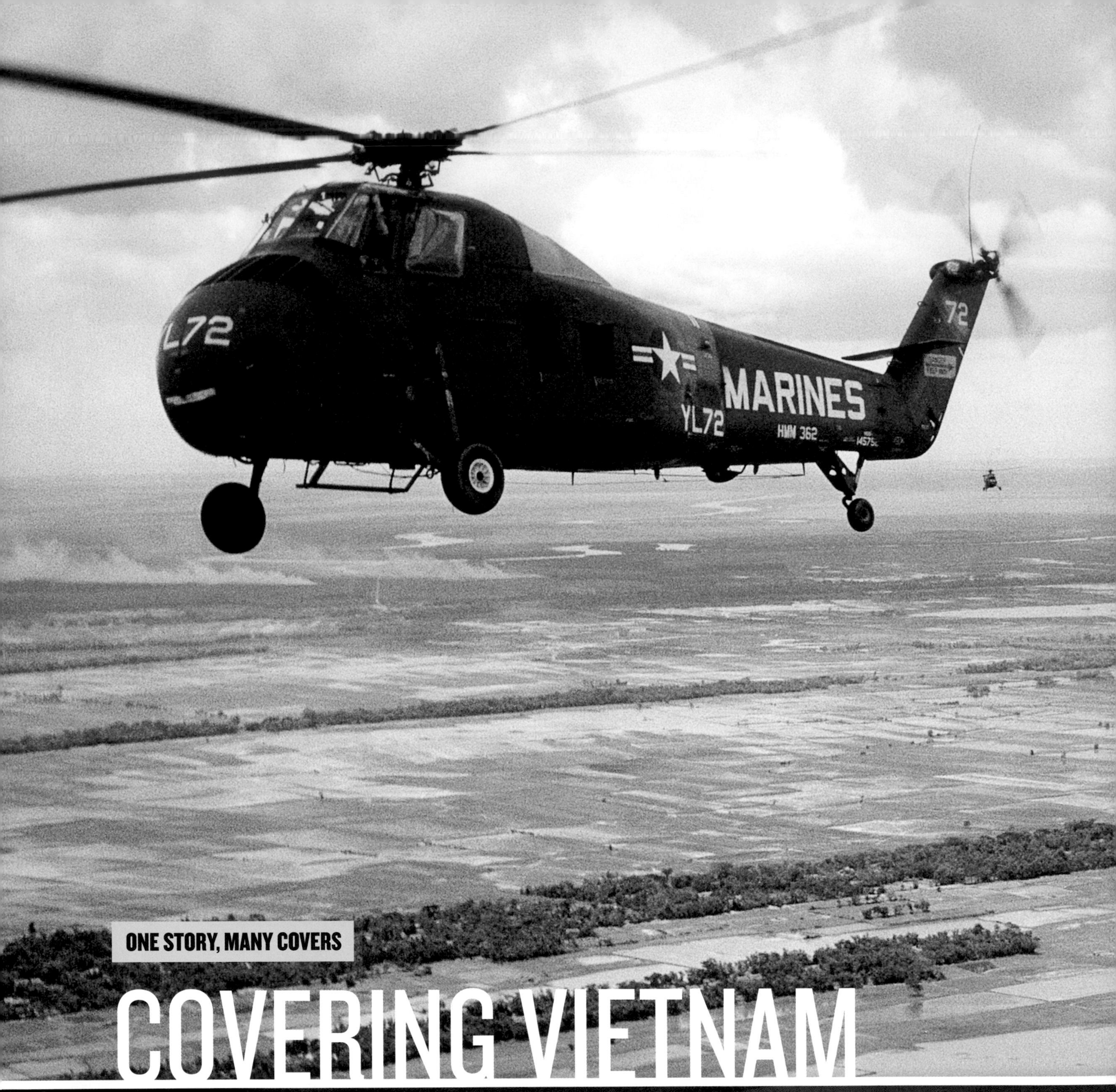

▲ NOVEMBER 1962 | DICKEY CHAPELLE
Dickey Chapelle's pictures were some of the first published anywhere to show American troops fighting in Vietnam.

SHE COVERED VIETNAM FROM its "helicopter war" to its "water war" for the *Geographic,* but in 1965 Dickey Chapelle was hit by shrapnel from an exploding grenade. She was dead by the time the chopper arrived—the first woman correspondent killed in that conflict. That was not the only precedent-rattling outcome of Vietnam for the magazine: In particular, the 11 articles on war in Southeast Asia published between 1961 and 1971 marked a turning point in the *Geographic's* photography toward more photojournalism.

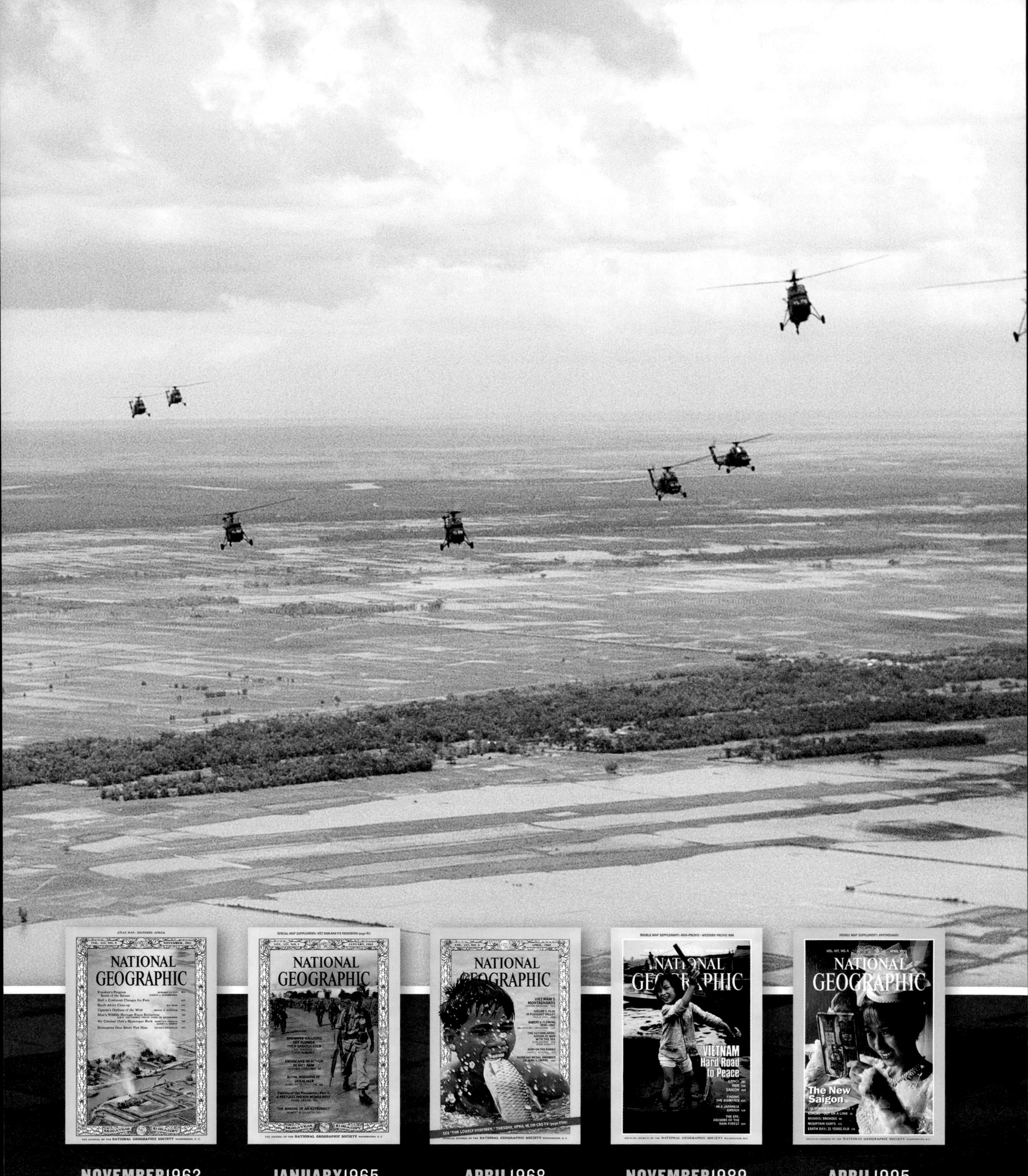
NATIONAL GEOGRAPHIC
NATIONAL GEOGRAPHIC
NATIONAL GEOGRAPHIC
VIET NAM'S MONTAGNARDS
NATIONAL GEOGRAPHIC
VIETNAM Hard Road to Peace
NATIONAL GEOGRAPHIC
The New Saigon
NOVEMBER 1962
JANUARY 1965
APRIL 1968
NOVEMBER 1989
APRIL 1995

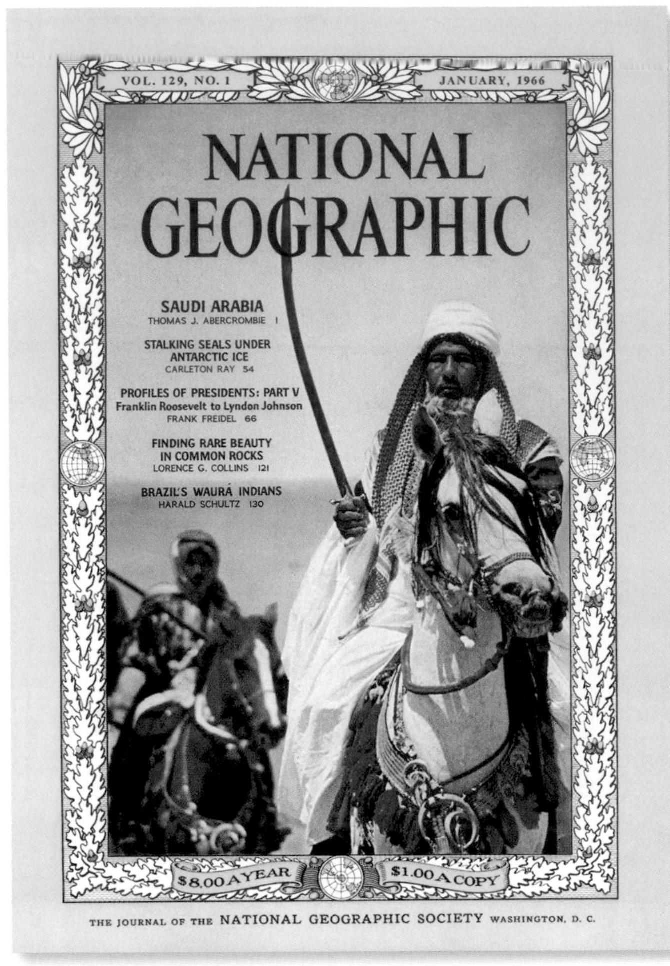

JANUARY | THOMAS J. ABERCROMBIE

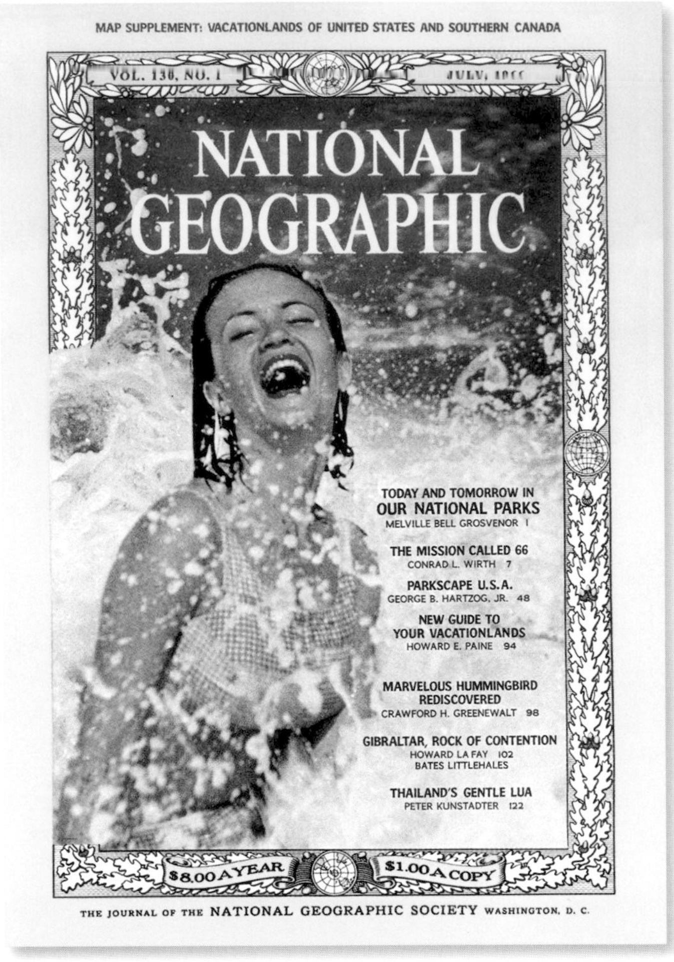

JULY | EMORY KRISTOF

▲ **ABERCROMBIE IN ARABIA** A scimitar-wielding Bedouin on a caparisoned Arabian steed canters toward Thomas J. Abercrombie—but without menace, as the *Geographic* correspondent was attending a Saudi royal horse show. During the four months Abercrombie traveled across Saudi Arabia, armed with letters from King Faisal himself, tent flaps everywhere opened to welcome him. His conversion to Islam also won him permission to photograph the annual pilgrimage to Mecca.

▲ **BUBBLES AND SURF** What does this woman have to do with the National Park Service and the feature article on their Mission '66? Readers had the same reaction—some stronger than others. "Shame on you!" wrote one woman, aghast that her *Geographic* was sporting a bathing beauty in a wet swimsuit. "It looks like a soap ad!" opined another outraged subscriber. "Oh my G-d, not the NG, too," complained one man, while another asserted that the cover was "half Coney Island and half Madison Avenue, with all the sickening dental display of both." Actually the surf she was enjoying was at Cape Hatteras National Seashore, a national park.

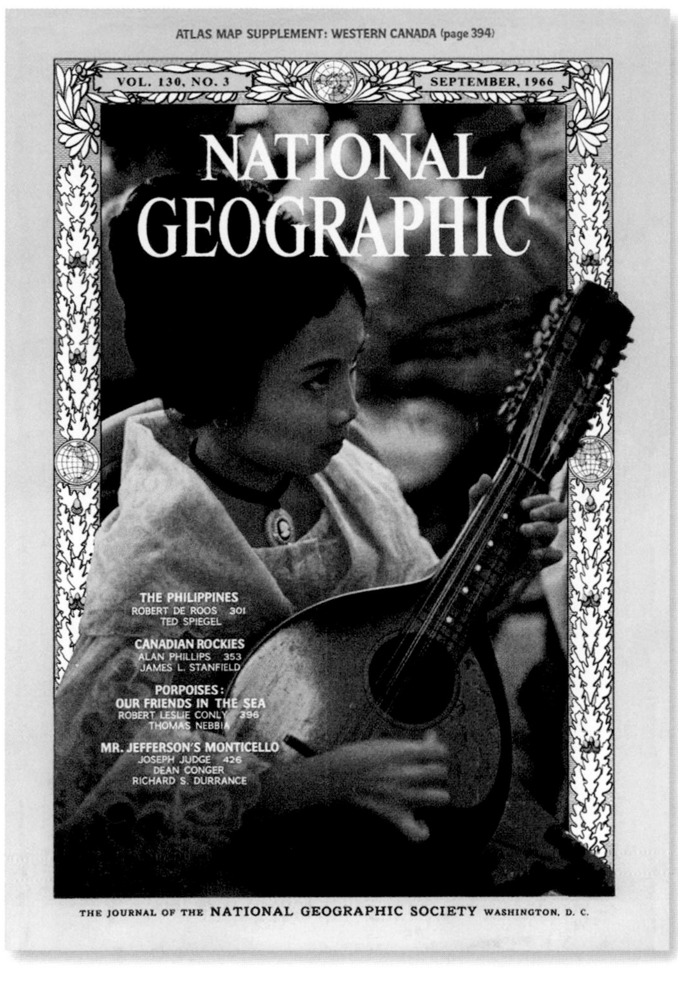

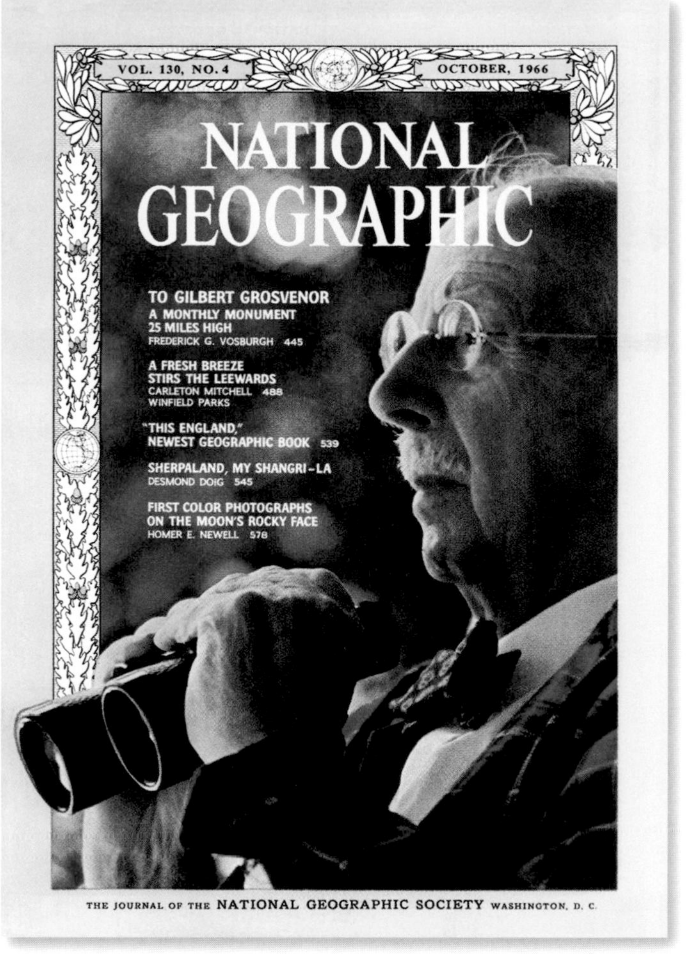

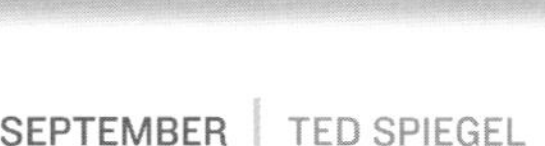

SEPTEMBER | TED SPIEGEL

OCTOBER | THOMAS NEBBIA

▲ **PATRIOTIC MUSICIAN** Her demure gaze reflecting a "pure soul," her fingers plucking her *bandurria,* this member of a *rondalla* orchestra in Manila's Luneta Park resembles María Clara, heroine of martyred Philippine patriot José Rizal's novel *Noli Me Tangere.* She even wears the full-sleeved blouse called, unsurprisingly, the María Clara. Following World War II, the newly independent Philippines, after centuries as a Spanish colony and decades under American rule, was forging a new national identity.

▲ **HONORING "MR. GEOGRAPHIC"** Gilbert H. Grosvenor (1875–1966), former *National Geographic* Editor in Chief, watches birds from his porch in Coral Gables, Florida.

"From the Golden Horn to the Potomac, from the year before the telephone to the year of testing the Apollo moonship, from a little group of scientists and scholars to a world-wide National Geographic Society of five million members—the long, busy life of Gilbert Hovey Grosvenor spanned all this."

—Frederick G. Vosburgh
from "To Gilbert Grosvenor"

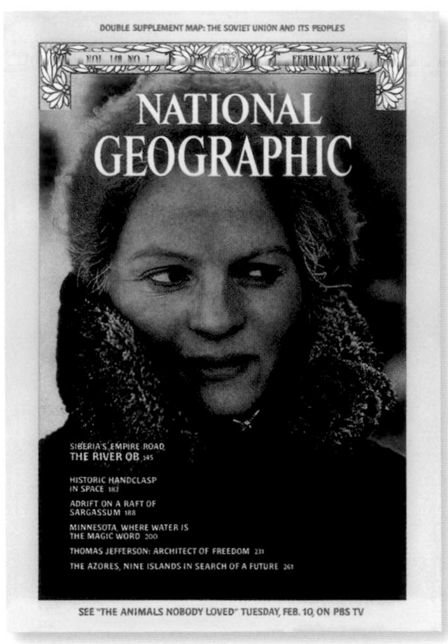

FEBRUARY 1976 | DEAN CONGER

1976 ▸▸▸▸ FAST FORWARD

A COLD WAIT Ten years later, while on another trip to the Soviet Union, Conger photographed this woman waiting for a department store to open in the Siberian city of Khanty Mansiysk—looking nonchalant despite the minus 40°F temperature. But to Conger's companion, *Geographic* author Bob Jordan, the cold "burned the face and tormented the lungs."

RUSSIAN REFLECTIONS ▸

Always and everywhere there was the escort. Dean Conger could not even make a picture of Red Square's multicolored, many-domed St. Basil's Cathedral without his official government-appointed guide hovering nearby.

Conger made nearly two dozen trips to the Soviet Union during the 1960s and '70s. As a result, his multifaceted portrait of that sprawling land and its people was unrivaled by any other American photojournalist of his era. But it came at a cost: For one thing, he was always ensnarled by red tape. The inescapable escort was one thing; the "Prohibited" list was another, for it stamped *nyet* across a broad swath of the country. He was forced to obtain a separate visa for each city he visited. Even the Russian winter conspired against him, fogging his lenses, cracking his film, and assaulting his nose and fingers with frostbite.

For another thing, it demanded a strong stomach—or perhaps a strong liver—for matching his hosts' vodka for vodka was a daily necessity:

> They want to feed you and give you a lot to drink. If you don't partake freely, you probably won't get to take your pictures. But if you do, you won't be in shape to take them . . . At times, the partying pressed upon the visitor is merely primitive hospitality. At other times, the parties mask the conspiracy to keep you from seeing anything. And if they can get you loaded, you won't care. "Dean, Dean, don't worry about the sun going down. It's all right." The guide's words are like a recording.
>
> —*From* Images of the World: Photography at the National Geographic, *Dean Conger*

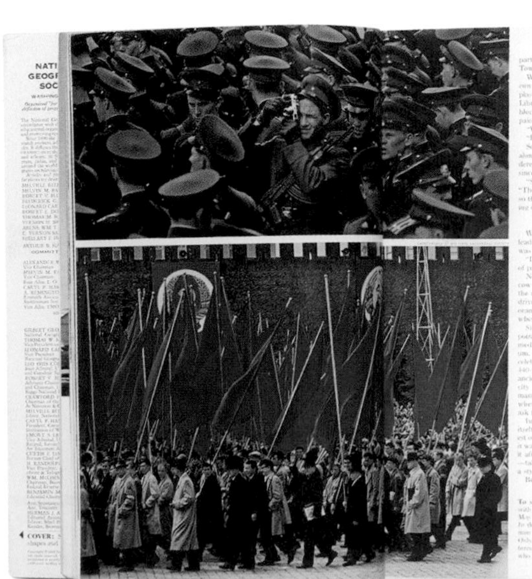

◂ MARCH 1966 | DEAN CONGER May Day in Red Square, when even soldiers wield cameras

▸ MARCH 1966 | DEAN CONGER St. Basil's Cathedral is reflected in a rain puddle.

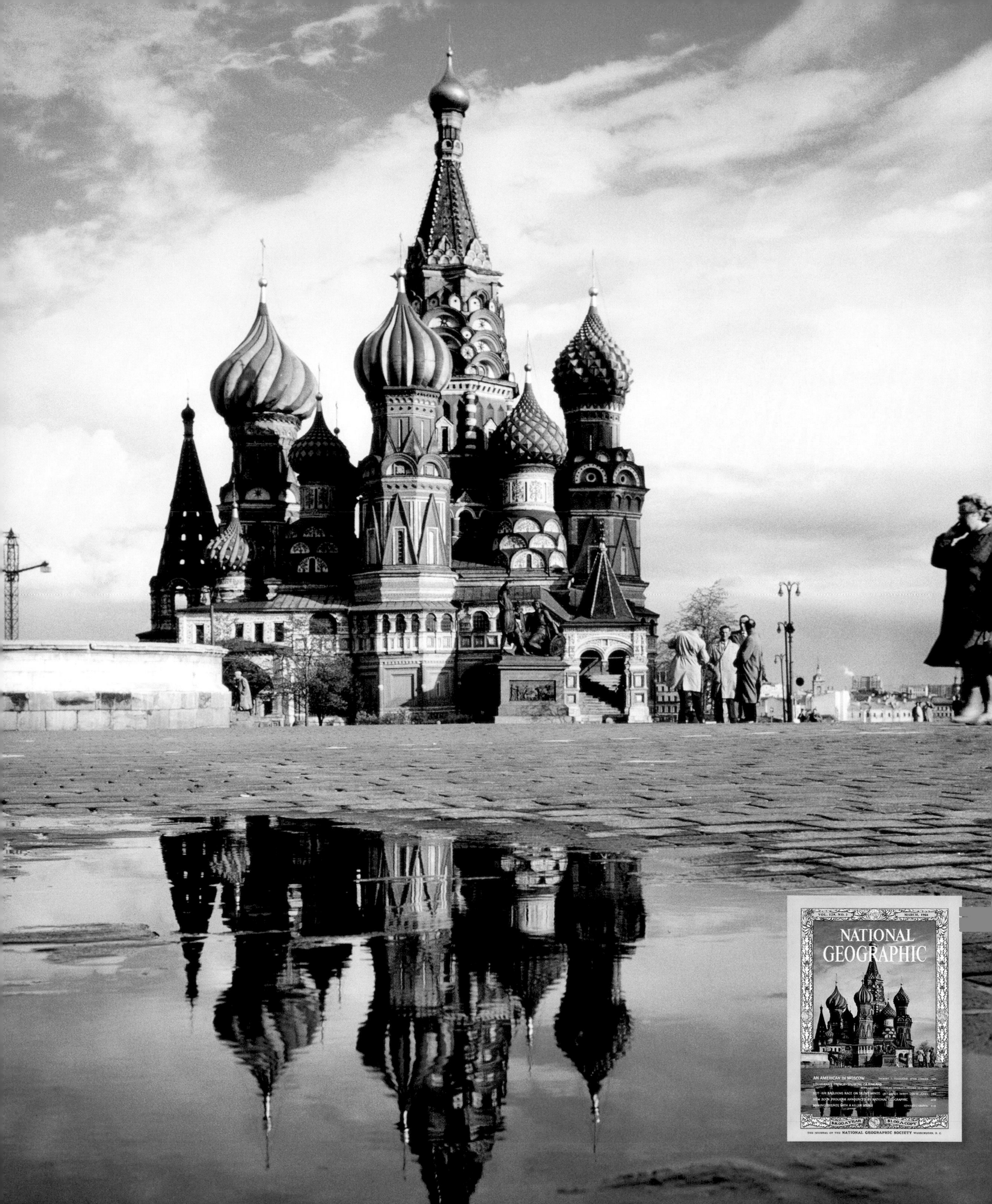
VOL. 129, NO. 3
MARCH, 1966
NATIONAL GEOGRAPHIC
AN AMERICAN IN MOSCOW
LOUISIANA'S FRENCH-SPEAKING CAJUNLAND
HOT-AIR BALLOONS RACE ON SILENT WINDS
NEW BOOK PROGRAM ANNOUNCED BY NATIONAL GEOGRAPHIC
MAKING FRIENDS WITH A KILLER WHALE
$8.00 A YEAR
$1.00 A COPY
THE JOURNAL OF THE NATIONAL GEOGRAPHIC SOCIETY WASHINGTON, D. C.

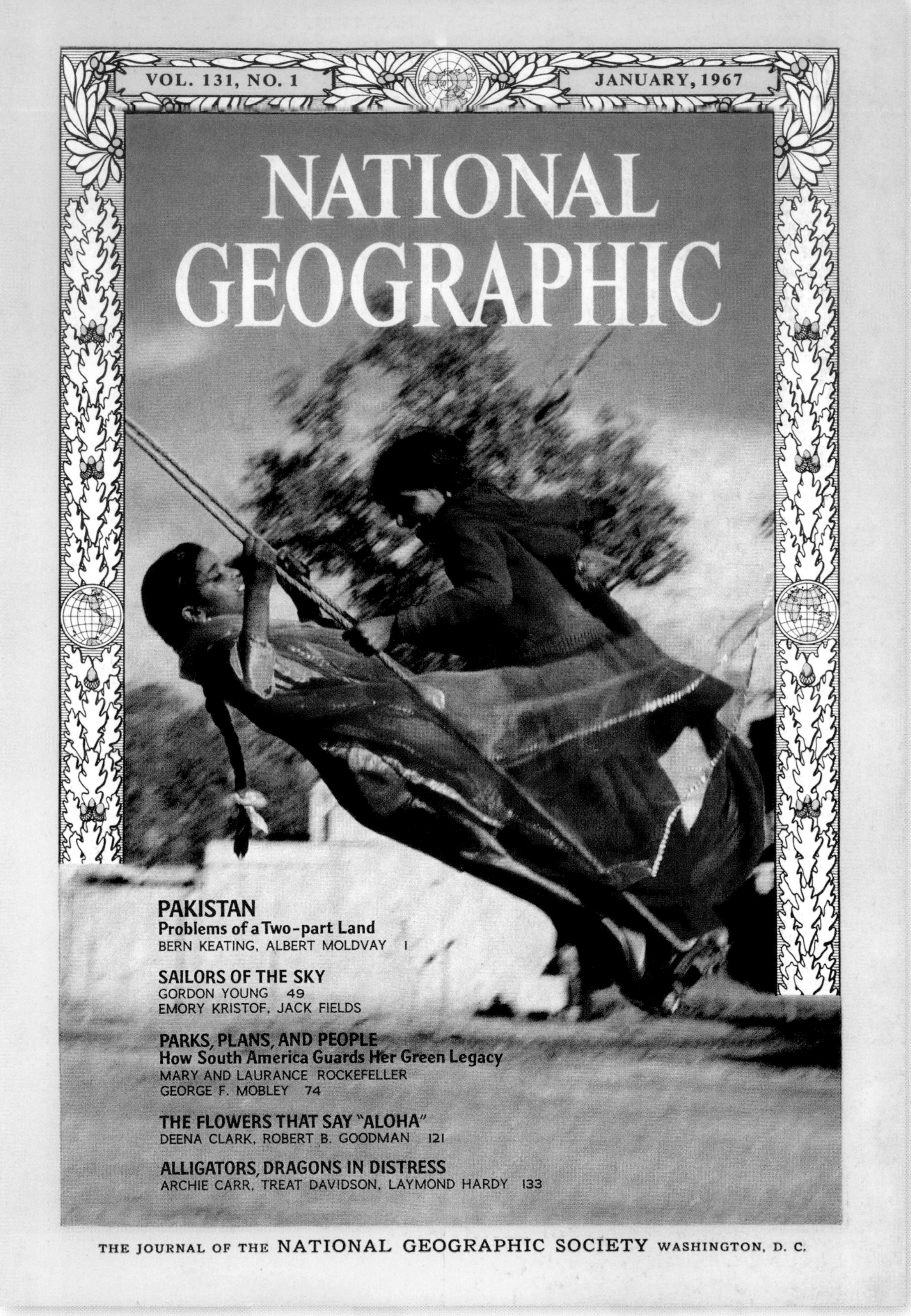
VOL. 131, NO. 1

JANUARY, 1967

NATIONAL GEOGRAPHIC

PAKISTAN
Problems of a Two-part Land
BERN KEATING, ALBERT MOLDVAY 1

SAILORS OF THE SKY
GORDON YOUNG 49
EMORY KRISTOF, JACK FIELDS

PARKS, PLANS, AND PEOPLE
How South America Guards Her Green Legacy
MARY AND LAURANCE ROCKEFELLER
GEORGE F. MOBLEY 74

THE FLOWERS THAT SAY "ALOHA"
DEENA CLARK, ROBERT B. GOODMAN 121

ALLIGATORS, DRAGONS IN DISTRESS
ARCHIE CARR, TREAT DAVIDSON, LAYMOND HARDY 133

THE JOURNAL OF THE NATIONAL GEOGRAPHIC SOCIETY WASHINGTON, D. C.

JANUARY | ALBERT MOLDVAY

UPSWING In matching dresses worn for a Muslim festival, these swinging girls seem an apt symbol for an article on Pakistan, still a twinned nation—East Pakistan and West Pakistan—separated by 1,500 miles of Hindu India. But trouble is coming: After a bitter 1971 civil war, East Pakistan will become independent Bangladesh.

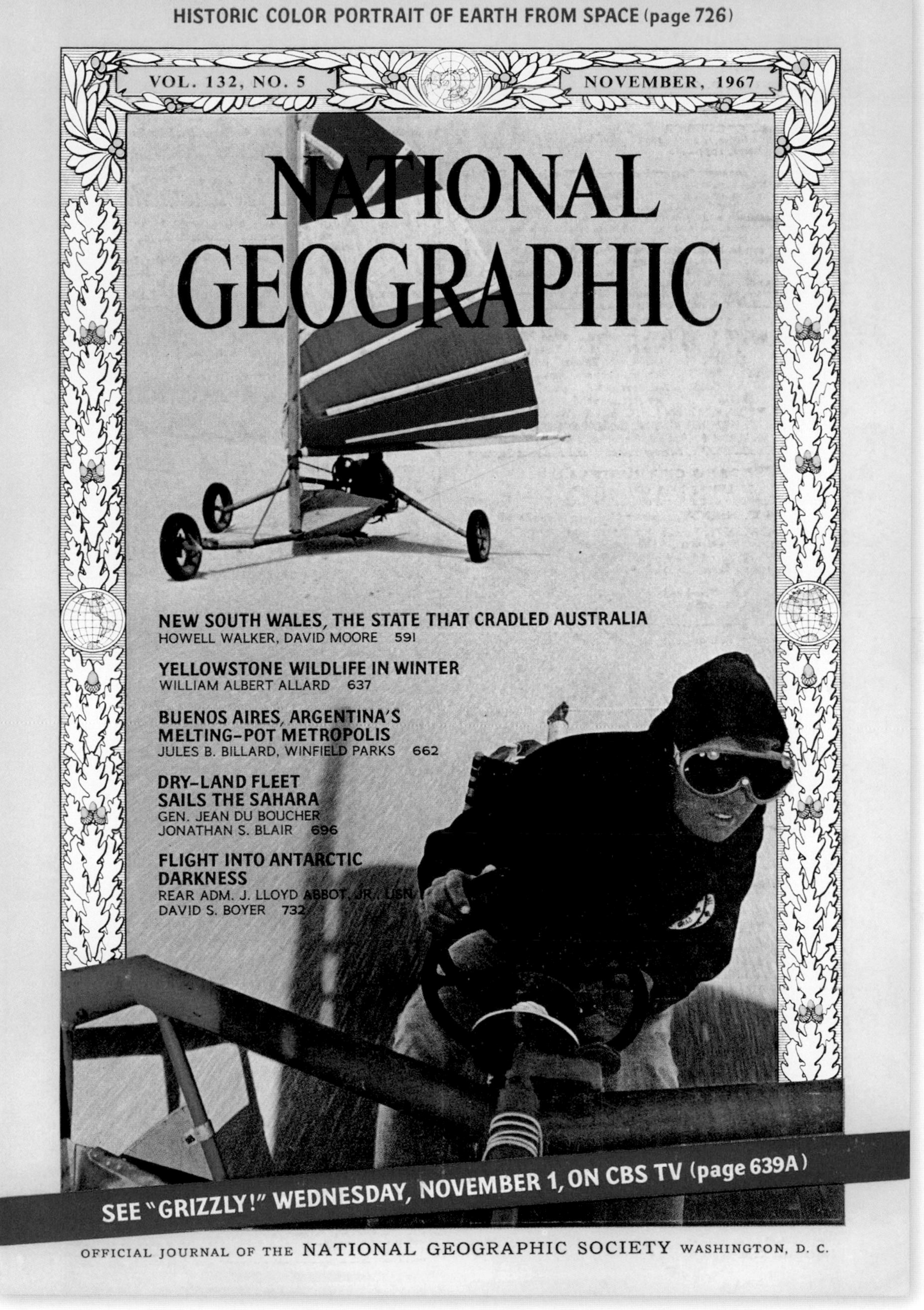

NOVEMBER | JONATHAN BLAIR

SEA OF SAND A camera gaffer-taped to the mast captured this image of "land yachts" being swept across the Sahara by gale-force winds. An international team spent 32 days under sail, crossing 1,700 desert miles; but wind-driven sand was so abrasive that photographer Blair was forced to use tightly sealed Nikonos underwater cameras.

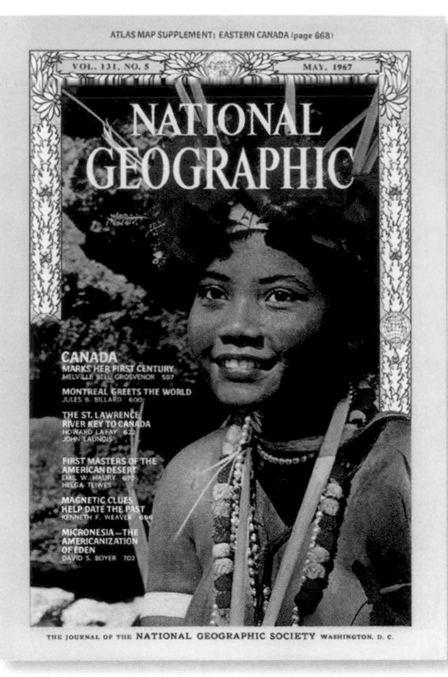

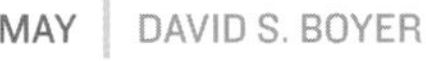

MAY | DAVID S. BOYER

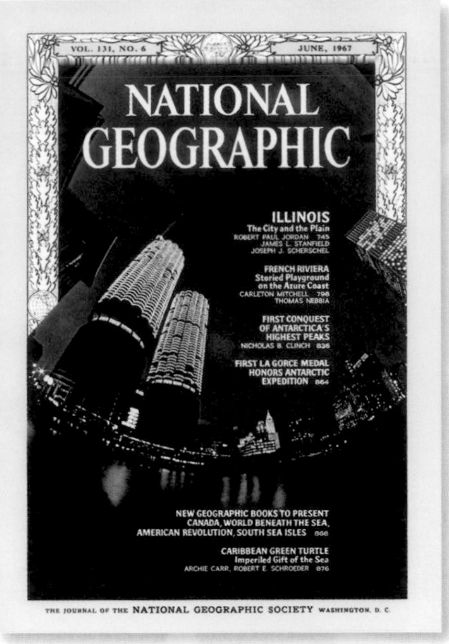

JUNE | BRUCE DALE

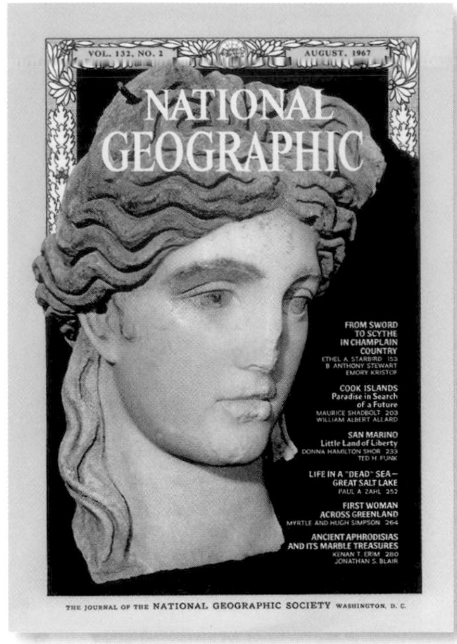

AUGUST | JONATHAN BLAIR

▲ **FESTIVE ADORNMENTS** A girl from the Micronesian island of Yap is garlanded with hibiscus and draped with pearls.

> *"If all the Micronesians in all this wide blue world were to come together, they wouldn't fill the stands of the Rose Bowl in Pasadena . . . Only 96 of the 2,100 islands and atolls, all but lost in three million square miles of ocean just north of the Equator, are inhabited."*
>
> —David S. Boyer
>
> *from "The Americanization of Eden"*

SNOWFLAKE, THE WHITE GORILLA ▶

NFUMU—WHITE—may have been his official name, but most everyone preferred Copito de Nieve, or Little Snowflake. When he was a fully grown star attraction in the Barcelona Zoo, the "Little" fell away. As a male lowland gorilla, he was not so little and could be as pugnacious as he was pug-nosed.

Back in 1966, however, he was only two years old and recently orphaned after a Fang tribesman killed Snowflake's mother for raiding his banana plantation. Naturalist Jorge Sabater Pi, director of the Barcelona Zoo's collecting station near the port of Bata in Spanish-controlled Rio Muni (today's Equatorial Guinea), bought the young albino and brought him to the station. That's also where Sabater—who coincidentally was assisting a National Geographic–funded study of lowland gorillas in the nearby forests—made the picture that appeared on the March 1967 cover.

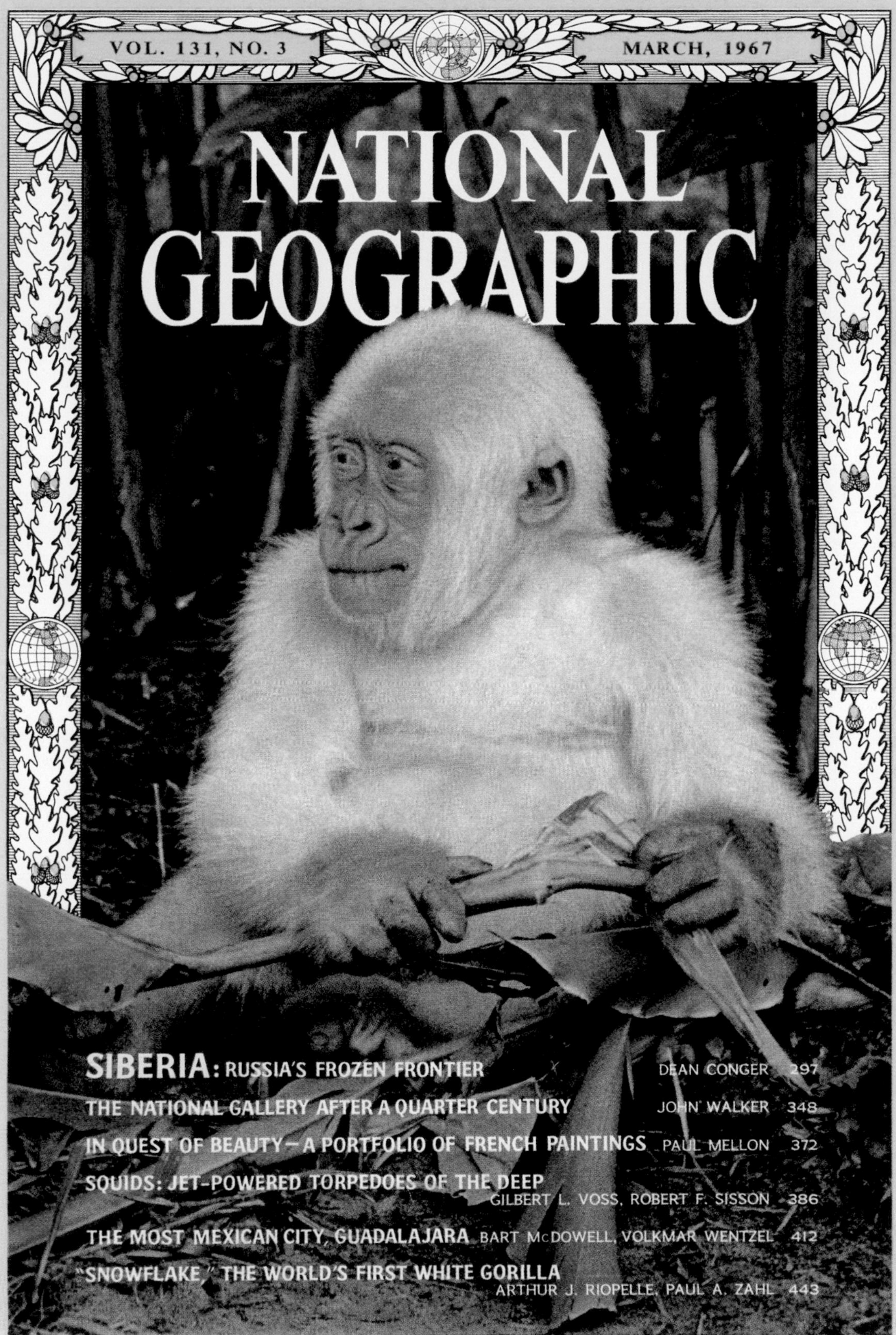

ATLAS MAP SUPPLEMENT: EASTERN SOVIET UNION (page 346)

VOL. 131, NO. 3 — MARCH, 1967

NATIONAL GEOGRAPHIC

SIBERIA: RUSSIA'S FROZEN FRONTIER — DEAN CONGER 297
THE NATIONAL GALLERY AFTER A QUARTER CENTURY — JOHN WALKER 348
IN QUEST OF BEAUTY—A PORTFOLIO OF FRENCH PAINTINGS — PAUL MELLON 372
SQUIDS: JET-POWERED TORPEDOES OF THE DEEP — GILBERT L. VOSS, ROBERT F. SISSON 386
THE MOST MEXICAN CITY, GUADALAJARA — BART McDOWELL, VOLKMAR WENTZEL 412
"SNOWFLAKE," THE WORLD'S FIRST WHITE GORILLA — ARTHUR J. RIOPELLE, PAUL A. ZAHL 443

THE JOURNAL OF THE NATIONAL GEOGRAPHIC SOCIETY WASHINGTON, D. C.

MARCH | JORGE SABATER PI Snowflake at ease among stalks of African wild ginger

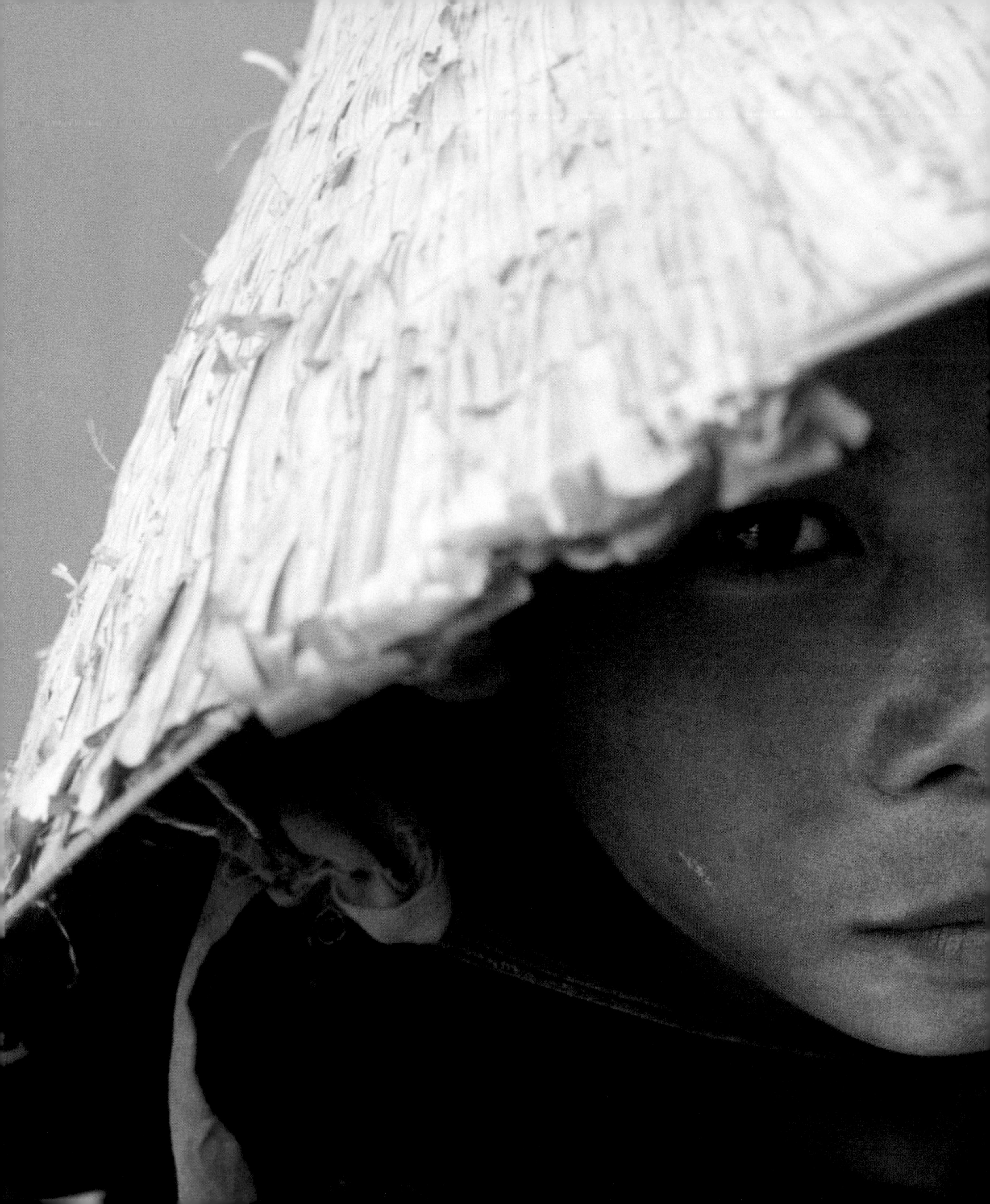

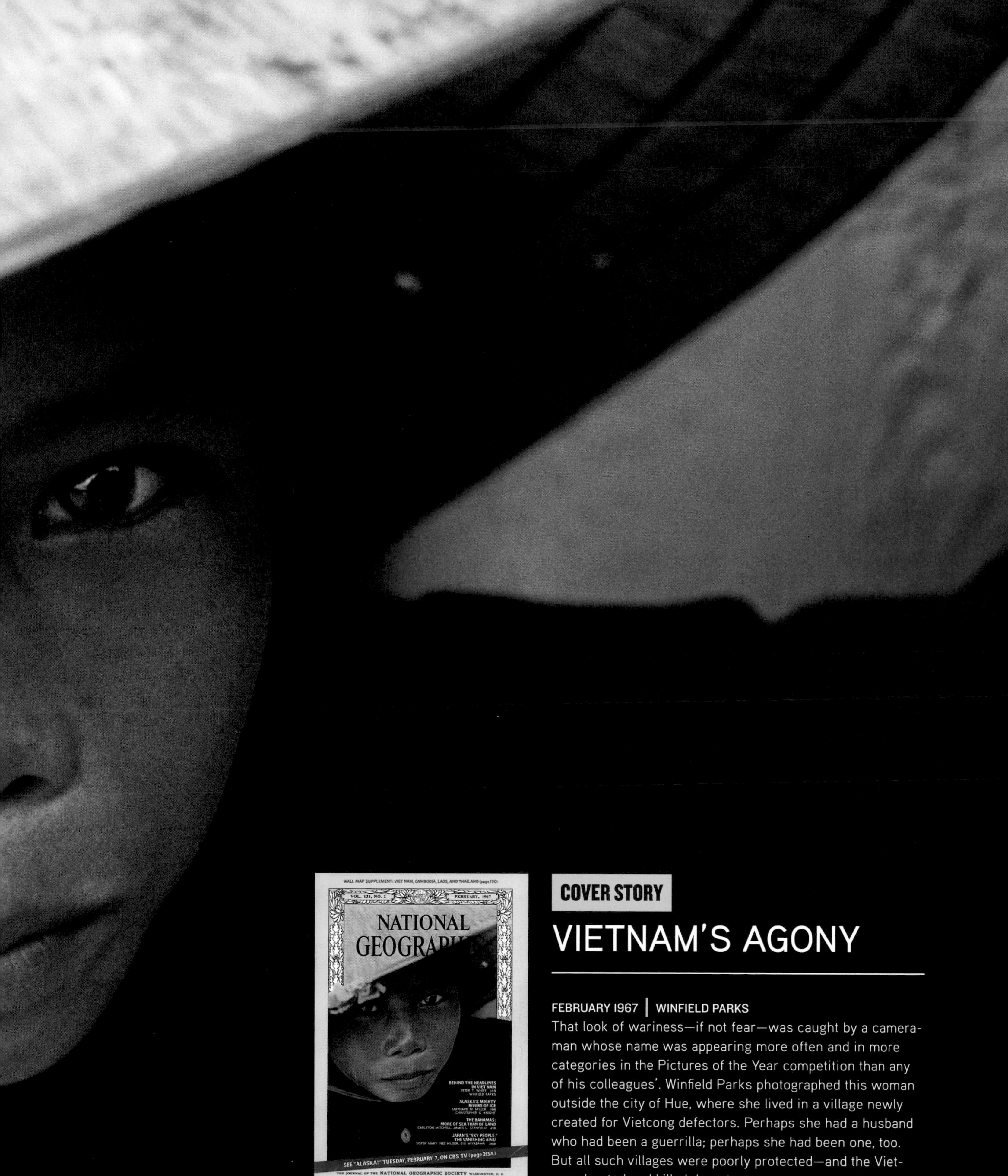

COVER STORY

VIETNAM'S AGONY

FEBRUARY 1967 | WINFIELD PARKS

That look of wariness—if not fear—was caught by a cameraman whose name was appearing more often and in more categories in the Pictures of the Year competition than any of his colleagues'. Winfield Parks photographed this woman outside the city of Hue, where she lived in a village newly created for Vietcong defectors. Perhaps she had a husband who had been a guerrilla; perhaps she had been one, too. But all such villages were poorly protected—and the Vietcong hunted and killed deserters.

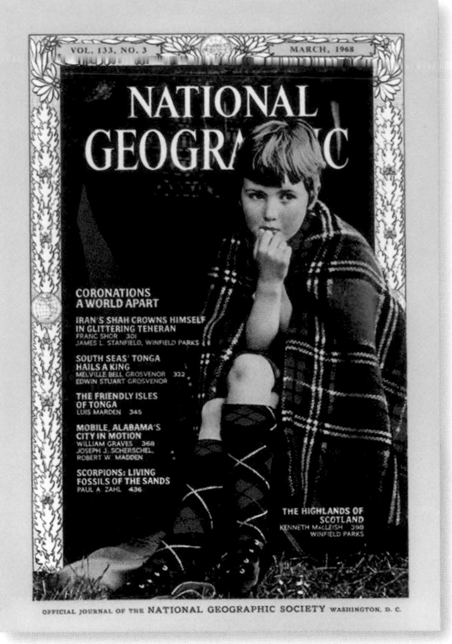

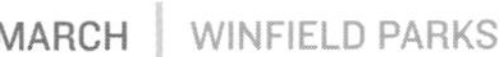

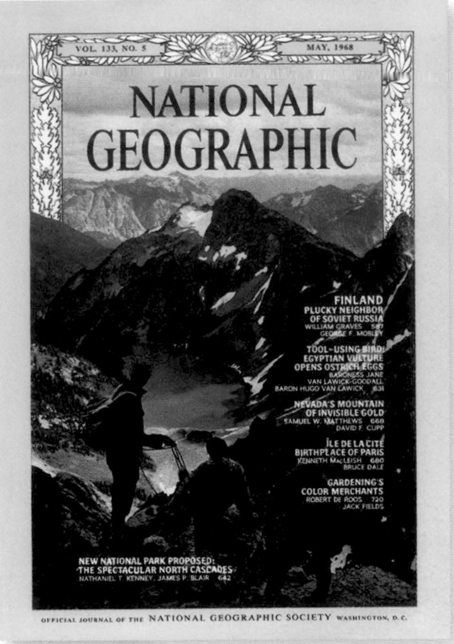

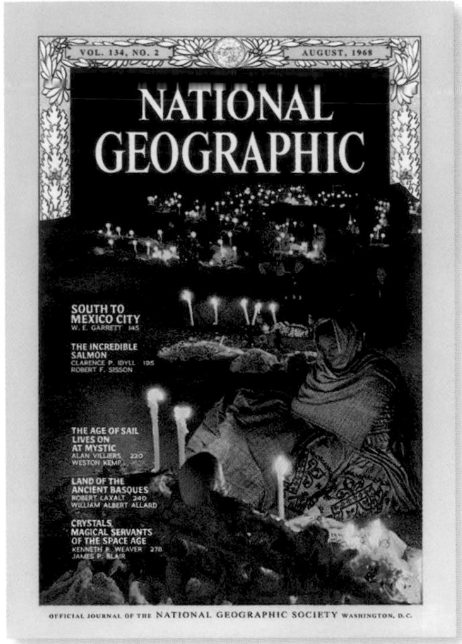

MARCH | WINFIELD PARKS

MAY | BOB AND IRA SPRING

AUGUST | WILBUR E. GARRETT

▲ **HIGHLANDER** Tightly wrapped in her tartan, a Highland girl belongs to one of the storied clans of northern Scotland.

> *"Among [the treasures of Clan MacPherson] was a broken fiddle which once belonged to a freebooting ancestor, one Jamie MacPherson, who played at his own hanging, then smashed the instrument over his knee and jumped from the scaffold to his death."*
>
> —Kenneth MacLeish
> *from "The Highlands of Scotland"*

MOROCCO'S BERBERS ▶

A FESTIVAL KINDLES HIGH spirits in the girls of Haodeguine, a village tucked into the folds of Morocco's High Atlas Mountains. Their amber necklaces and distinctive black-and-white striped robes mark them as belonging to the Ait Haddidou people, one of numerous Berber tribes whose earth-walled towns long repulsed both European colonizers and desert raiders alike—the last not being taken by the French Foreign Legion until the 1930s. Although most of these girls would be married by 15 or 16, they still caught the wandering eye of "Ahmed," the Marrakesh-based interpreter who led Belgian photojournalist Victor Englebert by mule through the snowbound passes:

> Ahmed speaks no more of Zuhra [his beloved]. The girls of Haodeguine are driving him out of his senses with their beauty. They are not shy with him; Berber women have more freedom than their Arab sisters.
>
> *—From "Trek by Mule Among Morocco's Berbers," Victor Englebert*

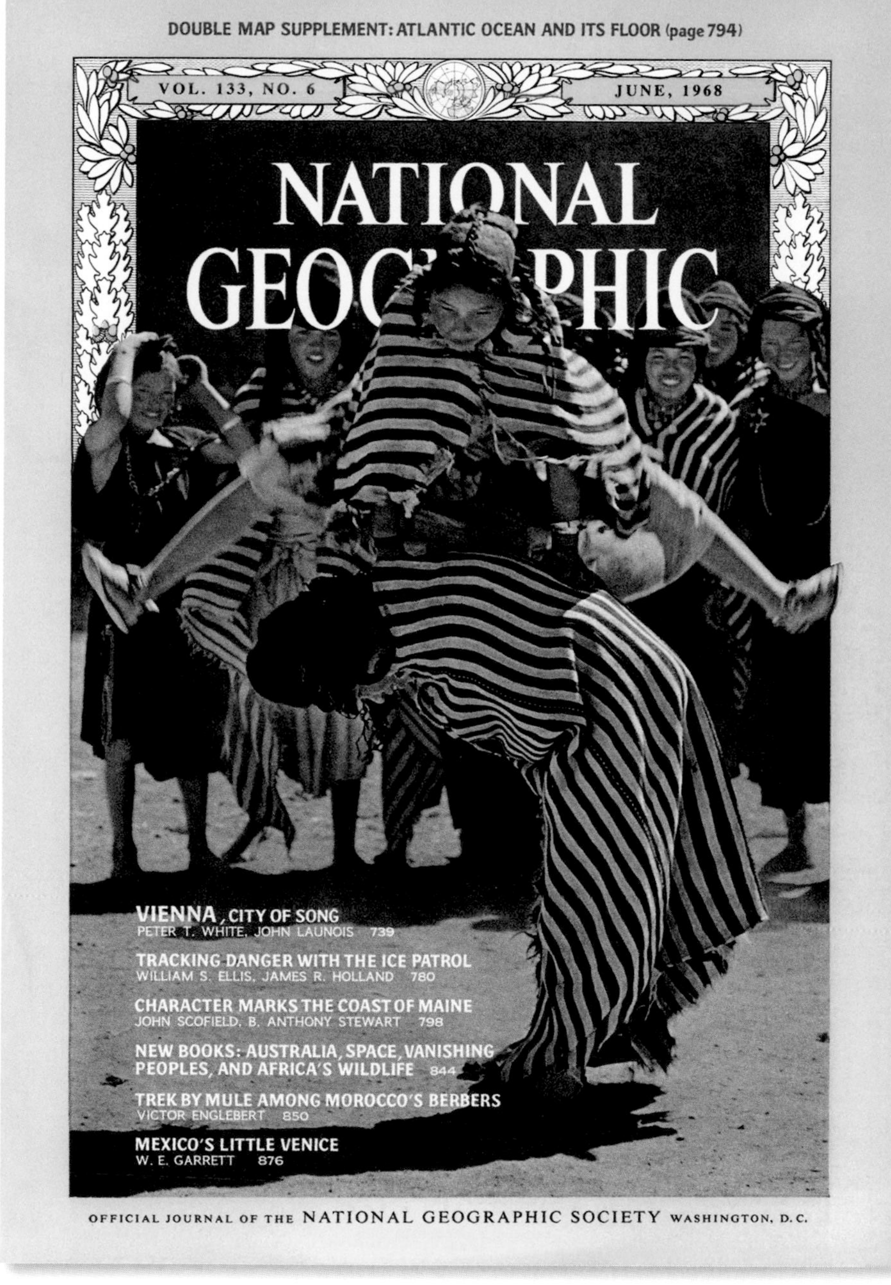

JUNE | VICTOR ENGLEBERT

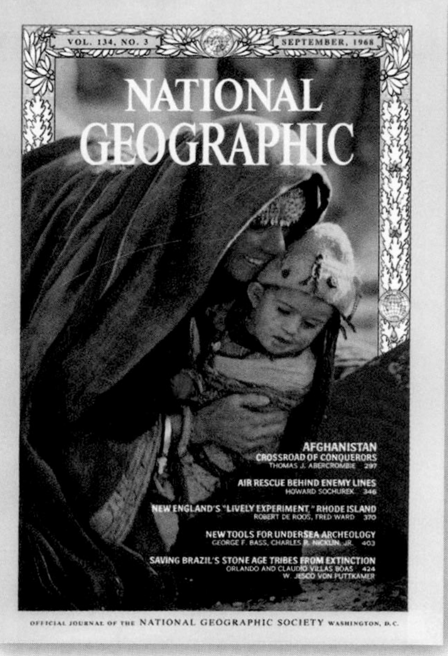

SEPTEMBER | THOMAS J. ABERCROMBIE

▲ **AFGHAN IDYLL** On a chill autumn dawn a Ghilzai mother wraps her child before fastening him to a camel for the day's march. Most prominent of the clans making up the nomadic Kuchi peoples, the Ghilzai were frequently encountered in the mountains of Afghanistan. Tom Abercrombie chanced upon this group north of Kandahar and remained with them for three days. Having left the cool summer pastures, all "90 nomads, 46 camels, 12 donkeys, five horses, and 600 sheep" were tramping south to spend the winter near the Dasht-e Margo, or Desert of Death.

"The countryside through which we passed was one of extraordinary beauty . . . Streams swollen with melted snow from the hoary peaks all around us raced through pleasant valleys. Unveiled women in clothes of bright colors worked in the grain fields."

—Victor Englebert
from "Trek by Mule Among Morocco's Berbers"

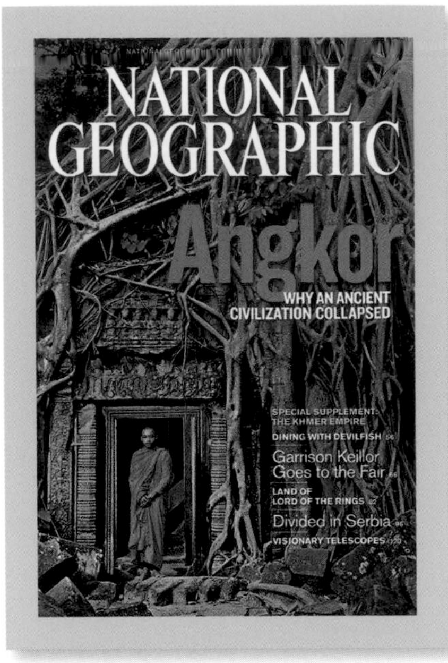

JULY 2009 | ROBERT CLARK

2009 ▸▸▸▸ FAST FORWARD

ANGKOR WAT Forty-one years after Bill Garrett visited Angkor during his Mekong River survey, the July 2009 *National Geographic* published a cover story on the famous Cambodian temple complex—which in the intervening decades had survived a civil war, the brutalities of the Khmer Rouge regime, widespread looting and vandalism, and, most recently, a dramatic resurgence of tourism.

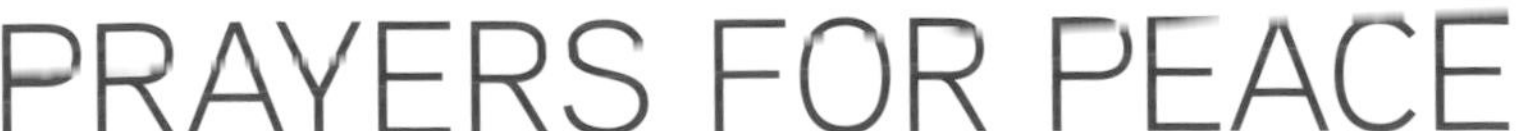

PRAYERS FOR PEACE ▸

THE MESSAGE WAS UNMISTAKABLE: Vietnamese children were praying for peace. And they were doing so on the cover of the December issue, a month in which most of the Society's members were singing carols of "peace on Earth." It was also the month that closed one of the bloodiest years of the Vietnam War.

Assistant Editor Bill Garrett photographed these children at a shrine of the Dao Dua sect, a hybrid of Buddhism and Christianity, which stood on an island in the Mekong Delta. He had been journeying up and down the length of that great river from the Chinese border to South Vietnam, stopping in Laos and a still peaceful Cambodia along the way. Yet he arrived in the Mekong Delta in the wake of the Tet offensive, when North Vietnamese soldiers and Vietcong irregulars struck more than a hundred South Vietnamese towns and cities. Fighting had raged not only in the streets of Saigon and Hue but also throughout the watery mazes of the many-fingered delta. Garrett accompanied Navy patrol boats, rode in helicopter gunships, and slogged through snaky thickets with foot patrols, hunting guerrillas among the booby-trapped paddies and groves.

In a year that also saw the assassinations of Martin Luther King, Jr., and Robert F. Kennedy and numerous international riots and protests, the National Press Photographers Association awarded Garrett one of its highest accolades, Magazine Photographer of the Year, largely on the strength of his Vietnam coverage but also to honor the man who had done so much to bring a harder-edged photojournalism to the pages of *National Geographic.*

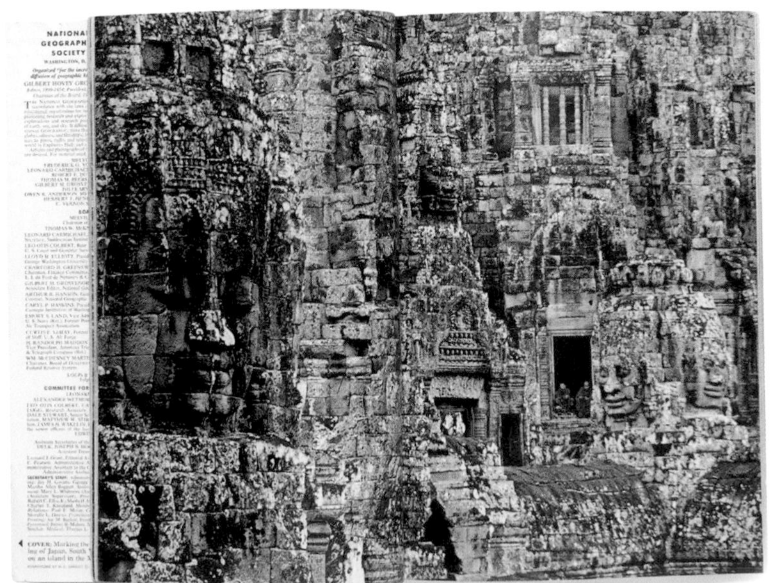

◂ DECEMBER 1968 | WILBUR E. GARRETT Monks peer from a doorway in the Bayon, the central temple of Angkor Thom.

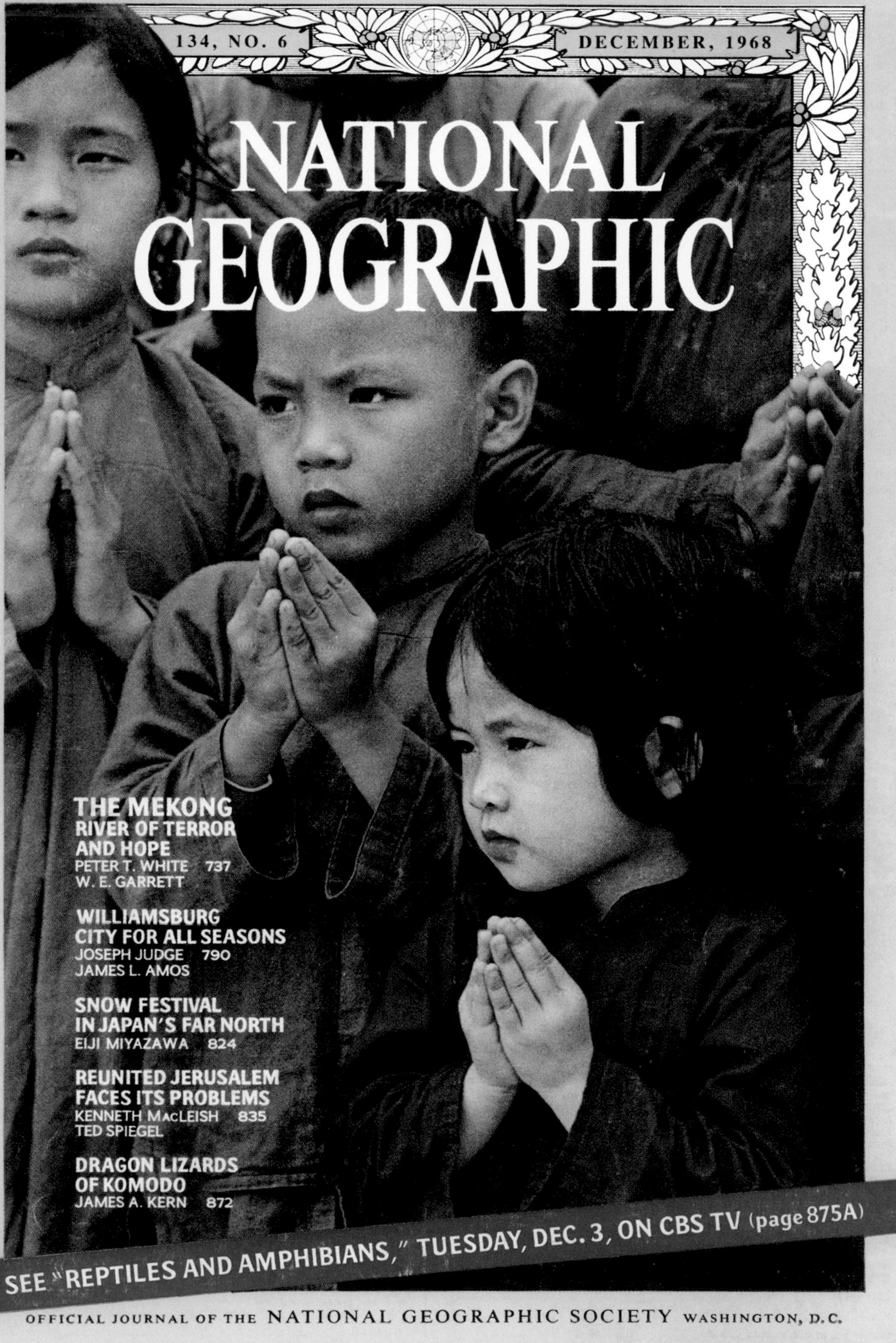

DECEMBER | WILBUR E. GARRETT Children pray for peace in the Mekong Delta.

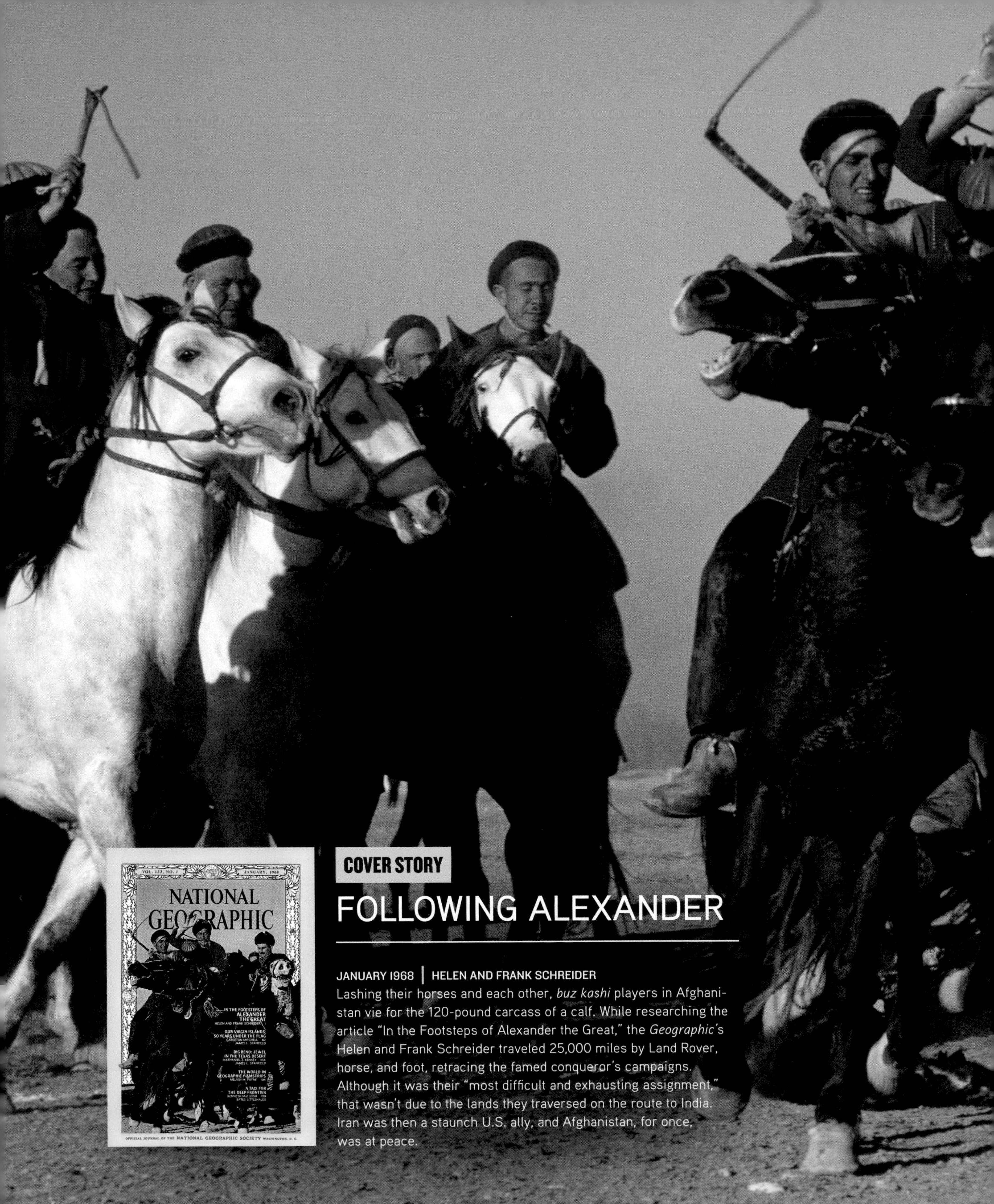

COVER STORY

FOLLOWING ALEXANDER

JANUARY 1968 | HELEN AND FRANK SCHREIDER

Lashing their horses and each other, *buz kashi* players in Afghanistan vie for the 120-pound carcass of a calf. While researching the article "In the Footsteps of Alexander the Great," the *Geographic*'s Helen and Frank Schreider traveled 25,000 miles by Land Rover, horse, and foot, retracing the famed conqueror's campaigns. Although it was their "most difficult and exhausting assignment," that wasn't due to the lands they traversed on the route to India. Iran was then a staunch U.S. ally, and Afghanistan, for once, was at peace.

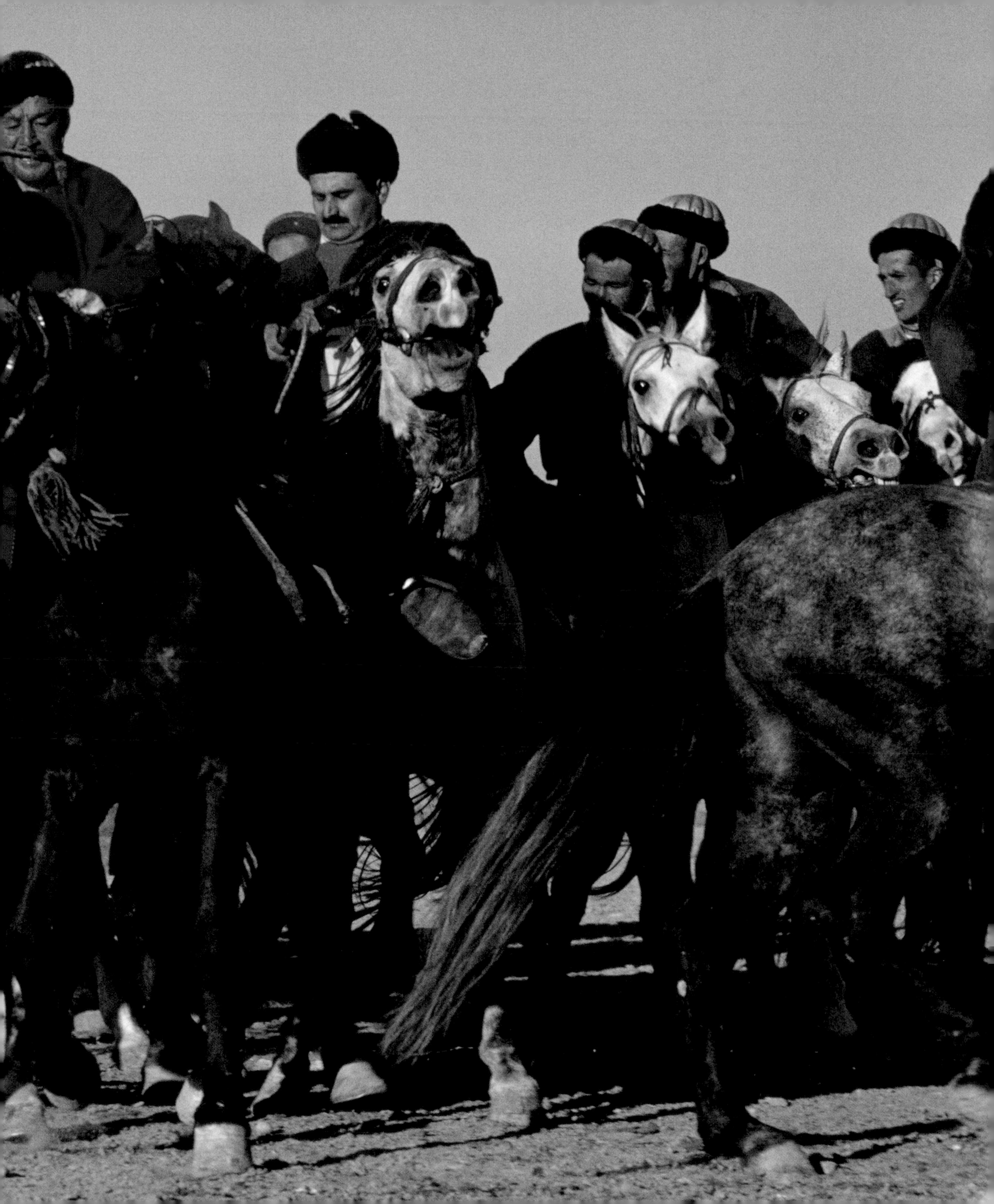

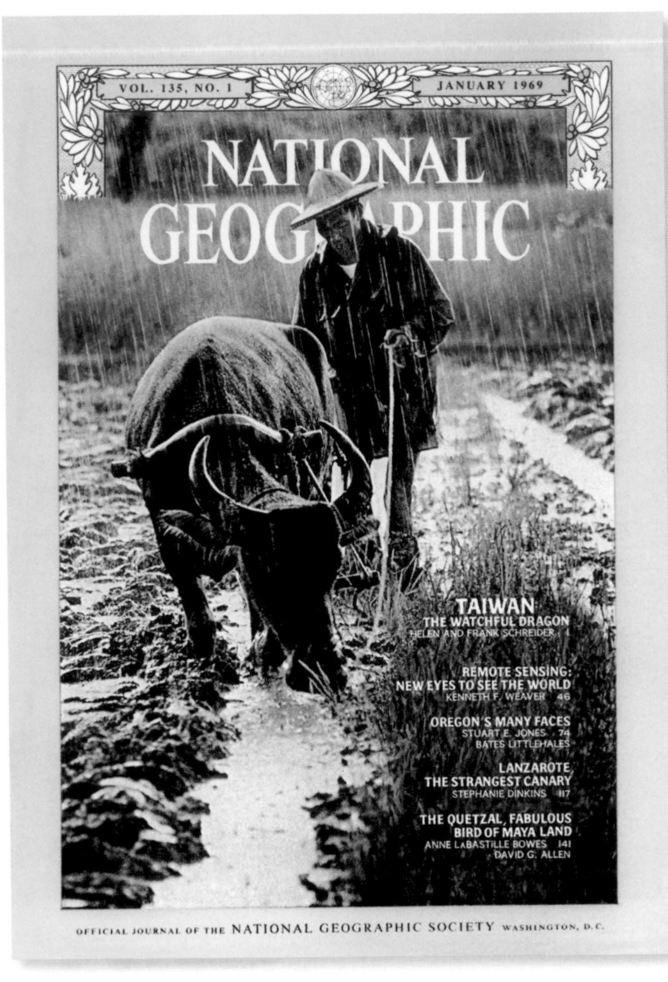

JANUARY | CHARLES MOORE

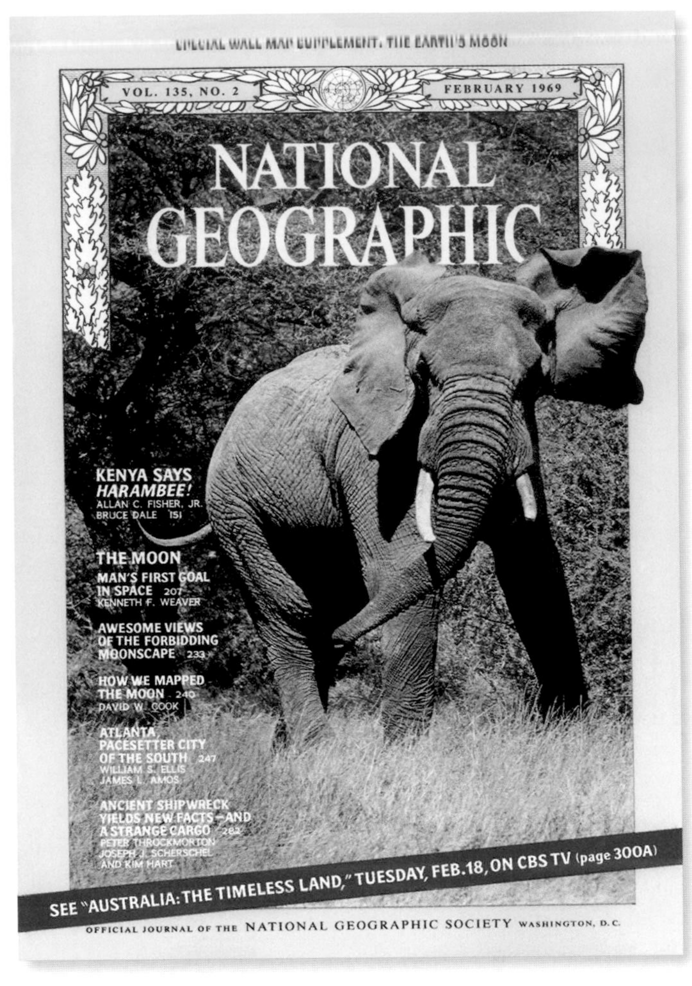

FEBRUARY | M. PHILIP KAHL

▲ **GETTING HIS FEET WET** Famous for depicting the civil rights struggles in the American South, photographer Charles Moore certainly had wet feet photographing this rice farmer—he never used long lenses.

▲ **HIGH ALERT** He had a reputation as a bit of a daredevil, so it would be no surprise if the late Philip Kahl was nowhere near a vehicle when he encountered this old tusker. An ornithologist by training, Kahl was actually in Kenya on a National Geographic grant to study flamingos in the alkaline lakes of the Great Rift Valley. But he eventually became an authority on elephants as well.

> *"Few years ago only rice fields here," Chang [the interpreter] said, waving toward the new high-rise hotels and office buildings. "Now too much cars. Too much motorcycles. Terrible, sir."*
>
> —Frank Schreider
>
> *from "Taiwan: The Watchful Dragon"*

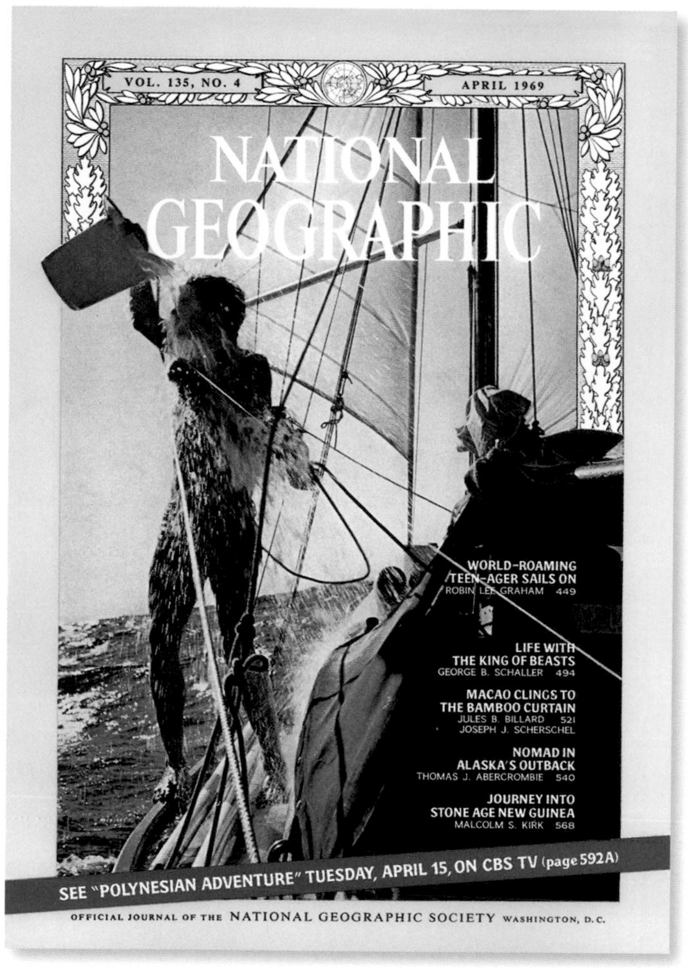

APRIL | ROBIN LEE GRAHAM

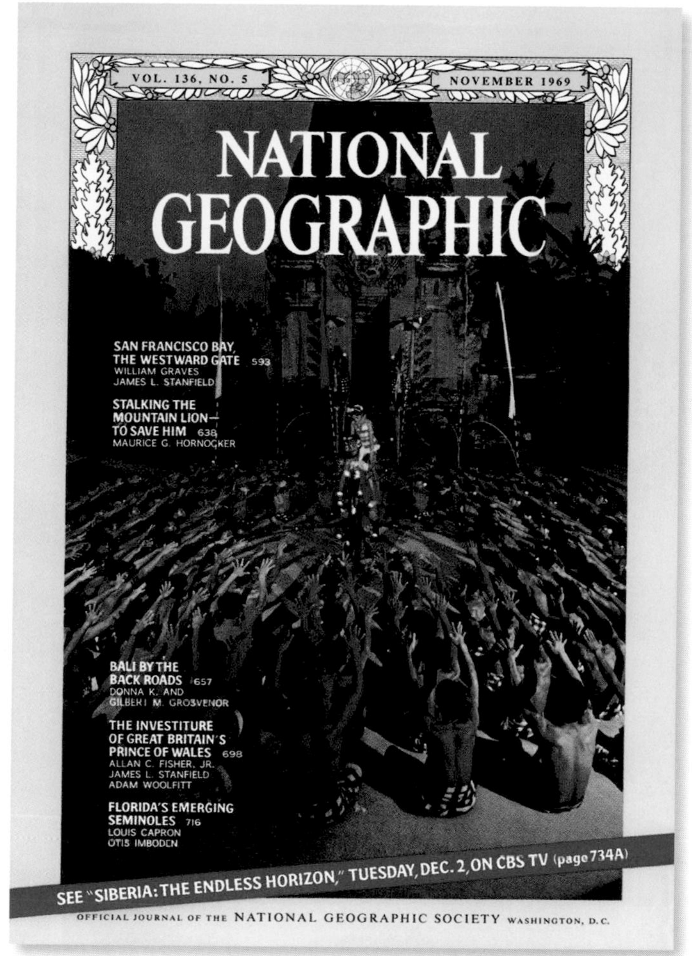

NOVEMBER | GILBERT M. GROSVENOR

▲ **HIGH-SEAS SELFIE** An impromptu shower in the warm South Atlantic cools off Robin Lee Graham, whose right hand hoists the bucket while his left pulls the string to a camera mounted aft on *Dove*, his famous 24-foot sloop. The "world-roaming teenager" was more than halfway through his solo voyage around the globe, and this cover story represented the second installment in his popular three-part *Geographic* odyssey. At previous landfalls staff photographers had met him, checked his cameras, retrieved his film, and vainly implored him to postpone marriage (to Patti Ratteree, a globe-trotting American he met in Fiji) until journey's end. His nuptials over, however, he indeed pushed on alone, homeward bound. His story was later told in two best-selling books and a Hollywood movie.

▲ **LIGHTS! CAMERA! ACTION!** Although the scene was inherently dramatic—villagers on Bali were reenacting an episode from the Hindu epic the *Ramayana*—Gil Grosvenor knew he could never impart drama to a picture taken beneath the blue skies of a tropical afternoon. "Then came a threatening storm," he later recalled, "and with it the shadow of the emotion I wanted." As palms bent to the gusts and clouds whipped overhead, a lurid light enveloped the sky just as 150 villagers, their voices barking in chorus and their arms waving in unison, urged the monkey army to once again save the princess. The resulting picture made the cover.

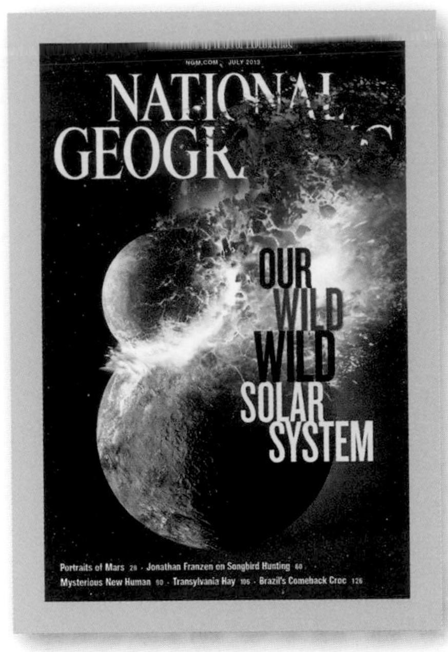

JULY 2013 | DANA BERRY

2013 ▸▸▸▸ FAST FORWARD

DEEP IMPACT Although commissioned for the magazine's pages, this rendering of the birth of the moon—possibly the result of a Mars-size protoplanet (a planet in the early stages of formation) colliding with Earth 4.5 billion years ago—is so dramatic that it made the cover as well. Paint flecked on paper and scanned into a computer added texture to the image.

WALKING ON THE MOON ▸

Of course they were golden moments, those 2 hours and 20 minutes on July 20, 1969, when human beings first walked on another world. But they were literally so, too, because the visors of the astronauts' helmets had been coated with gold to better block the sun's heat, glare, and radiation. And reflected in Buzz Aldrin's aureate dome stands Neil Armstrong, frozen in the very instant he snaps one of the iconic images of the space age.

The camera—a special Hasselblad 500EL Data Camera that was mounted via a bracket on Armstrong's chest—was left behind on the moon. But the image—officially AS11-40-5903, made on a 70mm Ektachrome frame—returned to Earth with the nine film magazines. Of the 550 color photographs taken on the lunar surface, most of which depicted rocks, moonscapes, and footprints, it was this portrait of Aldrin peering at the checklist sewn onto his left glove that captivated people here below, including the editors at *National Geographic*, who promptly put it on the cover of the December 1969 issue.

So excited, in fact, were those editors by what had transpired in the distant Sea of Tranquility that they not only filled those pages with four major articles but also included a record, "Sounds of the Space Age," 10 minutes and 51 seconds of excerpts from historic radio broadcasts and mission recordings. Such enthusiasm was understandable, for Apollo 11 was "a momentous adventure," wrote Kenneth Weaver in this issue, "the most widely shared adventure in all history."

◂ **DECEMBER 1969** | **OTIS IMBODEN** President Lyndon Johnson and officials watch Apollo 11 blast off for the moon.

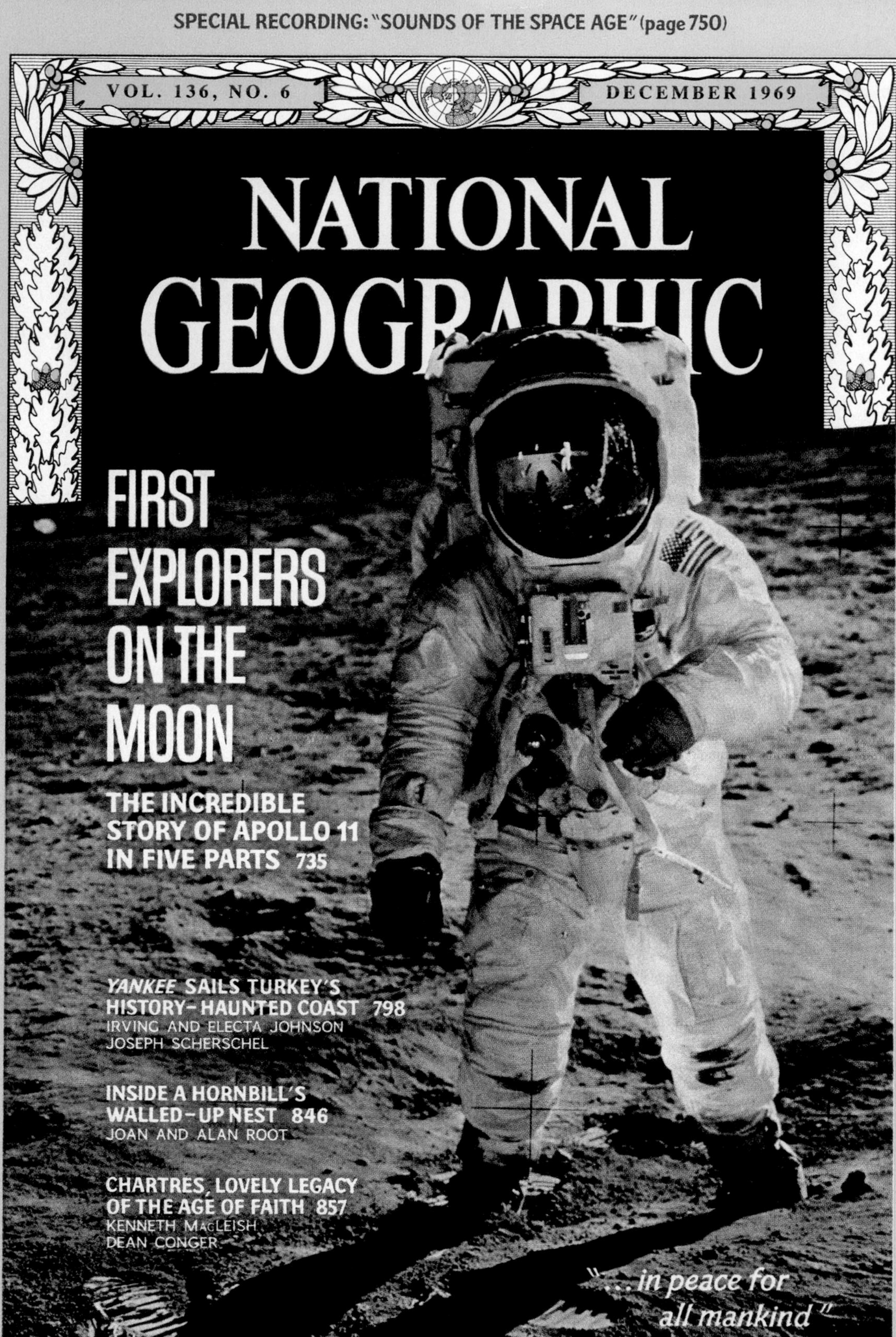

DECEMBER | **NEIL ARMSTRONG** Buzz Aldrin stands on the lunar surface.

1970-

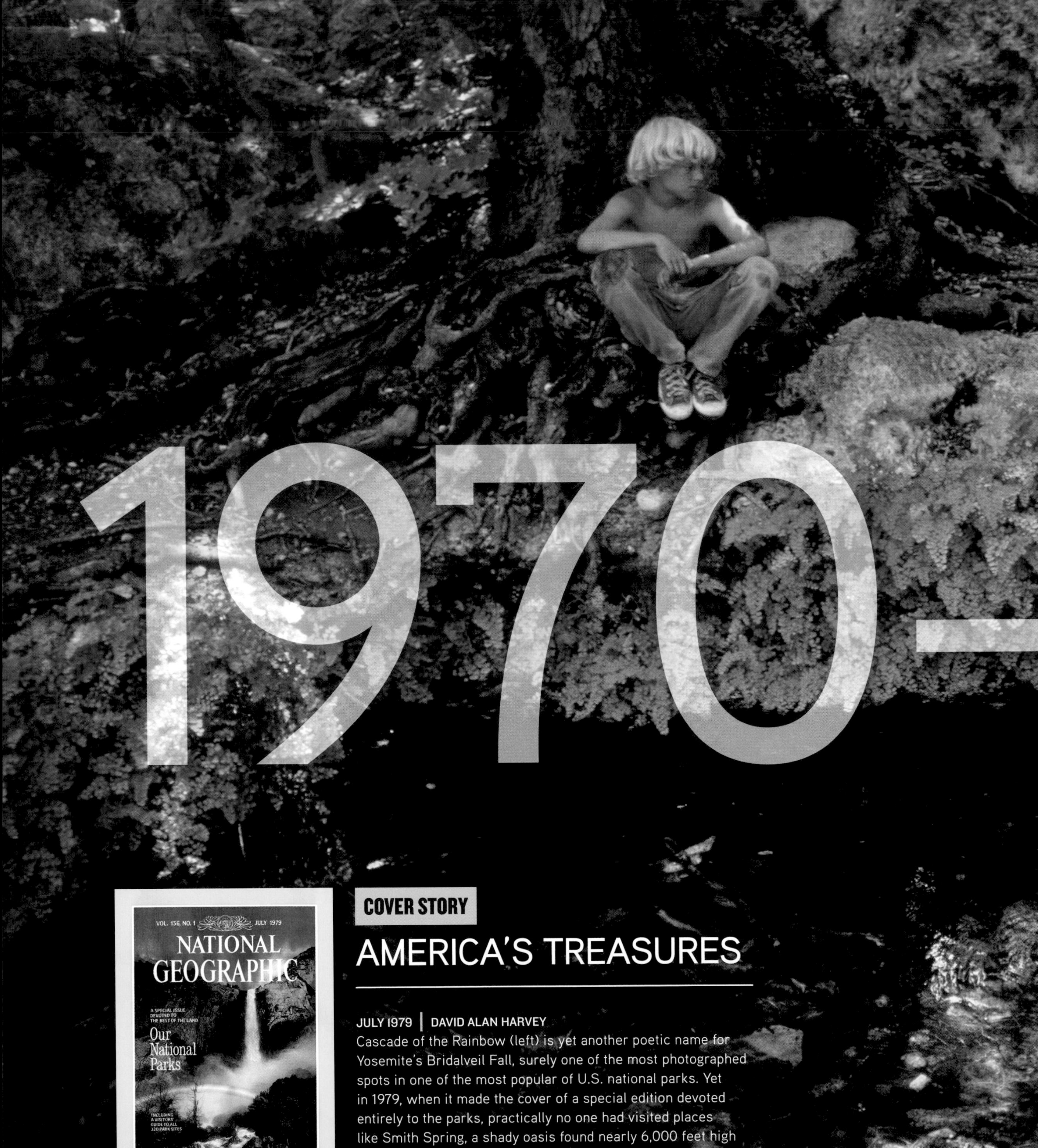

COVER STORY

AMERICA'S TREASURES

JULY 1979 | DAVID ALAN HARVEY

Cascade of the Rainbow (left) is yet another poetic name for Yosemite's Bridalveil Fall, surely one of the most photographed spots in one of the most popular of U.S. national parks. Yet in 1979, when it made the cover of a special edition devoted entirely to the parks, practically no one had visited places like Smith Spring, a shady oasis found nearly 6,000 feet high in Texas's spectacular Guadalupe Mountains National Park, described by nature writer Edward Abbey as otherwise being a "harsh, dry, bitter place, lonely as a dream."

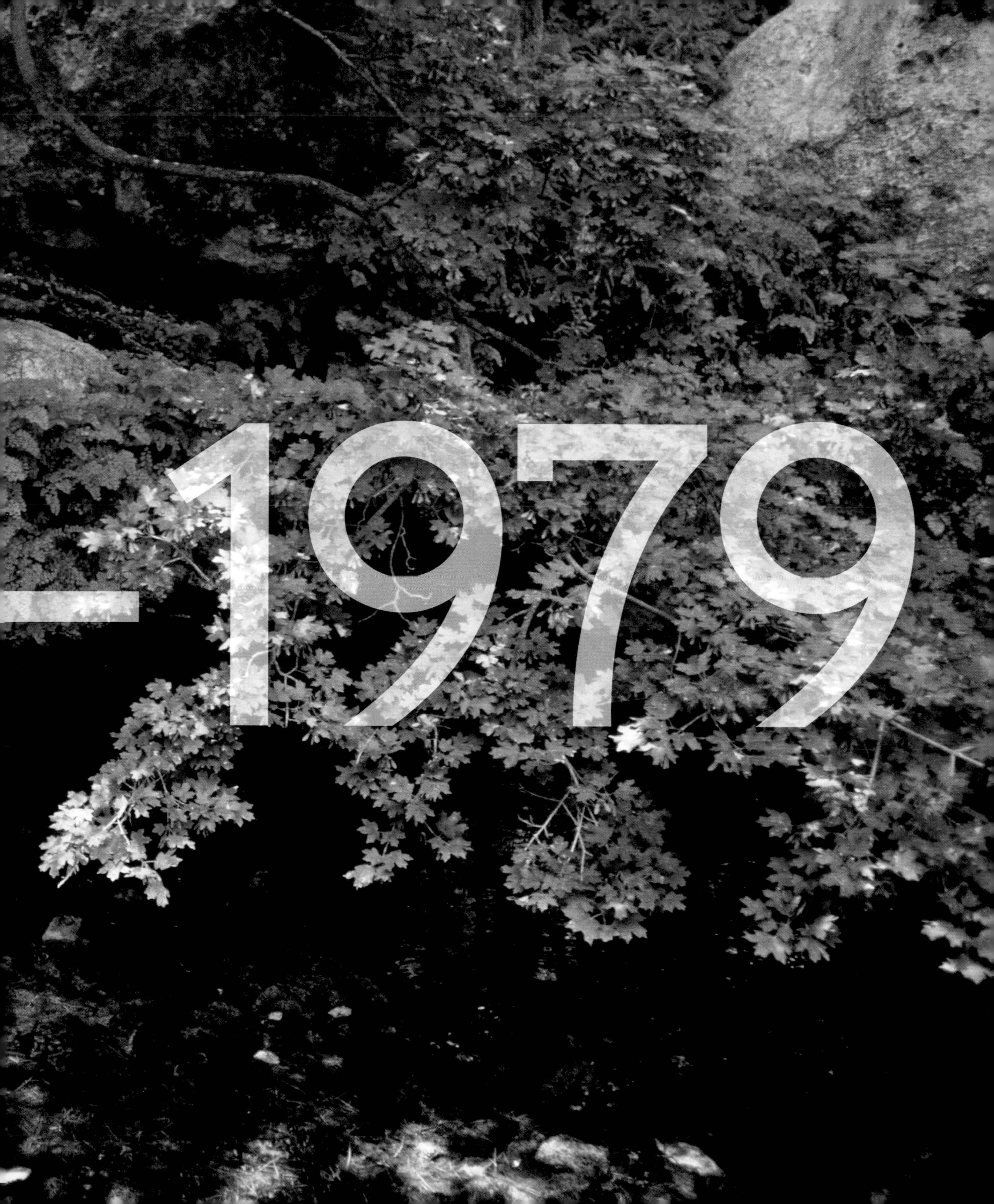
–1979

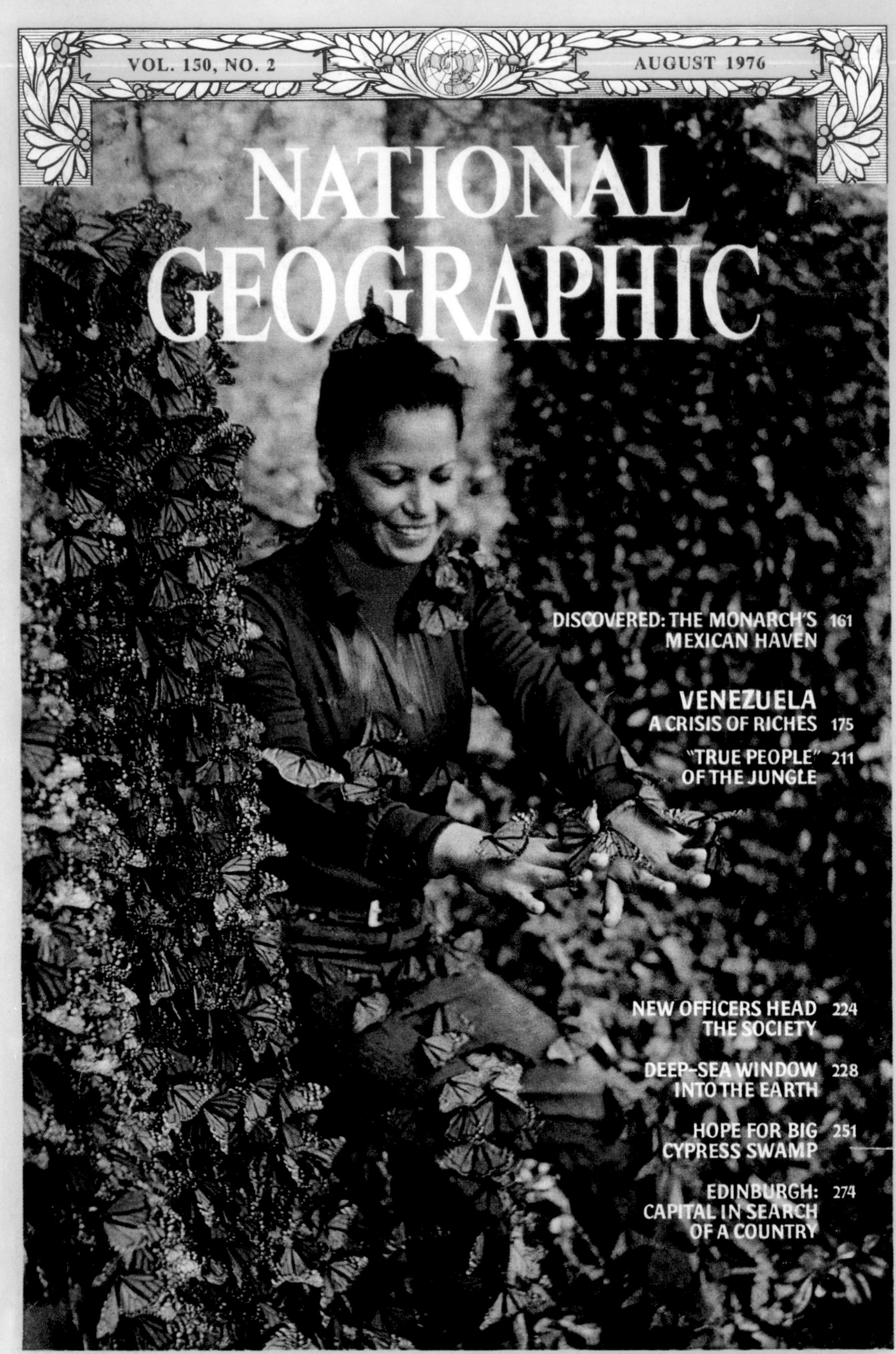

AUGUST 1976 | ALBERT MOLDVAY Monarch butterflies swarm researcher Catalina Aguado's turtleneck and bell-bottoms.

THE WORLD IN THE 1970S

"I gazed in amazement at the sight. Butterflies—millions upon millions of monarch butterflies."

—Fred Urquhart,
from "Discovered: The Monarch's Mexican Haven"

FOR MOST people, January 9, 1975, was probably just another ordinary day. But for Canadian entomologist Fred Urquhart, that particular Thursday was the culminating moment of a 38-year quest. Ear pressed to a telephone receiver, he listened as Kenneth Brugger, one of his field assistants in Mexico, excitedly told him that they had finally solved one of the oldest mysteries in North American biology: Where did the eastern population of monarch butterflies fly off to each autumn? They simply disappeared. But Brugger was saying that the team had finally tracked them down. The insects were congregating in the millions on several slopes in Mexico's Sierra Nevada. Former *National Geographic* photographer Al Moldvay, then living in Mexico City, was on hand to document a spectacle that had probably been happening for untold thousands of years.

Those monarchs moved to an entirely different rhythm of time, but for most human beings the 1970s were bell-bottoms, platform shoes, long hair, Sonny and Cher, the Bee Gees, "You Light Up My Life," and the Brady Bunch, as well as political disaster in the White House with the Watergate scandal and resignation of a U.S. president. The 1970s was also the decade of the inglorious finale of the Vietnam War as the last American helicopter left the roof of the abandoned U.S.

FACTS & FIGURES THE 1970s

- **14** covers featuring wildlife
- **10** covers featuring birds
- **10** covers featuring archaeological subjects
- **9** covers featuring boats or planes
- **7** covers featuring undersea subjects
- **4** covers featuring outer space
- **4** covers featuring primates

AROUND THE WORLD

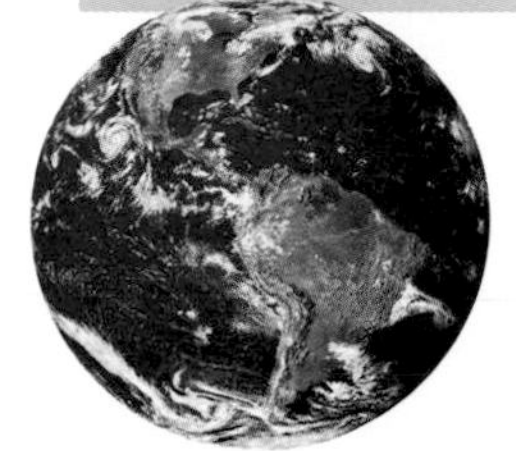

EARTH DAY 1970
The first one is held on either March 21 or April 22—depending on whom you talk to.

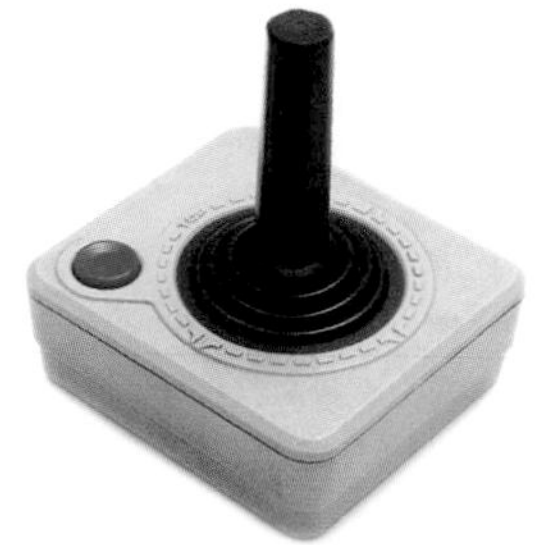

VIDEO GAMES 1971
Computer Space becomes the first commercially sold video game.

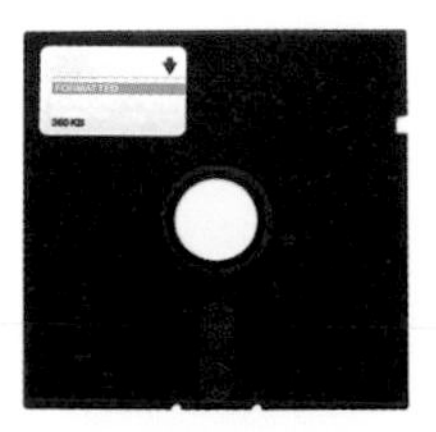

FLOPPY DISC 1971
The first floppy disks, eight inches in diameter, are sold commercially.

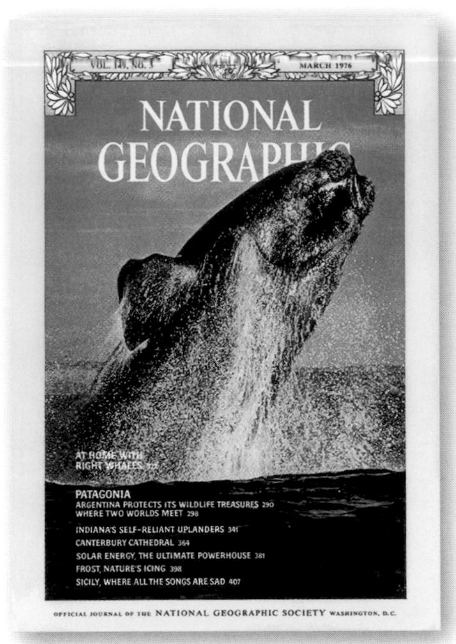

MARCH 1976 | DES AND JEN BARTLETT

▲ **THAR SHE BLOWS!** A right whale breaches off the coast of Patagonia. In the 1970s, National Geographic sponsored the first cameramen—Bill Curtsinger, Chuck Nicklin, and Al Giddings—brave enough to swim among whales while photographing them.

Embassy in Saigon; the death of Chairman Mao, when the People's Republic of China gradually reestablished relations with the Western democracies; and the beginning of the Cold War thaw known as détente. Tragedy marked the 1972 Munich Olympics when terrorists murdered some of the athletes. The following year, Israeli tanks faced off against those of Egypt and Syria in the Yom Kippur War. By the end of the decade, crowds in Tehran had celebrated the overthrow of the Shah of Iran. OPEC's oil embargoes, which led to the 1973 and '79 oil crises that stymied world economic growth gave rise to the era of "stagflation."

Those long queues at the filling stations only sharpened the edge of a burgeoning environmental movement. The groundswell of ecological concern that had been growing throughout the 1960s—leading in the United States to the Clean Air Act, Clean Water Act, and Wild and Scenic Rivers Act—soon gave rise to the Environmental Protection Agency, the first Earth Day, the Endangered Species Act, and by 1975 the Convention on International Trade in Endangered Species, or CITES. The movement adopted as its emblem the "blue marble," the photograph of our home planet floating in the black cosmos that returned with the Apollo 17 astronauts.

Ecological concern was also creeping into the pages of *National Geographic,* and increasingly appearing on its cover. The December 1970 issue, with its stark pictures of pollution, in effect announced that a younger cadre of environmentally attuned photojournalists were now in charge of the magazine: Gilbert M. Grosvenor was Editor in Chief throughout the decade, while Wilbur E. Garrett directed the illustrations. Well-researched coverages of controversial issues such as nuclear power and pesticides appeared in the magazine, but the editors were careful to maintain a balance in the *Geographic*'s article mix. For every piece on Castro's Cuba or South African apartheid, there was another on the ancient Maya or Dickens's England or the coral reefs of the Red Sea. Meanwhile, the magazine's trend of using a pretty woman's face

AROUND THE WORLD

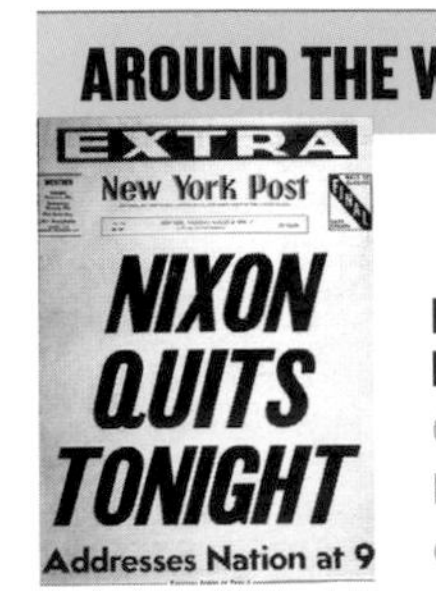
EXTRA
New York Post
NIXON QUITS TONIGHT
Addresses Nation at 9

NIXON RESIGNS 1974
On August 9 Richard Nixon becomes the first U.S. president to resign from office.

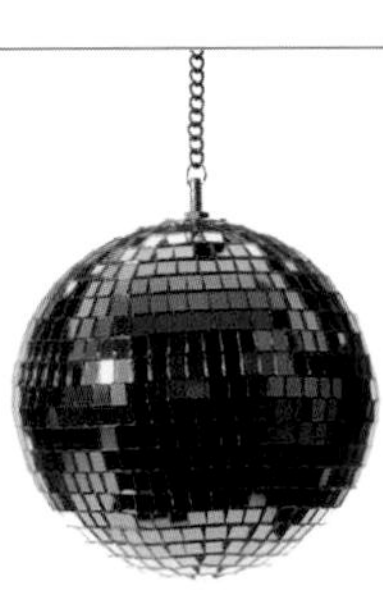

DISCO FEVER 1977
Box-office smash *Saturday Night Fever* is released, launching disco as the sound track of the '70s.

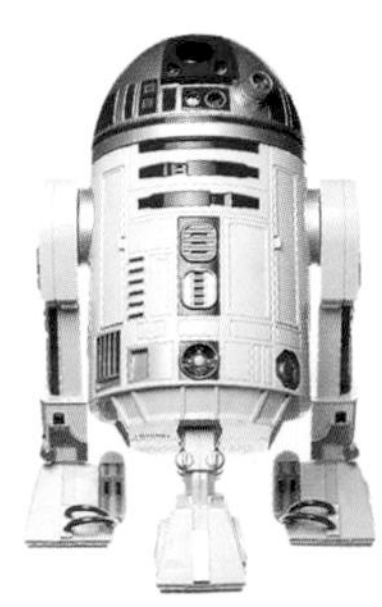

STAR WARS 1977
The derring-do of Luke Skywalker and Princess Leia introduces a blockbuster movie franchise.

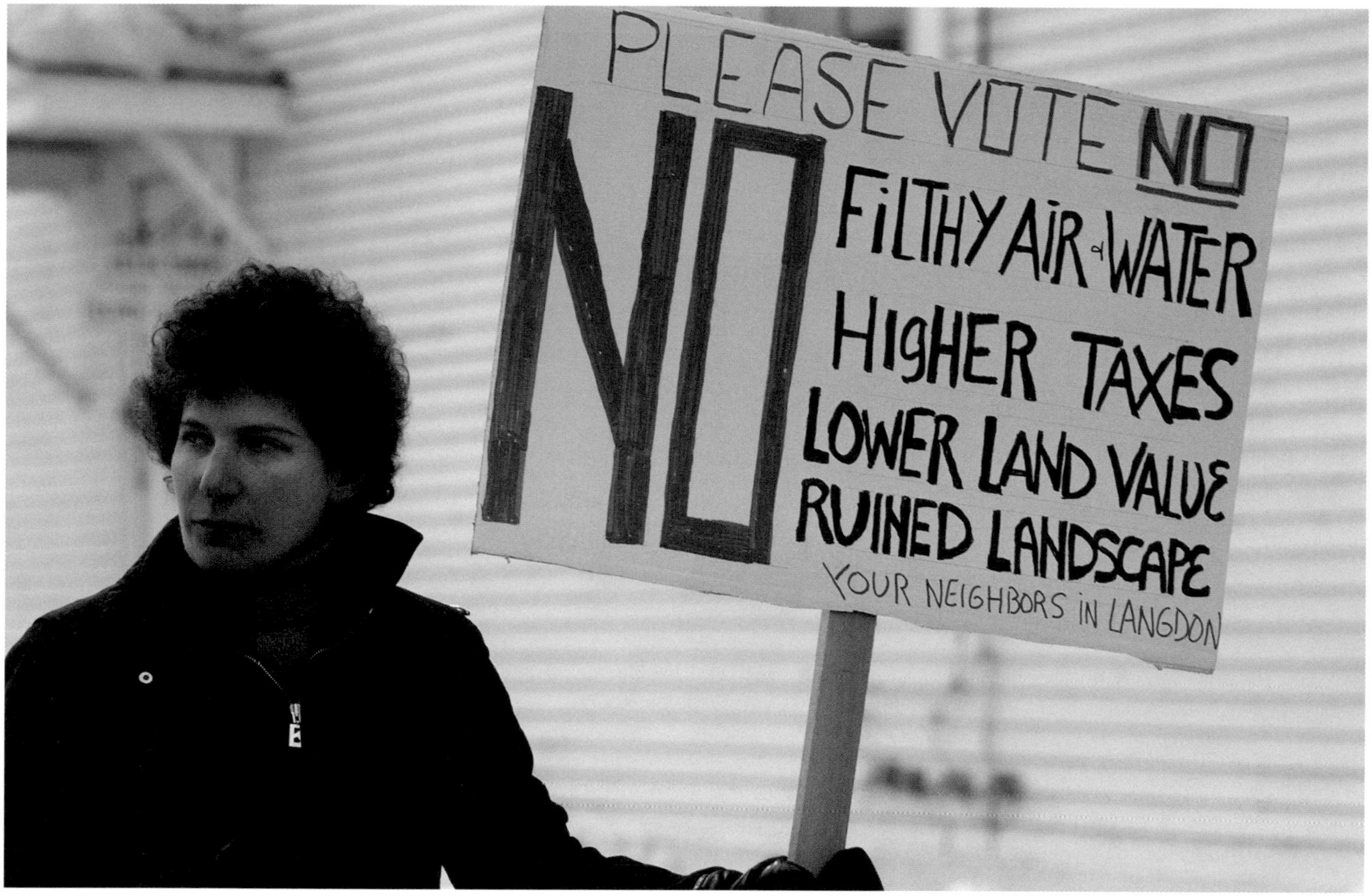

JULY 1976 | MARTIN ROGERS A New Hampshire resident does not want a paper mill anywhere near the town of Langdon.

to represent a culture or place (see page 32 for examples) builds pace throughout the 1970s.

Above all, with membership pushing toward ten million, and perhaps three or four times that number of readers, a cover story could have potential impact. That was one reason why Fred Urquhart chose *National Geographic* as his vehicle to announce to the world that the mysterious wintering grounds of that fabulous insect, the eastern North American monarch butterfly, had finally been discovered. ■

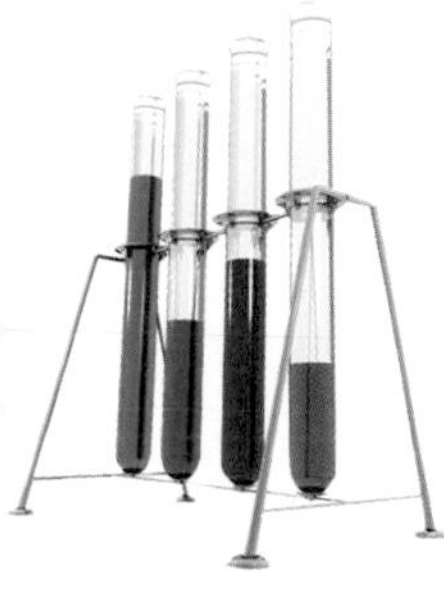

TEST-TUBE BABY 1978
Louise Brown becomes the first "test-tube baby," born as a result of in vitro fertilization.

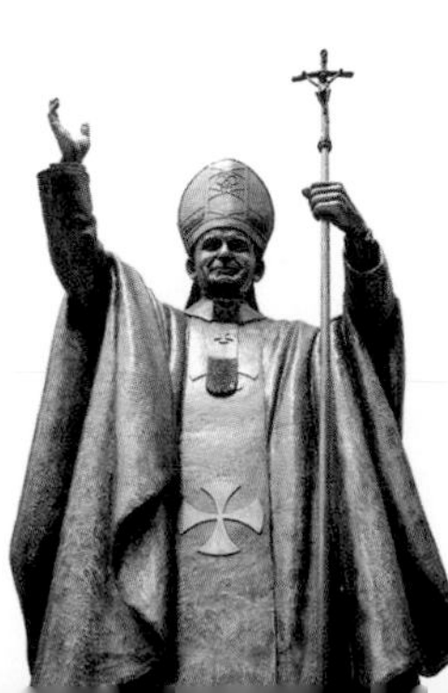

POPE JOHN PAUL II 1978
On October 16 Karol Józef Wojtyła becomes the Roman Catholic pontiff.

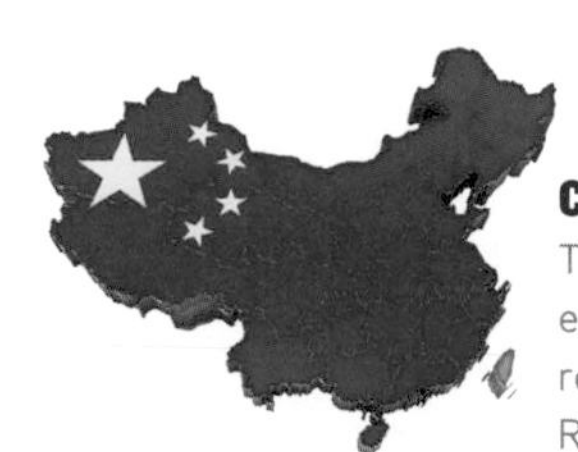

CHINA 1979
The United States finally establishes full diplomatic relations with the People's Republic of China.

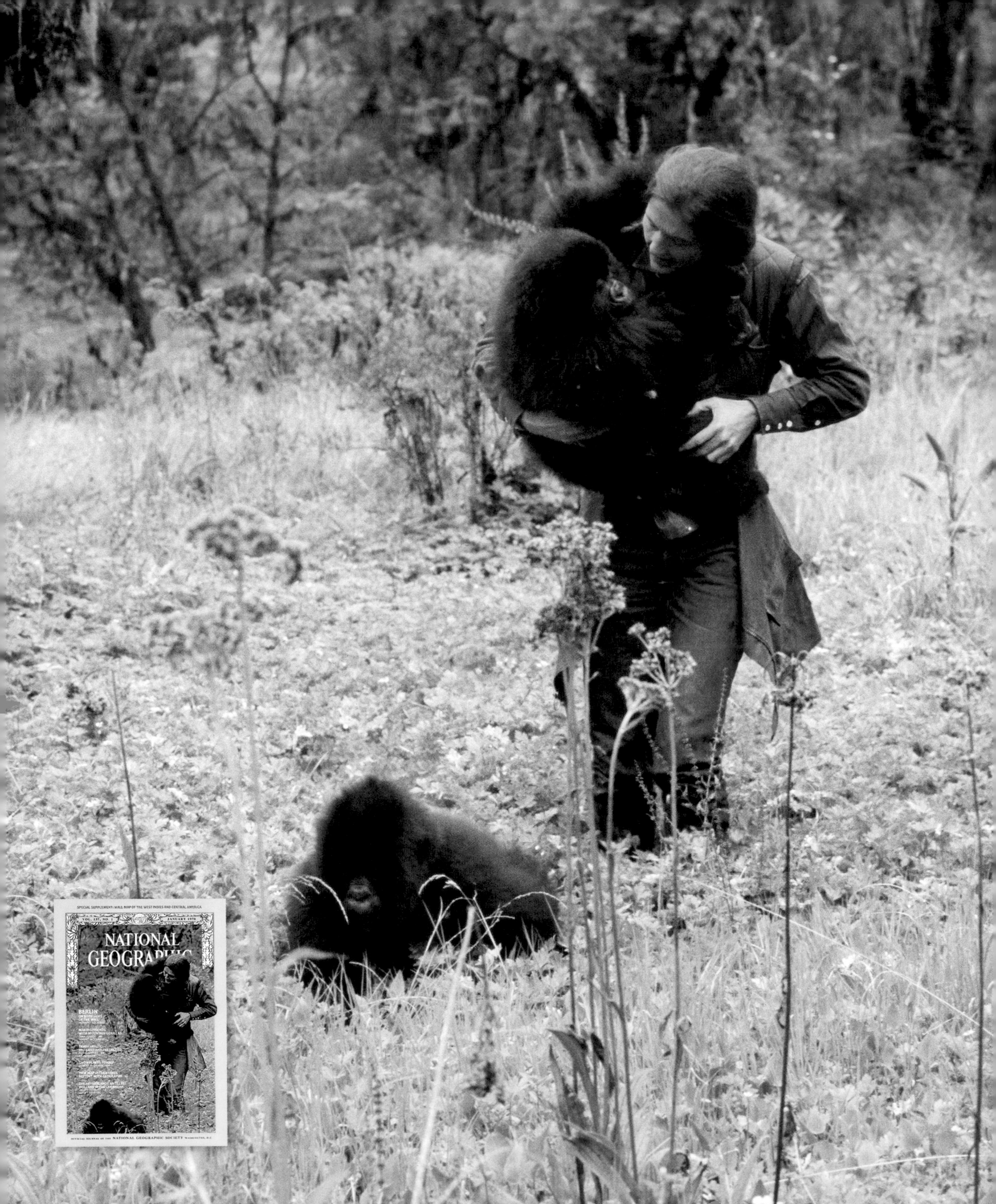
SPECIAL SUPPLEMENT: WALL MAP OF THE WEST INDIES AND CENTRAL AMERICA
VOL. 137, NO. 1
JANUARY 1970
NATIONAL GEOGRAPHIC
BERLIN
ON BOTH SIDES OF THE WALL
MAKING FRIENDS WITH MOUNTAIN GORILLAS
DEATH VALLEY, THE LAND AND THE LEGEND
SNOWFLAKES TO KEEP
NEW MAP INTERWEAVES HISTORY WITH GEOGRAPHY
THE NETHERLANDS ANTILLES: HOLLAND IN THE CARIBBEAN
OFFICIAL JOURNAL OF THE NATIONAL GEOGRAPHIC SOCIETY WASHINGTON, D.C.

LIFE AMONG GORILLAS

"MAKING FRIENDS WITH Mountain Gorillas" is a title with a promising ring to it, and the cover picture seems to reinforce that impression: Dian Fossey seems effortlessly at home with the primates.

That picture is one of many made in the spring of 1969 as Fossey—only the second researcher to study the endangered apes in the wild—tended to Coco and Pucker Puss at her cluster of cabins 10,000 feet up in Rwanda's cool, lushly forested Volcanoes National Park. She had been caring for these two orphans while they awaited shipment to a European zoo.

Yet, at that time, those were the only pictures that showed her actually engaging with gorillas. Although she had logged 2,000 hours observing and photographing the reticent wild apes, gradually habituating them to her presence, her solo work meant that there was no one to photograph her and the apes together. It was only when photographer Bob Campbell, needing more close-ups for the *Geographic,* pushed her to enter the frame with her gorillas that the magic happened: In the very month this issue was released—January 1970—he photographed "the touch," the outstretched finger of the male called Peanuts making contact with one of hers, the first instance of mutual friendship ever recorded between a wild mountain gorilla and a human being.

After her cover appearance Fossey earned her Ph.D. in zoology at Cambridge University, became one of the world's most famous primatologists, and wrote the book *Gorillas in the Mist,* later made into a movie.

Until the day she was murdered in 1985, many such pictures would follow; and the images of Fossey reclining amid gorillas would help convince the general public that these shy and gentle apes were not fearsome beasts, after all.

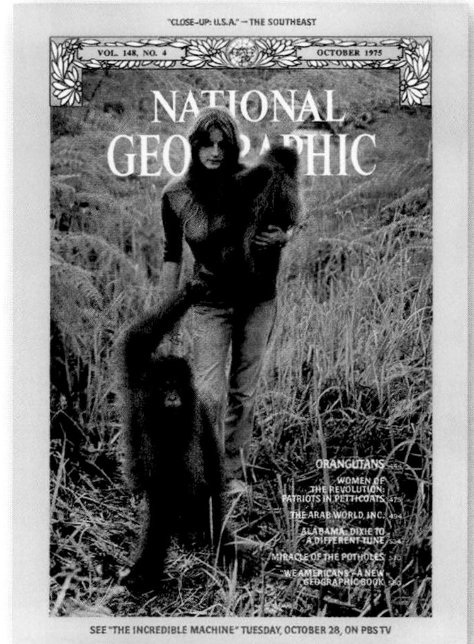

OCTOBER 1975 | ROD BRINDAMOUR

1975 ▸▸▸▸ FAST FORWARD

BIRUTÉ GALDIKAS Engaged in the first long-term study of orangutans in the wilds of Borneo, primatologist Biruté Galdikas (the third of the so-called Trimates, beside Fossey and Goodall) found that she spent half her time observing the habits of the reclusive adult apes, and the other half playing surrogate mother to orphaned youngsters.

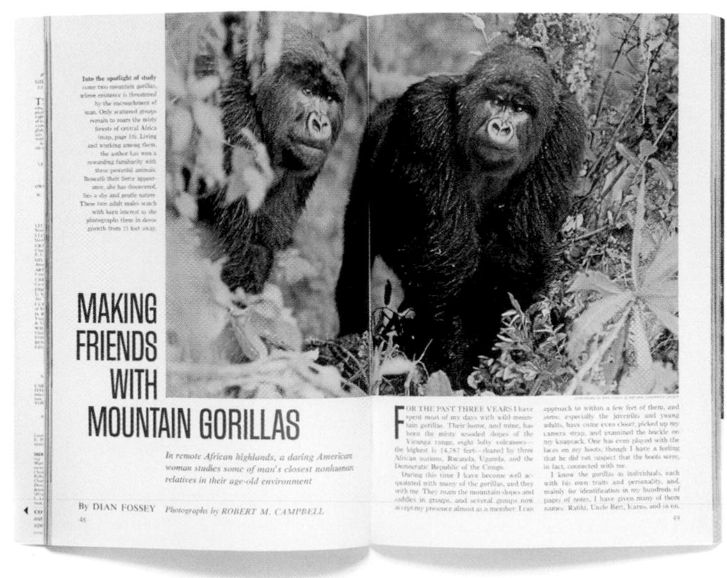

◀ **JANUARY 1970** | ROBERT I. M. CAMPBELL Dian Fossey romps with Coco and Pucker Puss.

▶ **JANUARY 1970** | DIAN FOSSEY Two mountain gorillas peer suspiciously at human intruders.

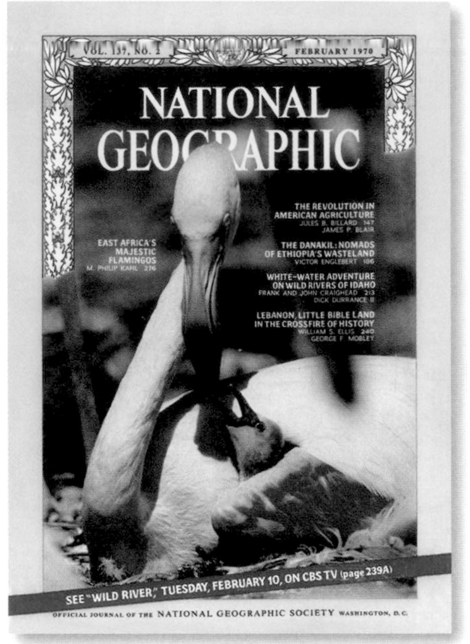

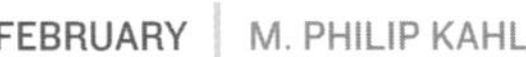

FEBRUARY | M. PHILIP KAHL

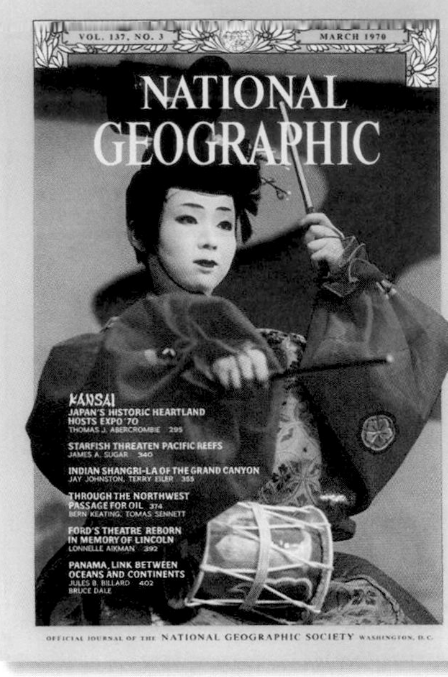

MARCH | THOMAS J. ABERCROMBIE

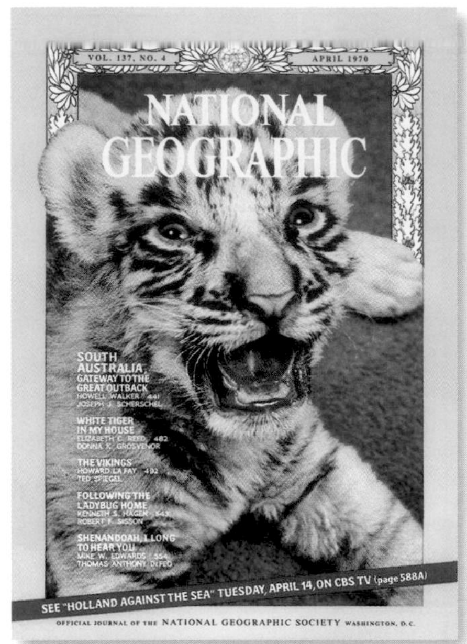

APRIL | DONNA K. GROSVENOR

▲ **CLOSE ENCOUNTER** This greater flamingo, feeding a week-old nestling on an island in Kenya's Lake Elmenteita, was photographed from Philip Kahl's "Trojan horse": a floating blind in which he eased into the midst of the breeding colony. The ornithologist used leg power to propel himself through the shallows, wearing hip boots as protection against soda burns from the caustic waters. In his opinion, the masses of flamingos congregating on East Africa's alkaline lakes constituted the "greatest show in the entire bird kingdom."

OUR ECOLOGICAL CRISIS ▶

IN THE EARLY MONTHS of 1969 staff photographer Bruce Dale was in southern California covering devastating mudslides caused by heavy rains. Then came the largest oil spill that had yet fouled U.S. waters, the blowout of Union Oil's Platform A in the Santa Barbara Channel.

He was not assigned to cover the spill. But Dale made the most of his proximity to Santa Barbara to walk out onto a pier overlooking the Pacific surf and see firsthand what damage the oil slick—which eventually tarred all the nearby beaches—had caused.

This bird simply swam out from beneath the pier. At first he thought it was a cormorant, for it was so smudged with oil it was hard to recognize a western grebe. He focused and shot—an unplanned, spontaneous image he little dreamed would become one of his "signature pictures." For just as public outrage at the spill helped engender some of the nation's formative environmental legislation, Dale's dying grebe, some 18 months later, was selected as the cover of one of *National Geographic*'s signature issues—the December 1970 "Our Ecological Crisis" issue, which announced the magazine's pivotal turn toward environmental photojournalism.

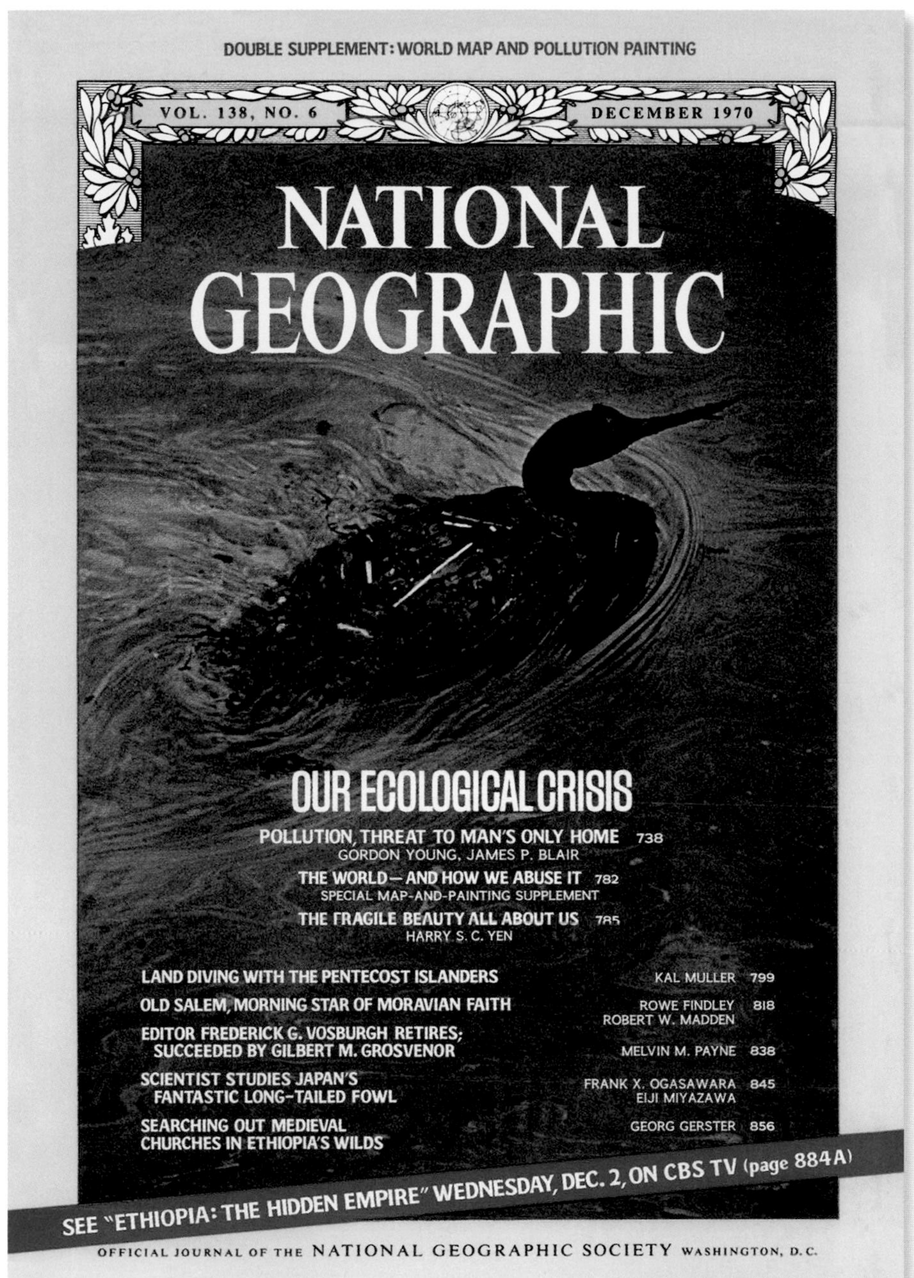

DECEMBER | BRUCE DALE

▲ **THE DAMAGE DONE** "That bird was doomed," said prominent ornithologist Dr. Alexander Wetmore (a National Geographic trustee) of this western grebe. "The oil so damaged his feathers that human help would be of no avail." For the photographer, the 35mm Kodachrome transparency mirrored a moment of "pure journalism"—but it also reflected an ironic beauty, the iridescent sheen of the deadly oil on the water.

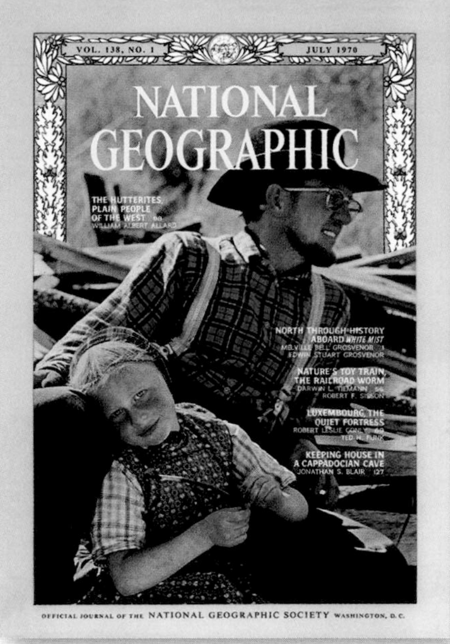

JULY | WILLIAM ALBERT ALLARD

▲ **FAMILY LIFE** On the Great Plains of Montana, a Hutterite father and daughter share a restful moment together.

"I'd wandered through this country before, and with each return it seemed more apparent that perhaps this was the way man was supposed to live. In a place where he could breathe deeply and drink from clear streams and rivers. In a place wide enough for eagles."

—William Albert Allard

from "The Hutterites: Plain People of the West"

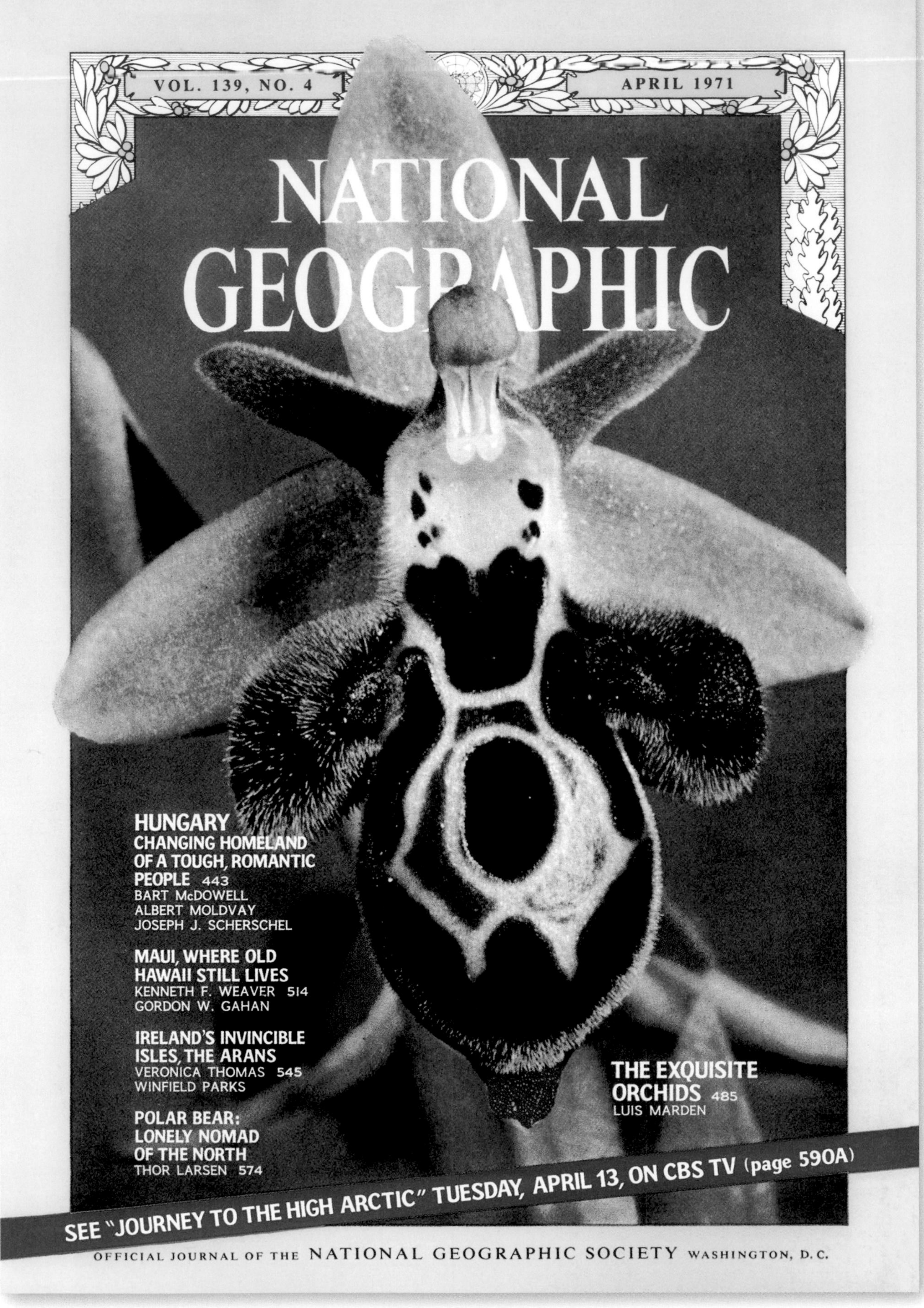

APRIL | **OTHMAR DANESCH** An orchid found on Crete mimics an insect to attract pollinators.

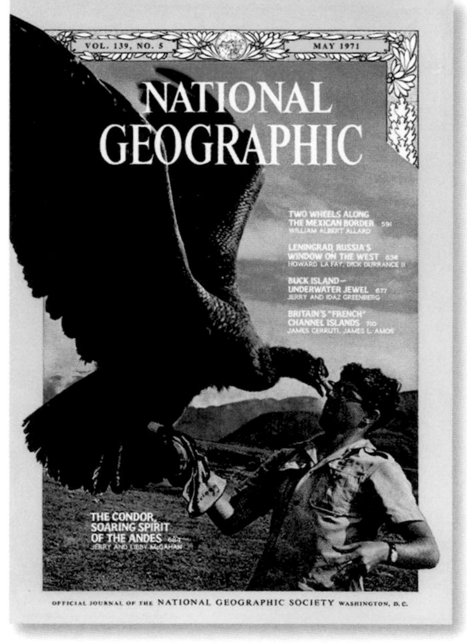
VOL. 139, NO. 5 MAY 1971

NATIONAL GEOGRAPHIC

TWO WHEELS ALONG THE MEXICAN BORDER 591
WILLIAM ALBERT ALLARD

LENINGRAD, RUSSIA'S WINDOW ON THE WEST 636
HOWARD LA FAY, DICK DURRANCE II

BUCK ISLAND—UNDERWATER JEWEL 677
JERRY AND IDAZ GREENBERG

BRITAIN'S "FRENCH" CHANNEL ISLANDS 710
JAMES CERRUTI, JAMES L. AMOS

THE CONDOR, SOARING SPIRIT OF THE ANDES
JERRY AND LIBBY McGAHAN

OFFICIAL JOURNAL OF THE NATIONAL GEOGRAPHIC SOCIETY WASHINGTON, D.C.

MAY | LIBBY MCGAHAN

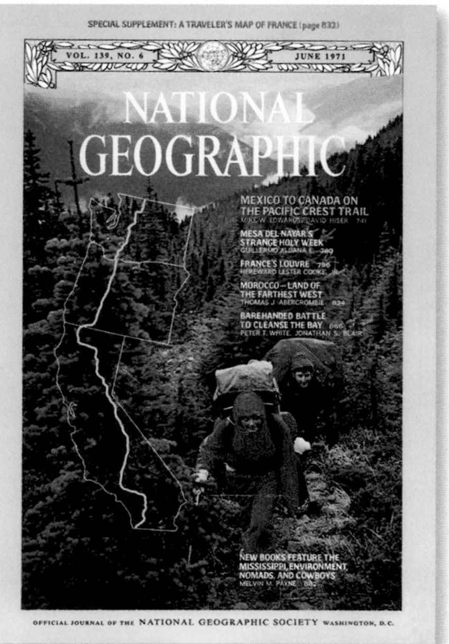
SPECIAL SUPPLEMENT: A TRAVELER'S MAP OF FRANCE (page 832)

VOL. 139, NO. 6 JUNE 1971

NATIONAL GEOGRAPHIC

MEXICO TO CANADA ON THE PACIFIC CREST TRAIL
MIKE W. EDWARDS, DAVID HISER 741

MESA DEL NAYAR'S STRANGE HOLY WEEK
GUILLERMO ALDANA E. 780

FRANCE'S LOUVRE 796
HEREWARD LESTER COOKE, JR.

MOROCCO—LAND OF THE FARTHEST WEST
THOMAS J. ABERCROMBIE 834

BAREHANDED BATTLE TO CLEANSE THE BAY 866
PETER T. WHITE, JONATHAN S. BLAIR

NEW BOOKS FEATURE THE MISSISSIPPI, ENVIRONMENT, NOMADS, AND COWBOYS
MELVIN M. PAYNE 882

OFFICIAL JOURNAL OF THE NATIONAL GEOGRAPHIC SOCIETY WASHINGTON, D.C.

JUNE | DAVID HISER

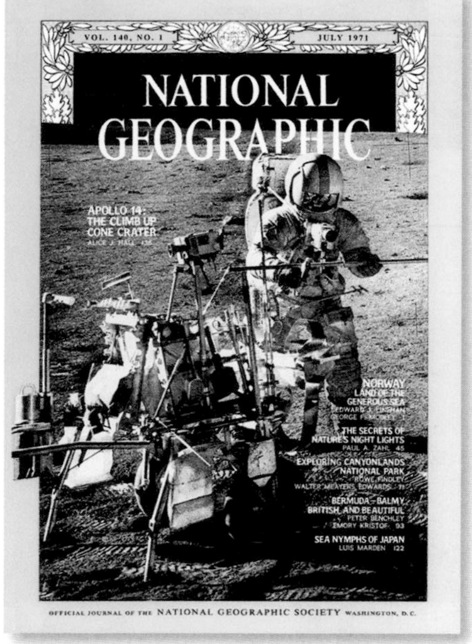
VOL. 140, NO. 1 JULY 1971

NATIONAL GEOGRAPHIC

APOLLO 14: THE CLIMB UP CONE CRATER

NORWAY LAND OF THE GENEROUS SEA

THE SECRETS OF NATURE'S NIGHT LIGHTS
PAUL A. ZAHL 45

EXPLORING CANYONLANDS NATIONAL PARK
ROWE FINDLEY
WALTER MEAYERS EDWARDS 71

BERMUDA—BALMY, BRITISH, AND BEAUTIFUL
PETER BENCHLEY
EMORY KRISTOF 93

SEA NYMPHS OF JAPAN
LUIS MARDEN 122

OFFICIAL JOURNAL OF THE NATIONAL GEOGRAPHIC SOCIETY WASHINGTON, D.C.

JULY | NASA

THE EXQUISITE ORCHIDS

One of the largest and most widespread plant families on Earth, the orchids—from those that can fit in a thimble to 100-foot vines—have been beguiling human beings for thousands of years.

> The word "orchid" projects at once an image of the clubwoman's resplendent purple blossom, but the variation of form and color among orchids is hard to believe even when seen. Some of them mimic bees, wasps, butterflies, or moths; some resemble swans or doves; others look like frogs or lizards, or miniature men; some even display perfectly-formed Arabic numerals . . . In between burgeon flowers in strange shapes and nearly every color: red, orange, yellow, green, purple, brown, white, and, rarely, blue. Despite legend there is no black orchid, though some come quite close.
>
> *—From "The Exquisite Orchids," Luis Marden*

▲ **LUNAR SCIENCE** Apollo 14 astronaut Edgar Mitchell made this portrait of Apollo 14's commander, Alan Shepard, assembling a core tube for sampling moon soil. This third lunar landing in craggy uplands was the most scientifically ambitious yet, capped by a mile-long trek to Cone Crater and back. This frame was one of 417 taken on this mission with the Hasselblad 70mm cameras bracket-mounted on the front of the astronauts' suits. Some of the 15 panoramas also made were published as gatefolds in this issue of the *Geographic*—one of the only magazines to do so.

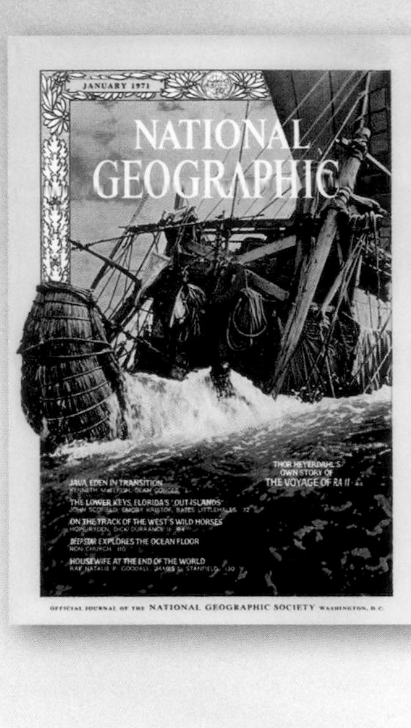

COVER STORY

THE *RA II*

JANUARY 1971 | CARLO MAURI

The sea crashes over—and through—the stern of adventurer Thor Heyerdahl's *Ra II,* nearly submerging a crewman. Made of papyrus reeds held together only with rope, the boat was modeled on those depicted in ancient Egyptian tomb reliefs. Although it nearly broke apart at times, in 1970 *Ra II* did cross the Atlantic from Morocco to Barbados in 57 days, demonstrating at least the feasibility of Heyerdahl's controversial contention that the pharaohs might have spread their pyramid-building culture to the Americas.

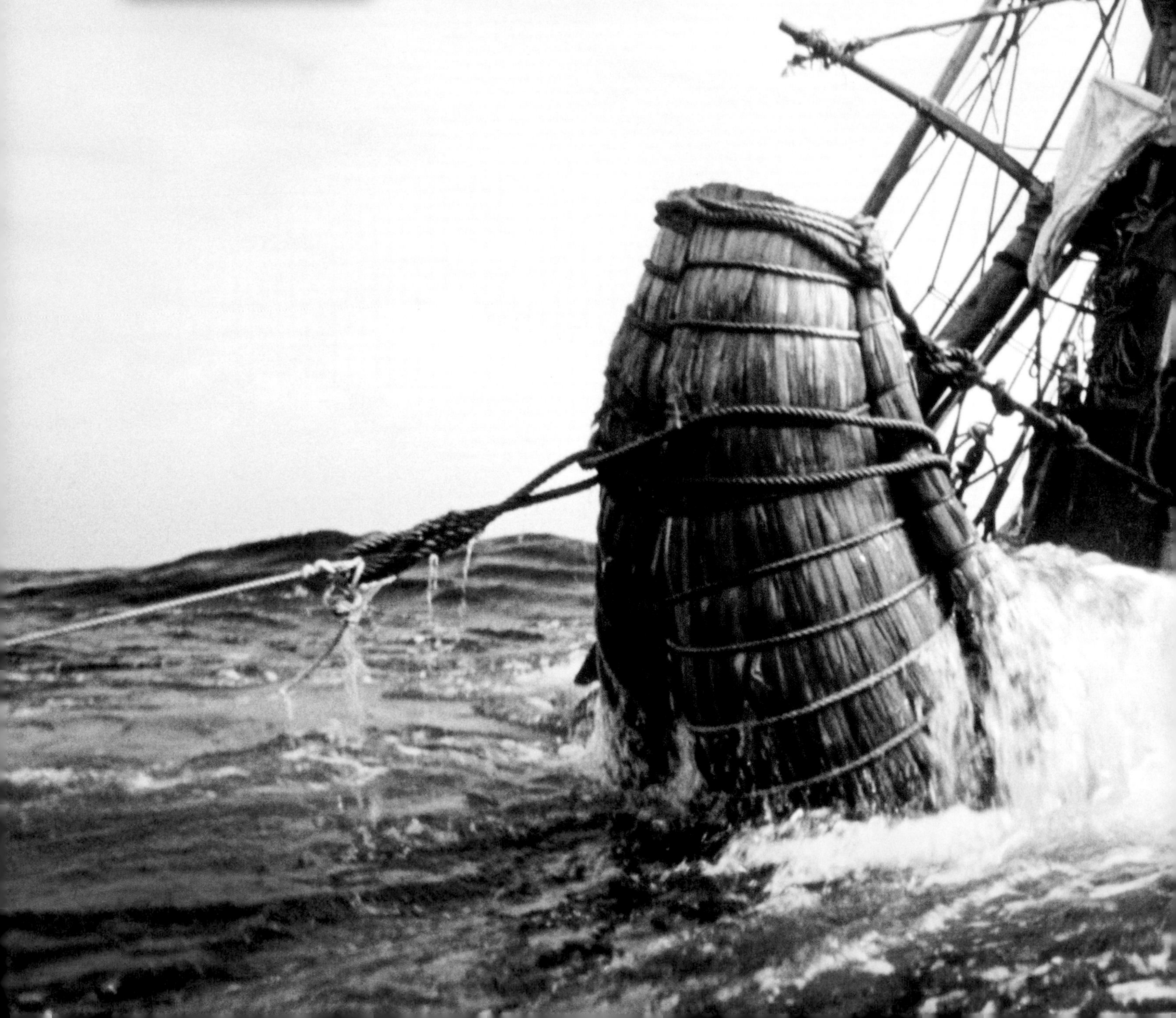

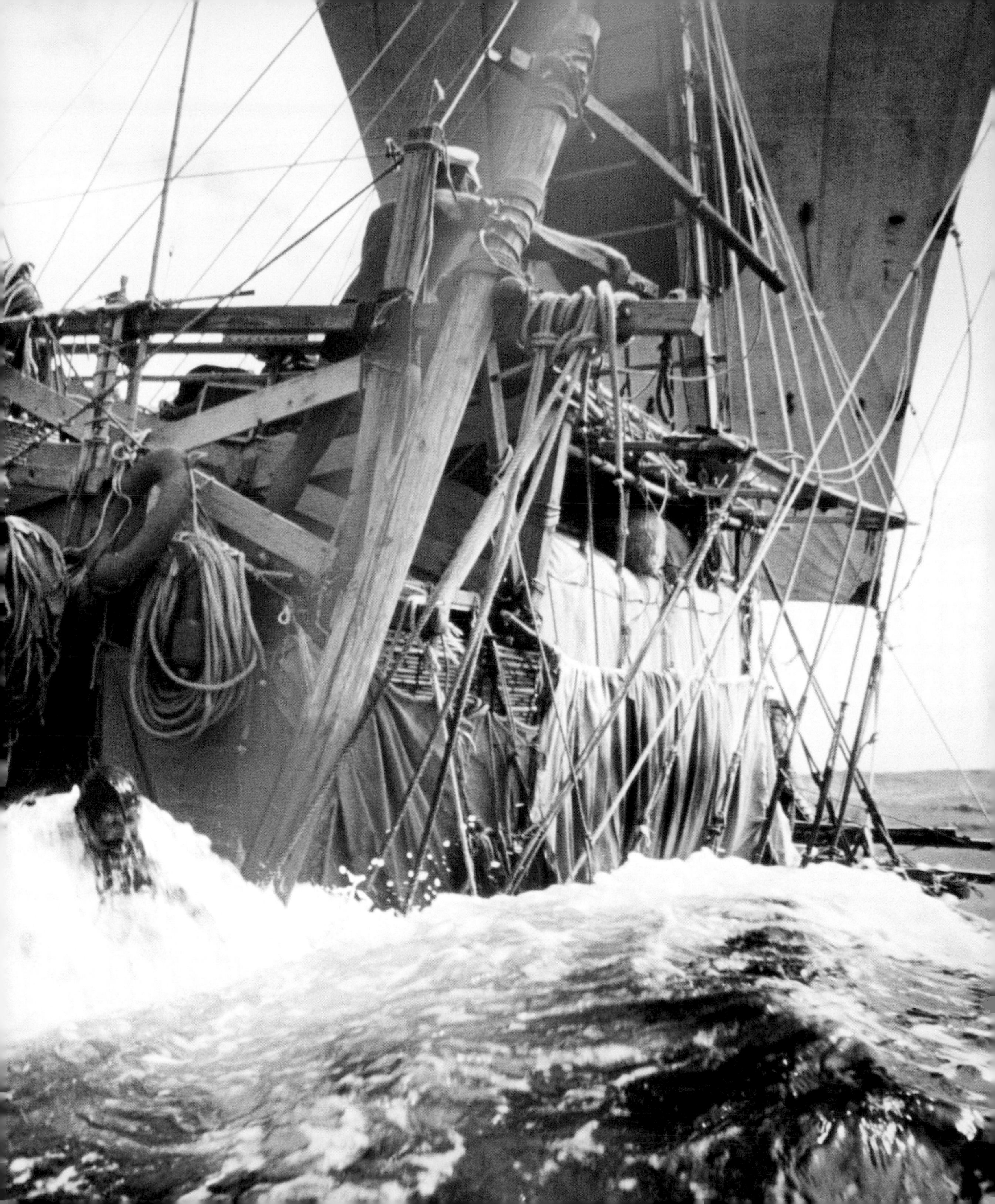

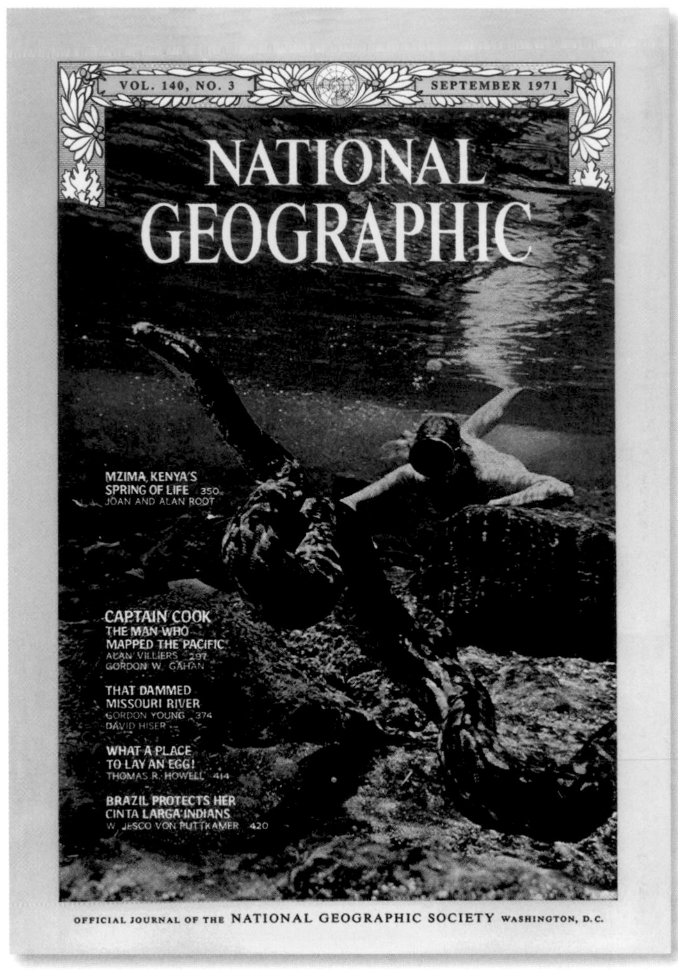

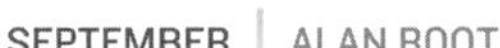
SEPTEMBER | ALAN ROOT

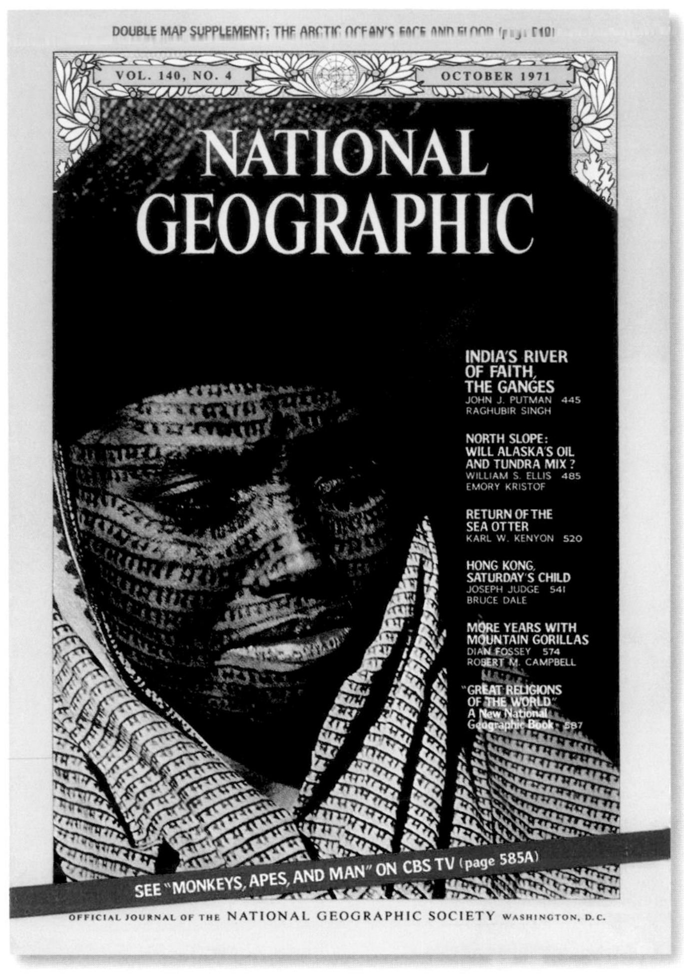

OCTOBER | RAGHUBIR SINGH

▲ **WATER SNAKE** A 14-foot rock python glides between photographer Alan Root and his wife, Joan, as they explore Kenya's Mzima Springs, a "desert-rimmed Eden" in arid Tsavo National Park.

> *"Like most residents of the springs, however, the hunter may quickly become the hunted. For all its awesome size, the python is fair game for Mzima's largest crocodiles."*
>
> —Alan Root
>
> *from "Mzima, Kenya's Spring of Life"*

▲ **TRUE BELIEVER** With the name of Rama, a Hindu god, stenciled in Sanskrit across her face and stitched into her sari, a woman arrives at Gangotri Temple carrying food, utensils, and clothing in a sack on her head. Standing near the source of the Ganges River in India, the temple has always drawn numbers of pilgrims, many trekking for weeks to get there. The devotees camp around its precincts, soliciting priestly blessings, filling jugs with the sacred waters, or simply touching the temple's walls.

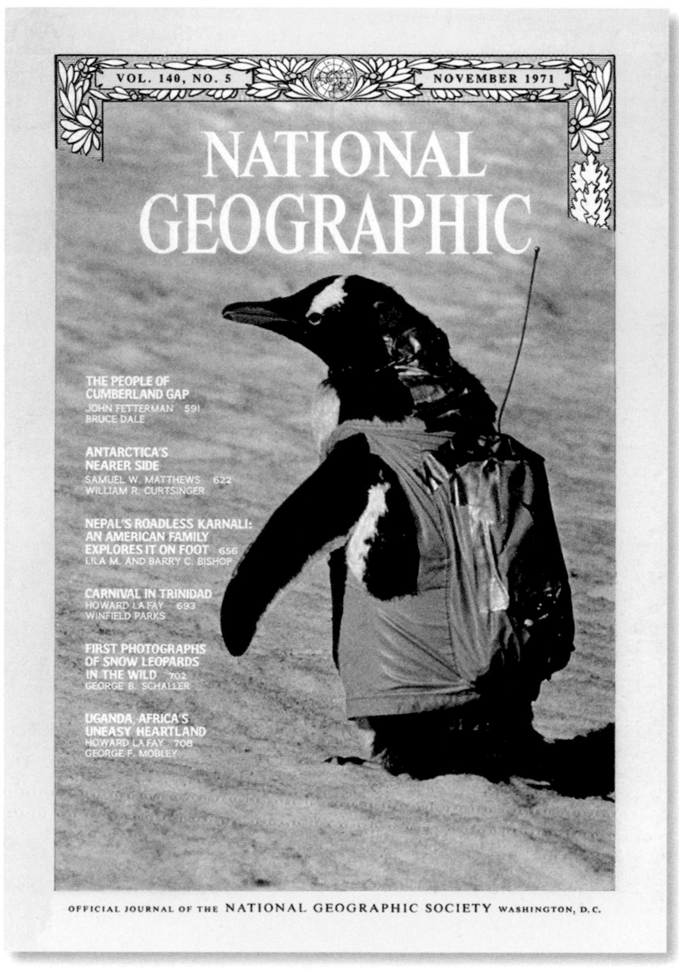

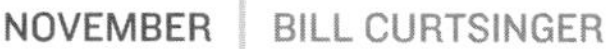
NOVEMBER | BILL CURTSINGER

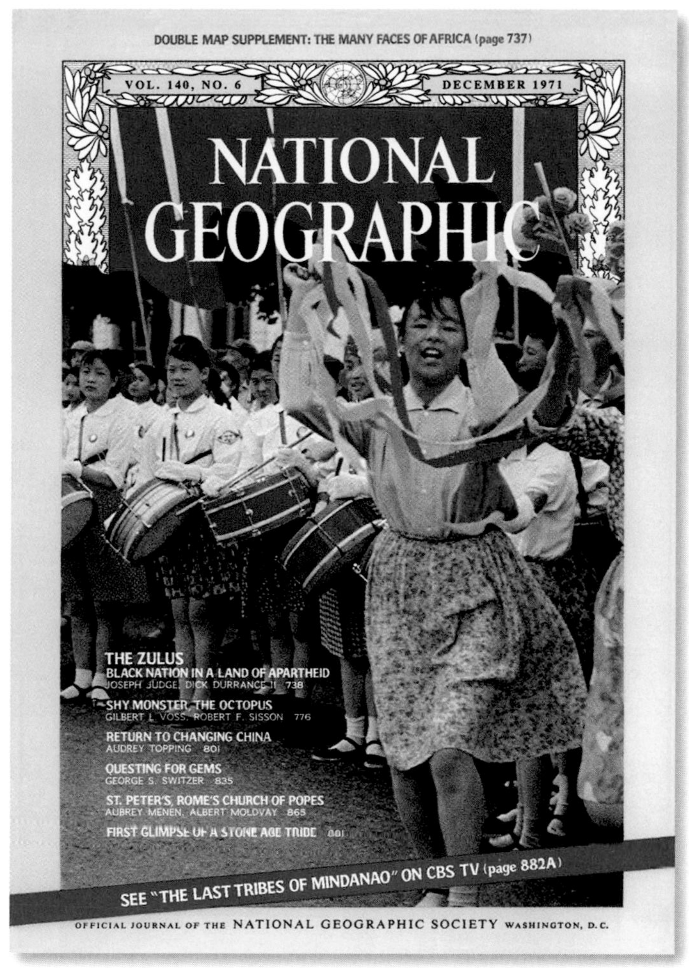

DECEMBER | AUDREY TOPPING

▲ **PROJECT: PENGUIN** Strolling across the Antarctic ice, a gentoo penguin wears a radio backpack providing biologists with data on its blood pressure and flow. Working from the 133-foot research vessel *Alpha Helix,* Scripps Institution of Oceanography scientists were placing penguins in pressurized diving chambers, measuring their body heat regulation, or watching them waddle on improvised treadmills. "Someday our human attempts to live and work deep in the oceans may be helped by knowing better how penguins and seals thrive in seas as cold as this," one biologist told *Geographic* writer Sam Matthews.

▲ **INSIDE RED CHINA** Journalist Audrey Topping's pictures—like this one of cheering schoolgirls in Beijing—provided a rare Western glimpse inside Communist China. Although her husband was Seymour Topping, a well-known *New York Times* correspondent, he could not gain admittance to that country because no American journalist had been permitted entry since the early 1950s. But Audrey Topping, who had been born in China, obtained a rare visa after applying as a "Canadian housewife." It helped that her father had once been a diplomat there—and that he still remained close to Premier Chou En-lai, Chairman Mao's chief lieutenant.

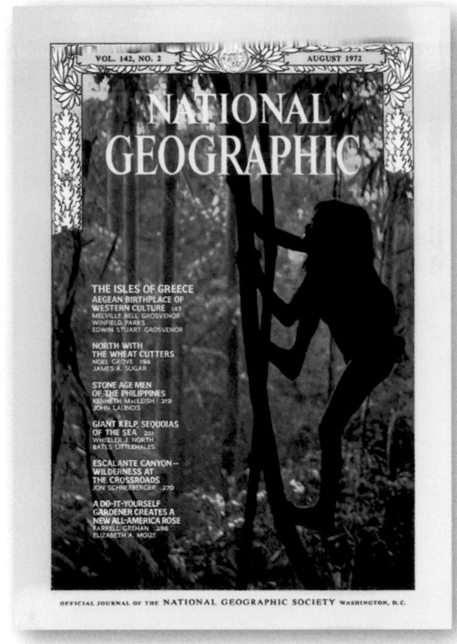

AUGUST 1972 | JOHN LAUNOIS

▲ **WILD CHILD** Lubu, a Tasaday boy, climbs a forest vine. "The Tasadays moved like monkeys," reported Launois, "swinging on vines from one slope to another." Nearby, trees soar over 200 feet.

THE TASADAYS ▶

TO THE END OF their lives *National Geographic*'s Kenneth MacLeish and freelance photographer John Launois believed that the four days they spent in the wilds of Mindanao had amounted to the space age encountering the Stone Age.

In March 1972, less than a year after an enthralled world first heard that a tribe, the Tasadays, had been discovered on that Philippine island—a tribe still living in caves without any knowledge of the outside world—MacLeish and Launois found themselves flying over an expanse of tropical forest so thick the helicopter had to drop them off on a platform in a treetop.

Theirs was seemingly a visit to a lost world. The Tasadays, all 24 of them, wearing only leaves, were shy hunter-gatherers who claimed they had lived in those caves since time immemorial. Launois shot 38 rolls of film, but that small number resulted in a *Geographic* cover story that garnered enormous international attention. Not long afterward, however, President Ferdinand Marcos banned further visitation, on the pretext of protecting the tribe.

Many anthropologists now think it was at least partially a hoax. The Tasadays might indeed have been hunter-gatherers, but they hadn't been completely isolated since the Stone Age. They knew about neighboring villages, they knew about clothes, they probably lived in thatched huts and only occasionally used those caves. Someone highly placed had persuaded them to drape themselves in leaves, perhaps to project an image of the Philippines as a primeval Eden.

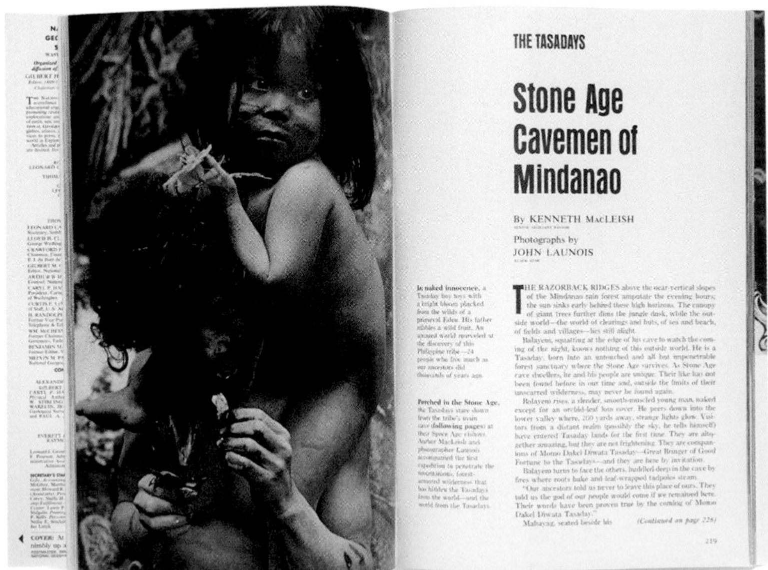

THE TASADAYS

Stone Age Cavemen of Mindanao

By KENNETH MacLEISH

Photographs by JOHN LAUNOIS

In naked innocence, a Tasaday boy toys with a bright bloom plucked from the wilds of a primeval Eden. His father nibbles a wild fruit. An amazed world marveled at the discovery of this Philippine tribe—24 people who live much as our ancestors did thousands of years ago.

Perched in the Stone Age, the Tasadays stare down from the tribe's main cave **(following pages)** at their Space Age visitors. Author MacLeish and photographer Launois accompanied the first expedition to penetrate the mountainous, forest-armored wilderness that has hidden the Tasadays from the world—and the world from the Tasadays.

THE RAZORBACK RIDGES above the near-vertical slopes of the Mindanao rain forest amputate the evening hours; the sun sinks early behind these high horizons. The canopy of giant trees further dims the jungle dusk, while the outside world—the world of clearings and huts, of sea and beach, of fields and villages—lies still alight.

Balayem, squatting at the edge of his cave to watch the coming of the night, knows nothing of this outside world. He is a Tasaday, born into an untouched and all but impenetrable forest sanctuary where the Stone Age survives. As Stone Age cave dwellers, he and his people are unique. Their like has not been found before in our time and, outside the limits of their unscarred wilderness, may never be found again.

Balayem rises, a slender, smooth-muscled young man, naked except for an orchid-leaf loin cover. He peers down into the lower valley where, 200 yards away, strange lights glow. Visitors from a distant realm (possibly the sky, he tells himself) have entered Tasaday lands for the first time. They are altogether amazing, but they are not frightening. They are companions of Momo Dakel Diwata Tasaday—Great Bringer of Good Fortune to the Tasadays—and they are here by invitation.

Balayem turns to face the others, huddled deep in the cave by fires where roots bake and leaf-wrapped tadpoles steam.

"Our ancestors told us never to leave this place of ours. They told us the god of our people would come if we remained here. Their words have been proven true by the coming of Momo Dakel Diwata Tasaday."

Mahayag, seated beside his (Continued on page 226)

219

◀ AUGUST 1972 | JOHN LAUNOIS "In naked innocence," a Tasaday father and son pluck flowers and eat fruit.

▶ AUGUST 1972 | JOHN LAUNOIS Lubu supposedly belonged to an isolated 24-person tribe.

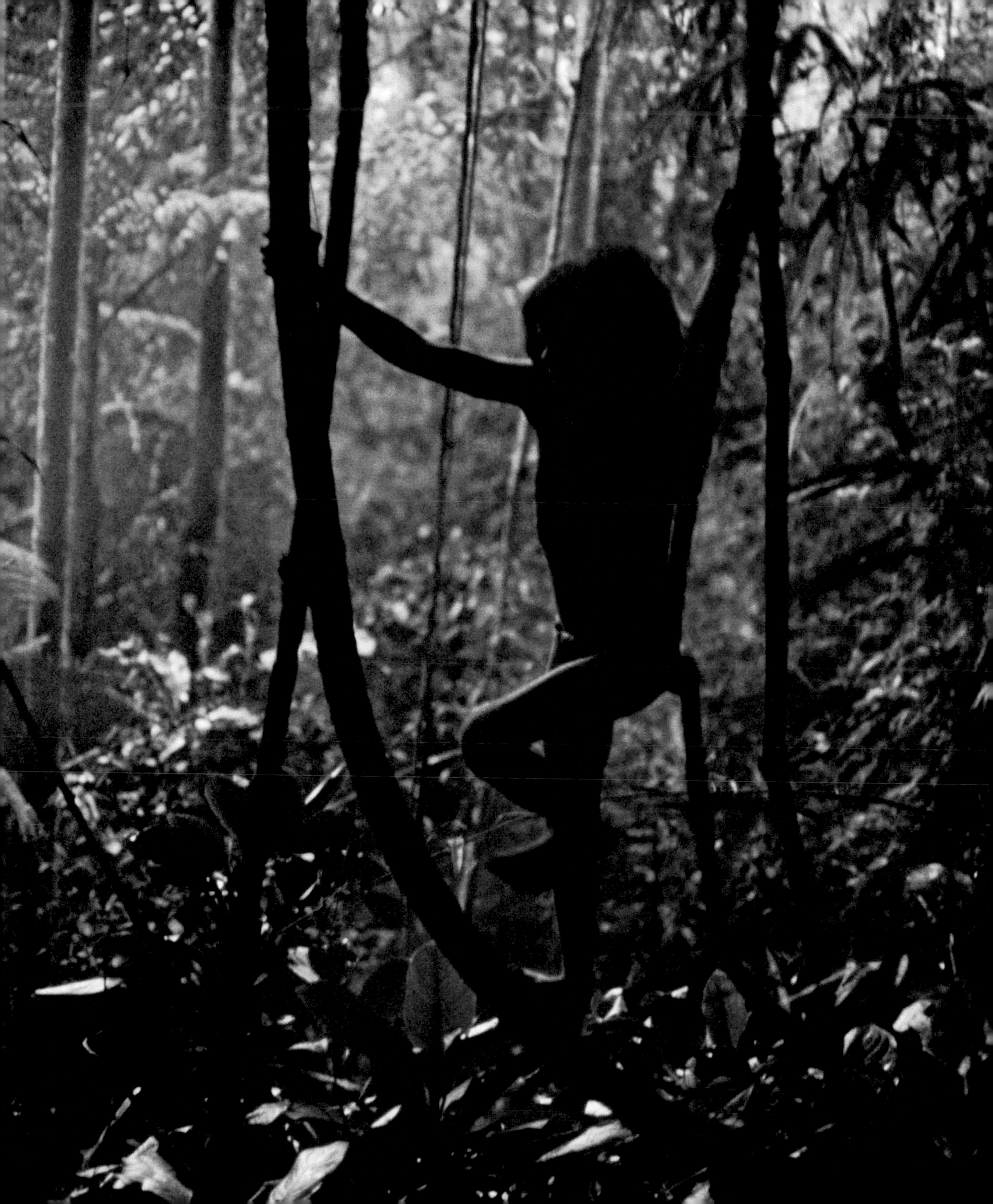

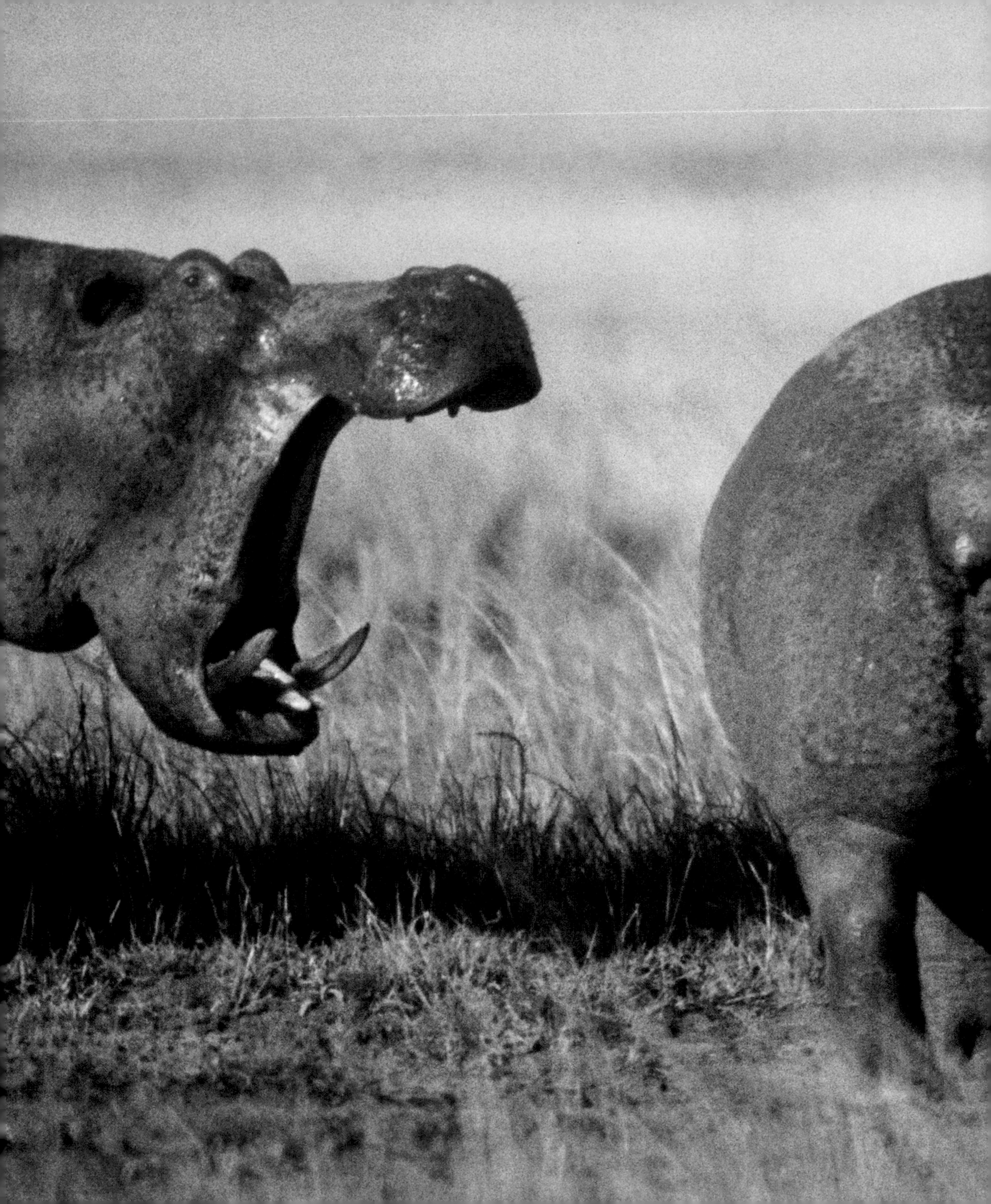

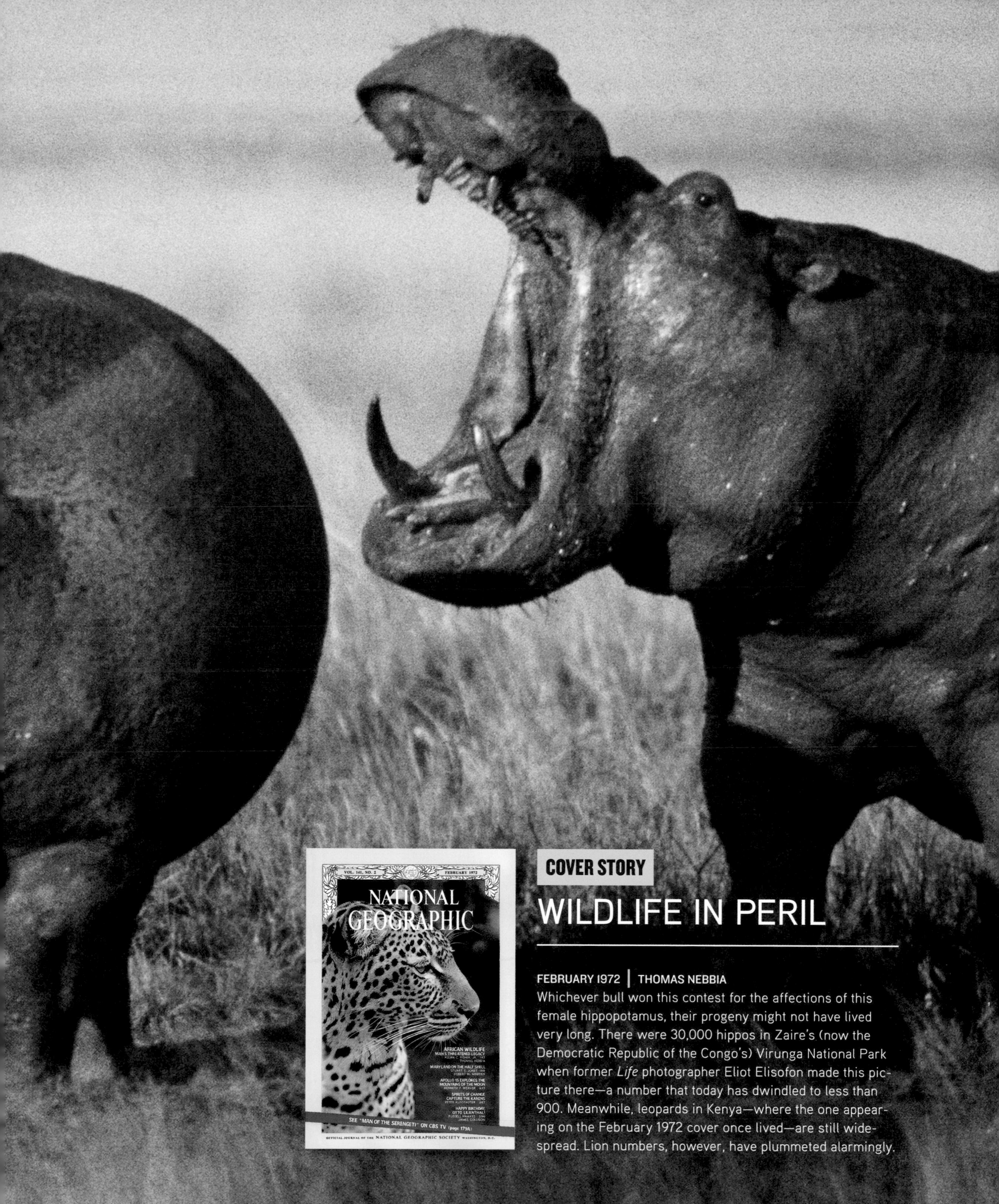

COVER STORY

WILDLIFE IN PERIL

FEBRUARY 1972 | THOMAS NEBBIA

Whichever bull won this contest for the affections of this female hippopotamus, their progeny might not have lived very long. There were 30,000 hippos in Zaire's (now the Democratic Republic of the Congo's) Virunga National Park when former *Life* photographer Eliot Elisofon made this picture there—a number that today has dwindled to less than 900. Meanwhile, leopards in Kenya—where the one appearing on the February 1972 cover once lived—are still widespread. Lion numbers, however, have plummeted alarmingly.

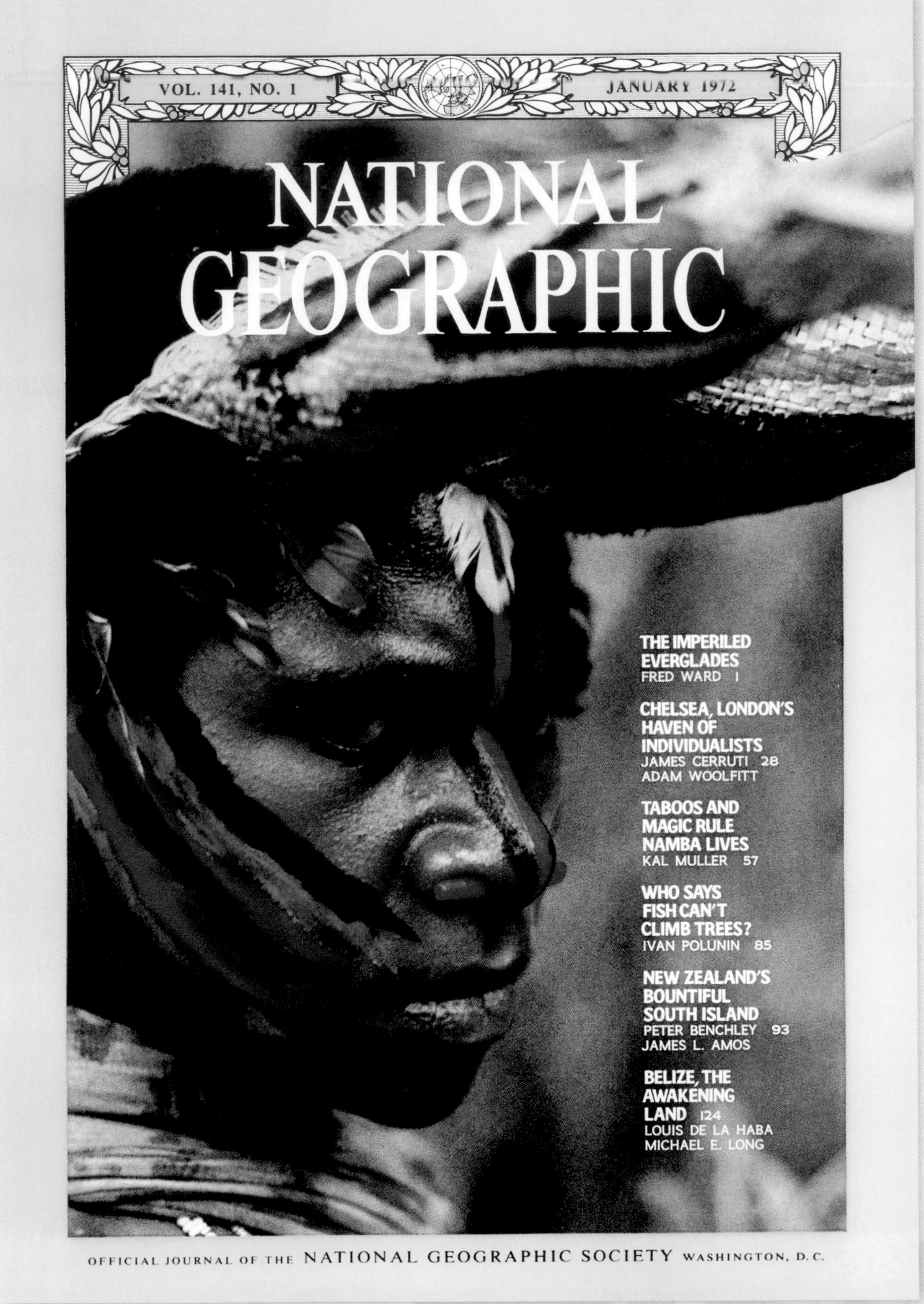

JANUARY | **KAL MULLER** A Small Namba woman prepares for a grading ceremony.

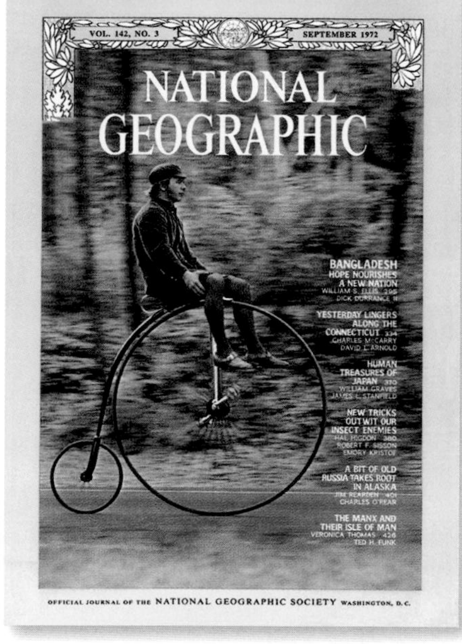

SEPTEMBER | DAVID L. ARNOLD

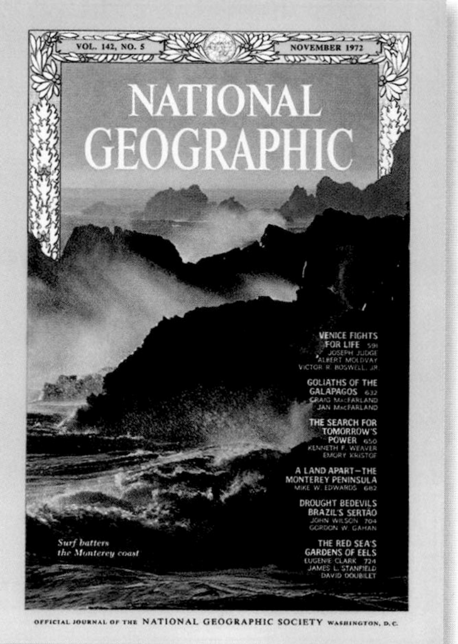

NOVEMBER | DECLAN HAUN

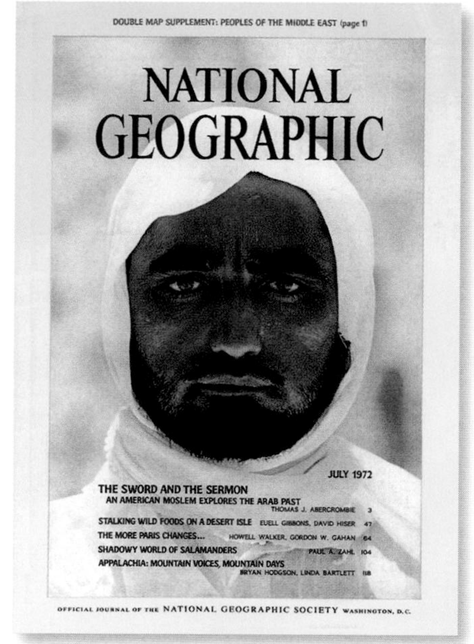

JULY | THOMAS J. ABERCROMBIE

KNOWING THE NAMBA

FEATHERS AND FIBER HORNS adorn a Small Namba woman on the island of Malakula in the New Hebrides (today called Vanuatu). Only about 125 members of her tribe still inhabited the rugged mountains of that 60-mile-long, jungle-clad island to the east of New Guinea, protected by terrain so severe that when Kal Muller arrived in the village called Lendombwey he was the first stranger ever to reach it.

Muller was one of those footloose self-taught anthropologists who drifted from island to island with battered cameras and torn notebooks, drawn to those tribes still living in traditional fashion.

He was permitted to photograph ceremonies never before seen by outsiders by promising the Namba that "people of the faraway United States would learn about their way of life." That worked because the New Hebrides had been a staging ground for U.S. troops fighting the Japanese during World War II. The islanders had not forgotten the "time man America allgetta he come long fight"—referring to, in pidgin, the arrival of the GIs in 1942.

▲ **ARRESTING GAZE** This cover, the first on a yellow-bordered *National Geographic* to appear without any oak leaves, featured a story on the Islamic world that won its author, Thomas J. Abercrombie, an Overseas Press Club Award. "I just took his picture—one shot—and walked on to something else," he recalled about that face in the crowd at Mecca, where in the early '70s cameras were still frowned upon, making photography an often surreptitious endeavor. "I didn't know him or talk to him. But his gaze is arresting and captures the fervor of Islam."

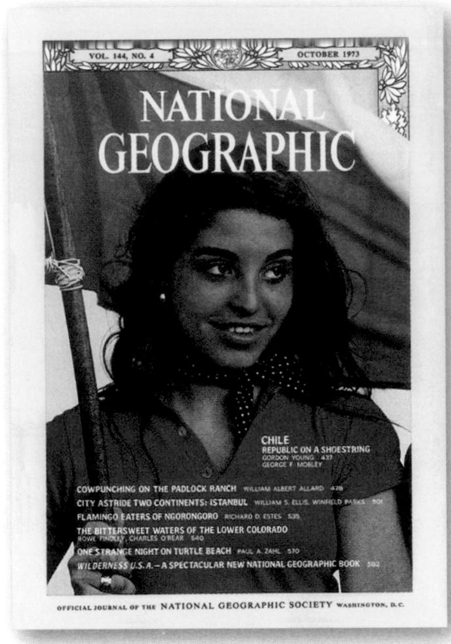

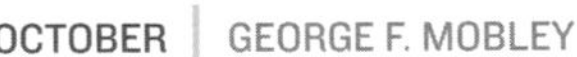
OCTOBER | GEORGE F. MOBLEY

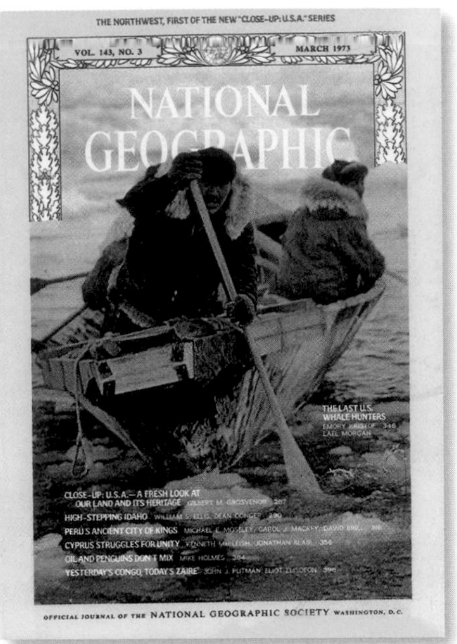

MARCH | EMORY KRISTOF

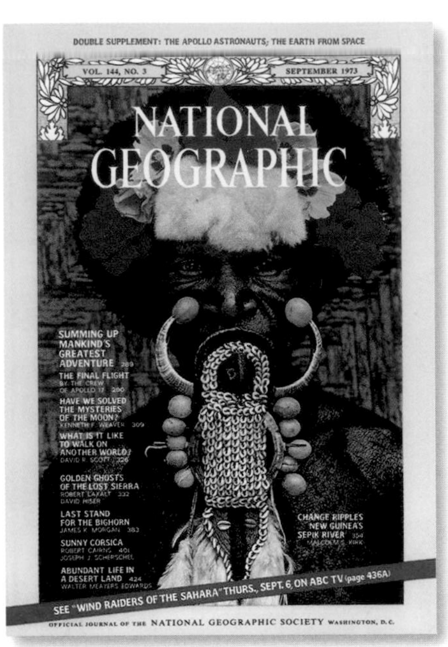

SEPTEMBER | MALCOLM S. KIRK

▲ **DANGEROUS POLITICS** Dressed in red and waving the red Chilean flag, this girl makes her allegiances obvious: They lay with left-wing President Salvador Allende—but this *Geographic* was hardly in the mail to members when in September 1973 Allende was deposed by coup d'état and killed. That left this *chilena*, and others pictured within the article, exposed to arrest by Gen. Augusto Pinochet's right-wing military government. For years photographer George Mobley agonized over her fate and that of the other *desaparecidos*—disappeared ones—whom he had photographed. To his relief, he later discovered that this girl, at least, was still alive and well.

ABORIGINAL ART ▶

SERPENT-HEADED IN A LAND that possesses some of the deadliest snakes in the world, a malignant female spirit called a *namarkain* weaves a string between her bony fingers—making it easier to pass from one sick person to another so as to steal their souls.

The 24-inch figure writhes up a stony wall at Cannon Hill, one of numerous Aboriginal rock art sites—including Bala-Uru, Obiri Rock, Kolondjuruk Creek, Nourlangie Rock—scattered about the bush country of Australia's Northern Territory. It was while they were photographing the plants and animals of the nearby Adelaide River that Stanley and Kay Breeden paused long enough to document some of the cliffs, caves, and shelters still retaining a shadow of that fusing of natural and spiritual worlds once called the Dreamtime.

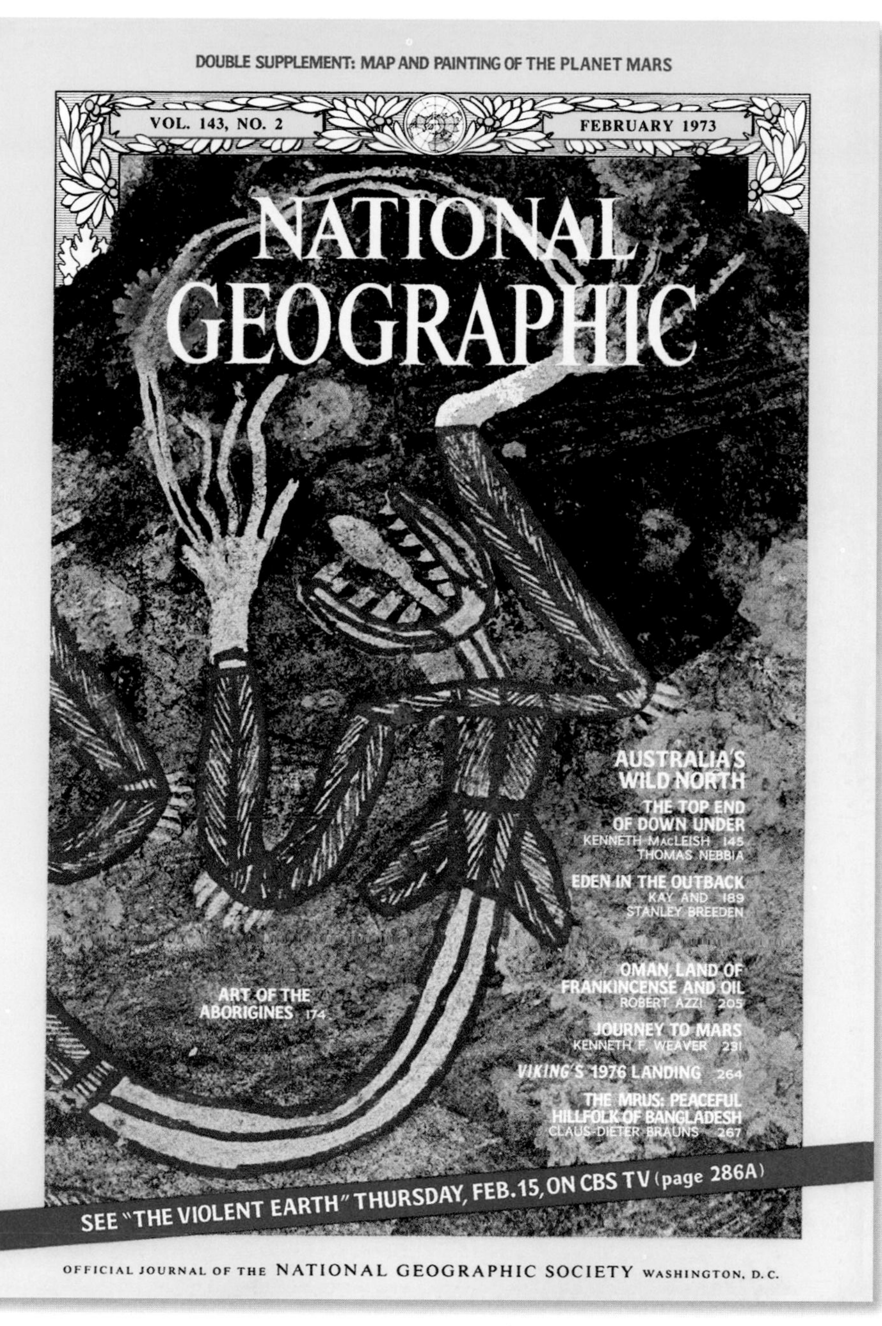
DOUBLE SUPPLEMENT: MAP AND PAINTING OF THE PLANET MARS

VOL. 143, NO. 2 — FEBRUARY 1973

NATIONAL GEOGRAPHIC

AUSTRALIA'S WILD NORTH
THE TOP END OF DOWN UNDER
KENNETH MacLEISH 145
THOMAS NEBBIA

EDEN IN THE OUTBACK
KAY AND 189
STANLEY BREEDEN

ART OF THE ABORIGINES 174

OMAN, LAND OF FRANKINCENSE AND OIL
ROBERT AZZI 205

JOURNEY TO MARS
KENNETH F. WEAVER 231

VIKING'S 1976 LANDING 264

THE MRUS: PEACEFUL HILLFOLK OF BANGLADESH
CLAUS-DIETER BRAUNS 267

SEE "THE VIOLENT EARTH" THURSDAY, FEB. 15, ON CBS TV (page 286A)

OFFICIAL JOURNAL OF THE NATIONAL GEOGRAPHIC SOCIETY WASHINGTON, D.C.

FEBRUARY | KAY AND STANLEY BREEDEN

> *"Decorating their stone canvases with pulverized rock mixed with water, nomads in Australia created a genesis in ocher with paintings dating from as long ago as 5,000 years."*
>
> —Kay and Stanley Breeden
> *from "Eden in the Outback"*

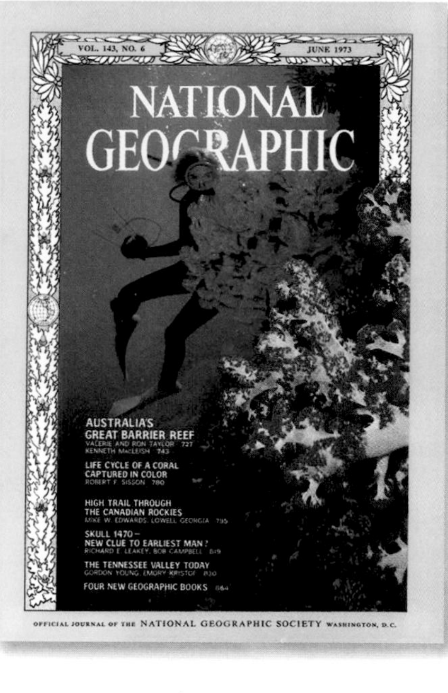
VOL. 143, NO. 6 — JUNE 1973

NATIONAL GEOGRAPHIC

AUSTRALIA'S GREAT BARRIER REEF
VALERIE AND RON TAYLOR 727
KENNETH MacLEISH 743

LIFE CYCLE OF A CORAL CAPTURED IN COLOR
ROBERT F. SISSON 780

HIGH TRAIL THROUGH THE CANADIAN ROCKIES
MIKE W. EDWARDS, LOWELL GEORGIA 795

SKULL 1470 – NEW CLUE TO EARLIEST MAN?
RICHARD E. LEAKEY, BOB CAMPBELL 819

THE TENNESSEE VALLEY TODAY
GORDON YOUNG, EMORY KRISTOF 830

FOUR NEW GEOGRAPHIC BOOKS 864

OFFICIAL JOURNAL OF THE NATIONAL GEOGRAPHIC SOCIETY WASHINGTON, D.C.

JUNE | RON TAYLOR

▲ **CORAL REEFER** Easing around the colorful coral, diver Valerie Taylor explores Australia's Great Barrier Reef. The former art student was fast becoming an expert underwater photographer, using cameras protected by waterproof housings designed and built by her husband, Ron Taylor. In 1969 the Australian couple had starred in the first hit shark movie, the documentary *Blue Water, White Death*. A year after this cover appeared, they would be filming much of the footage for an even bigger blockbuster: *Jaws*.

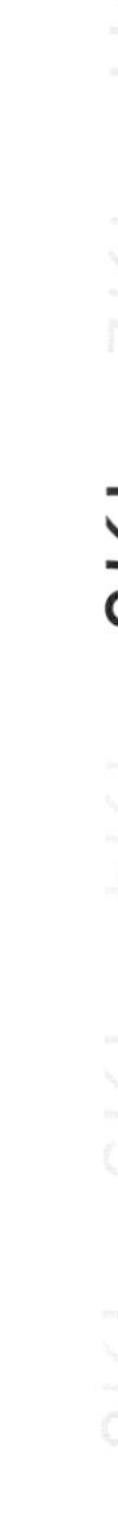

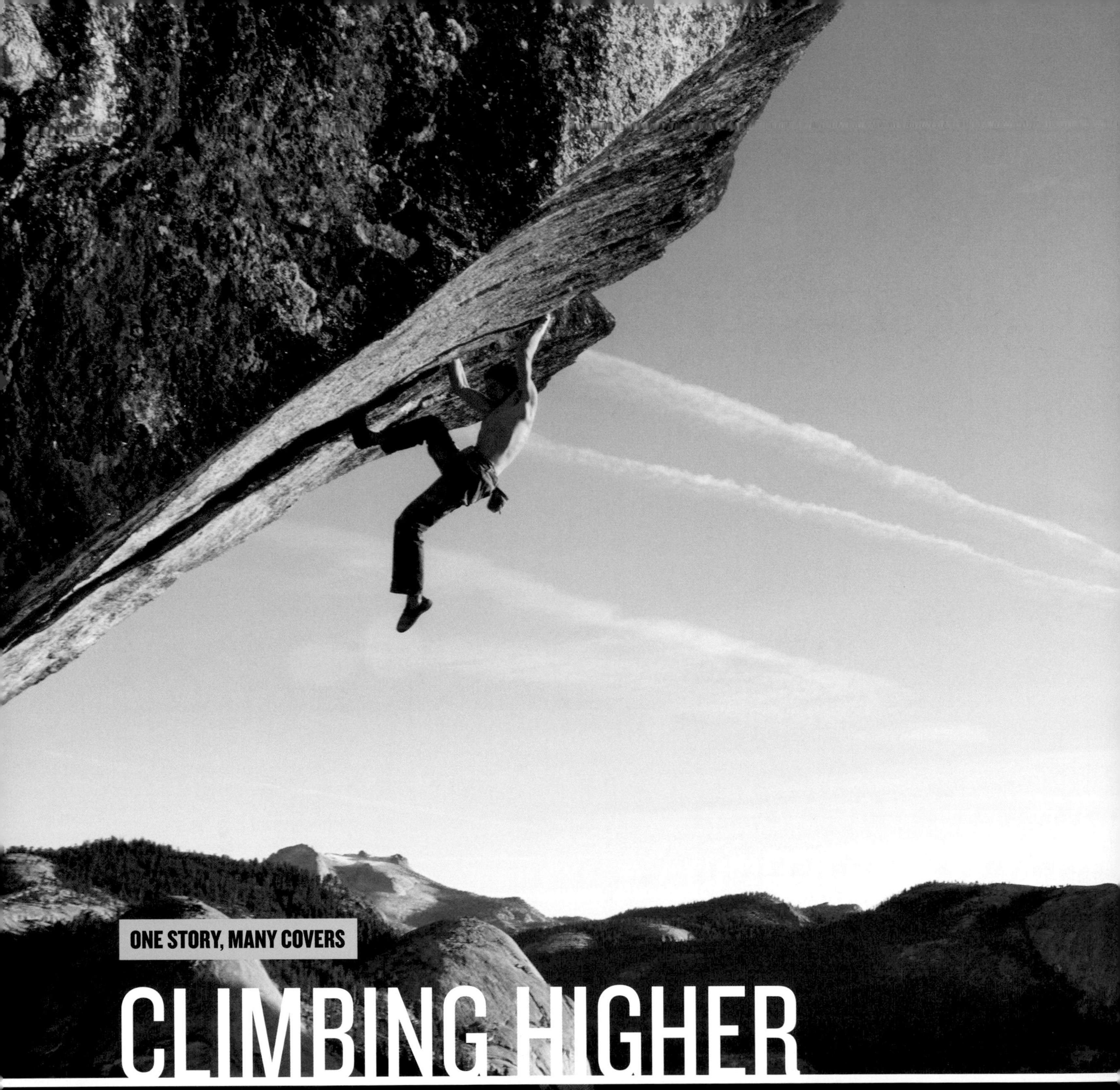

ONE STORY, MANY COVERS

CLIMBING HIGHER

▲ MAY 2011 | MIKEY SCHAEFER
Climbing Yosemite's Glacier Point without ropes is all in a day's work for Dean Potter.

"IN THIS VERTICAL WORLD you have to be prepared for sudden *oops* and downs," wrote the well-known climber and photographer Galen Rowell in the June 1974 *National Geographic*. Mountaineering narratives have been a staple in the magazine since 1891, when it published a captivating account of a failed attempt to summit Alaska's Mount St. Elias. Dozens of subsequent stories have carried readers to the iciest of heights and the most precipitous of slopes, enhanced by that head-spinning, stomach-churning photography

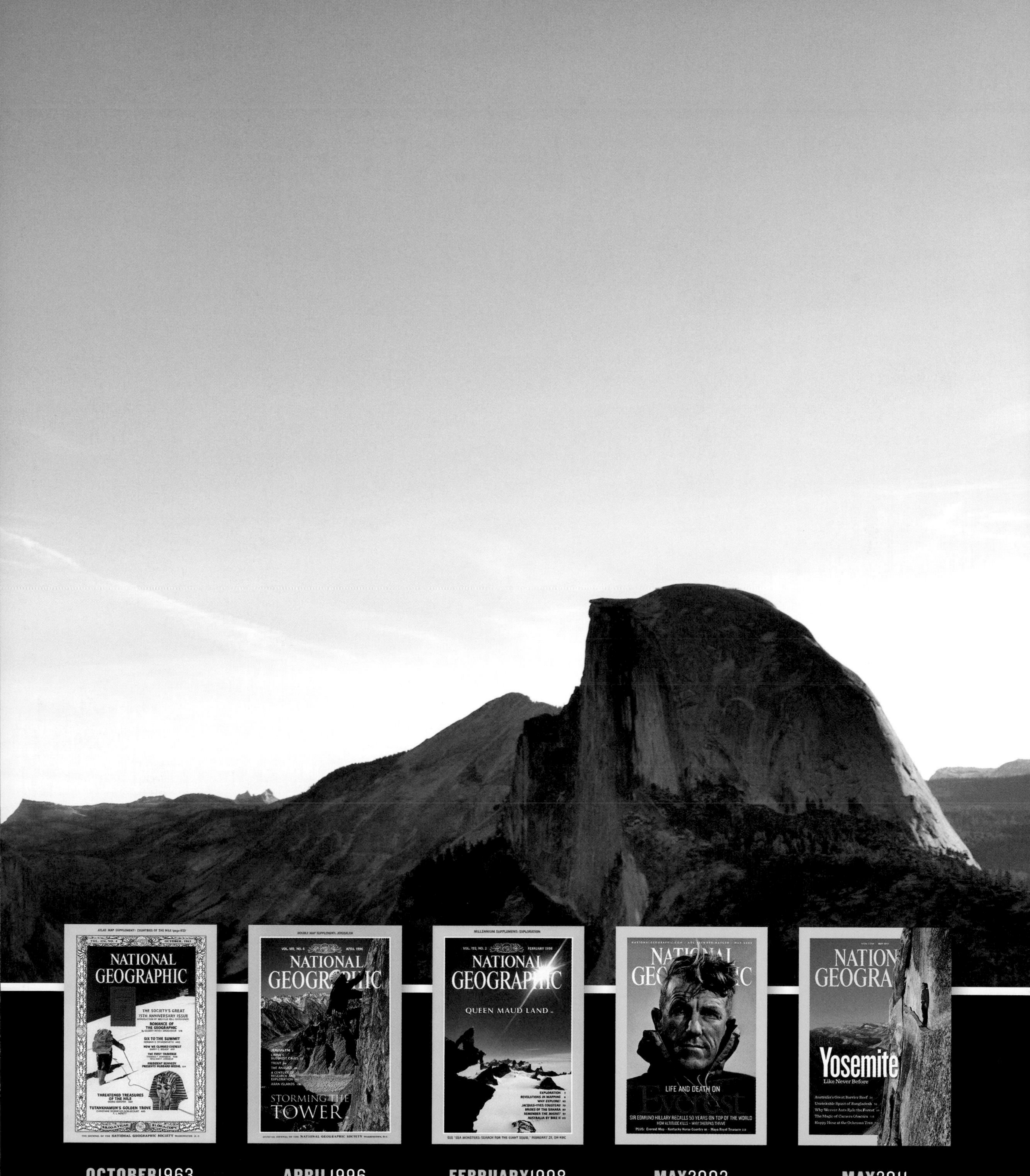

OCTOBER 1963 APRIL 1996 FEBRUARY 1998 MAY 2003 MAY 2011

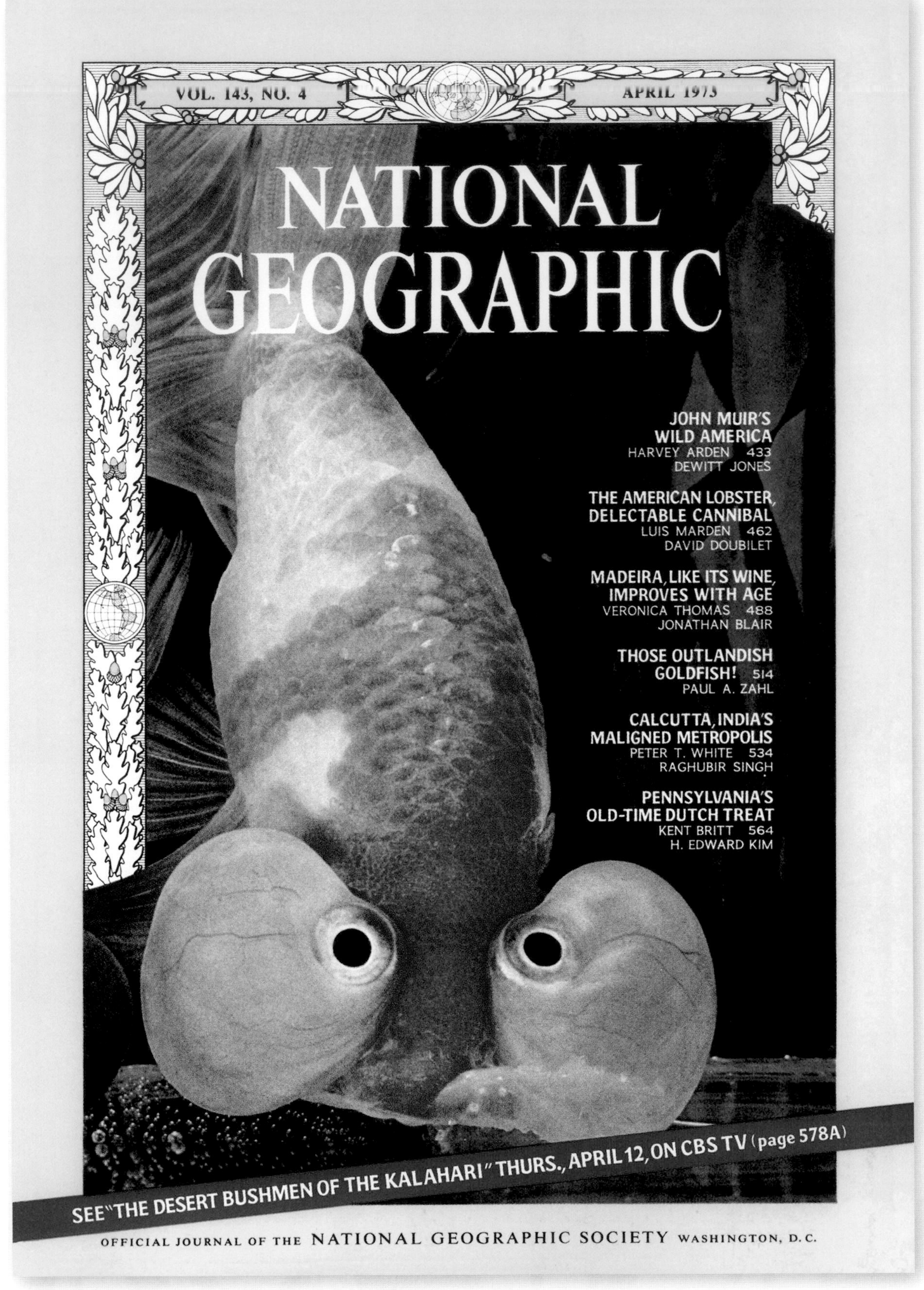

APRIL | PAUL A. ZAHL

BUBBLE EYE The bizarre-looking fish is really just a variety of goldfish with large fluid-filled eye sacs—one of numerous fanciful breeds popular in Asia. Paul Zahl, the *Geographic's* staff naturalist, specialized in biological oddities such as giant frogs, four-eyed fish, and fanged denizens of the deep.

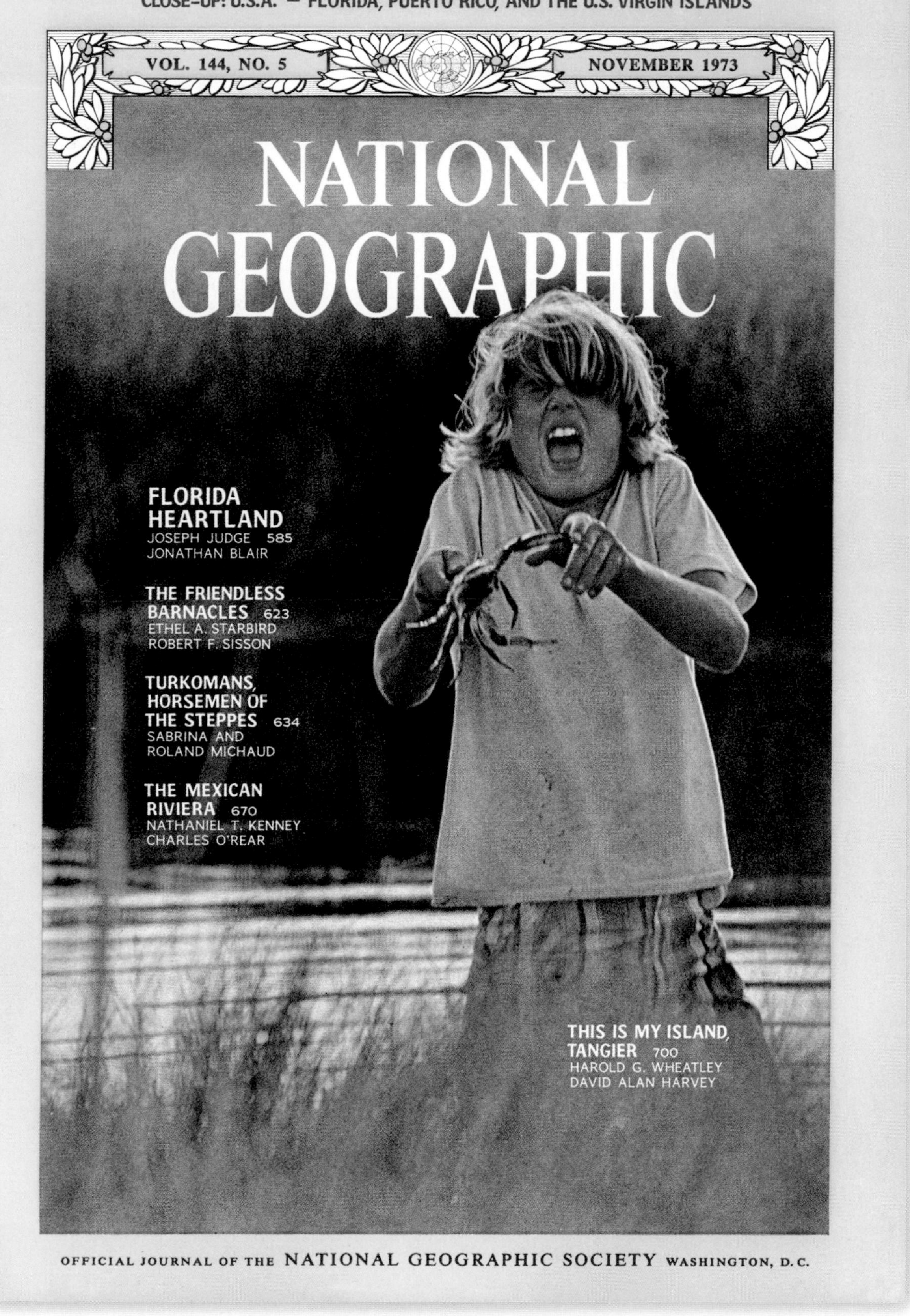

NOVEMBER | DAVID ALAN HARVEY

YOUCH! Not going gently into that good pot, a blue crab nips a youngster's finger on Virginia's Tangier Island, where crabbing was once a way of life. "Give him 40 rolls of film and see what he can do," runs an oft-told story of how Dave Harvey received this first *National Geographic* assignment—and began his legendary career.

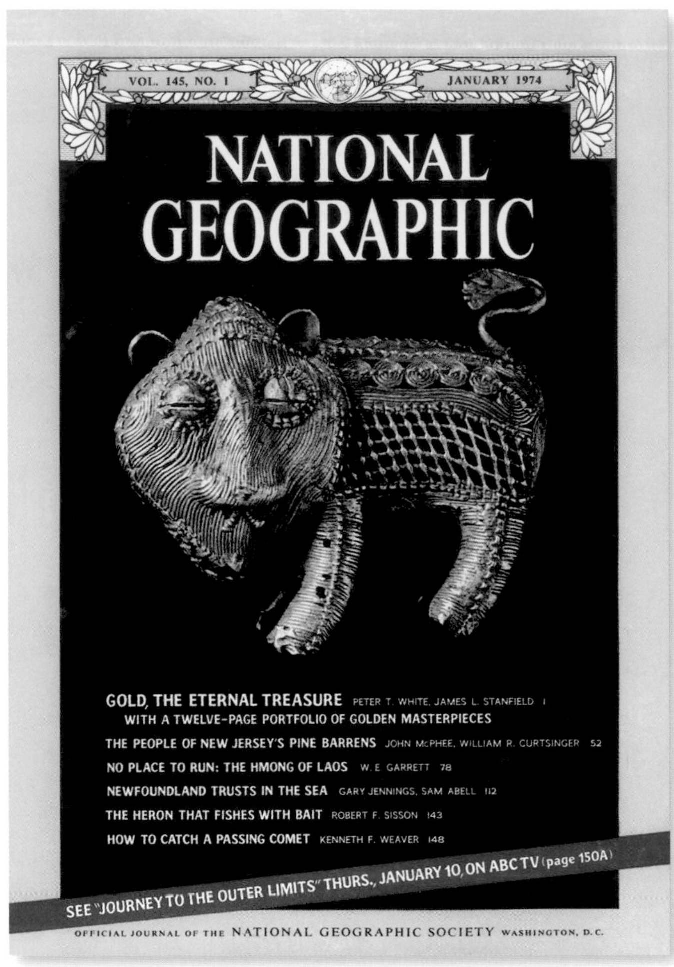

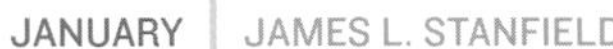
JANUARY | JAMES L. STANFIELD

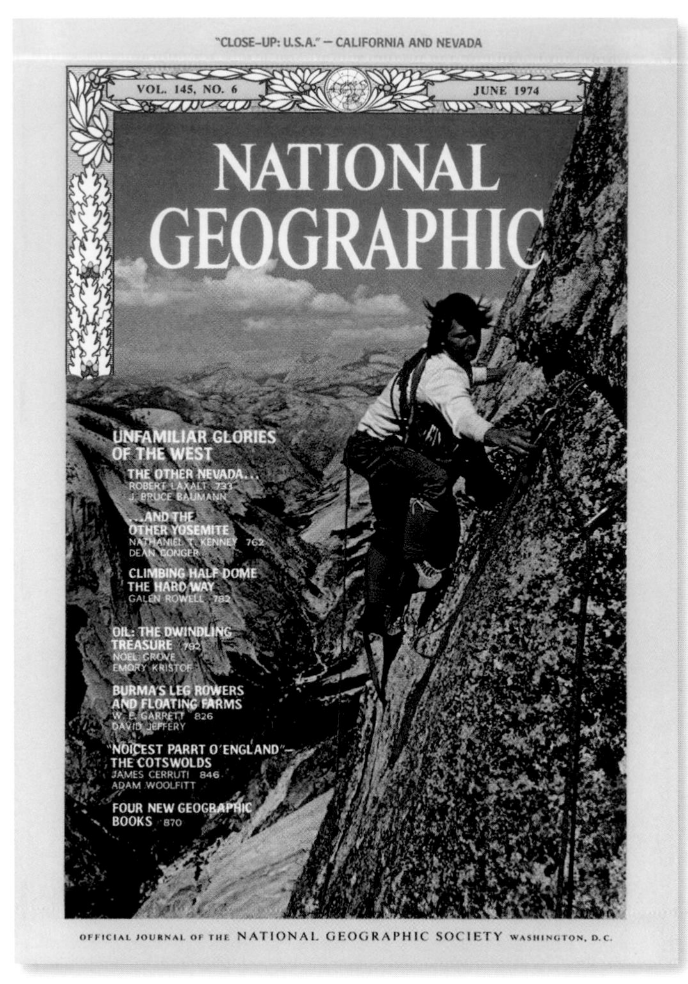

JUNE | GALEN ROWELL

▲ **GOLDEN LION** With its hooded eyes, latticed flanks, and cobra-like tail, this four-inch lion was made by a Twi-speaking Akan goldsmith of West Africa some two centuries ago.

"I've seen only one place where gold occupies even more exalted a place than in India. That is West Africa, in the Twi-speaking Ashanti Region in the Republic of Ghana, the land Europeans once called the Gold Coast."

—Peter White
from "Gold, the Eternal Treasure"

▲ **SKY HIGH** Climber Dennis Hennek carefully traverses the nearly vertical face of Yosemite's Half Dome, which soars nearly 5,000 feet above the valley below. He is leading the first "clean" ascent up that sheer granite wall, using only easily removed chocks and nuts instead of steel pitons, which permanently disfigure the rock into which they're hammered. This was the article that launched the already accomplished climber Galen Rowell on his celebrated career as a landscape and adventure photographer. It also helped spur a clean-climbing revolution among conservation-minded mountaineers.

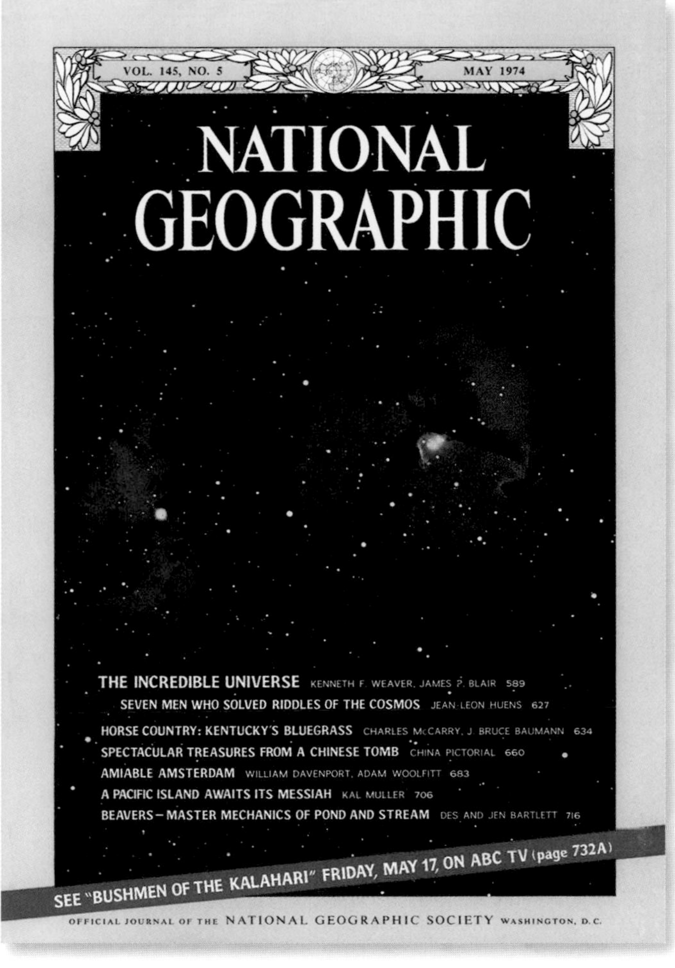

MAY | WILLIAM E. SCHOENING (KITT PEAK NATIONAL OBSERVATORY)

▲ **STAR DUST** The three-lobed Trifid Nebula, some 5,000 light-years distant, was a natural choice for a cover story on "The Incredible Universe" because it remains one of the most photogenic and colorful of the cosmic phenomena easily viewed with a telescope. Located in the constellation Sagittarius, this nursery of stars billows with clouds of luminescent dust and gas, the red portions emitting the heat of young stars, the blue regions reflecting the light of hot ones.

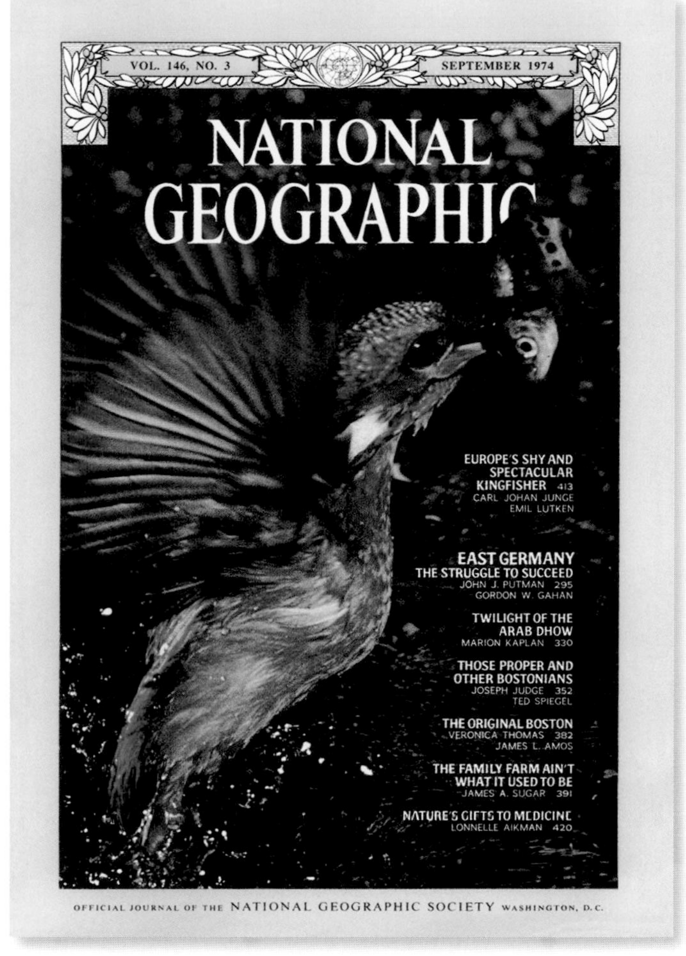

SEPTEMBER | CARL-JOHAN JUNGE AND EMIL LUTKEN

▲ **SLOW MOTION** Frozen in the instant it rockets out of a stream, a European kingfisher clamps a trout fingerling in its beak. Fascinated by the flash of cobalt that is the kingfisher in flight, Danish teachers Carl-Johan Junge and Emil Lutken spent two years attempting to capture its movements on film. From a blind set on a stream bank in Denmark's Jutland peninsula they documented the bird's hunting, courting, and nesting habits. Because the kingfisher's acrobatics are often too fast for human eyes to follow, they relied on strobes synchronized to shutter speeds set as high as 1/10,000 of a second.

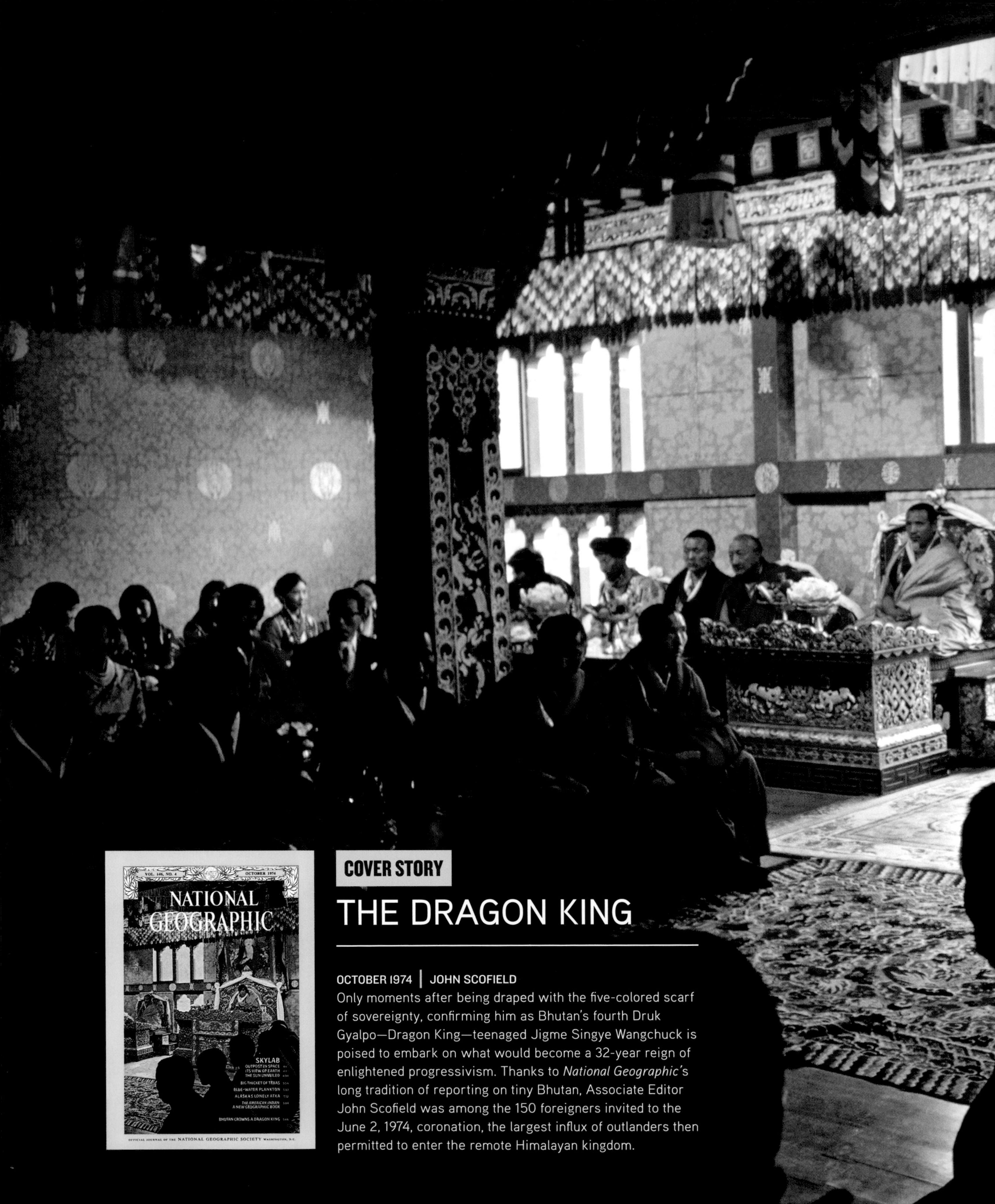

COVER STORY

THE DRAGON KING

OCTOBER 1974 | JOHN SCOFIELD

Only moments after being draped with the five-colored scarf of sovereignty, confirming him as Bhutan's fourth Druk Gyalpo—Dragon King—teenaged Jigme Singye Wangchuck is poised to embark on what would become a 32-year reign of enlightened progressivism. Thanks to *National Geographic*'s long tradition of reporting on tiny Bhutan, Associate Editor John Scofield was among the 150 foreigners invited to the June 2, 1974, coronation, the largest influx of outlanders then permitted to enter the remote Himalayan kingdom.

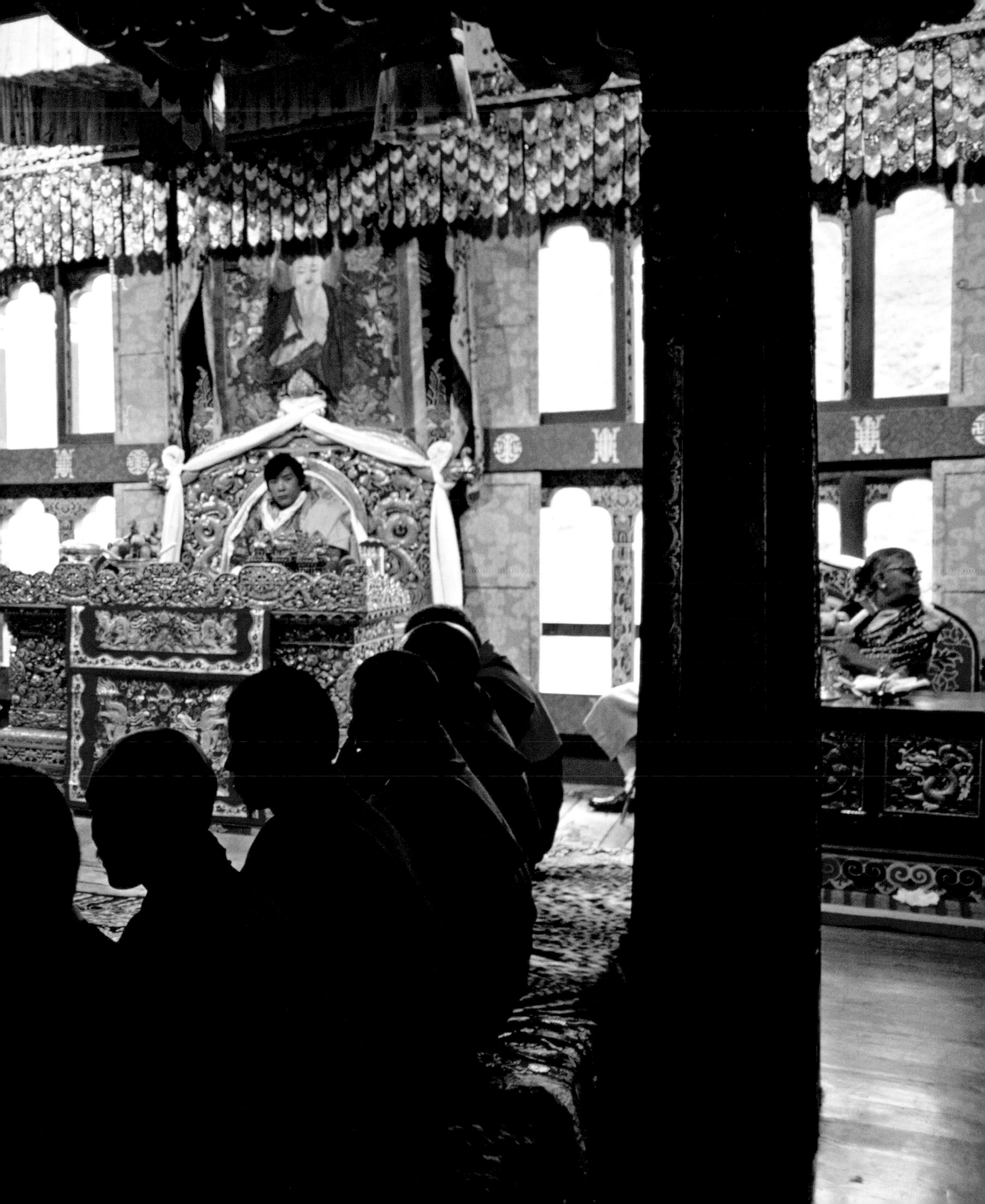

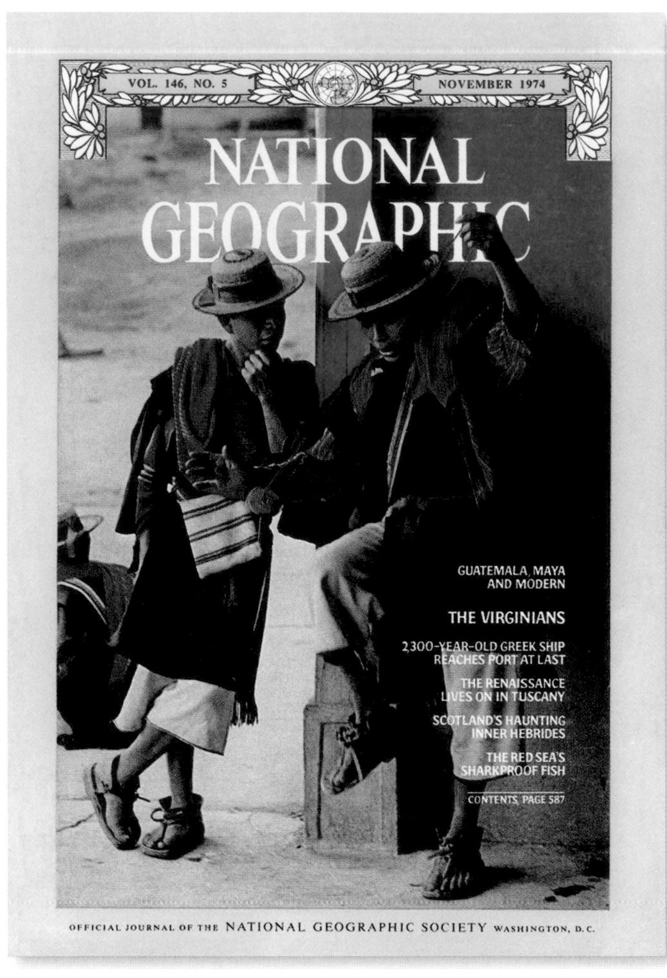

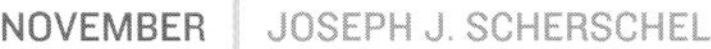
NOVEMBER | JOSEPH J. SCHERSCHEL

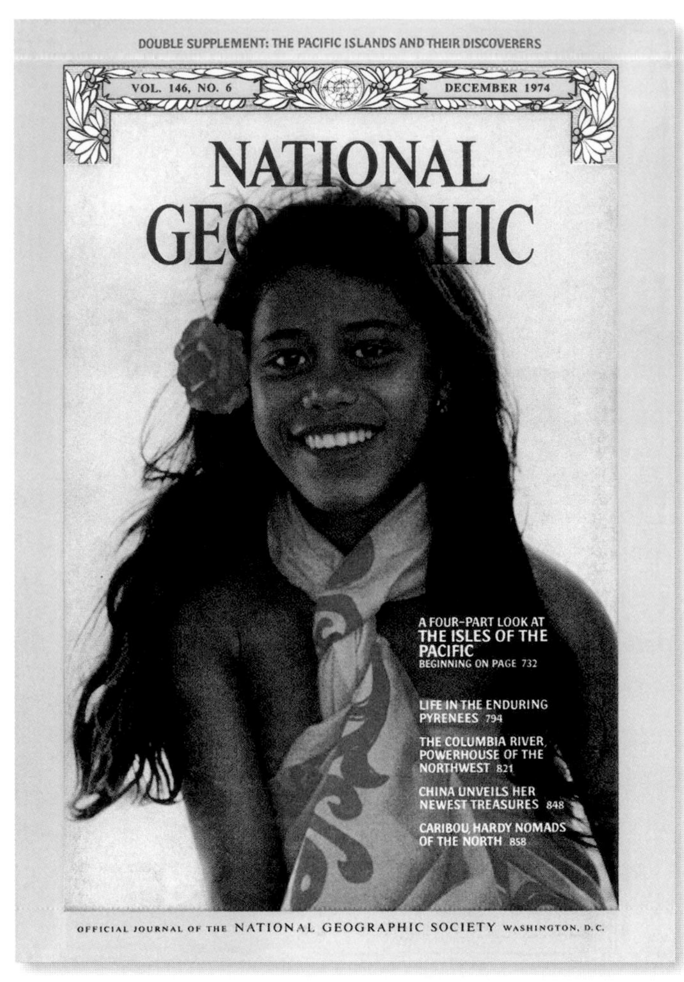

DECEMBER | H. EDWARD KIM

▲ **HARD AT WORK** In the highland village of San Juan Atitlán, Indian youths hang out while one spins thread for a homespun garment.

"In Guatemala's lofty highlands, far from the hubbub of the modern capital, Maya Indians and their pantheon of spirits dwell amid the cloud-ripping hulks of dead and dormant volcanoes."

—Louis de la Haba
from "Guatemala, Maya and Modern"

▲ **ALL SMILES** A girl from Bora Bora epitomizes the fabled beauty of Polynesian women. David Samwell, a surgeon's mate who accompanied Captain Cook to the South Seas, described "great Numbers of Girls . . . who in Symmetry & proportion might dispute the palm with any women under the Sun." *Bounty* mutineer James Morrison extolled "Eyes full and sparkling." Both 18th-century tributes were quoted in December 1974's four-part series, "The Isles of the Pacific."

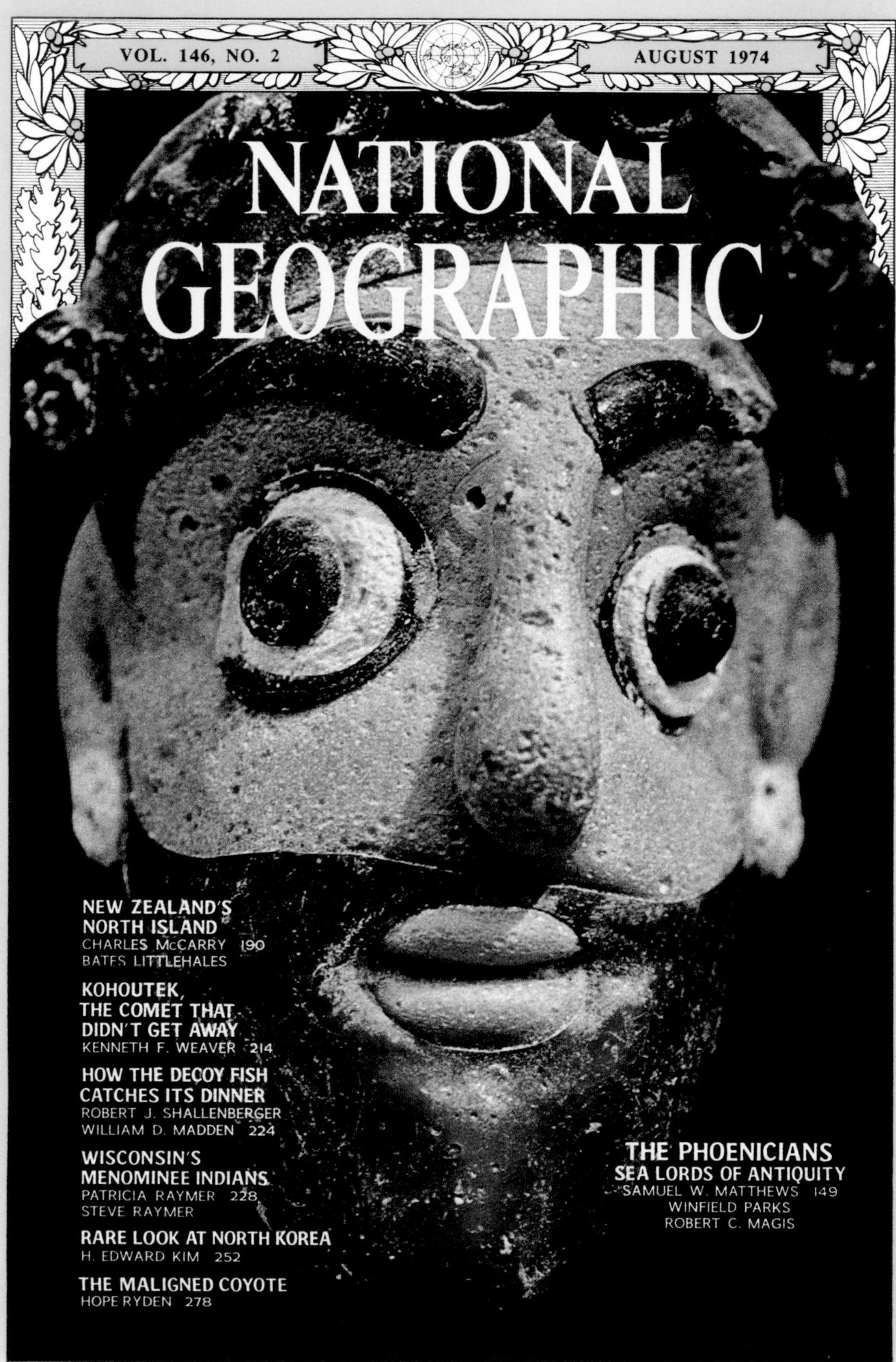

AUGUST | WINFIELD PARKS An inch-high amulet of colored glass captures the features of the Phoenician god Bes.

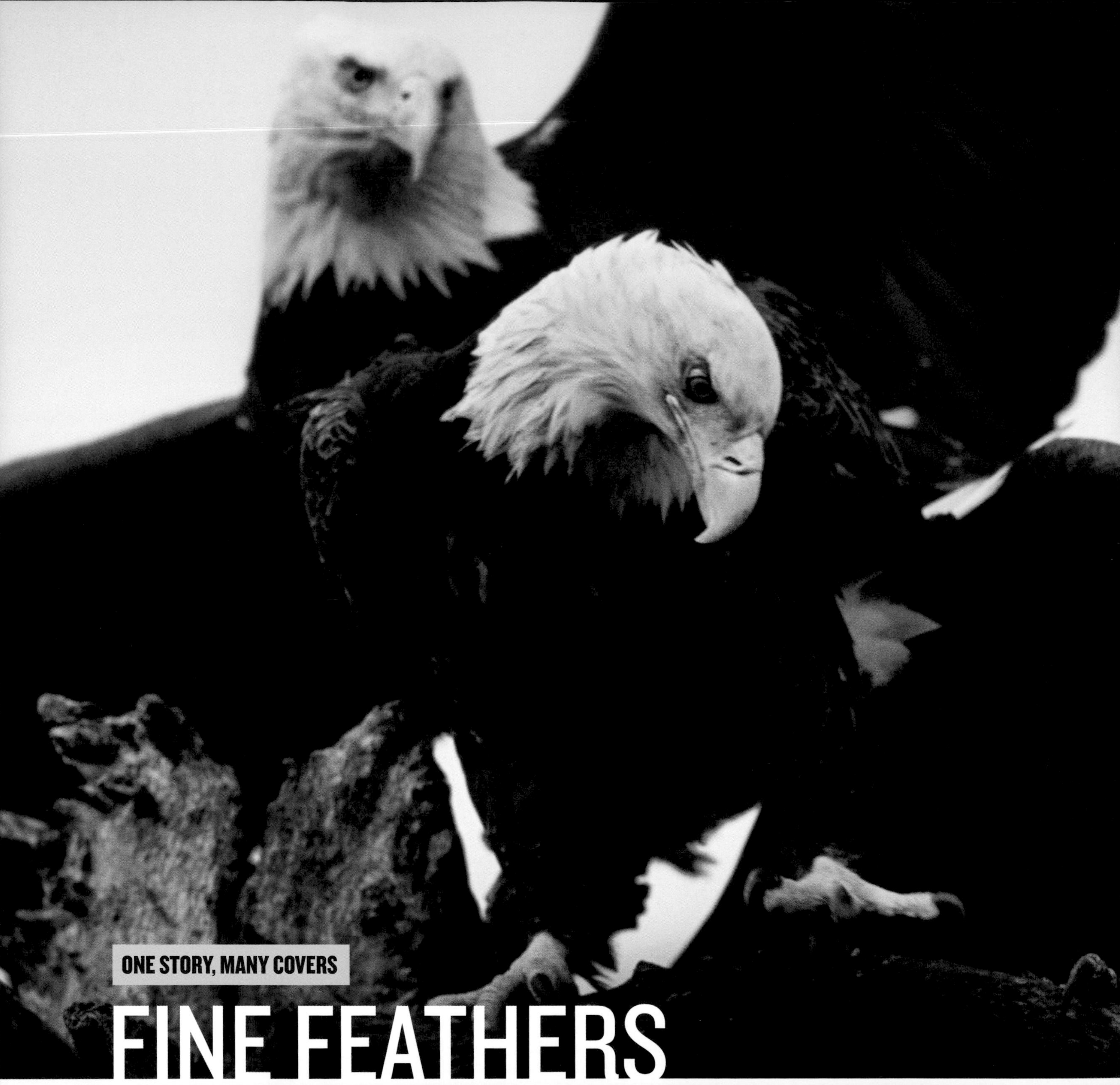

ONE STORY, MANY COVERS

FINE FEATHERS

▲ JULY 2002 | NORBERT ROSING
Bald eagles compete for handouts of fish in Homer, Alaska.

NATIONAL GEOGRAPHIC'S LOVE AFFAIR with birds began long before a picture was ever put on its cover. In 1913 Editor Gilbert H. Grosvenor discovered the pleasures of bird-watching, and over the succeeding decades not only did he fill the magazine with paintings of them but he also ensured that every advance in avian photography was included. Thus birds quite naturally migrated to the cover—and have preened, glared, and soared there ever since.

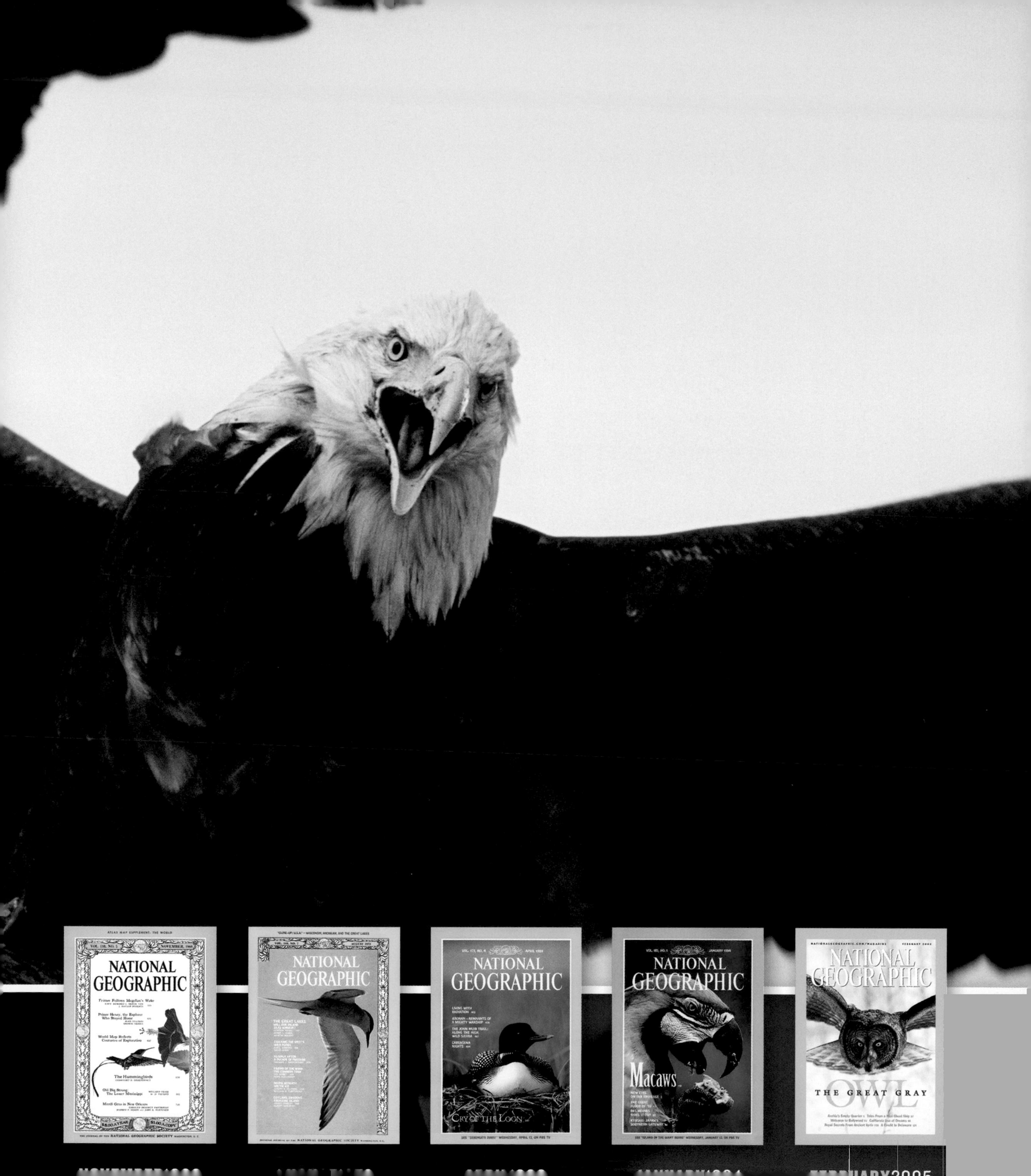

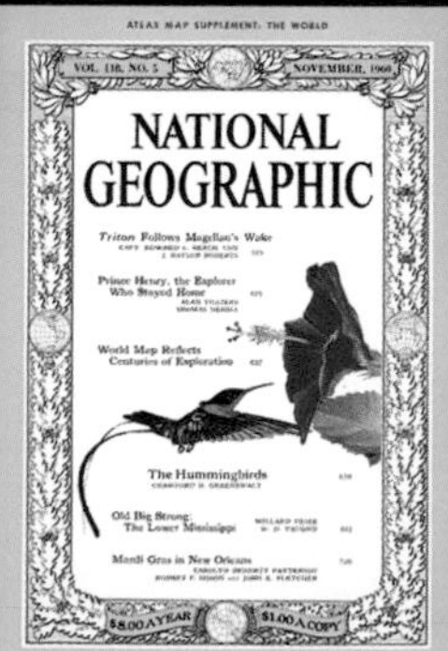
NATIONAL GEOGRAPHIC
The Hummingbirds

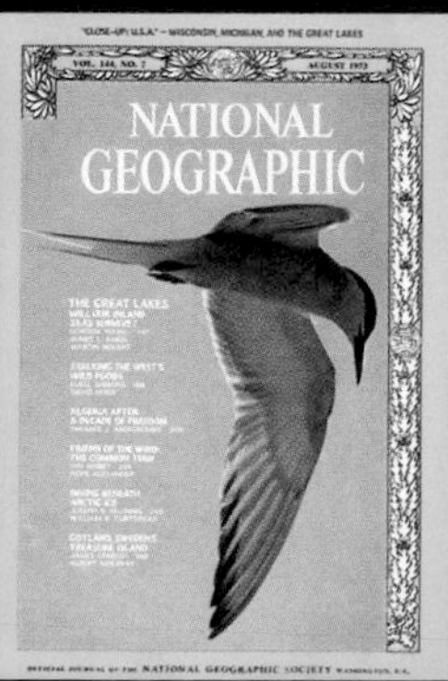
NATIONAL GEOGRAPHIC

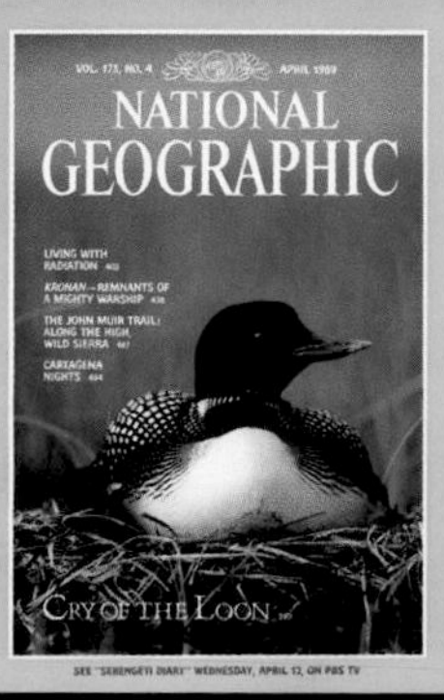
NATIONAL GEOGRAPHIC
CRY OF THE LOON

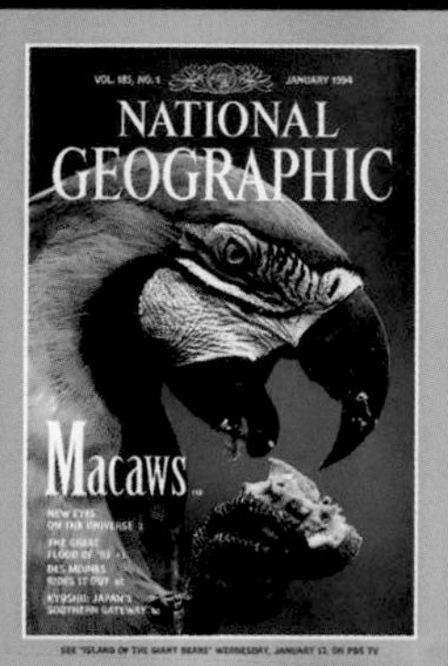
NATIONAL GEOGRAPHIC
Macaws

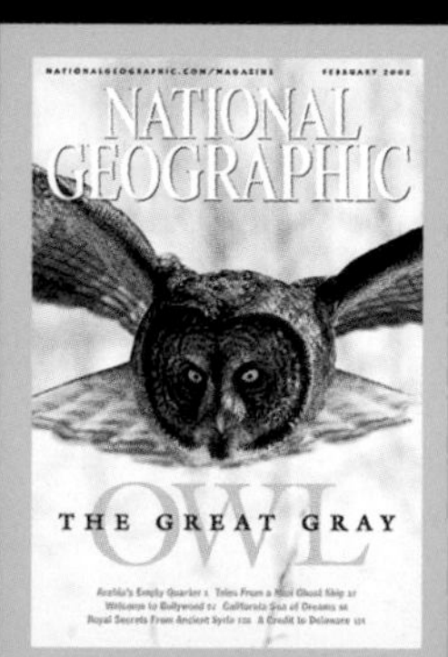
NATIONAL GEOGRAPHIC
OWL
THE GREAT GRAY

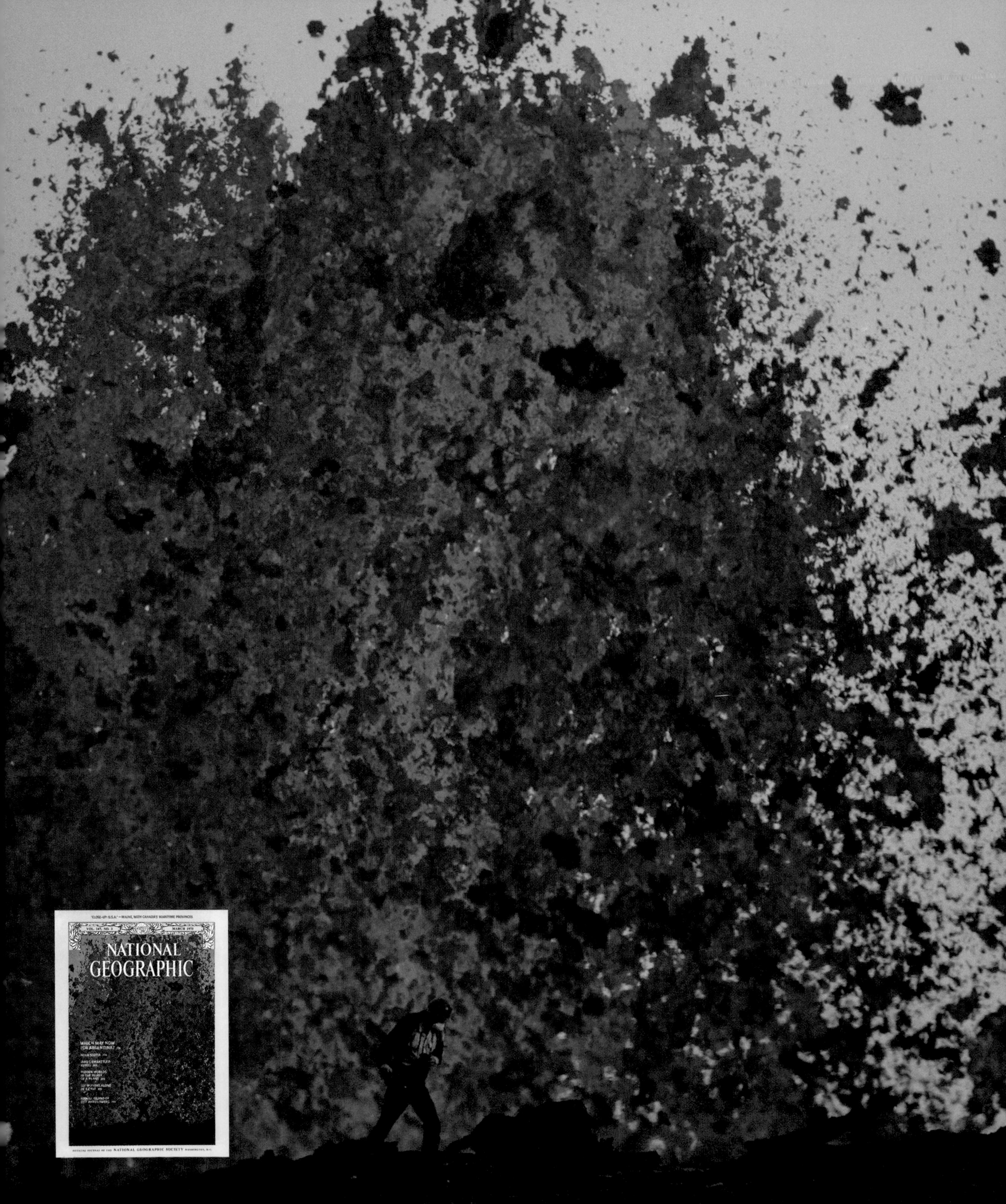
"CLOSE-UP: U.S.A." —MAINE, WITH CANADA'S MARITIME PROVINCES
VOL. 147, NO. 3
MARCH 1975
NATIONAL GEOGRAPHIC
WHICH WAY NOW FOR ARGENTINA?
NOVA SCOTIA
IRAQ'S EMBATTLED KURDS
HIDDEN WORLDS IN THE HEART OF A PLANT
SIX MONTHS ALONE IN A CAVE
NATIONAL GEOGRAPHIC SOCIETY

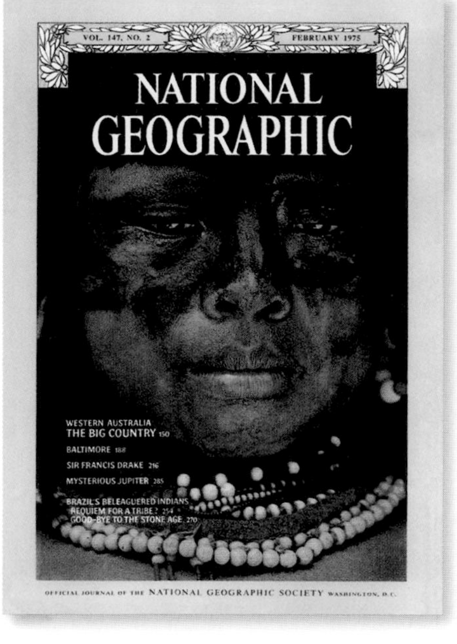

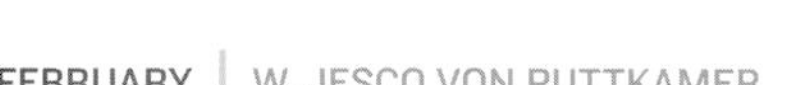
FEBRUARY | W. JESCO VON PUTTKAMER

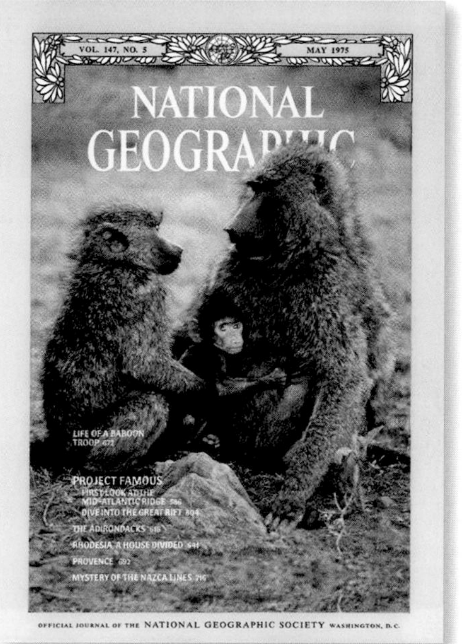

MAY | TIMOTHY W. RANSOM

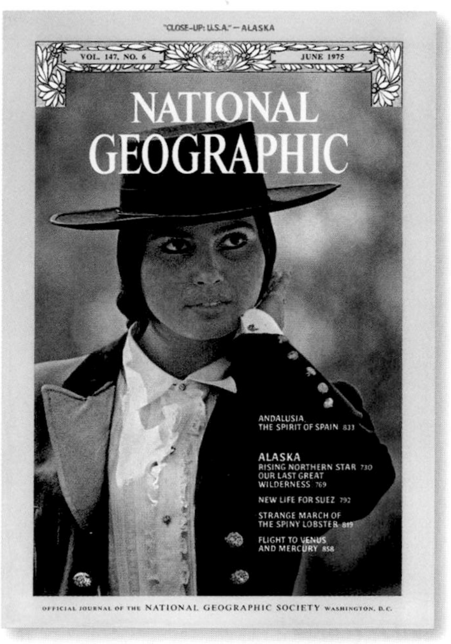

JUNE | JOSEPH J. SCHERSCHEL

HAWAII'S MOUNTAIN OF FIRE

PHOTOGRAPHER BOB MADDEN WAS close, but a telephoto lens makes this volcanologist keeping upwind of that exploding lava look much closer than the 200 or so feet he put between him and Kilauea's fiery fury. This eruption—which lasted from May 1969 to July 1974—was the longest flank eruption then recorded in Hawaii.

> Violent? Spectacular? Surely a volcano that can send fountains of lava 1,900 feet into the sky rates those terms. But Hawaii's volcanoes are normally well behaved. For proof, look at Volcano House, the latest in a succession of hotels that have perched on Kilauea's rim for more than a century. Never are the hotel's rooms more in demand than when the mountain erupts.
>
> *—From "Hawaii, Island of Fire and Flowers," Gordon Young*

▲ **PARADE DRESS** A traditionally dressed equestrienne rides in one of the celebrated processions of Spain's annual Seville Fair.

"For in Andalusia—ruled for almost 800 years by Moors who came to love this fair land as much as Allah—words and place-names, foods and customs hark back to an age of turbaned knights and gazelle-eyed maidens."

—Howard La Fay

from "Andalusia, the Spirit of Spain"

◄ MARCH | ROBERT W. MADDEN A volcanologist is in his element on Hawaii.

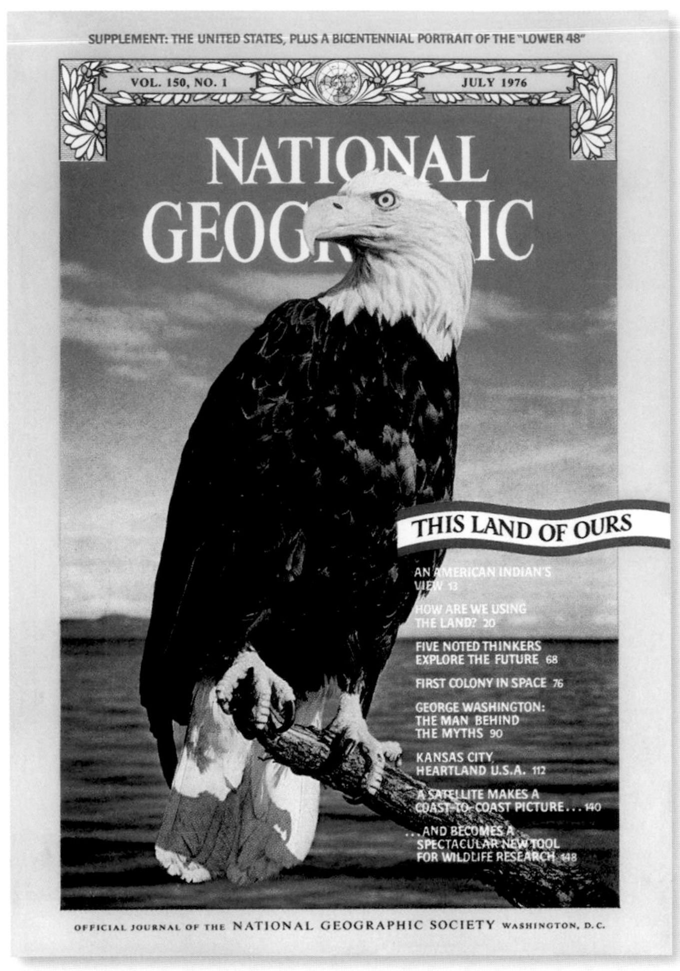

JULY | JEFF FOOTT

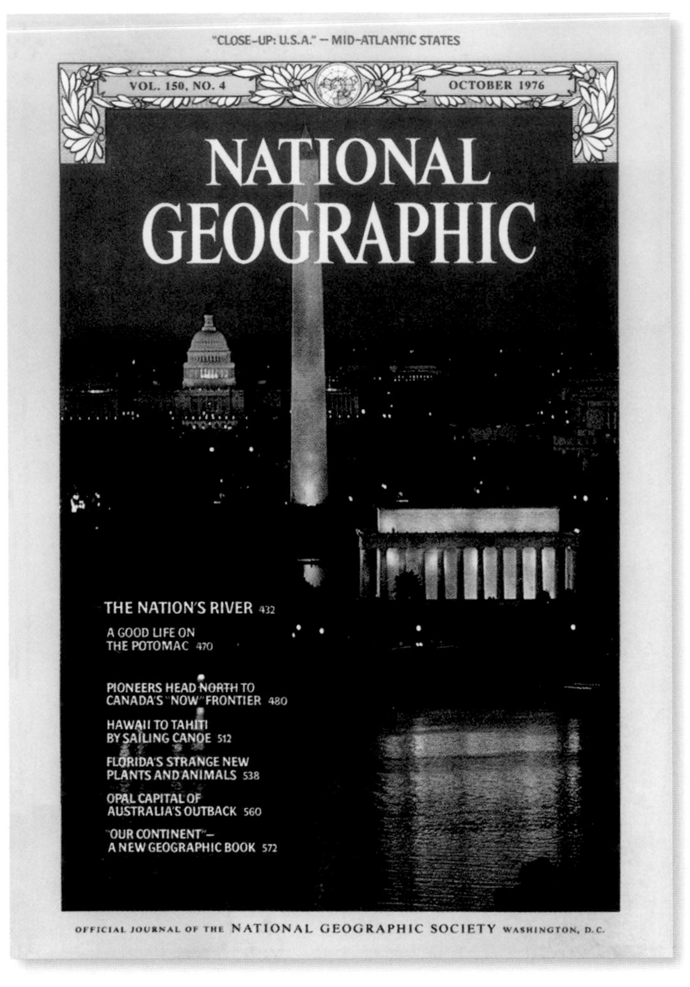

OCTOBER | JAMES L. STANFIELD

▲ **BICENTENNIAL BIRD** A bald eagle as symbol of America was a natural—if clichéd—choice for the Bicentennial cover celebrating "This Land of Ours."

▲ **SHINING CITY** Beacons to the world, three Washington, D.C., icons come into alignment via a telephoto lens: Two honor presidents—the needlelike Washington Monument commemorating the man who won the nation its independence, the columned Lincoln Memorial honoring the leader who preserved the Union—while the distant dome of the Capitol represents the fundamental arbiter of American democracy: "We, the People . . ."

"As an Indian I think: 'You say that I use the land, and I reply, yes, it is true; but it is not the first truth. The first truth is that I love the land; I see that it is beautiful; I delight in it; I am alive in it.'"

—N. Scott Momaday

from "This Land of Ours: An American Indian's View"

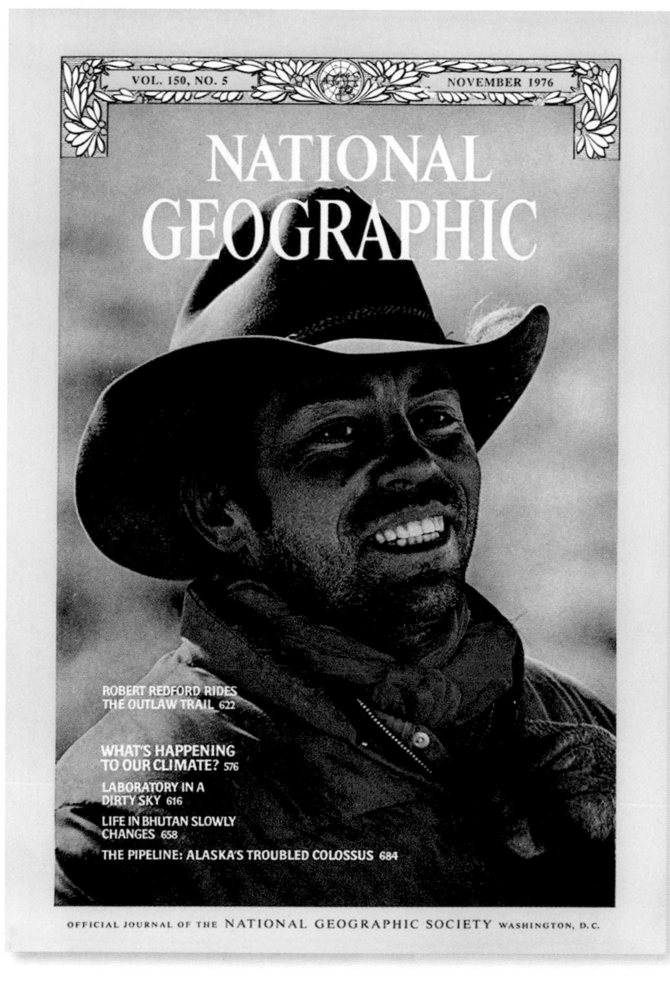

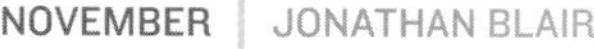
NOVEMBER | JONATHAN BLAIR

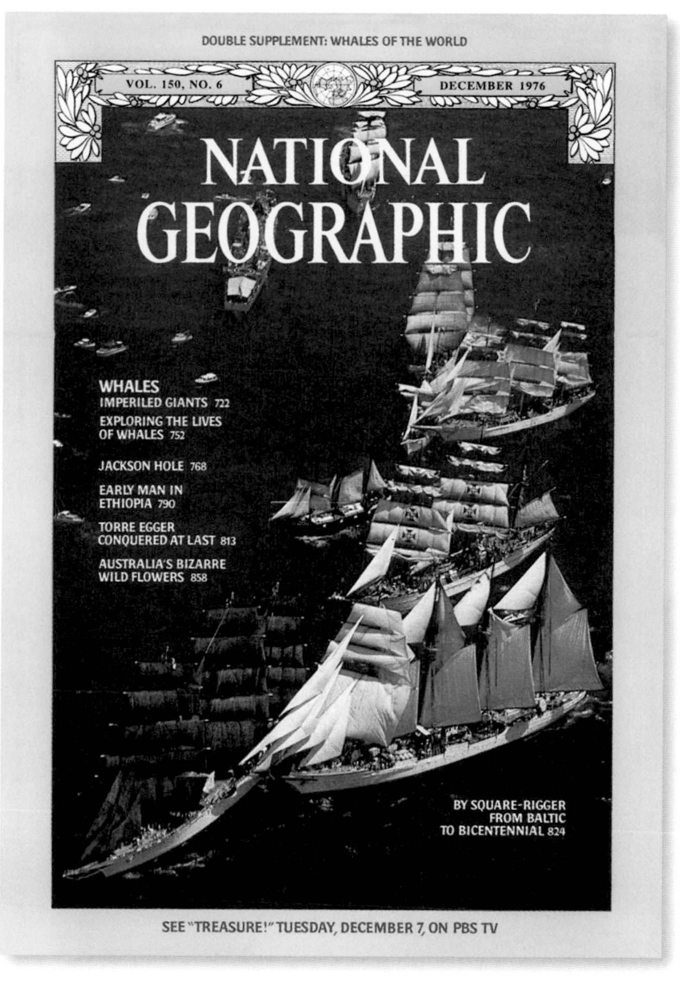

DECEMBER | GILBERT M. GROSVENOR

▲ **TRUE COWBOY** A tale of travel and adventure by Robert Redford, and he's not on the cover? That was a head-scratcher for many people, including photographer Jonathan Blair, who rode alongside the actor as they retraced the 600 winding miles between Montana and Texas, a route favored by the likes of Butch Cassidy and the Sundance Kid. But it was Redford who described the companion who did make the cover—A. C. Ekker—as epitomizing the old-time cowboy's "verve, strength, and enterprising spirit." Blair concurred: "He was a good wrangler, a good horseman." And a daredevil; a few years after this cover appeared, Ekker ran a plane into the ground and was killed.

▲ **CLOSE CALL** As *National Geographic* Editor Gil Grosvenor and staff photographer Joe Scherschel watched from a plane, tall ships leaving the narrow entrance to Hamilton, Bermuda, collided in the dramatic start of a Bermuda-to-Newport race. Then the plane, turning too tightly, began to stall. That meant a drop into the sea. Strapping on a life preserver, Grosvenor glanced at Scherschel—who, oblivious to his own safety, was instead slipping rolls of exposed film into a waterproof bag. "That is the difference between an editor and a professional photographer," Grosvenor thought as the pilot regained control of the aircraft.

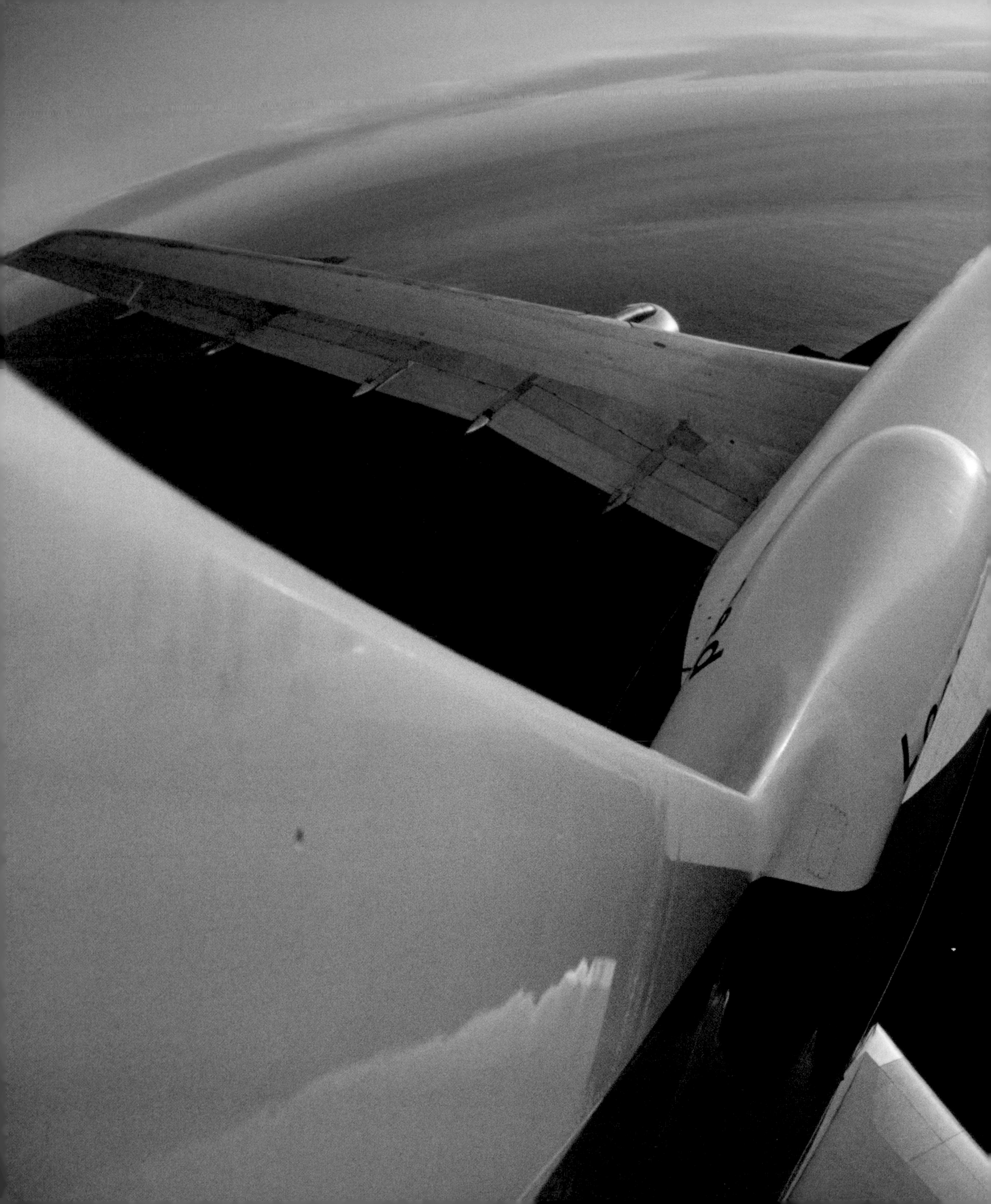

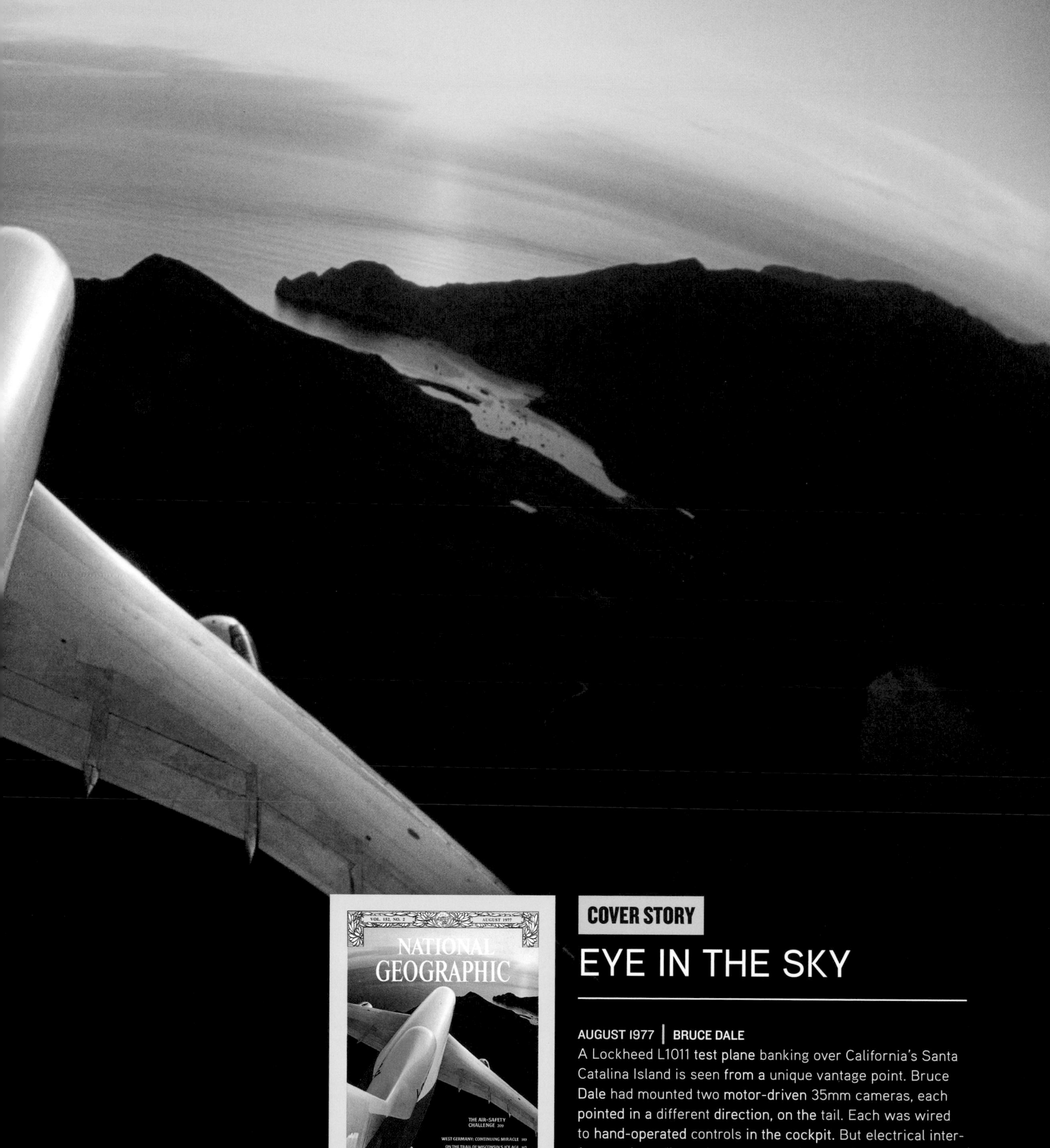

COVER STORY

EYE IN THE SKY

AUGUST 1977 | BRUCE DALE

A Lockheed L1011 test plane banking over California's Santa Catalina Island is seen from a unique vantage point. Bruce Dale had mounted two motor-driven 35mm cameras, each pointed in a different direction, on the tail. Each was wired to hand-operated controls in the cockpit. But electrical interference kept disrupting the setup. Solution? Sit an engineer beneath the tail and have him trigger the cameras by cable releases as Dale, eyeing the changing view from the cockpit, tells him over the intercom which one to fire.

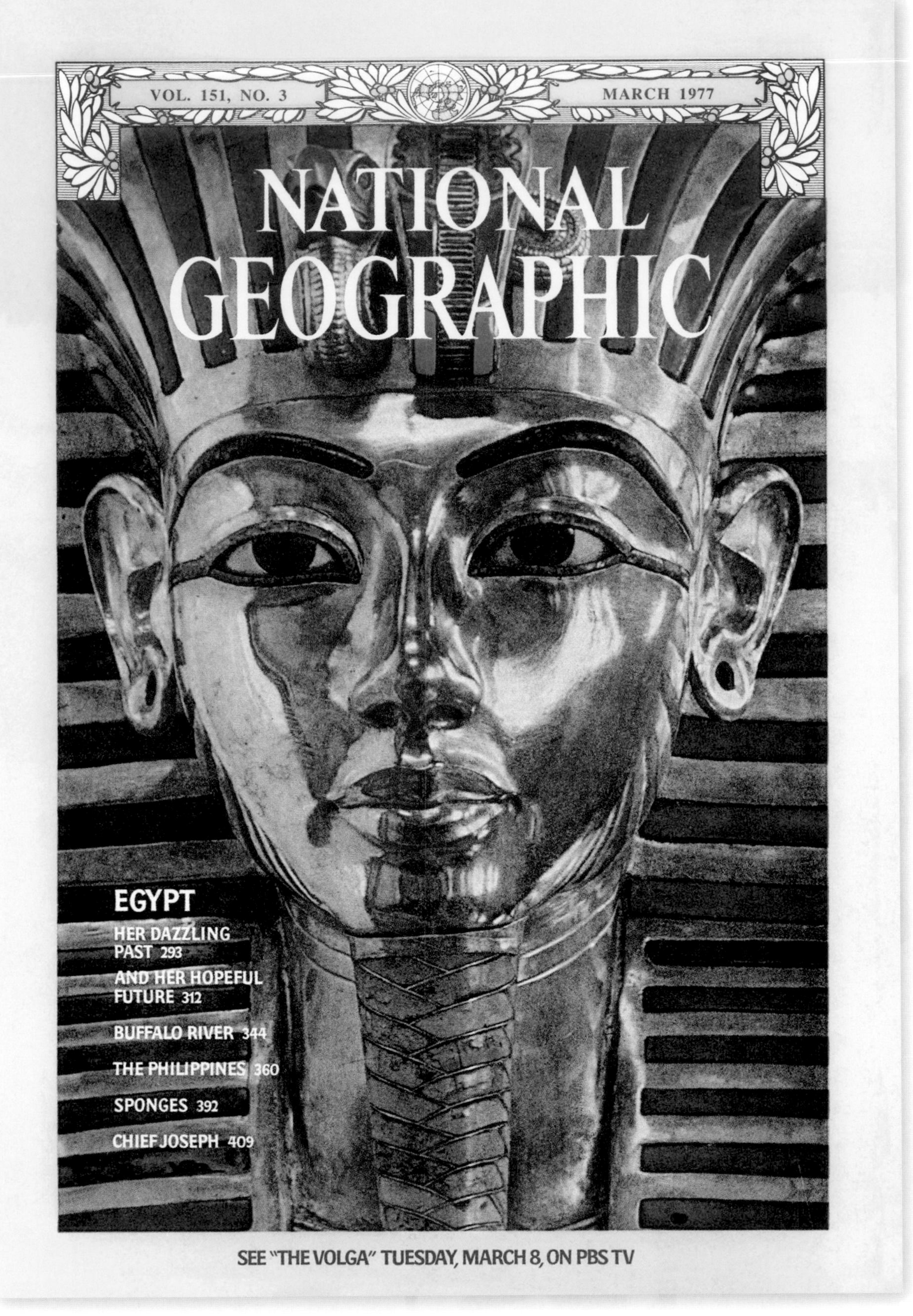

MARCH | JOHN G. ROSS

GOLDEN BOY By the time this picture of Tutankhamun's funeral mask appeared on the cover, more than 800,000 people had seen the real thing then on display in Washington's National Gallery of Art. The 53 pieces in Egypt's "Treasures of Tutankhamun" constituted the first "blockbuster" exhibit to attract millions of viewers worldwide.

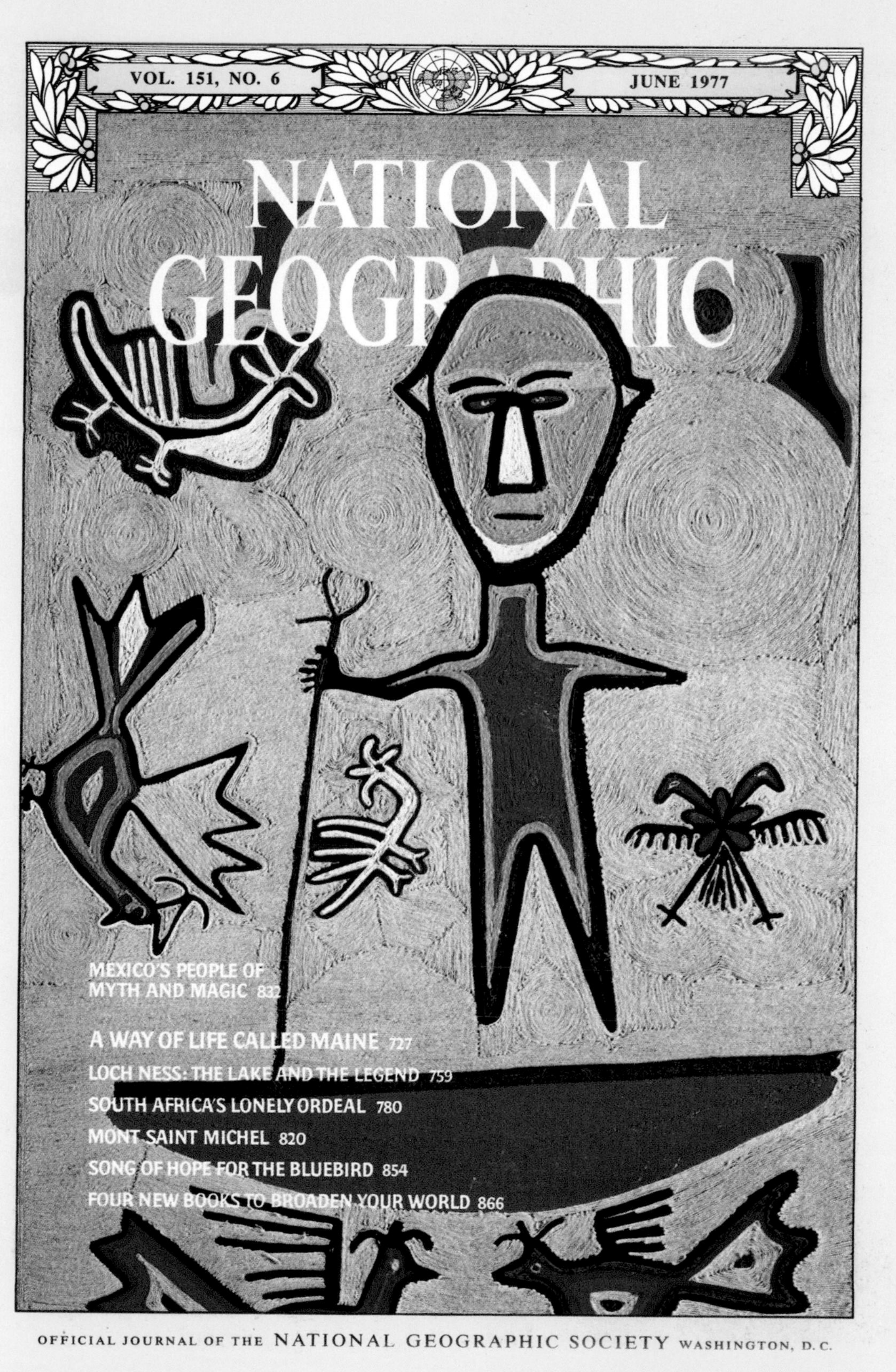

JUNE | JOSEPH H. BAILEY

ANCIENT ART FORM Noah stands in his ark while birds flock around him. Such *nieli'kas*—designs made from yarn pressed into warm beeswax—are produced by Mexico's Huichol people, who live in the Sierra Nevada mountains. Biblical subjects might appeal to tourists, but the Huichol's own shamanistic traditions stretch back thousands of years.

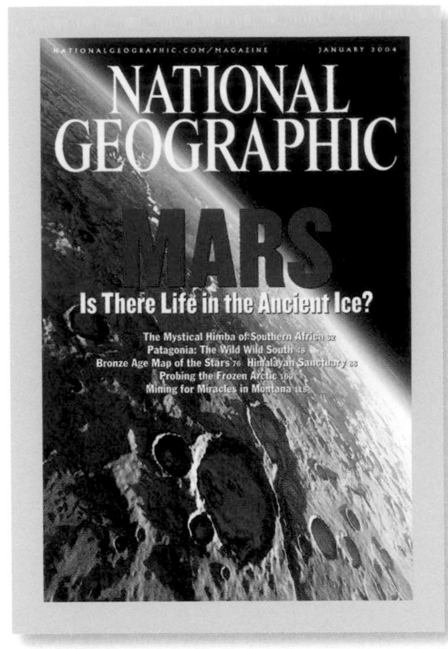

JANUARY 2004 | KEES VEENENBOS

2004 ▸▸▸▸ FAST FORWARD

WHITE PLANET Was Mars always red? Some scientists speculate that between 50,000 and 500,000 years ago it was white. Periodic changes in its obliquity, or angle to the sun, might encase it in a sheet of ice. Artist Kees Veenenbos draped a wintry mantle over topographic data provided by the Mars Global Surveyor to simulate the "white planet."

THE RED PLANET ▸

"I ALMOST EXPECTED TO see camels," quipped one scientist after the first images from Mars had flickered onto the monitors in NASA's Jet Propulsion Laboratory in Pasadena, California. The black-and-white pictures did indeed look like parts of Arabia; but on the next day, when the color images arrived, the rocks and sand were obviously coated with red iron oxide—rust.

Between July 20, 1976, the day that Viking 1 touched down on Mars, and November 11, 1982, when all contact with it was finally lost, this spacecraft and its sister lander, Viking 2, transmitted 4,500 images back to Earth. The one selected for the January 1977 *National Geographic* cover was made by "camera one," one of two pivoting cameras in tall cylindrical cases, mounted on Viking 1's base, that made 360-degree panoramas. Scientists dubbed the large boulder, the most prominent feature in the picture, "Big Joe"; and it was within yards of that eight-foot-wide stone that instruments conducted one of the first searches for life on Mars.

Unfortunately, despite human imagination always peopling Mars with alien beings, samples of that red dirt provided no incontrovertible evidence of living microorganisms. "Why pursue the question of whether life exists on Mars?" pondered the article's author, Rick Gore. "The existence of even microbes would mean, simply, that we are not alone in the universe. If life emerged and persisted on so hostile a spot, it must abound on other, more clement planets across the galaxies."

Despite such inconclusive results, the pictures retained their own fascination. After all, this was the surface of another planet, one never before seen. As Viking mission director Tom Young put it: "For the first time man has a beachhead on a world beyond his own."

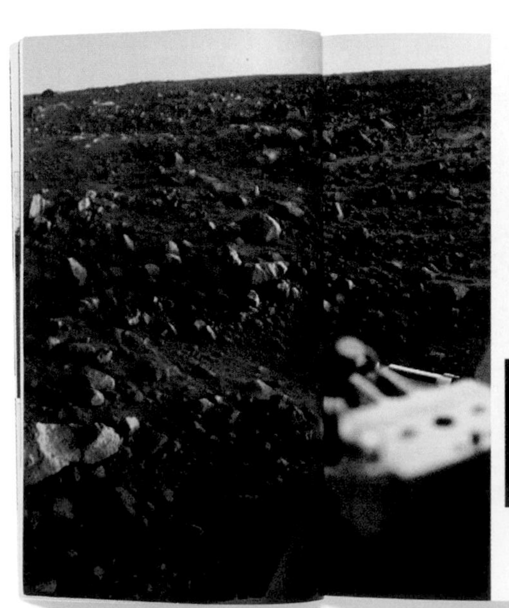

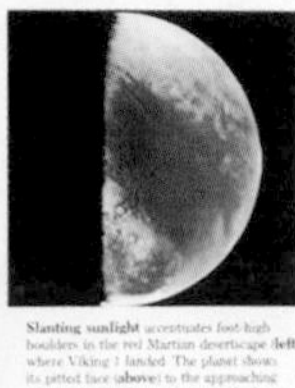

◂ JANUARY 1977 | NASA The red Martian desertscape where Viking 1 landed.

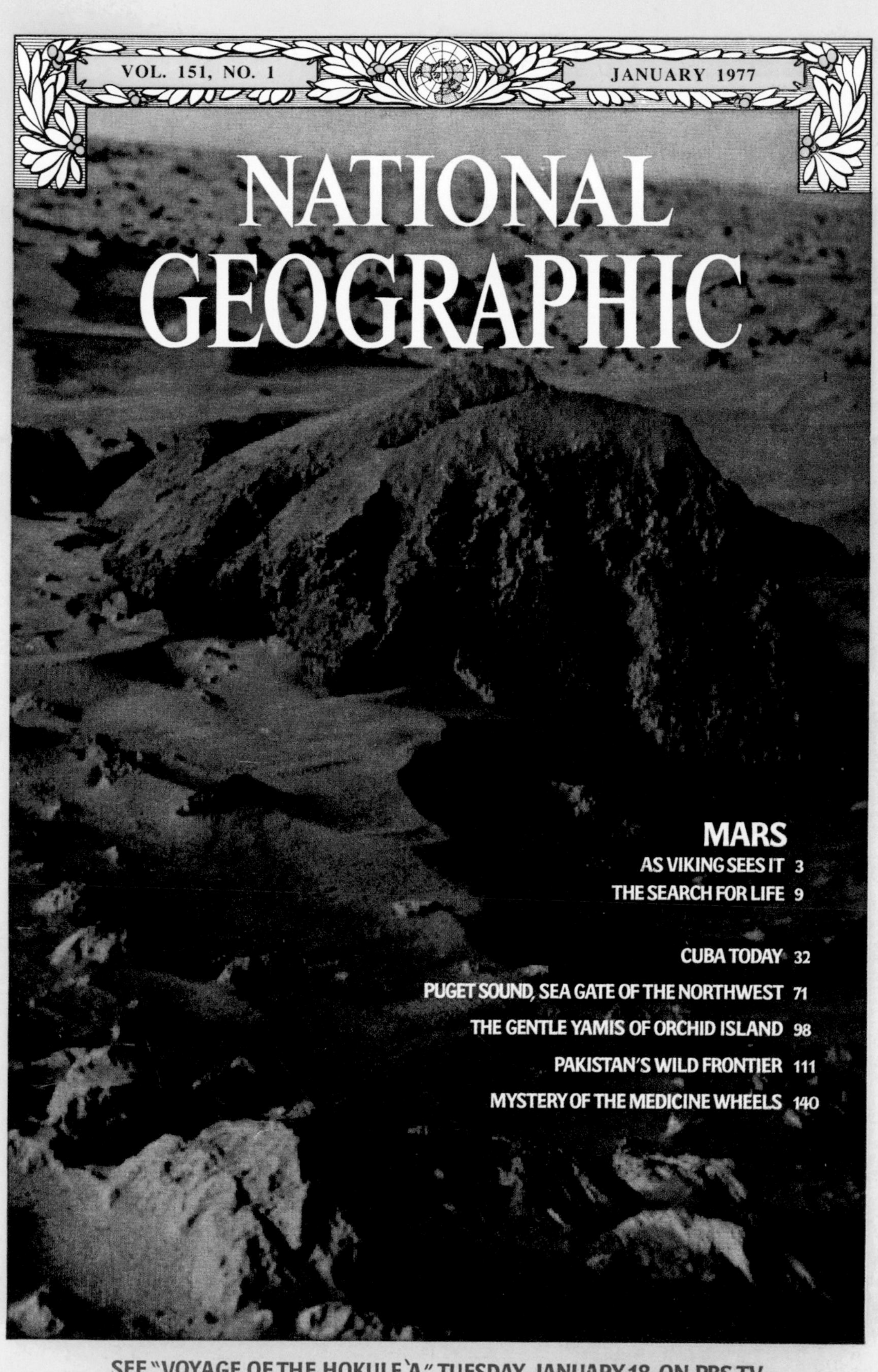

VOL. 151, NO. 1 JANUARY 1977

NATIONAL GEOGRAPHIC

MARS

AS VIKING SEES IT 3

THE SEARCH FOR LIFE 9

CUBA TODAY 32

PUGET SOUND, SEA GATE OF THE NORTHWEST 71

THE GENTLE YAMIS OF ORCHID ISLAND 98

PAKISTAN'S WILD FRONTIER 111

MYSTERY OF THE MEDICINE WHEELS 140

SEE "VOYAGE OF THE HOKULE'A," TUESDAY, JANUARY 18, ON PBS TV

JANUARY | NASA Although resembling a mountain, Big Joe is a Martian boulder.

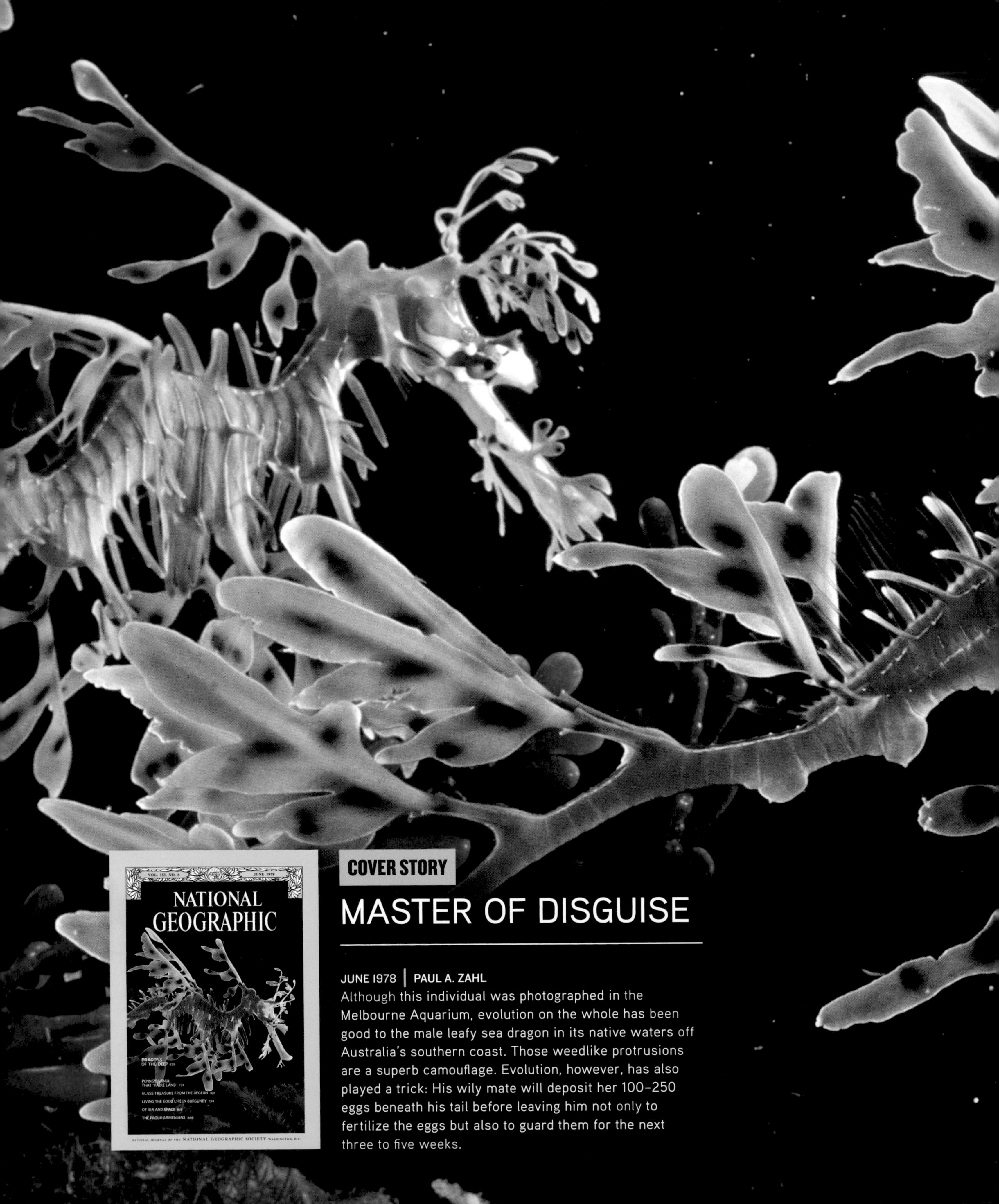

COVER STORY

MASTER OF DISGUISE

JUNE 1978 | PAUL A. ZAHL

Although this individual was photographed in the Melbourne Aquarium, evolution on the whole has been good to the male leafy sea dragon in its native waters off Australia's southern coast. Those weedlike protrusions are a superb camouflage. Evolution, however, has also played a trick: His wily mate will deposit her 100–250 eggs beneath his tail before leaving him not only to fertilize the eggs but also to guard them for the next three to five weeks.

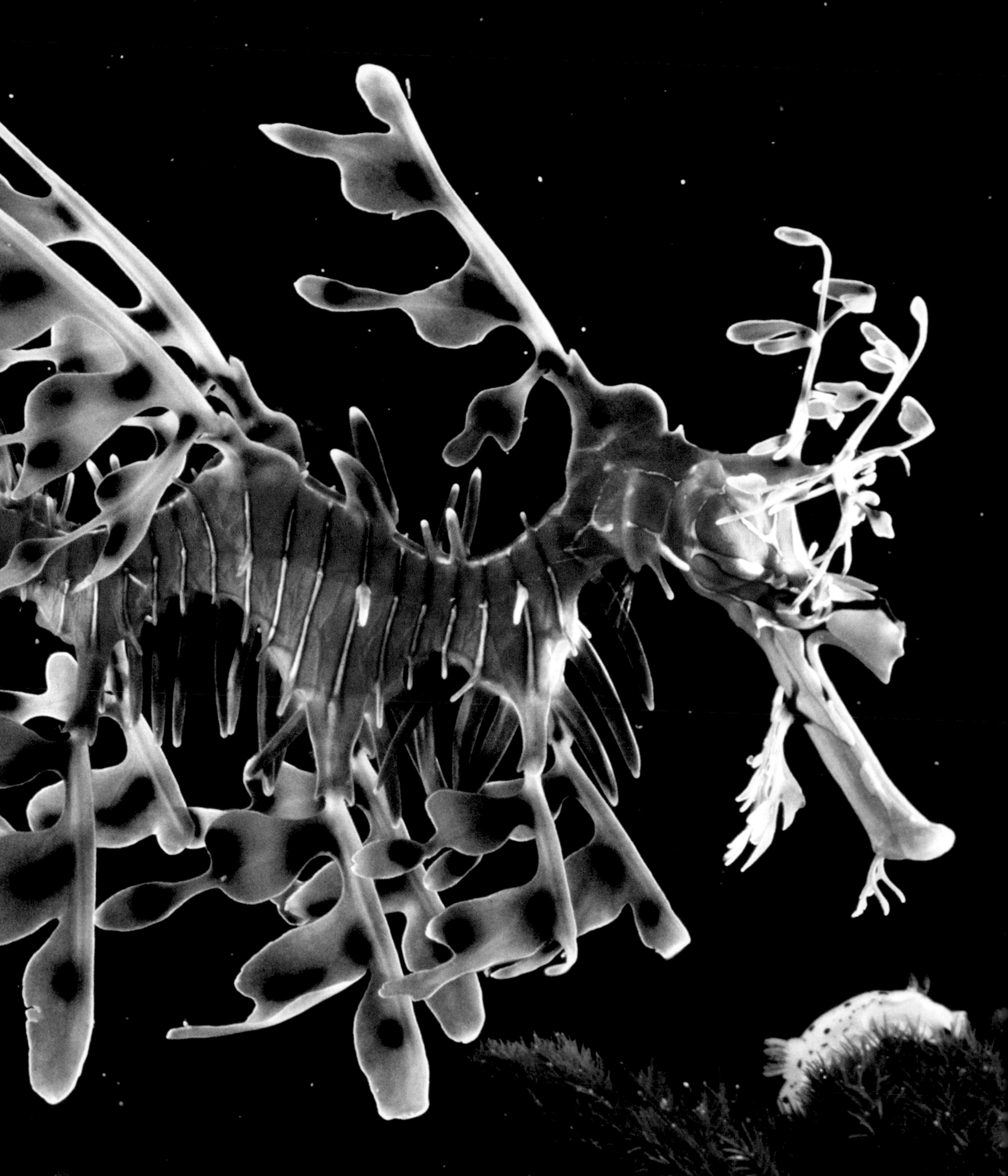

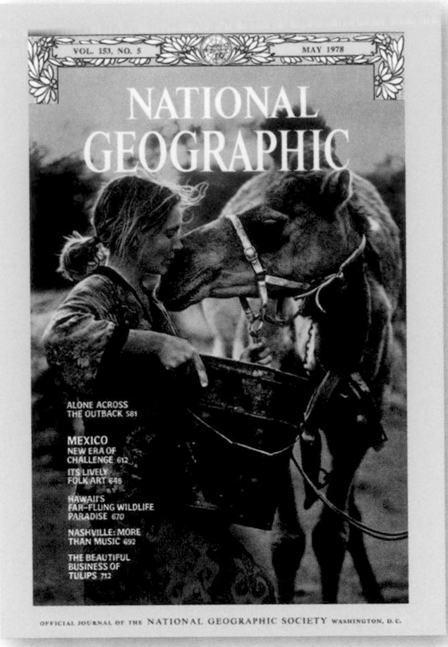

MAY | RICK SMOLAN

▲ **OUTBACK ODYSSEY** "Golden rule of making camp is: Attend to the animals first." And Robyn Davidson, who wrote those words in her diary, had four camels—Bub, Zeleika, Dookie, and Goliath—and one scamp of a sheepdog, Diggity, to attend to. With this entourage she set out to cross some 1,700 miles of Australian outback, an inner quest as much as an outer one, and a tale as beautifully told as it is poignant.

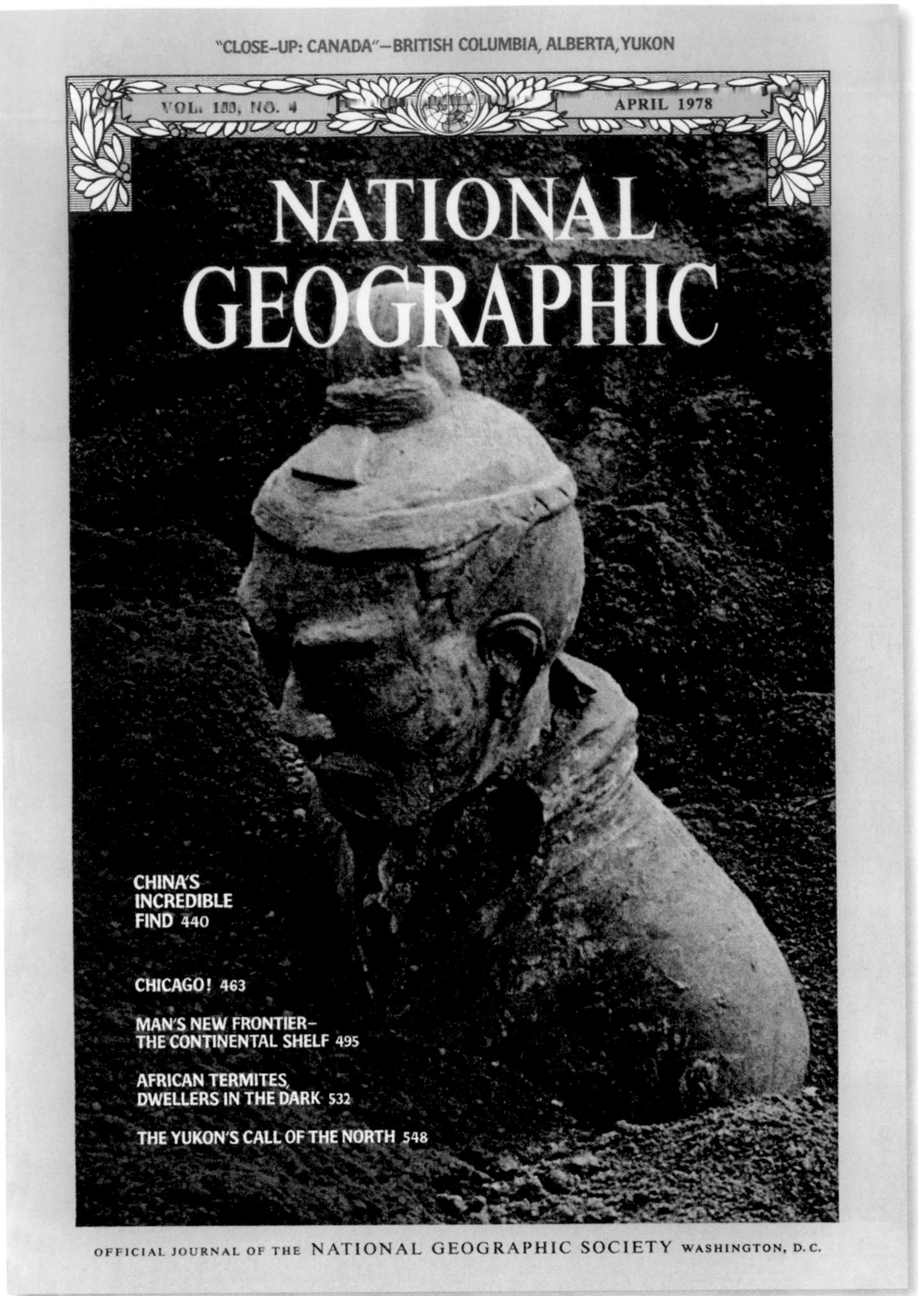

APRIL | HOWARD NELSON

▲ **SOLDIER FOR THE AFTERLIFE** A terra-cotta warrior emerges seemingly from the grave. Emperor Qin Shi Huang might have only symbolically reinstated the ancient practice of burying alive a royal retinue of warriors, women, servants, and horses, but millions actually died building his Great Wall, "longest cemetery in the world" in the third century B.C. Furthermore, Chairman Mao might have approved his crackdown on conservative Confucian scholars. The emperor executed 460 of them, burying some alive and others only up to their necks—before beheading them.

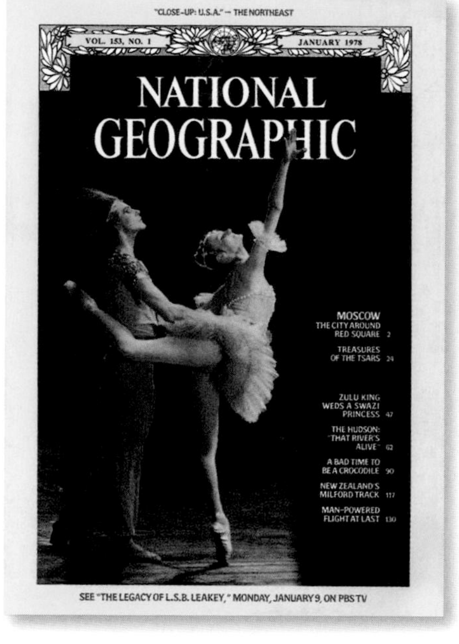

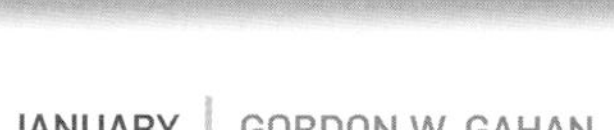

JANUARY | GORDON W. GAHAN

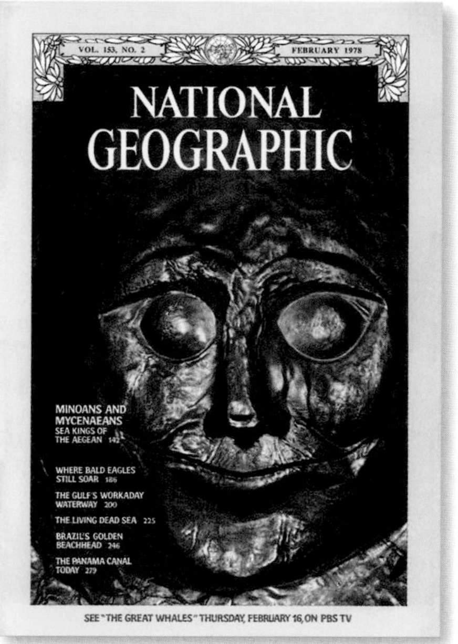

FEBRUARY | GORDON W. GAHAN

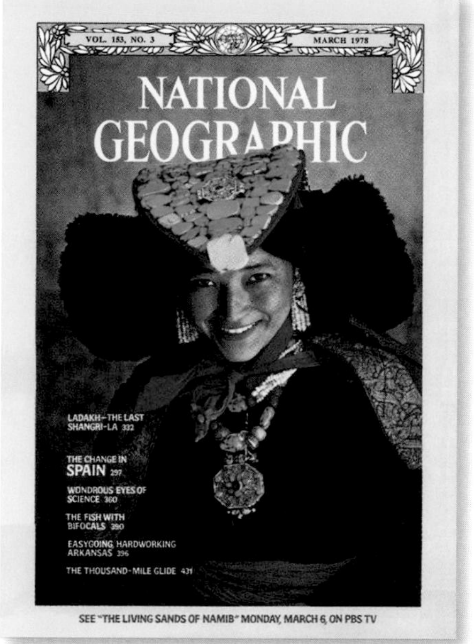

MARCH | THOMAS J. ABERCROMBIE

TERRA-COTTA WARRIORS

On March 29, 1974, peasants near Xi'an in Shaanxi Province began sinking shovels into the earth. But instead of digging a well of water, as they intended, they broke into a well of the past.

Chinese archaeologists soon arrived and began unearthing what was amazing then and continues to amaze today: an entire underground army, thousands of life-size terra-cotta statues of warriors, servants, and horses pulling war chariots. They had been buried 2,200 years ago in an enormous subterranean chamber so as to protect their emperor, Qin Shi Huang, the first unifier of China, whose tomb lay only a mile away.

> Some of the astonishingly realistic figures were upright, intact, and poised, as if waiting for a command to attack. Others lay pathetically smashed and scattered; they had been broken and their weapons stolen four years after the emperor's death, when soldiers of the succeeding reign looted and burned this part of the ruler's grave site.
>
> *—From "China's Incredible Find," Audrey Topping*

▲ **SPLASH OF COLOR** A girl from Ladakh wears a turquoise-covered *peyrak*, a traditional headpiece in her remote corner of India's Himalaya.

> *"I found it peopled by hardy mountain stock, proud, spirited, steeped in ancient traditions, not yet encumbered by modern gadgetry such as matches, gunpowder, or (except for mechanized prayer devices) the wheel."*
>
> —Thomas J. Abercrombie
> *from "Ladakh—The Last Shangri-La"*

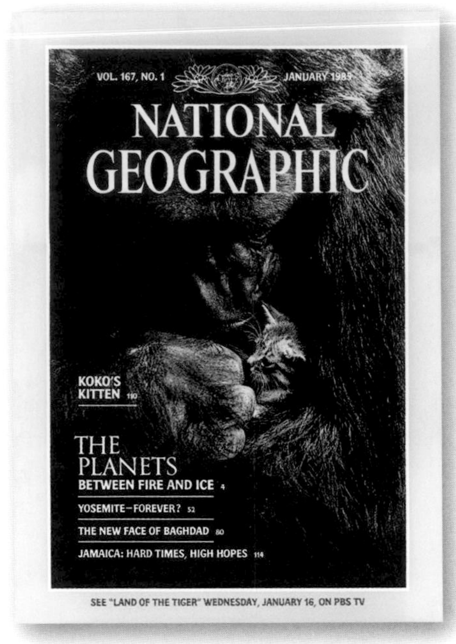

JANUARY 1985 | RONALD H. COHN

1985 ▸▸▸▸ FAST FORWARD

"BAD, SAD, BAD" Because *Puss in Boots* was one of her favorite picture books, Koko one day signed that she wanted a cat. When presented with a litter of abandoned kittens, she chose a young male and named him All Ball. She cherished her new friend and apparently tried to nurse him, as if he were a baby gorilla. Hardly had the January 1985 issue arrived in members' mailboxes, however, when All Ball escaped and was killed by a car. Upon being told, Koko signed "Bad, sad, bad" and "Frown, cry, frown, sad."

PHOTOS BY KOKO ▸

"IT'S ONLY FITTING for an educational magazine that the most popular cover girl we have ever had is known for her brains, not for her beauty," quipped Editor Bill Garrett in the April 1985 *National Geographic,* recalling the October 1978 issue in which Koko first appeared.

Koko is a female gorilla, born in the San Francisco Zoo in 1971, who from infancy has been taught American Sign Language by developmental psychologist Francine "Penny" Patterson. By the age of seven, Koko was using 375 signs on a regular basis and had an IQ of 95. She showed moral discernment (knowing when she had been "bad"), coined words of her own ("eye-hat" for mask), and described herself as a "fine animal gorilla." Patterson's project would become one of the longest-running studies of human-animal communication, shedding much light on the origins and nature of language.

In 1978, Koko was still living in a trailer on the Stanford University campus, the main room outfitted with a sleeping box, an exercise bar, a trapeze, picture books, a mirror, and some toys—including a Polaroid camera. It was by imitating photographer Ronald Cohn, who was documenting the project, that Koko learned how to handle her camera.

Word of that development soon reached the National Geographic Society, which was sponsoring Patterson's work. It wasn't long before Garrett, then the magazine's associate editor, turned up at the trailer.

Koko knew how to hold an Olympus OM-2 correctly, and it took no urging to have her press the shutter release, for she loved the flash of a strobe. All Garrett had to do was point her in the direction of that mirror and let her fire away.

Koko got the shot . . . and the cover as well. When the session ended she signed, "Love camera."

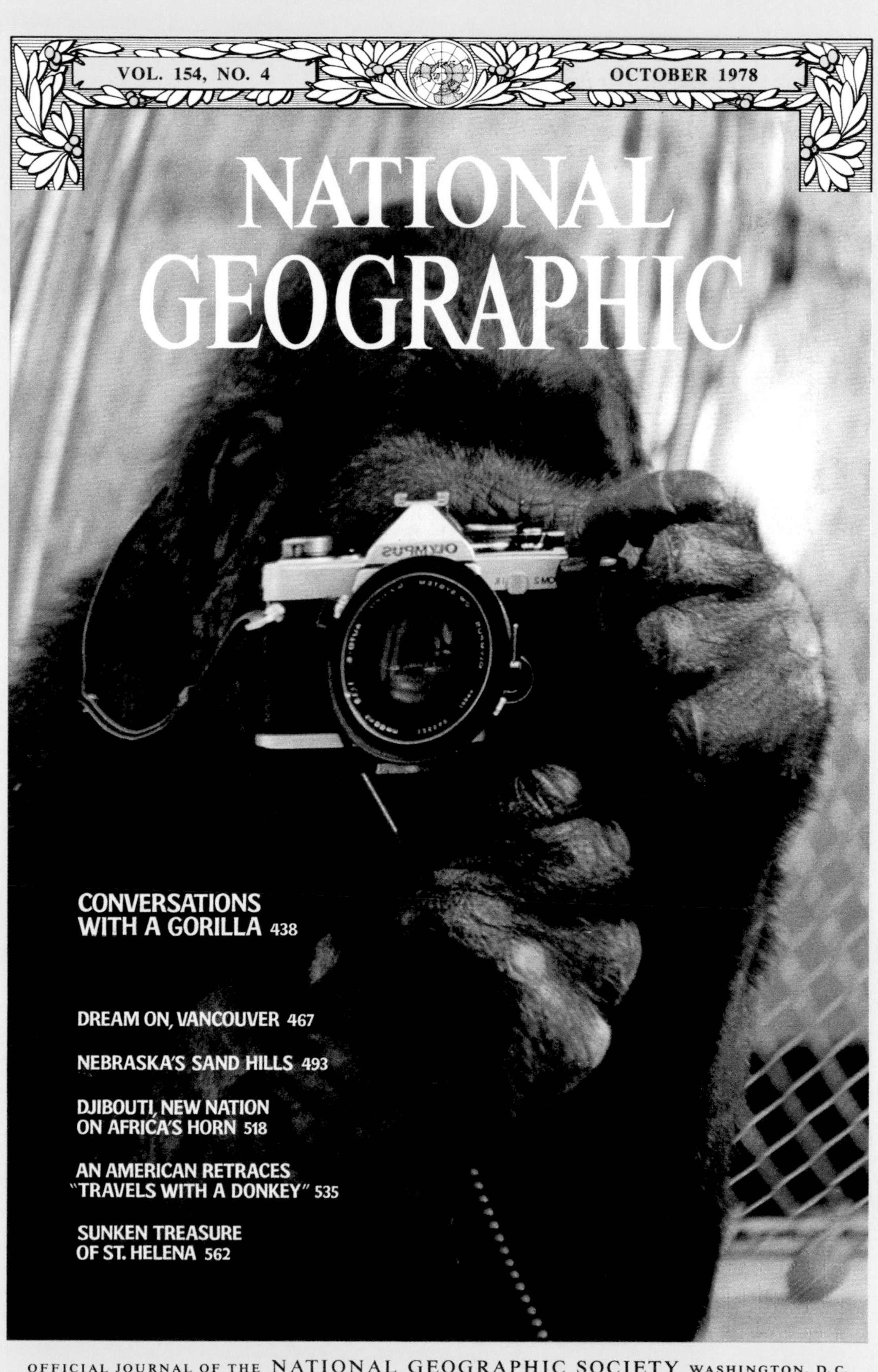

VOL. 154, NO. 4 OCTOBER 1978

NATIONAL GEOGRAPHIC

CONVERSATIONS WITH A GORILLA 438

DREAM ON, VANCOUVER 467

NEBRASKA'S SAND HILLS 493

DJIBOUTI, NEW NATION ON AFRICA'S HORN 518

AN AMERICAN RETRACES "TRAVELS WITH A DONKEY" 535

SUNKEN TREASURE OF ST. HELENA 562

OFFICIAL JOURNAL OF THE NATIONAL GEOGRAPHIC SOCIETY WASHINGTON, D.C.

OCTOBER | **KOKO** A newly minted *National Geographic* photographer makes her own self-portrait.

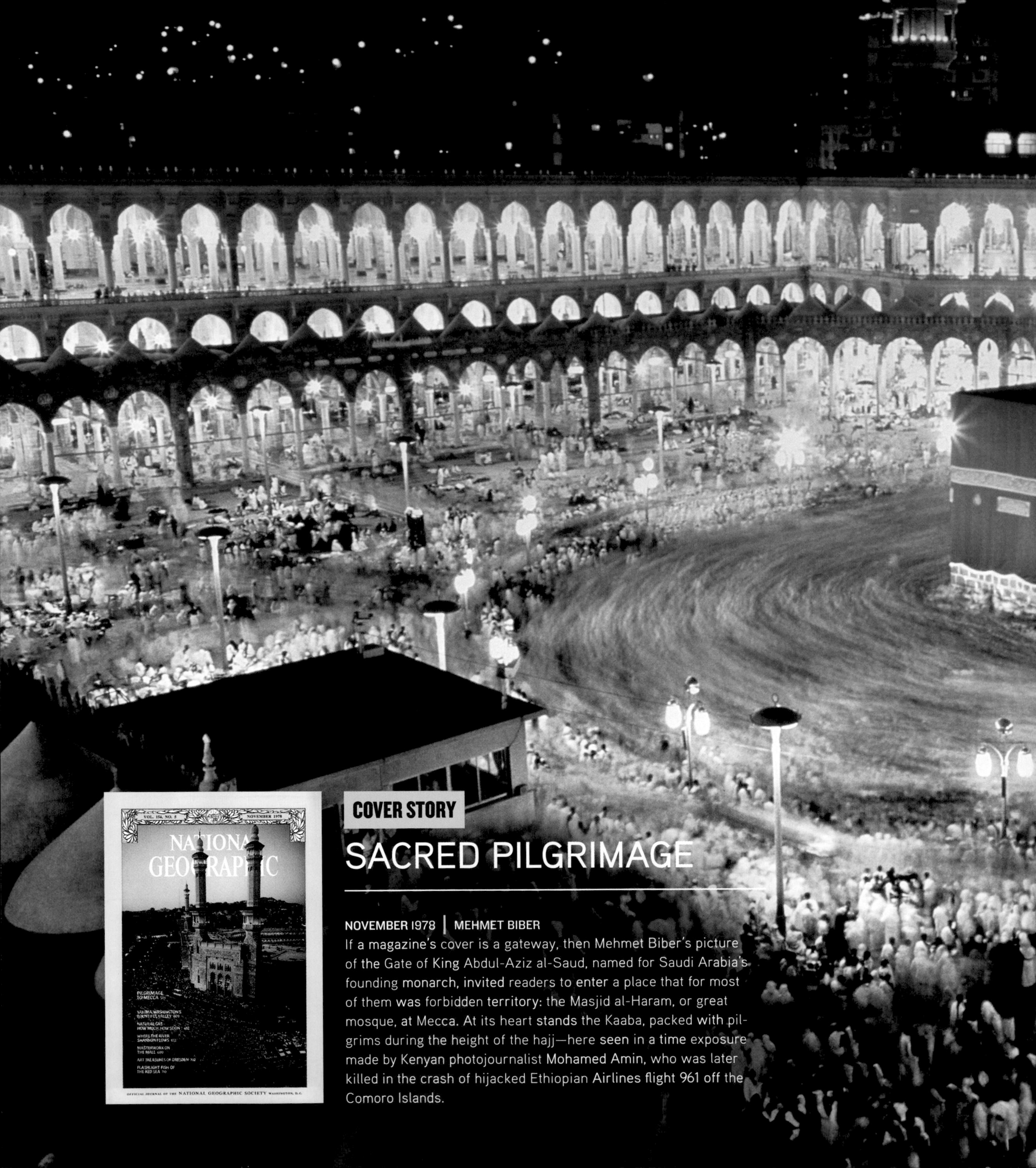

COVER STORY

SACRED PILGRIMAGE

NOVEMBER 1978 | MEHMET BIBER

If a magazine's cover is a gateway, then Mehmet Biber's picture of the Gate of King Abdul-Aziz al-Saud, named for Saudi Arabia's founding monarch, invited readers to enter a place that for most of them was forbidden territory: the Masjid al-Haram, or great mosque, at Mecca. At its heart stands the Kaaba, packed with pilgrims during the height of the hajj—here seen in a time exposure made by Kenyan photojournalist Mohamed Amin, who was later killed in the crash of hijacked Ethiopian Airlines flight 961 off the Comoro Islands.

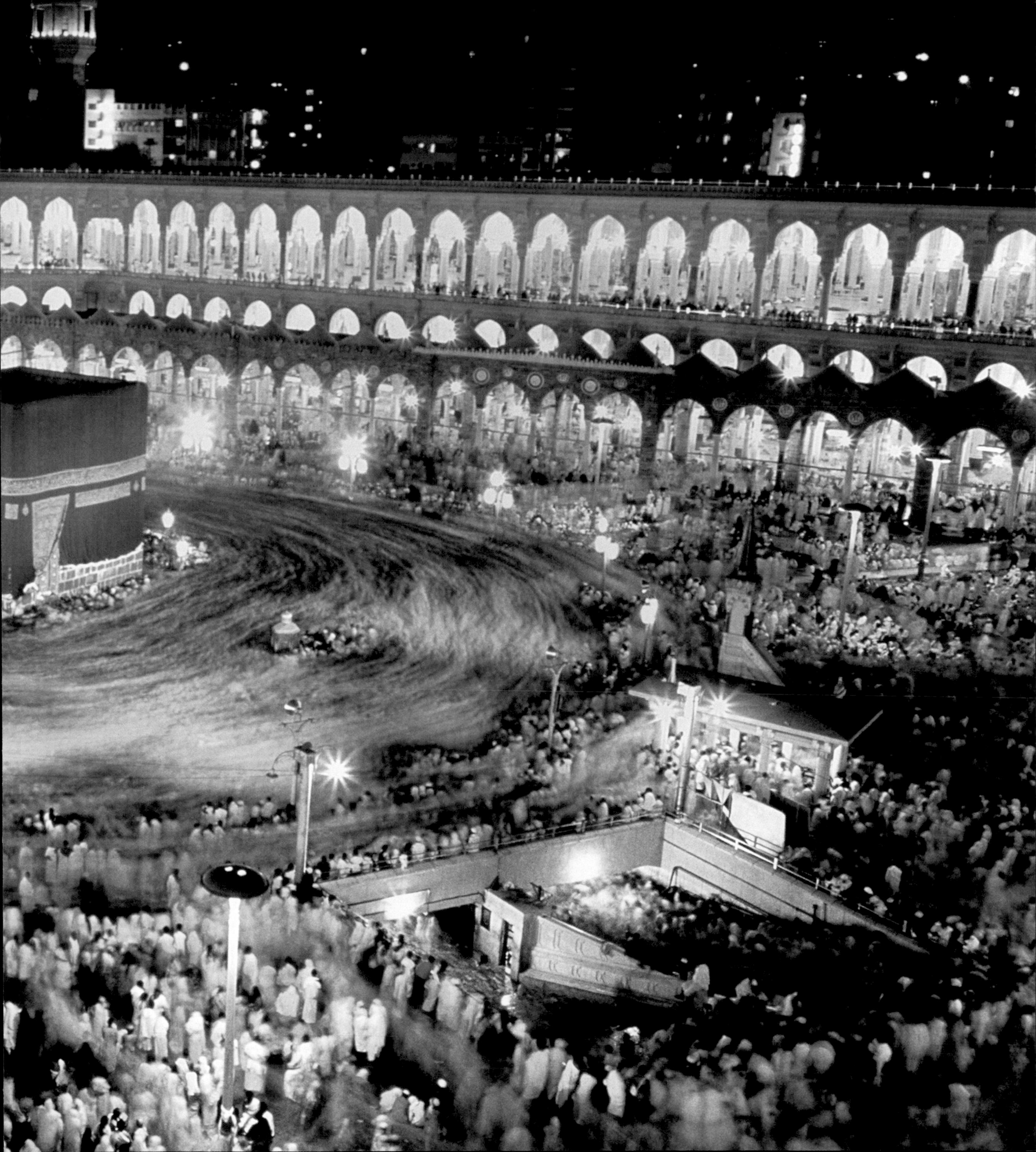

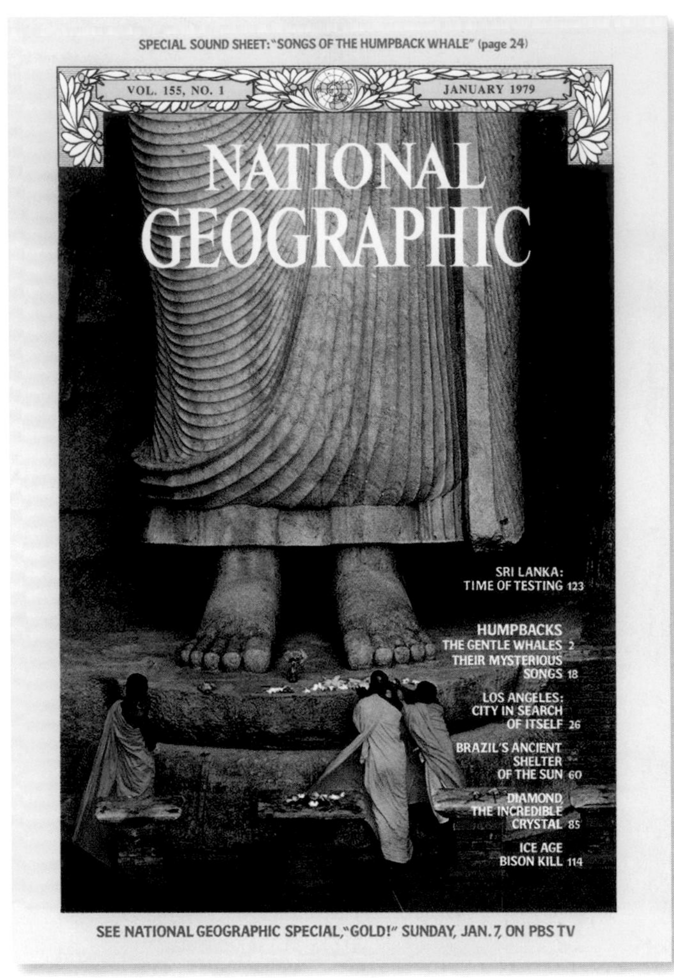

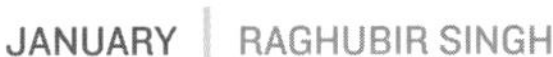
JANUARY | RAGHUBIR SINGH

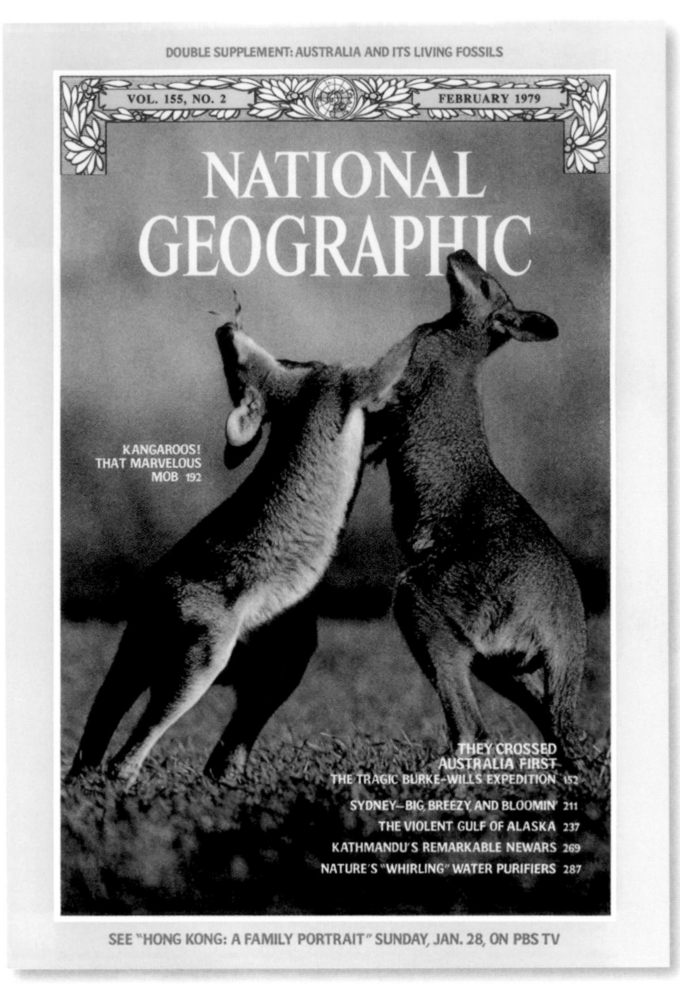

FEBRUARY | DES AND JEN BARTLETT

▲ **GIANT BUDDHA** Monks present flowers to the great Buddha of Avukana, carved out of a Sri Lankan cliff nearly 1,500 years ago.

> *"Time can seem suspended in a land like this. Once I stood among silent worshippers in an ancient Buddhist temple, watching as they strewed blossoms . . . My escort, a bronze-skinned philosopher in a sarong, froze the moment in words: 'Life is like the flowers,' he whispered. 'They are born fresh. In one day they die.'"*
>
> —Robert P. Jordan
> *from "Sri Lanka: Time of Testing"*

▲ **ROUGHHOUSING** Two red-necked wallabies sport with each other on an Australian golf course. The photographers, Des and Jen Bartlett, met while he was shooting wildlife documentaries and she was tennis star Jen Edmondson. They married and soon she took on most of the still photography projects. Although working largely in Africa, they roamed the globe, and spent over a year in their native Australia covering kangaroos.

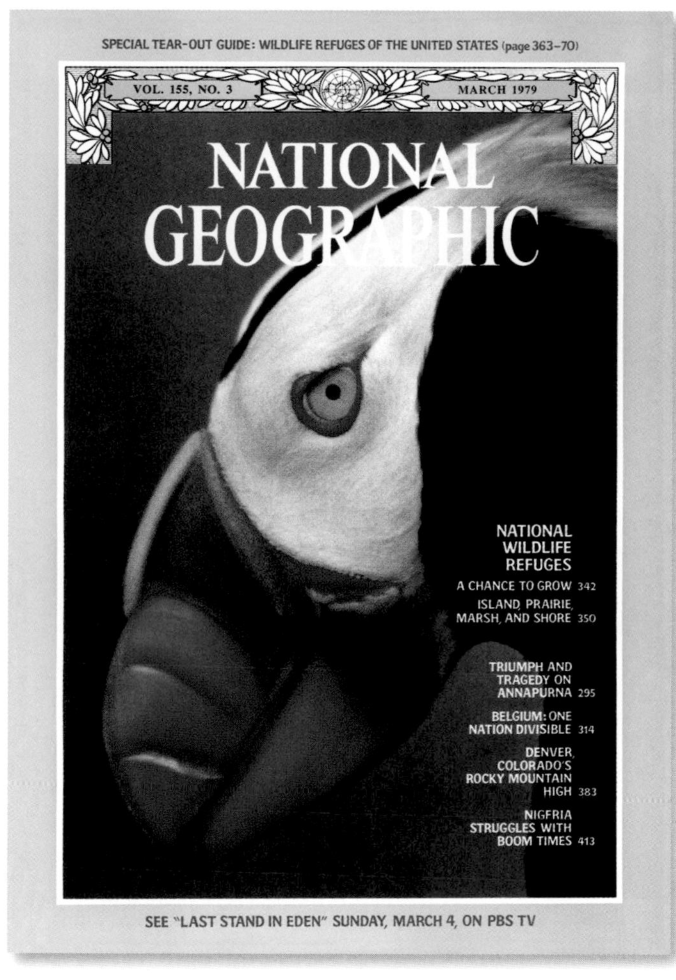

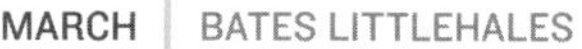

MARCH | BATES LITTLEHALES

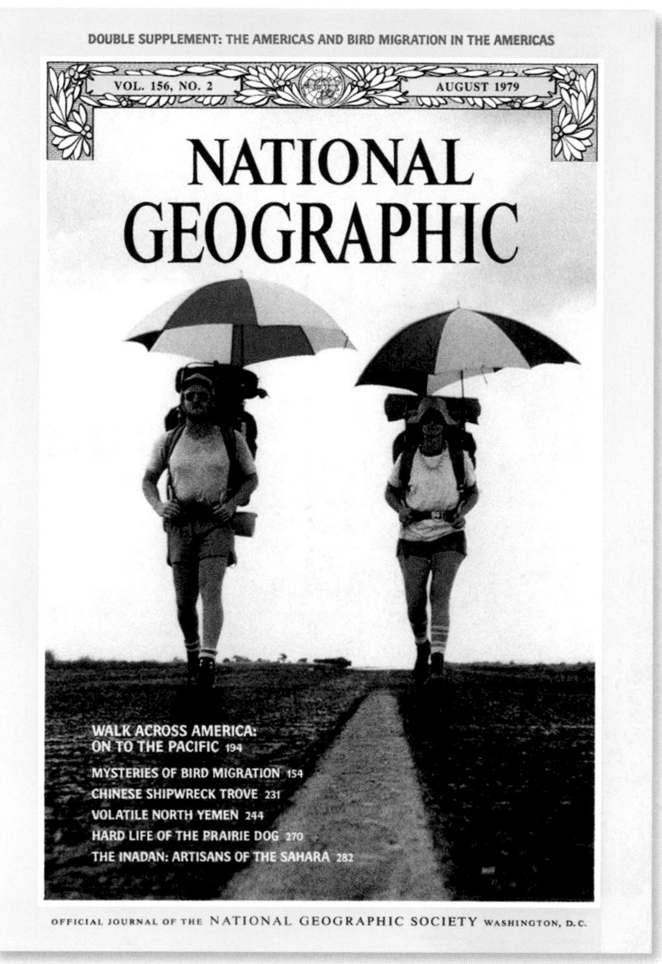

AUGUST | SKEETER HAGLER

▲ **PUFFIN PICTURES** When photographing birds became his specialty, staff photographer Bates Littlehales found that often a car not only got him places but also made a good shooting platform, as birds sometimes fled men but ignored automobiles. When he made this picture of a tufted puffin, however, the closest car was in San Francisco, some 28 miles away. Littlehales was visiting the Farallon Islands National Wildlife Refuge, where seabird colonies congregated on craggy, surf-beaten rocks—some of them so steep that he had to be hoisted ashore by crane.

▲ **EPIC STROLL** One-hundred-degree Texas heat doesn't stop Peter Jenkins, seen here with his new bride, Barbara, from taking a few more steps on his 4,751-mile trek across the country. It was six years earlier when he and his Alaskan malamute walked unannounced into *Geographic* Editor Gilbert M. Grosvenor's office and left with an assignment to chronicle his walk. When he resumed his journey Jenkins was on track to write a phenomenally popular two-part article, "Walk Across America," in the April 1977 and August 1979 issues, which led to a best-selling book.

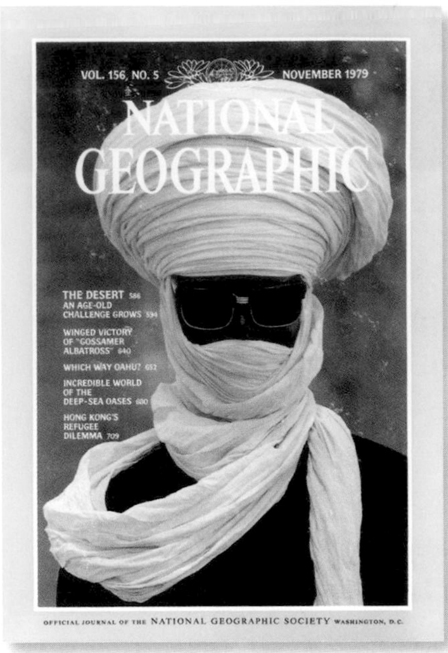

NOVEMBER 1979 | GEORG GERSTER

▲ **COOL IN ANY CULTURE** Dressed for the desert, a Bella tribesman in Upper Volta (today's Burkina Faso) combines old and new with flair. His stylish turban cools his head when the sun is high while those shades protect his eyes from the solar glare. He covers his mouth, however, for the same reason as do the Sahara's Tuareg: Men, not women, are traditionally veiled, believing it wards off evil spirits.

CHALLENGING K2 ▶

WITH CAMP IV HUDDLED behind him and Camp V somewhere up ahead, Rick Ridgeway climbs a knife-edged ridge between Pakistan, the sunlit slopes to his left, and China, falling off into shadow on his right. He's probably 23,000 feet high at this point; nearly a mile higher still is this American expedition's goal, the summit known by its old surveyor's designation: K2.

K2—it's "just the bare bones of a name, all rock and ice and storm and abyss," as Italian climber Fosco Maraini once famously put it. It is also one of the most daunting names in mountaineering, for this dagger of the Karakorams is steeper than Everest, the only peak in the world that stands taller. It was Charles Houston, who led a failed 1953 attempt that became an epic of endurance, who gave it another deadly sobriquet: the "savage mountain."

Only two teams had ever gained its summit: the Italians in 1954 and the Japanese in 1977, the year before this American team laid siege to its slopes. Led by Jim Whittaker and including, besides Ridgeway, the first women ever to set foot upon K2, it had everything to prove. Five previous American attempts to climb it had failed; five of the seven mountaineers so far killed on its flanks had been U.S. citizens.

In the event, the team did prove itself equal to the task. Despite bad weather, waist-high snow, and frequent avalanches, on September 6–7, 1978, four men—Ridgeway, Louis Reichardt, Jim Wickwire, and John Roskelley—reached the summit. They had pioneered a new route to the top. They had reversed decades of bad luck. And nobody died.

▶ **MAY 1979** | **JOHN ROSKELLEY** Rick Ridgeway wears a metal mask to deflect sun and cold.

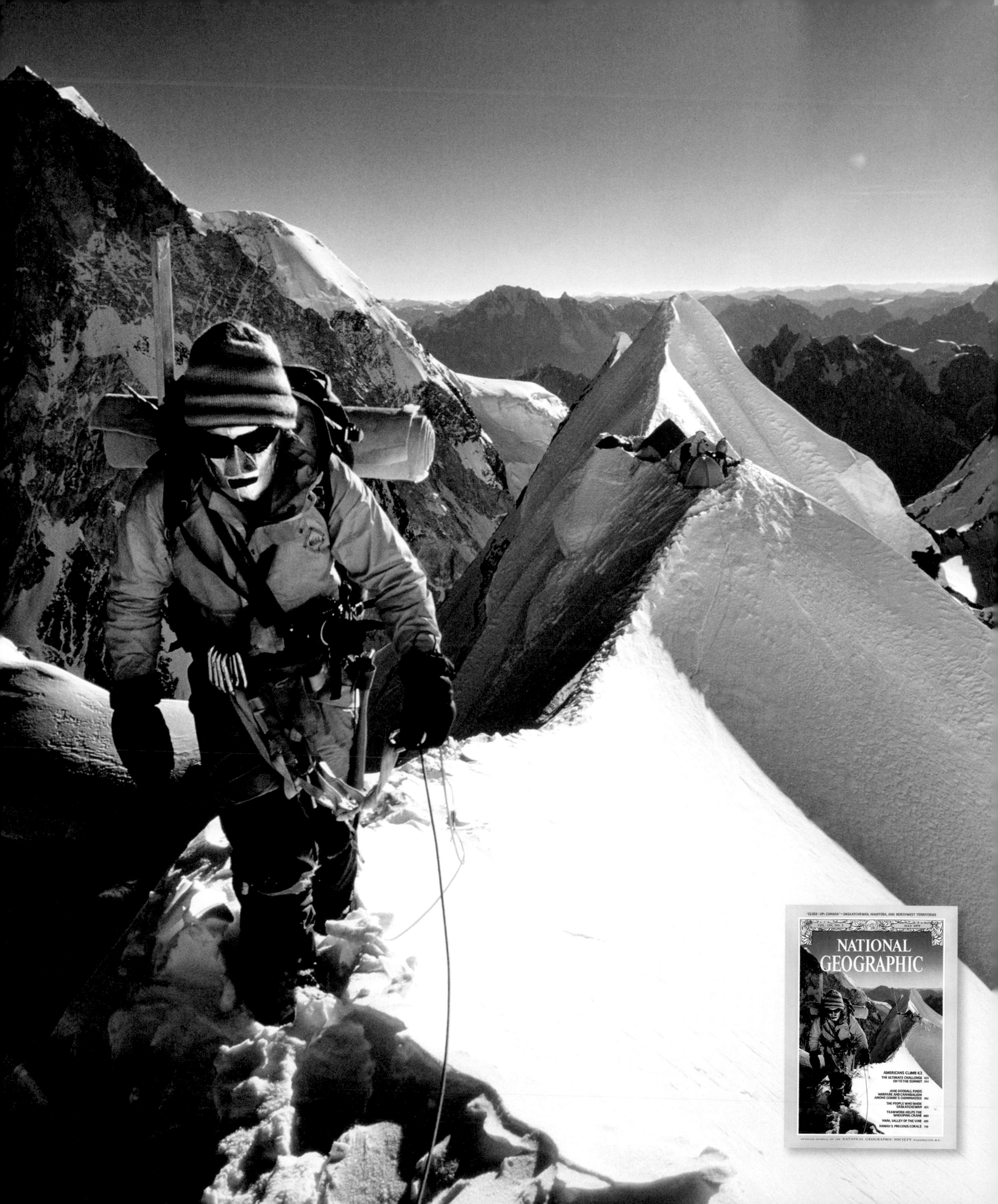
"CLOSE-UP: CANADA"—SASKATCHEWAN, MANITOBA, AND NORTHWEST TERRITORIES
MAY 1979
NATIONAL GEOGRAPHIC
AMERICANS CLIMB K2
THE ULTIMATE CHALLENGE 623
ON TO THE SUMMIT 641
JANE GOODALL FINDS WARFARE AND CANNIBALISM AMONG GOMBE'S CHIMPANZEES 592
THE PEOPLE WHO MADE SASKATCHEWAN 651
TEAMWORK HELPS THE WHOOPING CRANE 680
NAPA, VALLEY OF THE VINE 695
HAWAII'S PRECIOUS CORALS 719
NATIONAL GEOGRAPHIC SOCIETY

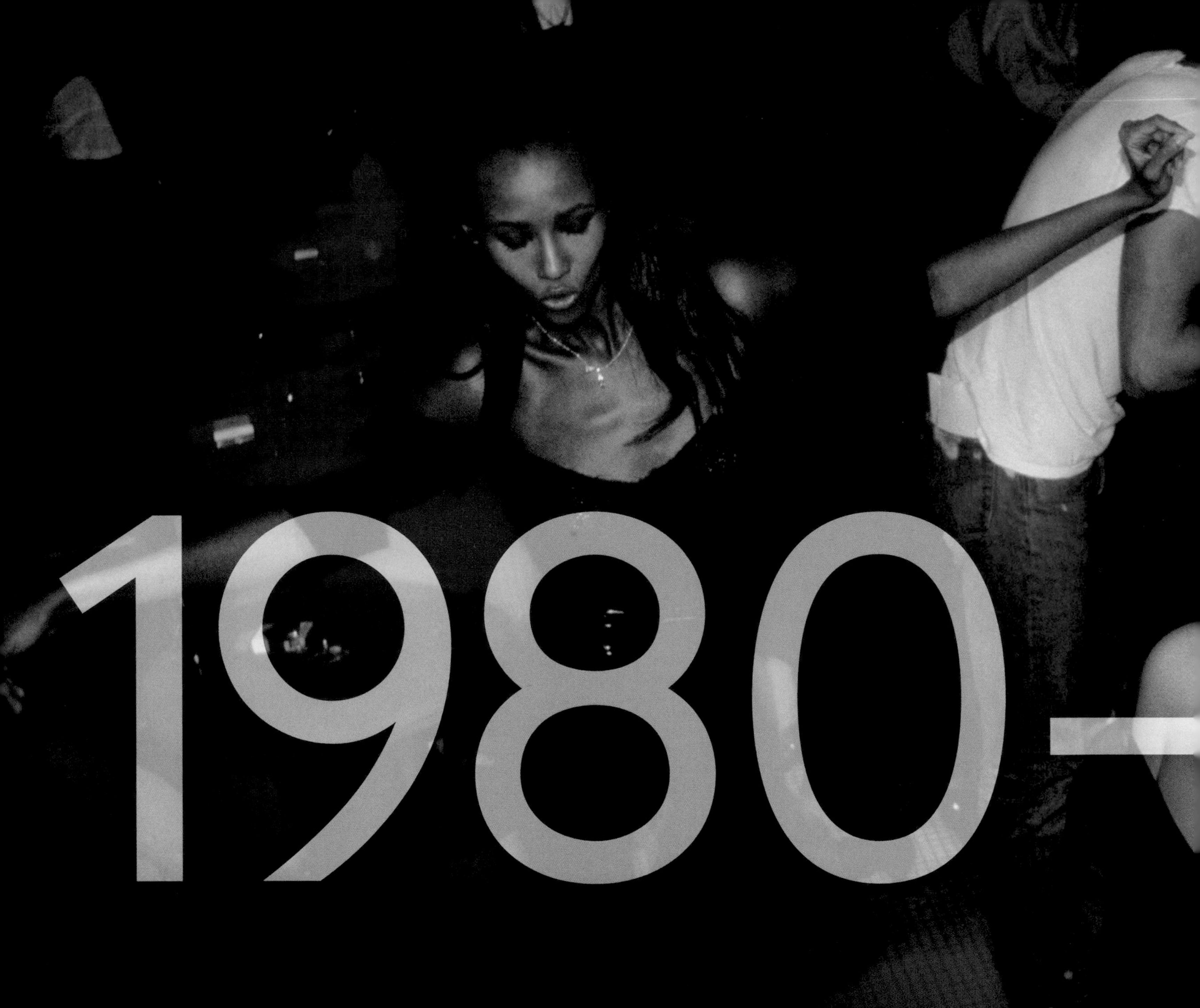

1980–

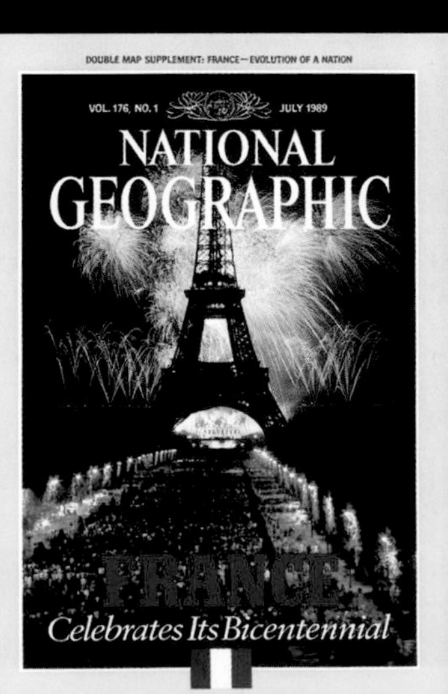

COVER STORY

BON ANNIVERSAIRE!

JULY 1989 | JAMES L. STANFIELD

The chicest club in town in the late 1980s, Les Baines was *the* Paris watering hole if you liked to see, be seen, and depart with someone different than the one you arrived with. Photographer Jim Stanfield, covering France's 1989 bicentennial, attended a party held there by fashion designer Christian Lacroix. So did Russian-born singer Iness, standing in the spotlight; and Somali-born supermodel Iman, cavorting on the dance floor. Only a few years later Iman would be a cosmetics entrepreneur and the wife of David Bowie.

1989

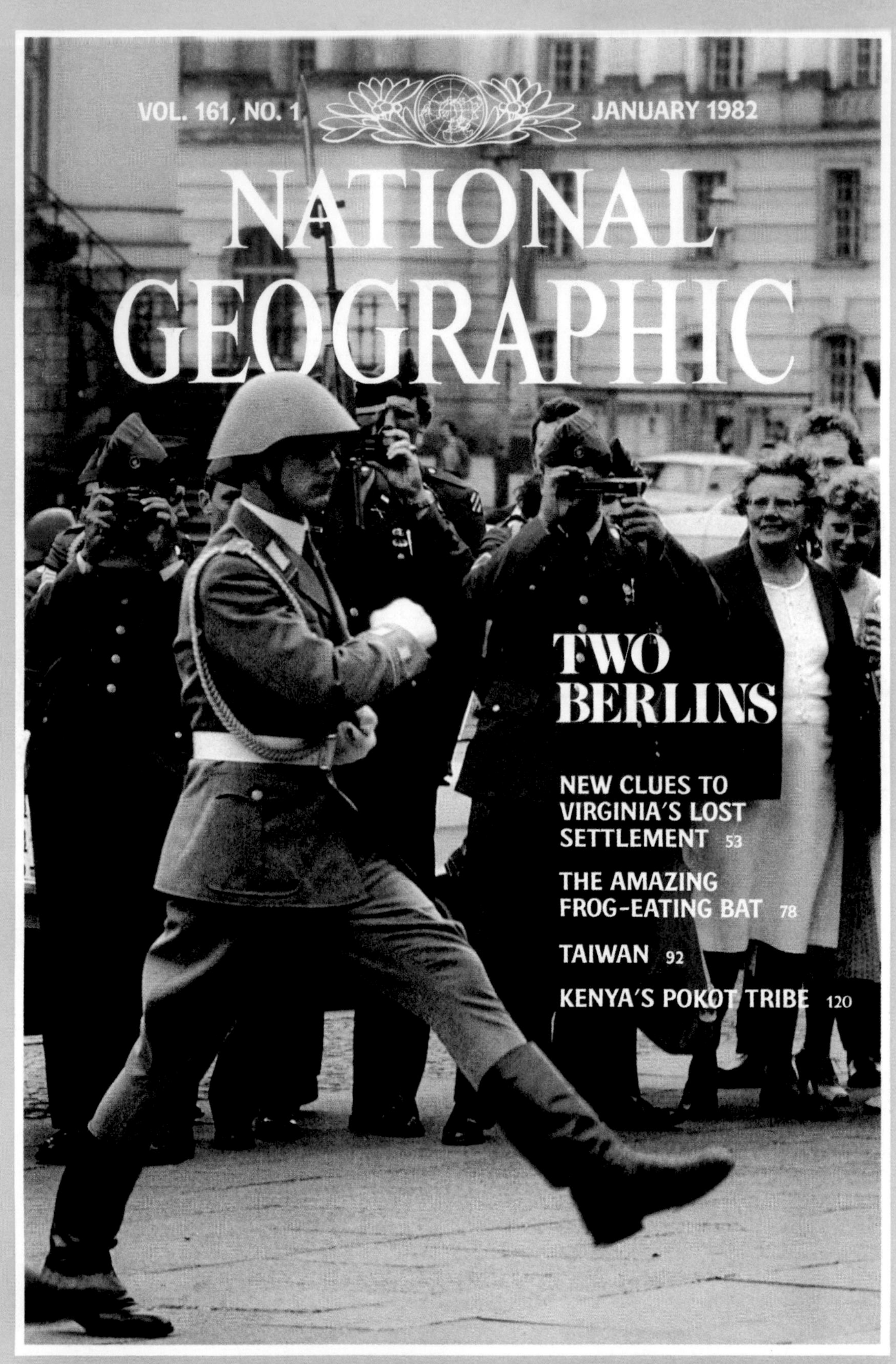

JANUARY 1982 | COTTON COULSON An East German border guard, or "Vopo," patrols a border crossing to West Berlin.

THE WORLD IN THE 1980S

"'What would happen,' I asked, 'if the Wall were taken down?'"

—Priit Vesilind, from "Two Berlins"

ALTHOUGH HE could not have known it at the time, that East German border guard was slowly but surely goose-stepping his way off the cover and into the history books. Before the 1980s ran their course the four-decade standoff that was the Cold War would collapse with a suddenness that matched the ease with which sledgehammers demolished the Berlin Wall.

As Eastern Europeans began emerging from their grimy cities to test the air of freedom, the regime in Deng Xiaoping's China—where everyone at that time still rode bicycles—was relaxing its economic constraints but not its iron political grip. The odes to joy may have swelled in Berlin in November 1989 when the Wall came down; but five months earlier Chinese tanks had crushed democratic yearnings in Beijing's Tiananmen Square.

Night may have fallen again on Asia, but it was still morning in America—Ronald Reagan's America, that is. The genial, avuncular Reagan, with his slicked-back pompadour and brown suits, incarnated for many in the United States the virtues of a simpler and more innocent era. Not even a would-be assassin's bullet could stop him; Reagan was making quips from his hospital bed soon after the failed March 30, 1981, attempt. But if he personified the sunnier side of the decade for

FACTS & FIGURES THE 1980s

- **13** covers on archaeological subjects
- **11** covers featuring wildlife
- **11** covers on historical or biographical subjects
- **7** covers taken underwater
- **4** covers on space
- **3** hologram covers
- **3** covers featuring skeletons or mummies
- **2** covers on natural disasters

AROUND THE WORLD

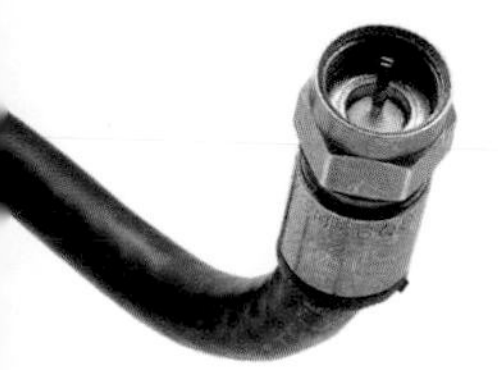

CABLE TV 1980
At least 28 cable programming networks are entertaining U.S. television viewers.

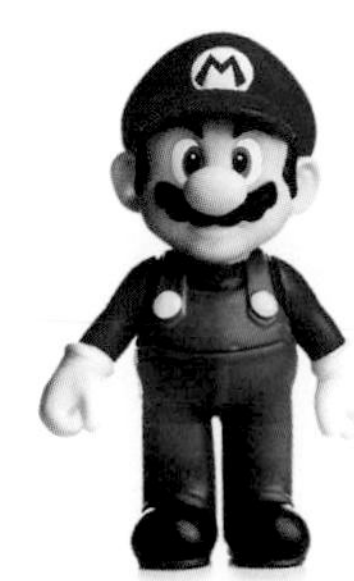

NINTENDO 1980
Nintendo launches the world's first video game console in Japan.

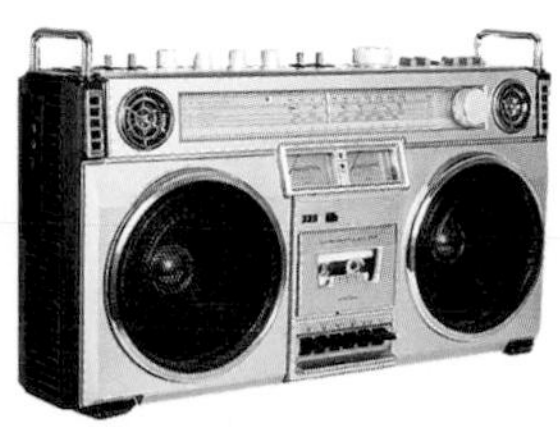

BOOM BOX 1981
Portable stereos become a status symbol among urban youth.

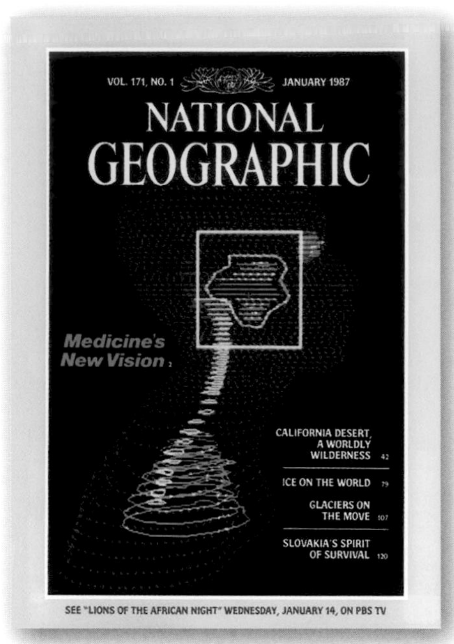

JANUARY 1987 | HOWARD SOCHUREK

▲ **MEDICINE'S NEW VISION** Longtime *National Geographic* contributor Howard Sochurek spent much of the 1960s reporting from the battlefields of Vietnam. Two decades later, he was pioneering new computer-assisted imaging technologies.

Americans, its darker aspect was ruled over by the fictional Gordon Gekko, the cinematic epitome of the "go-go eighties," the emblem of the Wall Street greed that produced the real-life Michael Milken and the junk bond crisis.

Reagan's willingness to outspend the Russians on defense may have hastened the end of the Cold War. But it was Soviet leader Mikhail Gorbachev's reforms—glasnost and perestroika—that had already been reorienting the strategic goals of the Communist colossus. For one thing, he oversaw Soviet withdrawal from Afghanistan, ending a decade of fruitless occupation that had claimed a million Afghan lives and sent an additional six million refugees to camps in Iran and Pakistan (including one 12-year-old girl who would leave a very deep imprint on *National Geographic*).

Meanwhile, equally savage conflicts were being fought around the globe. Saddam Hussein's 1980 invasion of Iran triggered an eight-year war that in sheer carnage—and the use of chemical weapons—rivaled anything seen in World War I. Lebanon collapsed in chaos while El Salvador and Nicaragua were each plunged into vicious civil wars. Even Britain fought Argentina over the sovereignty of the Falkland Islands.

Elsewhere the wars were being fought for wildlife. Poaching of elephants for their tusks and rhinos for their horns approached genuine crisis. Tree wars also claimed a share of the headlines as debates raged over the destruction of forests, whether in Amazonia or the Pacific Northwest. Additional crises—Bhopal in India, where in 1984 Union Carbide's accidental release of methyl isocyanate gas, used in pesticides, killed 3,000 people outright and thousands more subsequently; and the nuclear meltdown at Chernobyl in 1986, which contaminated much of Europe with radioactive fallout and may still be causing thyroid cancer in the worst afflicted areas—only strengthened the environmental movement.

Articles on environmental topics garnered even more *National Geographic* pages in the 1980s than they did in the '70s. This was, after all, Bill Garrett's decade as Editor in Chief (1980–1990): The committed environmentalist had perhaps the most envied Rolodex in the magazine

AROUND THE WORLD

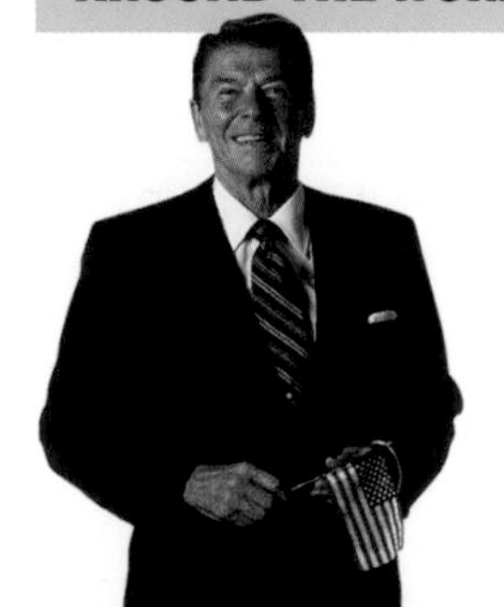

REAGAN 1981
Ronald Reagan begins two terms as the 40th U.S. president.

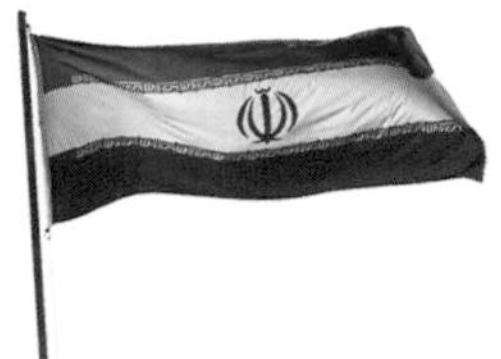

IRAN HOSTAGES 1981
52 Americans held hostage in the American Embassy in Tehran are released.

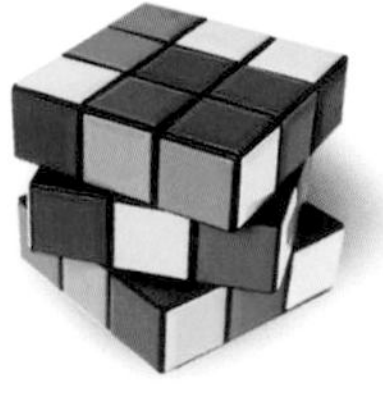

RUBIK'S CUBE 1982
Ernö Rubik's perplexing puzzle flummoxes millions of people worldwide.

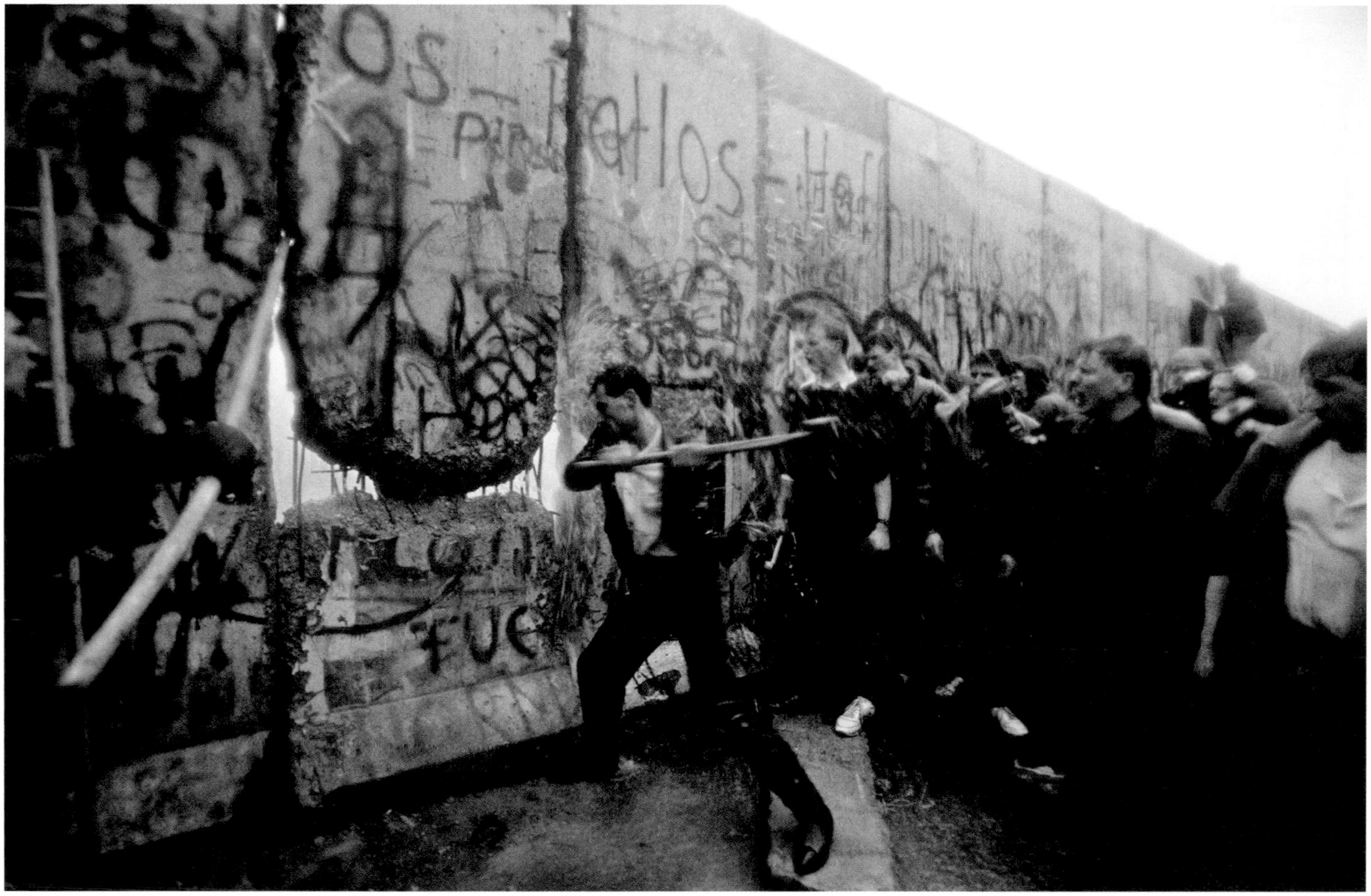

1989 | ANTHONY SUAU The Berlin Wall comes tumbling down . . .

business, and there were few talented photojournalists anywhere that he could not quickly contact. With a strong photographic staff and a talented outer circle of contract photographers he could always rely on, Garrett continually broadened the *Geographic's* editorial scope and in return saw the Society's membership hit the highest levels in its history.

Throughout this decade rolls of film poured into headquarters by the tens of thousands and typewriters continually clattered throughout the editorial offices. Change, however, lurked just over the horizon. ■

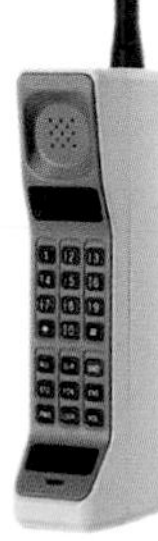

DYNATAC 1984
The Motorola DynaTAC 8000X is the first cell phone ever sold commercially.

CHERNOBYL 1986
The April 26 explosion at the Chernobyl plant becomes one of the worst nuclear disasters in history.

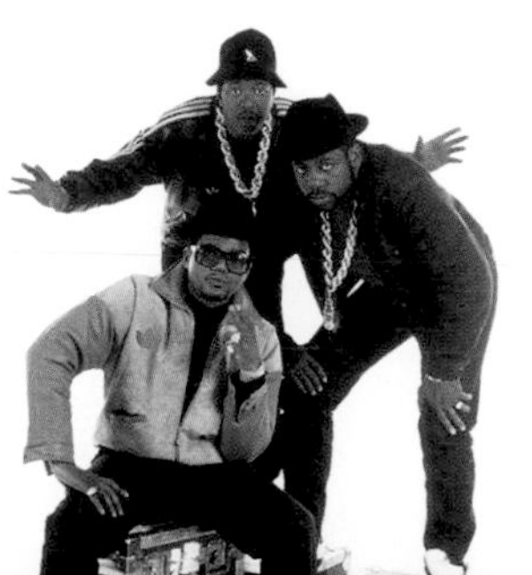

RUN-DMC 1987
The boys from Queens become the first hip-hop group to be nominated for a Grammy.

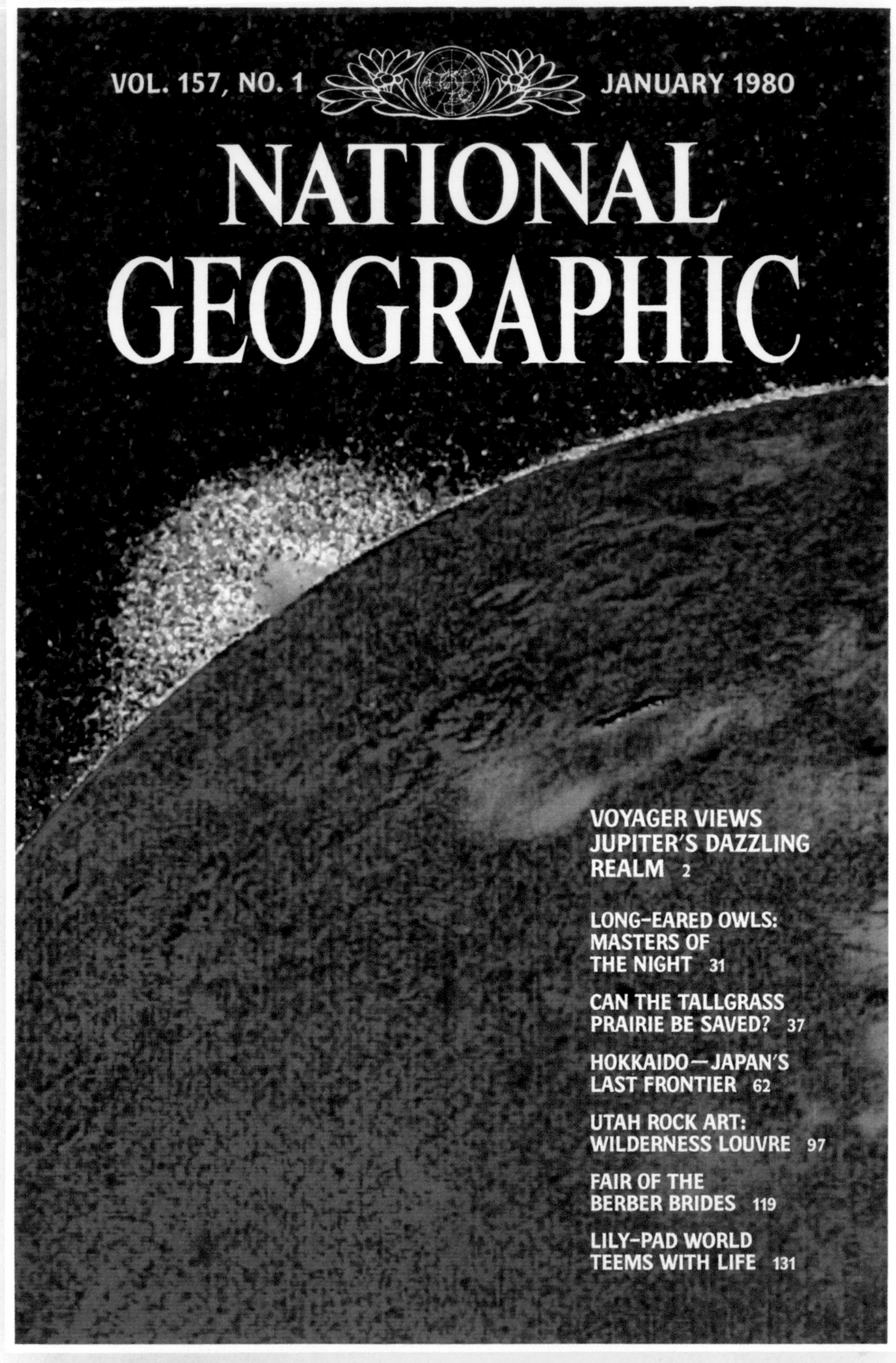

JANUARY | NASA A volcano erupts on Jupiter's moon Io.

MAGNIFICENT VOYAGERS

THAT PLUME ON THE edge of Jupiter's moon Io, seen in this high-contrast image, marks this picture as being among the most significant in the annals of space exploration.

Snapped by a rearward-facing camera on the unmanned probe Voyager 1, then speeding away from Io, it had made its own long journey. First it was saved onto an onboard reel-to-reel tape, then broadcast via antenna some 390 million miles to Earth as a string of numbers, and ultimately forwarded to Building 264 at the Jet Propulsion Laboratory in Pasadena, California. There a sharp-eyed technician recognized that plume as being a volcanic eruption, the first ever discovered elsewhere in the solar system.

More revelations would come from Voyager 1 and its sister probe, Voyager 2, both of which had launched in 1977. Voyager 1 reached Jupiter and Saturn first and discovered that Saturn's moon Titan was covered with lakes of liquid methane. Titan's gravity then spun the spacecraft onto a track leading out of the solar system.

Voyager 2, meanwhile, not only reached Saturn but two years later passed Uranus, glimpsing canyons on its moon Miranda that were 12 miles deep. By August 1989 it was grazing Neptune, finding it perpetually scoured by winds reaching an astounding 1,200 miles an hour.

The Grand Tour was over, but the journey only continues. In 38,000 years Voyager 1 might arrive at another star; in 256,000 more years so might Voyager 2, on its own path through the cosmos.

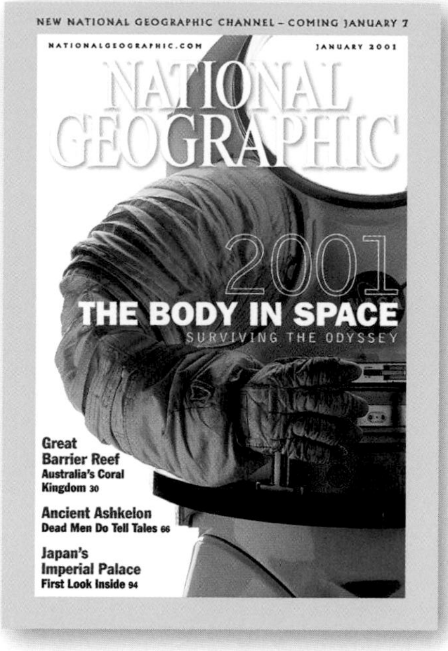

JANUARY 2001 | IRA BLOCK

2001 ▸▸▸▸ FAST FORWARD

MANNED MISSION Twenty-one years later, 2001 had arrived and no astronauts had yet been lost on a voyage to Jupiter, as they were in the film *2001: A Space Odyssey*. Yet NASA had been facing the formidable challenges of sending manned missions at least as far as Mars—including the development of space suits, like this MK III (H-1), which promised to make the trip a safer and more comfortable one.

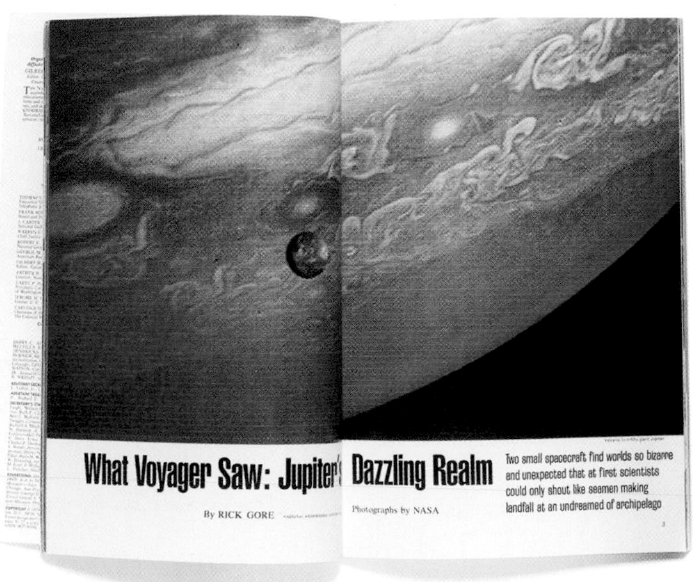

▸ JANUARY 1980 | NASA Tiny Io is buffeted by the tremendous gravitation of its gigantic neighbor, Jupiter.

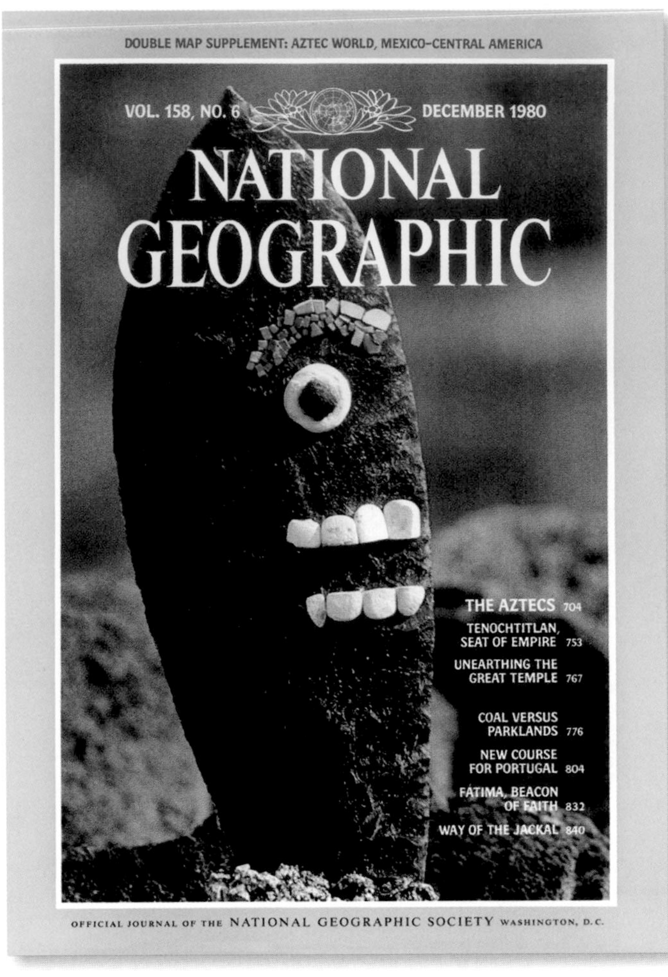

DECEMBER | DAVID HISER

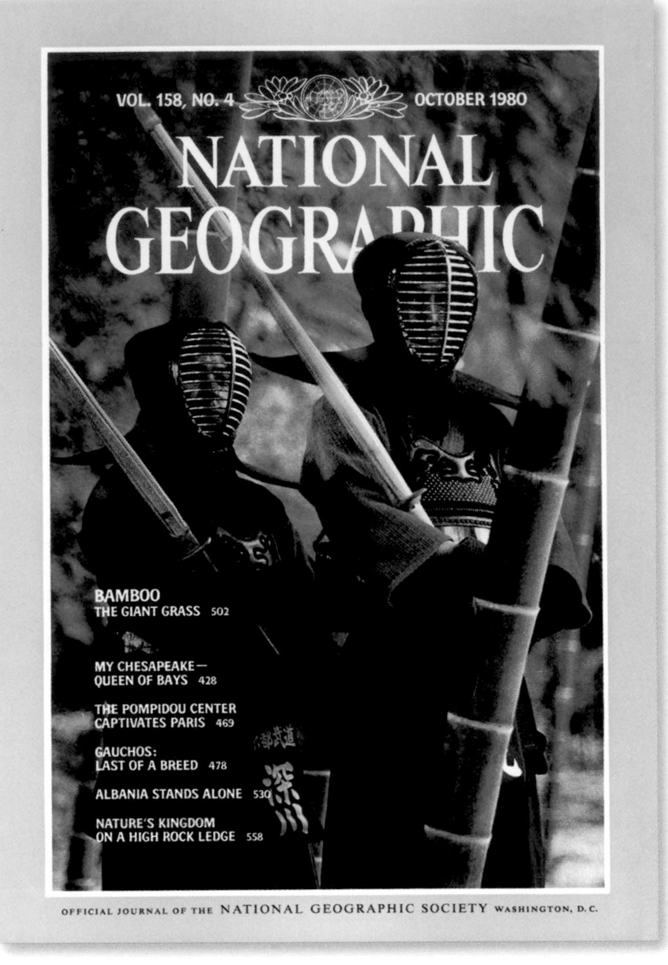

OCTOBER | JIM BRANDENBURG

▲ **SACRIFICIAL KNIFE** Its single eye crowned with a jade eyebrow, its ghastly teeth fixed in a fiendish grin, this decorated obsidian knife might have been one of those used to carve out the hearts of human sacrifices. The six-inch-long ritual blade was part of a cache unearthed at the Great Temple in Tenochtitlan, the Aztec capital now lying beneath Mexico City.

▲ **BAMBOO BLADES** Japanese fencers, emulating samurai warriors, practice dueling with bamboo swords, employing one of the most versatile plants on Earth.

"Bamboo is all things to some men; and some things to all men. It enriches the soil; binds the earth against raging floods and the shocks of earthquakes; gives man tools to work with, instruments to make music, toys to divert his children, and weapons with which to fight his fellow creatures."

—Luis Marden

from "Bamboo: The Giant Grass"

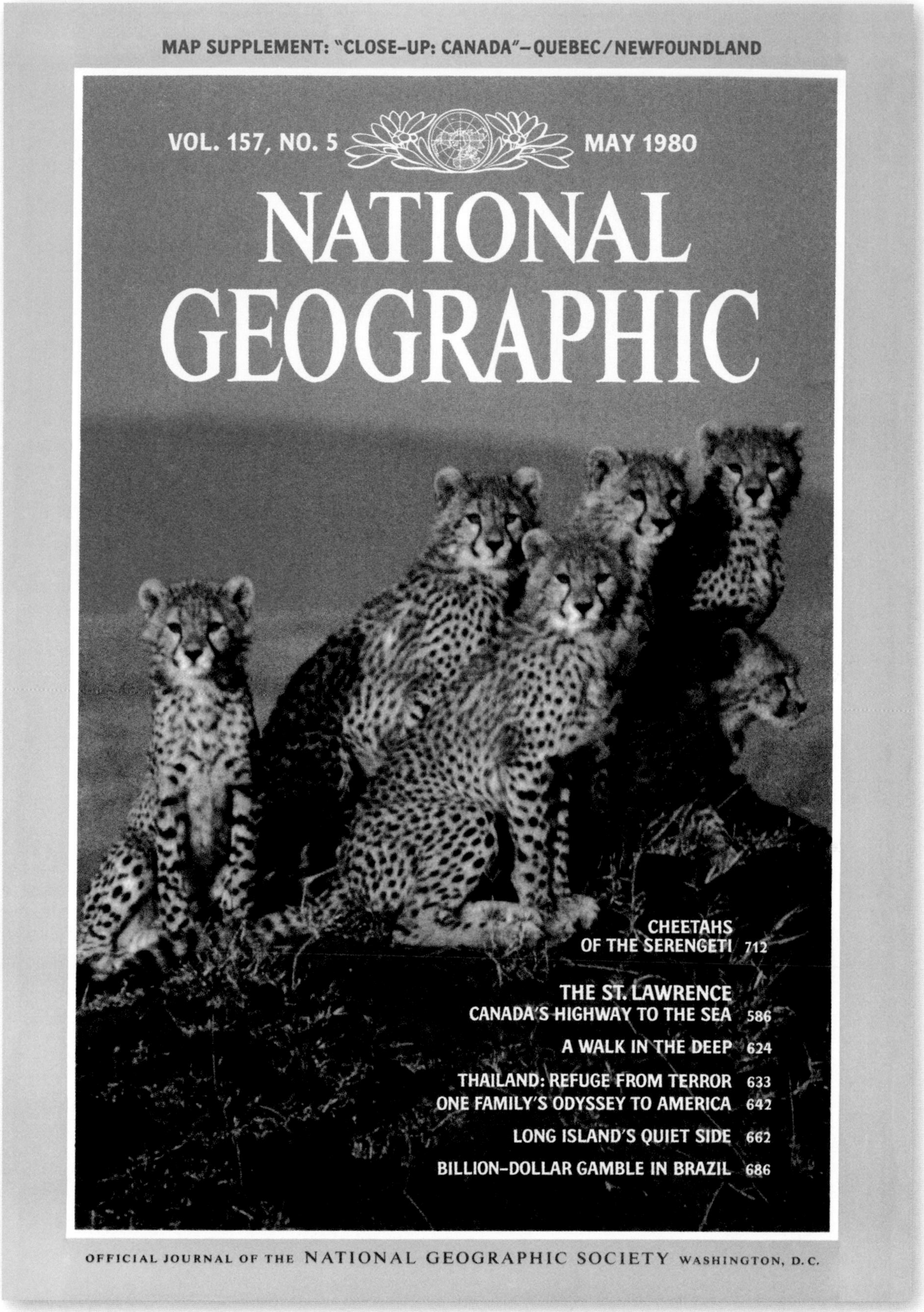

MAP SUPPLEMENT: "CLOSE-UP: CANADA"–QUEBEC/NEWFOUNDLAND

VOL. 157, NO. 5 MAY 1980

NATIONAL GEOGRAPHIC

CHEETAHS OF THE SERENGETI 712

THE ST. LAWRENCE CANADA'S HIGHWAY TO THE SEA 586

A WALK IN THE DEEP 624

THAILAND: REFUGE FROM TERROR 633

ONE FAMILY'S ODYSSEY TO AMERICA 642

LONG ISLAND'S QUIET SIDE 662

BILLION-DOLLAR GAMBLE IN BRAZIL 686

OFFICIAL JOURNAL OF THE NATIONAL GEOGRAPHIC SOCIETY WASHINGTON, D.C.

MAY | GEORGE AND LORY FRAME

CHEETAHS OF THE SERENGETI Identical even to the point of alertness, a group of cheetah cubs surveys its famous grassland home. Swiftest of all mammals, the graceful cats were already declining alarmingly in numbers by the time this picture was made.

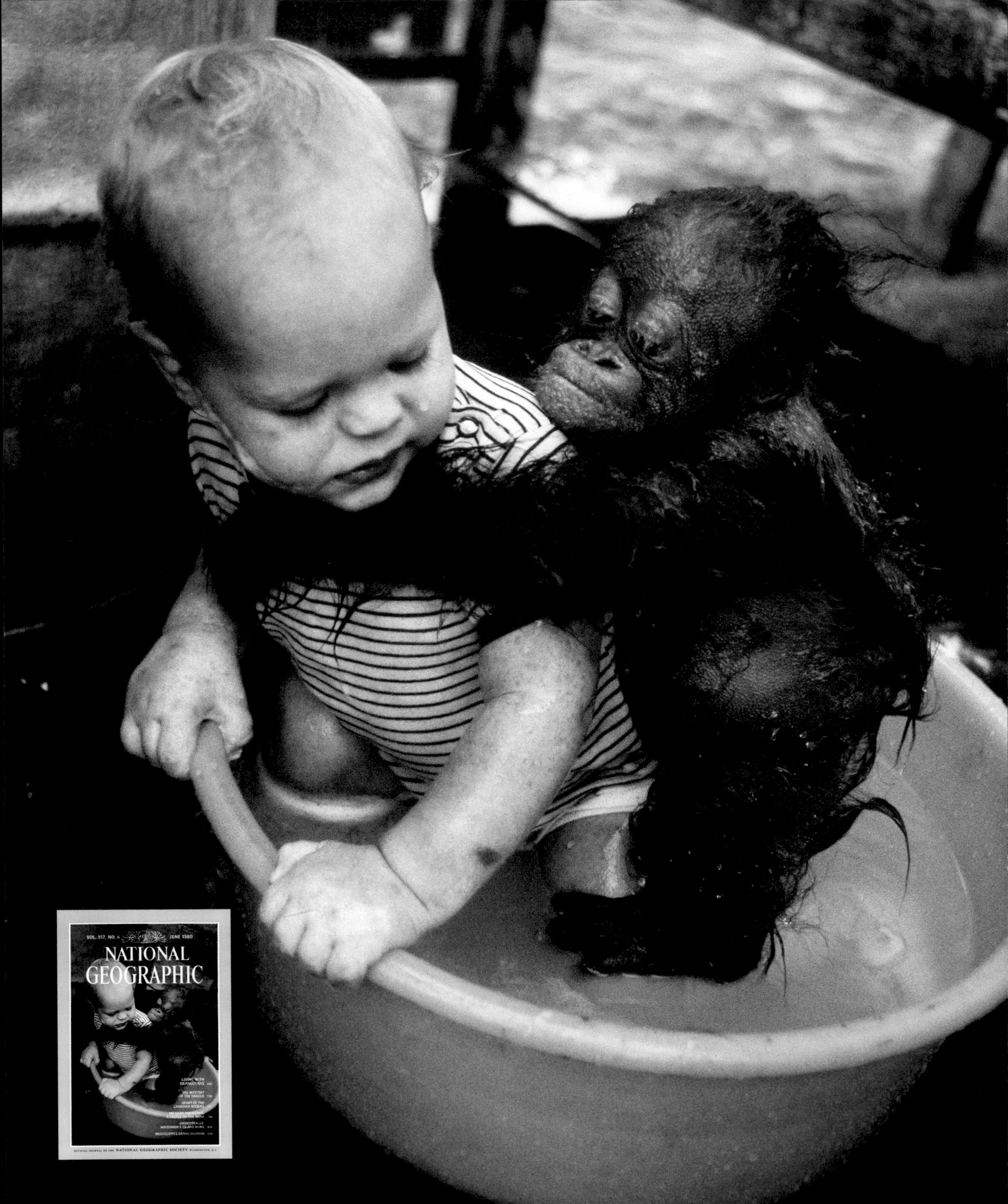
VOL. 157, NO. 6
JUNE 1980
NATIONAL
GEOGRAPHIC
LIVING WITH
ORANGUTANS
THE MYSTERY
OF THE SHROUD
HEART OF THE
CANADIAN ROCKIES
CHINCOTEAGUE
WATERMEN'S ISLAND HOME
NATIONAL GEOGRAPHIC SOCIETY

BORN FREE, RAISED WILD

Born in Borneo's Tanjung Puting National Park, Binti Paul Galdikas Brindamour was the only human child in a forest camp surrounded by hundreds of square miles of tropical rain forest.

Bin's development during his first year helped his mother, primatologist Biruté Galdikas, clarify some of her ape and human theories. For five years she had been immersed in orangutan existence: eating with them, sleeping with them, watching them give birth, watching them die.

After Bin was born, she worried that he would become the prototypical wild child of fable. But the child's behavior that first year highlighted only the differences between human babies and orangutan newborns. Unlike Princess, a one-year-old orang that Biruté was concurrently raising, Bin showed little interest in food—but he was greatly interested in implements. He did pick up sign language from his distant primate cousins. He imitated Princess's facial expressions and noises. He dangled his arms when carried and could hoot like an orang at the age of three. The parents began to worry that he was choosing the wrong role models.

But they had no need to worry, after all. More scientists arrived in Tanjung Puting; and when Bin began hanging out with their children, he swiftly gave up orangutan ways altogether.

> *"Sometimes I felt as though I were surrounded by wild, unruly children in orange suits who had not yet learned their manners."*
>
> —Biruté Galdikas
>
> *from "Living With Orangutans"*

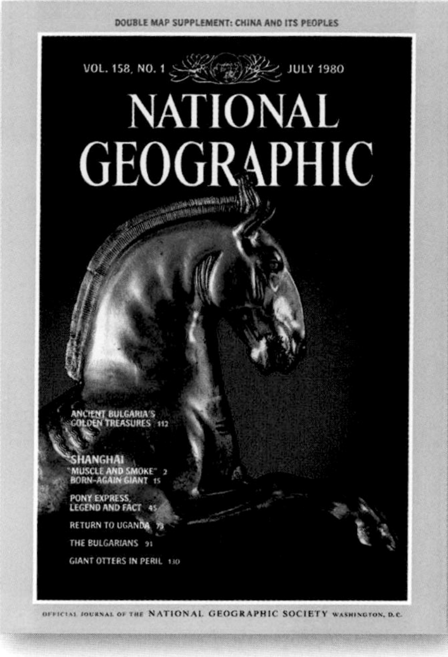

JULY | JAMES L. STANFIELD

▲ **THRACIAN GOLD** An eight-inch-high horse of silver and gold attests the wealth of the Thracians who once occupied what is today Bulgaria. Author Colin Renfrew, writing in "Ancient Bulgaria's Golden Treasures," surveyed a recently discovered trove of copper and gold artifacts and found that they vindicated his theory that Bronze Age metallurgy, far from being a Near Eastern import, had evolved independently in Europe.

◄ **JUNE** | **ROD BRINDAMOUR** Galdikas's one-year-old son, Bin, has second thoughts about sharing his camp bath with Princess.

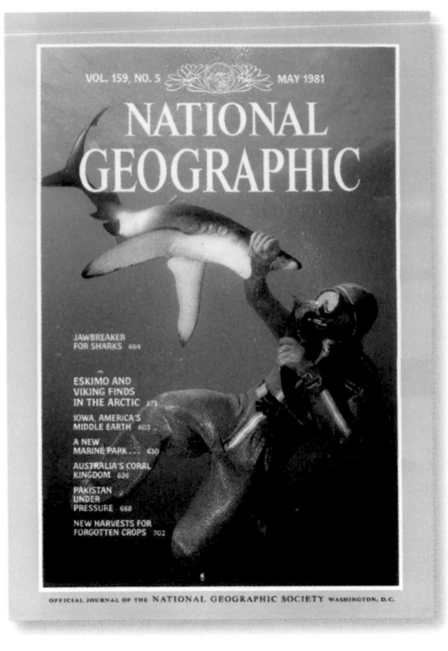

MAY | RON TAYLOR

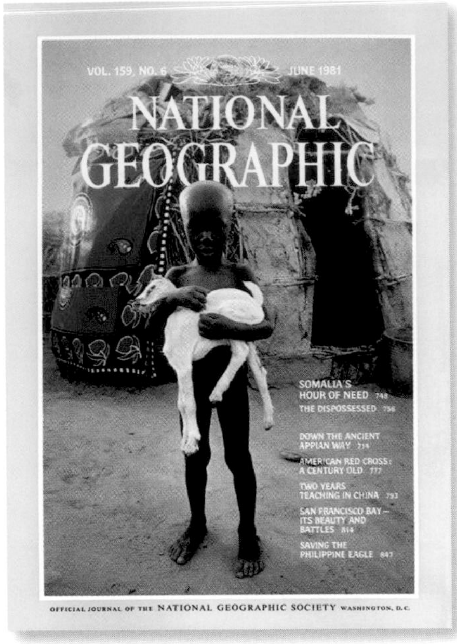

JUNE | KEVIN FLEMING

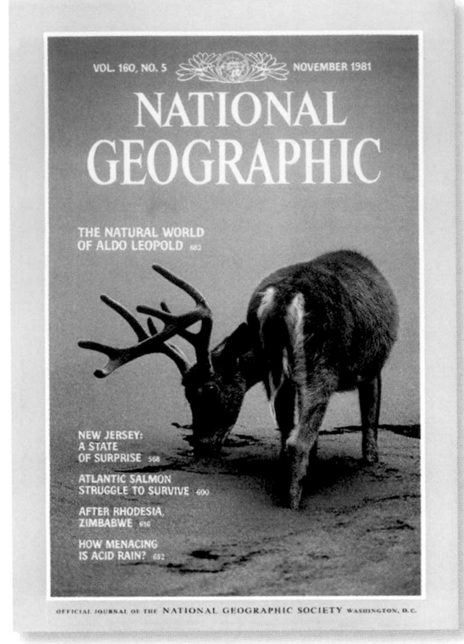

NOVEMBER | JIM BRANDENBURG

▲ **JAWBREAKER** Clad in a chain mail antishark diving suit, Valerie Taylor takes on a blue shark. Ron Taylor came up with the idea, but the prototype was too small for him. It fell to his wife, Valerie, to test its effectiveness. It worked; yet on one occasion, a gray reef shark simply bit her face instead, leaving four puncture wounds in her chin. A tiny chip of shark tooth remains embedded in her jaw.

MOUNT ST. HELENS ▶

At precisely 8:32 a.m. on Sunday, May 18, 1980, Mount St. Helens erupted with the fury of a ten-megaton bomb, killing 61 people, two million animals, and perhaps billions of plants, and covering much of the Northwest in cindery ash.

> The entire mountainside falls as the gases explode out with a roar heard 200 miles away. The incredible blast rolls north, northwest, and northeast at aircraft speeds. In one continuous thunderous sweep, it scythes down giants of the forest, clear-cutting 200 square miles in all. Within three miles of the summit, the trees simply vanish—transported through the air for unknown distances . . . Then comes the ash—fiery, hot, blanketing, suffocating . . .
>
> *—From "Mountain With a Death Wish," Rowe Findley*

▼ **JANUARY 1981** | GARY ROSENQUIST
A wall of ash rolls forward at 200 miles an hour during the 1980 Mount St. Helens eruption.

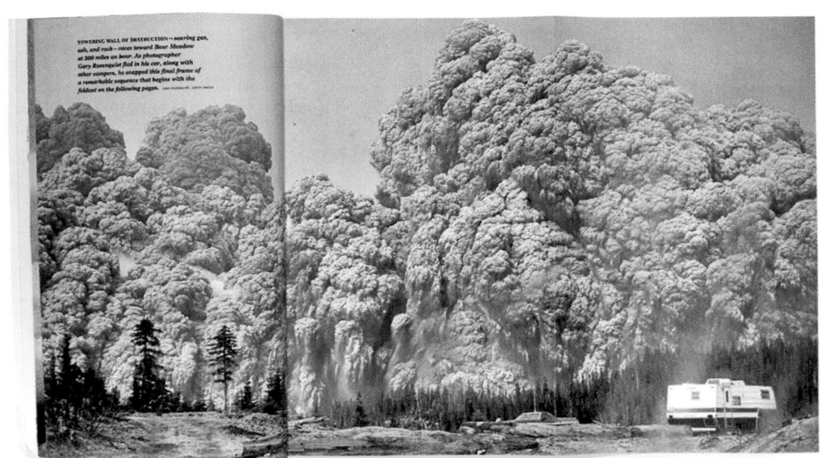

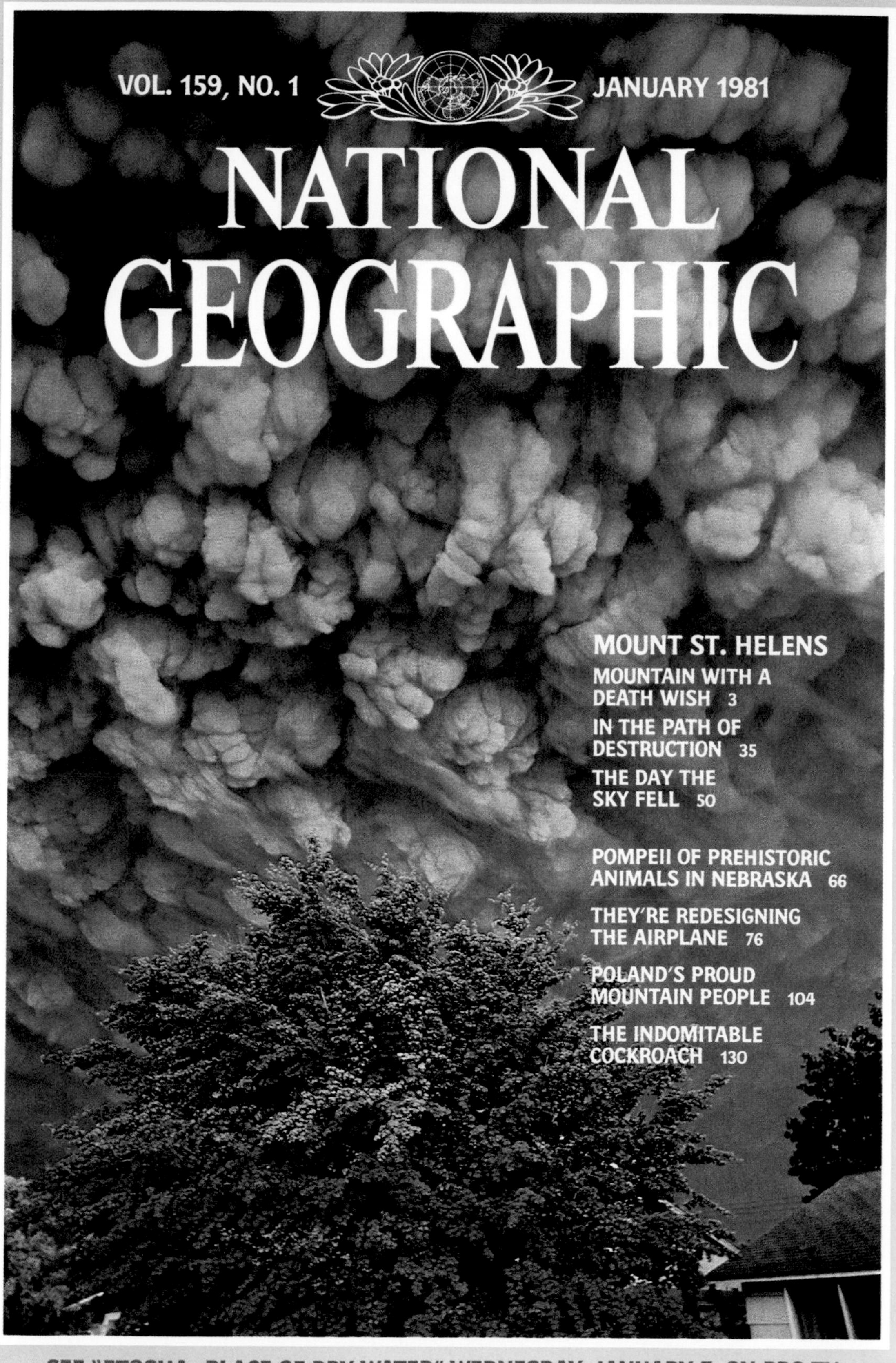

JANUARY | DOUGLAS MILLER Ash swirls above Ephrata, Washington, three hours after the eruption.

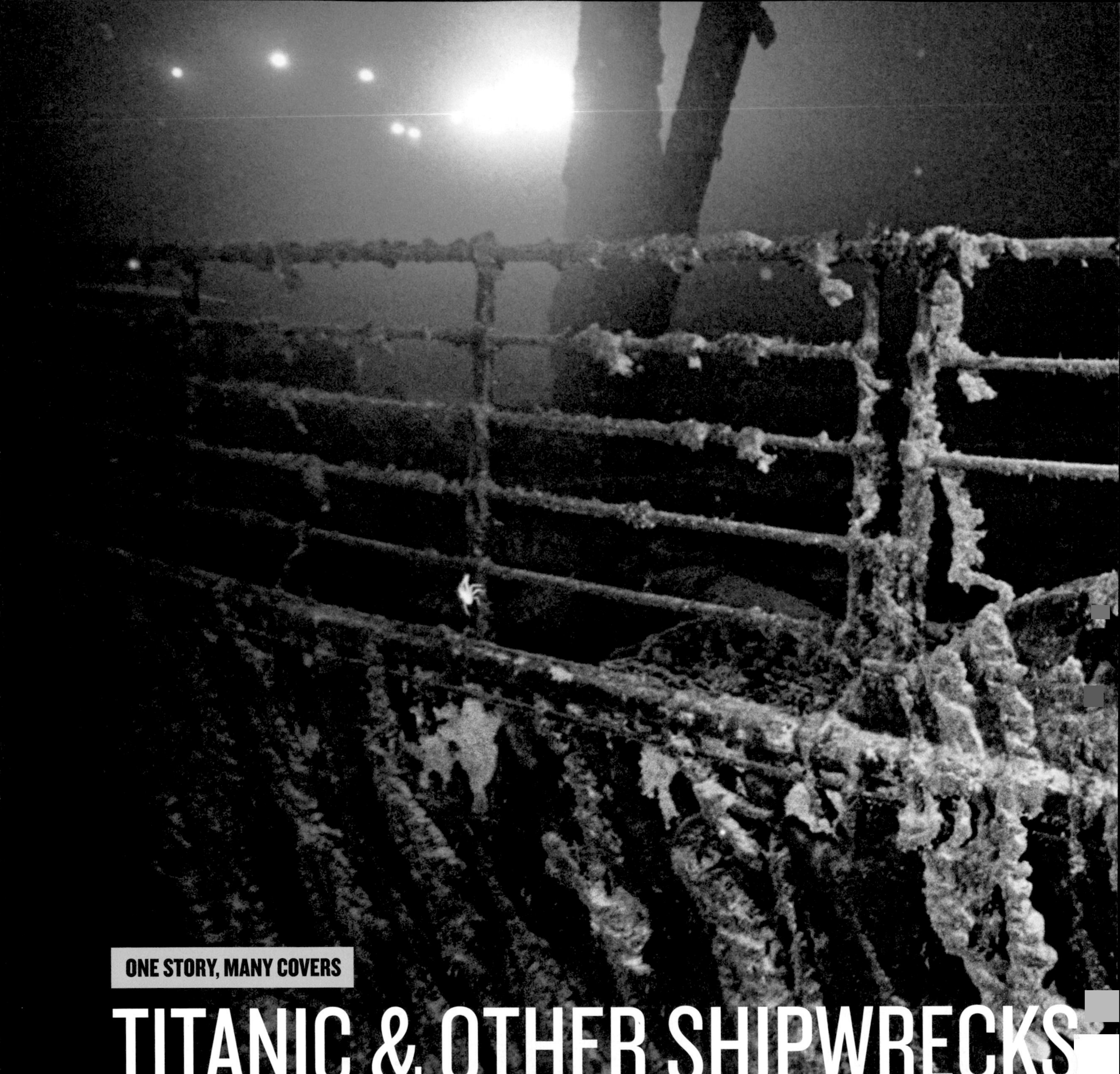

ONE STORY, MANY COVERS

TITANIC & OTHER SHIPWRECKS

▲ **AUGUST 2001 | EMORY KRISTOF**
Former staff photographer Emory Kristof managed to light up *Titanic*—more than 12,000 feet deep—a feat that impressed movie director

WHEN "EPILOGUE FOR *TITANIC*," the third article on that subject in less than two years, was published in the October 1987 *National Geographic*, it proved to be no epilogue. More articles inevitably followed. Since the days of Jacques-Yves Cousteau and Luis Marden—who discovered scattered remnants of the *Bounty* in 1957—the magazine has filled its pages with images of sunken ships, scuba-clad archaeologists gridding off seafloor

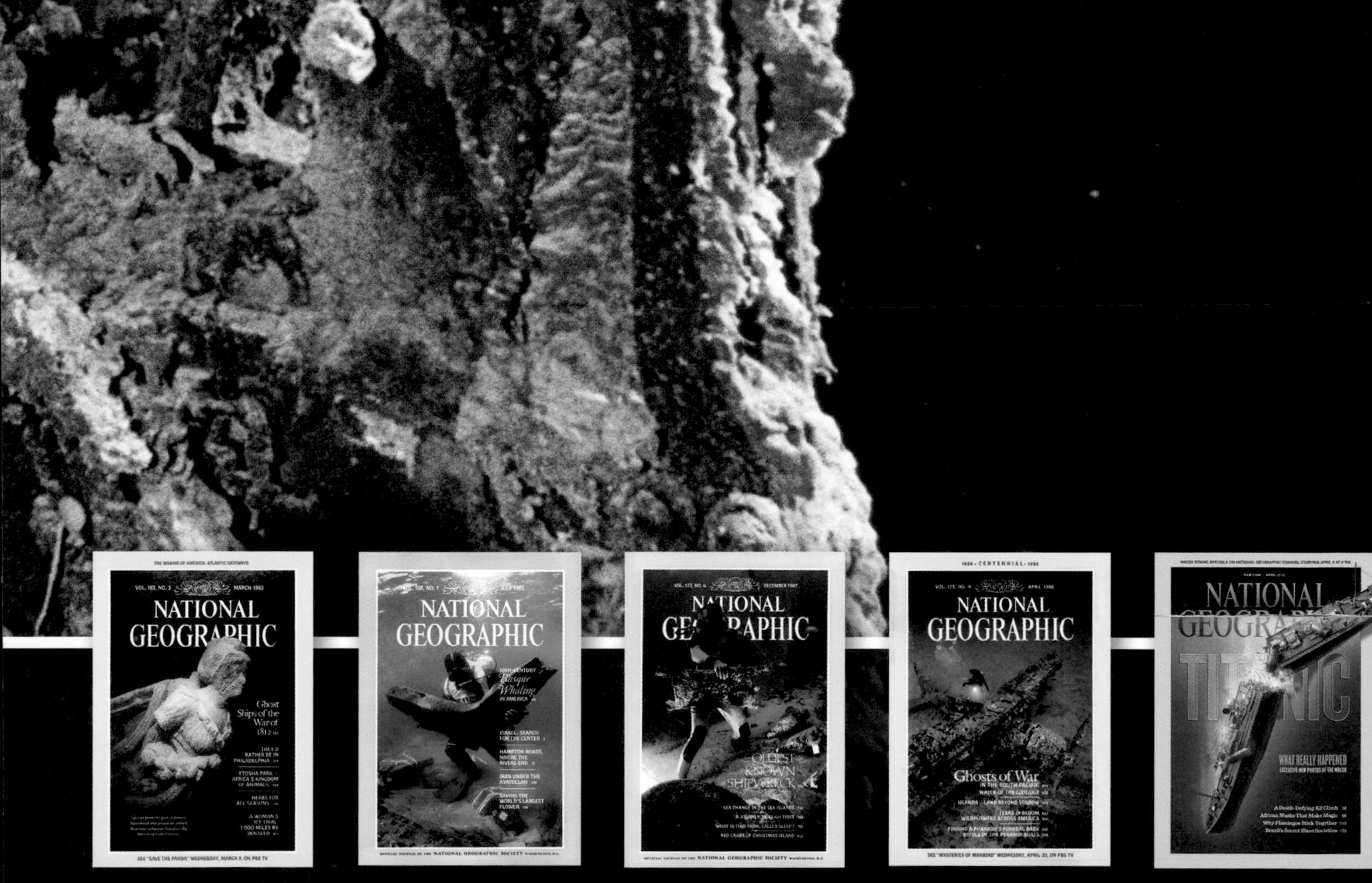
NATIONAL GEOGRAPHIC
Ghost Ships of the War of 1812
NATIONAL GEOGRAPHIC
Basque Whaling
NATIONAL GEOGRAPHIC
OLDEST KNOWN SHIPWRECK
NATIONAL GEOGRAPHIC
Ghosts of War
NATIONAL GEOGRAPHIC
TITANIC
WHAT REALLY HAPPENED
A Death-Defying K2 Climb
African Masks That Make Magic
Why Flamingos Stick Together
Brazil's Secret Slave Societies

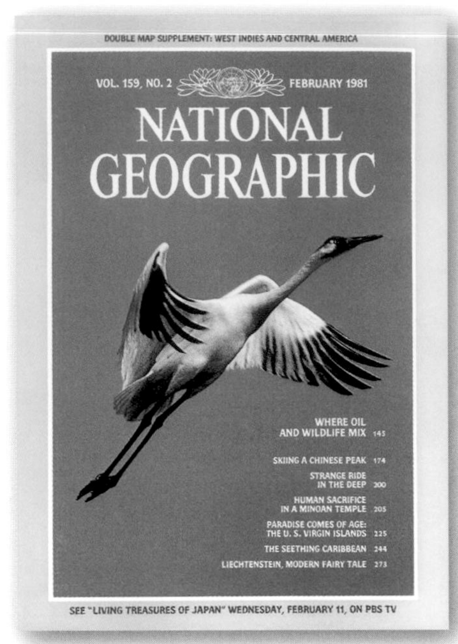

FEBRUARY | STEVEN C. WILSON

▲ **RARE BIRD** On their unlucky days, Steven Wilson and Karen Hayden often spent an hour waist-deep in mud of Texas's Aransas Reserve pushing a boat ever closer to some of the 76 whooping cranes then left in the world. One lucky day, however, the biologists were hiding in tall grass when a pair of the critically endangered birds landed only 20 feet away. For nearly half an hour the cranes stood there and groomed each other. Eventually they flew away, but the awed humans got their picture, and it made the cover.

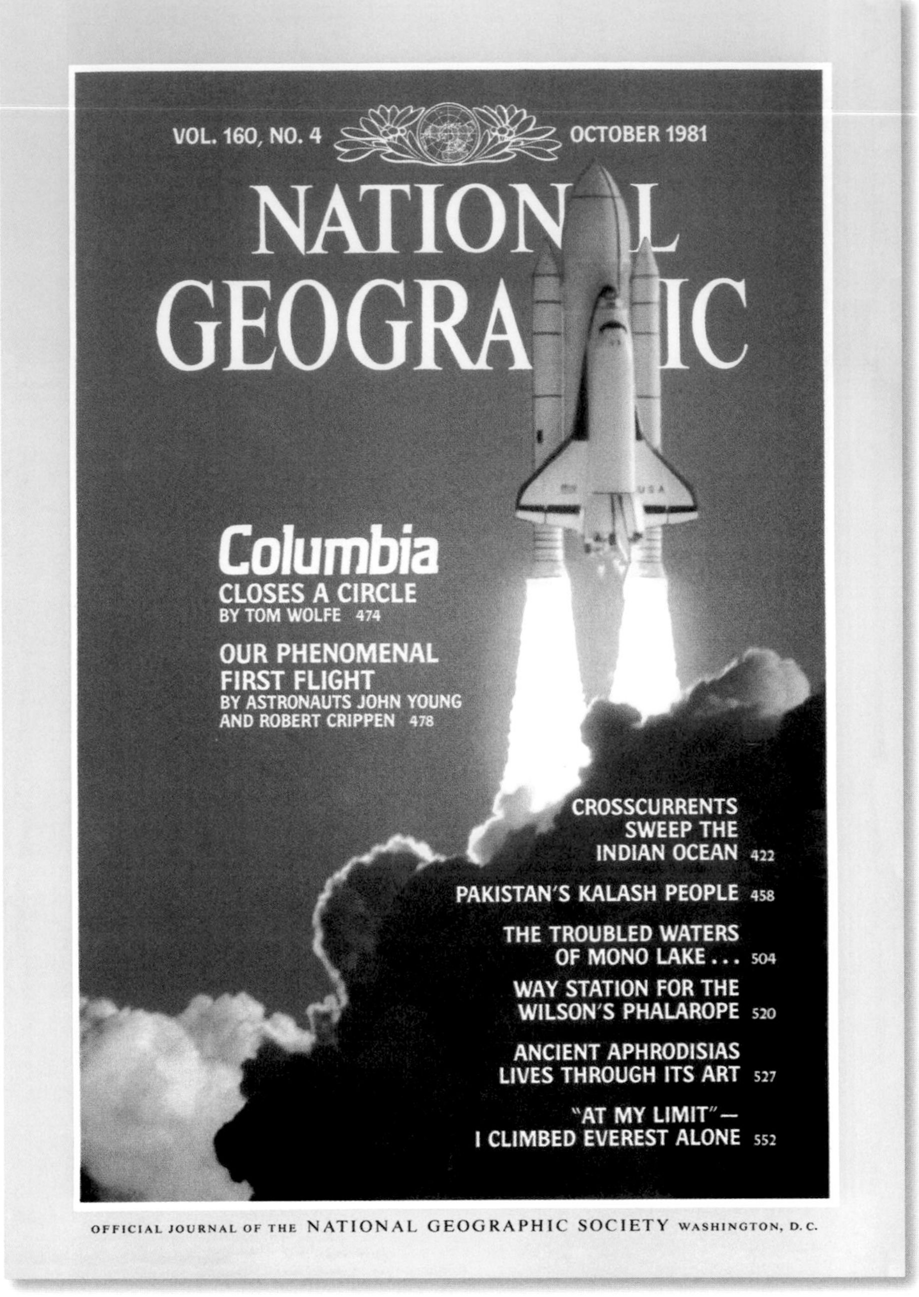

OCTOBER | JON SCHNEEBERGER

▲ **LIFTOFF** Since no one would be allowed within miles of the pad when *Columbia* blasted off from Cape Canaveral, a *National Geographic* team led by Illustrations Editor Jon Schneeberger set up a ring of strategically located, remotely triggered, shock-resistant cameras to make dramatic photographs of the liftoff—one of which appeared on this October 1981 cover.

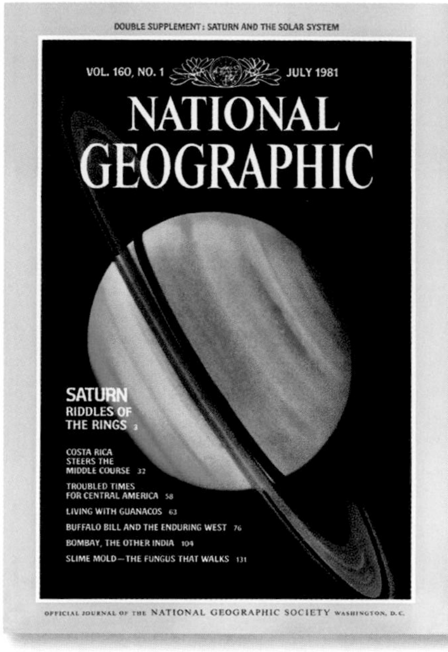

JULY | NASA

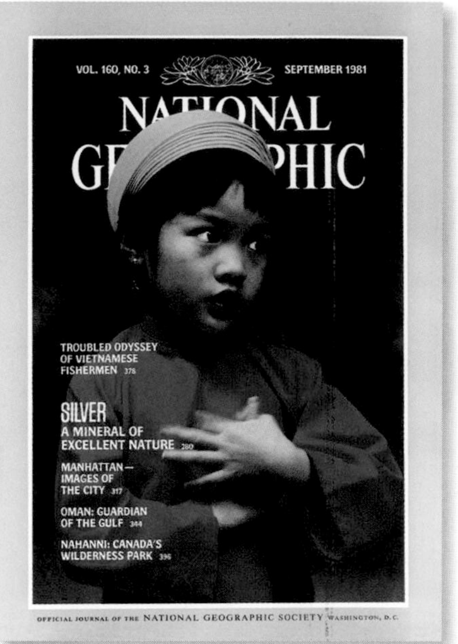

SEPTEMBER | STEVE WALL

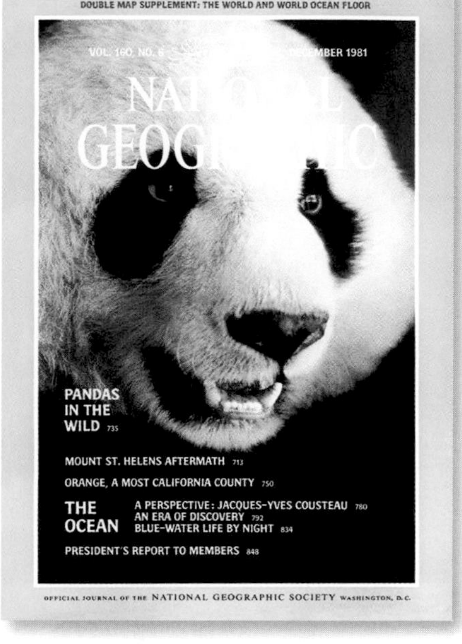

DECEMBER | GEORGE B. SCHALLER

HAIL, *COLUMBIA!*

On April 12, 1981, nearly 80,000 people were present while millions more watched on television as *Columbia* lifted off from Cape Canaveral on the first flight of a space shuttle. Perhaps no one fully realized how dangerous that high frontier would prove to be—because two decades after that historic first flight, on February 1, 2003, *Columbia* would disintegrate and its seven crew members would perish.

> It is this, the unspeakable danger—and the term "danger" is itself taboo among the pilots—that has always given the phrase *the first flight* such a righteous aura among test pilots. And what great first flights remain? It has been 18 years since Milt Thompson, for NASA, and Yeager, for the Air Force, made the first flights of a wingless aircraft (lifting body) at Edwards. It has been 13 years since the X-15 made its final flight. The flight of *Columbia* in April may prove to be the last historic first flight in this century.
>
> —*From* "Columbia *Closes a Circle,*" *Tom Wolfe*

▲ **PANDA-MONIUM** Although in 1980 George Schaller became the first Western biologist invited to China to study the rare giant panda in the wild, the *Geographic*'s editors chose one of his pictures of a panda living in a captive-breeding facility for the cover. The wild bears proved elusive targets in the thick bamboo clothing the hillsides on the Wolong National Nature Reserve. Nevertheless, Schaller was soon proving that panda populations were plummeting largely due to their being captured for zoos, and not because of periodic bamboo diebacks, as was formerly believed.

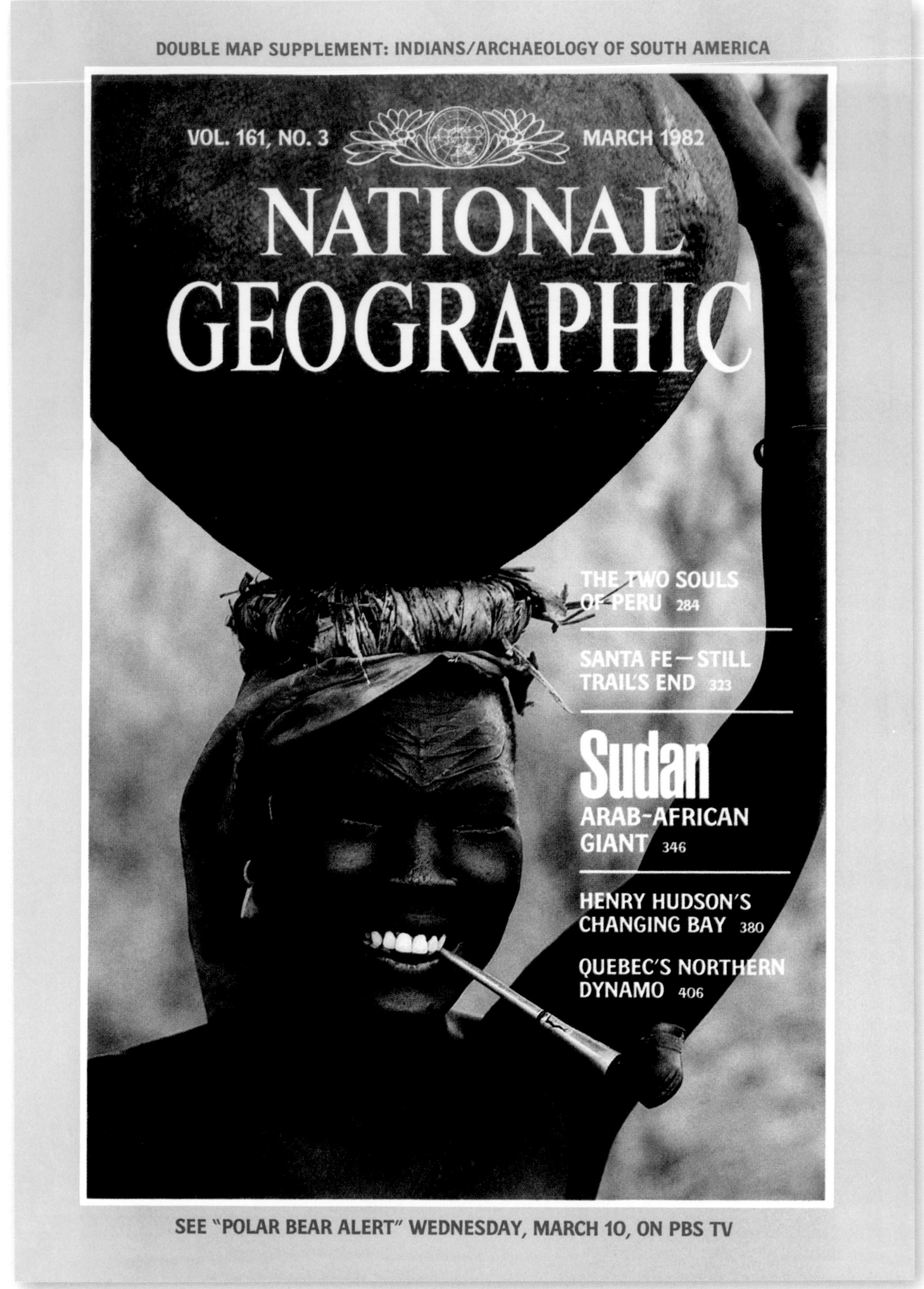

MARCH | ROBERT CAPUTO

SUDANESE SMILE Her face adorned with the chevron-like scar of the Mondari tribe, this Sudanese woman seems amused by the presence of writer-photographer Bob Caputo. He visited her cattle-herding people during his journey across a country a third the size of the contiguous U.S. but with only 800 miles of paved roads.

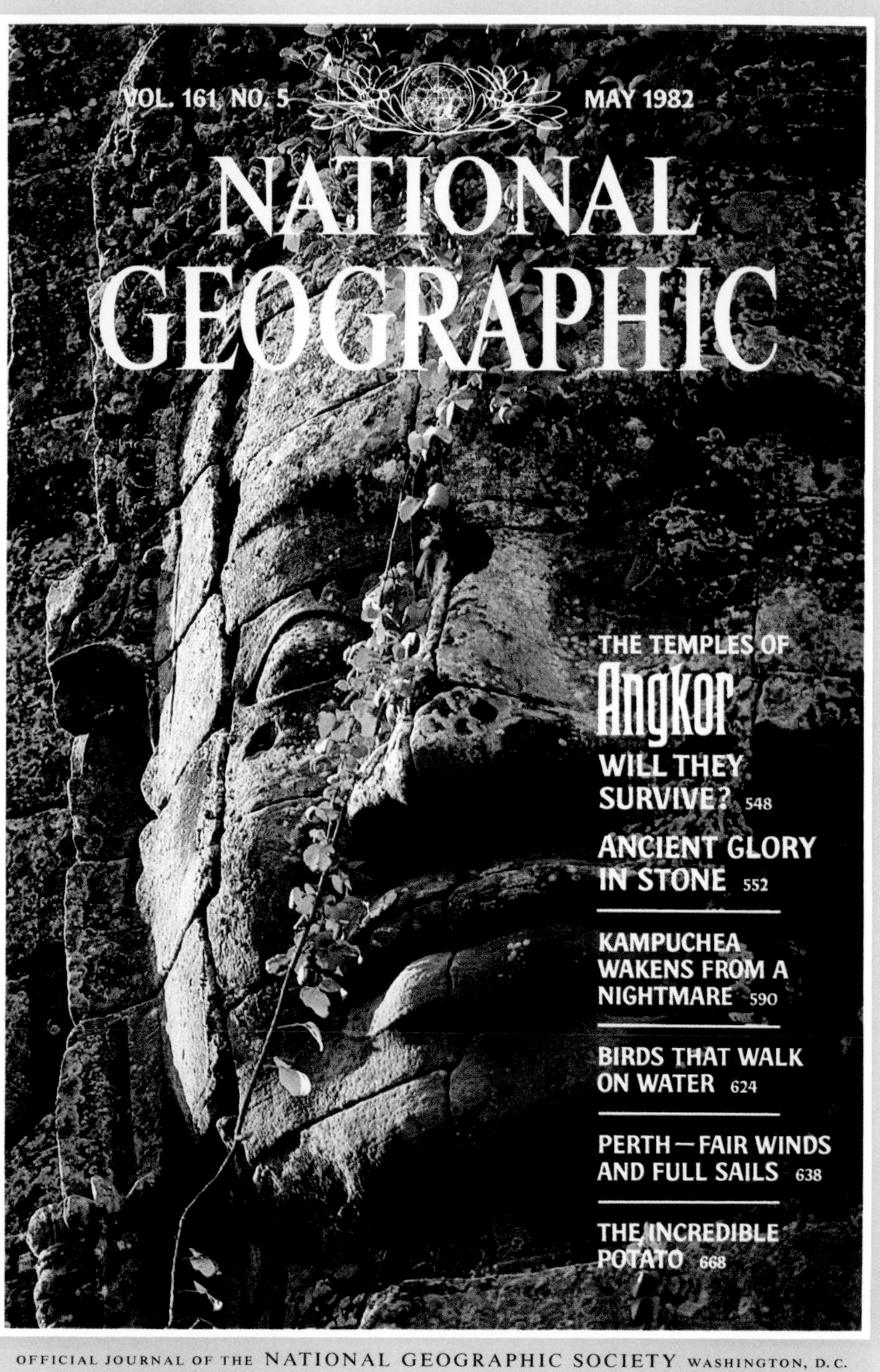

MAY | DAVID ALAN HARVEY

RISKING IT ALL A stone face at Angkor might seem the image of blissful repose, but the journey to the famous Cambodian temples was a nerve-wracking one for David Alan Harvey. The Khmer Rouge had recently been toppled, but mass graves were still everywhere and menacing ex-soldiers were always lurking in the nearby jungles.

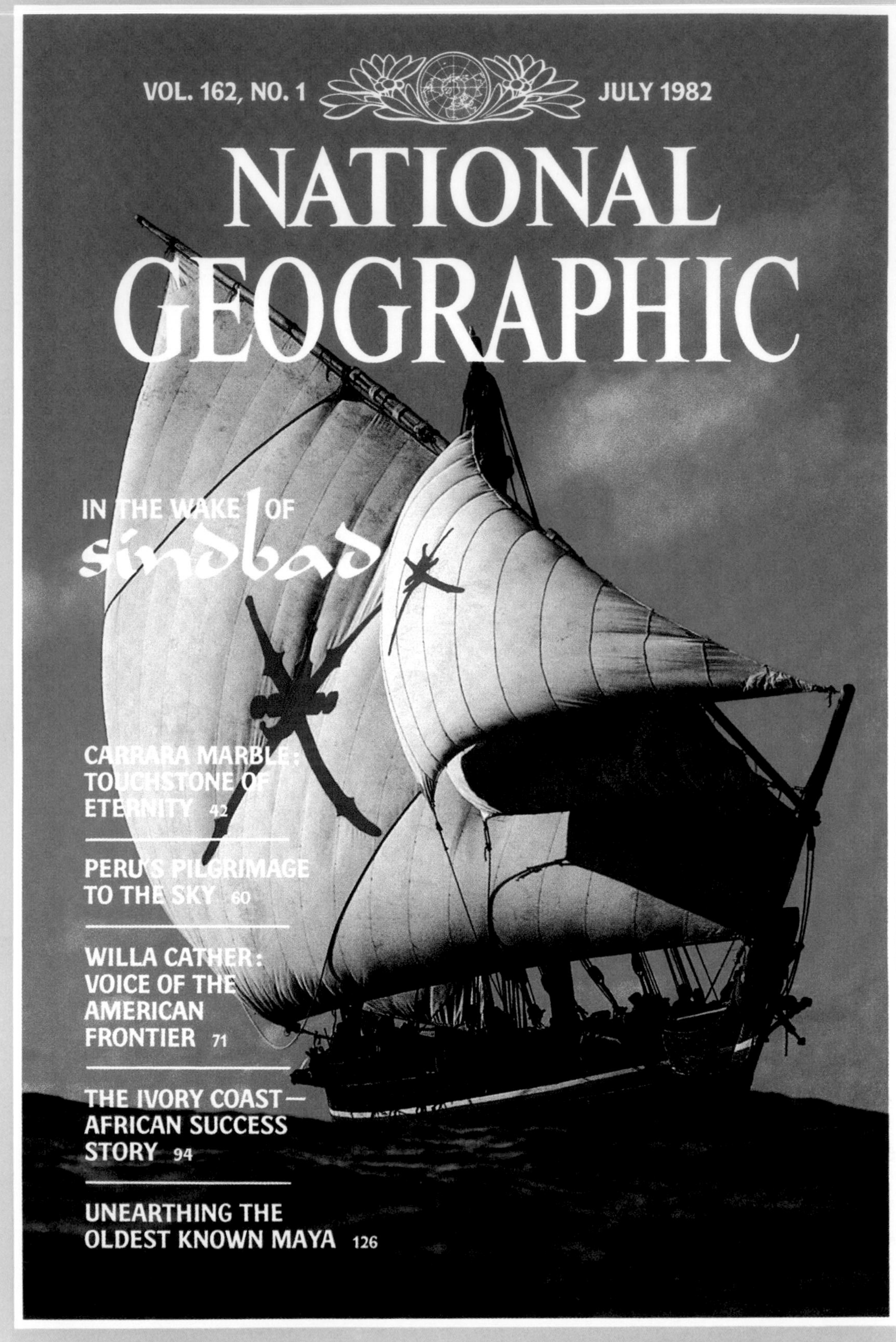

JULY | RICHARD GREENHILL A replica of an Arab dhow that Sinbad might recognize puts to sea.

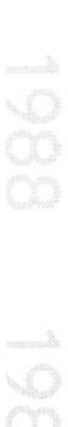

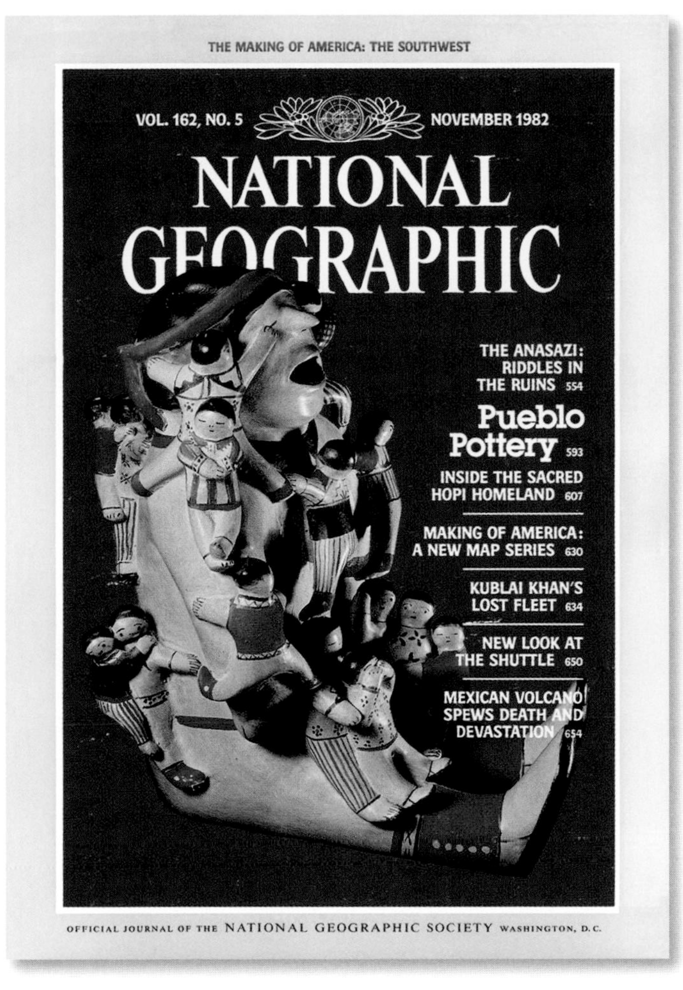

NOVEMBER | JERRY D. JACKA

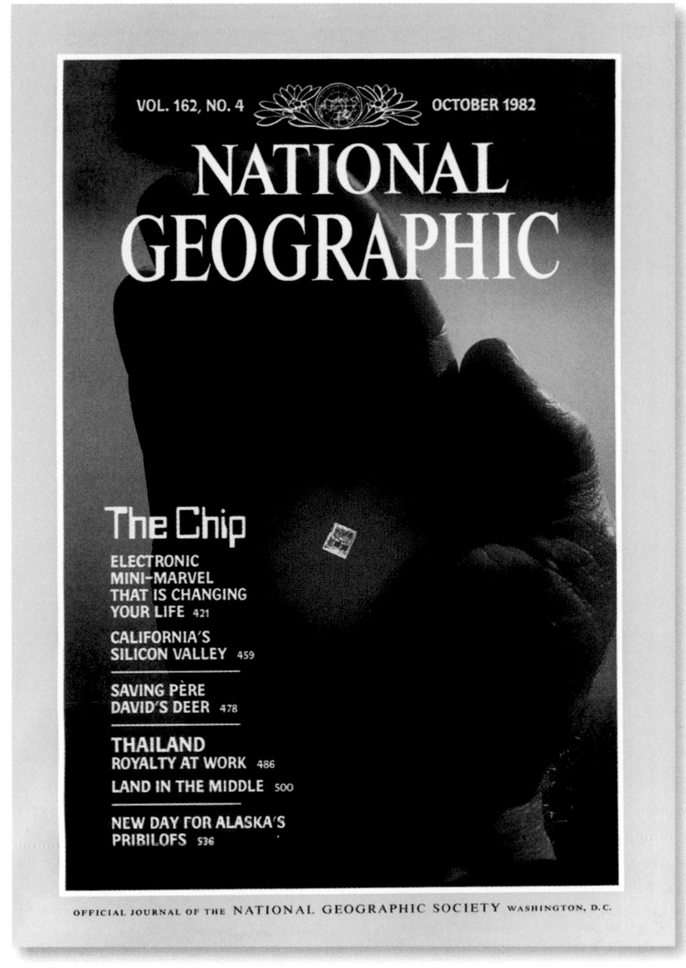

OCTOBER | CHARLES O'REAR

▲ **TELL US A STORY** A ceramic storyteller surrounded by eager children—a motif perhaps thousands of years old—was made using ancient methods by the celebrated artist Helen Cordero (1915–1994) of New Mexico's Cochiti Pueblo.

> *"Cordero's storyteller model was her grandfather. Recalling with affection the tales he told in her youth, she models him with clinging listeners wearing expressions of rapture or fright, depending on the story."*
>
> —David L. Arnold
> *from "Pueblo Pottery"*

▲ **SMALL WONDER** A chip in the palm might be worth two or more old mainframes, even in 1982, only a year after the IBM PC appeared and two years before the first Apple Macintosh debuted. It also makes a simple but striking cover for a story that took Charles O'Rear a year to photograph and flooded the office with more than 18,700 pictures. The ability of the integrated circuit, or "chip," to embody logic and memory gave it, according to author Allen Boraiko, the "essence of human intellect . . . and much the same potential to alter life fundamentally." To O'Rear, speaking of his coverage in a different vein but just as prophetically, "At times it was like stepping into the 21st century."

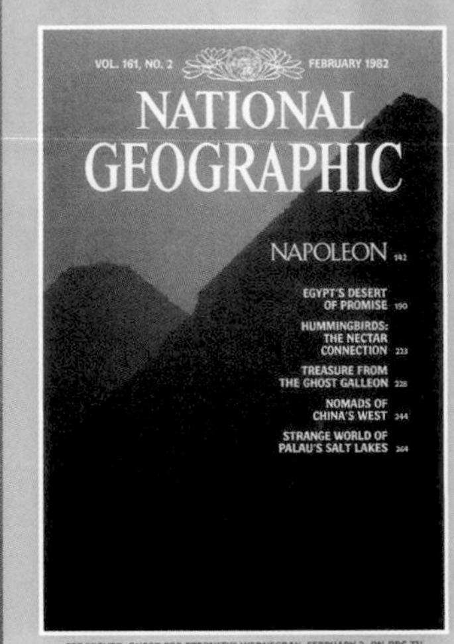

COVER STORY

MOVING THE PYRAMIDS

FEBRUARY 1982 | GORDON W. GAHAN

See the Pyramids—and now look again. It's the same picture, only they appear differently on the cover, thanks to some early digital manipulation. Editor Bill Garrett defended the controversial step. "The effect was the same as if the photographer had moved over a few feet," he wrote three years later. Nevertheless, such experiments were quickly abandoned, and *National Geographic* soon renounced all manipulation of elements in photographs—moving things around, in other words—a pledge it remains committed to today.

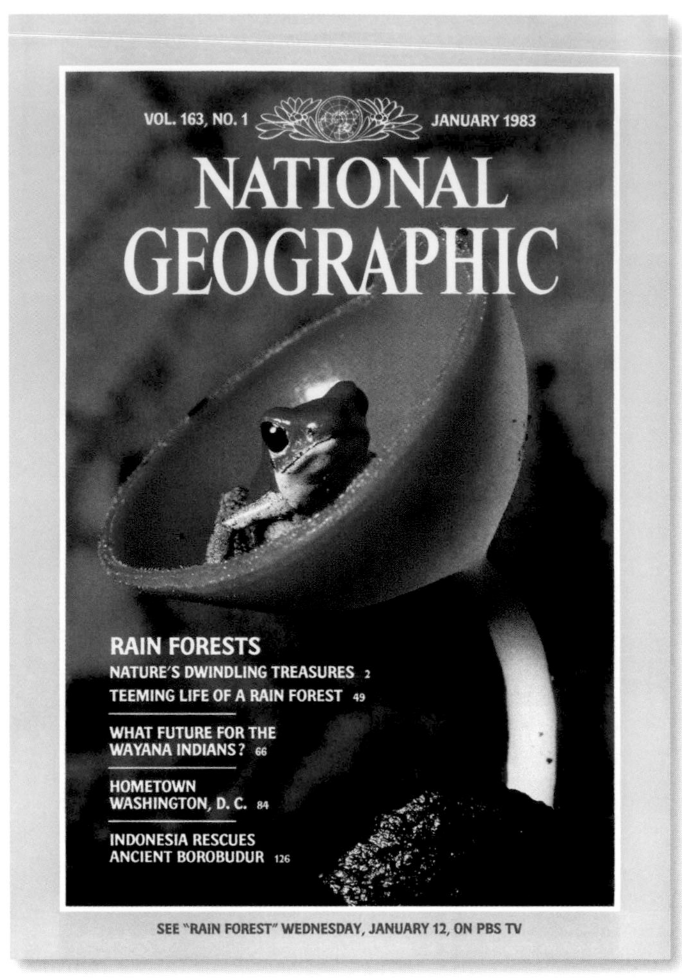

JANUARY | CAROL AND DAVID HUGHES

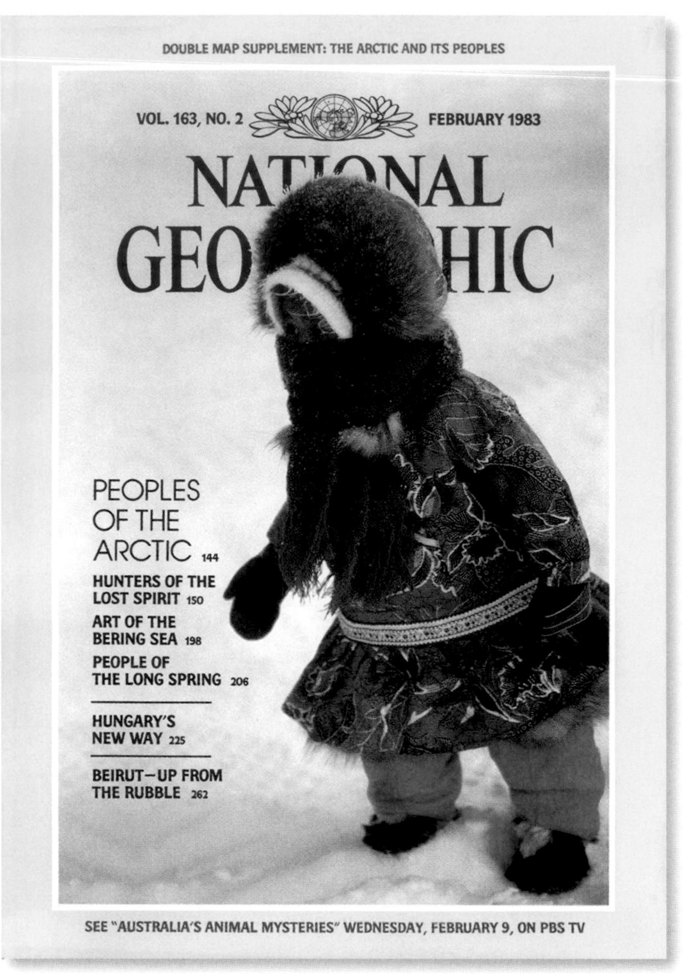

FEBRUARY | DAVID ALAN HARVEY

▲ **KING OF THE JUNGLE** A poison dart frog, about the size of a thumbnail, finds a mushroom's cup makes a suitable throne in Costa Rica's Corcovado National Park. The males of *Oophaga granulifera* seek out such high perches to better trumpet their love songs, the amatory *zeet, zeet, zeets* sounding, to Carol and David Hughes, like "tiny saws rasping wood." It rained every day of the 18 months that the filmmaking couple worked in those damp forests, but drenched as they were they still managed to document most aspects of the tiny amphibian's courtship and breeding rituals.

▲ **KEEP WARM!** An Inupiat child in Kiana, Alaska, might be dressed for subzero weather, but her eyes blaze with the observant look of the hunter.

> *"Many Alaska natives consider themselves under cultural siege. They find their fulfillment on the land and fear the day new laws put limits on their harvest. For them hunting and fishing are not only essential, but are also powerful psychological needs."*
>
> —Priit Vesilind
> *from "Hunters of the Lost Spirit"*

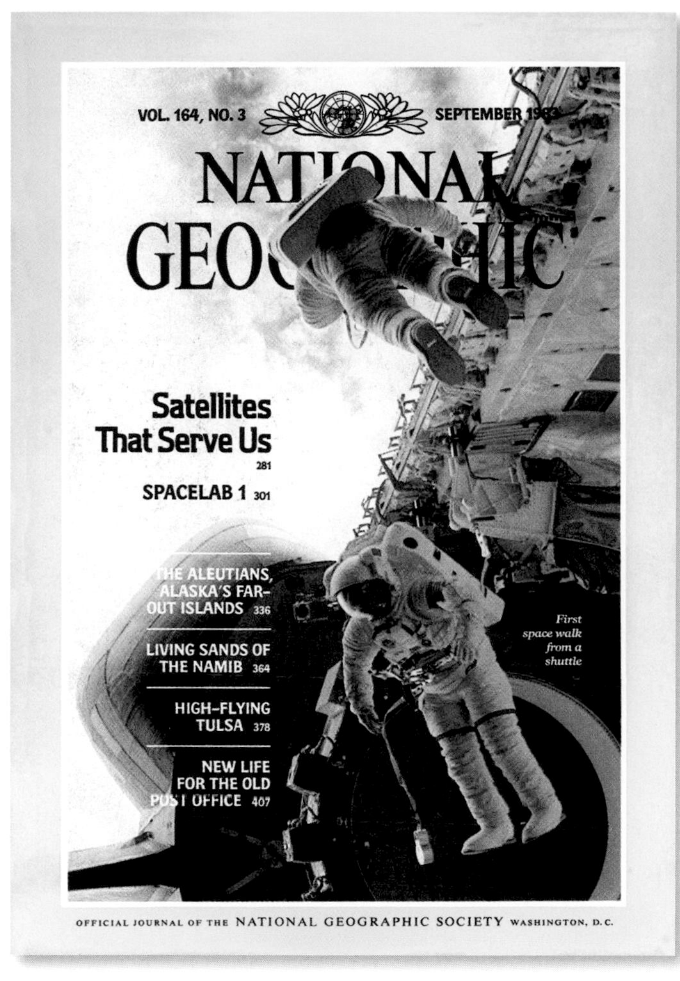

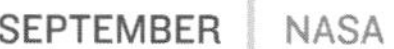
SEPTEMBER | NASA

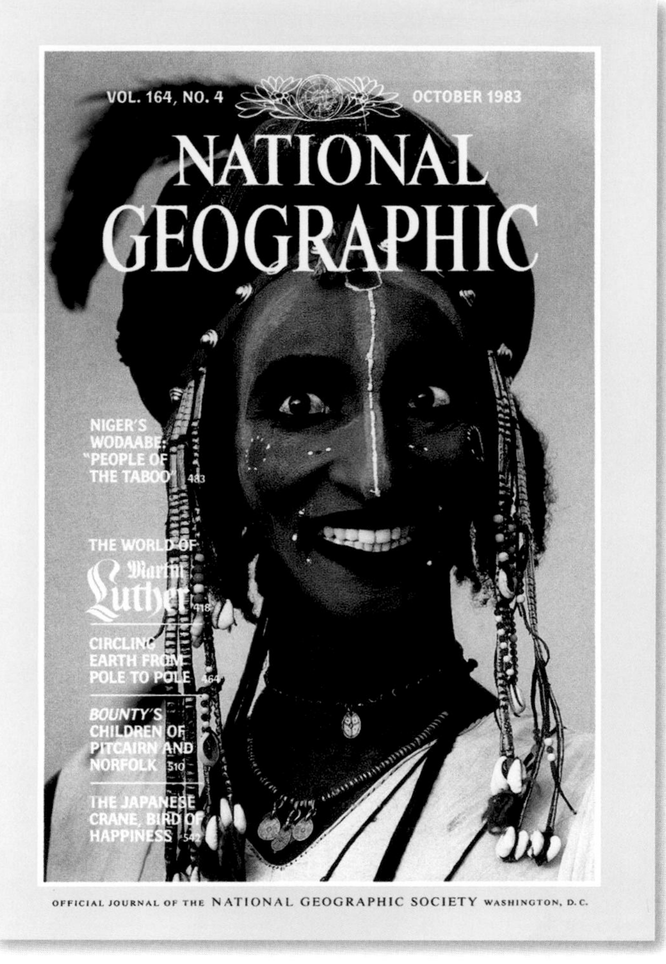

OCTOBER | CAROL BECKWITH

▲ **THE GRANDEST VIEW** "It's so bright out here!" were the first words spoken on the first space walk ever made from a shuttle. They came from Dr. Story Musgrave—the lower figure on the cover, in the cargo bay alongside Donald Peterson, seen above, both men being photographed from the aft widow of *Challenger*'s flight deck—and were spoken at the beginning of a four-hour test of suits and techniques. Earth was neither up nor down for Musgrave on that April 7, 1983, sortie; it was just everywhere, affording an eyeball-filling vision of the "totality of humanity within a single orbit. It's a history lesson and a geography lesson; a sight like you've never seen."

▲ **FAIREST OF THEM ALL** The winner of a Wodaabe beauty contest preens for the camera. He—yes, he—must have impressed the judges, especially the women, with his attractively rolling eyes. Most of the year the nomadic Wodaabe drove their zebu cattle across the dusty Sahel of Niger, and the men looked suitably lean, mean, and thoroughly masculine to Carol Beckwith, who lived with the tribe for 18 months. Yet whenever the rains broke it was festival time, and the herdsmen engaged in a week-long marathon of painting, primping, and dancing, each competing for various prizes. This beauty contest winner's equally charming cousin offered to make Beckwith his second wife and inquired about the number of cattle he should offer her Boston-based father. She politely declined.

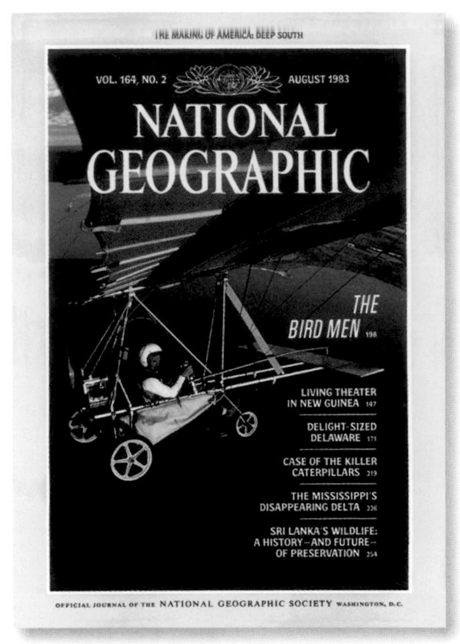

AUGUST | CHARLES O'REAR

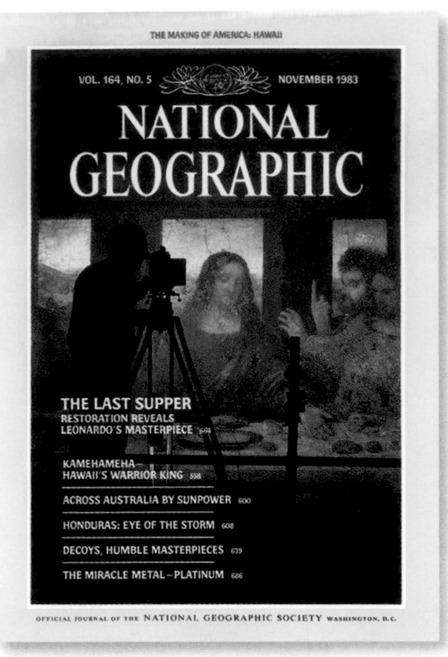

NOVEMBER | O. LOUIS MAZZATENTA

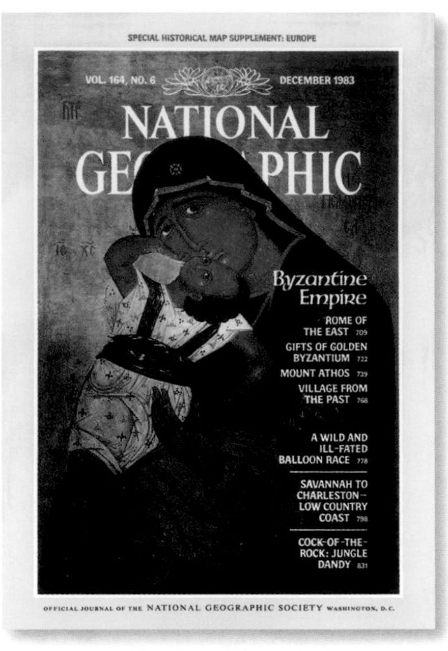

DECEMBER | JAMES L. STANFIELD

▲ **SOARING** High above Chase Lake, North Dakota, photographer Charles O'Rear—assigned to illustrate an article on ultralight aircraft—makes a self-portrait with a camera mounted on his wing tip.

> *"To fly like a bird, to cast off the bonds of gravity and soar free, wheeling through the sky with the wind rustling past our outstretched wings—who has not done so in his dreams?"*
>
> —Luis Marden
> *from "The Bird Men"*

ICY PLUNGE ▶

No, it's not something from an old science-fiction film. It's instead an "atmospheric diving suit," allowing humans to work on the seafloor in relative safety and comfort. Wearing it is underwater engineer Phil Nuytten, one of many specialists gathered on the six-foot-thick sea ice near Canada's Beechey Island, 500 miles north of the Arctic Circle. Chris Nicholson, designer of small underwater robots carrying video and still cameras, is also there. So is *National Geographic*'s Emory Kristof, a leading photographer of the deep dark abyss. Joining them is Dr. Joseph MacInnis, who discovered what lies 340 feet beneath their tent: the remains of H.M.S. *Breadalbane*, crushed by ice in 1853.

Divers wearing the suit recovered artifacts for museums. Meanwhile, Nicholson piloted a robot via joystick as Kristof, a video screen his viewfinder, remotely took footage and snapped hundreds of still photographs. The images depicted a ship, thanks to the cold water, still in immaculate condition, its planking, rudder, wheel, even its copper-sheathed hull appearing pristine—the best preserved wooden ship ever found on the seafloor.

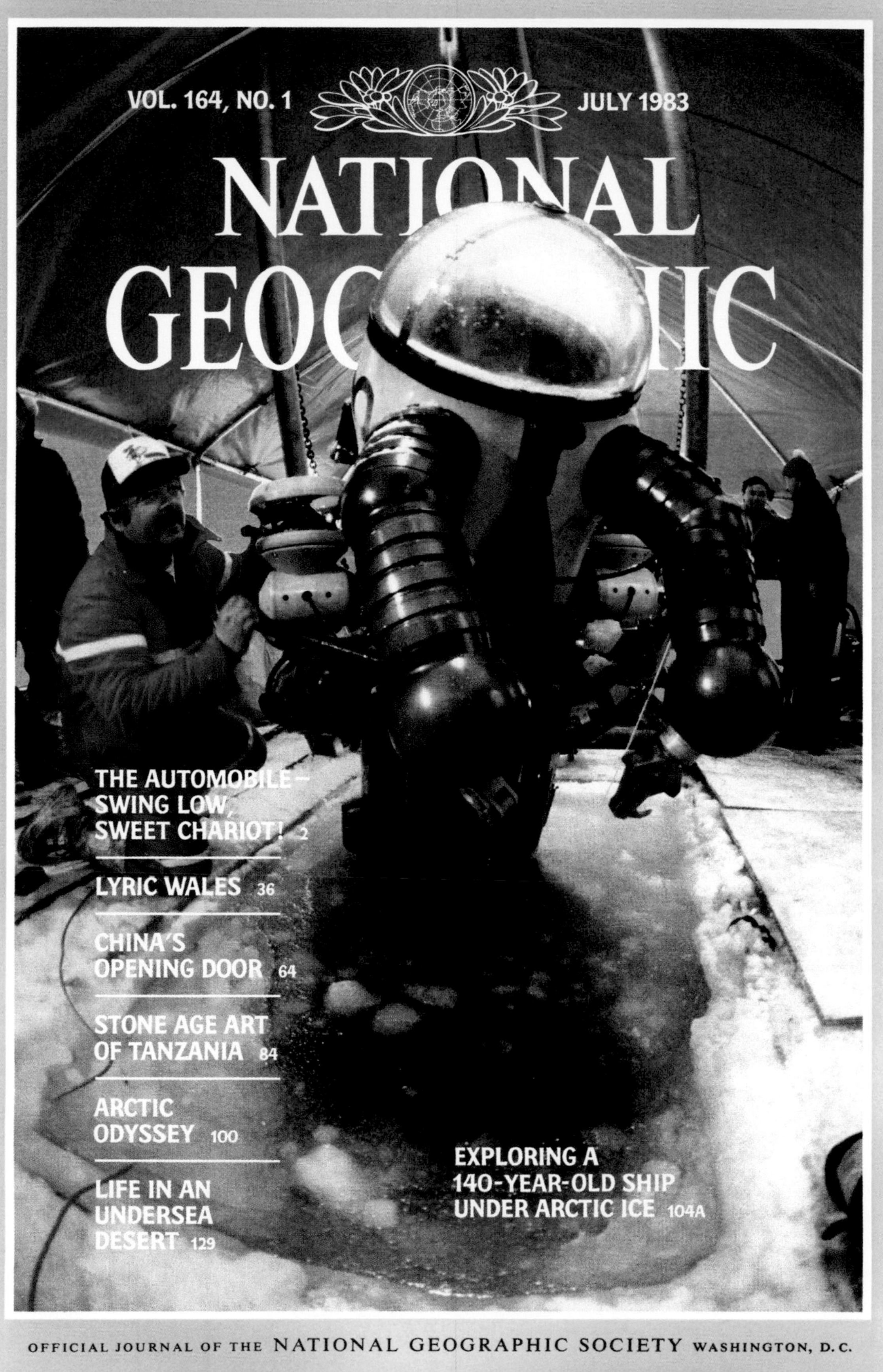

JULY | EMORY KRISTOF Phil Nuytten suits up to explore a 340-foot-deep Arctic shipwreck.

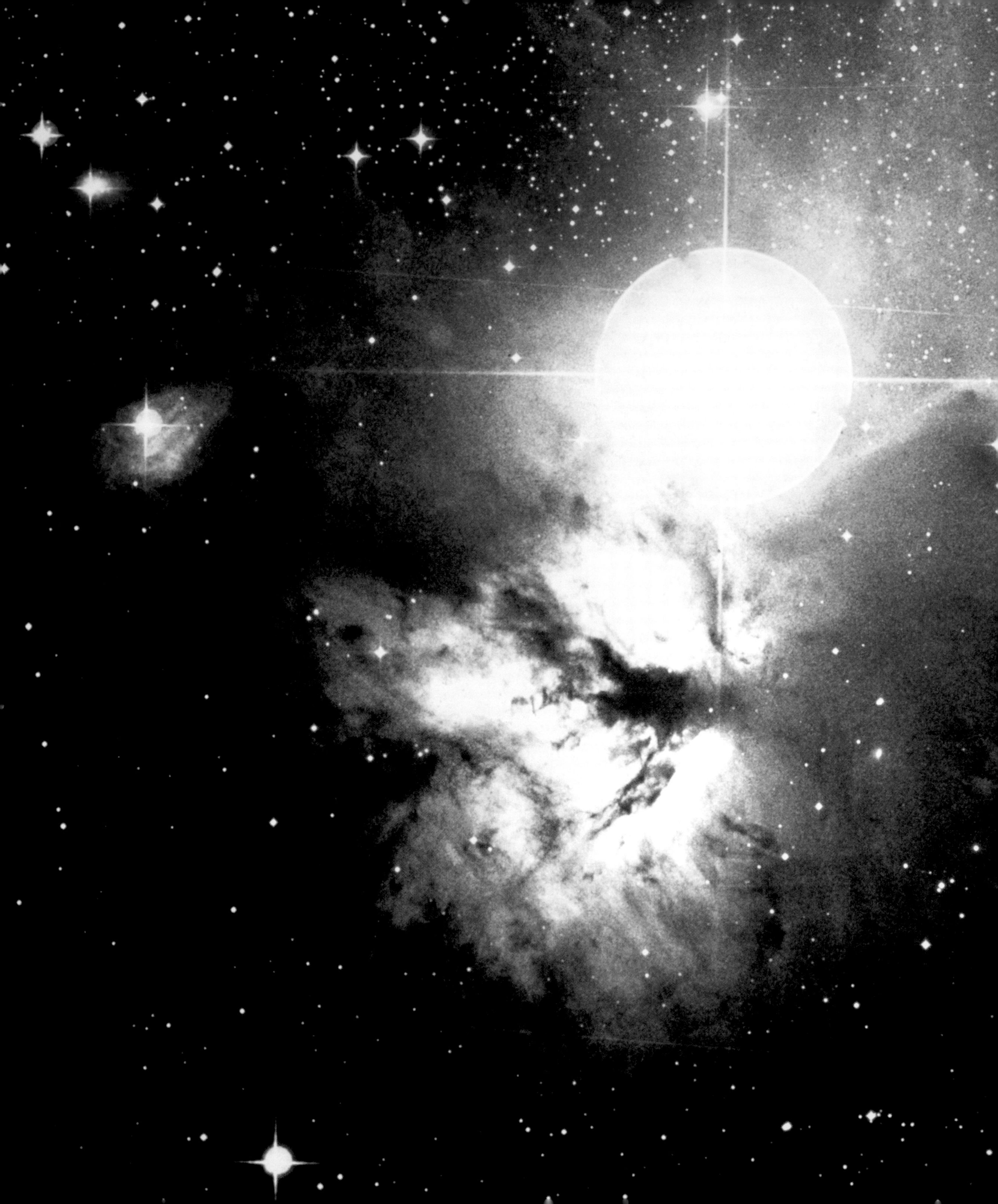

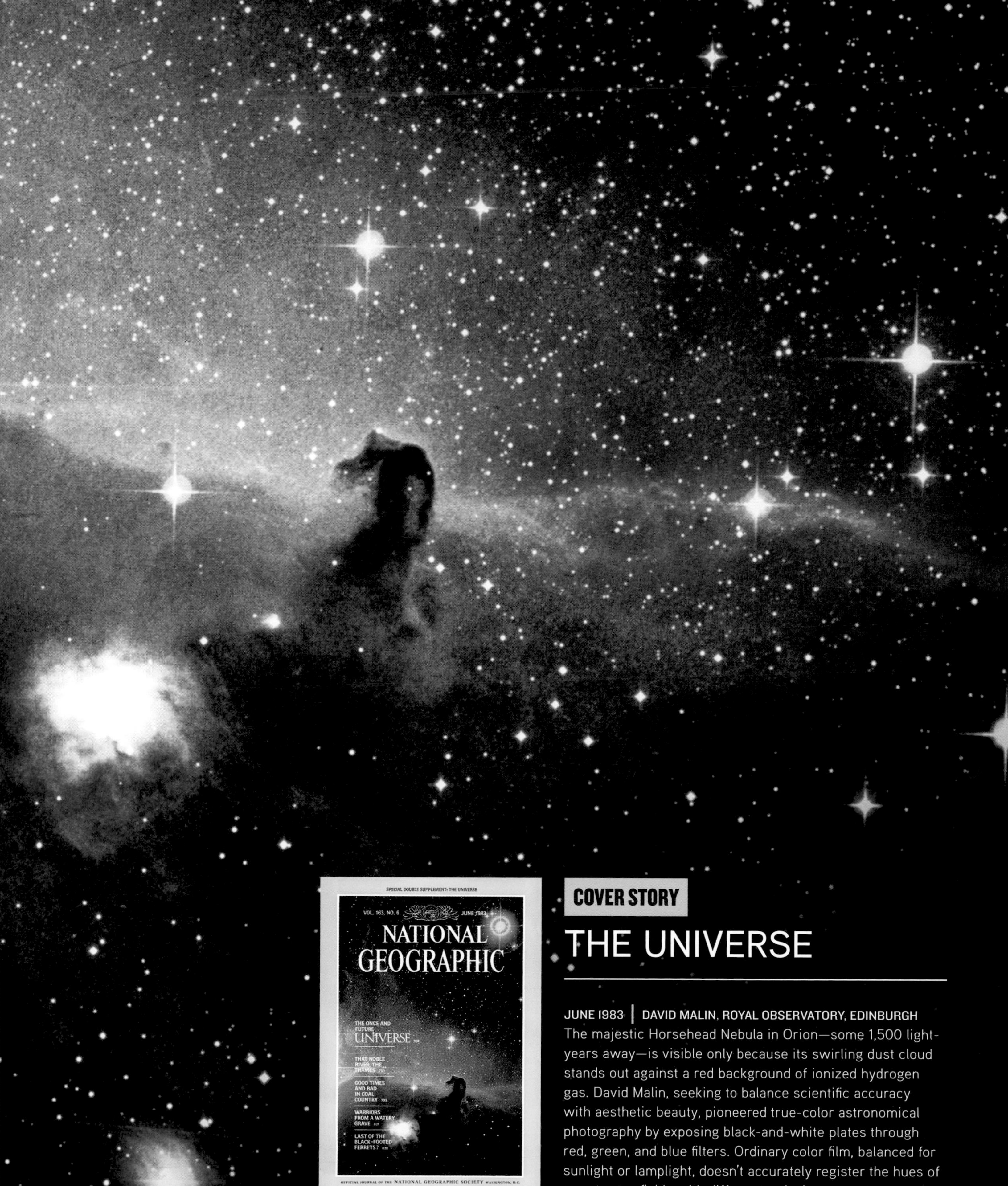

COVER STORY

THE UNIVERSE

JUNE 1983 | DAVID MALIN, ROYAL OBSERVATORY, EDINBURGH
The majestic Horsehead Nebula in Orion—some 1,500 light-years away—is visible only because its swirling dust cloud stands out against a red background of ionized hydrogen gas. David Malin, seeking to balance scientific accuracy with aesthetic beauty, pioneered true-color astronomical photography by exposing black-and-white plates through red, green, and blue filters. Ordinary color film, balanced for sunlight or lamplight, doesn't accurately register the hues of remote star fields with different emission spectra.

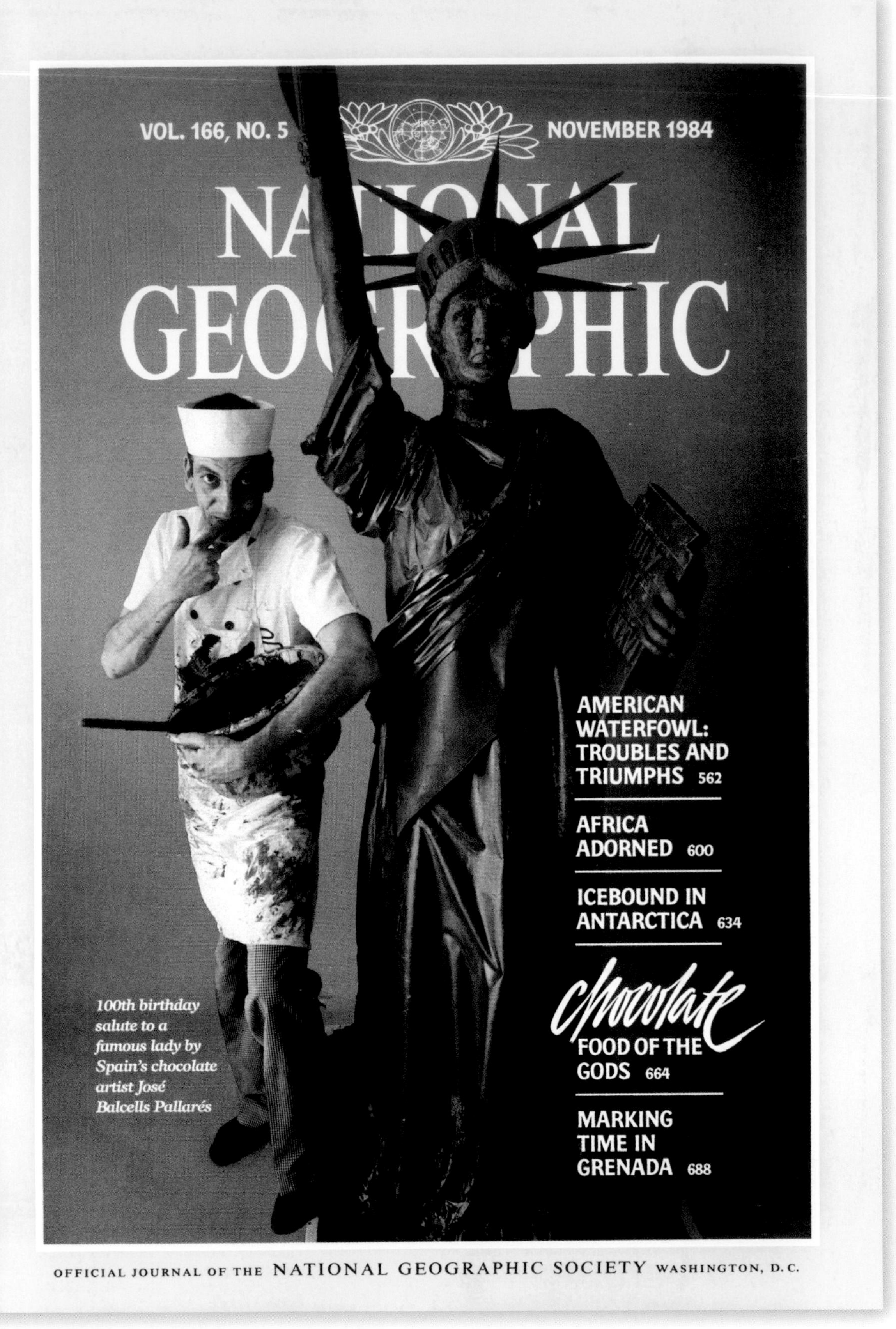

NOVEMBER | JAMES L. STANFIELD

SWEET LIBERTY Barcelona chocolatier José Balcells Pallarés, sculpting a 229-pound Statue of Liberty in honor of the monument's upcoming centennial, samples a portion of his specialty. Photographer Jim Stanfield roamed the cacao groves of West Africa as well as the confectionaries of Europe to depict the world's favorite delicacy, chocolate.

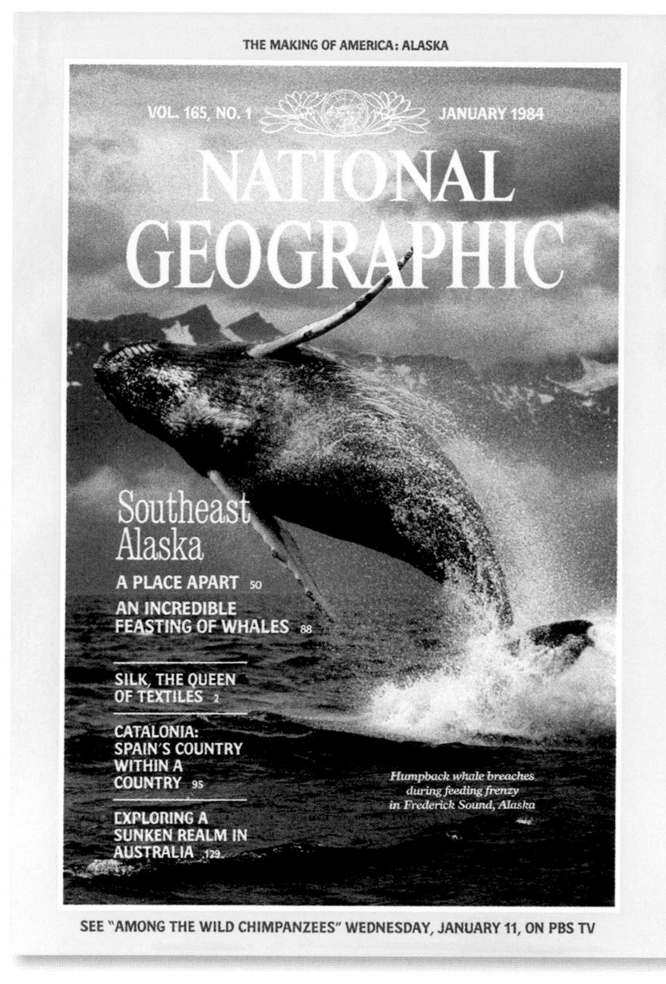

JANUARY | AL GIDDINGS

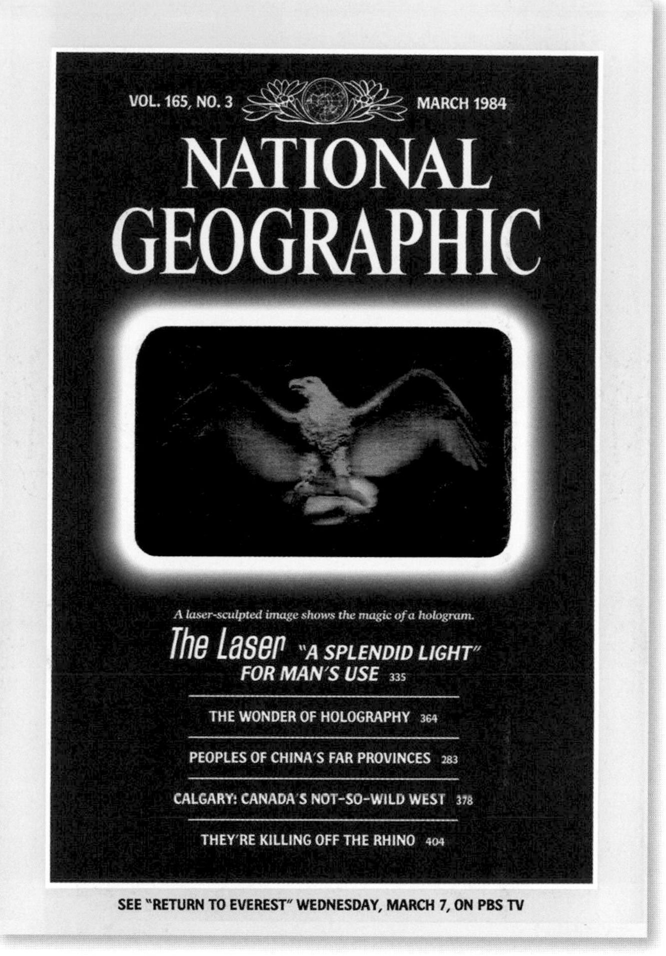

MARCH | AMERICAN BANK NOTE COMPANY

▲ **ONE GIANT LEAP** A humpback whale caught in mid-breach was only one of the dramatic sights witnessed by Al Giddings and his crew as they filmed the cetaceans in Alaska's Frederick Sound. They found themselves in the midst of a "bubble net," a cooperative feeding strategy employed by the whales. As one group circled around a school of prey, tighter and tighter, another one drove up beneath the "net," blowing bubbles and forcing the small fry to congregate near the surface where they were more easily swallowed by the leaping humpbacks.

▲ **IN 3-D** Sculpted by intersecting laser beams, a 3-D holographic image of a model eagle becomes the first hologram ever printed by any major magazine.

"Striking as he is, our little eagle offers more than graphic novelty—he gives us a peek into an onrushing technological storm based on the marriage of computer sciences and the laser beam."

—Wilbur E. Garrett

from Editor's Page, National Geographic, *March 1984*

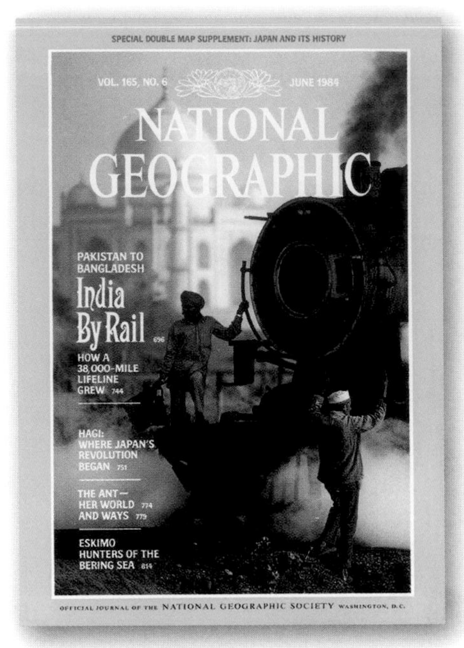

JUNE 1984 | STEVE MCCURRY

▲ **LOST LOVE** The Taj Mahal shimmering in the distance might have been an everyday sight to railroad workers in industrial Agra. But it was never so to its builder, Shah Jahan, fifth Mogul emperor of India, who raised the marble mausoleum to honor a late lamented wife, Mumtaz Mahal. Later imprisoned by a usurper in Agra's Red Fort, he was said to have gazed out of his window at the glorious structure day after day, until came the day when he, too, was laid in its crypt.

▶ **JUNE 1984** | **STEVE MCCURRY** Breakfast between Peshawar and Lahore means passing trays from the dining car to first class.

INDIA BY RAIL ▶

THE UNEXPECTED. It met Steve McCurry everywhere he went during the four months he spent riding Indian railways from Pakistan to Bangladesh. Cows and monkeys wandering through crowded, monumental railway stations. Barbers plying their trade on train platforms. Waiters passing trays between the dining car and first class because the inside doors were locked for security. And in the gritty, industrial city of Agra, the dreamlike domes of the Taj Mahal floating above the smokestacks.

He spent five days in Agra, hoping to make an image of railroad life juxtaposed against those shimmering domes. He spent one of those days following a local track inspector, who even rode a handcar past the Taj. But the best shot came by chance. As he was walking down the track from Agra Fort Station, he saw engineers shunting old steam engines around the rail yard. It was just a matter of getting in the right position and waiting. Eventually they moved a steam locomotive into just the right position along just the right track where those floating domes could be seen to best advantage—and he got his picture (left).

> *"India. How does this vast overpopulated subcontinent manage to run, and even to prosper? For 130 years the chief reason has been the railway. Dusty and monumental, its trains often seem as ancient as India itself . . . Much of Indian life is lived within sight of the tracks or the station, and often next to the tracks, or inside the station."*
>
> —Paul Theroux
> *from "India By Rail"*

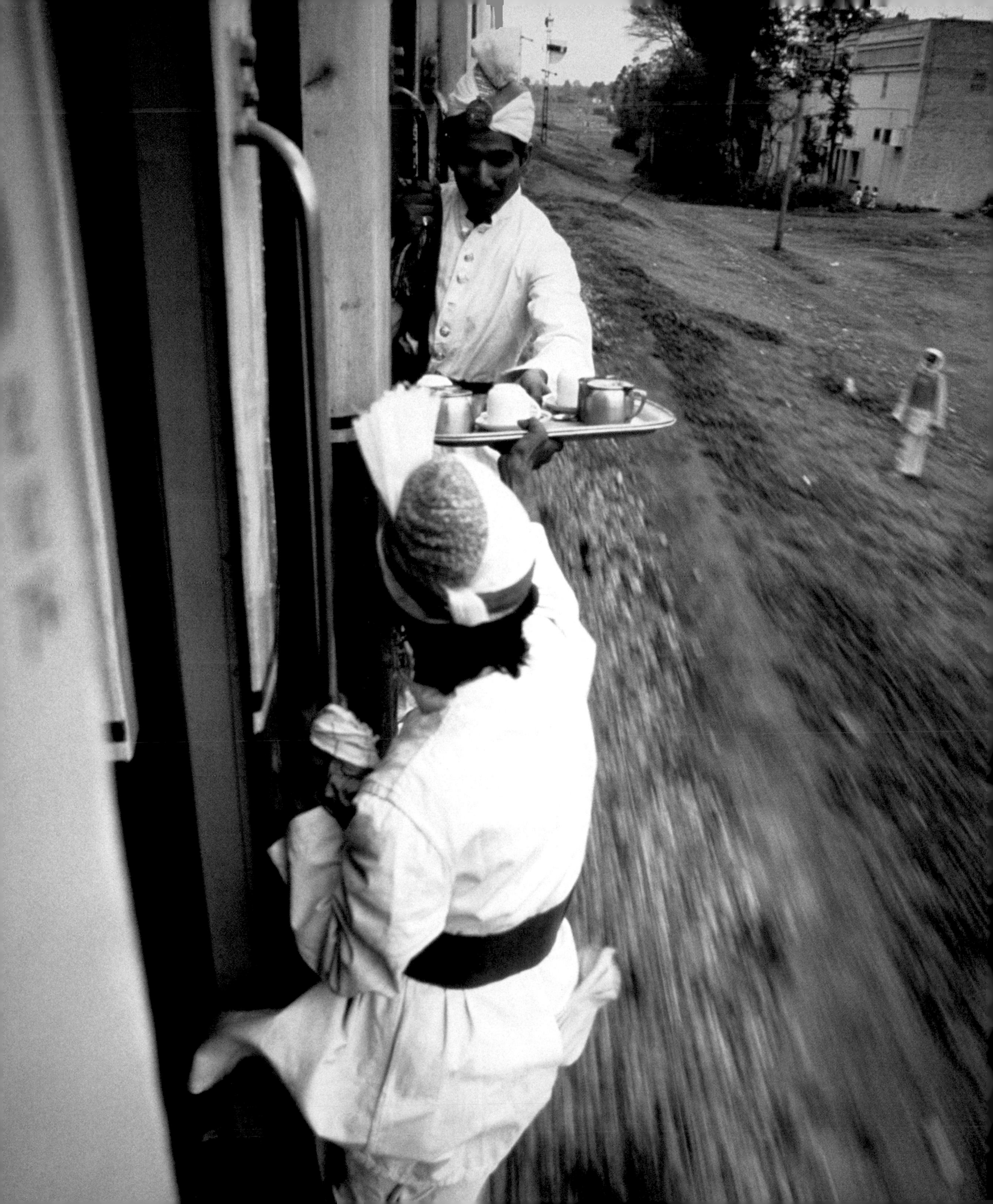

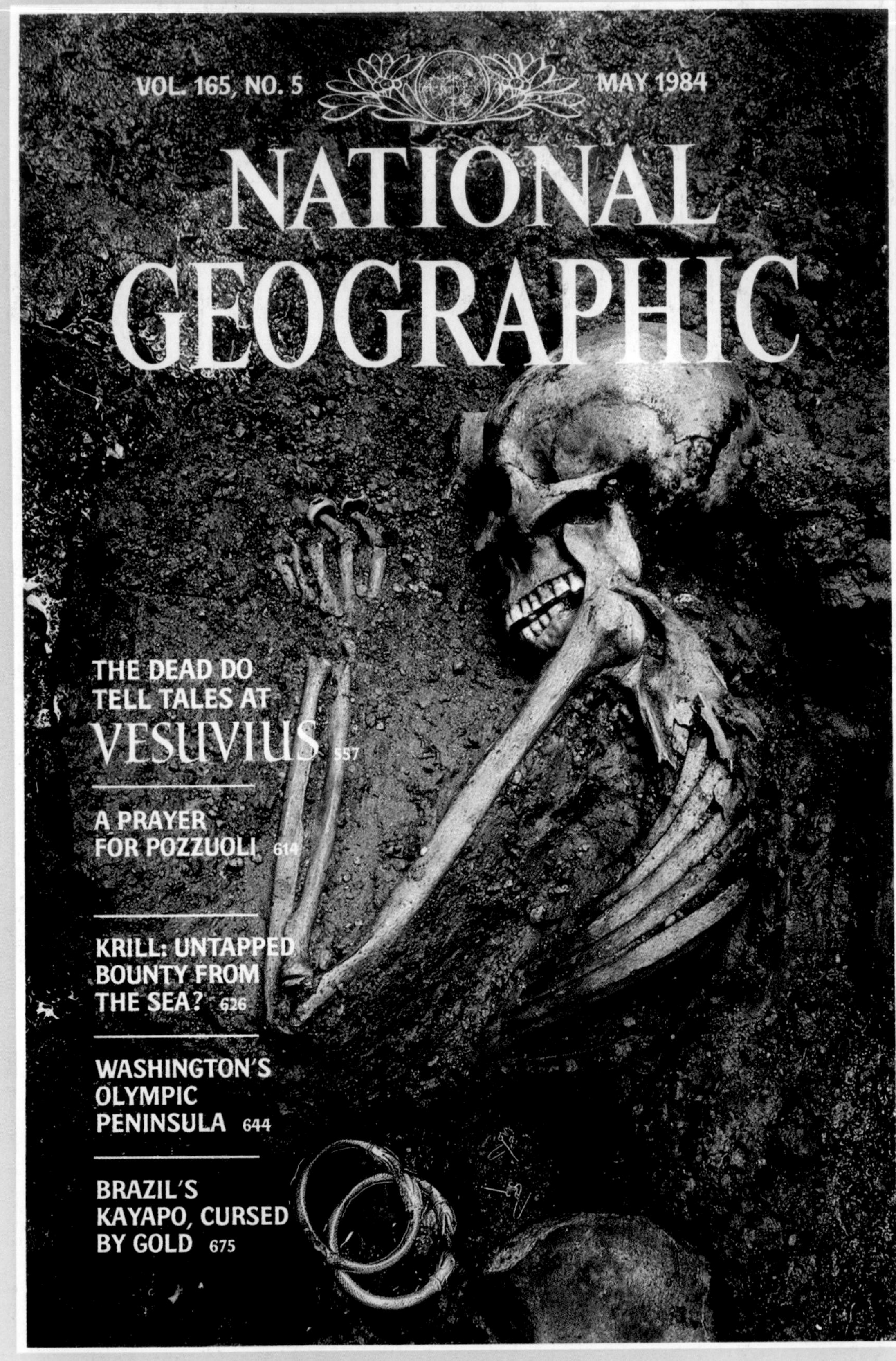

MAY | O. LOUIS MAZZATENTA A skeleton unearthed at Herculaneum, found with gold rings, bracelets, and earrings

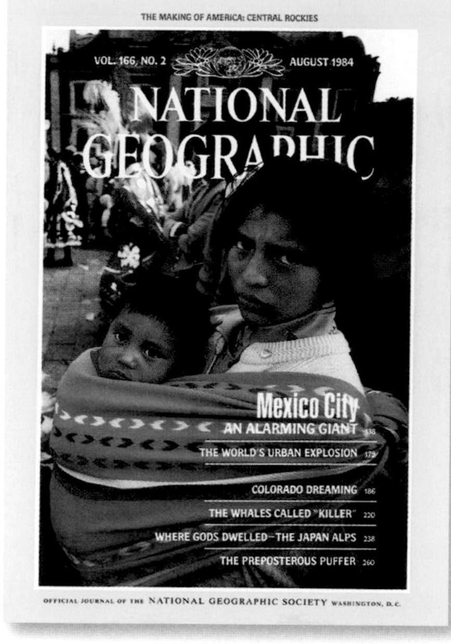

AUGUST | STEPHANIE MAZE

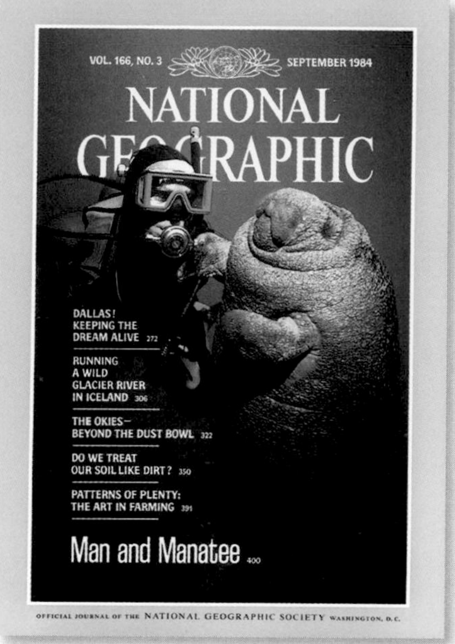

SEPTEMBER | FRED BAVENDAM

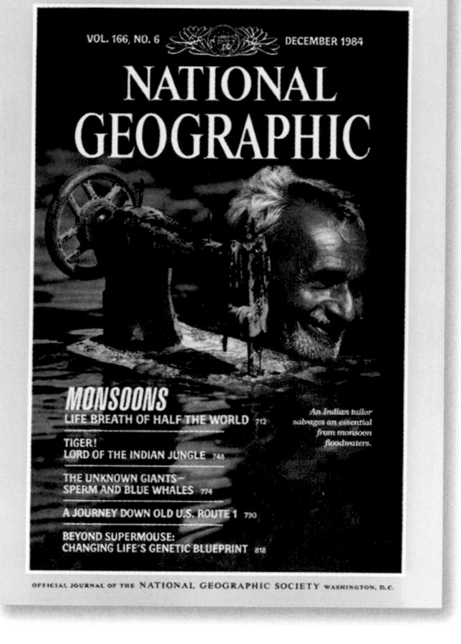

DECEMBER | STEVE MCCURRY

TALES OF THE DEAD

A TREASURE OF JEWELS was found with the skeleton of a 45-year-old woman, killed when Italy's Vesuvius erupted in A.D. 79, burying Herculaneum and Pompeii in burning ash.

> Amid death's shades the glint of gold . . . and the echo of love. "She was certainly homely, but someone cared enough to give her beautiful things," said physical anthropologist Sara Bisel . . . A bird struts across the carnelian set in one of her two gold rings, while jasper enhances the other. Jasper also gleamed as eyes on the snake heads of her two gold bracelets. Pearls probably adorned the golden tips of earrings, made for pierced ears.
>
> *—From "The Dead Do Tell Tales at Vesuvius," Rick Gore*

▲ **FLOODWATERS** Monsoon floodwaters don't bother this tailor, hoisting his antique sewing machine in Porbander, India. Even tea vendors hawked their beverages while practically swimming in the annual inundation. Steve McCurry spent four days in those chest-deep waters with floating garbage, sewage, and dead animals, and every night he picked leeches off his legs.

▼ **MAY 1984** | **O. LOUIS MAZZATENTA**
Another skeleton at Herculaneum

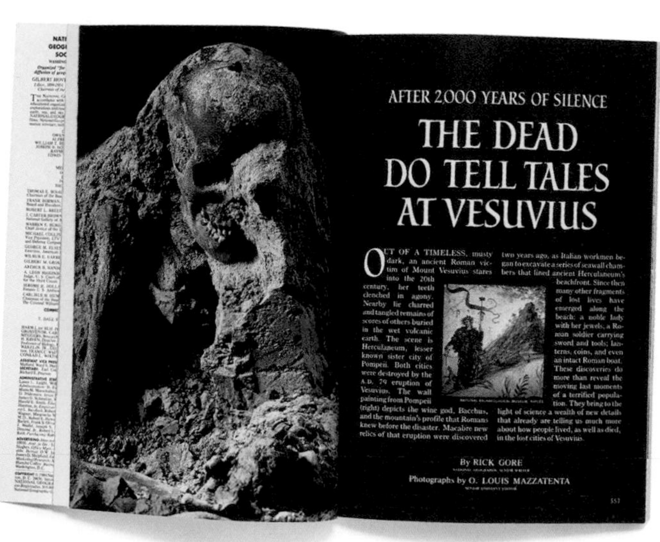

AFTER 2,000 YEARS OF SILENCE

THE DEAD DO TELL TALES AT VESUVIUS

OUT OF A TIMELESS, musty dark, an ancient Roman victim of Mount Vesuvius stares into the 20th century, her teeth clenched in agony. Nearby lie charred and tangled remains of scores of others buried in the wet volcanic earth. The scene is Herculaneum, lesser known sister city of Pompeii. Both cities were destroyed by the A.D. 79 eruption of Vesuvius. The wall painting from Pompeii (right) depicts the wine god, Bacchus, and the mountain's profile that Romans knew before the disaster. Macabre new relics of that eruption were discovered two years ago, as Italian workmen began to excavate a series of seawall chambers that lined ancient Herculaneum's beachfront. Since then many other fragments of lost lives have emerged along the beach: a noble lady with her jewels, a Roman soldier carrying sword and tools; lanterns, coins, and even an intact Roman boat. These discoveries do more than reveal the moving last moments of a terrified population. They bring to the light of science a wealth of new details that already are telling us much more about how people lived, as well as died, in the lost cities of Vesuvius.

By RICK GORE

Photographs by O. LOUIS MAZZATENTA

553

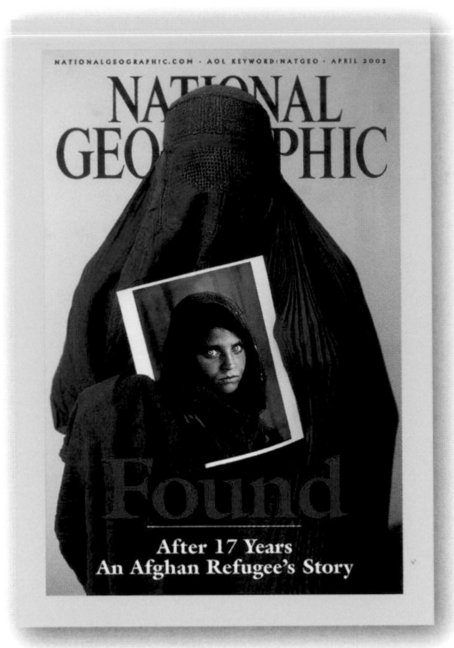

APRIL 2002 | STEVE MCCURRY

2002 ▸▸▸▸ FAST FORWARD

SEVENTEEN YEARS LATER he found her. The "Afghan Girl" had remained the unknown daughter of a distant tribe until the American invasion of her homeland in late 2001 scattered the Taliban. In January 2002 a National Geographic Television film crew helped McCurry locate her. Pictures handed to the elders at the Nasir Bagh refugee camp, just before it closed, helped track down her brother. Her name was Sharbat Gula—Sharbat meaning "sweet-water flower girl" in Pashto—and she was 28 to 30 years old, a married mother living in the mountains of Afghanistan. After being persuaded through intermediaries to journey to Peshawar, the veiled Sharbat and McCurry were briefly reunited. He photographed her, with her husband's permission, but otherwise they didn't have much to say. She was no longer a girl, but she still had those eyes—behind the usual burka.

THE AFGHAN GIRL ▸

LOOK ONCE MORE INTO those eyes: Is it a haunted gaze? A fearful one? A look of defiance? People have seen all manner of things in those mesmerizing eyes. In her own words, spoken many years later, she said she had been angry about being photographed.

Those eyes, of course, were the first things Steve McCurry noticed when invited into the tent turned makeshift girls' classroom in the overcrowded Nasir Bagh refugee camp near Peshawar. It was late 1984, and he was covering the plight of Afghans who had fled the Soviet gunships raining death and destruction upon their villages. The girl with the green eyes, a teacher told him, was still traumatized—her parents had been killed in a Soviet raid.

She was about 12 years old, only a year or so away from going behind the veil. She *did* permit him to photograph her, but she kept her robe pulled up to those eyes until the teacher allowed her to drop it. It all happened in the next instant. She looked straight into the lens, he squeezed off two shots—no strobes—and then she was up and gone.

Months later, leaning over a light table in Washington, McCurry saw the slides for the first time. He recalled that it had been a "powerful moment," but could not have guessed just how powerful an impact the portrait would have. The picture editor, in fact, thought it too strong and didn't include it in his final cut. Bill Garrett, the Editor in Chief, remembered retrieving it from the "seconds"; McCurry insists that it was included in what Bill was finally shown. Either way, whenever he did eventually see it, Garrett leaped out of his chair, declaring, "There's our next cover!"

> Names have power, so let us speak of hers. Her name is Sharbat Gula, and she is Pashtun, that most warlike of Afghan tribes. It is said of the Pashtun that they are only at peace when they are at war, and her eyes—then and now—burn with ferocity.
>
> *—Cathy Newman, from "A Life Revealed,"* National Geographic, *April 2002*

▸ JUNE 1985 | STEVE MCCURRY Iconic *National Geographic:* The Afghan Girl

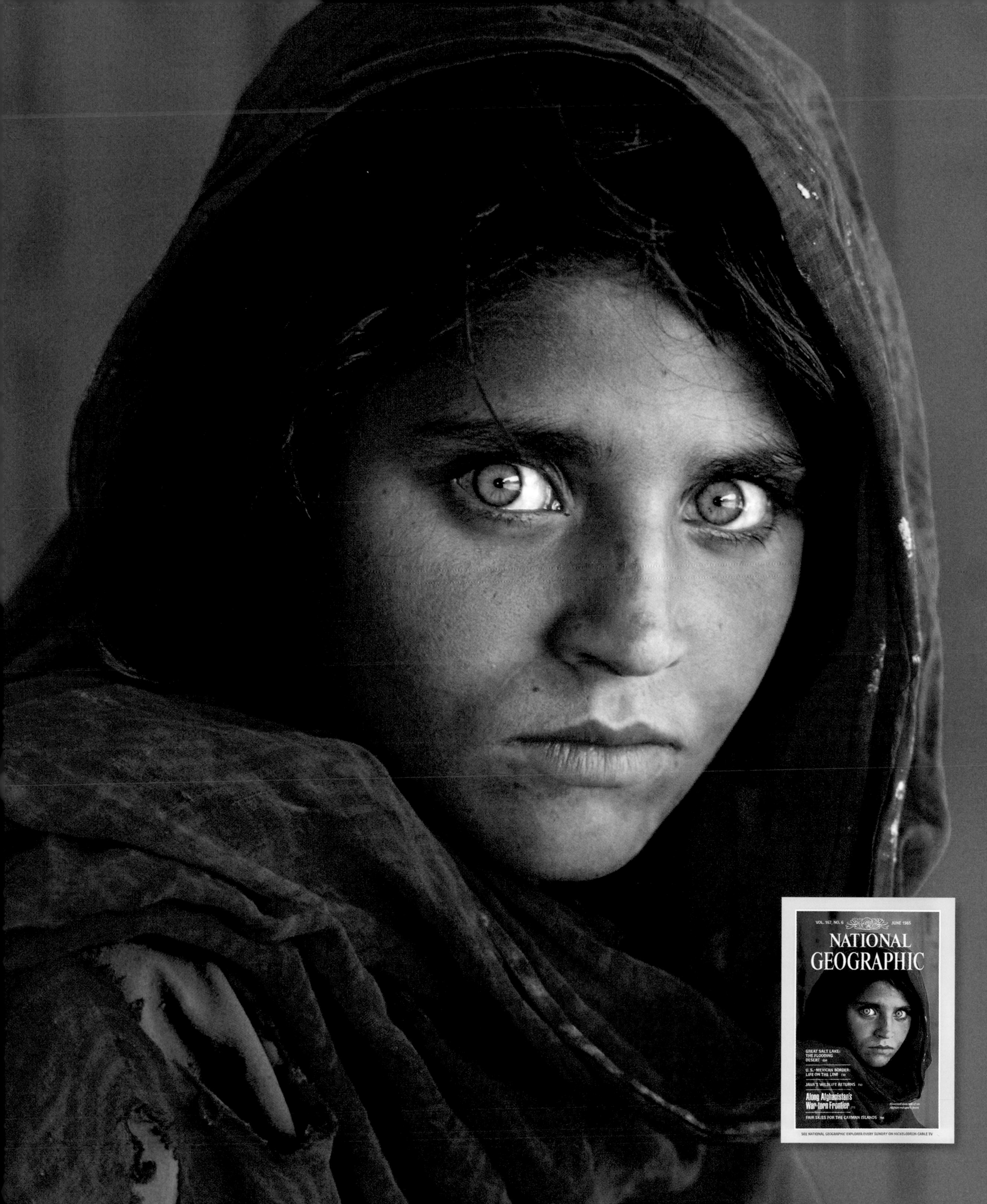
VOL. 167, NO. 6
JUNE 1985
NATIONAL GEOGRAPHIC
GREAT SALT LAKE: THE FLOODING DESERT
U.S.-MEXICAN BORDER: LIFE ON THE LINE 730
JAVA'S WILDLIFE RETURNS
Along Afghanistan's War-torn Frontier
FAIR SKIES FOR THE CAYMAN ISLANDS
SEE NATIONAL GEOGRAPHIC EXPLORER EVERY SUNDAY ON NICKELODEON CABLE TV

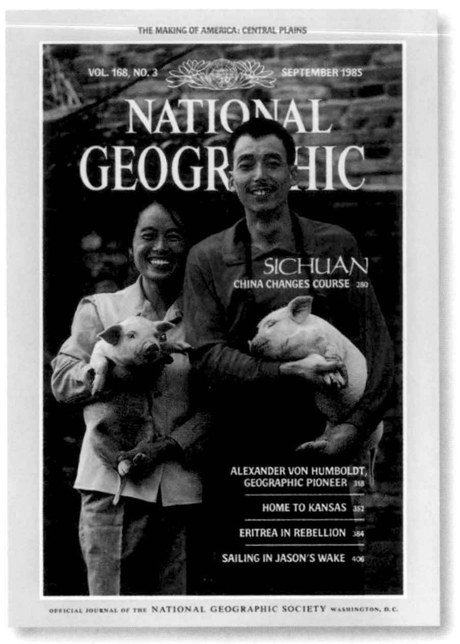

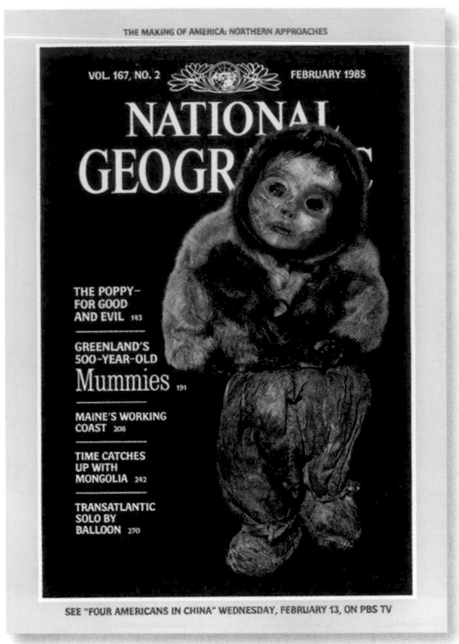

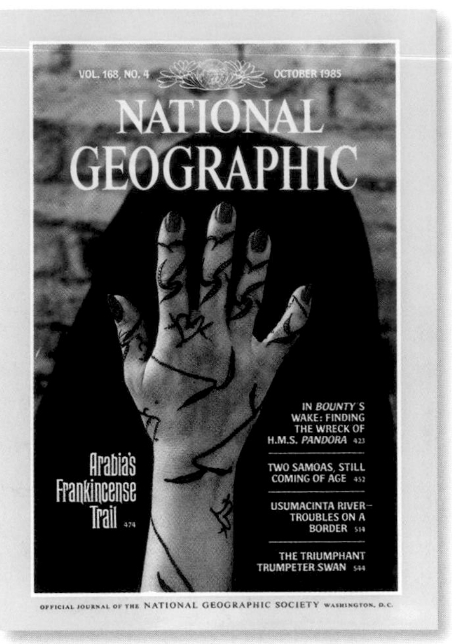

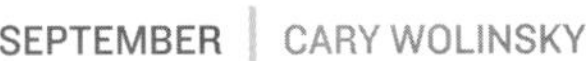
SEPTEMBER | CARY WOLINSKY

FEBRUARY | JOHN LEE

OCTOBER | LYNN ABERCROMBIE

▲ **PROMISING PIGS** Thanks to Premier Deng Xiaoping's selection of Sichuan Province as a place to experiment with limited capitalism, a Chinese couple's pig farm is earning them some welcome cash. Cary Wolinsky had made valuable contacts in China when shooting an earlier story on wool; he used them to gain entrance to Sichuan—long closed to foreigners—once that province began opening its doors.

FINDING *TITANIC* ▶

THE SINKING OF *TITANIC* on that night to remember, April 15, 1912, had been the maritime disaster of the 20th century. Finding it on the seafloor 73 years later—on September 1, 1985—likewise became the most celebrated shipwreck discovery of its time. To Bob Ballard, leader of the successful expedition, mounted in partnership with the U.S. Navy and IFREMER, the French undersea exploration office, it was akin to a successful moon landing. For *National Geographic,* which had first U.S. magazine rights to the only valuable artifacts the ship returned with—the photographs—it meant pushing deadlines to the limit in order to remake the December issue. It went on the press at the very last minute—with Ballard's "How We Found *Titanic*" on the cover.

> I cannot believe my eyes. From the abyss two and a half miles beneath the sea the bow of a great vessel emerges in ghostly detail.
>
> —*From "How We Found* Titanic,*" Robert Ballard*

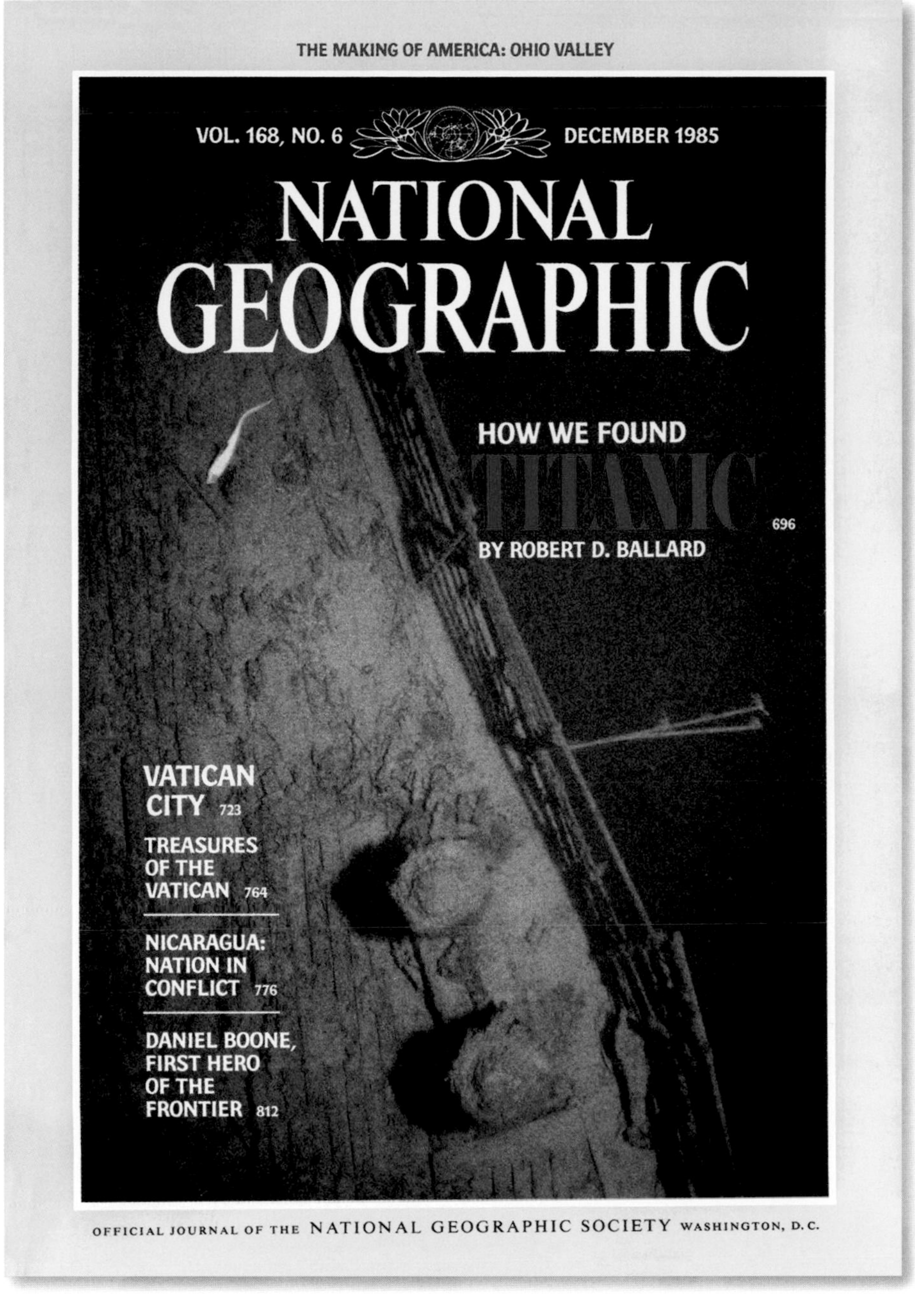

DECEMBER | WHOI, IFREMER, AND ROBERT D. BALLARD

▲ **FIRST LOOKS** This image of a rattail fish gliding over *Titanic*'s debris-coated foredeck and port rail was one of 20,000 frames of film shot by the expedition's underwater cameras in the four days they were deployed above the famous wreck. Most of the still pictures were made by ANGUS, a "blind" camera sled on a 13,000-foot tether that was guided by sonar across the seafloor. It had to be hoisted back to the surface for its film to be developed—and only then could anyone see the results.

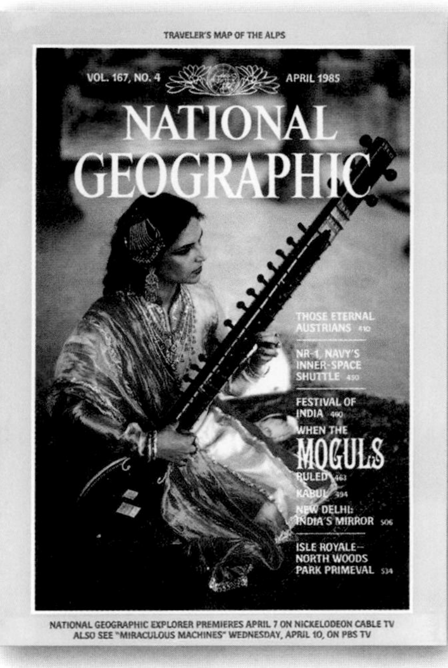

APRIL | ROLAND MICHAUD

▲ **COOL RETREAT** Sitting beneath a pavilion in Lahore's Shalimar Gardens, Pakistani folk musician Tahira Syed plays a sitar and sings a *ghazal*, a traditional ballad of love and loss. Built in the 17th century and exhibiting Persian influence, the gardens with their 410 fountains mark an apogee of Mogul artistic expression, the most enduring legacy of the Muslim dynasty that ruled much of the Indian subcontinent for three centuries.

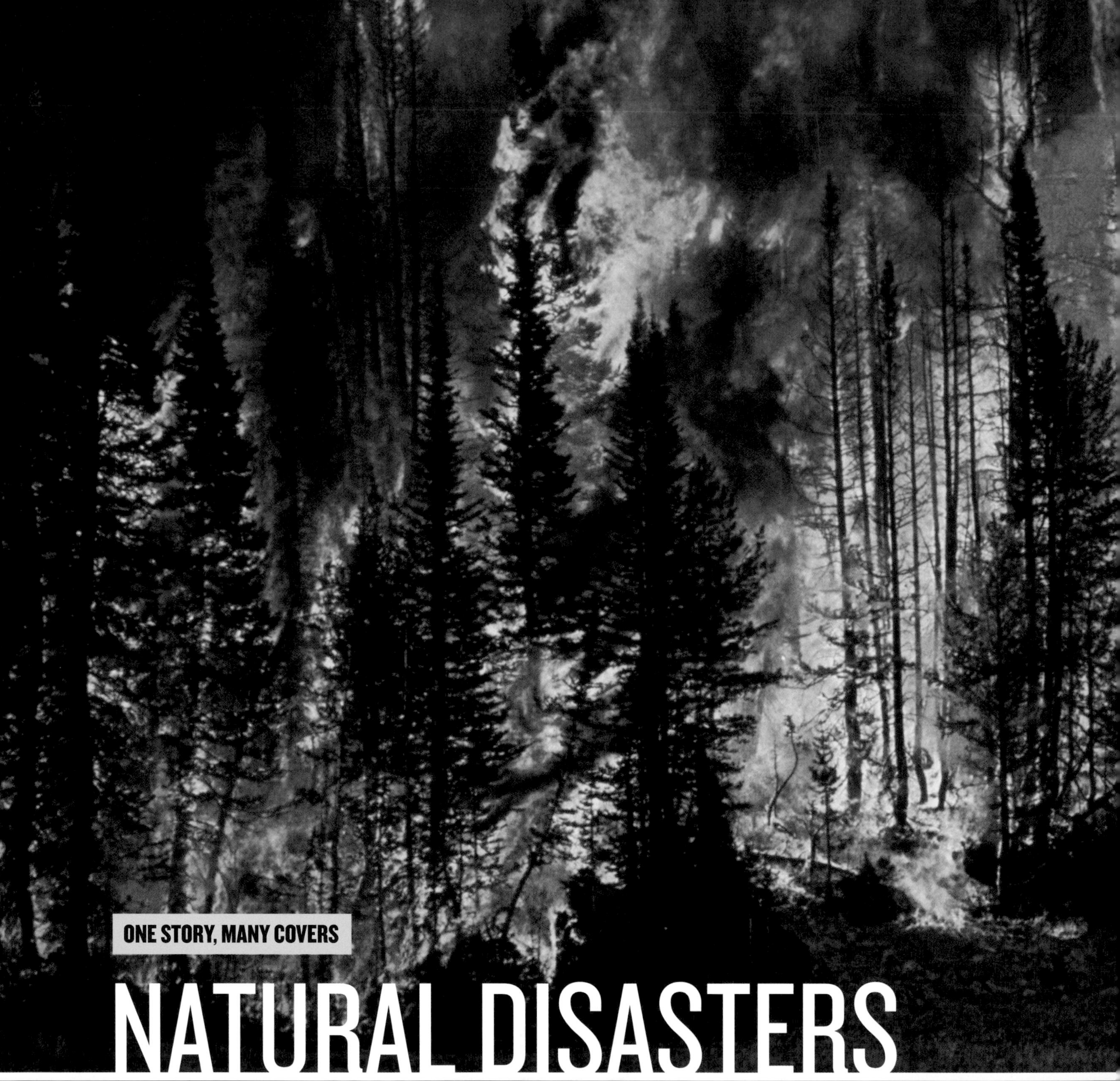

ONE STORY, MANY COVERS

NATURAL DISASTERS

▲ FEBRUARY 1989 | CRAIG FUJII, THE *SEATTLE TIMES*
Tired firefighters can do little more to stem the onrushing Yellowstone inferno.

FIRE, FLOOD, EARTHQUAKE, STORM, and volcanic eruption are five apocalyptic horsemen who have ridden through the pages of *National Geographic* since at least 1902, when the magazine published an account of the disastrous eruption of Martinique's Mount Pelée. The January 1981 story on Mount St. Helens was long ranked the most popular in the journal's history; and an October 2004 article on New Orleans predicted the devastating consequences of a direct hit from a major hurricane—a year before Katrina.

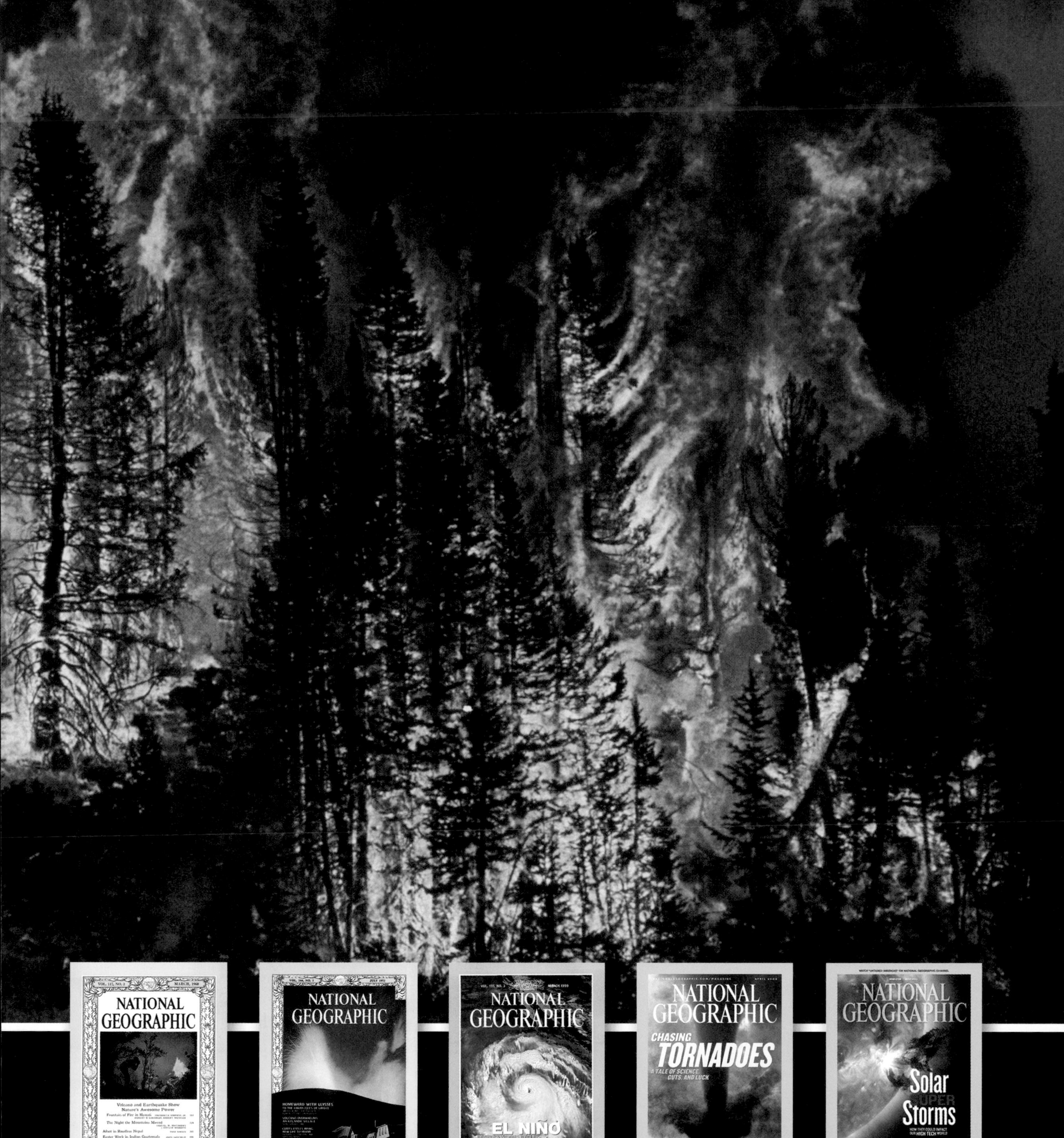

VOL. 117, NO. 3
MARCH, 1960
NATIONAL GEOGRAPHIC
Volcano and Earthquake Show Nature's Awesome Power
Fountain of Fire in Hawaii
The Night the Mountains Moved
Afoot in Roadless Nepal
Easter Week in Indian Guatemala
Waterway to Washington, the C & O Canal
Colleague of the Golden Years: John Oliver La Gorce
$8.00 A YEAR
$1.00 A COPY
NATIONAL GEOGRAPHIC SOCIETY
NATIONAL GEOGRAPHIC
HOMEWARD WITH ULYSSES
NATIONAL GEOGRAPHIC SOCIETY
MARCH 1999
NATIONAL GEOGRAPHIC
EL NIÑO
LA NIÑA
NATIONAL GEOGRAPHIC SOCIETY
NATIONAL GEOGRAPHIC
CHASING
TORNADOES
A TALE OF SCIENCE, GUTS, AND LUCK
Cranes: The Long Way Home
Africa's City of Hope and Fear
It's All Good in the Badlands
Tigers in the "Valley of Death"
Worm Capital of the World
PLUS Bird Migration Map
NATIONAL GEOGRAPHIC
Solar
SUPER
Storms
HOW THEY COULD IMPACT OUR HIGH-TECH WORLD

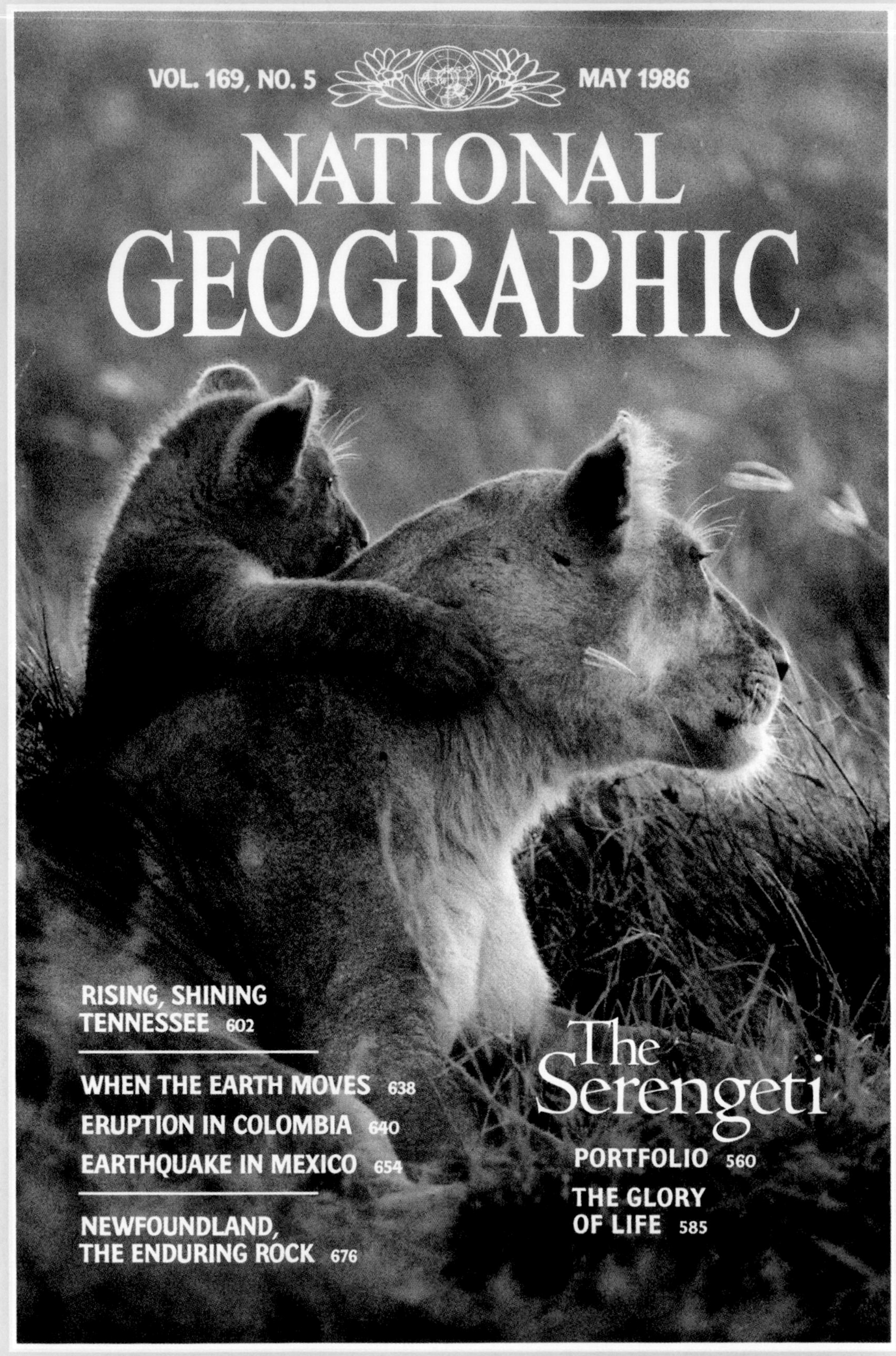

MAY | MITSUAKI IWAGO One cub remains hidden in the grass while the other bonds with its mother.

SERENGETI SERENITY

Sunrise on the Serengeti—and the lioness is alert but content to remain with her cubs. Perhaps six weeks old, they spar with each other, tug at her tail, suckle at her teats. Soon enough she must leave her lair and introduce them to the nearby pride. For the moment, however, she watches; and one of the cubs pauses long enough to watch with her, for in the Serengeti something is always moving, if only the wind in the grass.

Although Mitsuaki Iwago made thousands of photographs during his 18 months there, it was this idyllic image, appearing on the May 1986 *National Geographic* cover, that touched millions of readers worldwide. Countless letters flooded into headquarters—usually from mothers or daughters—wondering if copies of the picture might be purchased.

Highly esteemed as a wildlife photographer in his native Japan, the 32-year-old Iwago had arrived in Tanzania in August 1982, his wife and four-year-old daughter in tow. Despite his early success, he had grown frustrated with a life that saw too many airports and too few animals. He wanted to pause in one place long enough to become intimately familiar with its environment, and found what he was looking for in the 5,700-square-mile Serengeti National Park.

Whether by day or by night, in the rainy season or the dry, Iwago roamed the grasslands, photographing lions, cheetahs, hyenas, vultures, zebras, and the wildebeests whose annual migration was the most dramatic feature of the ecosystem. Watching through his viewfinder the drama of predator and prey he saw both the glory of life and the inevitability of death as aspects of the same ceaselessly turning wheel. In no other place was what the Japanese call *okite*—natural law or natural order—so abundantly on display.

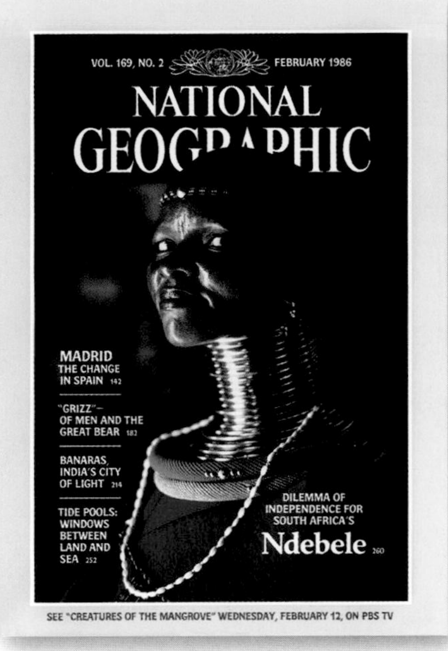

FEBRUARY | PETER MAGUBANE

▲ **BRASS RINGS** Copper or brass neck-rings were once universally worn by married Ndebele women of South Africa. Such *iindzila* were donned soon after a girl wed, around the age of 12. The custom was fast fading, though, when Peter Magubane documented their troubled lives under apartheid—a coverage in which he was also hit by 17 pellets of bird shot fired from a policeman's riot gun.

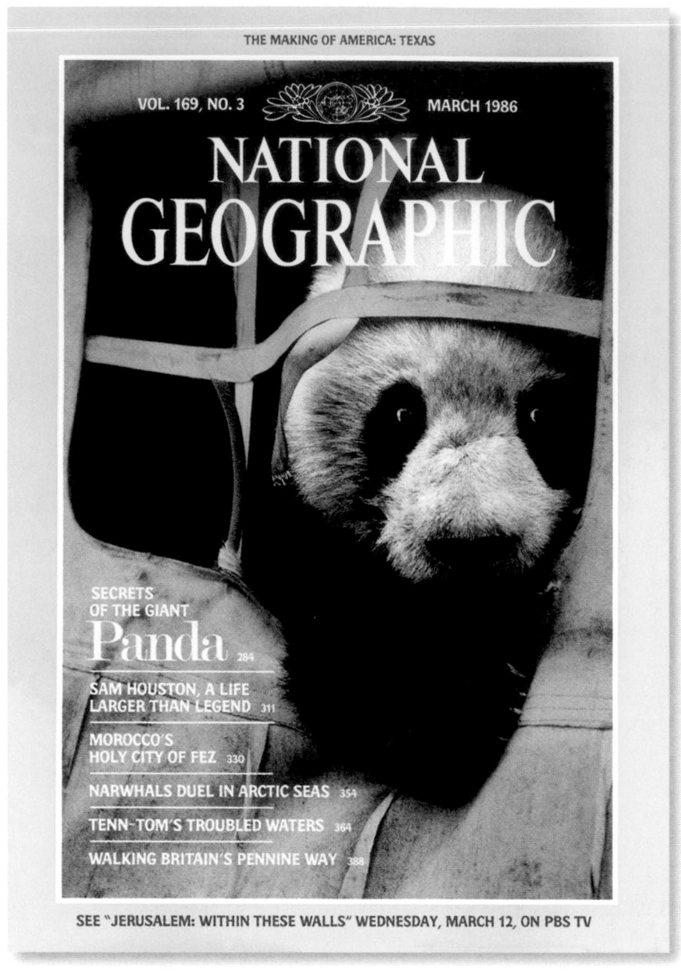

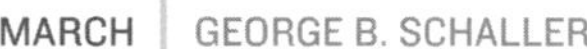
MARCH | GEORGE B. SCHALLER

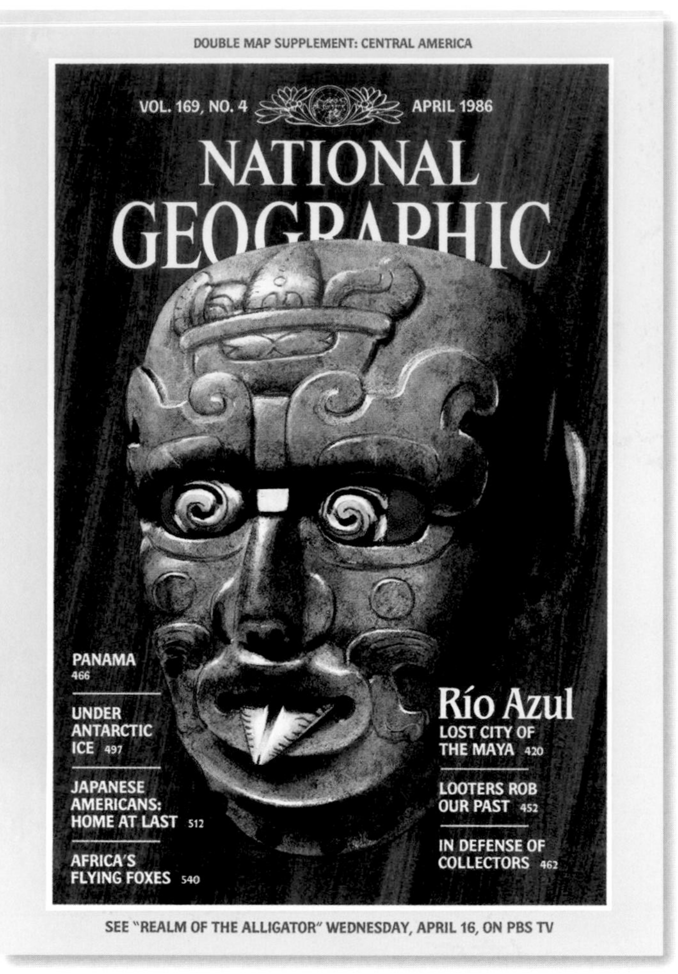

APRIL | WILLIAM H. BOND

▲ **WHERE IS EVERYBODY?** Zhen-Zhen looks endearing as she peeks out of a study team's tent in China's Wolong National Nature Reserve. Though at times she proved to be a nuisance around the camp, she had been the first giant panda that biologist George Schaller and his Chinese colleagues successfully radio-collared. After her death in 1985 at about 14, Schaller wrote that by "protecting her and her kind, we create an awareness that every species is valuable, that even a panda may shine for only a moment and then no more."

▲ **STOLEN TREASURE** This Classic Maya funerary mask was presented as a painting for the simple reason that no good photograph was obtainable. And that's because this treasure—which seems to have been the death mask of a high-ranking lord—was almost certainly looted from the Guatemalan site of Río Azul and illegally sold to a shadowy collector in the United States. In an attempt to smoke out the smugglers, *National Geographic* and the Guatemalan Institute of Anthropology and History offered $10,000 for a photograph that depicted the artifact in its original location—to no avail. Cloak-and-dagger investigations tracked the mask from the United States to a museum in Europe, but it has since disappeared.

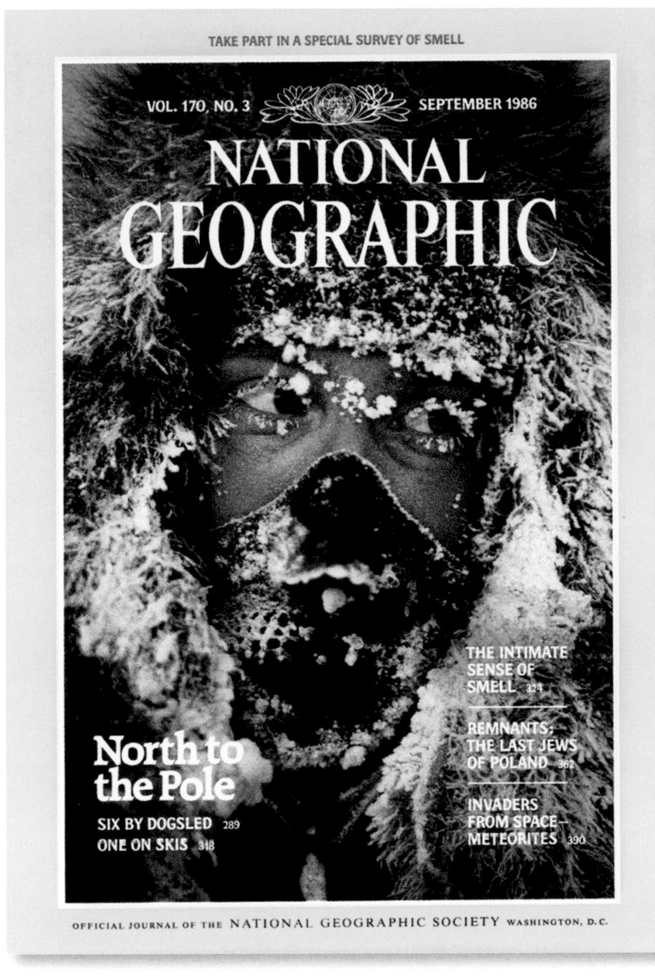

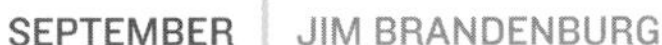
SEPTEMBER | JIM BRANDENBURG

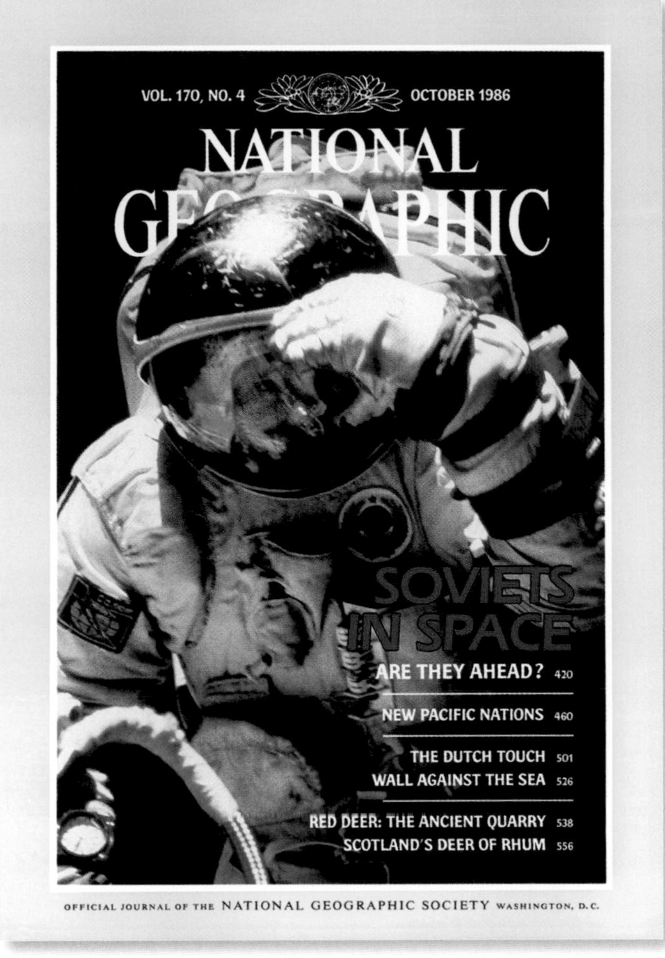

OCTOBER | ITAR-TASS

▲ **SNOW MAN** Badge of the true Arctic explorer, a face mask encrusted with ice graces Brent Boddy's handsome features during a historic 1986 trek to the North Pole. Led by Will Steger, the four men, one woman, and 21 dogs composed the first confirmed expedition to reach 90 degrees north without resupply of any sort. Boddy was also one of the first two Canadians ever to set foot on the fabled spot.

▲ **SPACE DIPLOMAT** With a smart salute to the camera, and through it to the National Geographic Society's largely American membership, Soviet cosmonaut Col. Leonid Kizim ventures outside the Salyut 7 space station.

> *"Exploits in space stir the Soviet soul like a religion—stirrings fanned by a government immensely proud of space successes."*
>
> —Thomas Y. Canby
>
> *from "Soviets in Space: Are They Ahead?"*

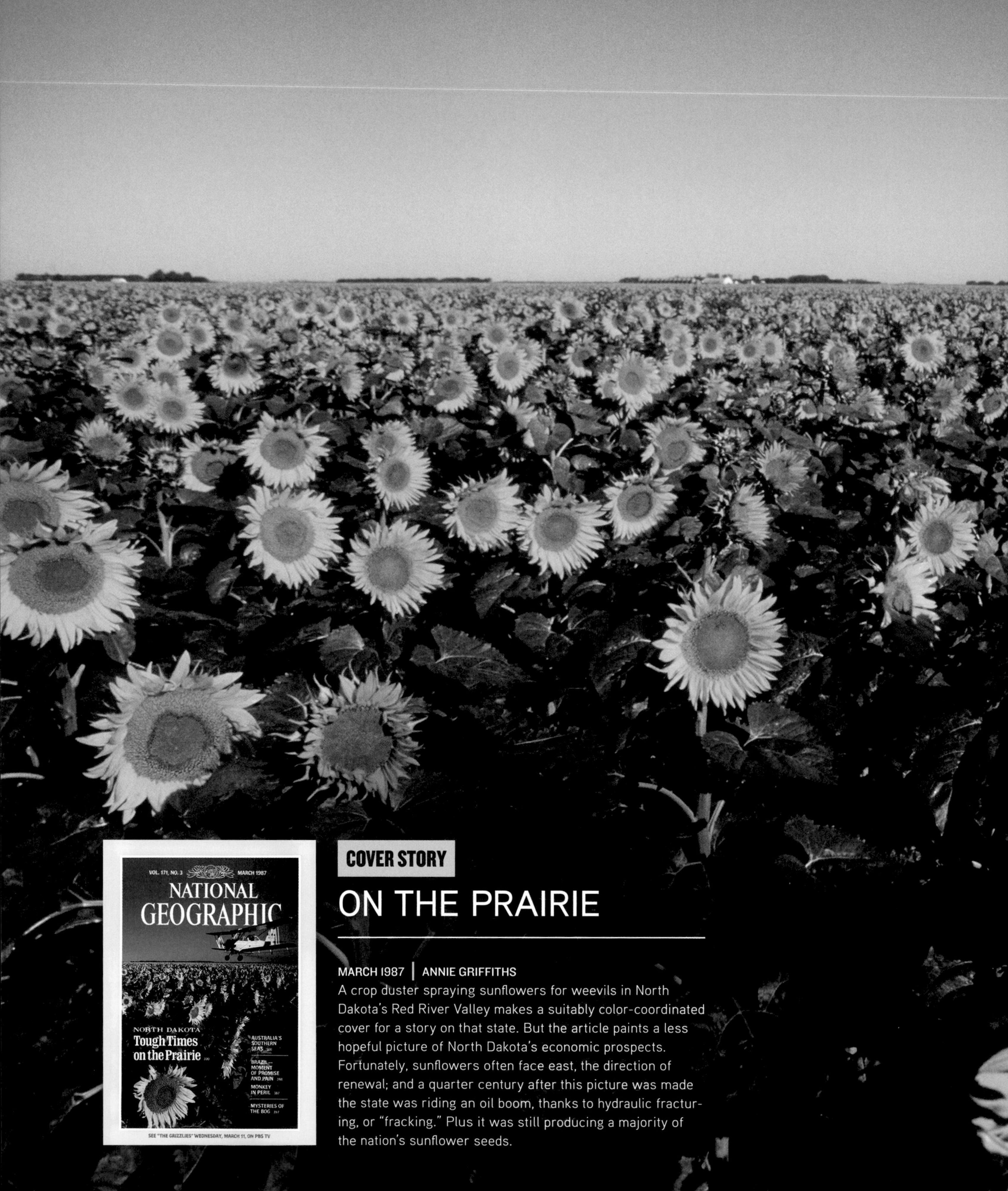

COVER STORY

ON THE PRAIRIE

MARCH 1987 | ANNIE GRIFFITHS

A crop duster spraying sunflowers for weevils in North Dakota's Red River Valley makes a suitably color-coordinated cover for a story on that state. But the article paints a less hopeful picture of North Dakota's economic prospects. Fortunately, sunflowers often face east, the direction of renewal; and a quarter century after this picture was made the state was riding an oil boom, thanks to hydraulic fracturing, or "fracking." Plus it was still producing a majority of the nation's sunflower seeds.

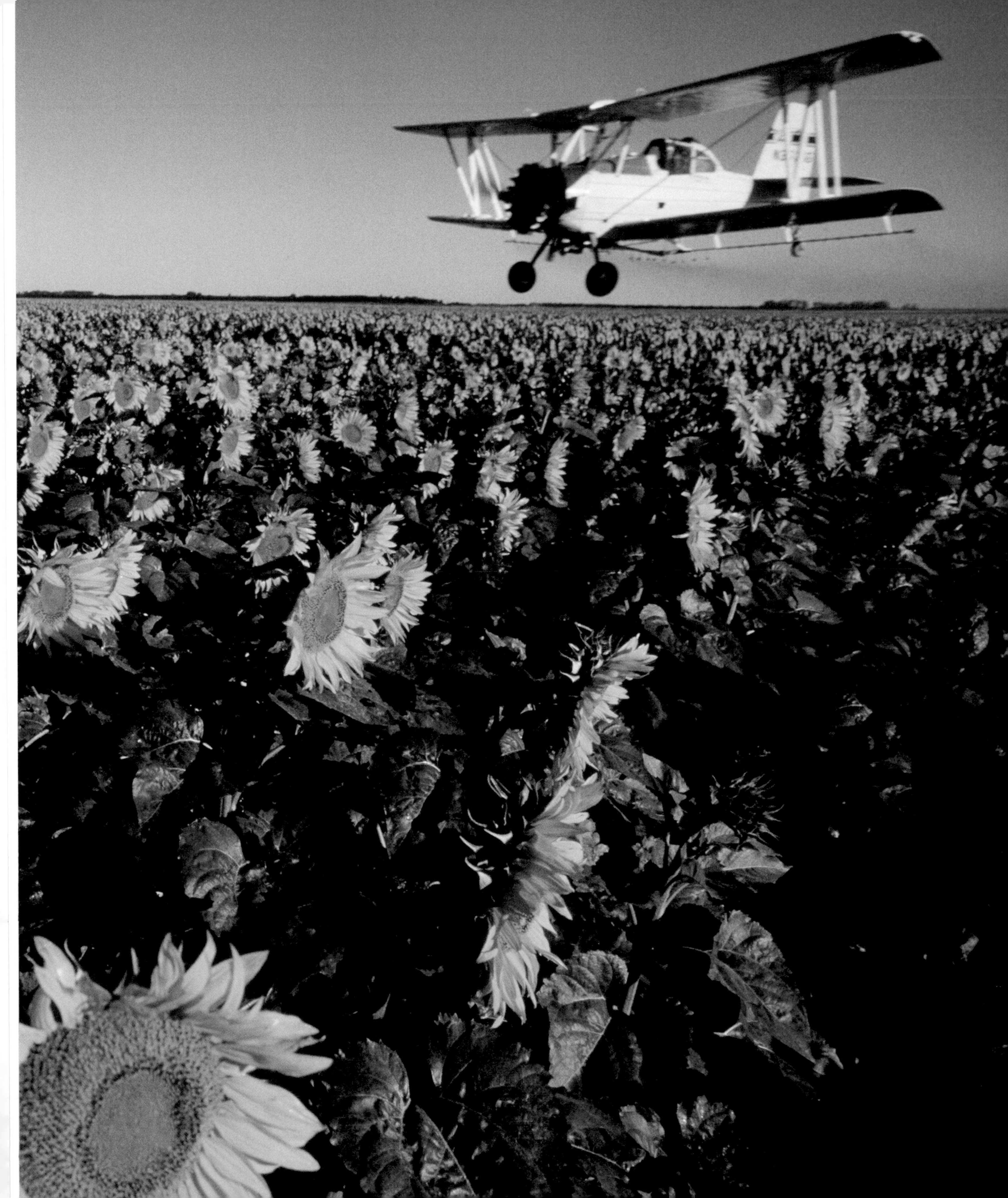

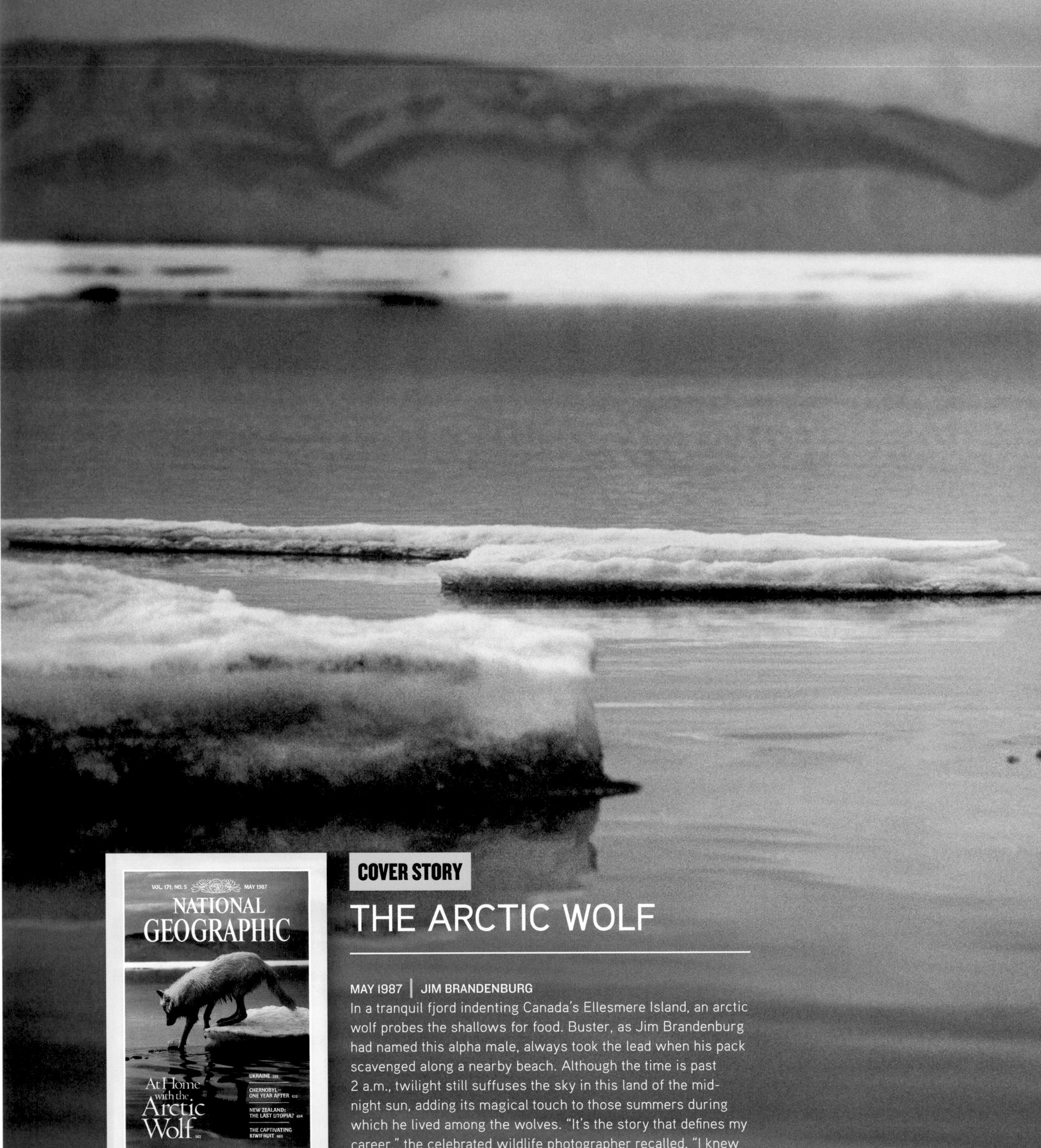

COVER STORY

THE ARCTIC WOLF

MAY 1987 | JIM BRANDENBURG

In a tranquil fjord indenting Canada's Ellesmere Island, an arctic wolf probes the shallows for food. Buster, as Jim Brandenburg had named this alpha male, always took the lead when his pack scavenged along a nearby beach. Although the time is past 2 a.m., twilight still suffuses the sky in this land of the midnight sun, adding its magical touch to those summers during which he lived among the wolves. "It's the story that defines my career," the celebrated wildlife photographer recalled. "I knew I would never top it."

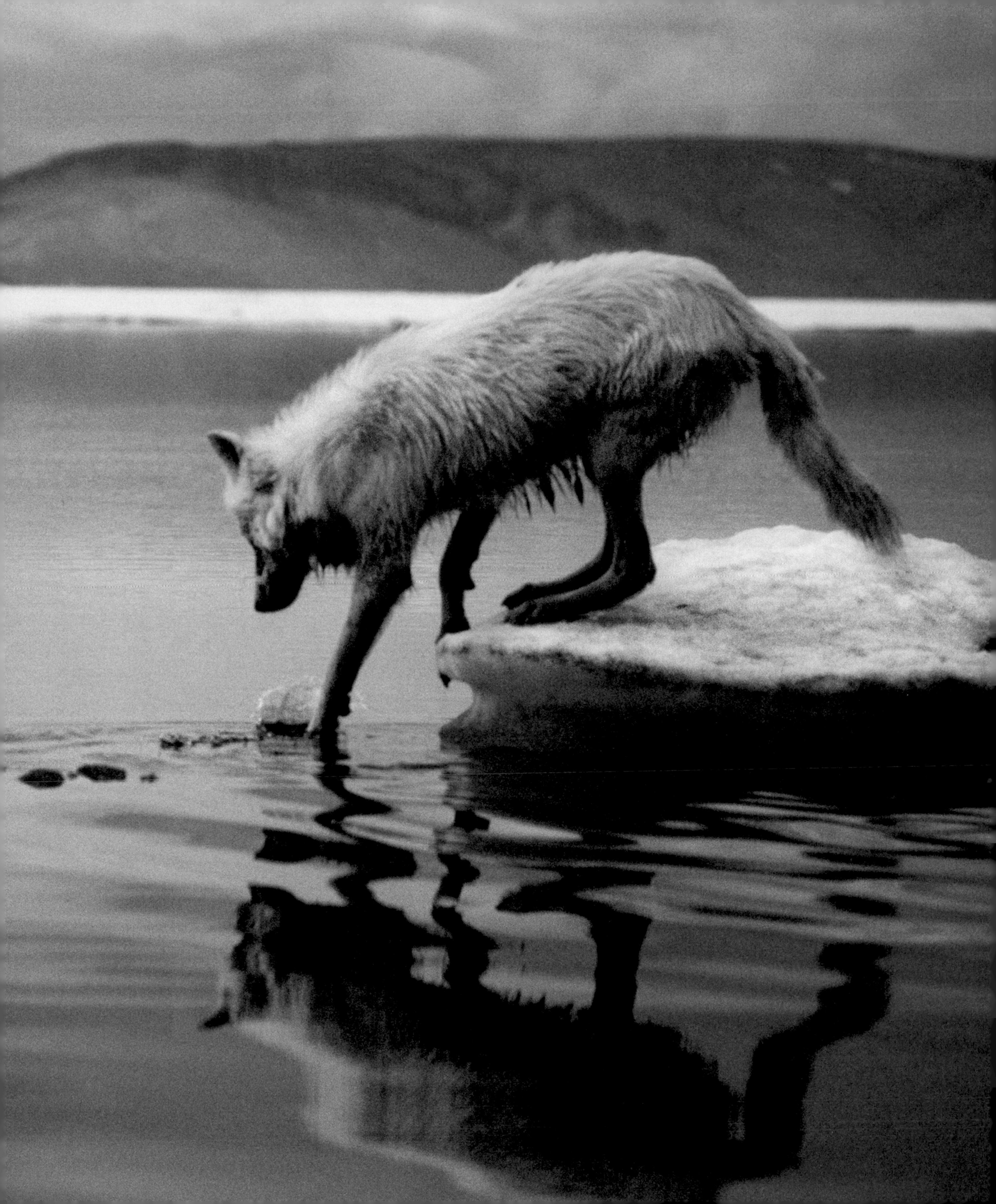

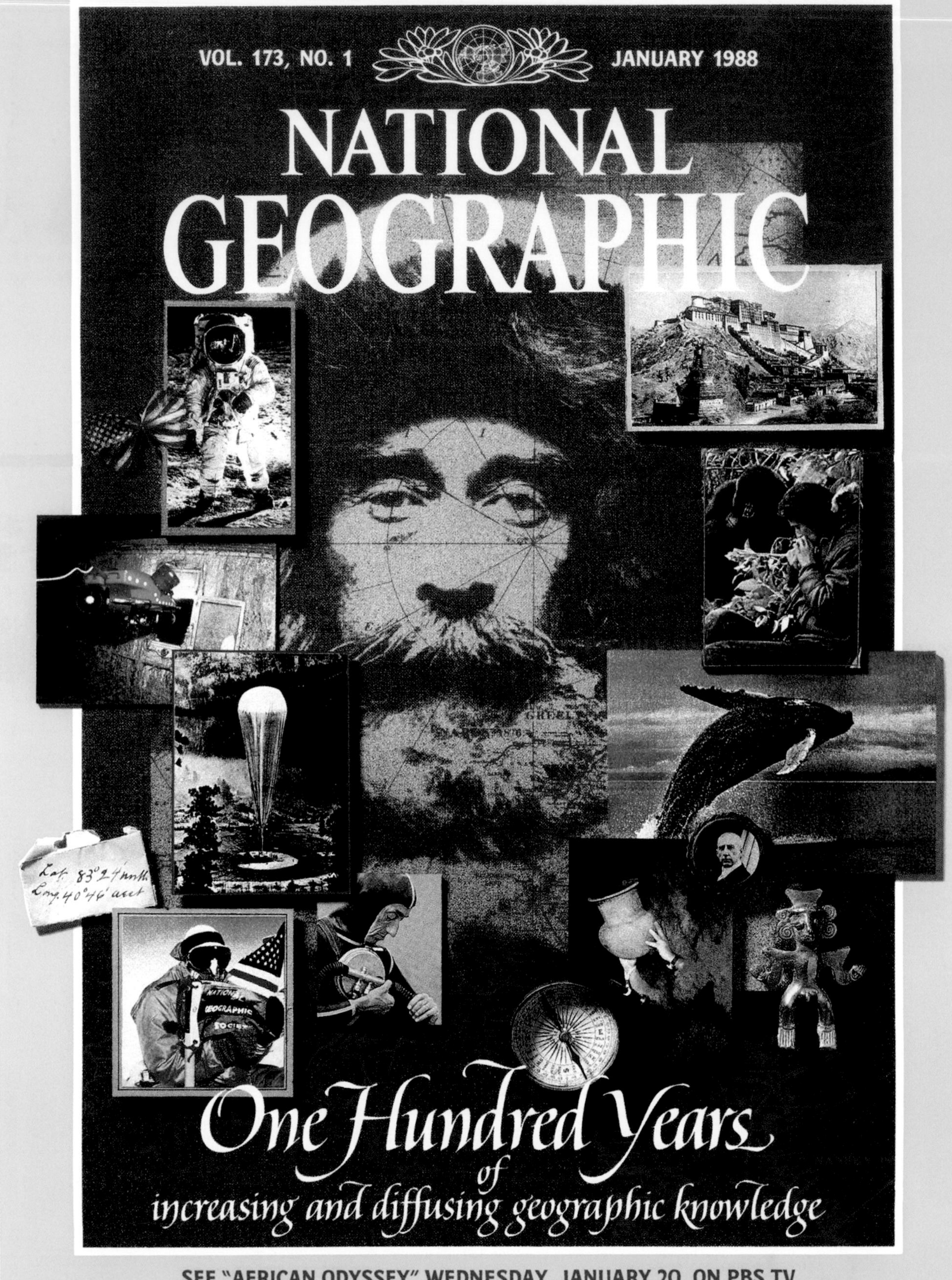

JANUARY | FRED OTNES Famous explorers mix and mingle on the cover of the Centennial issue.

ANNIVERSARY ISSUES

LOOKING BACK, ON THE occasion of its centennial, the "magazine of adventure and discovery" hews to a tradition 100 years in the making. That is not only the gist of a promotional piece in the January 1988 *National Geographic* but it is also the theme of its cover.

There, in collage, are some of the great moments in the making of the Society and its magazine: the excavation of Machu Picchu, its first foray into archaeology; the support of Dian Fossey's studies of mountain gorillas in Africa's Virunga mountains; its sponsorship of whale research or Jacques-Yves Cousteau's underwater explorations or Bob Ballard's venturing ever deeper. There is also Barry Bishop on the top of Mount Everest, the aeronauts of *Explorer II* reaching new heights in the stratosphere, and Buzz Aldrin bouncing across the surface of the moon—expeditions that all carried the National Geographic flag.

Behind all of them lingers the figure of Robert E. Peary, once the face of the heroic age of Arctic exploration, still looming large but also fading behind the cast of more recent heroes.

How different is the cover gracing the January 2013 *Geographic*, the 125th Anniversary Special Issue. It looks not past but forward, featuring an artist's rendition of a spacecraft—exploring an Earthlike planet—that, based on 1970s designs drawn up for the British Interplanetary Society, might be able to reach the nearest stars within a human lifetime. And whereas the former collage was old multimedia, this cover was new multimedia: On the iPad version, readers could steer that spacecraft in whichever direction they'd like.

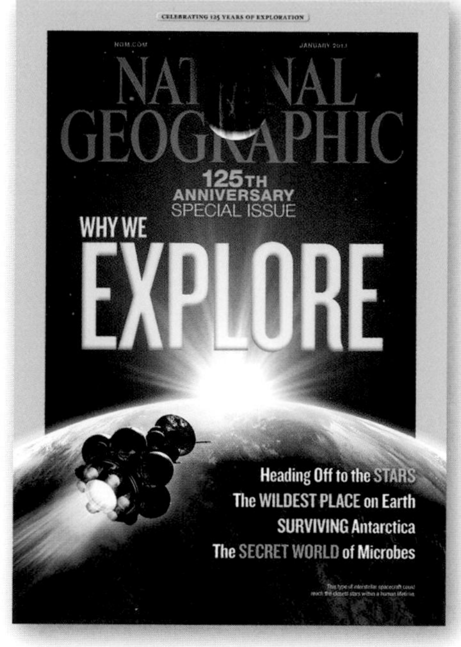

JANUARY 2013 | DANA BERRY

2013 ▸▸▸▸ FAST FORWARD

FIELDS OF EXPLORATION Twenty-five years later the cover and the first three pages were actually four different covers produced for the January issue: Beneath the topmost spaceship appeared covers depicting monkeys, microbes, and mountaineer Cory Richards, each representing a different field of exploration.

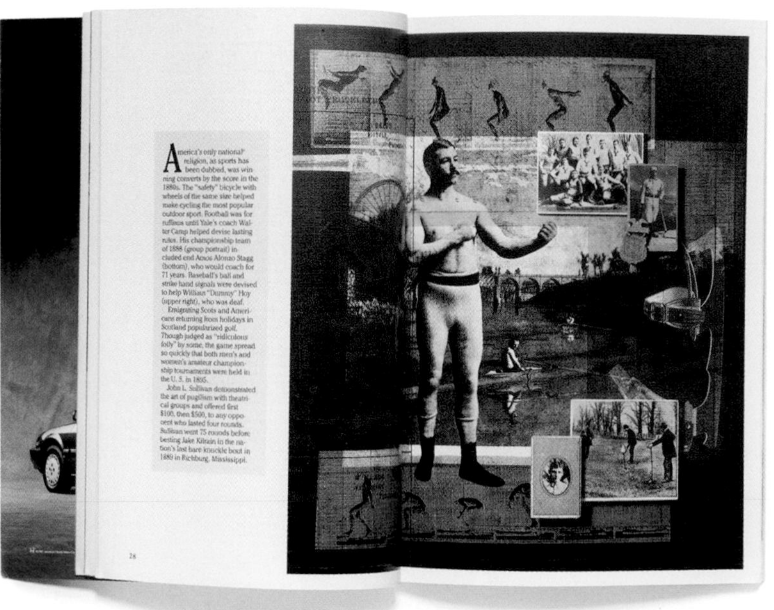

▸ **JANUARY 1988 | FRED OTNES** Boxer John L. Sullivan dominates other sports stars of the 1880s.

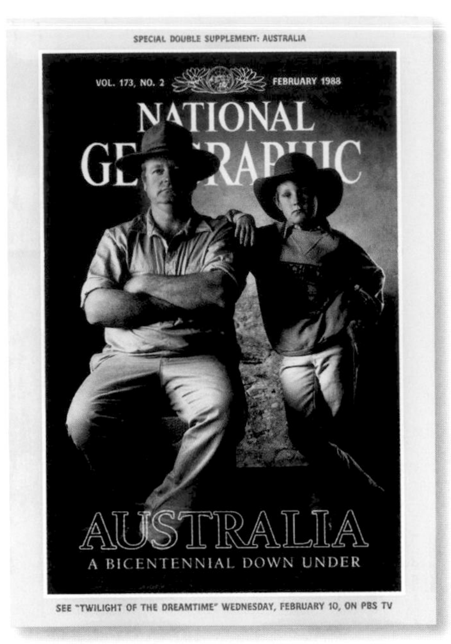

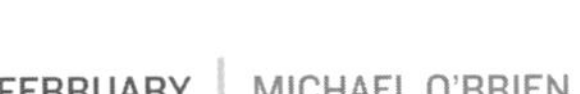

FEBRUARY | MICHAEL O'BRIEN

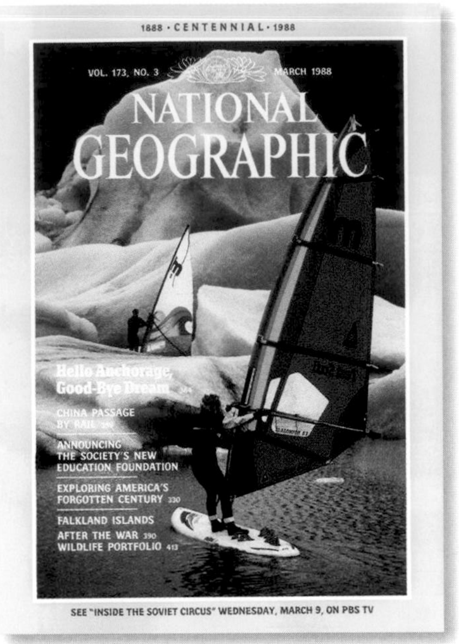

MARCH | CHRIS JOHNS

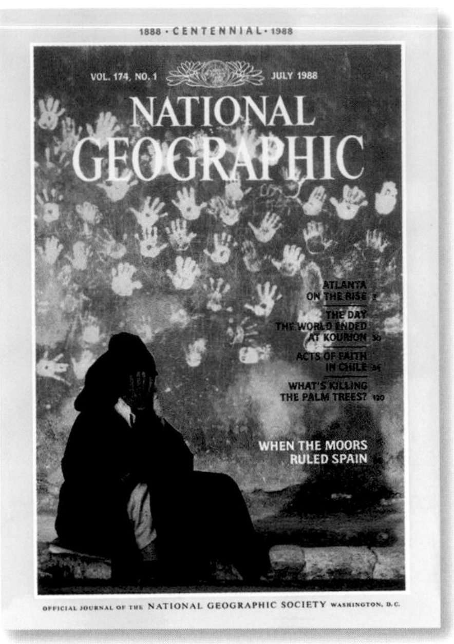

JULY | BRUNO BARBEY

▲ **BICENTENNIAL DOWN UNDER**
From the toes of their shoes to the brims of their hats, sheep-man Sandy McTaggart and son Boots typify the spirit of Australia, which in 1988 celebrated its bicentennial.

"Aussie blokes have dinkum reasons for thinking their land is bonzer, so shout them a drink, mate, and wish them a happy anniversary."

—Ross Terrill
from "Australia at 200"

EARTH-SHATTERING ▶

After choosing "Can Man Save This Fragile Earth?" as the theme for the culminating issue of its centennial year, Editor Bill Garrett decided it should be introduced by one of the most elaborate—and expensive—covers in the magazine's history. He wanted not one but two holograms. From one angle you'd see an intact Steuben crystal globe (four of them were made for the shoot at $3,500 apiece). From another angle, you'd see that globe shatter, a graphically compelling image of irretrievable ecological damage.

Photographer Bruce Dale set to work. Two pulsed lasers created the 3-D hologram. Four electronic timers synchronized the dropping of a globe (oriented so that the Soviet Union was not the target) into the firing line of an air pistol, the triggering of the air pistol, and the releasing and closing of the camera shutter—precisely 27.5 milliseconds after the pellet's impact—when the fractured globe began to break apart. The globes had to be dropped rather than mounted so that the mount wouldn't be visible in the final image. A second hologram was then made of an identical but intact globe, the two images being merged to form the "action" seen on the cover.

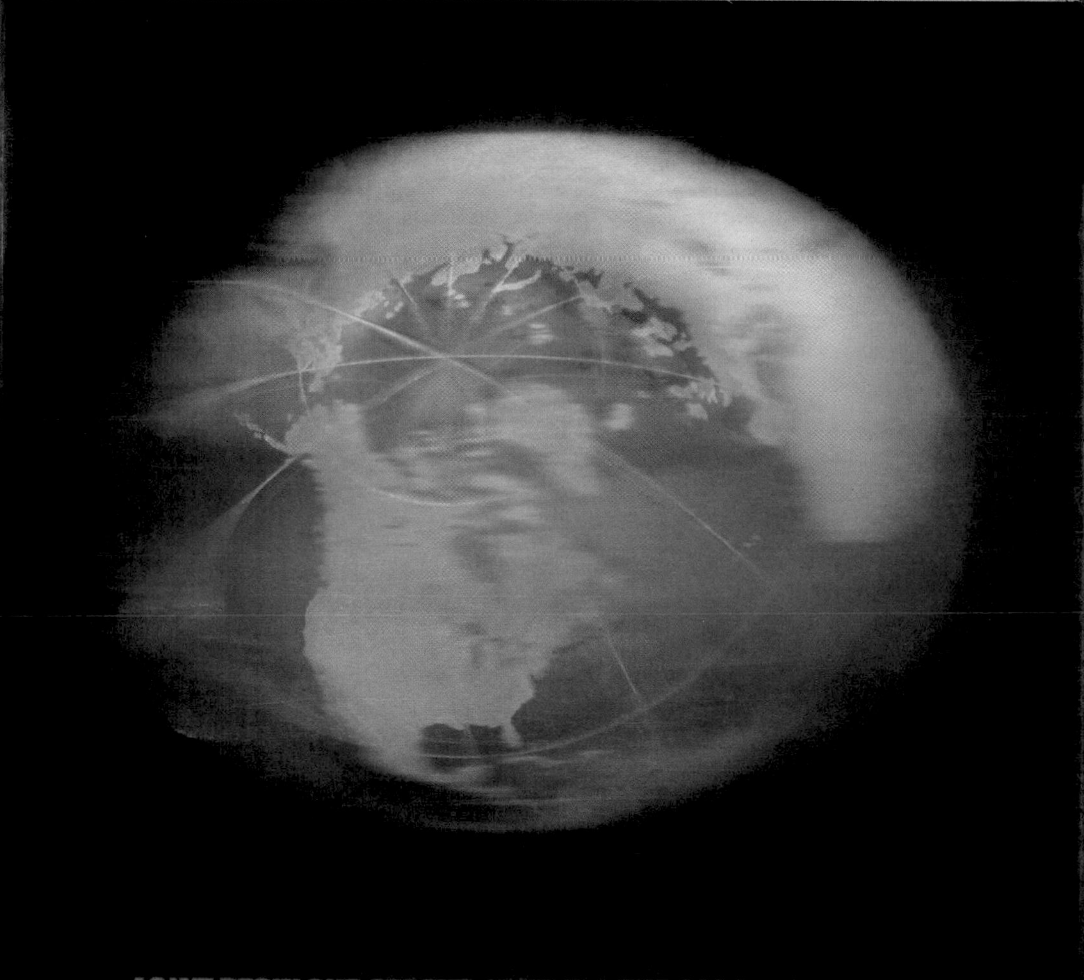

DECEMBER | BRUCE DALE, AMERICAN BANK NOTE HOLOGRAPHICS One of the two hologram views of a crystal globe

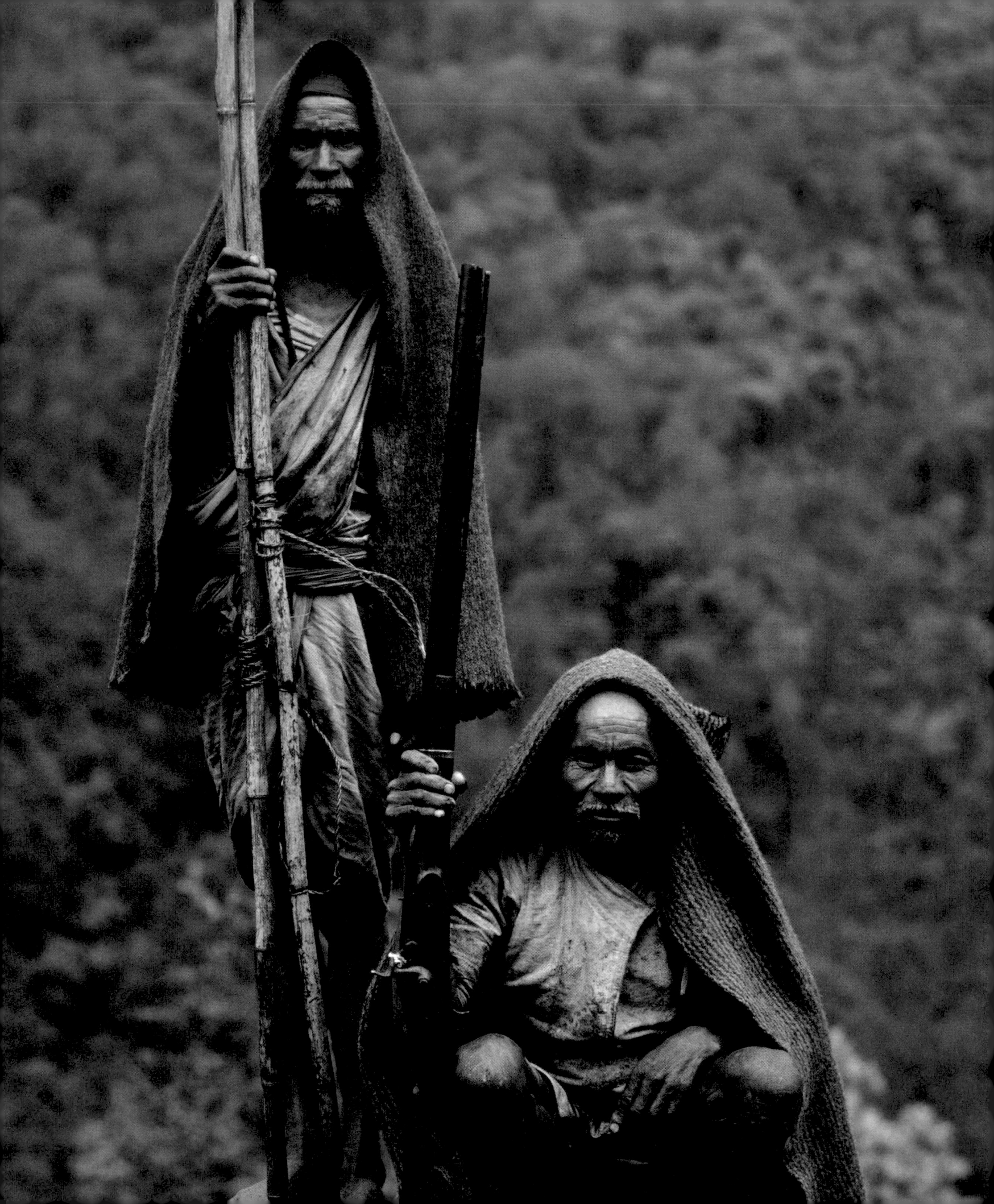

THE HONEY HUNTERS

THERE WERE TIMES WHEN ERIC VALLI, rappelling down a 395-foot cliff in the wilds of central Nepal, had to go into a Zen-like trance—not because of the height, even though one slip of the nylon rope meant certain death—but because of the bees.

The French-born Valli and his wife, Diane Summers, had long sought out the ancient ways of the Nepali hill people. For months they had tracked down rumors that honey hunters, practicing methods many thousands of years old, still worked sheer cliff faces in the forested foothills of the Himalaya. In 1986 they met 63-year-old Mani Lal, a Gurung tribesman and master honey hunter, and perhaps the last of his clan to practice the knowledge of extracting honey from inaccessible hives, a knowledge that had been passed from father to son since time immemorial.

Eventually the journalists were allowed to accompany Mani Lal on one of his twice-yearly honey-collecting expeditions. They documented every phase of the operation, from the initial offerings to placate the gods to the triumphant comb-bearing return to the village. But it was while dangling from the ropes—while Lal, clinging precariously to a handmade ladder, protected only by a cloak and the smoke of fires lit by assistants below, braved the swarms of angry bees to collect the combs—that Valli made his most dramatic pictures.

They were indeed quite breathtaking, and won the photographer a World Press Photo award even before they were published in the *Geographic*. They also stimulated an interest in the Gurung honey hunters that today brings hordes of tourists to those once remote hills.

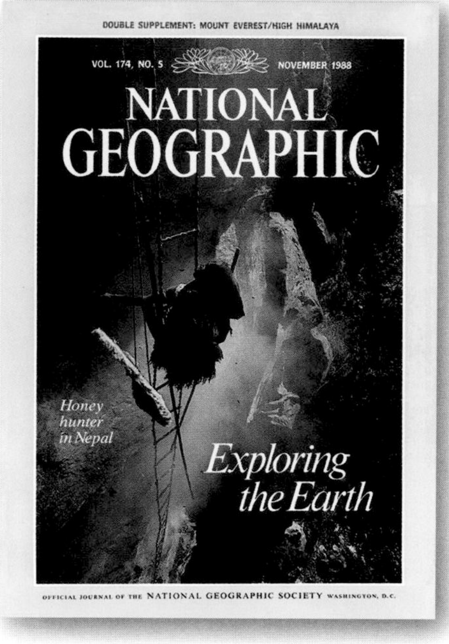

NOVEMBER | ERIC VALLI

▲ **EXPLORING THE EARTH** Eric Valli's portrayal of honey hunters represented the ethnographical component of a special issue devoted to exploration. Other articles included the mapping of Mount Everest, diving on the Caribbean's 3,200-foot-deep Cayman Wall, and plans for a manned mission to Mars.

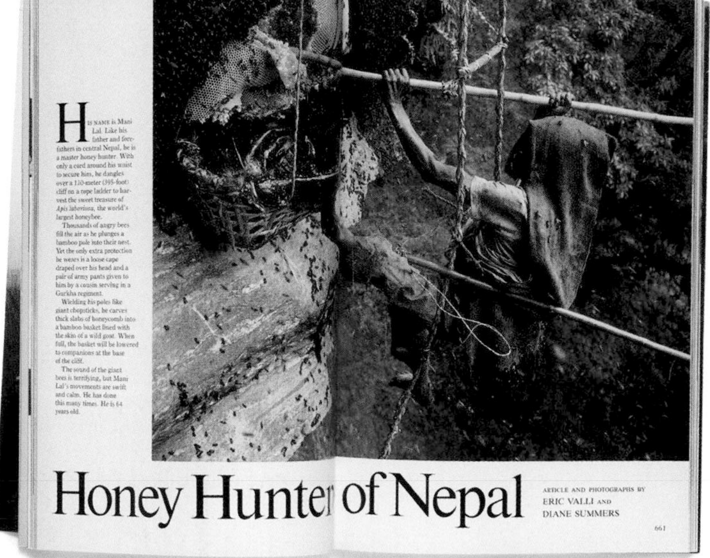
Honey Hunter of Nepal

ARTICLE AND PHOTOGRAPHS BY ERIC VALLI AND DIANE SUMMERS

▶ **NOVEMBER 1988** | **ERIC VALLI** Mani Lal braves the bees to collect the honey.

◀ **NOVEMBER 1988** | **ERIC VALLI** Mani Lal is joined by his musket-toting brother.

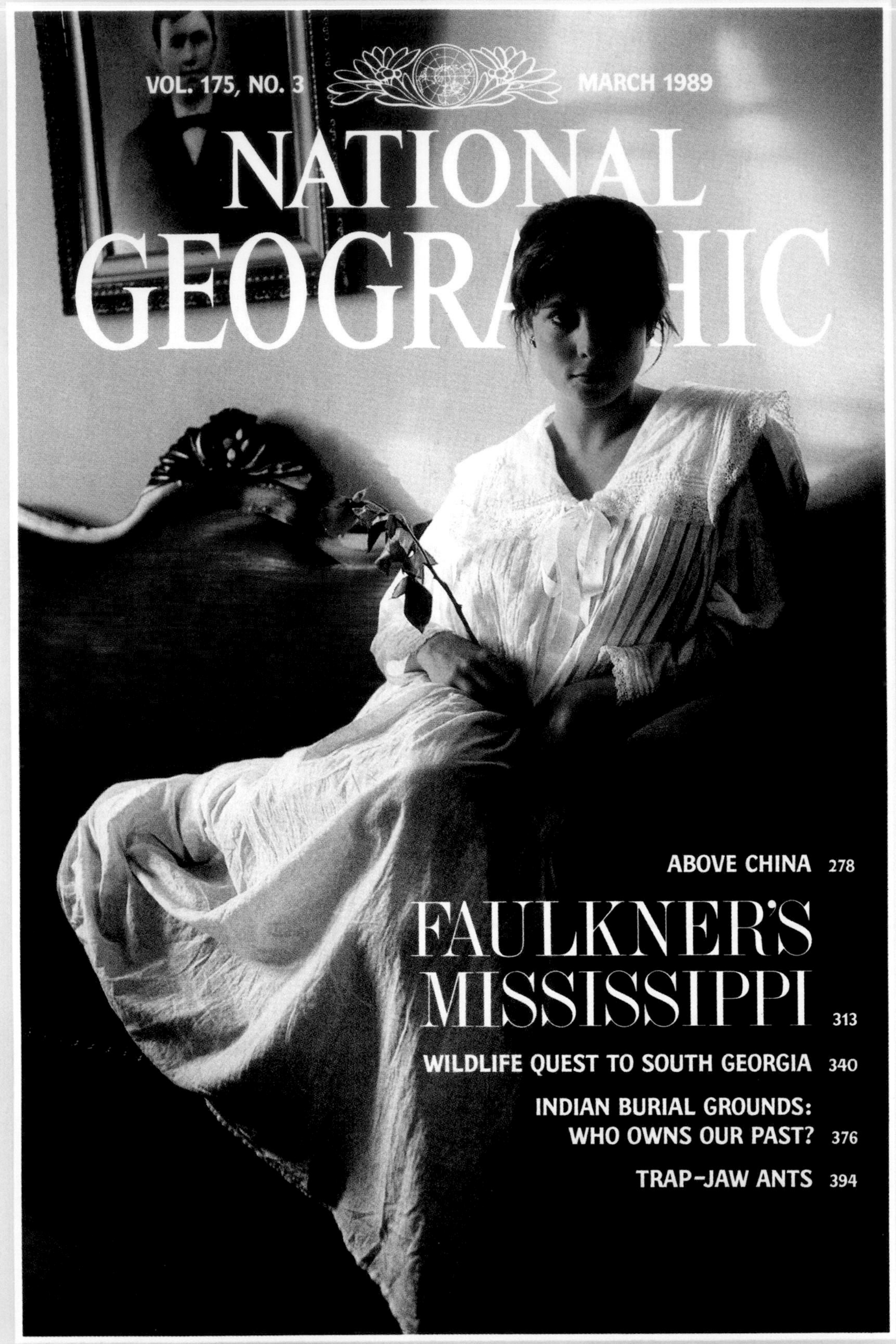

MARCH | WILLIAM ALBERT ALLARD An Ole Miss senior recalls William Faulkner's story "A Rose for Emily."

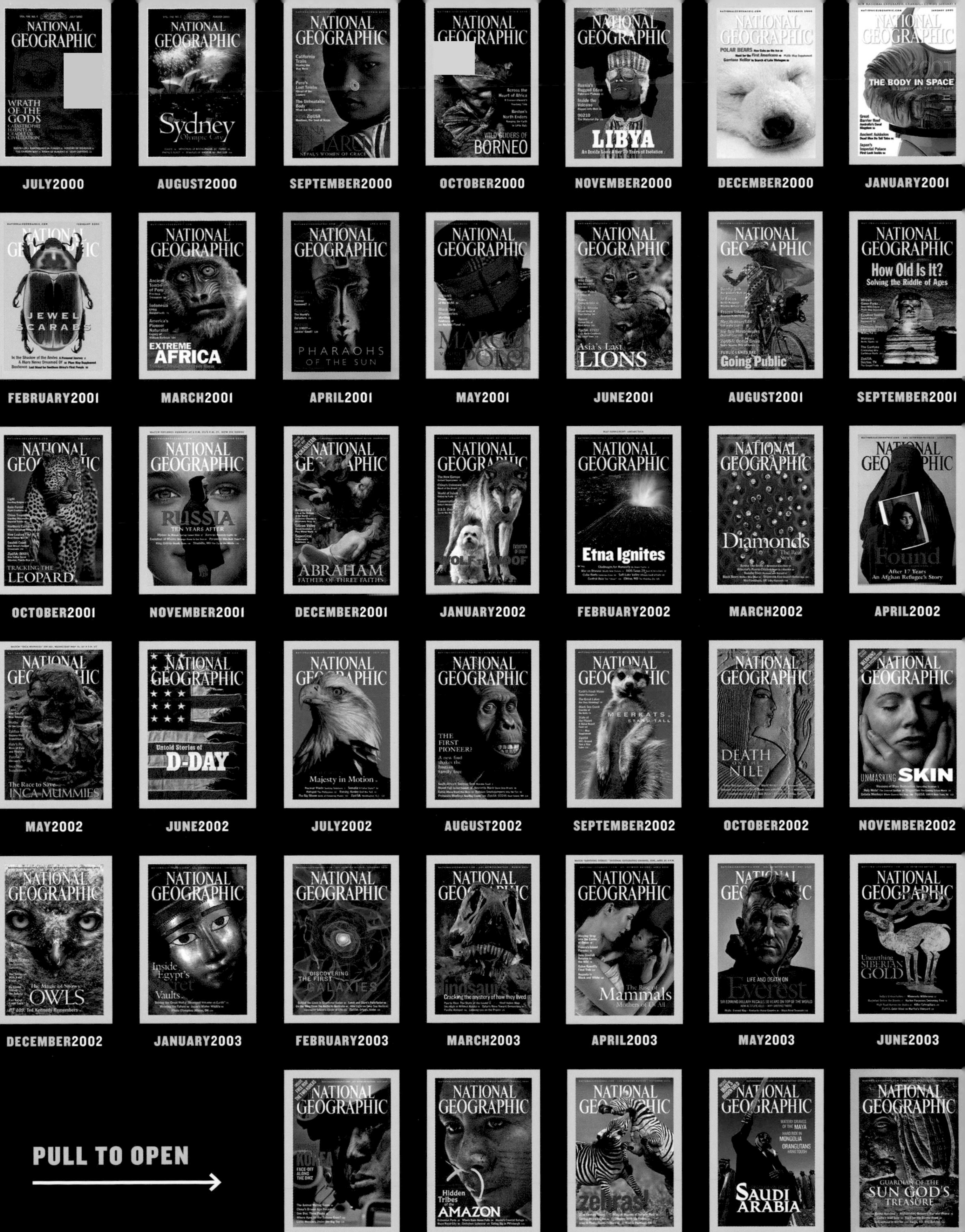

JULY2000
AUGUST2000
SEPTEMBER2000
OCTOBER2000
NOVEMBER2000
DECEMBER2000
JANUARY2001
FEBRUARY2001
MARCH2001
APRIL2001
MAY2001
JUNE2001
AUGUST2001
SEPTEMBER2001
OCTOBER2001
NOVEMBER2001
DECEMBER2001
JANUARY2002
FEBRUARY2002
MARCH2002
APRIL2002
MAY2002
JUNE2002
JULY2002
AUGUST2002
SEPTEMBER2002
OCTOBER2002
NOVEMBER2002
DECEMBER2002
JANUARY2003
FEBRUARY2003
MARCH2003
APRIL2003
MAY2003
JUNE2003
PULL TO OPEN
JULY2003
AUGUST2003
SEPTEMBER2003
OCTOBER2003
NOVEMBER2003

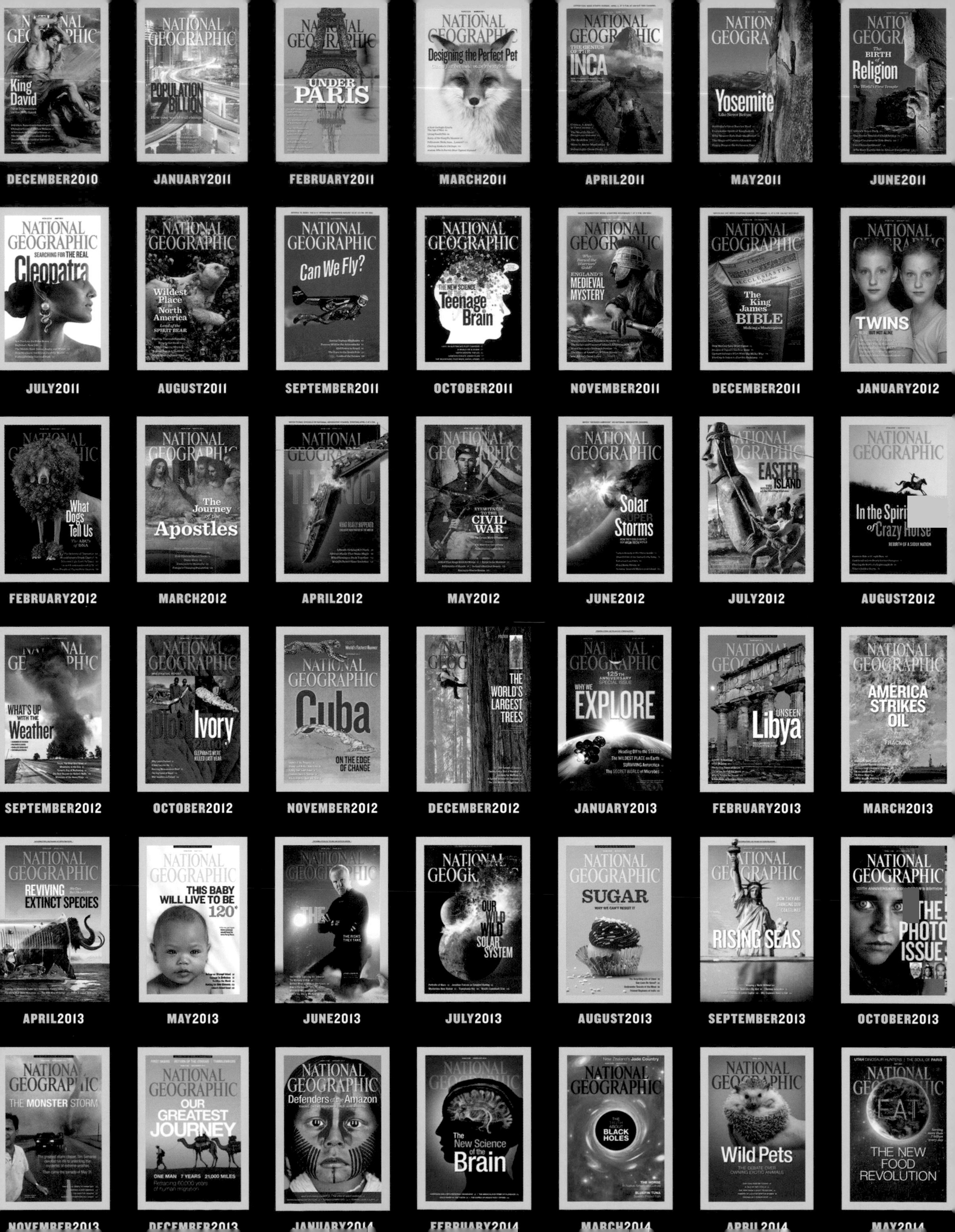
NATIONAL GEOGRAPHIC
King David
DECEMBER2010
POPULATION 7 BILLION
JANUARY2011
UNDER PARIS
FEBRUARY2011
Designing the Perfect Pet
MARCH2011
INCA
APRIL2011
Yosemite
MAY2011
The Birth of Religion
JUNE2011
Cleopatra
JULY2011
Wildest Place in North America
AUGUST2011
Can We Fly?
SEPTEMBER2011
Teenage Brain
OCTOBER2011
ENGLAND'S MEDIEVAL MYSTERY
NOVEMBER2011
The King James BIBLE
DECEMBER2011
TWINS
JANUARY2012
What Dogs Tell Us
FEBRUARY2012
The Journey of the Apostles
MARCH2012
TITANIC
APRIL2012
CIVIL WAR
MAY2012
Solar Super Storms
JUNE2012
EASTER ISLAND
JULY2012
In the Spirit of Crazy Horse
AUGUST2012
WHAT'S UP WITH THE Weather
SEPTEMBER2012
Blood Ivory
OCTOBER2012
Cuba
NOVEMBER2012
THE WORLD'S LARGEST TREES
DECEMBER2012
WHY WE EXPLORE
JANUARY2013
Libya
FEBRUARY2013
AMERICA STRIKES OIL
MARCH2013
REVIVING EXTINCT SPECIES
APRIL2013
THIS BABY WILL LIVE TO BE 120*
MAY2013
JUNE2013
OUR WILD WILD SOLAR SYSTEM
JULY2013
SUGAR
AUGUST2013
RISING SEAS
SEPTEMBER2013
THE PHOTO ISSUE
OCTOBER2013
THE MONSTER STORM
NOVEMBER2013
OUR GREATEST JOURNEY
DECEMBER2013
Defenders of the Amazon
JANUARY2014
The New Science of the Brain
FEBRUARY2014
BLACK HOLES
MARCH2014
Wild Pets
APRIL2014
EAT
THE NEW FOOD REVOLUTION
MAY2014

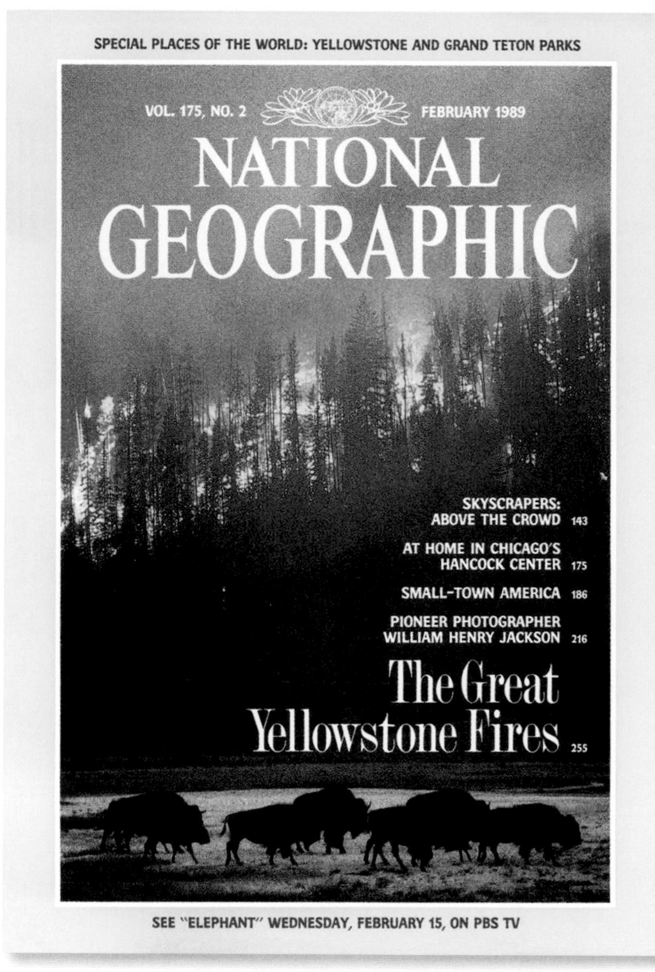

SPECIAL PLACES OF THE WORLD: YELLOWSTONE AND GRAND TETON PARKS

VOL. 175, NO. 2 FEBRUARY 1989

NATIONAL GEOGRAPHIC

SKYSCRAPERS: ABOVE THE CROWD 143

AT HOME IN CHICAGO'S HANCOCK CENTER 175

SMALL-TOWN AMERICA 186

PIONEER PHOTOGRAPHER WILLIAM HENRY JACKSON 216

The Great Yellowstone Fires 255

SEE "ELEPHANT" WEDNESDAY, FEBRUARY 15, ON PBS TV

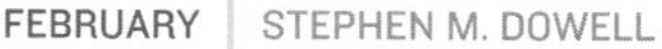

FEBRUARY | STEPHEN M. DOWELL

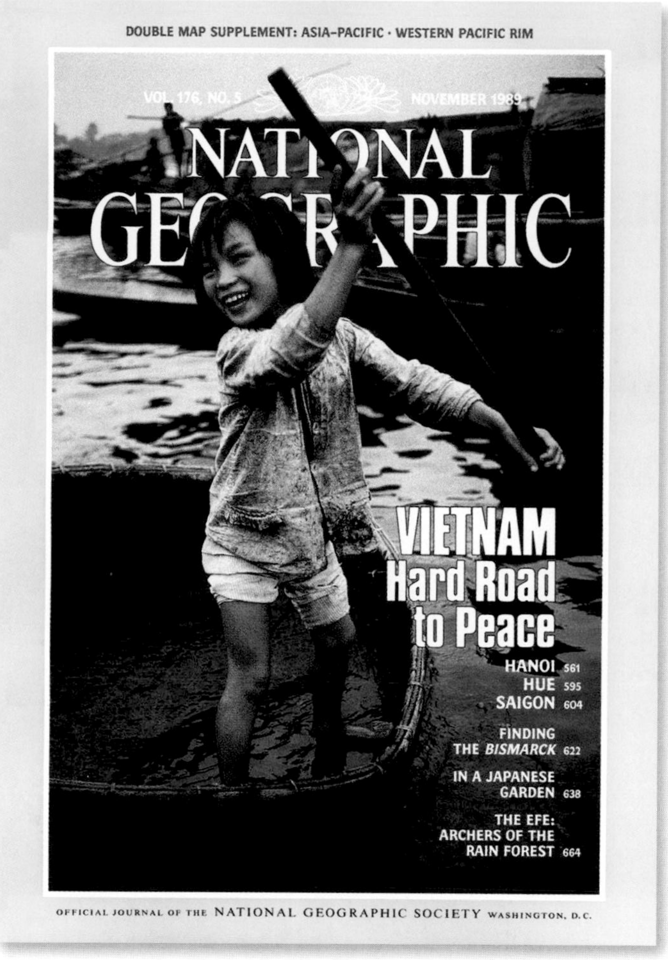

DOUBLE MAP SUPPLEMENT: ASIA-PACIFIC · WESTERN PACIFIC RIM

VOL. 176, NO. 5 NOVEMBER 1989

NATIONAL GEOGRAPHIC

VIETNAM Hard Road to Peace

HANOI 561

HUE 595

SAIGON 604

FINDING THE *BISMARCK* 622

IN A JAPANESE GARDEN 638

THE EFE: ARCHERS OF THE RAIN FOREST 664

OFFICIAL JOURNAL OF THE NATIONAL GEOGRAPHIC SOCIETY WASHINGTON, D.C.

NOVEMBER | DAVID ALAN HARVEY

▲ **YELLOWSTONE IN FLAMES** Bison peacefully grazing while one of the worst wildfires in the nation's history blazes behind them offers a pointed contrast. Despite the efforts of some 10,000 firefighters, the inferno that ravaged nearly a million acres of Yellowstone National Park in the summer and autumn of 1988 incinerated nearly half of the protected area's territory. To some people the Park Service's refusal to fight natural fires—a policy turnabout dating from the 1960s—was directly responsible for the disaster. To others, as author Dave Jeffery put it, the fires "seemed nature's signature written with a grand flourish on an awesome scale."

▲ **CAPTAIN OF THE SHIP** Fourteen years after the end of the Vietnam War, a dutiful daughter of a sampan-based family maneuvers her reed boat through the harbor at Hue.

> "*In Vietnam a person lives, works, suffers, succeeds, sacrifices not for the self but for the home, the nuclear family, the extended family including the dead and the unborn, for the village, for the nation.*"
>
> —Tran Van Dinh
>
> *from "Vietnam: Hard Road to Peace"*

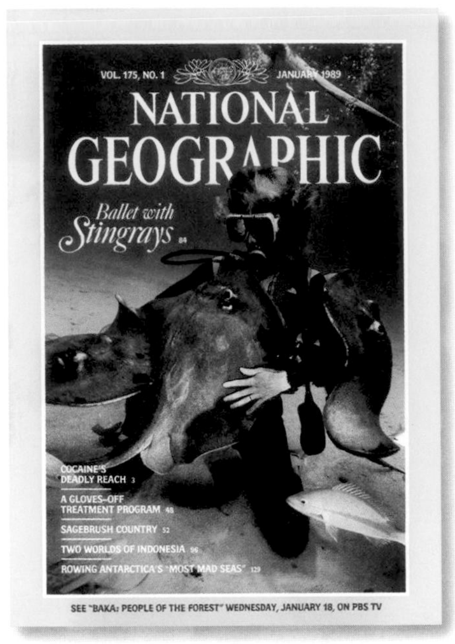

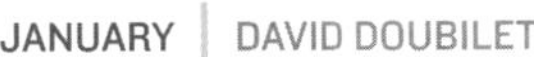

JANUARY | DAVID DOUBILET

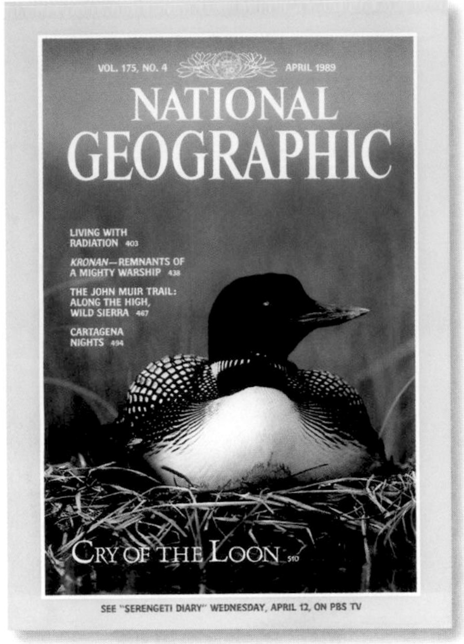

APRIL | MICHAEL S. QUINTON

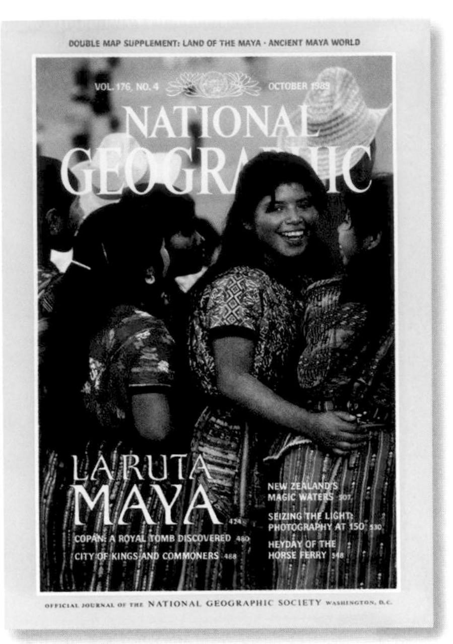

OCTOBER | KENNETH GARRETT

▲ **DANCES WITH STINGRAYS** To David Doubilet, the stage set was as interesting as the actors. The flats near Grand Cayman Island were elemental in their simplicity: all white sand, clear water, and blue sky. It made the perfect backdrop for the wonderful moment when a human embraced a once greatly feared sea creature—the stingray—in that creature's domain. Penny Hatch, who was one of the first to tame those fish, just rocked back on her heels and welcomed the advances of her barbed friend. When Doubilet captured that moment, only seven or eight people were diving with the rays; today several hundred tourists can be found there every day.

THE ULTRASAURS ▶

Stomping off into an uncertain future, both juvenile and adult "ultrasaurs" cross a western Colorado plain 140 million years ago. Ninety-nine percent of all species that ever walked the Earth have gone extinct. It was only in the 1980s that once outlandish theories about mass extinctions began to be taken seriously.

> The scenario is straight out of a science-fiction movie. Giant meteorite strikes earth, setting the planet afire. Volcanoes erupt, tsunamis crash into the continents. The sky grows dark for months, perhaps years. Unable to cope with the catastrophic changes in climate, countless species are wiped off the face of the planet. Yet that is the apocalyptic scene scientists suggest, as evidence grows that comets or meteorites may indeed be agents of mass destruction on earth . . . [Some] extinctions, however, were so rapid—within five hundred to a thousand years—that many scientists suspect an alternate—or at least an assistant—villain: . . . *Homo sapiens.*
>
> *—From "The March Toward Extinction," Rick Gore*

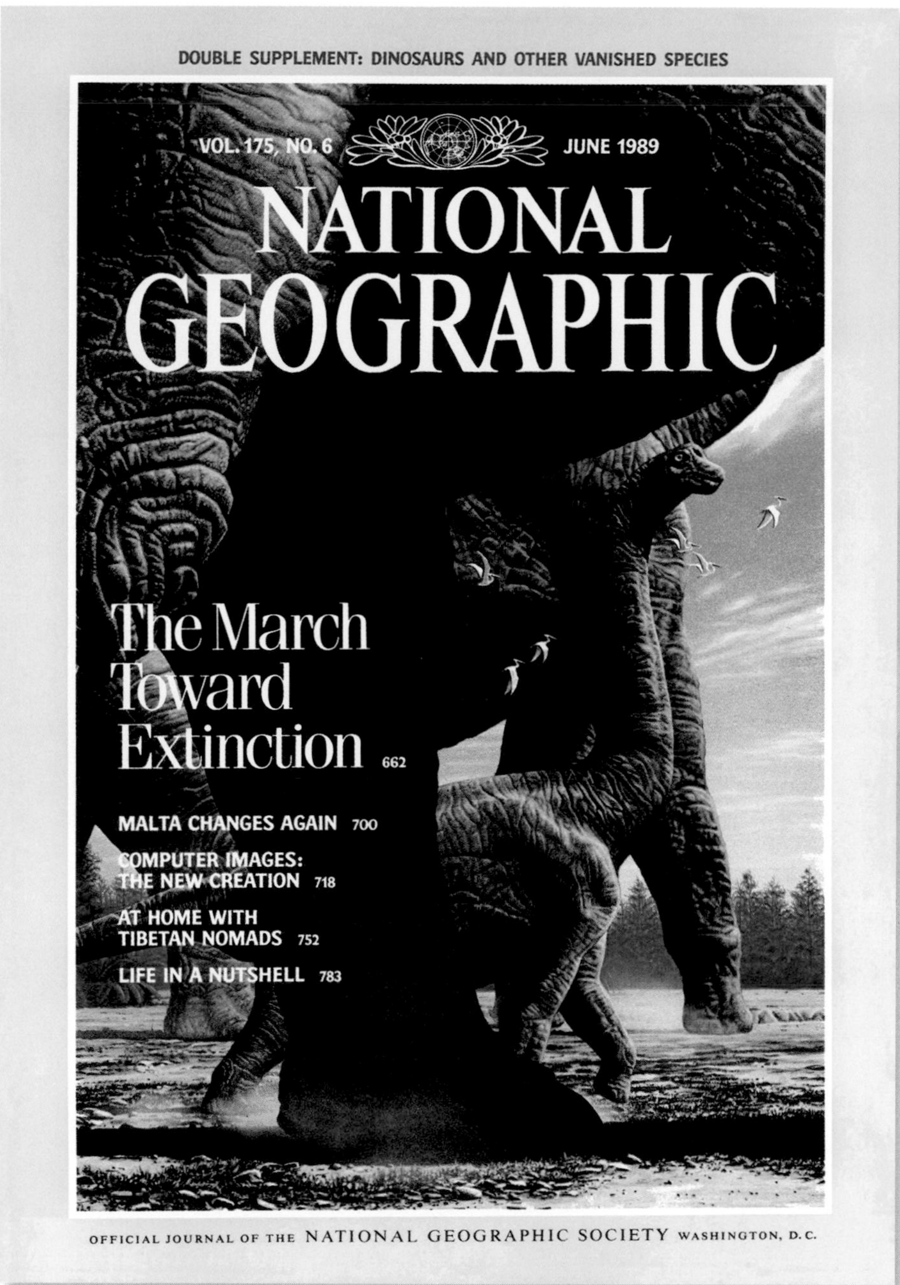

JUNE | JOHN GURCHE

▲ **INEVITABLE EXTINCTION?** John Gurche's "ultrasaurs" were doomed to go extinct much sooner than their creator had imagined. They had less than ten years left. It seems that the shoulder blade, vertebrae, and hip discovered by James Jensen in the 1970s in Colorado's Dry Mesa Quarry and subsequently christened *Ultrasaurus* were in the '90s determined to be bits of another dinosaur found in the same place and called *Supersaurus*. Nor did it help that a Korean researcher had already snagged the name Ultrasaurus for another beast altogether, having beaten Jensen into print.

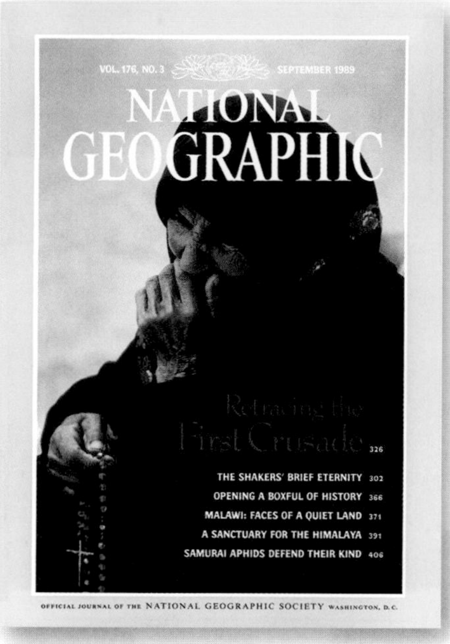

SEPTEMBER | PETER ESSICK

▲ **PORTRAIT OF FAITH** A pilgrim stands lost in prayer at Medjugorje, where in 1981 a series of Marian apparitions soon brought millions of Catholics to the Yugoslav town. While retracing the route of the First Crusade, photographer Peter Essick made a detour to visit the site. Upon seeing this woman, he fixed a 180mm telephoto lens to his camera, mindful of the advice given him at the *Geographic* "to remember to take a cover photograph." He thought it silly then, but seeing her crucifix and her emotion he also saw a cover for the Crusades story. So he made a vertical shot, even leaving room at the top for the cartouche. When Editor Bill Garrett saw the result, "it sailed right through."

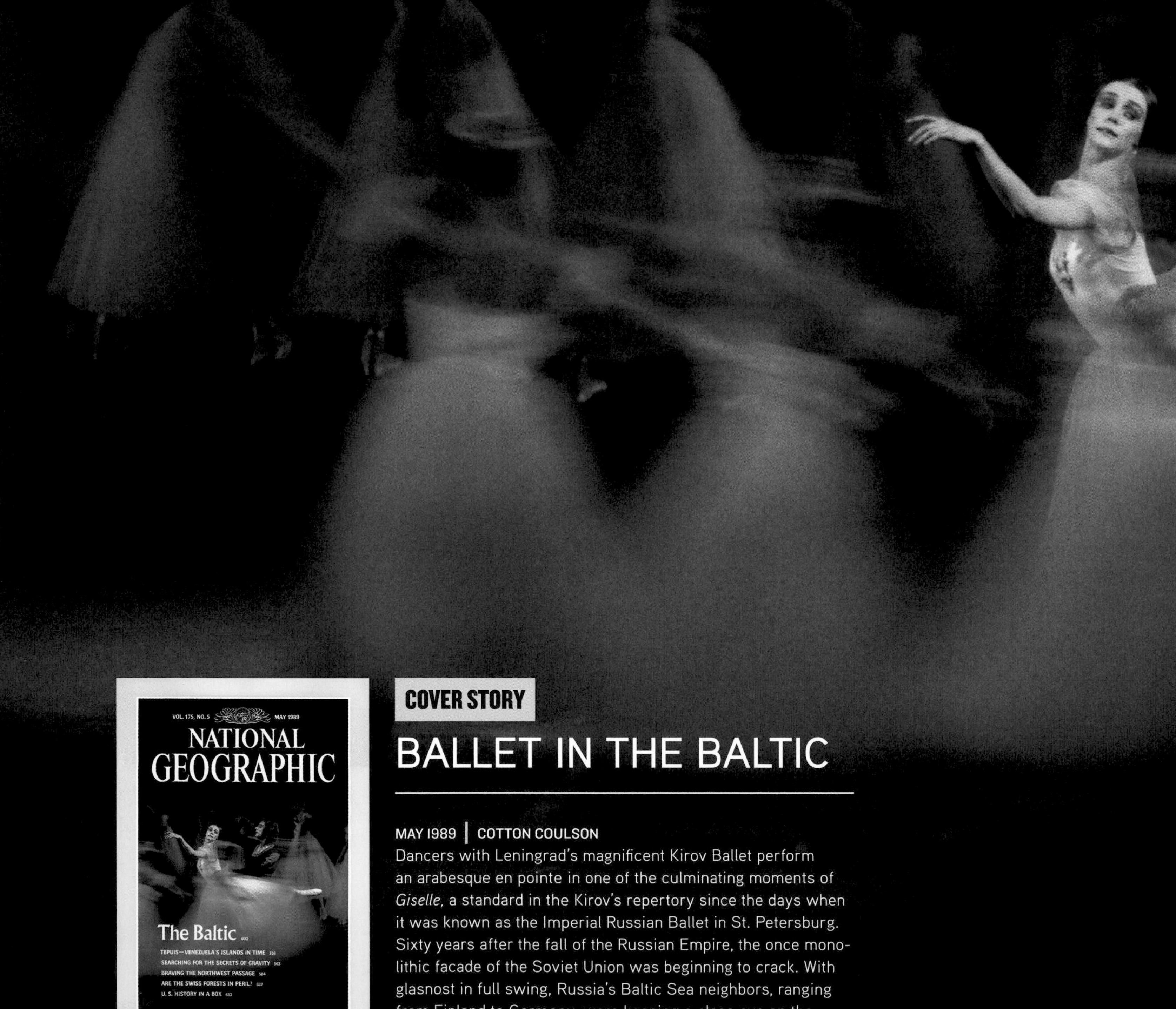

COVER STORY

BALLET IN THE BALTIC

MAY 1989 | COTTON COULSON

Dancers with Leningrad's magnificent Kirov Ballet perform an arabesque en pointe in one of the culminating moments of *Giselle*, a standard in the Kirov's repertory since the days when it was known as the Imperial Russian Ballet in St. Petersburg. Sixty years after the fall of the Russian Empire, the once monolithic facade of the Soviet Union was beginning to crack. With glasnost in full swing, Russia's Baltic Sea neighbors, ranging from Finland to Germany, were keeping a close eye on the unfolding drama to their east.

1990–

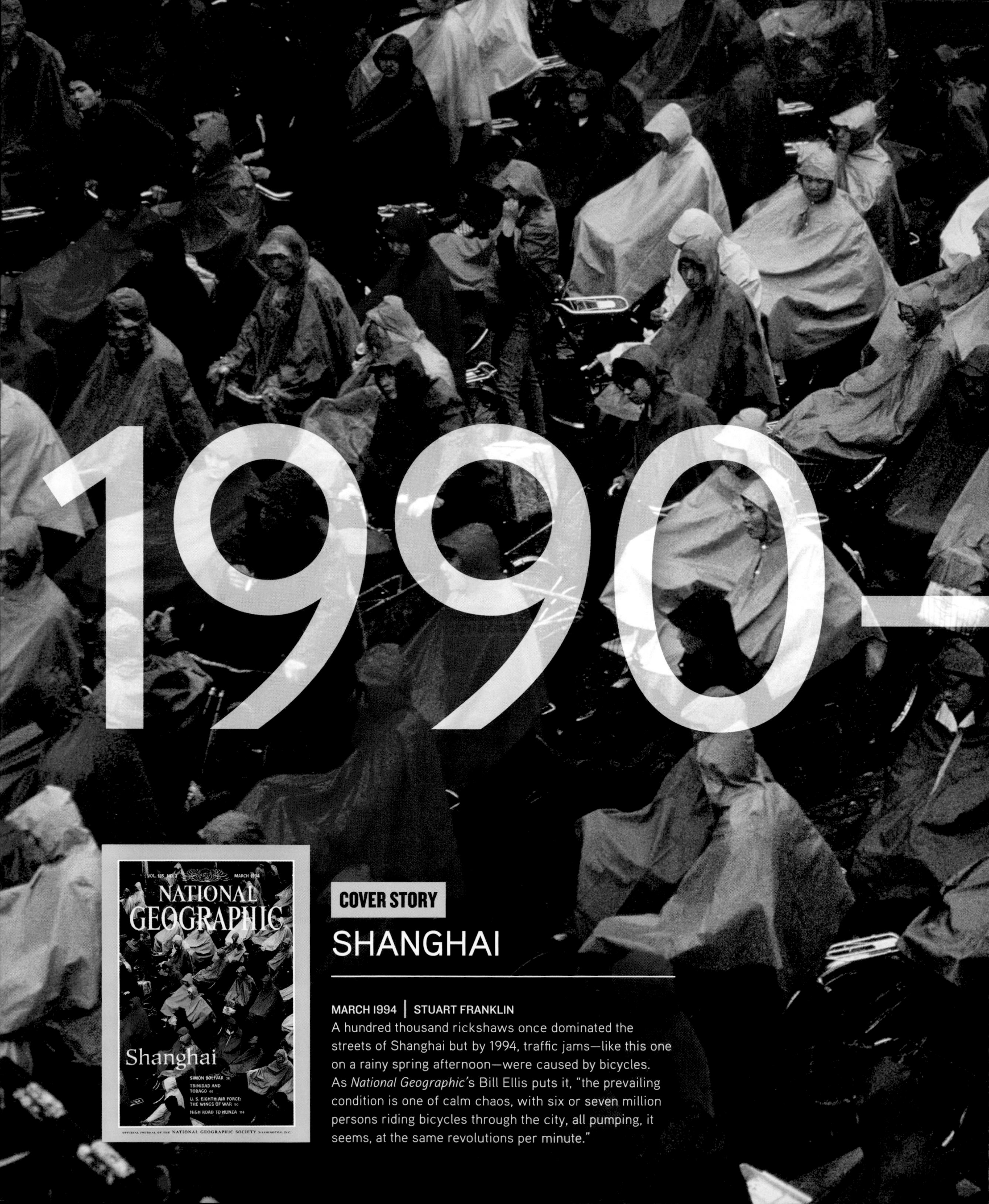

COVER STORY

SHANGHAI

MARCH 1994 | STUART FRANKLIN

A hundred thousand rickshaws once dominated the streets of Shanghai but by 1994, traffic jams—like this one on a rainy spring afternoon—were caused by bicycles. As *National Geographic*'s Bill Ellis puts it, "the prevailing condition is one of calm chaos, with six or seven million persons riding bicycles through the city, all pumping, it seems, at the same revolutions per minute."

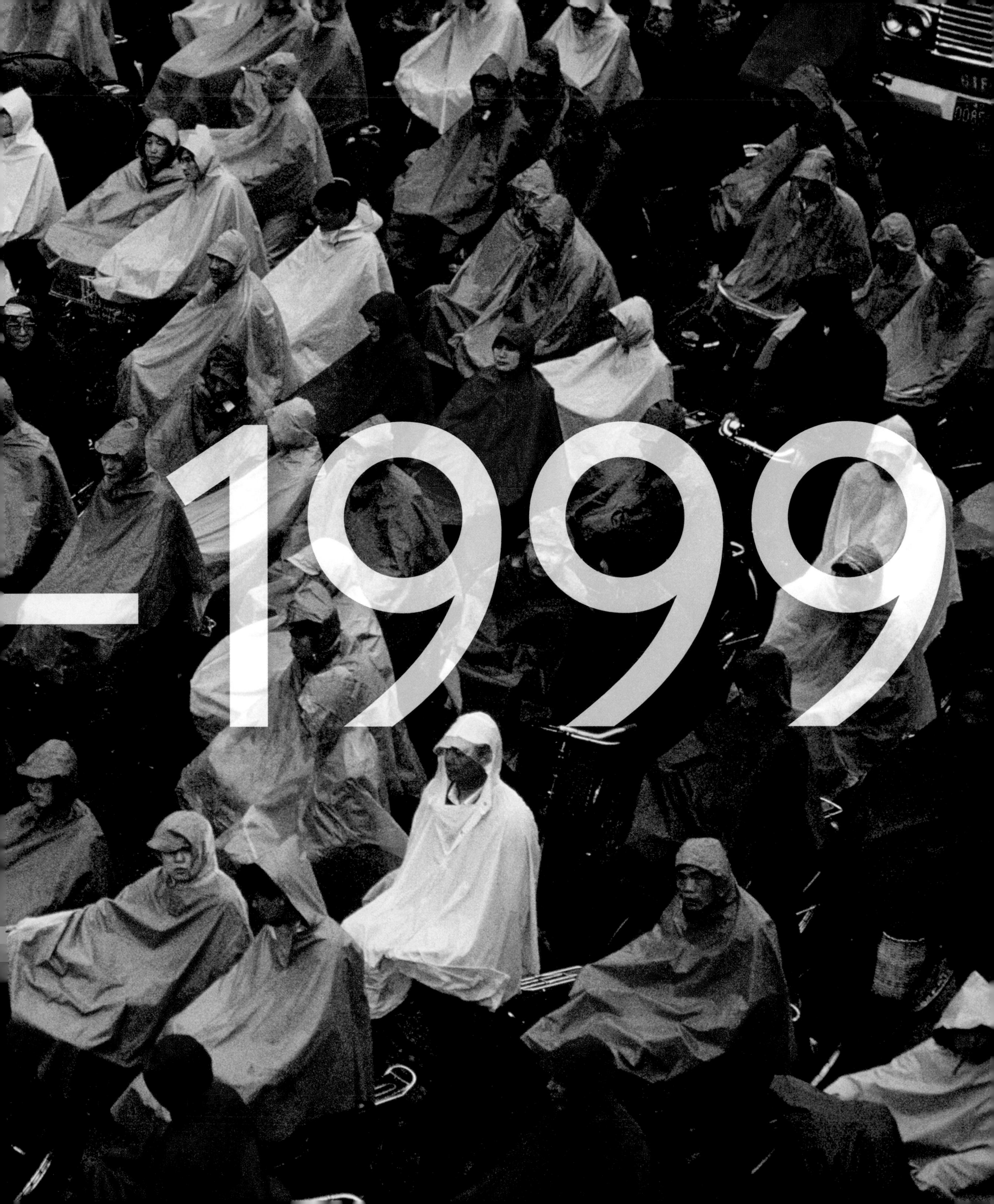
–1999

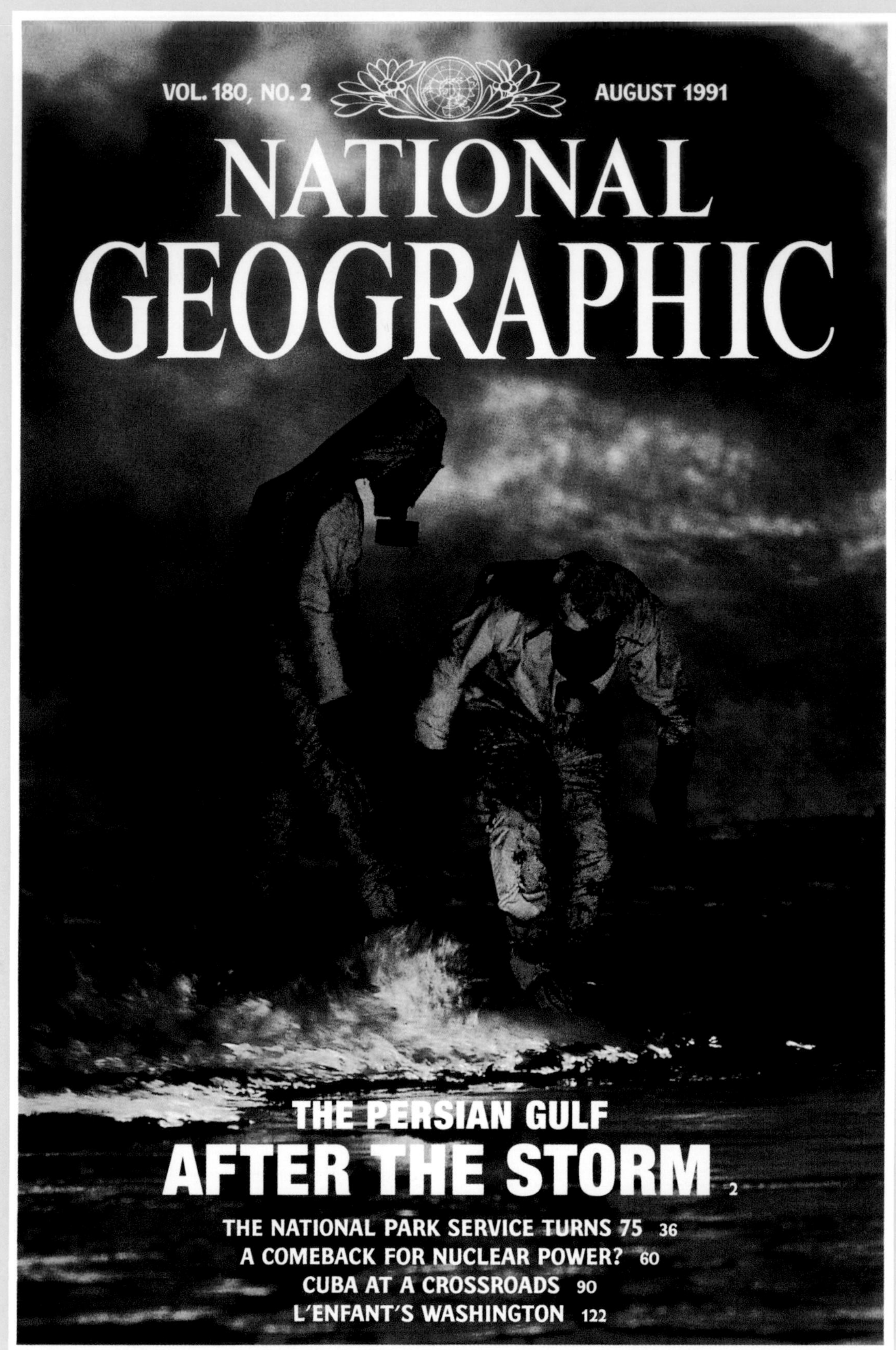

AUGUST 1991 | STEVE MCCURRY Earthtrust's Michael Bailey and Rick Thorpe examine burning oil at the al-Ahmadi field.

[THE WORLD IN THE 1990S]

"The photos I brought back show the black, hellish landscape—yet they cannot convey the fine mist of oil particles that hangs in the air, nor the deafening roar of the wildly burning wells."

—Steve McCurry, from "In the Eye of Desert Storm"

THEY LOOK like aliens on some infernal planet, but Earthtrust's Michael Bailey and Rick Thorpe were among the first environmentalists to don protective suits, brave the land mines, and see for themselves the nightmarish aftermath of war.

Steve McCurry photographed them as they examined ground soaked with burning oil at the al-Ahmadi field, one of 700 Kuwaiti wells torched by Saddam Hussein's retreating troops at the end of the 1991 Gulf War. The exposure settings on McCurry's camera were probably a quarter of a second at f2.8, usually reserved for low light. That's where he kept them, for the smoke from the burning wells turned day into night.

In December 1990, four months after Iraqi forces had invaded Kuwait, *National Geographic* had commissioned McCurry to photograph the environmental consequences of the coming struggle. When the U.S.-led coalition launched Desert Storm, initially an aerial offensive but eventually a full-scale attack that drove the Iraqi army out of Kuwait in only four days, McCurry was embedded with the 42nd Field Artillery Brigade. His pictures of the appalling ecological damage riveted readers of the August 1991 issue.

The '90s had started with a bang with the Gulf War flaring, but another one quietly burned out: On October 3, 1990, Germany was officially

FACTS & FIGURES THE 1990s

- **26** covers featuring wildlife
- **13** covers on tribes or cultures
- **12** covers on underwater subjects
- **6** covers featuring big cats
- **4** covers featuring primates
- **4** covers on archaeological subjects
- **4** covers with birds
- **3** covers in space

AROUND THE WORLD

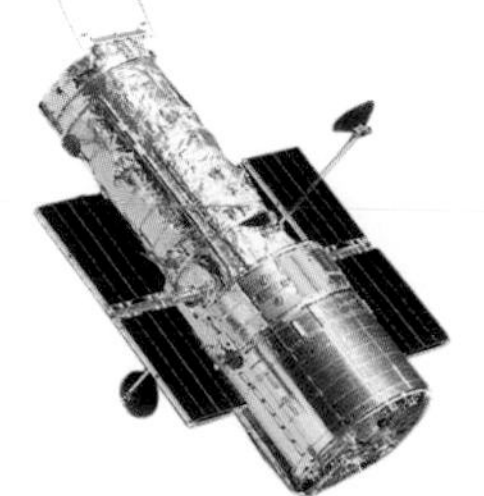

HUBBLE 1990
The Hubble Space Telescope is launched into orbit.

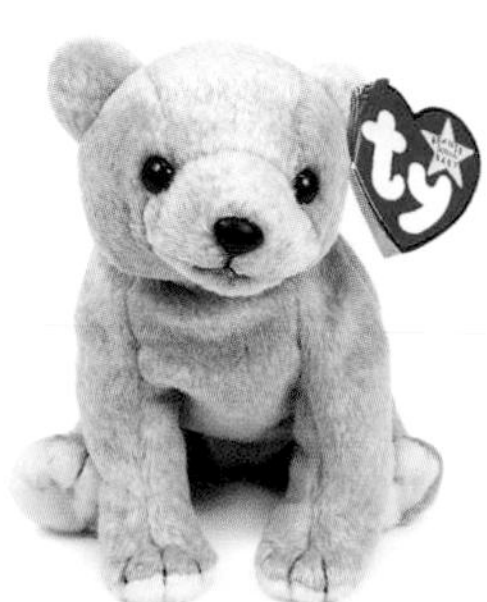

BEANIE BABIES 1993
The first of a long series of wildly popular stuffed animals by Ty Inc. appears.

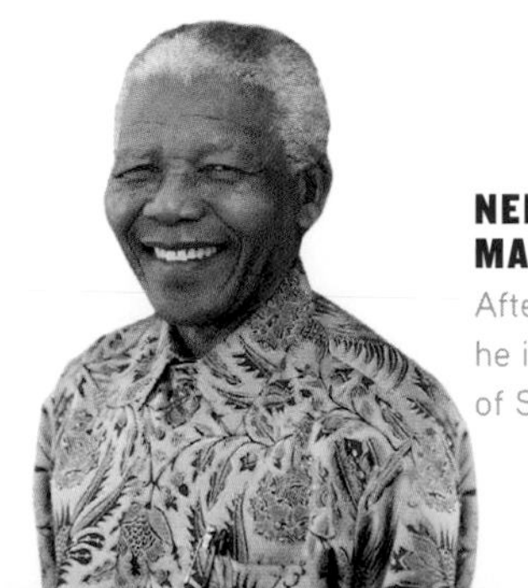

NELSON MANDELA 1994
After 27 years in prison, he is elected president of South Africa.

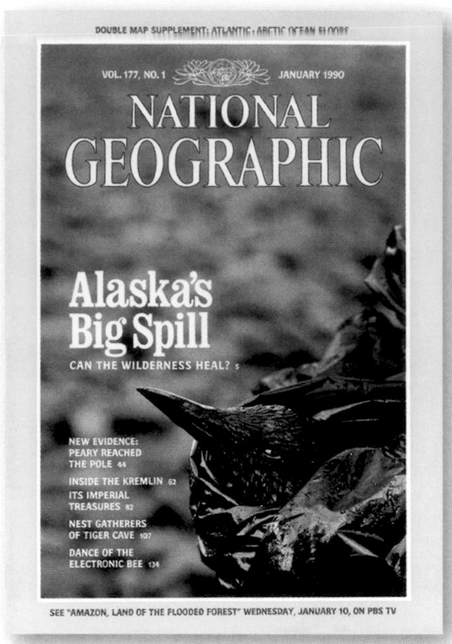

JANUARY 1990 | NATALIE FOBES

▲ **A DYING BIRD** This pigeon guillemot was one of at least 100,000 seabirds killed by the massive oil spill following the March 24, 1989, wreck of the *Exxon Valdez* in Alaska's Prince William Sound. Over a half million barrels of crude fouled the shores of the once pristine bay.

reunited, and Mikhail Gorbachev's Soviet Union did nothing to stop it, for its days were numbered, too. All of its constituent republics soon declared their independence, and by December 1991, when Gorbachev resigned, the Soviet Union had ceased to exist.

Hot wars, however, didn't end just because a cold one had. In June 1991, while those fires were still burning in Kuwait, Yugoslavia began breaking up. First Slovenia, then Croatia and Bosnia fought Serbia in an escalating series of massacres, reprisals, and other atrocities that went by the name of ethnic cleansing. Eventually all of Yugoslavia's former republics would go their own way, but not before another round of bloodletting devastated Kosovo, only ended by NATO air strikes on Belgrade.

In 1994 a 100-day Rwandan rampage saw Hutu mobs kill upward of a million Tutsis in a genocide that horrified the world. Hardly had order been restored in Rwanda when in 1996 the first of a series of wars broke out in neighboring Zaire (today the Democratic Republic of the Congo)—wars that eventually involved nine nations, nearly two dozen armed groups, and eventually was called simply the Great War of Africa. By the time it ended in 2008 over five million people had lost their lives, most of them victims of famine and disease, making that conflict one of the deadliest since 1945.

But that bloodshed was largely out of sight, and so out of mind for most Americans. For them the '90s were a prosperous decade, average personal incomes doubling while the U.S. economy enjoyed its longest peacetime expansion. Many people thanked President Bill Clinton for their good fortune; others preferred to see him removed from office as a consequence of the Monica Lewinsky scandal. The House, in fact, did impeach him; but the Senate acquitted him.

Millions followed such developments on cable television news channels—when they weren't watching *Seinfeld* or *Friends* or *The Simpsons*. Or perhaps they turned on their home PCs, booted up Windows 98, and dialed up access to the World Wide Web. For the '90s were also the decade when the digital revolution gained momentum. Websites were proliferating and cell phones were increasingly seen in city streets. New

AROUND THE WORLD

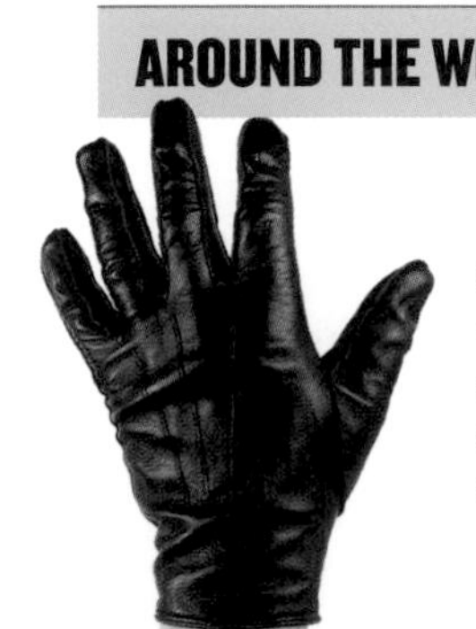

O. J. TRIAL 1995
After more than a year, the murder "trial of the century" ends with O. J. Simpson's controversial acquittal.

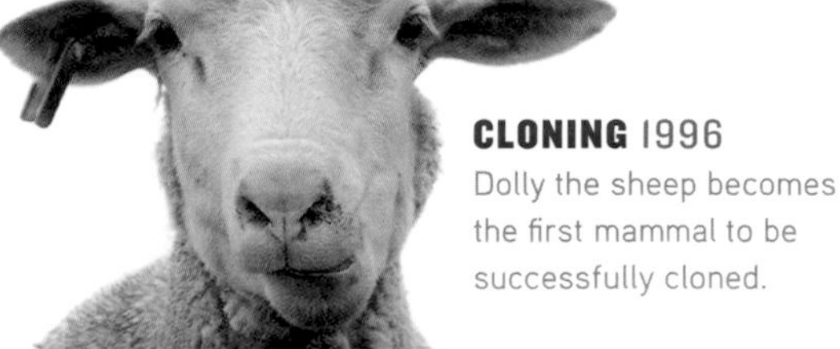

CLONING 1996
Dolly the sheep becomes the first mammal to be successfully cloned.

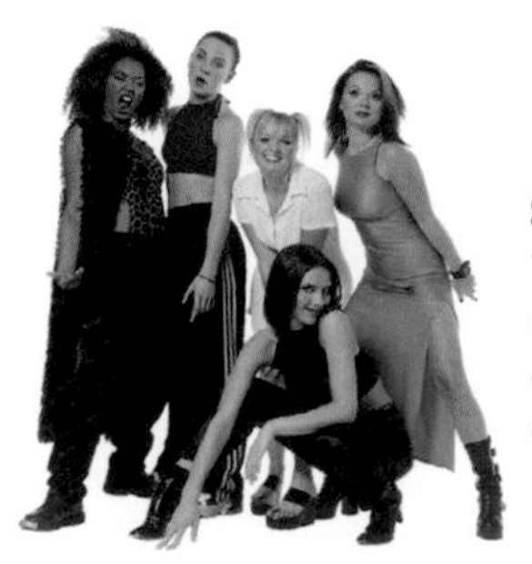

SPICE GIRLS 1996
The all-female pop group rockets to superstardom on the strength of their debut album, *Spice*.

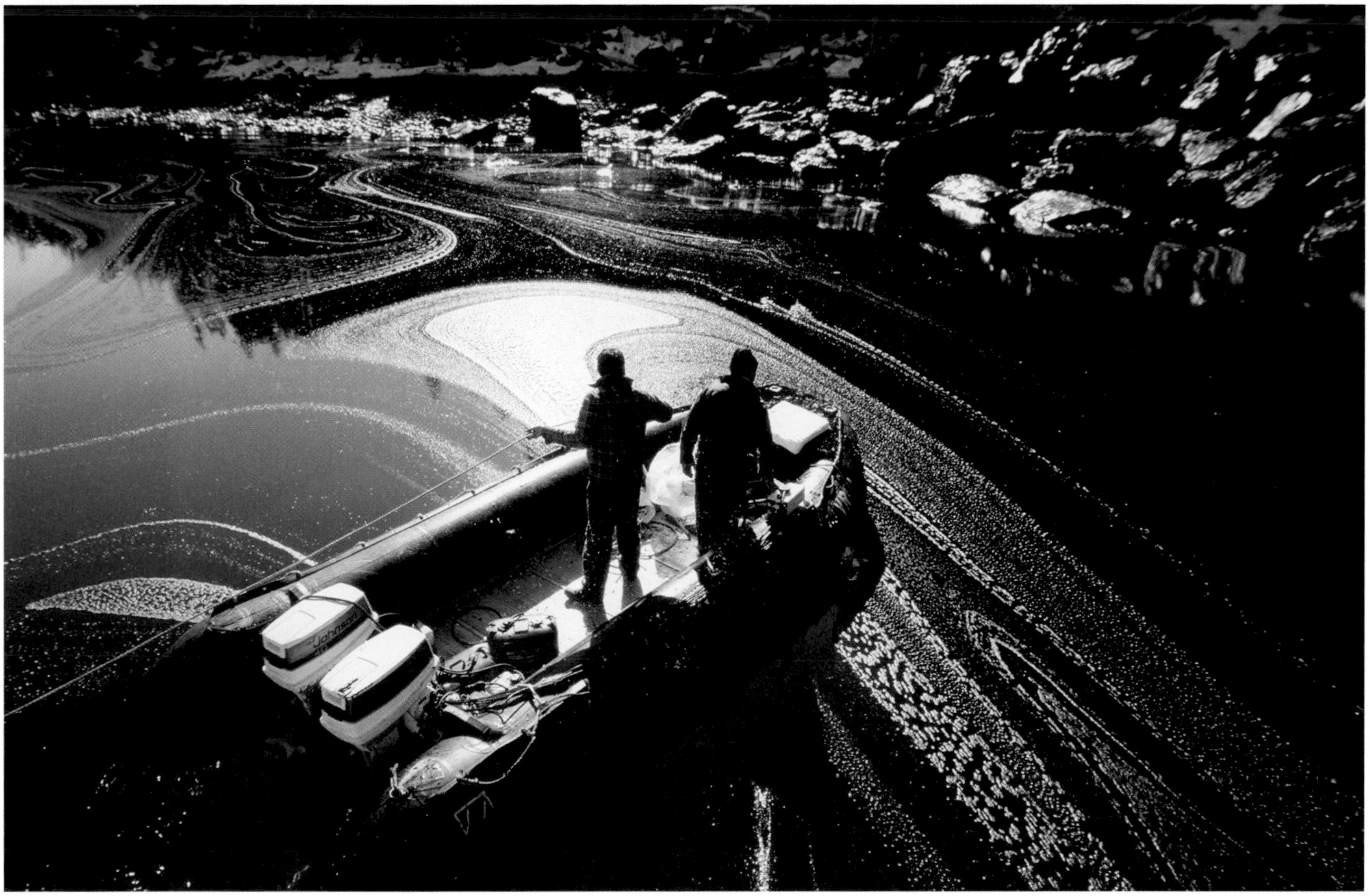

JANUARY 1990 | NATALIE FOBES Fishermen encounter an oil slick 35 miles from the site of the *Exxon Valdez* spill.

media began to outpace old; the music industry was the first to falter, but print publishing would not be far behind.

Thanks largely to Editor Bill Allen, who took the helm in 1995, *National Geographic* continued to win awards for its photojournalism. It also took an important new step: For nearly a century the Society's journal had been available only to members, but in 1998 it began appearing on newsstands as well. That meant more attention would soon be paid to cover appeal. ■

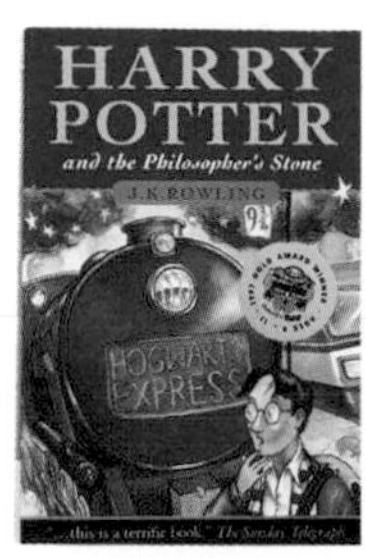

HARRY POTTER 1997
The first of seven immensely popular novels is published.

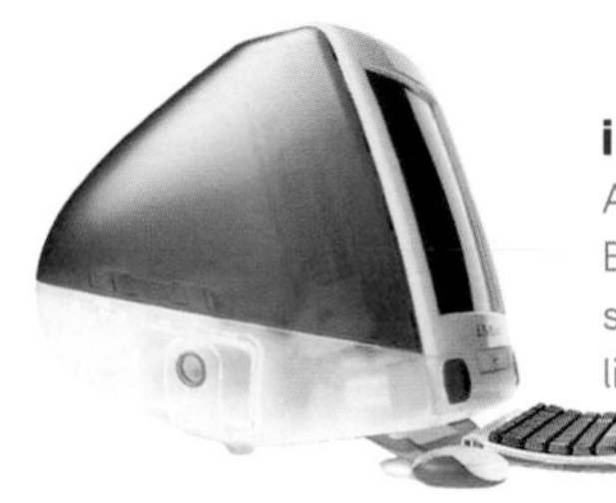

iMAC 1998
Apple releases iMac in Bondi Blue, the first version of its most popular line of desktop computers.

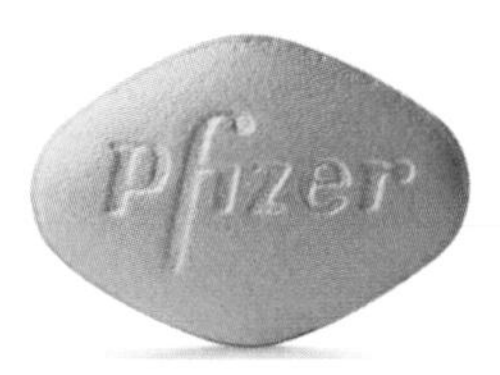

VIAGRA 1998
The blue pill for guys in need of a lift is approved.

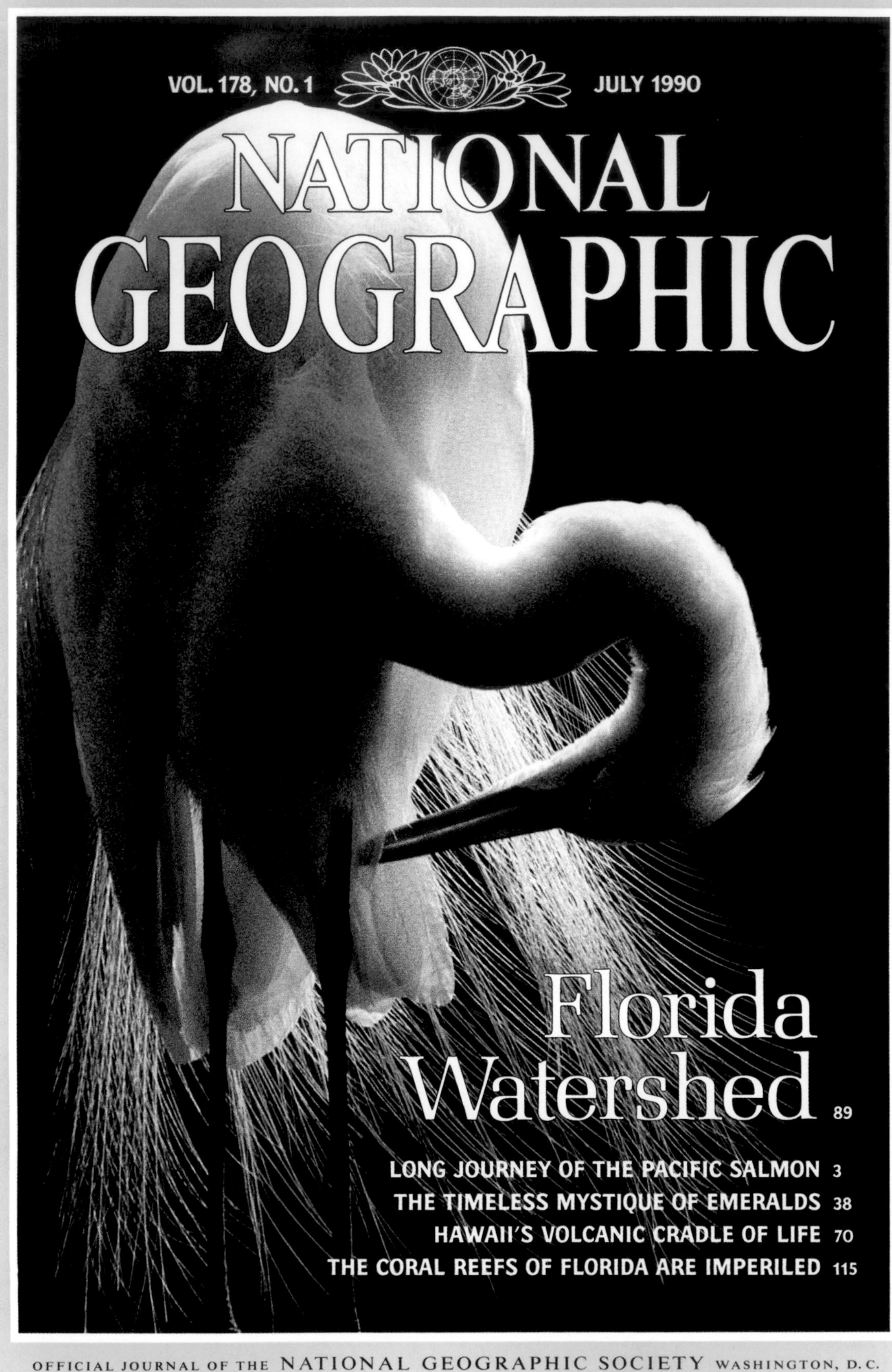

JULY | FARRELL GREHAN A great egret displays its breeding plumage.

FLORIDA'S WETLAND WARS

IN 1960 300,000 WADING BIRDS nested in the Everglades. Thirty years later, that number was down to 15,000. Meanwhile, South Florida had seen a boom in the population of *Homo sapiens*, and marshes had been diked and drained and replaced by tomato fields, sugarcane plantations, and cattle ranches. Agricultural and industrial runoff was contaminating the waters while the real estate market and encroaching urbanization hastened the disappearance of more vulnerable wetlands. Ultimately, it was this looming battle between urban water needs and those of the Everglades ecosystem—typified by that great egret—which the *Geographic* highlighted in its July 1990 issue.

A great egret displaying its breeding plumage in the Florida Everglades like this one was no stranger to threat. It had survived decimation just a century earlier when those long white plumes were more valuable than gold. There was not a fashionably dressed woman in the Western world who did not want egret feathers—or any other feathers, for that matter; or even entire stuffed birds—adorning her hat. That entailed an unprecedented avian slaughter, especially of the more ornamental species of shorebirds. Poachers were even willing to murder game wardens to secure the plumes.

Thanks to changes in fashion and public opinion, the efforts of the Audubon Society (its emblem is a great egret), as well as the establishment in 1934 of Everglades National Park, that slaughter was halted. Although bird populations quickly recovered, and egrets once again frequented the saw grass and mangroves, they were soon exposed to the even more insidious enemy: development.

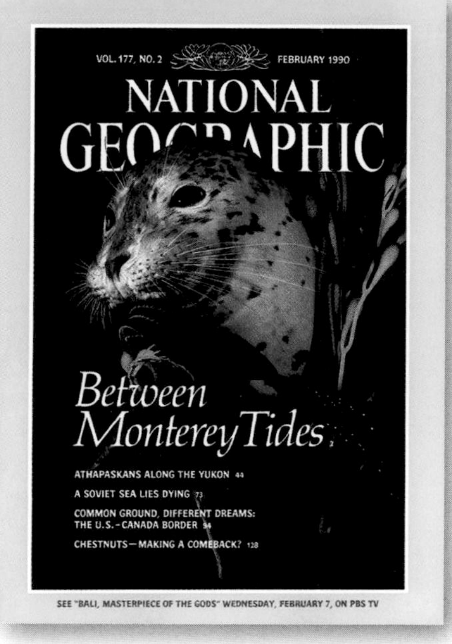

FEBRUARY | DAVID DOUBILET

▲ **SLY SMILE** "A warm face in a cold sea" is how David Doubilet characterized this portrait of a curious harbor seal peeking out of a submerged kelp forest in California's Monterey Bay. It played hide-and-seek with Doubilet the entire time he worked in the bay.

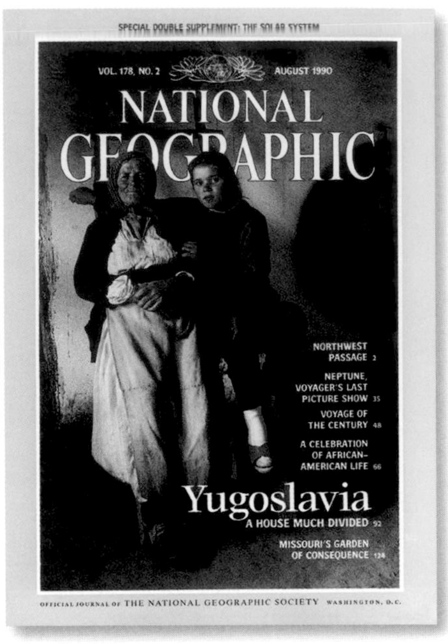

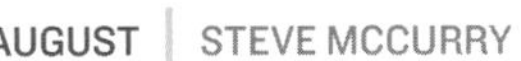
AUGUST | STEVE MCCURRY

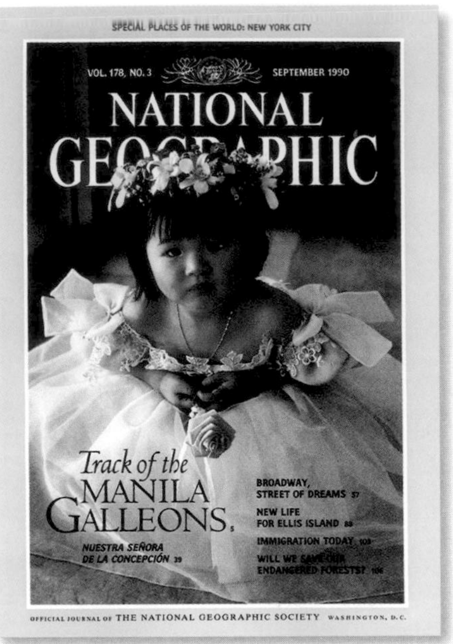

SEPTEMBER | SISSE BRIMBERG

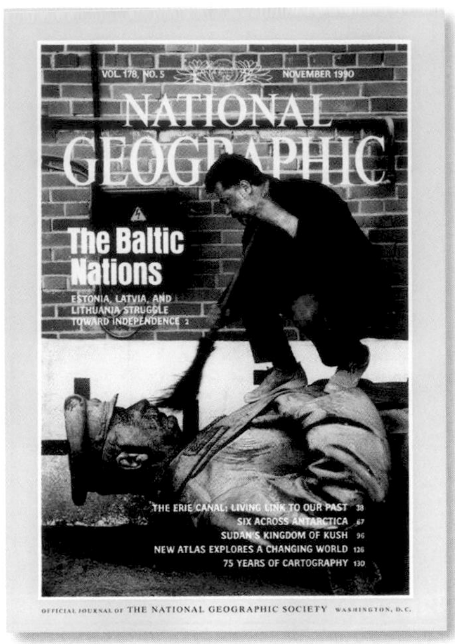

NOVEMBER | LARRY C. PRICE

▲ **GROWING APART** At first glance what looks like a portrait of a Yugoslav generation gap—an ethnic Albanian farm woman in Macedonia wearing the traditional Muslim *dimite*, or culotte, while her granddaughter prefers a more contemporary look—may also be seen as the emblem of an increasingly divided nation. After the death of strongman Marshal Tito in 1981, the center was no longer holding. Yugoslavia was about to descend into the horrific series of wars that marked its disintegration, with Serbs fighting Croats, Bosnians, and ethnic Albanians until what was one state became seven independent nations.

TOUGH LIFE IN SPANISH HARLEM ▶

CLUTCHING A FRIEND, A young girl faces a grim future from a shadowed East Harlem hallway. She did not face it alone—as documentary photographer Joseph Rodriguez showed in a gritty, unsparing, and compassionate coverage, the 120,000 residents of *el barrio,* also called Spanish Harlem, were confronting an epidemic of drugs and crime.

> We heard what sounded like gunfire coming from outside. José's wife, Therese, turned up the television. "The walls have ears," she said as she lit up a joint. Acrid marijuana smoke filled the room. José got up, picked up a vial, walked into the back room. He talked as he went away, then was quiet for a few seconds. When he came back, his eyes were glassy, his movements quicker. I was uneasy. Crack sends you up, makes you fearless, unpredictable.
>
> *—From "Growing Up in East Harlem," Jere Van Dyk*

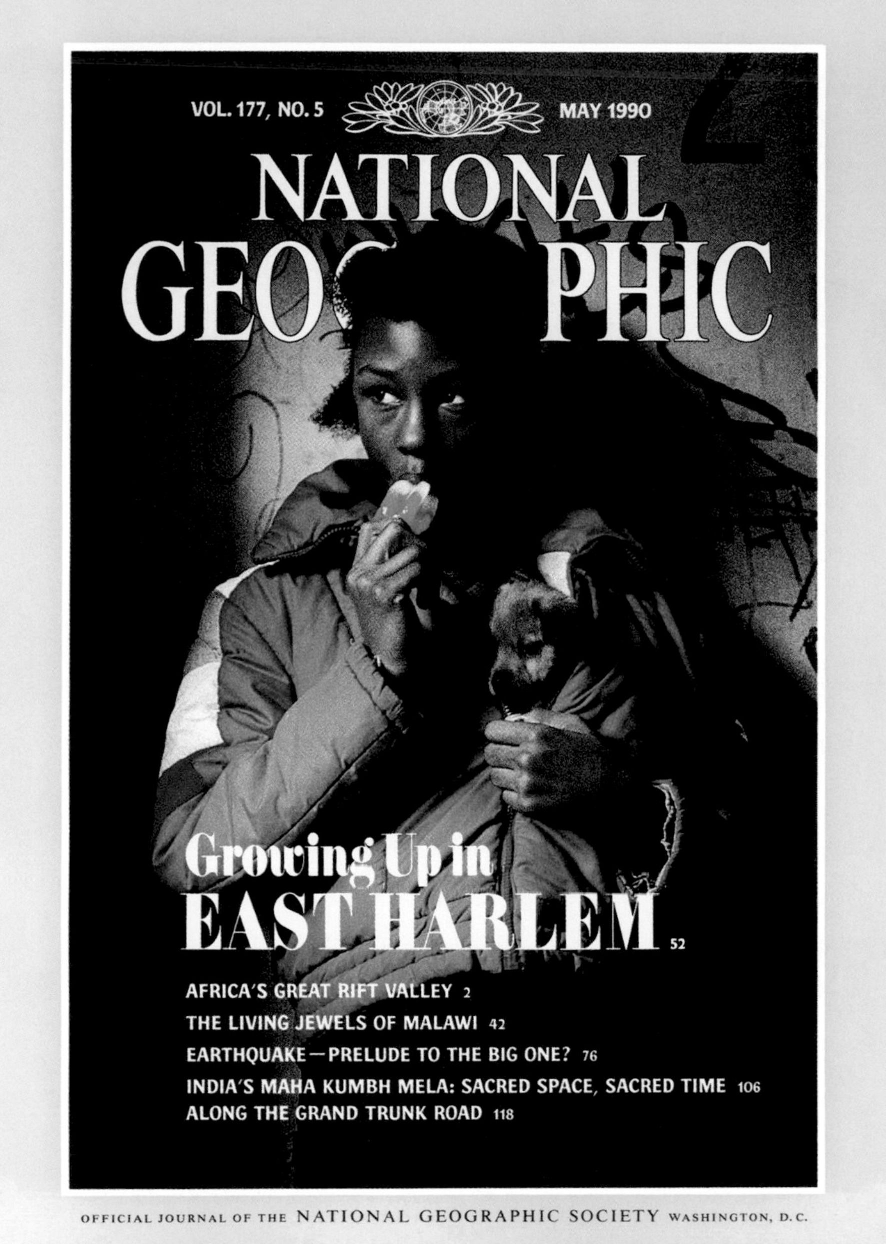

MAY | JOSEPH RODRIGUEZ

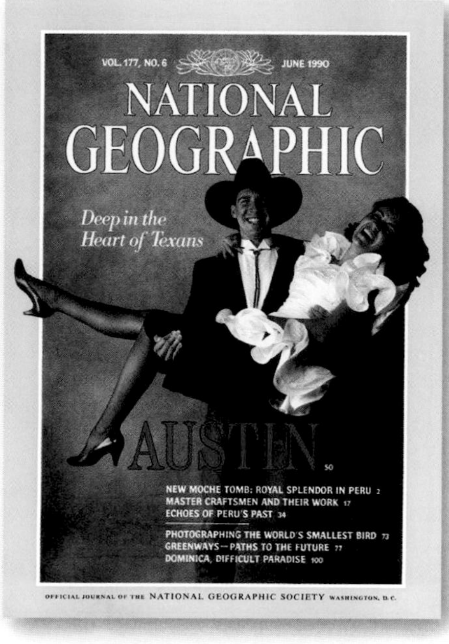

JUNE | MICHAEL O'BRIEN

▲ **PROM NIGHT** Dancing partners Sloan Teeple and Tracy Hanslık cavort at the Austin High School prom.

"There are three kinds of people in this world, according to citizens of Austin, Texas. Those who know Austin and love it. Those who want to go there and haven't. And the poor benighted souls who don't know what they're missing."

—Elizabeth A. Moize
from "Austin: Deep in the Heart of Texans"

"Brownstone tenements, housing projects, vacant lots, burned-out buildings, shattered windows—200 square blocks where 120,000 people live beset by drugs, crime, and despair but also in a cousinship of hope, love, and optimism . . ."

—Jere Van Dyk
from "Growing Up in East Harlem"

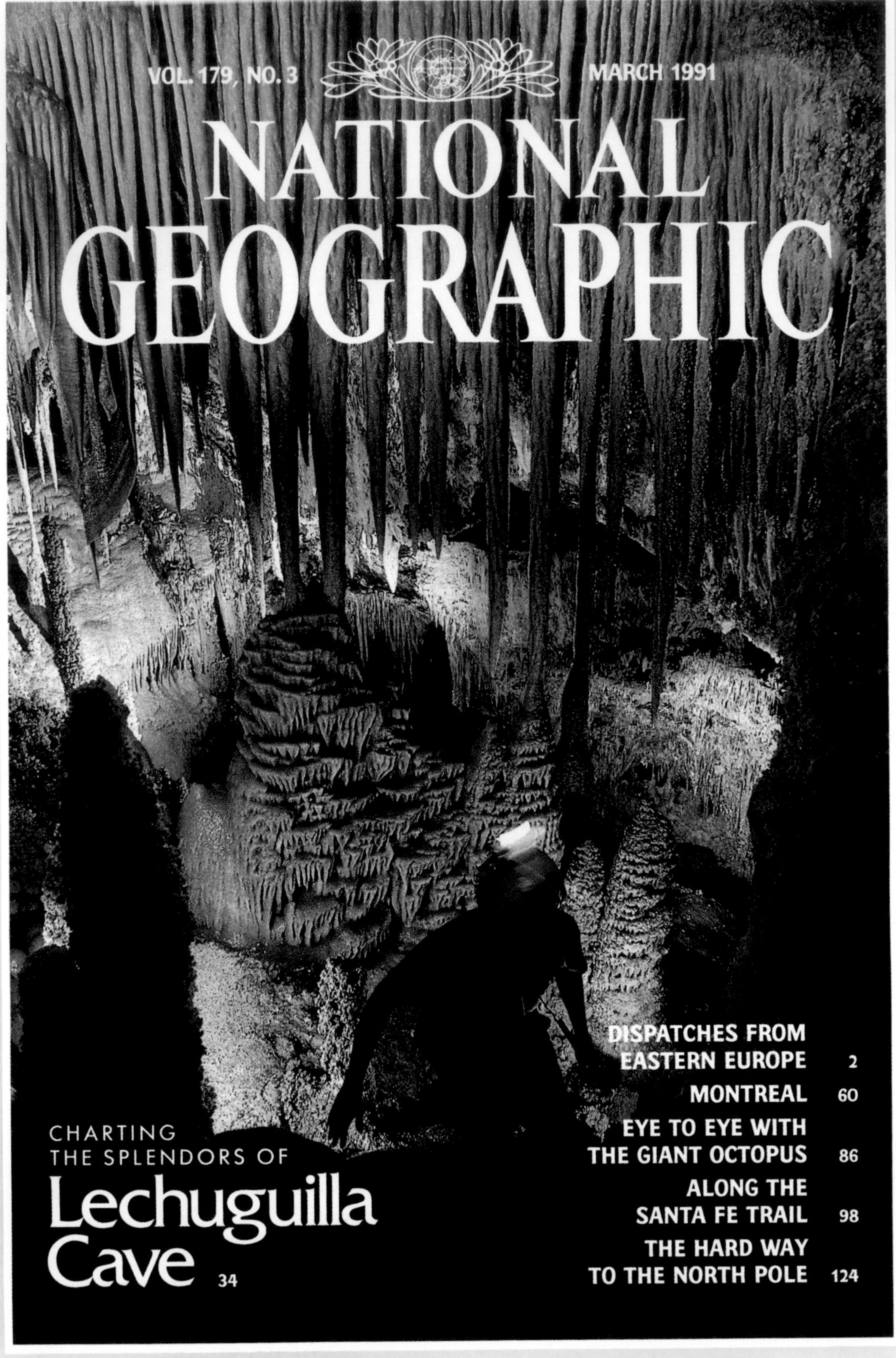

MARCH | MICHAEL NICHOLS A spelunker explores the wonders of one of America's deepest caves.

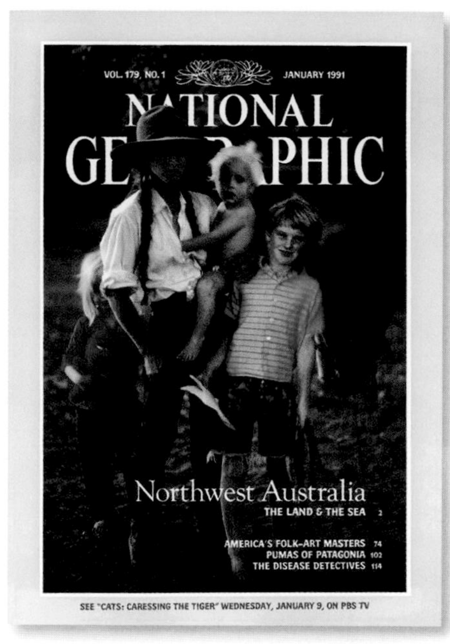

JANUARY | SAM ABELL

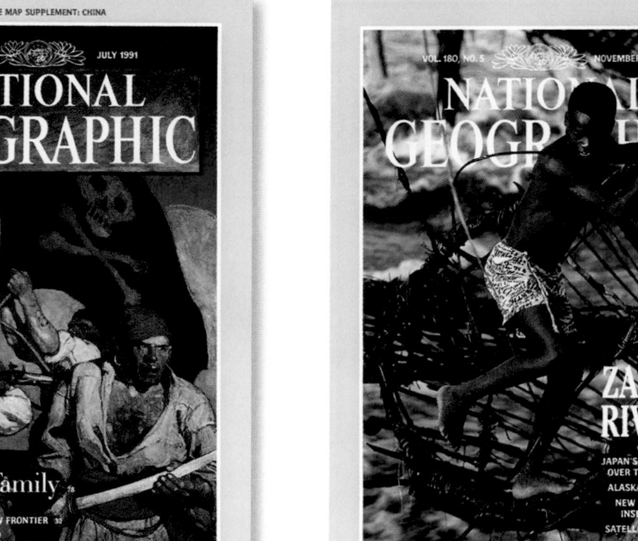

JULY | N. C. WYETH, COURTESY OF THE BRANDYWINE RIVER MUSEUM

NOVEMBER | ROBERT CAPUTO

SUBTERRANEAN GRAND CANYON

It was "Neil Armstrong stuff," reported one of Michael "Nick" Nichols's comrades, describing what it was like to explore the newly discovered underground wonderland called Lechuguilla Cave. That thought had occurred to Nichols, too, as he dragged his cameras and six battery-powered flashes past subterranean features newly christened with evocative names such as Freakout Traverse, Chasm Drop, Death Pit, and the Void. There were more than 130 miles of labyrinthine passageways in this extremely deep American cave, and it took a solid day to reach one of the beautiful chambers, with their flowstone formations and hanging stalactites, which he intended to photograph. It took most of another day to place those flashes. Twelve hours, perhaps, for two good exposures. One was a horizontal, and thinking he might get a cover shot, the second was a vertical—the one you see here.

▲ **ZAIRE JOURNEY** A young fisherman keeps his balance on one of the snare traps suspended above the rapids of the Congo River, which was then called the Zaire. Bob Caputo, an old "Africa hand," traveled to Zaire (today the Democratic Republic of the Congo) to undertake a voyage up the length of this continental lifeline. But it took him longer to get permission than it did to make the journey. He spent six exasperating weeks waiting in Kinshasa, the capital, for a government-issued press permit to proceed—and hardly was it in his pocket before he was arrested for making photographs. In the end, however, he completed the nearly 6,000-mile round-trip.

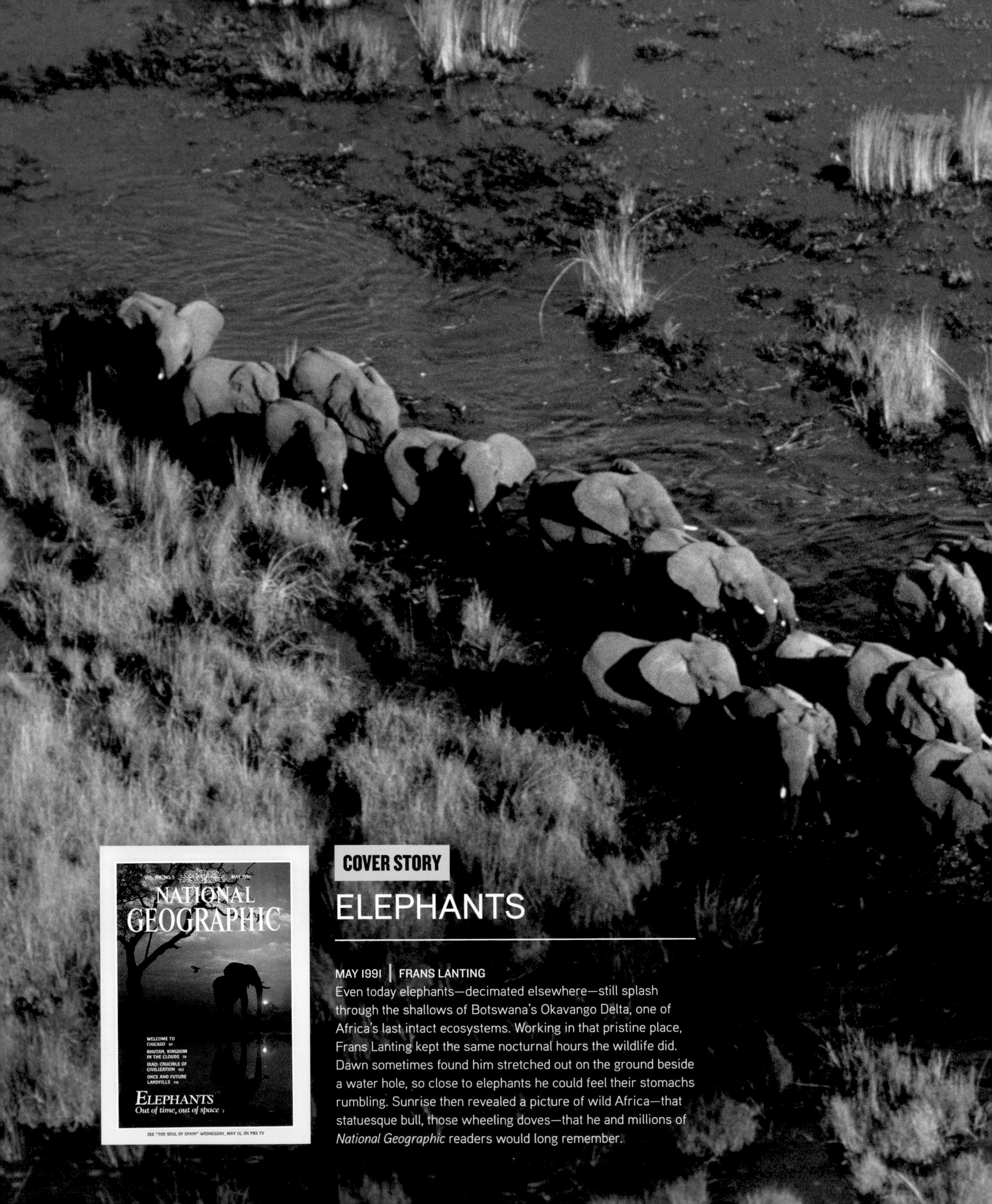

COVER STORY

ELEPHANTS

MAY 1991 | FRANS LANTING

Even today elephants—decimated elsewhere—still splash through the shallows of Botswana's Okavango Delta, one of Africa's last intact ecosystems. Working in that pristine place, Frans Lanting kept the same nocturnal hours the wildlife did. Dawn sometimes found him stretched out on the ground beside a water hole, so close to elephants he could feel their stomachs rumbling. Sunrise then revealed a picture of wild Africa—that statuesque bull, those wheeling doves—that he and millions of *National Geographic* readers would long remember.

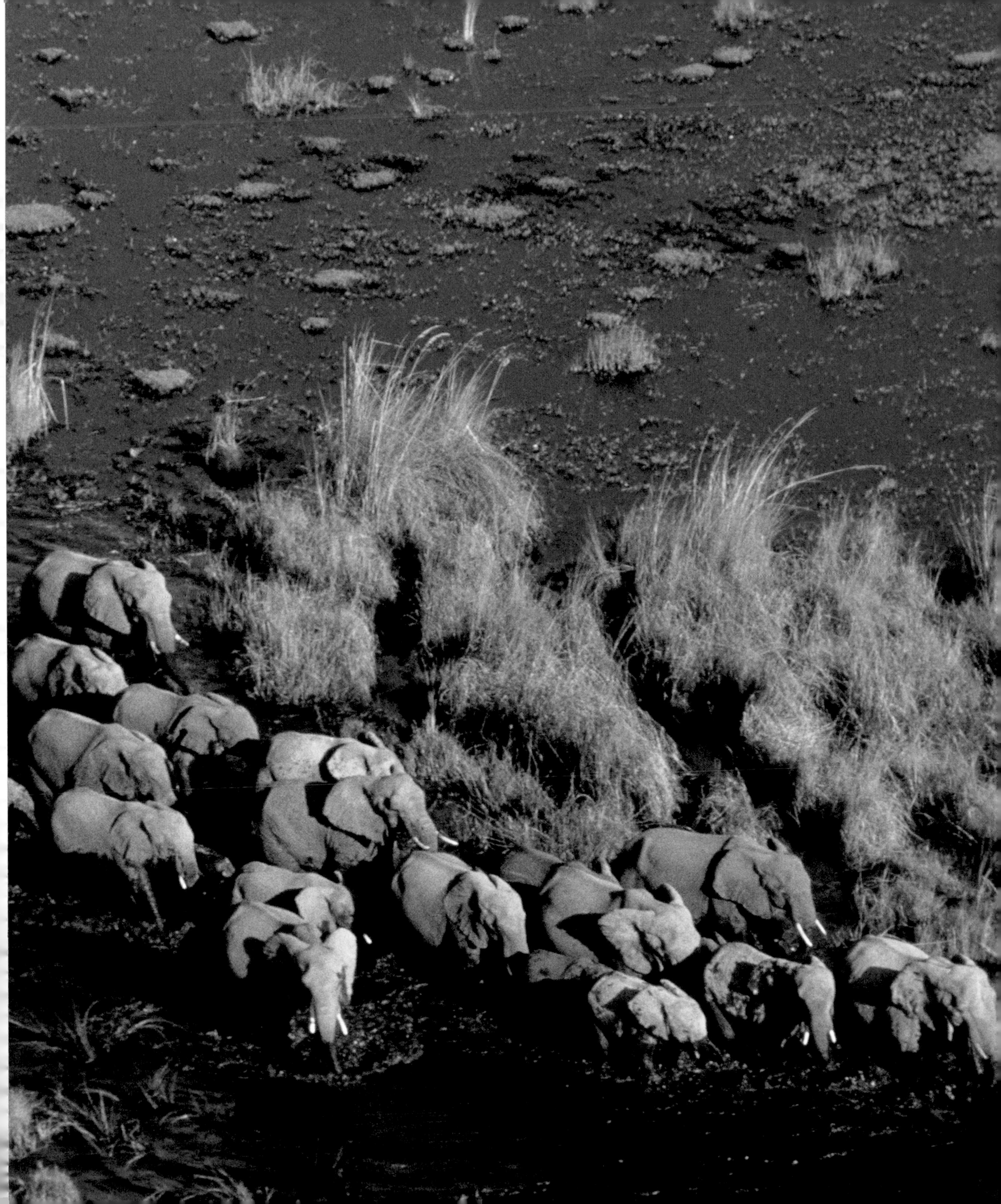

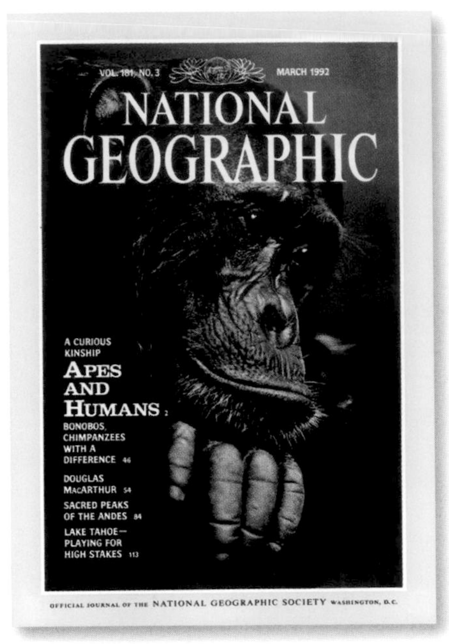

MARCH | MICHAEL NICHOLS

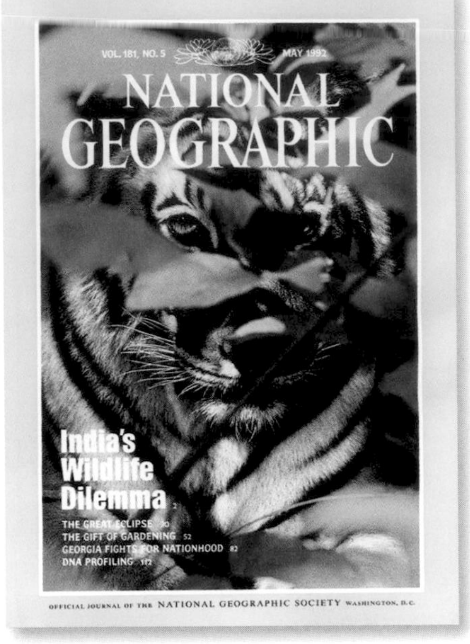

MAY | RAGHU RAI

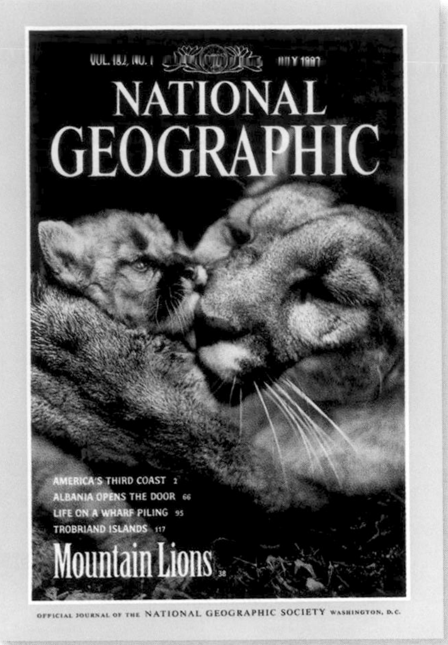

JULY | JIM DUTCHER

▲ **PRIMATE AT PEACE** Frodo looks pensive in this portrait, but Jane Goodall could attest that the large chimpanzee, which lived at her Gombe Stream study area in Tanzania, was more likely to be aggressive and intimidating—he once attacked and beat her savagely. Within five years he would become the alpha male, lording over his troop until the day he was overthrown by a coalition of his fellows. In 2002 he barely avoided execution by the Tanzanian authorities after he killed a 14-month-old human child who had been carried into his territory.

DISAPPEARING WETLANDS ▶

THIS AMERICAN BULLFROG MIGHT be the first to croak if wetlands continue vanishing at an alarming rate. Frogs are indicator species when determining the health of aquatic ecosystems: Their thin skin can absorb any toxins accumulating in their surroundings—making them among the first species to disappear.

> In a report to Congress last year the U.S. Fish and Wildlife Service announced that between the mid-1970s and mid-1980s the nation suffered a net loss of some 2.6 million acres of wetlands. That's 4,000 square miles, an area twice the size of Delaware. "On average," the report noted, "the lower 48 states have lost over 60 acres of wetlands for every hour between the 1780s and the 1980s."
>
> *—From "Our Disappearing Wetlands," John G. Mitchell*

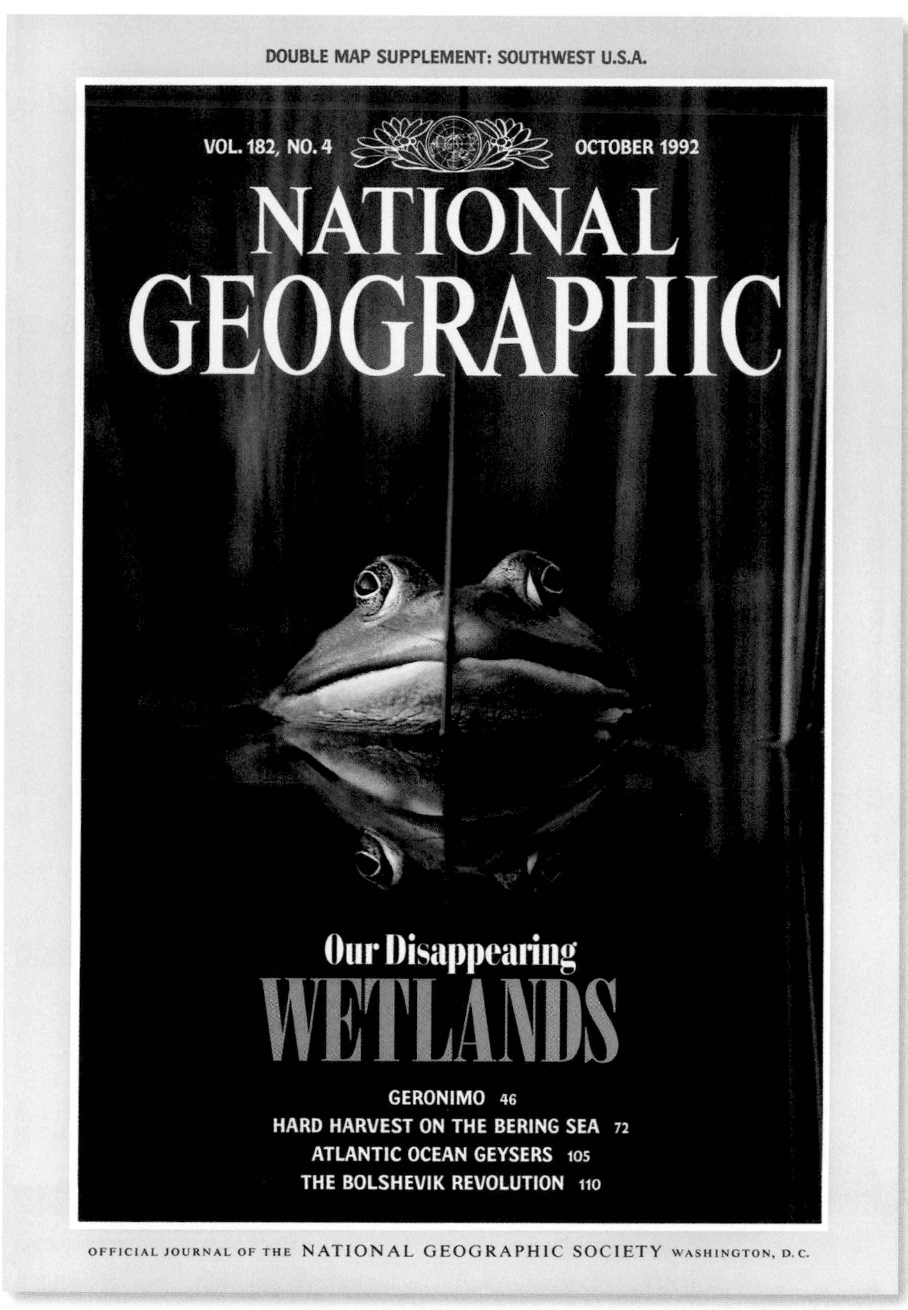

OCTOBER | MARK WILSON

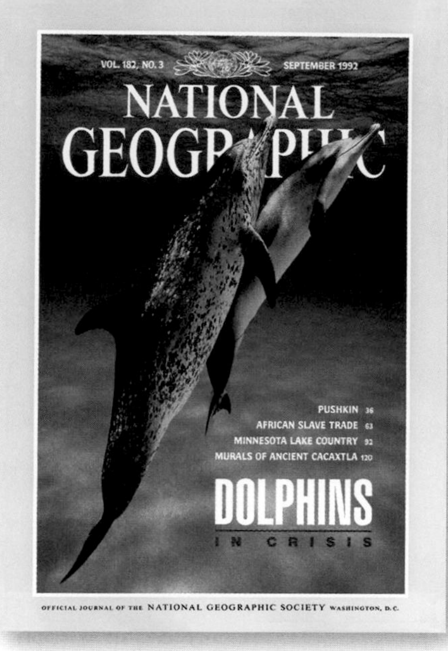

SEPTEMBER | FLIP NICKLIN

▲ **DOLPHIN ENCOUNTERS** There were few bright moments in the year that Flip Nicklin and marine biologist Kenneth Norris traveled the globe reporting on the status of various dolphin populations. Many thousands of individuals, they confirmed, were dying each year, trapped in drift nets and purse seines. But in the Bahamas, the Atlantic spotted dolphins (above) welcomed the human visitors. They swam up, peered into face masks, and caressed wet suits with their fins. "There was no trace of dolphin fear in all this," Norris wrote, "just a reaching across the barrier between our two kinds."

"Yet what could be more useful than biological productivity? Wetlands are producers of life, some being equal in output to a same-size chunk of tropical rain forest . . ."

—John G. Mitchell
from "Our Disappearing Wetlands"

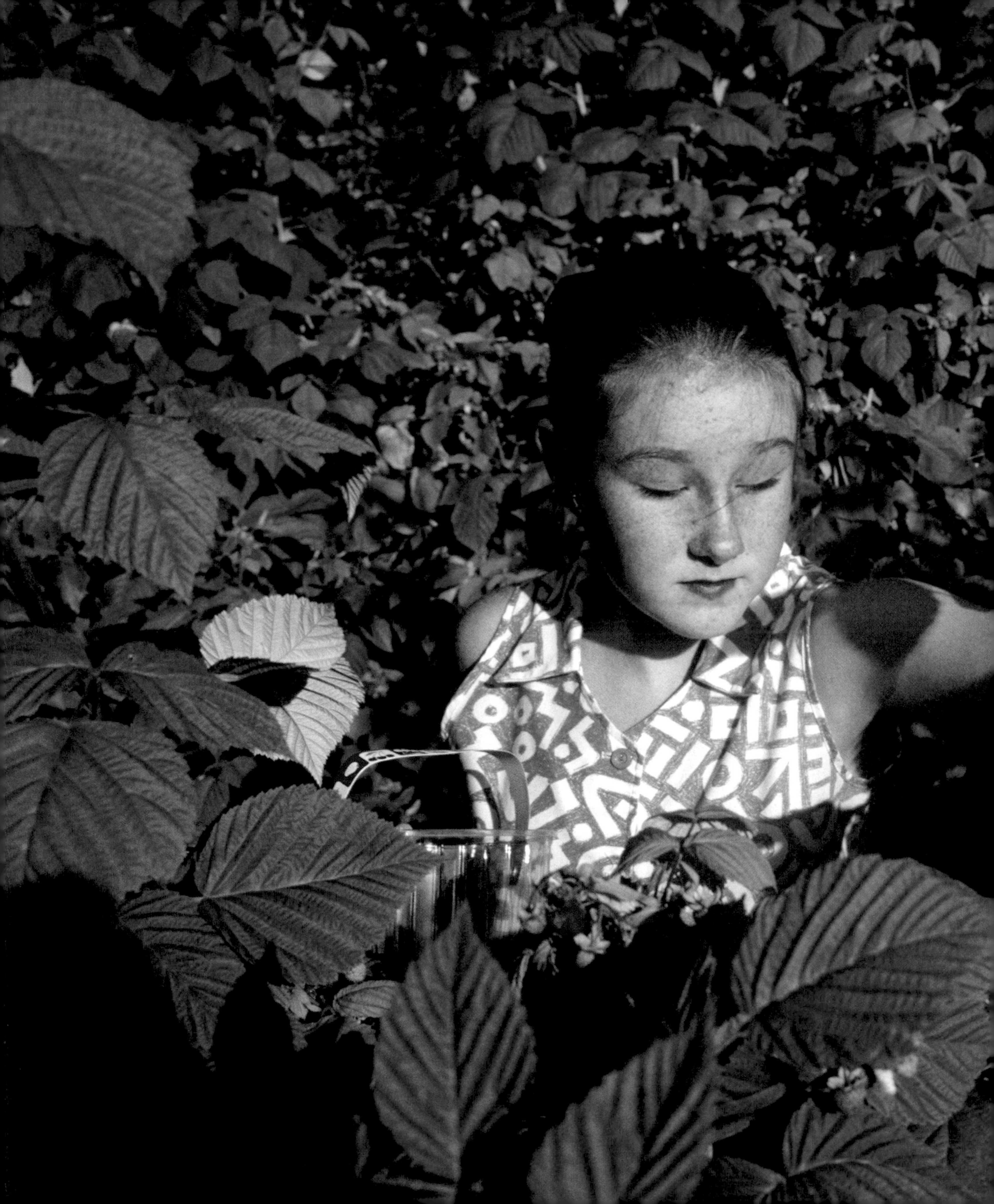

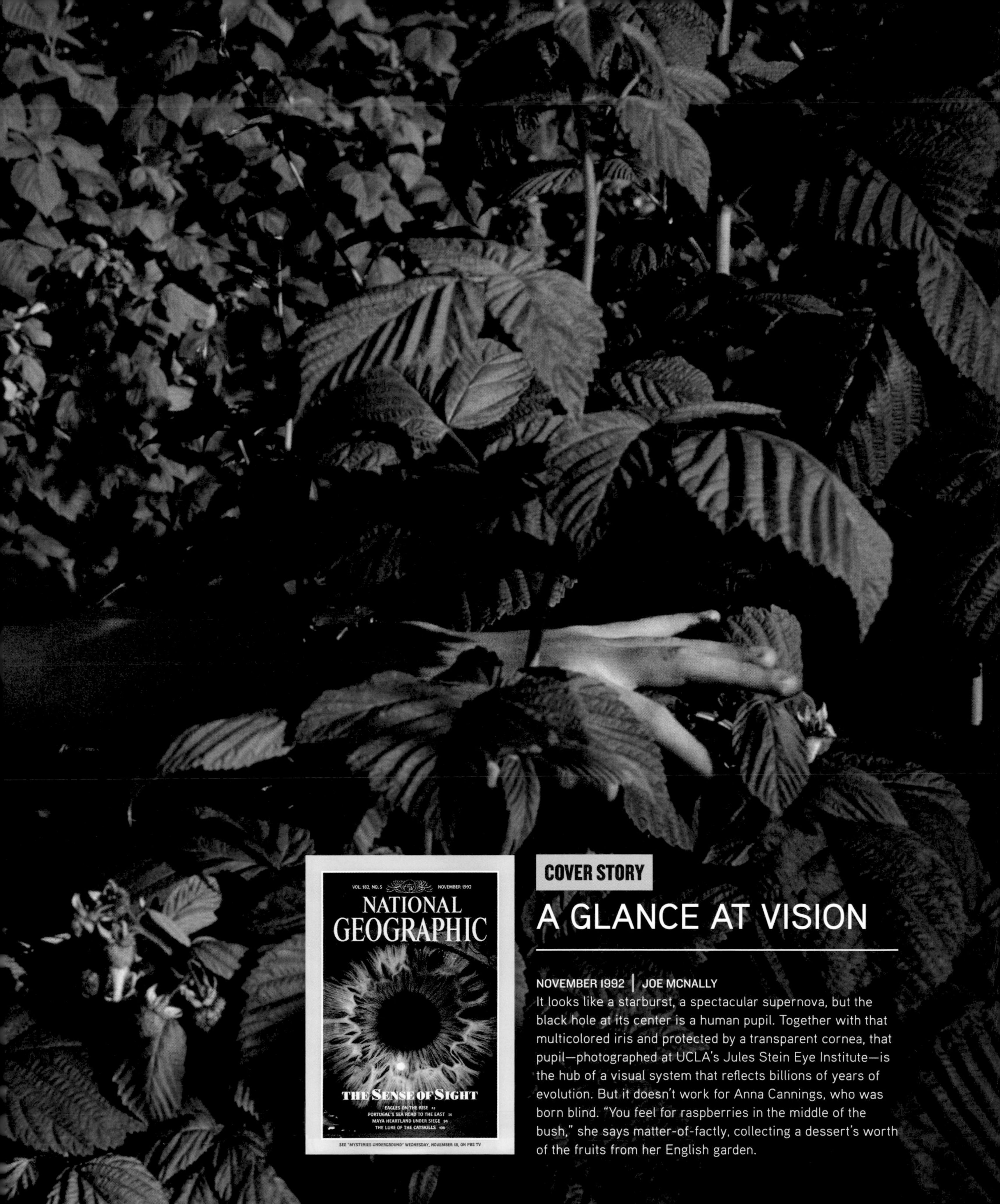

COVER STORY

A GLANCE AT VISION

NOVEMBER 1992 | JOE MCNALLY

It looks like a starburst, a spectacular supernova, but the black hole at its center is a human pupil. Together with that multicolored iris and protected by a transparent cornea, that pupil—photographed at UCLA's Jules Stein Eye Institute—is the hub of a visual system that reflects billions of years of evolution. But it doesn't work for Anna Cannings, who was born blind. "You feel for raspberries in the middle of the bush," she says matter-of-factly, collecting a dessert's worth of the fruits from her English garden.

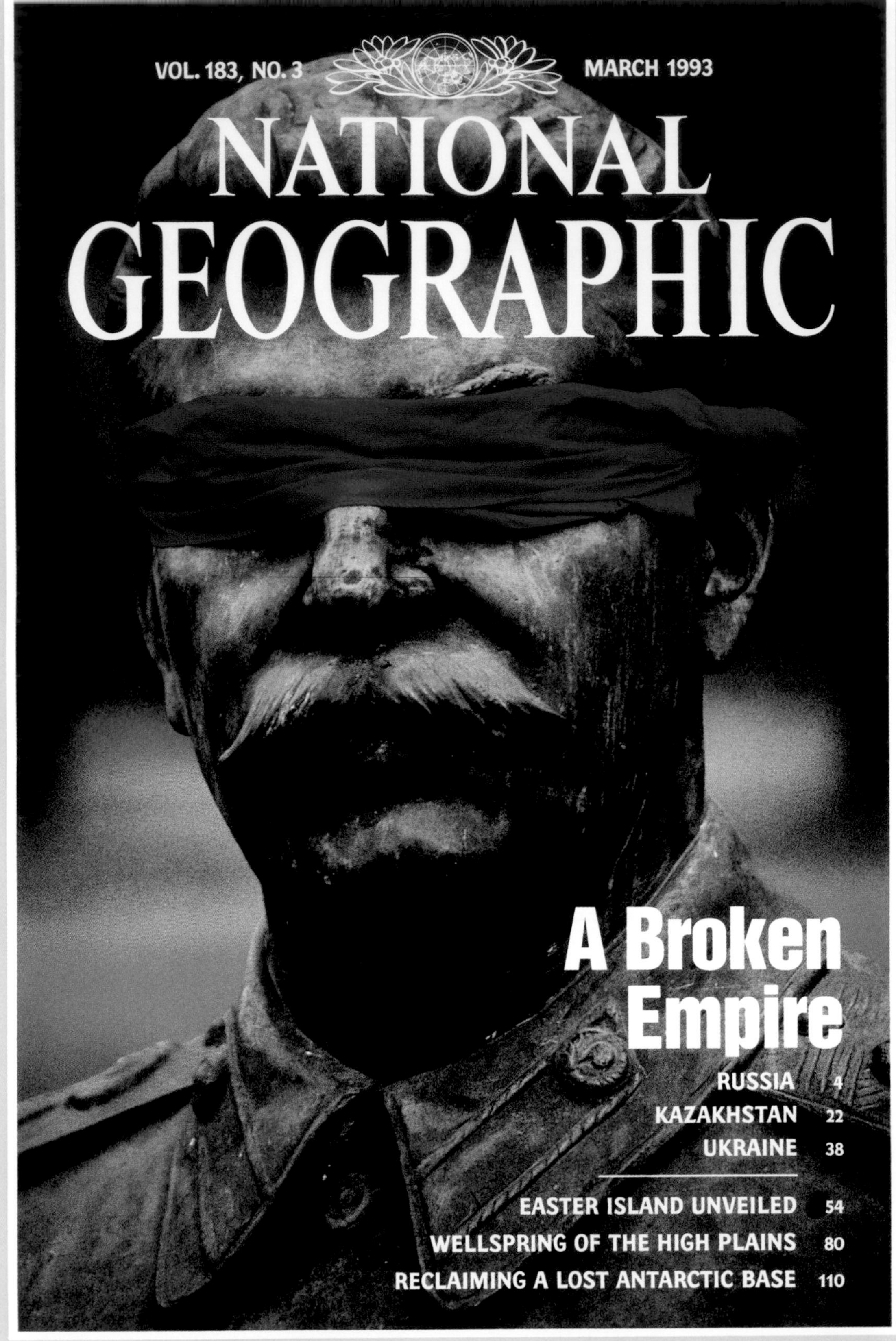

MARCH | **GERD LUDWIG** Blindfolded by a schoolgirl, a statue of Josef Stalin symbolizes the wreck of the Soviet Union.

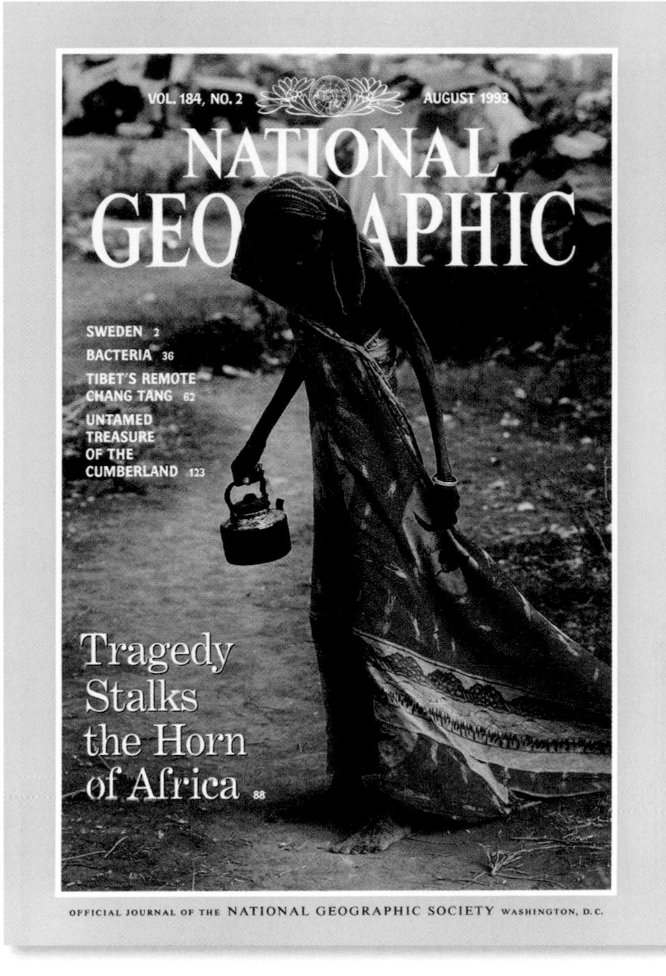

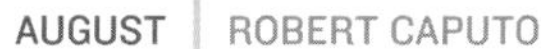

AUGUST | ROBERT CAPUTO

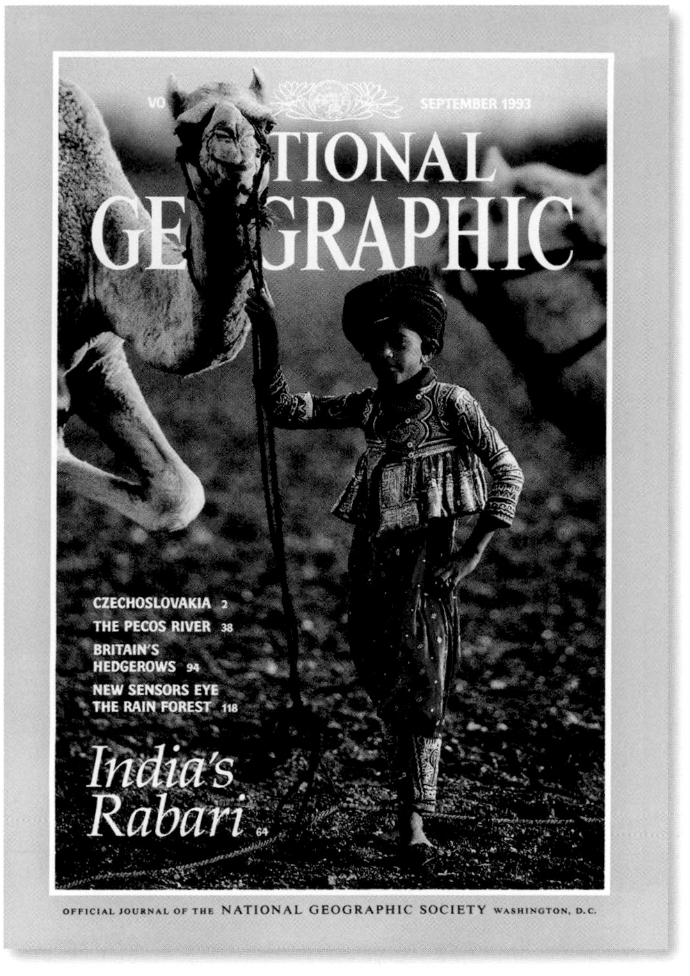

SEPTEMBER | DILIP MEHTA

▲ **ANGUISH OF FAMINE** A starving girl can barely stagger to the relief center at Baidoa, Somalia.

> *"Drought alone rarely causes mass starvation. War is the true plague of the region. 'God makes drought,' an old saying goes. 'Man makes famine . . .'"*
>
> —Robert Caputo
>
> *from "Tragedy Stalks the Horn of Africa"*

▲ **PASSAGE TO INDIA** Looking after the family camels is still a proud task for this turbaned son of India's Rabari people. Formerly a caste devoted to camel breeding, many of the 250,000 nomadic Rabari, stymied by the increasing number of fences crossing India's northwestern plains, have been reduced to selling sheep and goats. Nevertheless, "there was nothing servile about them," asserted author Robyn Davidson, who traveled for 75 days with one of their bands. "They asked for neither charity nor an easy life, only recognition of the value of their expertise and the same kind of government support that Indian farmers automatically receive."

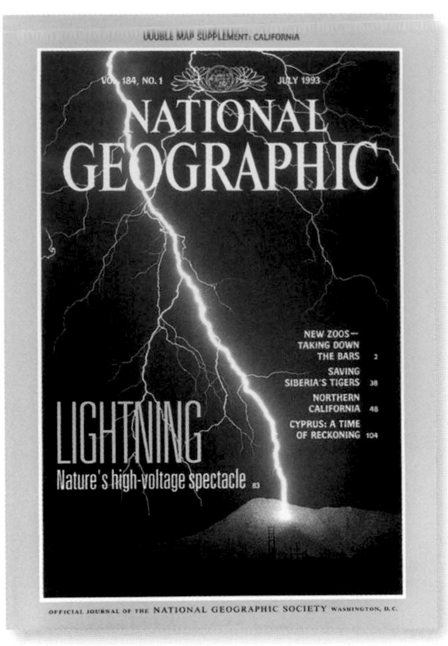

JULY | THOMAS H. IVES

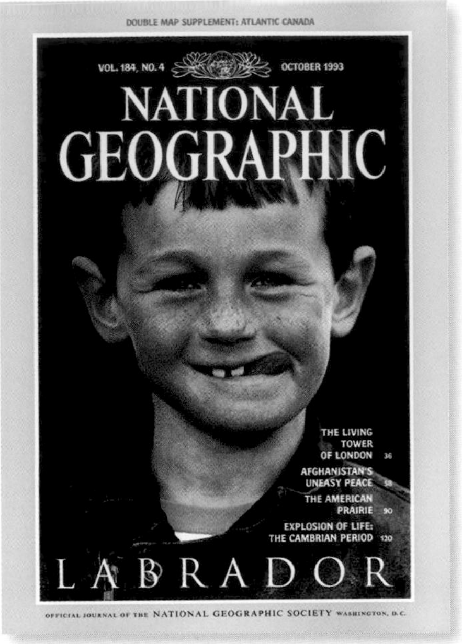

OCTOBER | RICHARD OLSENIUS

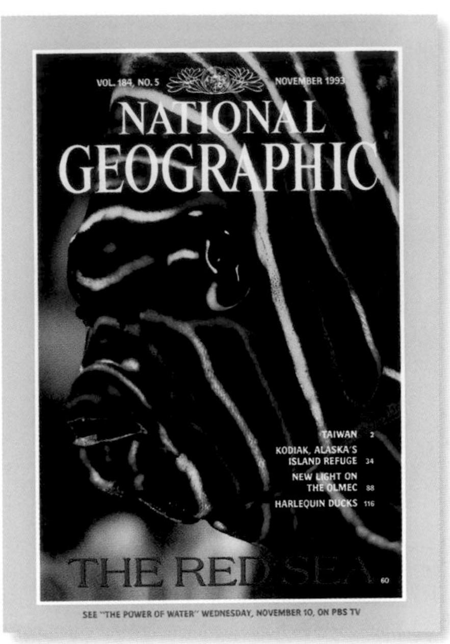

NOVEMBER | DAVID DOUBILET

▲ **BOLT FROM THE BLUE** A lightning strike—its jagged profile indicating a cloud-to-ground strike—electrifies Arizona's Tucson Mountains.

"It is a river of electricity rushing through a canyon of air. Careering as fast as 100,000 miles a second, lightning sears wild and unstoppable through twisted channels as long as ten miles."

—William R. Newcott
from "Lightning: Nature's High-Voltage Spectacle"

GLASS ▶

Lightning striking a beach can create it. Paleolithic hunters made spear points from it. Fiber-optic cables use it to convey information. Whether found as fulgurites (formed by lightning) in the sand, as obsidian in rock, as soaring iridescent windows in cathedrals, or in a cable connecting to your house, glass has always been a useful, beautiful, and magical material.

> It helps light the darkness, screen the elements, sharpen the acuity of vision, magnify the infinitesimal, and plumb the heavens. It transmits electronic signals across continents and may someday spawn a superbreed of ultrafast computers. Protean glass can also soar with a sculptor's imagination, as in Dominick Labino's nine-inch-high rhapsody in rosy hues titled "Emergence Four-Stage."
>
> *—From "Glass: Capturing the Dance of Light," William S. Ellis*

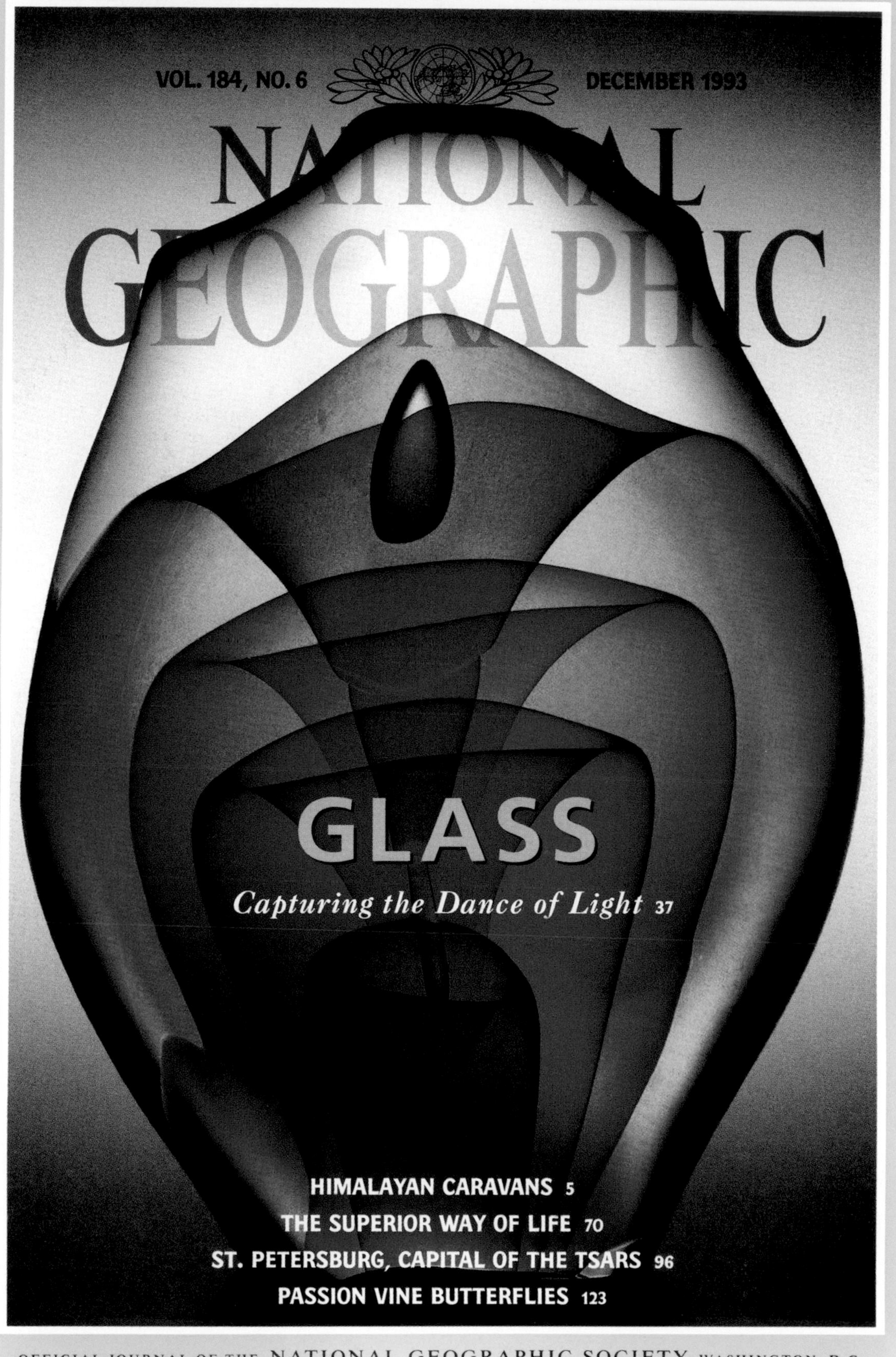

DECEMBER | JAMES L. AMOS Dominick Labino's "Emergence Four-Stage," photographed at the Corning Museum of Glass

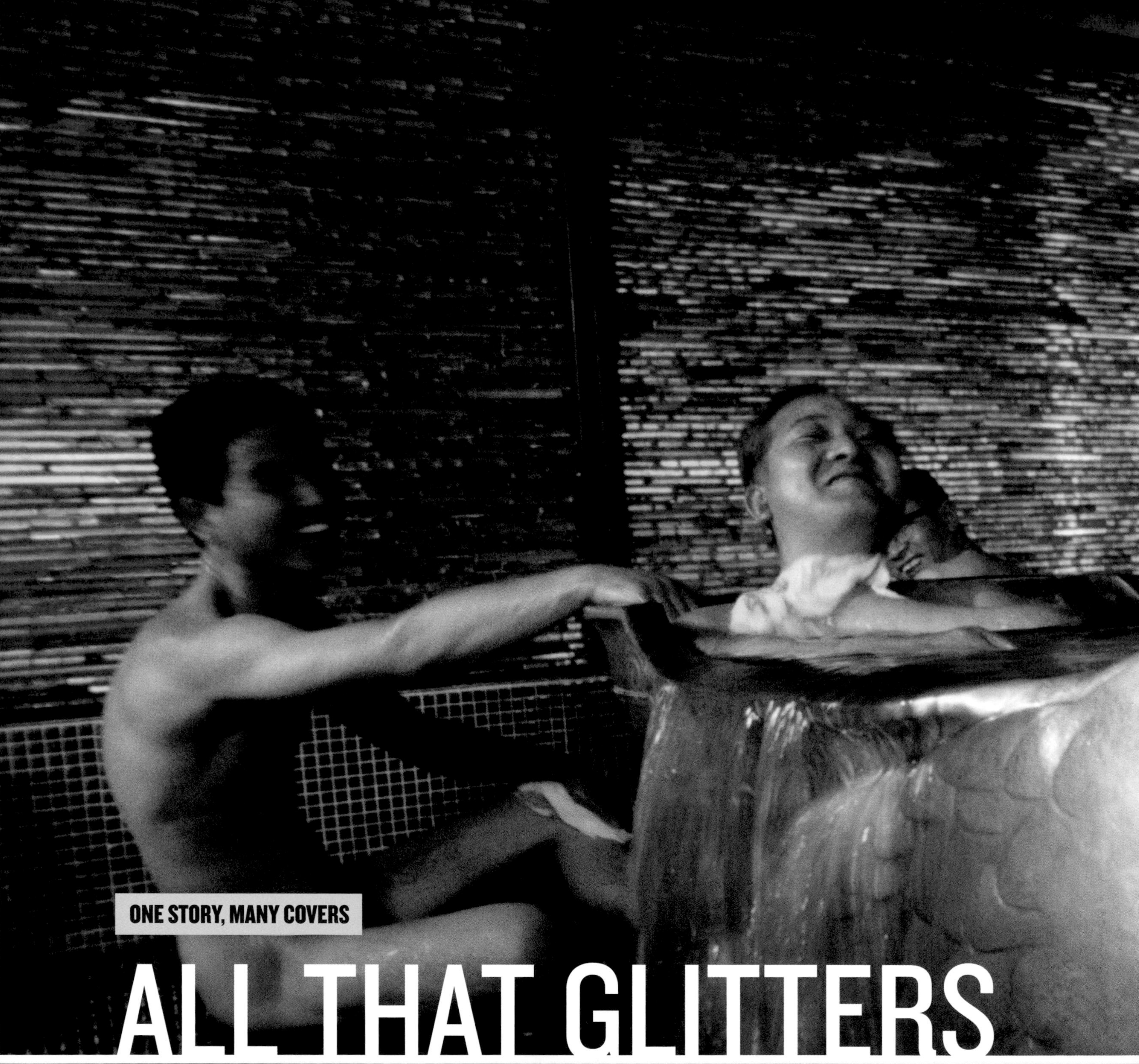

ONE STORY, MANY COVERS

ALL THAT GLITTERS

▲ JANUARY 1974 | JAMES L. STANFIELD
Businessmen at a Japanese hotel relax in a solid-gold tub.

PHOTOGRAPHER JIM STANFIELD AND writer Peter White couldn't resist a $2-a-minute dip in that tub. After all, they worked for *National Geographic,* which has never been immune to the lure of gold. Along that yellow-brick road its correspondents have met prospectors, smugglers, street hucksters, museum curators, treasure hunters, poachers, and princes. Coveting images of the gold might come at a price, however: Deep in a South African mine, Stanfield lost three cameras to the 115-degree heat—"the most strenuous day of my life."

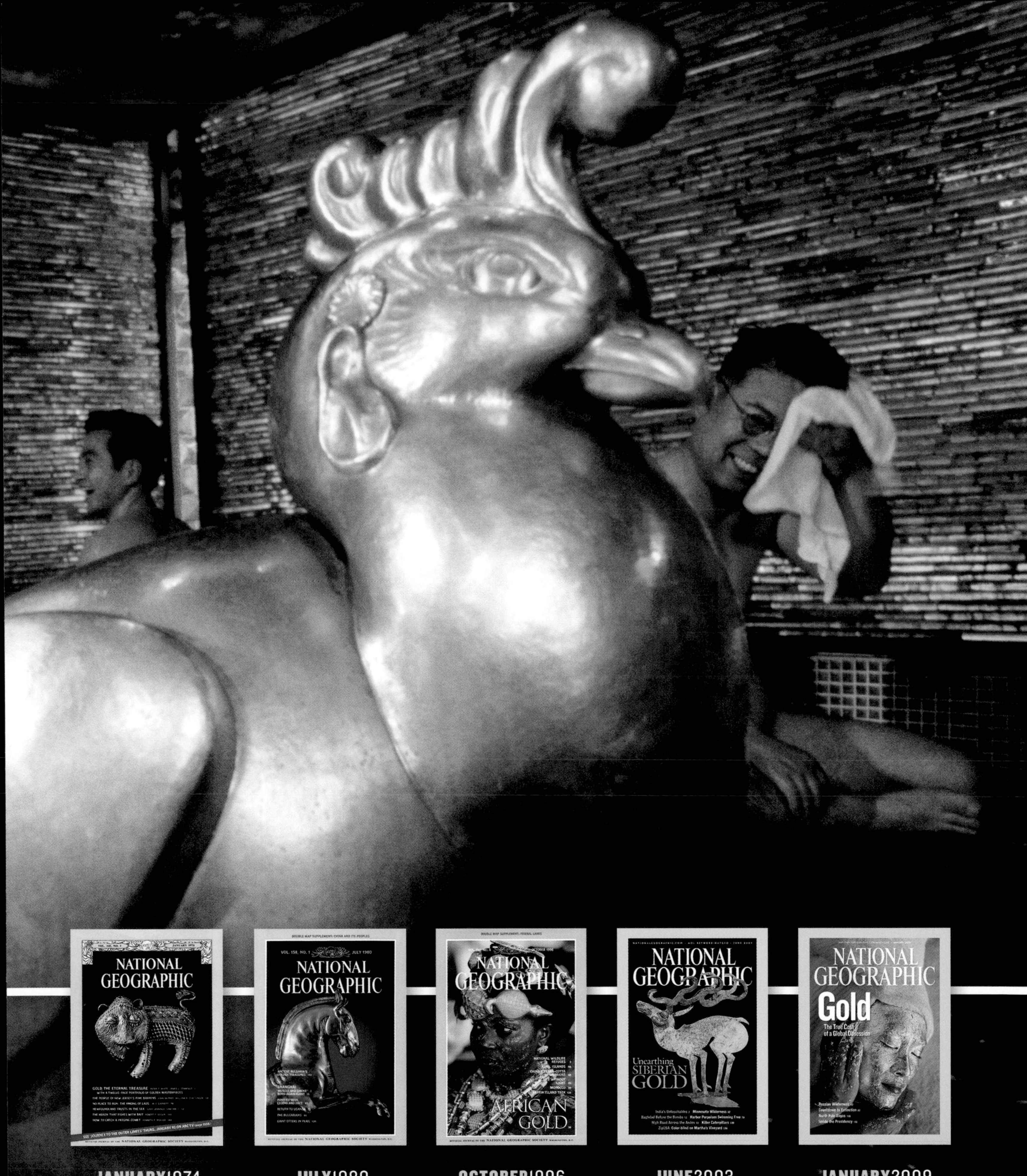
NATIONAL GEOGRAPHIC
GOLD: THE ETERNAL TREASURE
JANUARY 1974
NATIONAL GEOGRAPHIC
JULY 1980
NATIONAL GEOGRAPHIC
AFRICAN GOLD.
OCTOBER 1996
NATIONAL GEOGRAPHIC
Unearthing SIBERIAN GOLD
JUNE 2003
NATIONAL GEOGRAPHIC
Gold
The True Cost of a Global Obsession
JANUARY 2009

ANIMALS AT PLAY

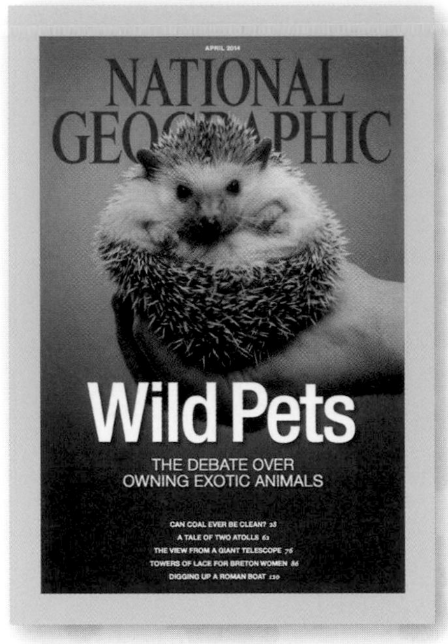

APRIL 2014 | VINCENT J. MUSI

2014 ▸▸▸▸ FAST FORWARD

EXOTIC PETS It wasn't all work and no play, but photographer Vince Musi did spend two days in Brandon Harley's parents' living room—turned into an impromptu studio—taking more than 3,000 photographs of hedgehogs. It was a picture of 11-month old Jade—whom Harley, a college student who already owned a pet business, used as a breeder—that made the April cover.

ONE WINTER DAY PHOTOGRAPHER Mitsuaki Iwago discovered that it was business as usual at Joshinetsu Plateau National Park near Nagano—monkey business, that is, for the young Japanese macaques were busy making snowballs.

Although adult macaques might toy with a ball of packed ice, they preferred simply hanging out in places like the Jigokudani hot springs. But the young macaques couldn't get enough of snowball making. They appeared to love rolling them around. Sometimes they just carried their treasures about, showing them off. Iwago even saw one little fellow standing on his snowball, balancing first on one foot, then on the other.

Puppies and juvenile macaques aside, many species of wild animals and birds have been observed playing. Chimpanzees, unsurprisingly, are according to Jane Goodall "champions" at amusing themselves; but elephants, lions, dolphins, and many other wild animals also frolic, gambol, spar, tug, romp, roughhouse, and chase one another, all seemingly for fun. At least that was the conclusion reached by Dr. Stuart L. Brown, author of an article on animal play in the December 1994 *National Geographic*. "I think of play as spontaneous behavior that has no clear-cut goal and does not conform to a stereotypical pattern," he wrote. "To me the purpose of play is simply play itself; it appears to be pleasurable."

It also appears to be necessary. Animals deprived of play when young—like some humans—can become psychotic adults.

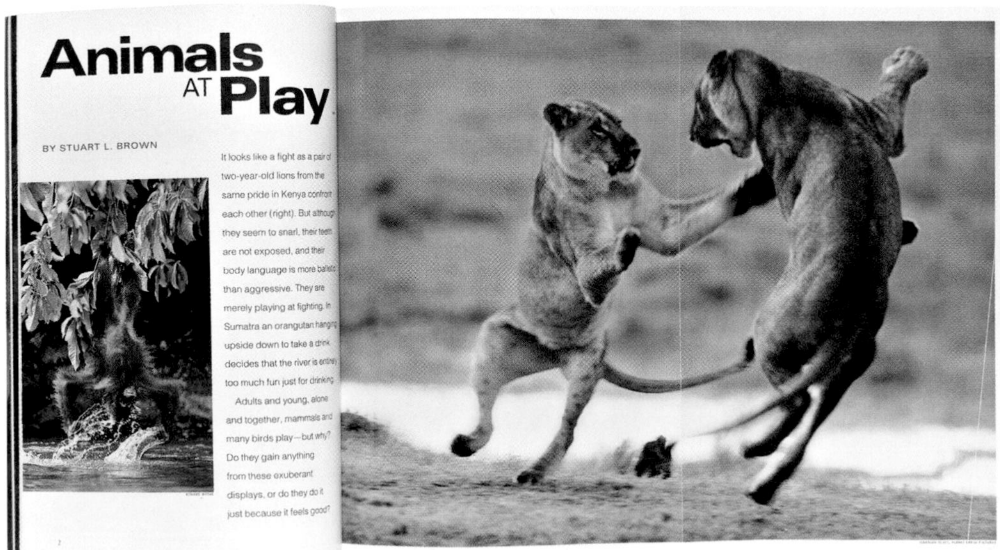
Animals AT Play

BY STUART L. BROWN

It looks like a fight as a pair o two-year-old lions from the same pride in Kenya confron each other (right). But althoug they seem to snarl, their teeth are not exposed, and their body language is more balletic than aggressive. They are merely playing at fighting. In Sumatra an orangutan hanging upside down to take a drink decides that the river is entirely too much fun just for drinking.

Adults and young, alone and together, mammals and many birds play—but why? Do they gain anything from these exuberant displays, or do they do it just because it feels good?

◂ **DECEMBER 1994** | KONRAD WOTHE, JONATHAN SCOTT Two juvenile lions roughhouse on a Kenyan plain.

DOUBLE MAP SUPPLEMENT: PRAIRIE PROVINCES

VOL. 186, NO. 6 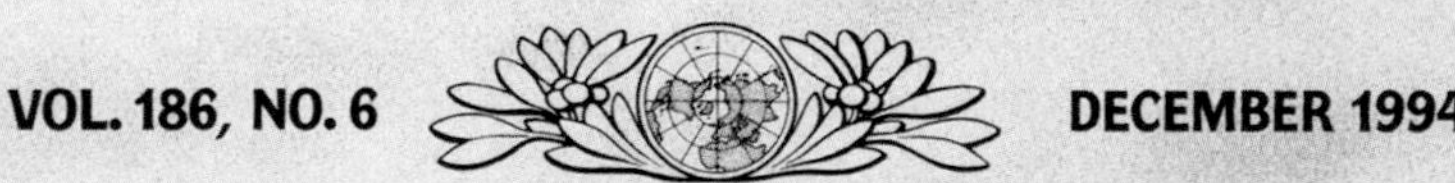 DECEMBER 1994

NATIONAL GEOGRAPHIC

CANADA'S HIGHWAY OF STEEL 36

C.S.S. *ALABAMA* 67

BUENOS AIRES 84

AMERICA'S POET: WALT WHITMAN 106

Animals AT Play

OFFICIAL JOURNAL OF THE NATIONAL GEOGRAPHIC SOCIETY WASHINGTON, D.C.

DECEMBER | MITSUAKI IWAGO A young Japanese macaque carries its snowball.

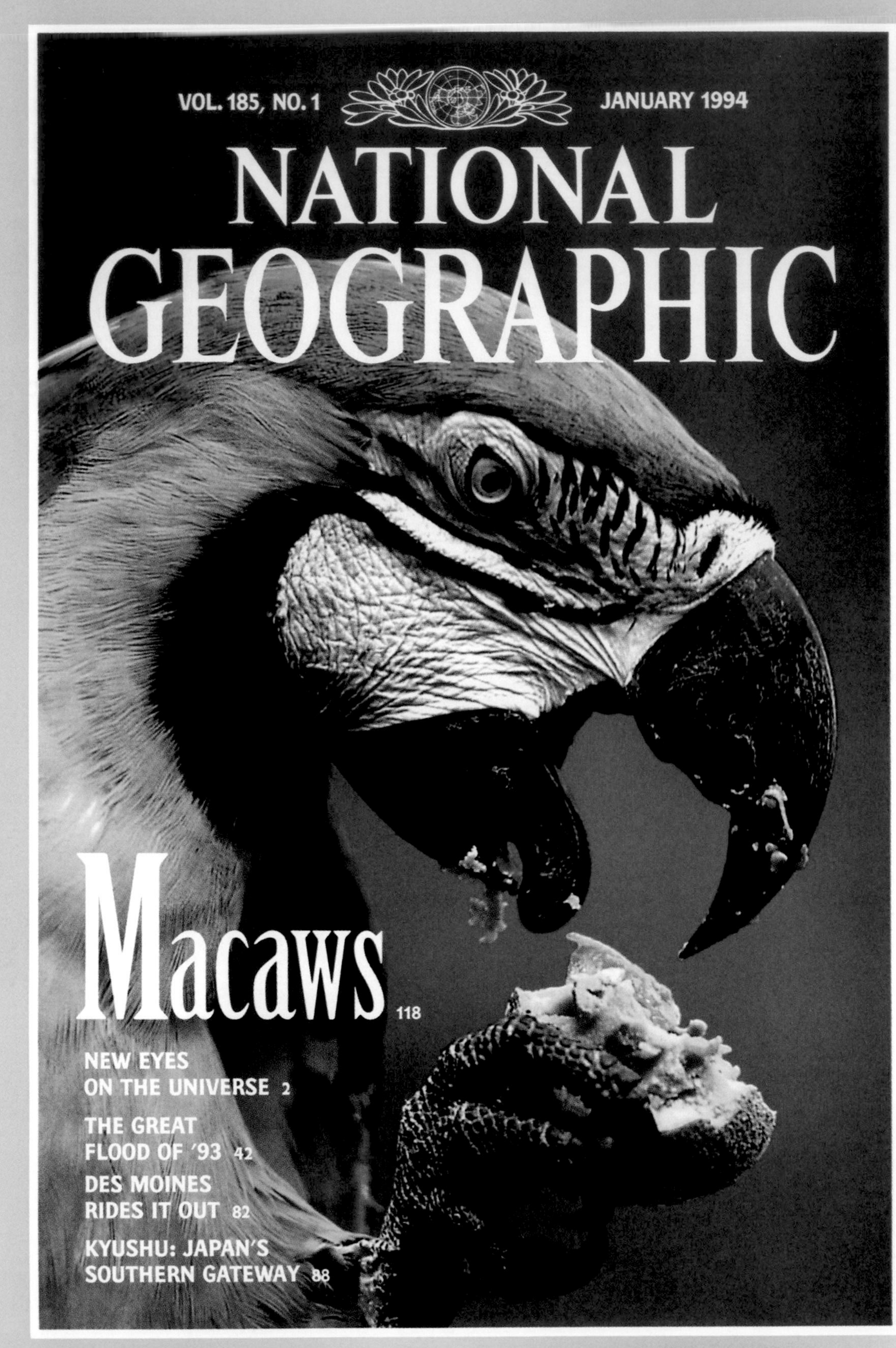

JANUARY | FRANS LANTING A macaw demonstrates its considerable seed-eating abilities.

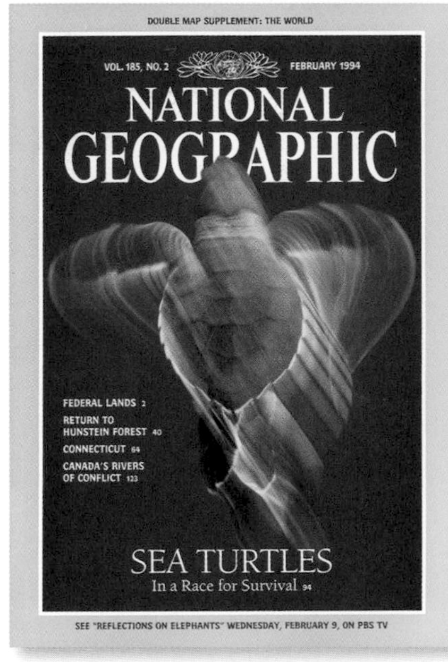

FEBRUARY | BILL CURTSINGER

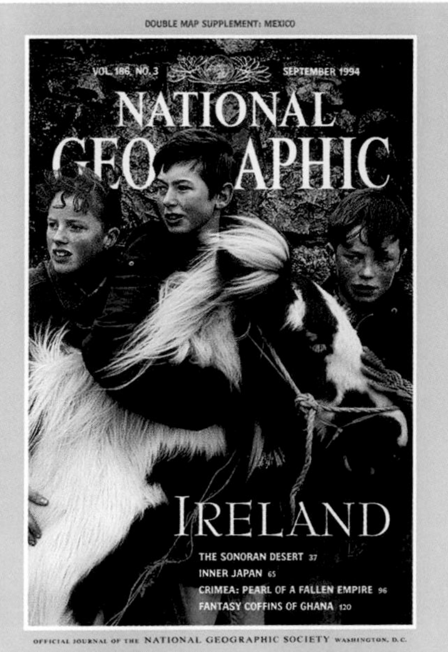

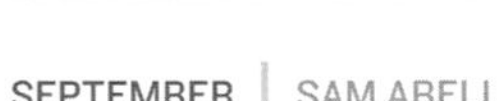
SEPTEMBER | SAM ABELL

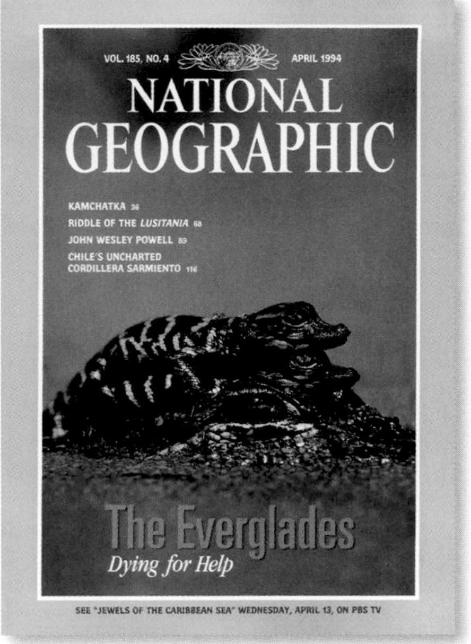

APRIL | CHRIS JOHNS

BRILLIANT MACAWS

Eye-to-eye in the treetops was the only way to photograph South American macaws, but for Frans Lanting, sitting 80 feet high in makeshift blinds in the rain forests of eastern Peru was often a frightening experience. Nevertheless, the pictures this wildlife photographer made of these most intelligent of birds combined a breathtaking beauty with ornithological rigor. Above all, by portraying macaws in their natural environment, those pictures would help advance Lanting's primary goal, to "turn wild creatures into ambassadors for whole ecosystems."

So it was ironic that when one of his macaw pictures was selected for the cover of the January 1994 issue, it was not of a wild one, taken eye-to-eye in the treetops, but instead this photograph of a hand-reared bird. This shot illustrates the macaw tool kit: its dexterous claw, conspicuous tongue, and massive beak. It is a clear statement of biological fact: Here is a bird curious enough to handle and mouth everything it encounters; a resplendent creature that, as ornithologist Charles Munn puts it, possesses the "most powerful bite in the bird world."

▲ **PIGGYBACK RIDE** How to get people to care about what many thought was just a swamp? That question was often at the forefront of Chris Johns's mind as he photographed the Everglades for a *Geographic* article. Surprisingly, he found one answer not in a sweeping landscape shot but rather while documenting the stages of an alligator raising her young. He photographed the nest and the hatching of the eggs, but it was only when two newborns, unable to swim yet, climbed atop their mother's crown that he found just that touch of unexpected warmth he needed.

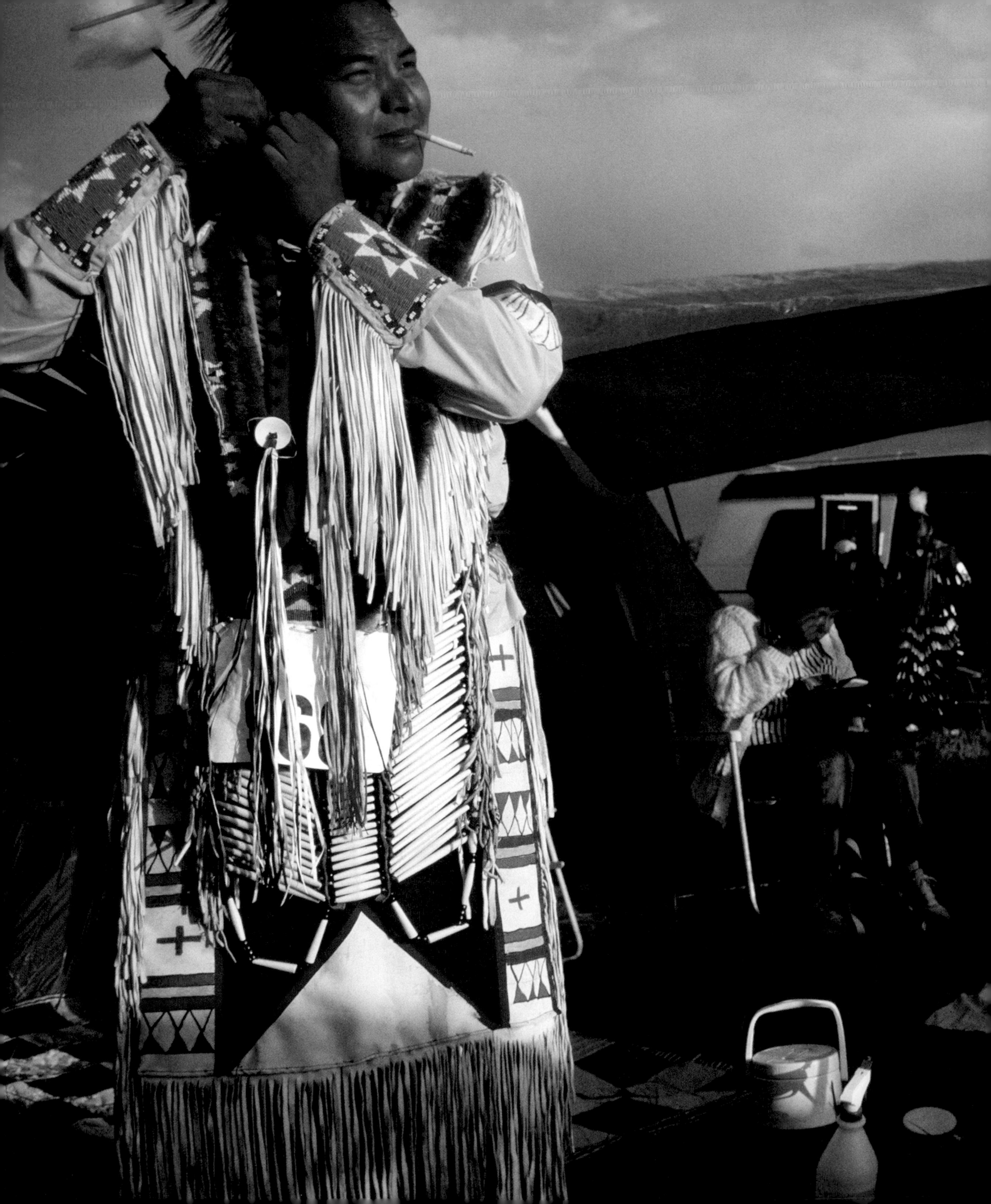

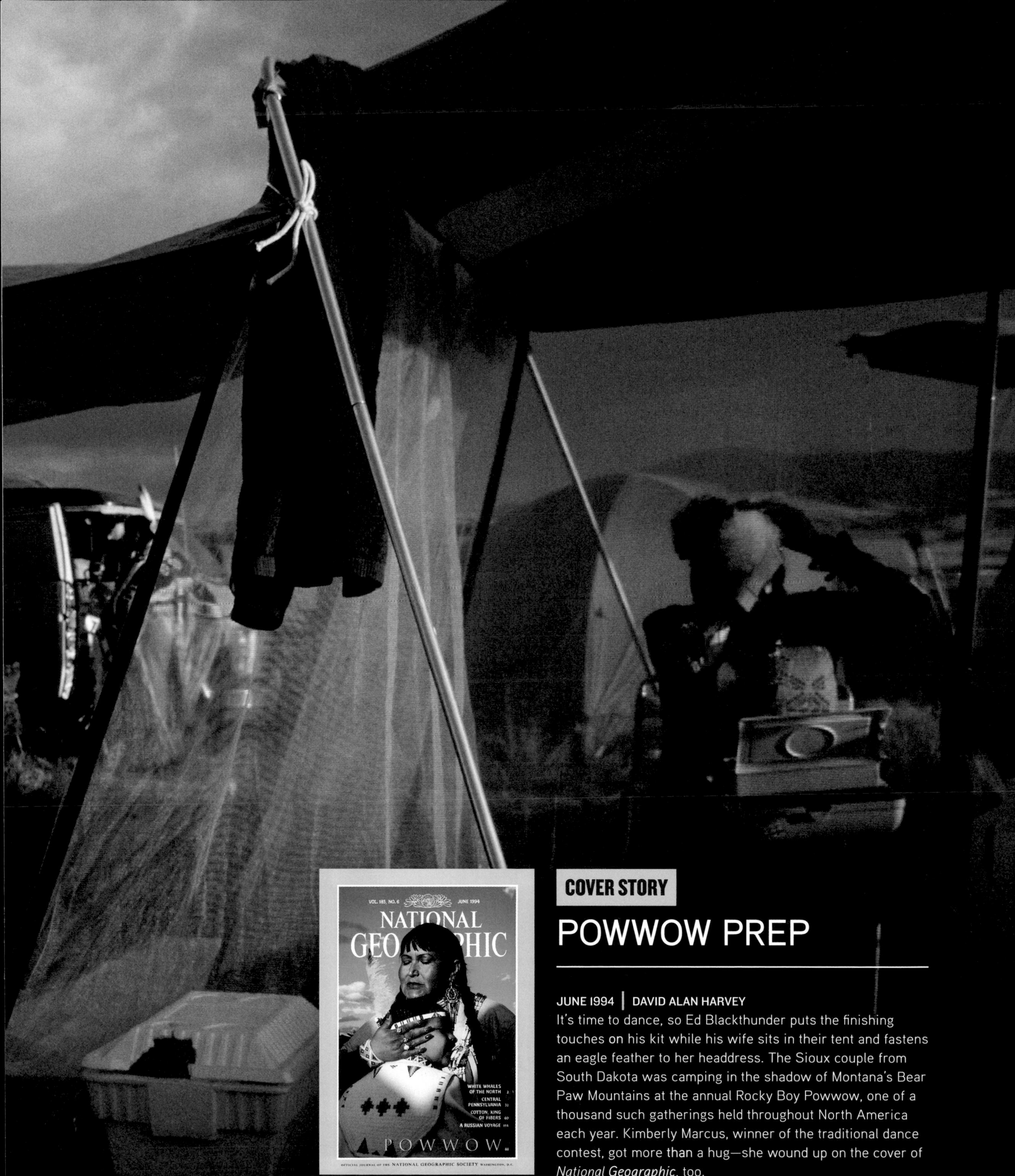

COVER STORY

POWWOW PREP

JUNE 1994 | DAVID ALAN HARVEY

It's time to dance, so Ed Blackthunder puts the finishing touches on his kit while his wife sits in their tent and fastens an eagle feather to her headdress. The Sioux couple from South Dakota was camping in the shadow of Montana's Bear Paw Mountains at the annual Rocky Boy Powwow, one of a thousand such gatherings held throughout North America each year. Kimberly Marcus, winner of the traditional dance contest, got more than a hug—she wound up on the cover of *National Geographic*, too.

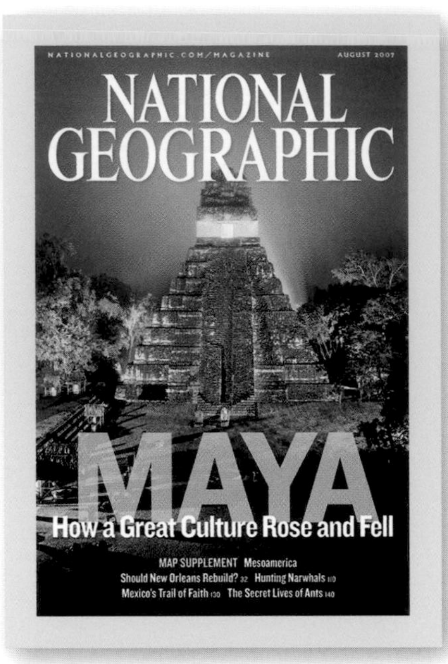

AUGUST 2007 | SIMON NORFOLK

BONAMPAK MURALS ▶

CLAD IN A TERRIFYING jaguar headdress, Maya ruler Chaan Muan topples an enemy. Painted circa A.D. 650 on the walls of a small temple at Bonampak, Mexico, this scene was quite faded when discovered in 1946. Nevertheless, because it was one of six sumptuous murals that shed new light on interpretations of Maya society, in 1992 *National Geographic* embarked on a groundbreaking project to restore it—digitally.

First it engaged Italian photographer Enrico Ferorelli, an expert at documenting archaeological sites, to set up his tripod inside the little temple and photograph the panels. A year later, in 1993, graphic artist Doug Stern and Yale professor Mary Miller spent three days there, laying acetate sheets over enlargements of Ferorelli's photographs. Stern traced onto the acetate every line he saw on the original murals. Back in D.C., he used an electronic pen to transfer his acetate lines onto scanned versions of both Ferorelli's pictures and infrared studies.

Digital enhancement, although familiar today, was still novel in the mid-1990s. "Because our reconstructions are based largely on photographs, they capture without alteration the murals' original hues, mottled flesh, distinctive style, and even mistakes," an editorial note stated in the February 1995 issue. "We included only what we saw. And what we saw was magnificent."

2007 ▸▸▸ FAST FORWARD

NIGHT AT THE TEMPLE Twelve years later Tikal's Temple of the Great Jaguar stands floodlit at night, thanks to the creativity of landscape photographer Simon Norfolk. Working at night, he found, cleared the ruined Maya cities of Central America of tourists and allowed him to better control contrast and emphasis. It also meant meticulous planning. Even a single picture exposed on the film of one of his mahogany-and-brass-encased view cameras, each shooting large-format sheet film, could take all night. Moreover, teams of local workers had to set up a dozen or more flood lamps in places that had little or no electricity. (The Geographic donated seven generators to the various sites.)

> *"The resulting computer reconstructions—showing about one-fifth of the murals—are as close to the originals as anyone could come without actually having been there as the paint dried."*
>
> —Mary Miller
>
> *from "Maya Masterpiece Revealed at Bonampak"*

▶ **FEBRUARY 1995** | DOUG STERN AND ENRICO FERORELLI A digitally restored mural at Bonampak portrays an ancient Maya battle.

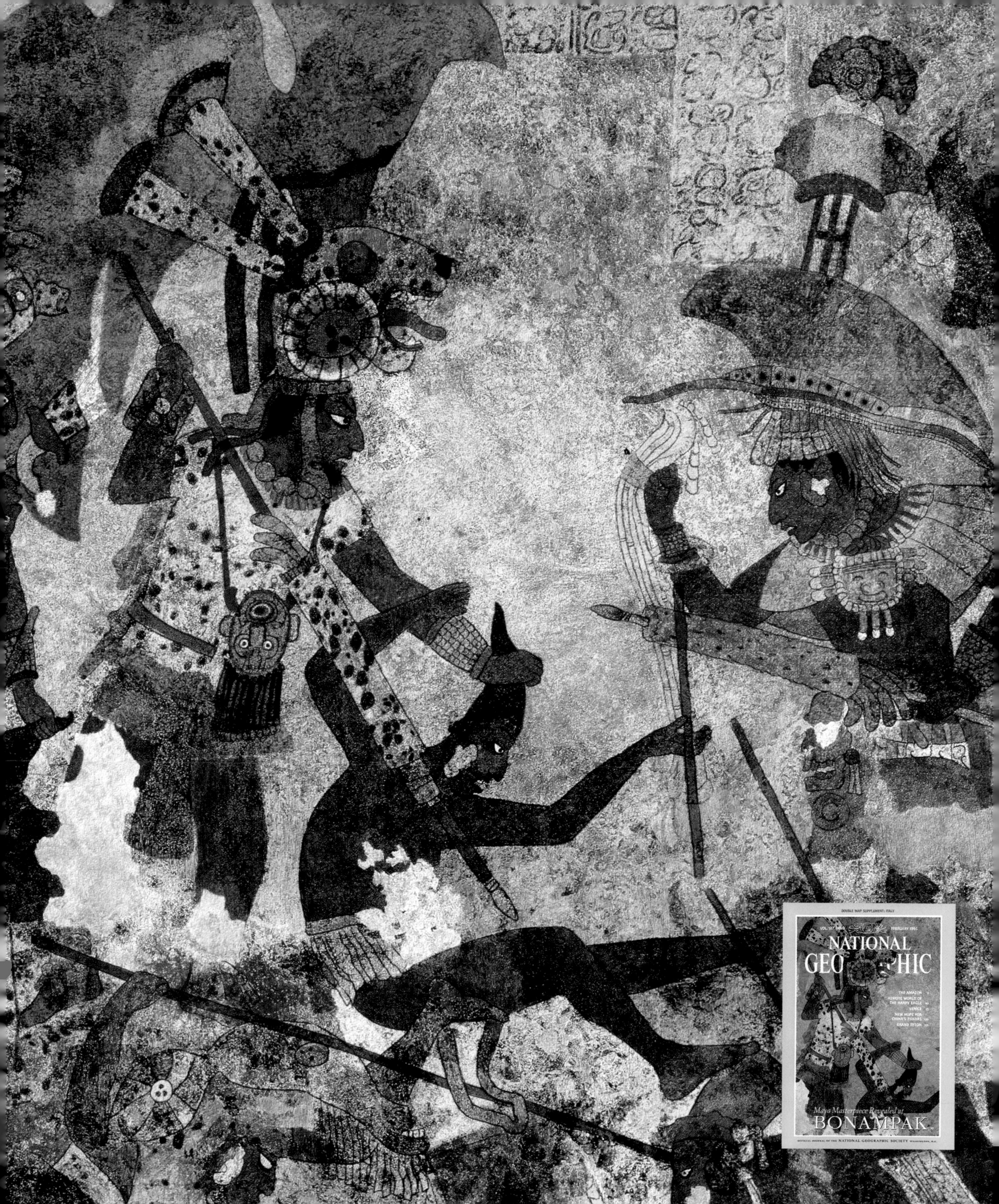
DOUBLE MAP SUPPLEMENT: ITALY
FEBRUARY 1995
NATIONAL
GEO PHIC
THE AMAZON
REMOTE WORLD OF THE HARPY EAGLE
VENICE
NEW HOPE FOR CHINA'S PANDAS
GRAND TETON
Maya Masterpiece Revealed at
BONAMPAK
OFFICIAL JOURNAL OF THE NATIONAL GEOGRAPHIC SOCIETY WASHINGTON, D.C.

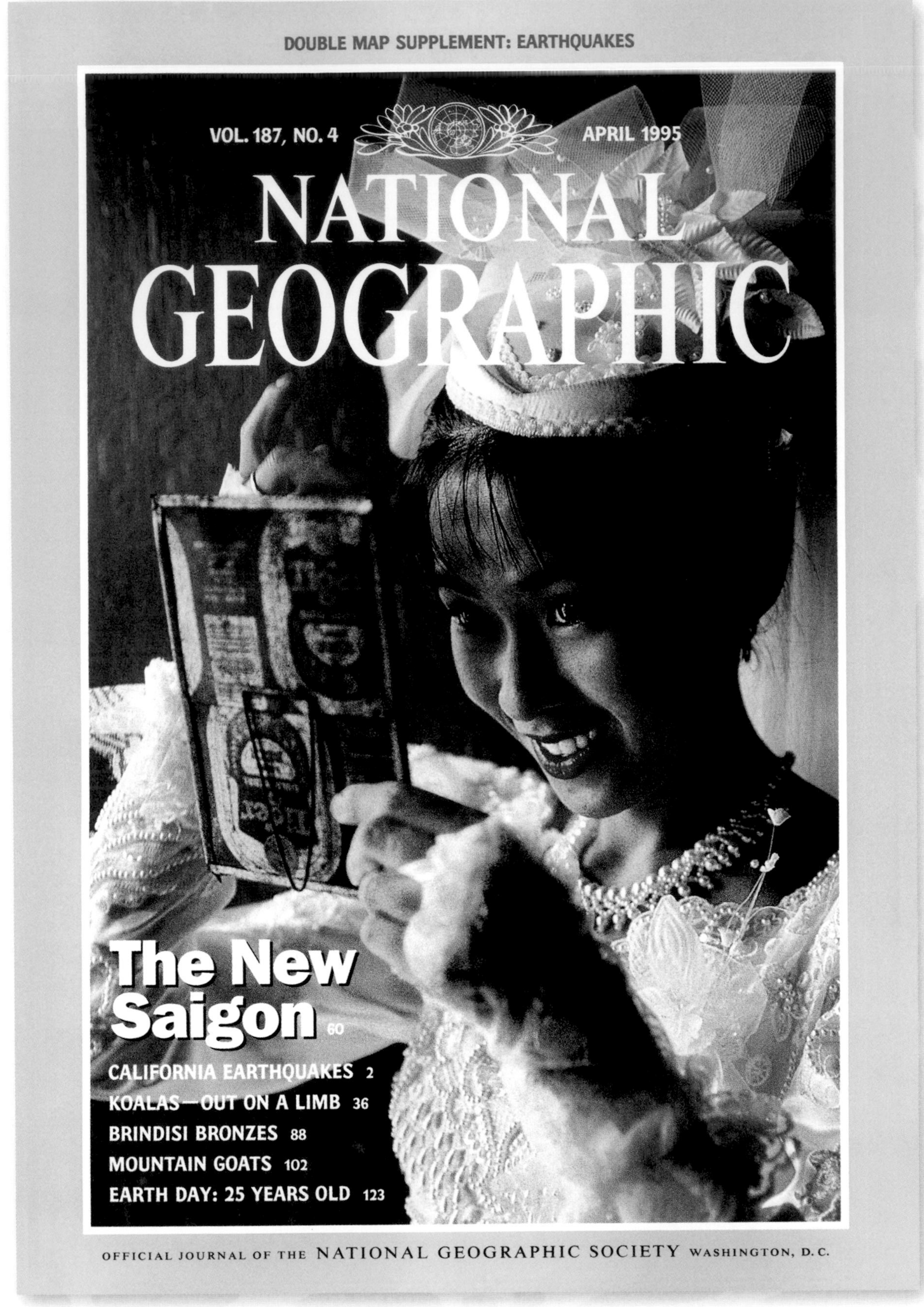

APRIL | KAREN KASMAUSKI

BRIDE TO BE Her mirror may be worn, but this produce vendor in Ho Chi Minh City has been so successful as an entrepreneur that she can afford to rent a Hong Kong–made, Western-style wedding gown. To Karen Kasmauski, she epitomized a postwar Vietnam beginning to refashion itself after years of austerity.

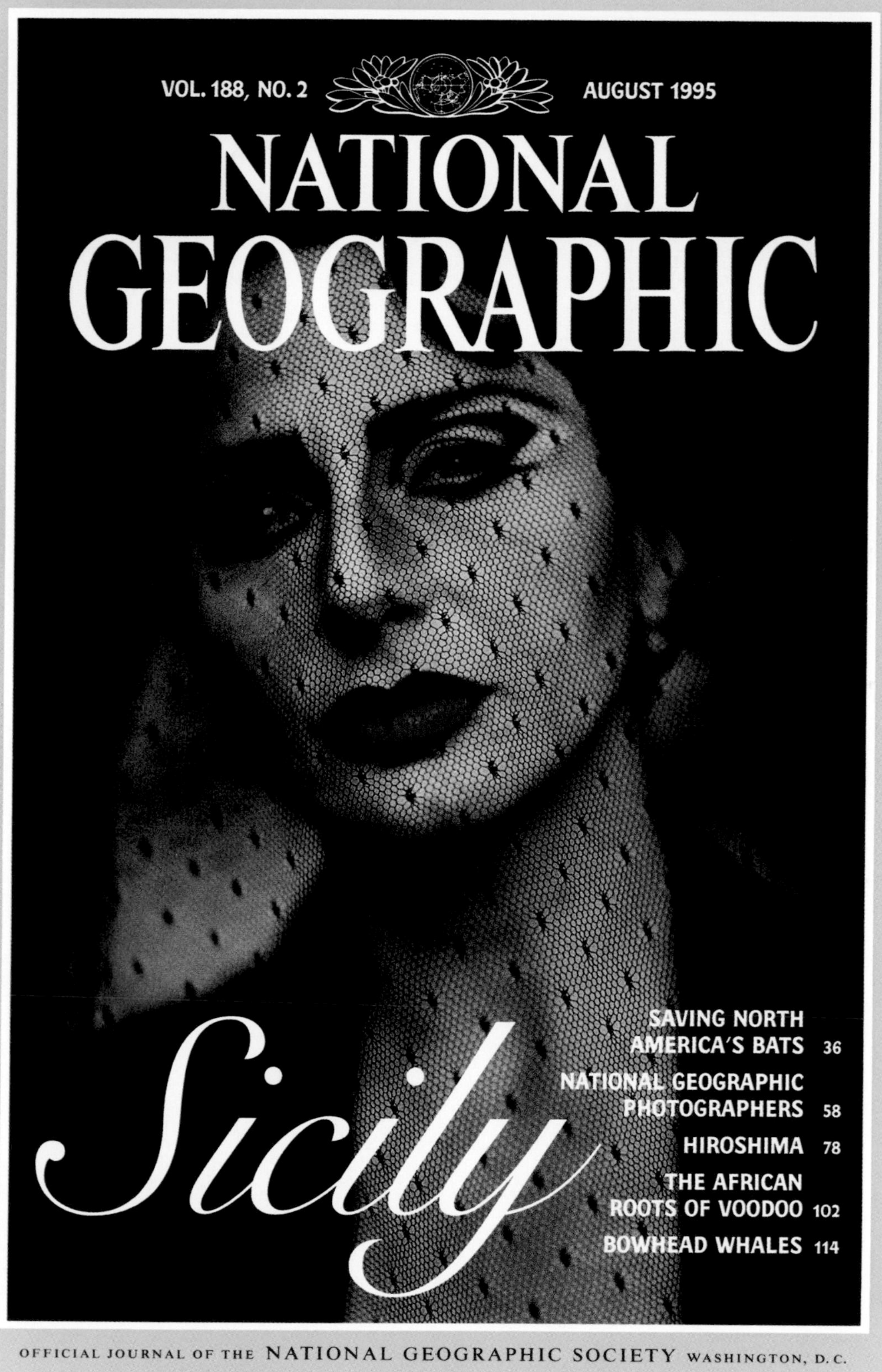

AUGUST | WILLIAM ALBERT ALLARD

DRESS REHEARSAL Dusk was falling on the ancient Greek outdoor theater in Syracuse, Sicily, as Italian actress Benedetta Buccellato, preparing for an upcoming role, took a few turns behind the set. Bill Allard stepped into her path, walked backward, photographed her, and said *"Grazie"* as she passed. She nodded, but never spoke a word.

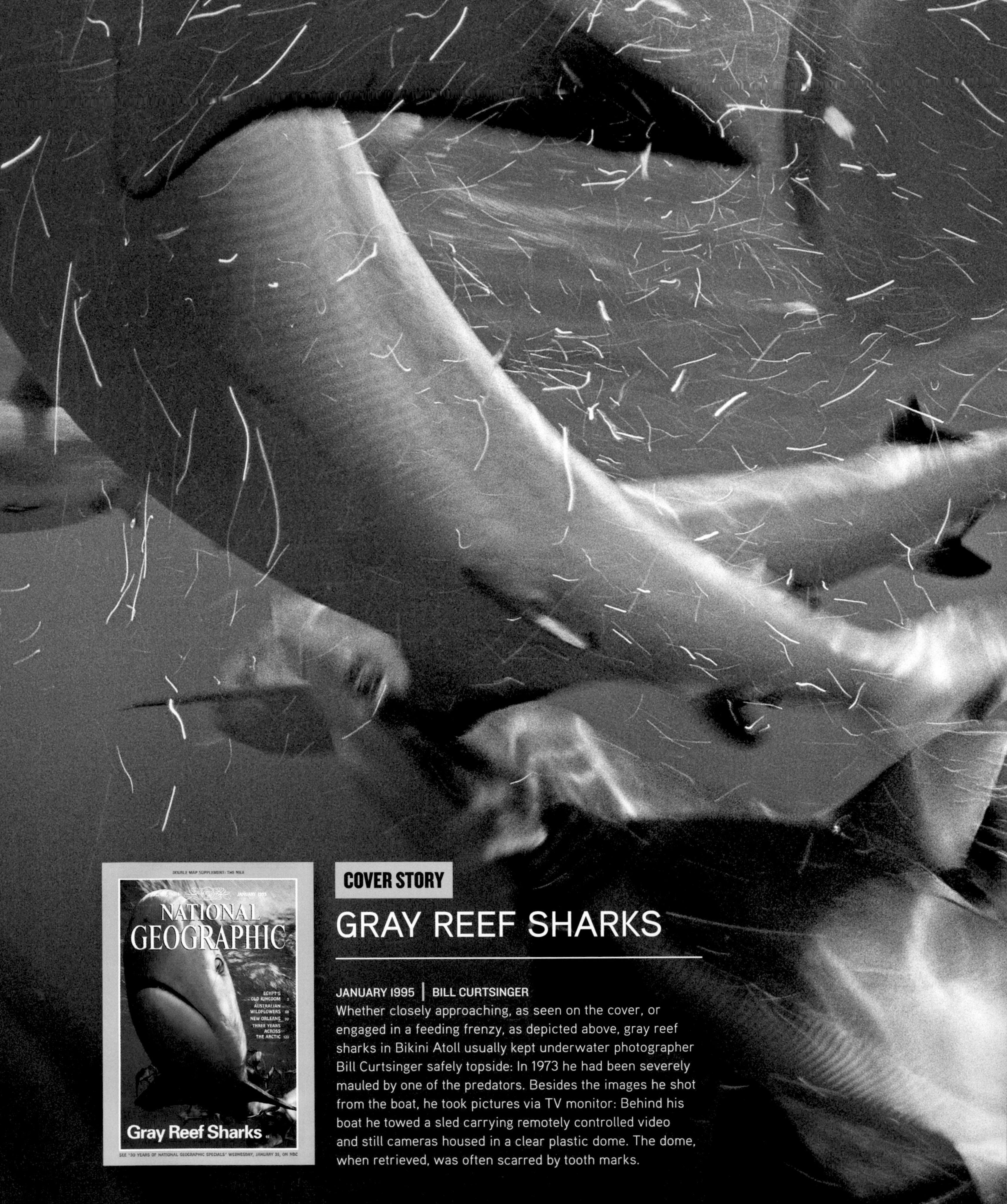

COVER STORY

GRAY REEF SHARKS

JANUARY 1995 | BILL CURTSINGER

Whether closely approaching, as seen on the cover, or engaged in a feeding frenzy, as depicted above, gray reef sharks in Bikini Atoll usually kept underwater photographer Bill Curtsinger safely topside: In 1973 he had been severely mauled by one of the predators. Besides the images he shot from the boat, he took pictures via TV monitor: Behind his boat he towed a sled carrying remotely controlled video and still cameras housed in a clear plastic dome. The dome, when retrieved, was often scarred by tooth marks.

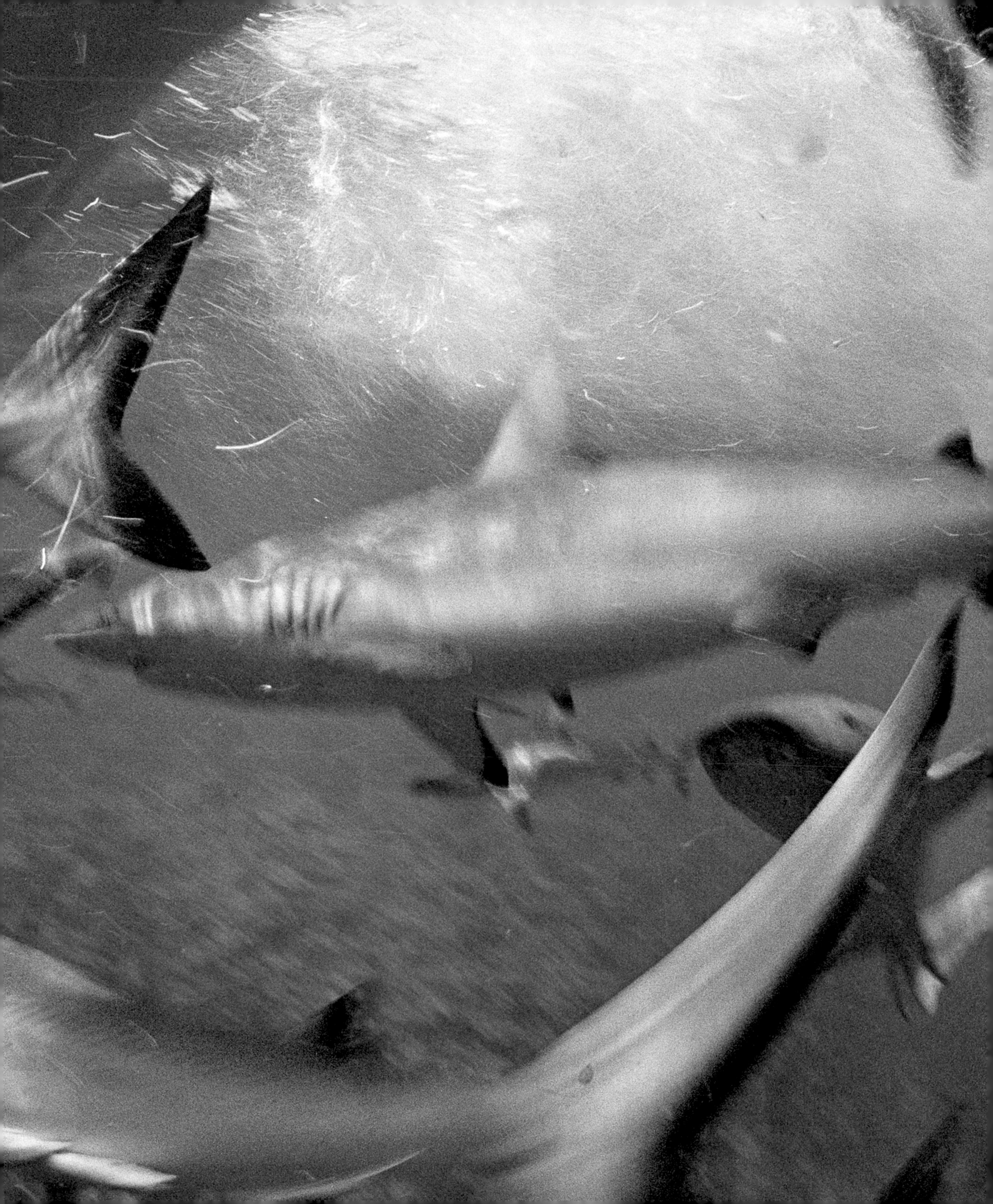

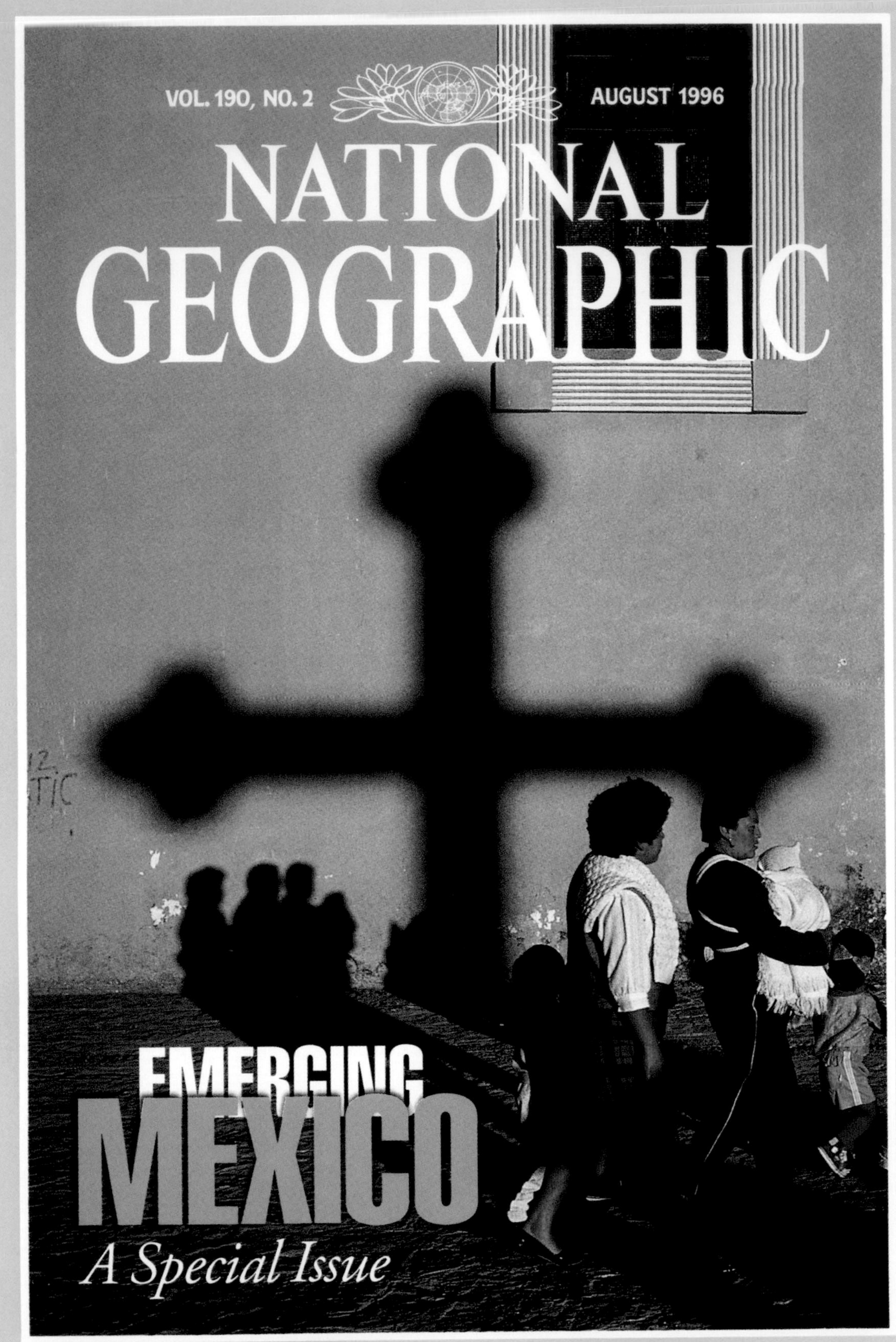

AUGUST | **TOMASZ TOMASZEWSKI** A family walks past the cathedral in San Cristóbal de las Casas.

MEXICAN PROGRESS, MEXICAN PROBLEMS

A SETTING SUN THROWS the shadow of a freestanding cross over a family passing the cathedral in San Cristóbal de las Casas, a town in Mexico's southernmost state, Chiapas.

The jungle-clad hills of Chiapas, as Michael Parfit put it in the August 1996 *National Geographic,* possessed a "soul of cross and mountain." In Mexico "religion colors life," he continued, "but in these hills it paints life blood red"—a reference to Chiapas's long history of rebellions, the most recent of which had occurred two years earlier. Several hundred people were killed in the 1994 Zapatista revolt that began in San Cristóbal and was supported by the left-leaning bishop of that very cathedral.

The failed Zapatista uprising—the name honors Emiliano Zapata, a hero of the 1910–1920 Mexican Revolution and a champion of the oppressed peasantry—was one reason that the *Geographic* published a special issue entirely devoted to a survey of that land. "We set out not to produce a tourist's guide to Mexico nor to revisit the nation's archaeological treasures, which have accounted for no less than 40 titles in *National Geographic,*" wrote Editor Bill Allen. "Instead we wanted to explore how our neighbors are facing the current economic and political crisis and to gauge how they are shaping their own future."

What amounted to a special task force spent most of 1995 in the field. While six journalists fed stories to the issue's chief writer, Michael Parfit, five photographers sent 2,850 rolls of film to Geographic headquarters. Out of those 102,600 individual frames, around 100 were published. Only one, of course—Tomasz Tomaszewski's picture of that church-bound family in Chiapas—made it as far as the cover. And if that were not honor enough, it also appeared as a gatefold next to the editor's introduction.

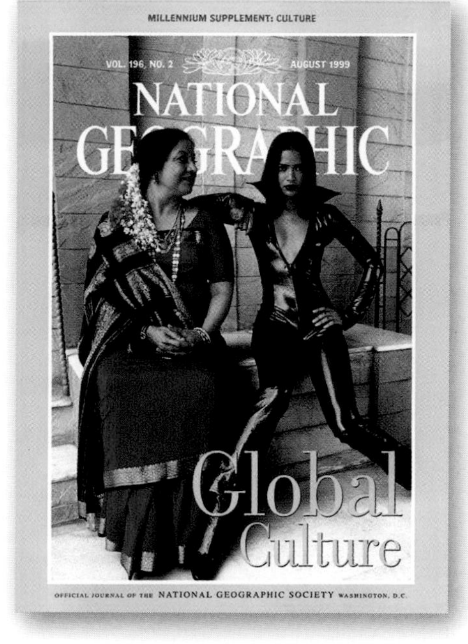

AUGUST 1999 | JOE MCNALLY

1999 ▸▸▸▸ FAST FORWARD

CHANGE IN INDIA Three years later another special issue surveyed the emergence of a new world culture—a well-educated, technologically savvy, cosmopolitan one shared by elites around the globe and typified by biochemist Nakshatra Reddy of Mumbai, who prefers wearing traditional clothing, and her daughter Meghana, a model more comfortable in a catsuit of her own design.

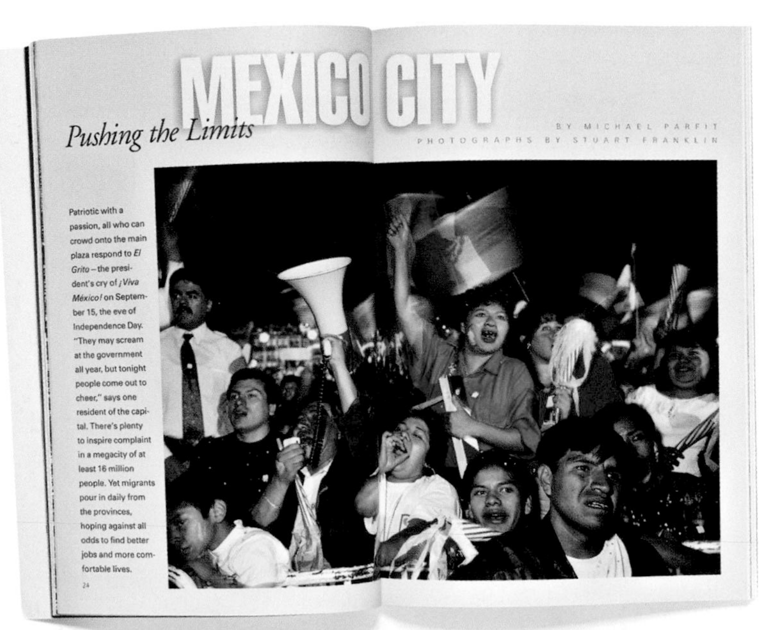

MEXICO CITY

Pushing the Limits

BY MICHAEL PARFIT

PHOTOGRAPHS BY STUART FRANKLIN

Patriotic with a passion, all who can crowd onto the main plaza respond to *El Grito*—the president's cry of *¡Viva México!* on September 15, the eve of Independence Day. "They may scream at the government all year, but tonight people come out to cheer," says one resident of the capital. There's plenty to inspire complaint in a megacity of at least 16 million people. Yet migrants pour in daily from the provinces, hoping against all odds to find better jobs and more comfortable lives.

24

▸ AUGUST 1996 | STUART FRANKLIN Crowds gather in Mexico City on the eve of Independence Day.

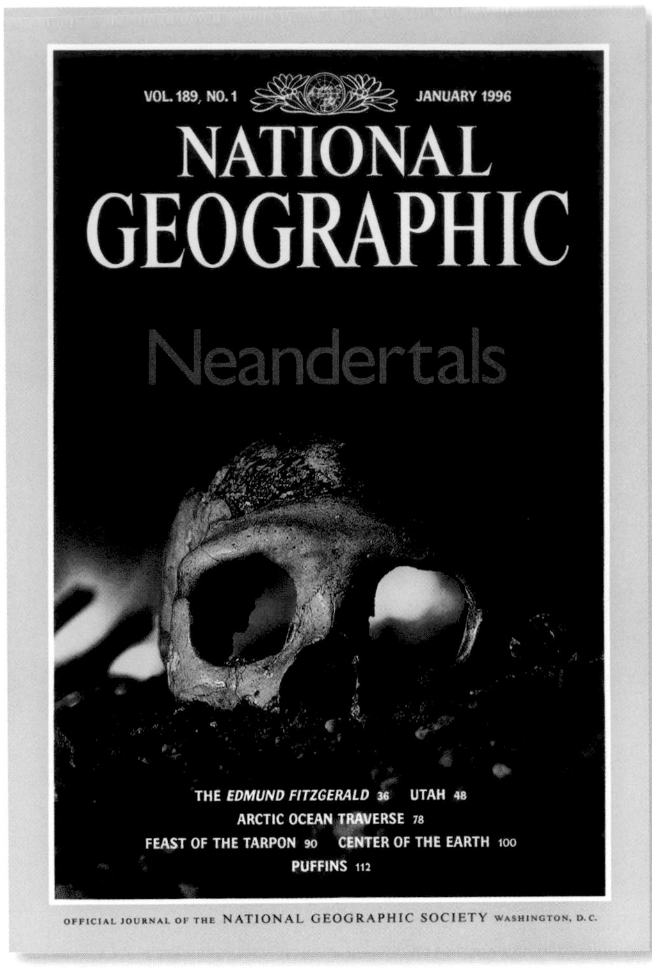

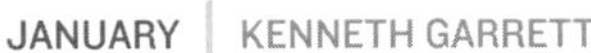
JANUARY | KENNETH GARRETT

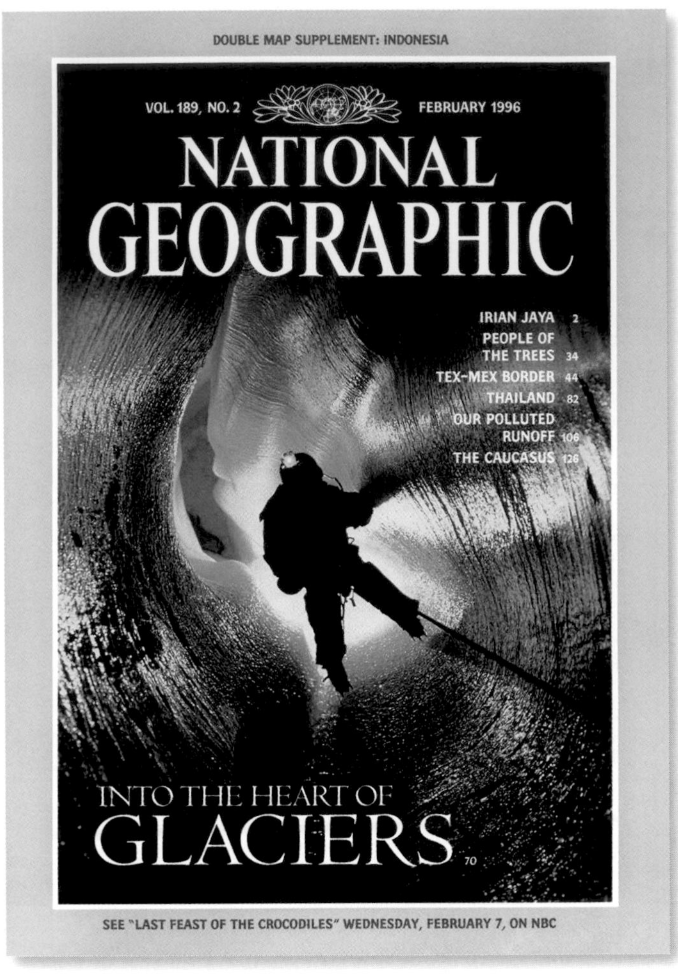

FEBRUARY | CARSTEN PETER

▲ **ANCIENT GLOW** When Kenneth Garrett, photographing a story on Neandertals, discovered that fossils of *Homo neanderthalensis* found in Croatia's Krapina Cave showed cut marks suggesting cannibalism, he came up with an idea. After persuading officials at the Natural History Museum in Zagreb to remove certain of the items, he then built a fire in the courtyard—which took some persuading in a nation that had recently fought a devastating war with neighboring Serbia. The fire was 15 feet away from "Krapina 3"—a 130,000-year-old Neandertal woman's skull—but a telephoto lens pulled them together. That smoldering look put the picture on the cover.

▲ **ICE CAVERNS** Autumn sunlight won't melt the frozen walls of this ice shaft. Each summer melting water creates a labyrinth of passages in the Greenland ice sheet, but the routes freeze again by the time cavers arrive to explore their blue depths. Unlike their terrestrial cousins, ice caves "change all the time," photographer Carsten Peter reports, having spent a decade exploring meltwater tunnels all over Europe and Greenland. Since the networks are reconfigured each summer, such icy passages, he says, "are the chameleons of caves."

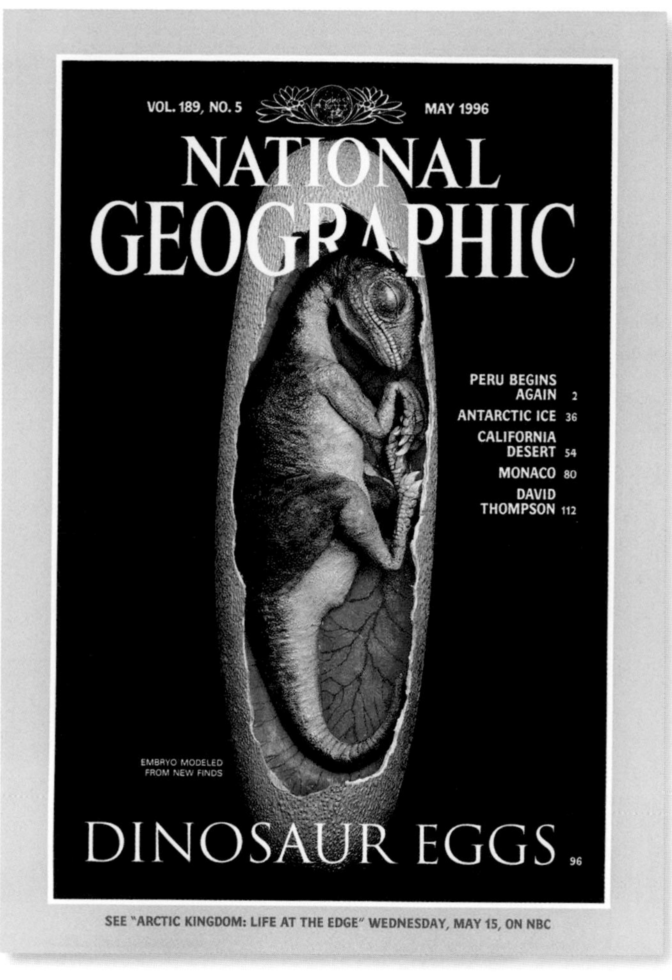

MAY | LOUIE PSIHOYOS AND BRIAN COOLEY

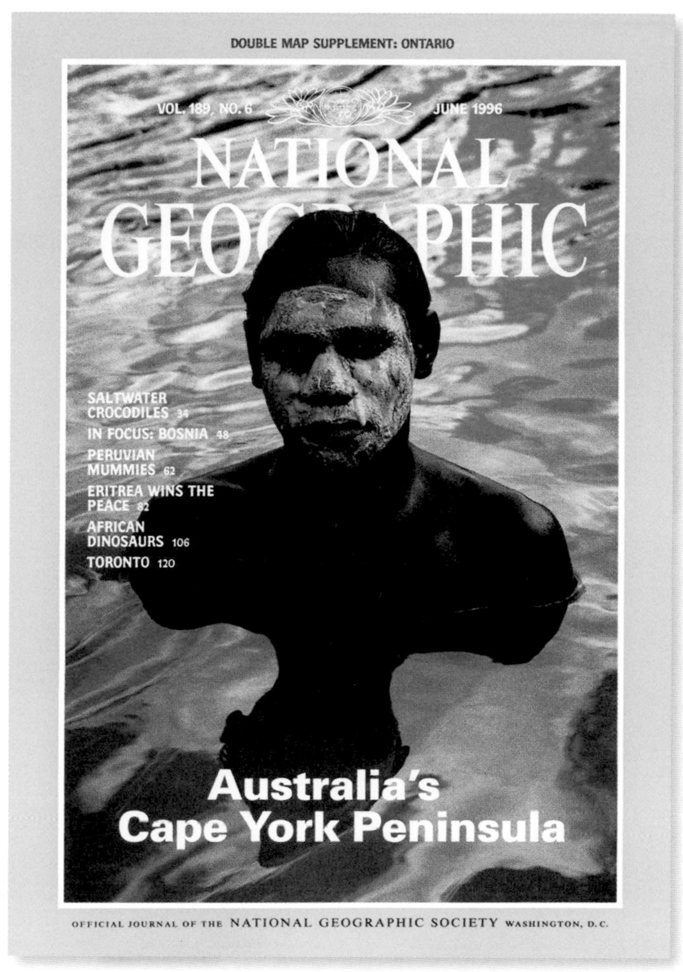

JUNE | SAM ABELL

▲ **DINOSAUR DEVELOPMENT** This model of a dinosaur embryo in an 18-inch egg, made by Brian Cooley, was based on an extraordinary fossil found in China.

"The study of embryos could reveal more about the link between the dinosaurs and their descendants, the birds . . . [But] the most intriguing idea—cloning a dinosaur from DNA, a scenario featured in the book and movie Jurassic Park*—is also the most outlandish."*

—Philip Currie
from "Dinosaur Eggs"

▲ **COOL STARE** Bushfires engulfing untold acres of Strathburn Station only made Sam Abell's weeklong visit to the sprawling cattle ranch all the more sweltering. Summer heat in the Cape York Peninsula—the far tip of Australia's "tropic north"—was so scorching that even a dip in a billabong was tempting, despite the possibility that crocodiles might lurk beneath the surface. One young Aboriginal man plunged in anyway. He "smeared clay on his face, stared at me for a moment, then swam off," Abell remembered.

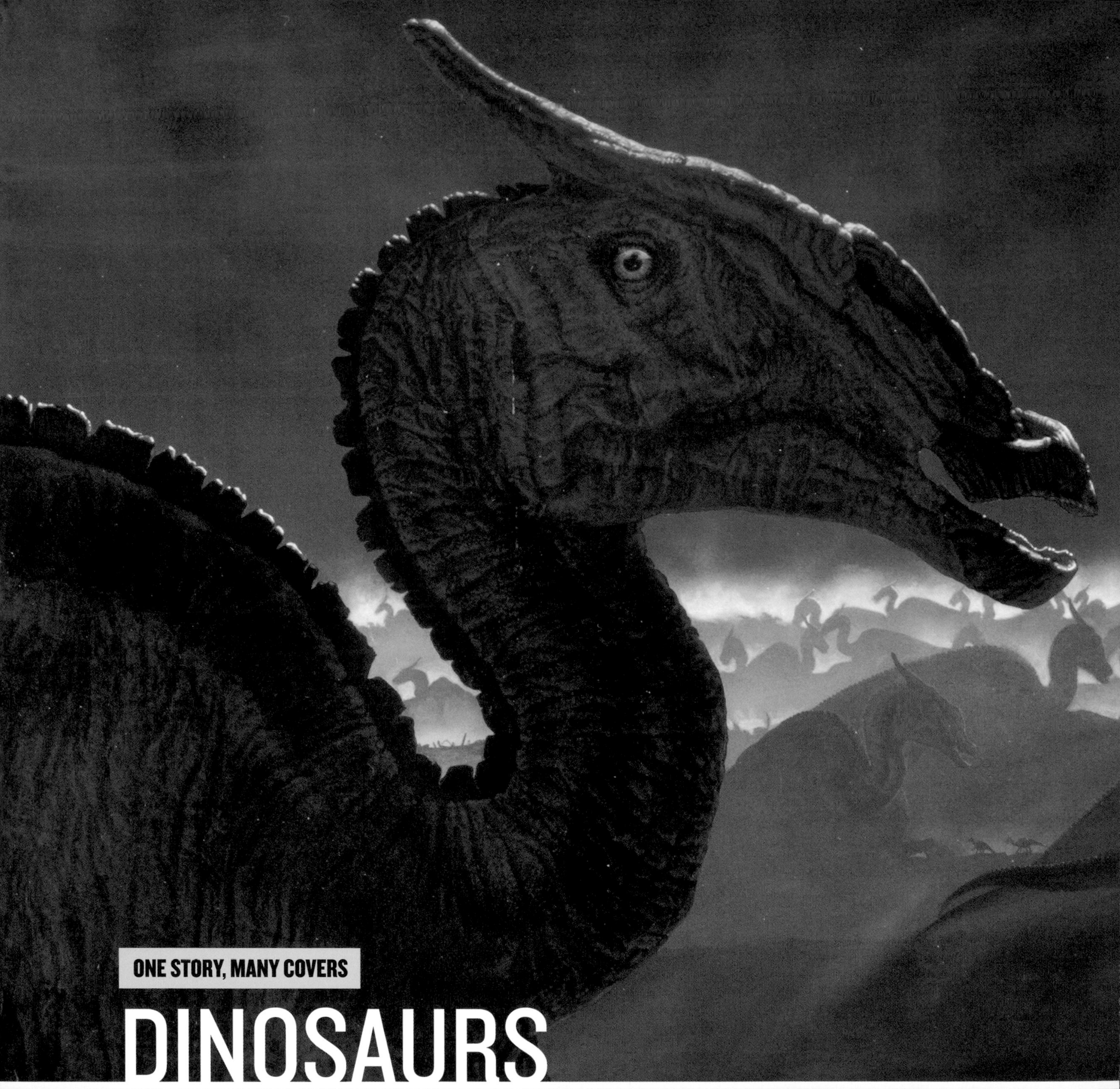

ONE STORY, MANY COVERS

DINOSAURS

▲ JANUARY 1993 | JOHN GURCHE
An illustration shows dawn light of the late Cretaceous—70 million years ago—illuminating a resting herd of *Saurolophus* in what is today Mongolia.

ONCE UPON A TIME they were only lumbering cold-blooded brutes. But the dinosaurs that have thrilled generations of *National Geographic* readers have also included quick, agile, warm-blooded, and feathered lizards. Paleontologists may find the fossils, but in the *Geographic* it's primarily the artists—including well-known painters such as Charles R. Knight and John Gurche—who have summoned the "terrible lizards" forth from their stony beds, sheathed them in flesh and blood, and restored them to a richly imagined primeval world.

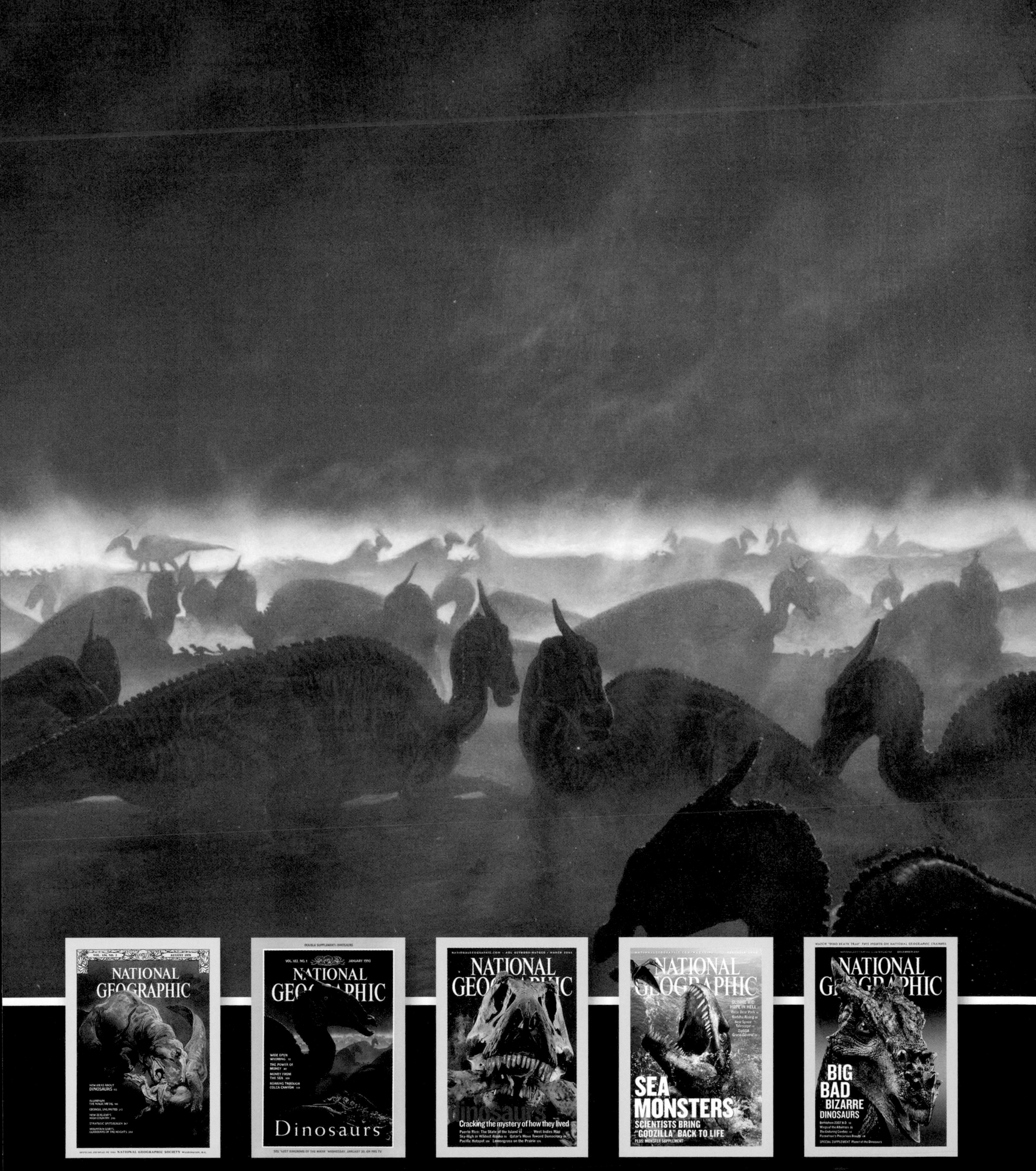

AUGUST 1978 | **JANUARY** 1993 | **MARCH** 2003 | **DECEMBER** 2005 | **DECEMBER** 2007

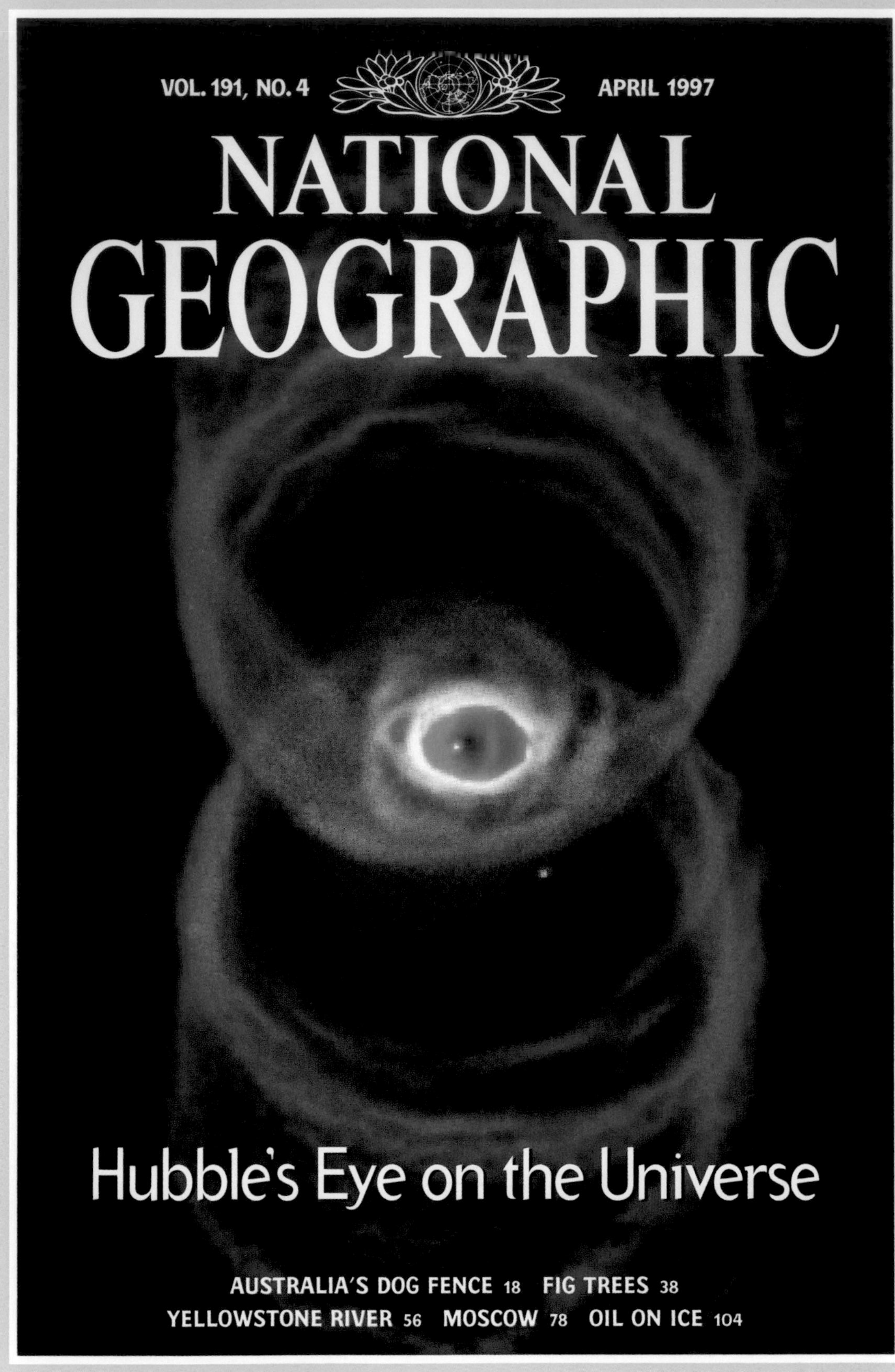

APRIL | RAGHVENDRA SAHAI, JOHN TRAUGER, NASA Hourglass Nebula

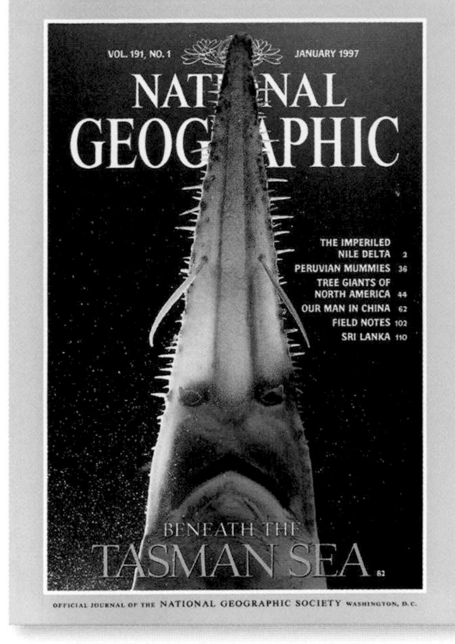

JANUARY | DAVID DOUBILET

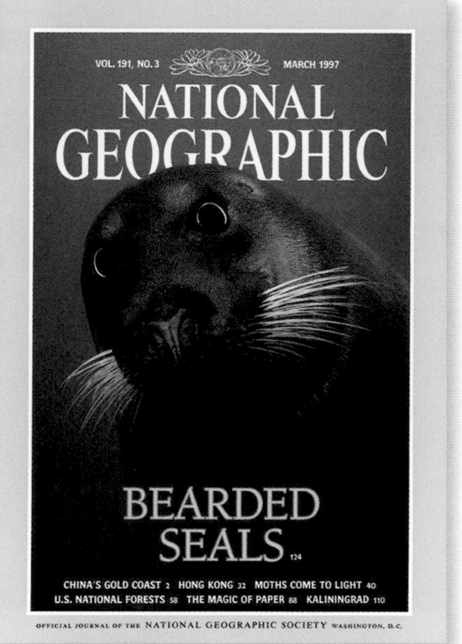

MARCH | FLIP NICKLIN

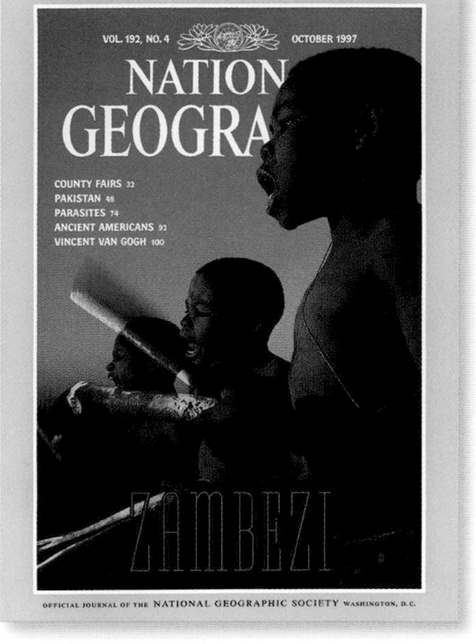

OCTOBER | CHRIS JOHNS

HUBBLE'S LONG VIEW

Editor Bill Allen liked visual puns. So it was no surprise, upon turning from that cover, to encounter this opening sentence: "Astronomers looked 8,000 light-years into the cosmos with the Hubble Space Telescope, and it seemed that the eye of God was staring back."

It was thanks to the eye of Hubble, however, that astronomers were at last able to gaze at what previously had been only a faint smudge in earthbound telescopes. In early 1996 scientists finally photographed the stunning Hourglass Nebula in all its glory using Hubble's Wide Field and Planetary Camera 2. Previous to the camera's installation by space shuttle astronauts in December 1993, the orbiting telescope had been effectively blind, a spherical aberration in its primary mirror blurring its images.

By applying corrective optics, the piano-size WFPC2 became the "camera that saved Hubble." For the next 16 years—until replaced in 2009—it was this eye in the sky that produced all those dazzling images of exploding stars and colliding galaxies that so entranced the general public and won it a well-deserved spot in the Smithsonian's National Air and Space Museum.

▲ **BOYS NO MORE** It was a cold dawn in Lukulu, western Zambia, but Chris Johns was so moved by the scene playing out before him that he ignored the chill. He was witnessing a culminating moment of the Luvale people's "Makishi festival." Weeks earlier vulnerable boys had been sent out to live in the bush, where elders instructed them in the lore of the tribe and the responsibilities of adult life. On the morning after their ritual circumcision, these newly minted men were greeting the dawn with traditional songs and drumbeats—and doing so with compelling fervor.

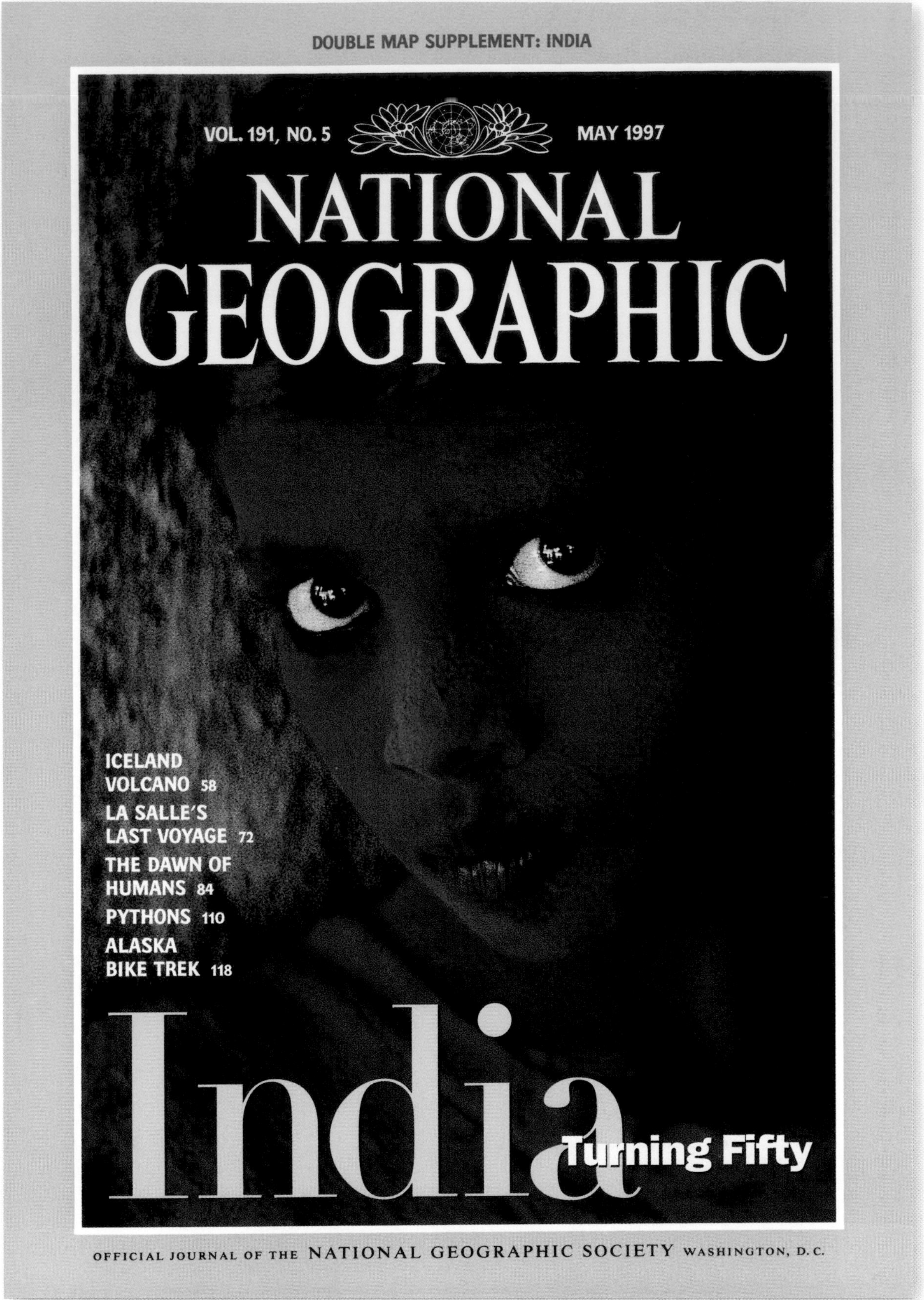

MAY | STEVE MCCURRY

PORTRAIT IN RED In Mumbai, says Steve McCurry, "images are almost instantaneous" because "nothing stands still." This boy—coated in the red powder that covers everything during the Hindu festival Ganesh Chaturthi—stood still long enough for the photographer to make one of his most memorable and well-known portraits.

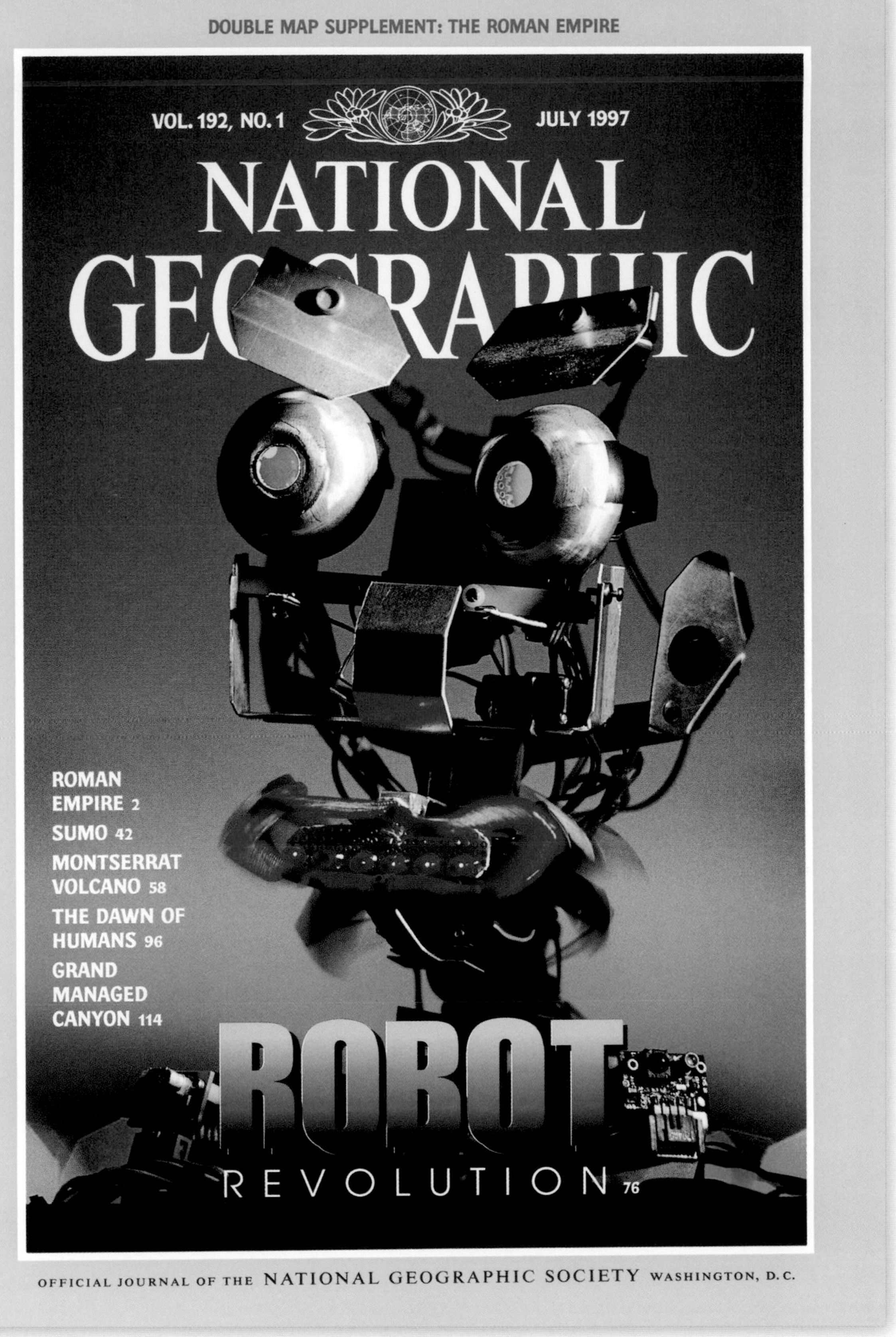

JULY | GEORGE STEINMETZ

ANDROID INTELLIGENCE The robot IT—designed by Artificial Creatures in Boston—was programmed to read outward signs of human emotions and react accordingly. Here it is not only smiling in the presence of people but it can also be seen speaking, thanks to a time exposure that emphasizes the movement of those lips.

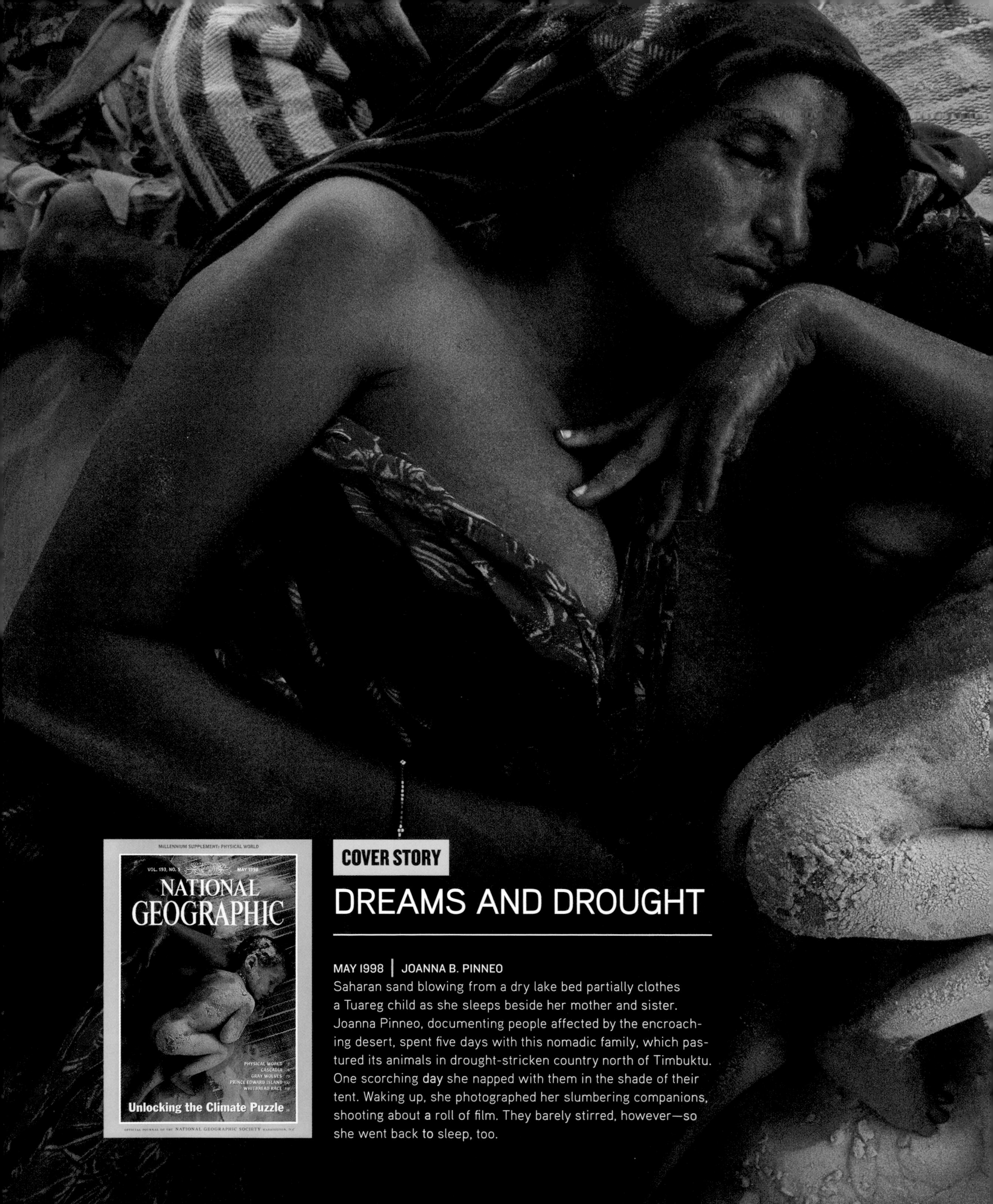

COVER STORY

DREAMS AND DROUGHT

MAY 1998 | JOANNA B. PINNEO

Saharan sand blowing from a dry lake bed partially clothes a Tuareg child as she sleeps beside her mother and sister. Joanna Pinneo, documenting people affected by the encroaching desert, spent five days with this nomadic family, which pastured its animals in drought-stricken country north of Timbuktu. One scorching day she napped with them in the shade of their tent. Waking up, she photographed her slumbering companions, shooting about a roll of film. They barely stirred, however—so she went back to sleep, too.

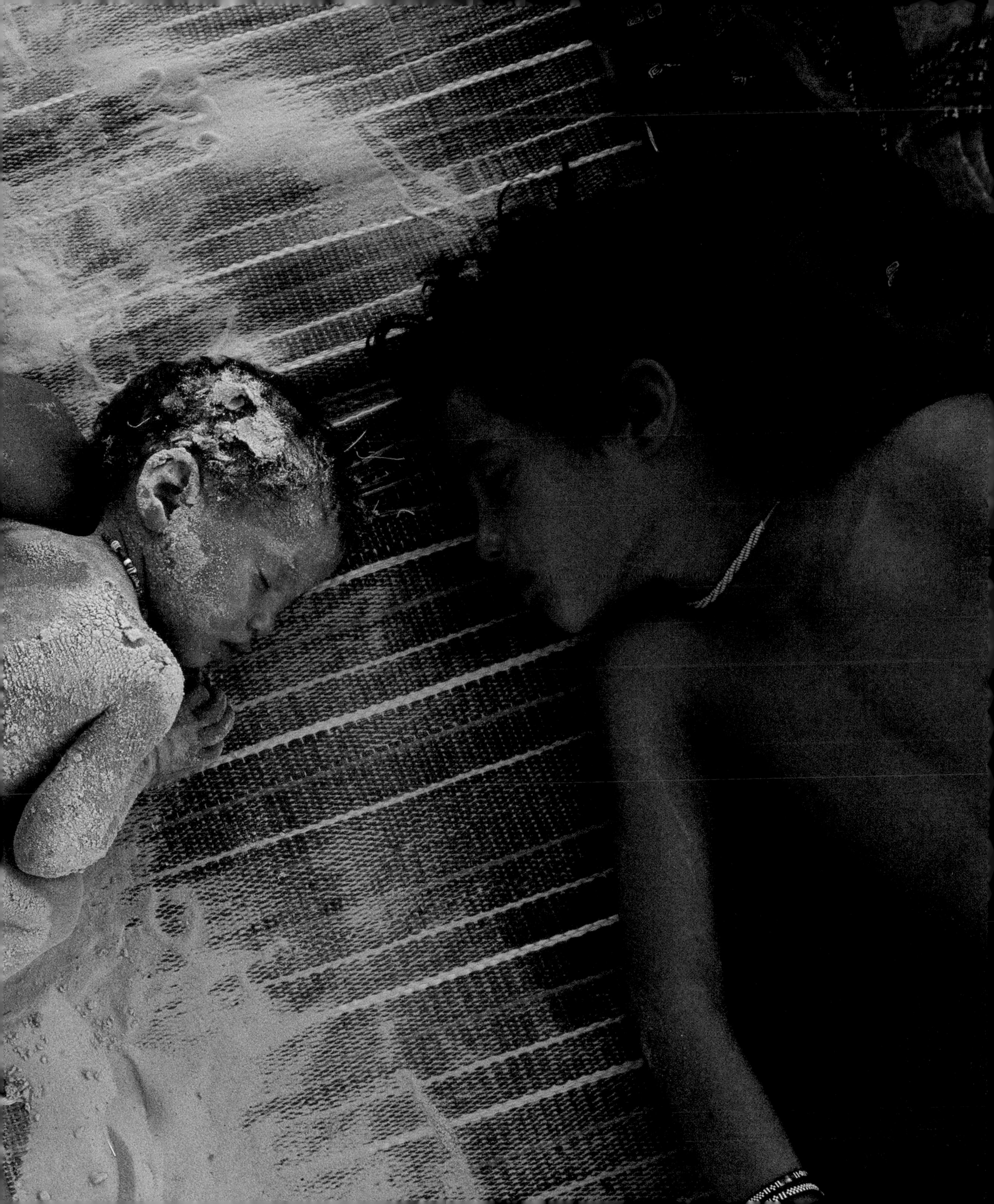

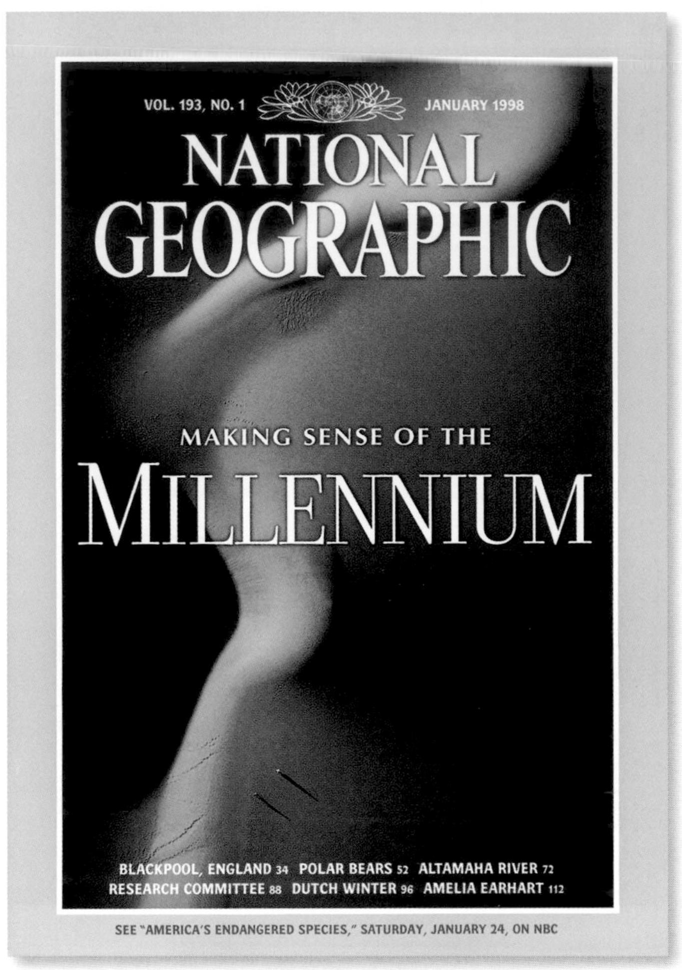

JANUARY | GEORGE STEINMETZ

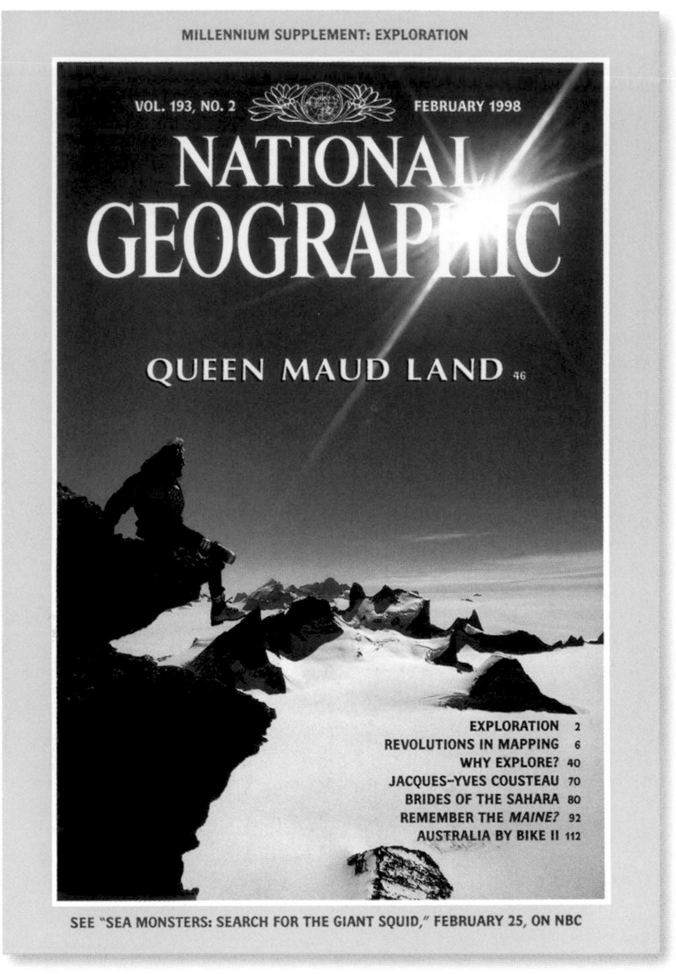

FEBRUARY | GORDON WILTSIE

▲ **SANDS OF TIME** Tiny figures appear to be travelers on the sands of time, an appropriate enough image for an issue devoted to preparing readers for a new millennium. George Steinmetz, when he took this picture, had actually hoped to photograph a camel caravan journeying to the old dune-encircled Saharan town of Chinguetti in Mauritania. When none appeared and evening was turning to dusk, he persuaded the pilot to make one more pass—and that was when he made this "grab shot" of two people taking an after-dinner stroll at the edge of town.

▲ **FRIGID AIR** Epitome of exploration, a mountaineer on one of the highest peaks in the loneliest of continents views a sublime panorama.

> *"Nowhere on Earth has the terra remained more incognita than Antarctica—and perhaps nowhere in Antarctica is the aura more palpable than in the mountains of Queen Maud Land."*
>
> —Jon Krakauer
> *from "Queen Maud Land"*

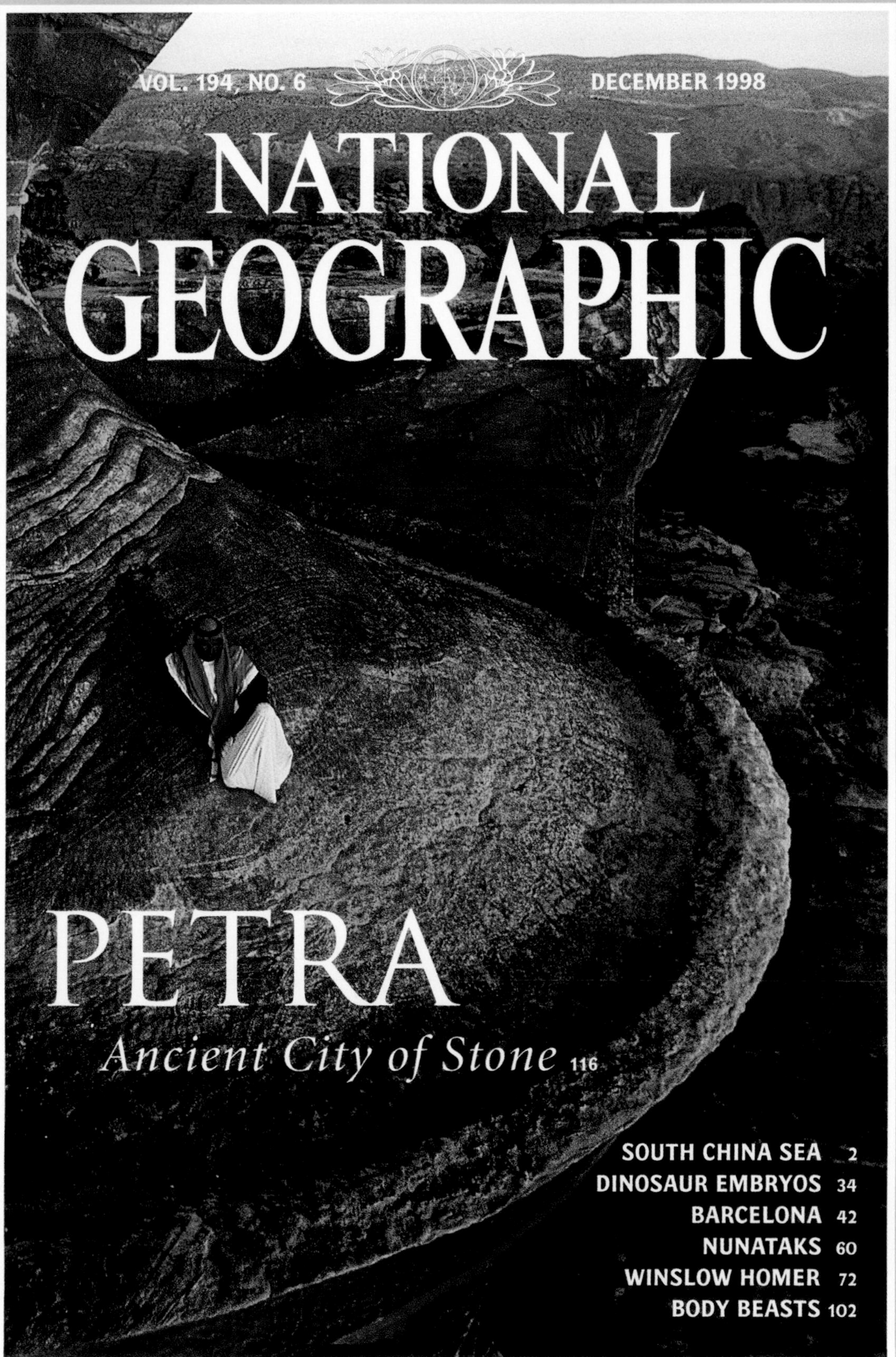

1990 1991 1992 1993 1994 1995 1996 1997 **1998** 1999

DECEMBER | ANNIE GRIFFITHS A Jordanian surveys his country's "rose-red city," ancient Petra.

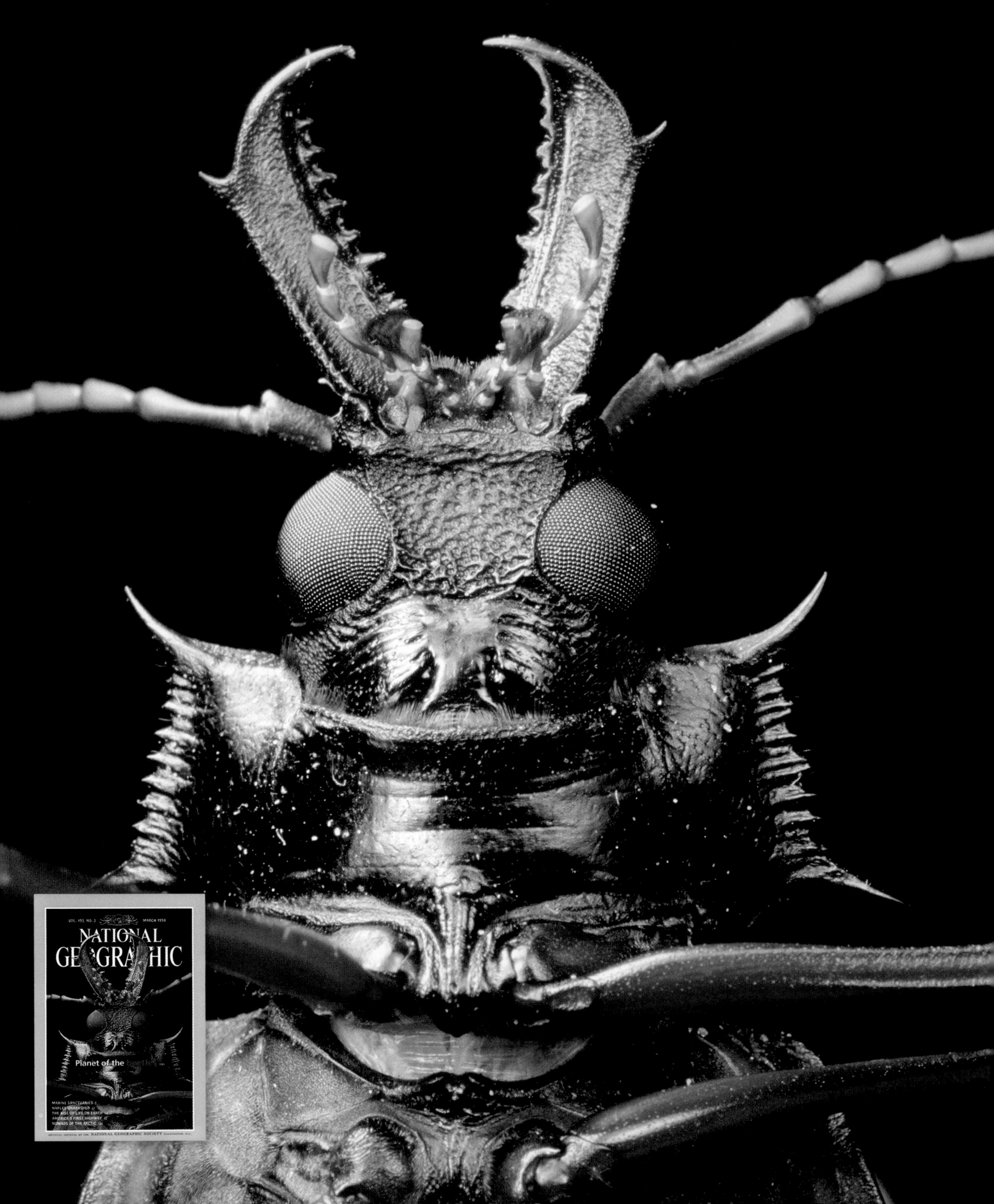

VOL. 193, NO. 3
MARCH 1998
NATIONAL GEOGRAPHIC
Planet of the
MARINE SANCTUARIES
NAPLES UNABASHED
THE RISE OF LIFE ON EARTH
AMERICA'S FIRST HIGHWAY
NOMADS OF THE ARCTIC
NATIONAL GEOGRAPHIC SOCIETY

BEETLEMANIA

IT MIGHT LOOK LIKE something out of *Star Wars*, but *Macrodontia cervicornis* is actually a long-horned beetle from French Guiana. While it makes a spectacular cover shot, some of the red is not a natural part of its coloring. That comes instead from human blood—the beetle slashed the photographer's hand.

That's all in a day's work for Mark Moffett. Somewhere along his eventful trail he was dubbed the "Indiana Jones of entomology" for his jungle adventures that resembled those of a character out of fiction: Once he accidentally sat on a fer-de-lance, the deadliest snake in the New World; another time he dined on giant spiders with Amazonian shamans; and on another occasion, he kept Colombian drug smugglers at bay with a blowgun. A favorite guest on late-night talk shows, Moffett is always pulling out a tarantula or a giant African bullfrog to impress his hosts.

But Moffett is first and foremost a Harvard-trained scientist, who spends most of his field time stalking ants in the tropics, often by climbing high into the rain forest canopy. (He did discover two new ant species, however, while touring a Balinese temple.) Beetles—which account for one in four animal species—are just some of the numerous small fry that the self-taught photographer has documented for *National Geographic*. "If you photograph an elephant or a whale, all you can do is make it look smaller than life," he once told an interviewer. "The fun thing with insects is you can make people forget their size and turn them into things that are the equivalent of science fiction . . . Even the small can be dramatic."

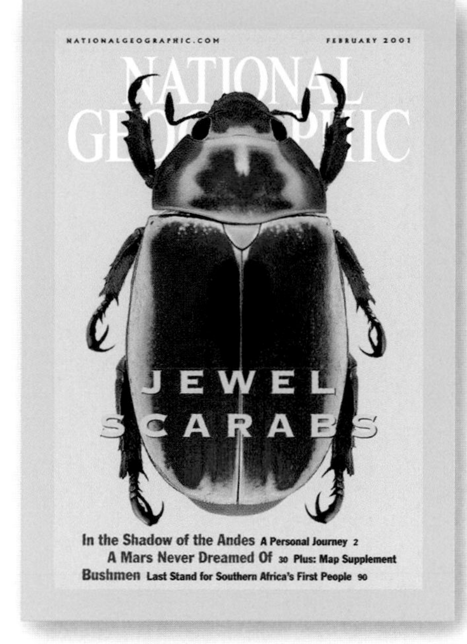

FEBRUARY 2001 | DAVID HAWKS

2001 ▸▸▸▸ FAST FORWARD

TREASURE BUGS Three years later another beetle would grace the *Geographic*'s cover. Jewel scarabs, found in montane forests in Mexico and Central America, are so iridescent—often verging on metallic silver and gold—that they have become collectors' items. Populations remain stable, though, as most of the eggs and larvae remain hidden underground. Only adults are taken.

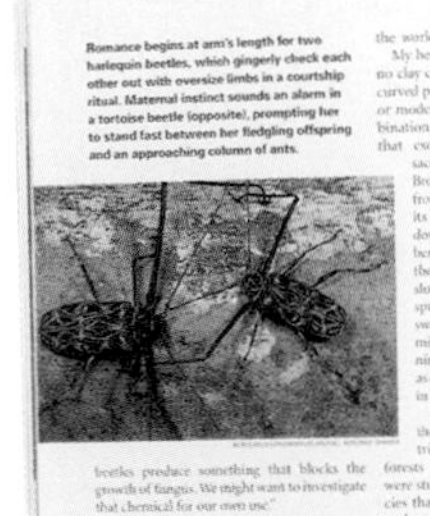

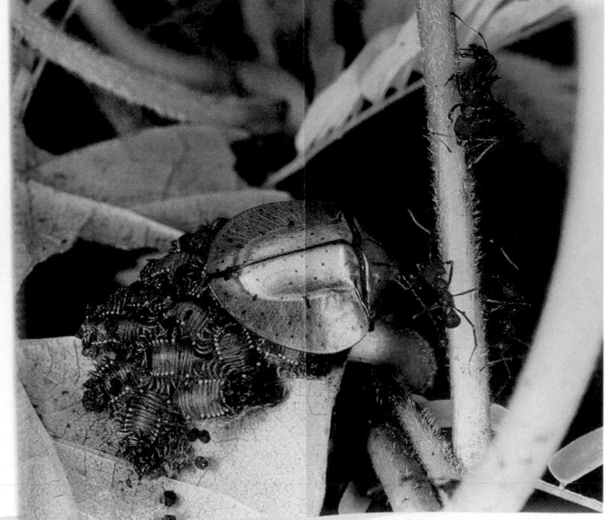

▸ MARCH 1998 | MARK W. MOFFETT A tortoise beetle protects her offspring from marauding ants.

◂ MARCH 1998 | MARK W. MOFFETT An alien-looking long-horned beetle from French Guiana.

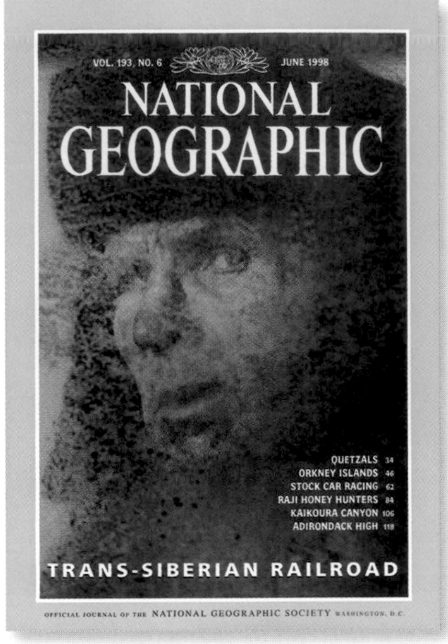

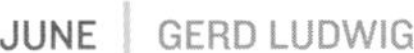

JUNE | GERD LUDWIG

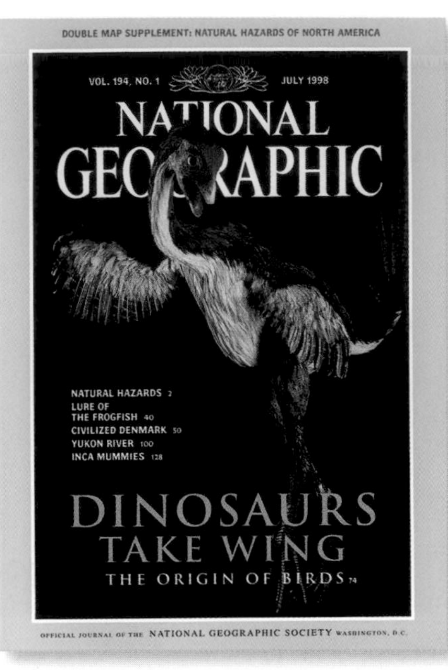

JULY | O. LOUIS MAZZATENTA AND BRIAN COOLEY

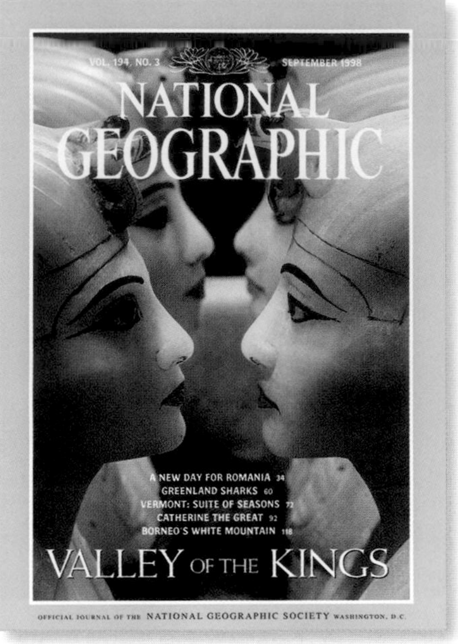

SEPTEMBER | KENNETH GARRETT

▲ BACKWARD GLANCE Peering through a frosted window, a citizen of Krasnoyarsk, Russia, rides an *electrichka,* a local electric train, wearing, Ludwig says, "the only defense against the cold, a fur *shapka.*" For the German-born photographer, covering the Trans-Siberian Railway—which runs from Moscow to distant Vladivostok on the Sea of Japan, a staggering 5,772 miles—was the "most physically difficult story I've ever done." To get the right shots, he often dangled from the sides of trains, secured only by a rope, while temperature plunged to minus 100 degrees Fahrenheit.

A CROWDED WORLD ▶

PUBLISHED AT A TIME when the world population was just hitting six billion—it's over seven billion now—this issue of *National Geographic* examined various problems facing families, communities, and nations posed by the sheer quantity of fellow human beings sharing the same planet.

> Population: We know it's a problem . . . But, if the problem were only numbers, these stories would have no power to touch or perplex us. Nor would we race to bring food to famine-stricken countries, or blanch to read of newborn babies being thrown into trash bins, or fall silent upon hearing of the pregnant mother who refused cancer treatments that could damage her baby, gave birth, and died. Even as some fear for our species' survival, we instinctively sense mysteries that transcend statistics. "Don't look at people like an ant heap," one expert urged. "These are individuals."
>
> *—From "Women and Population," Erla Zwingle*

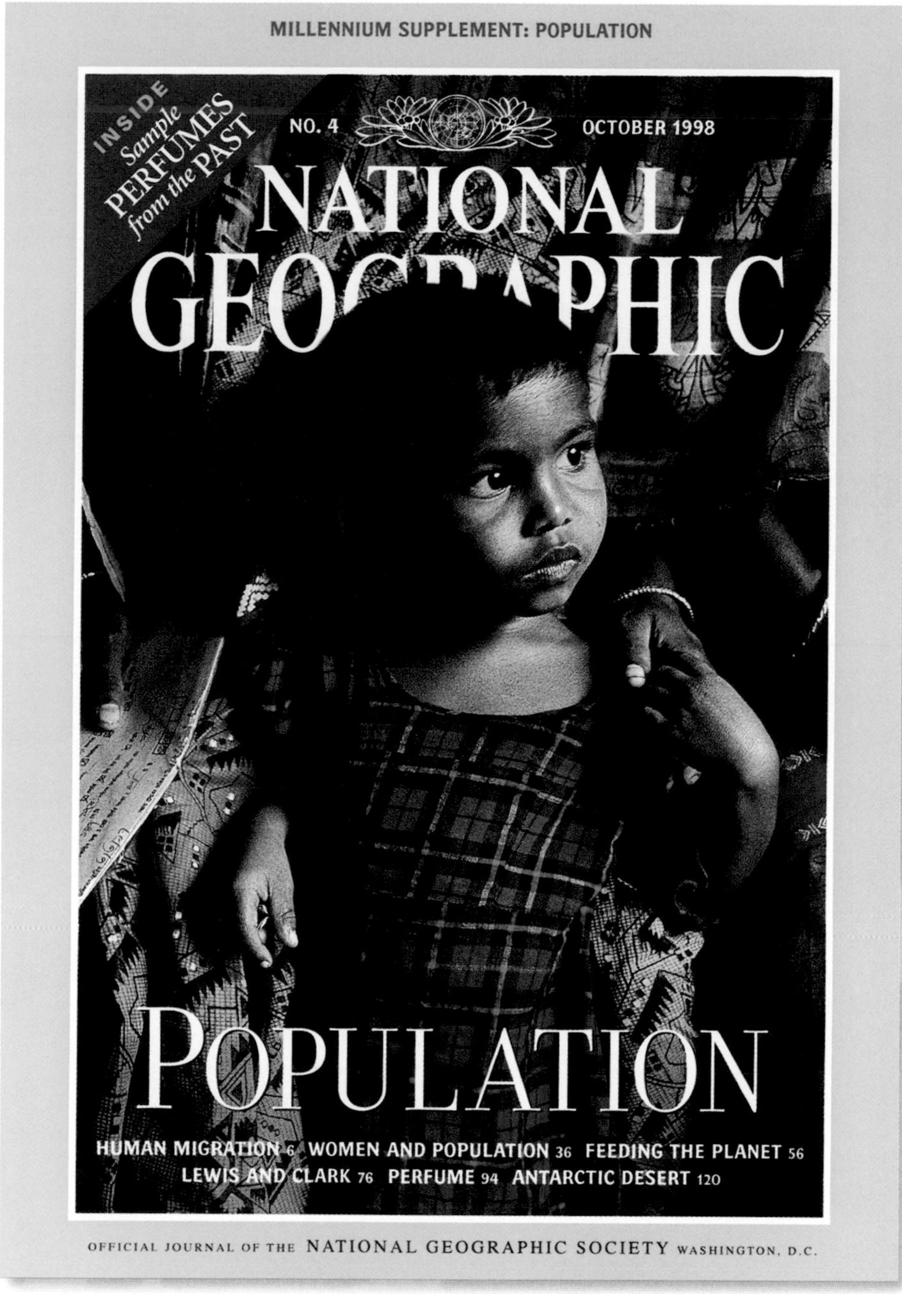

OCTOBER | KAREN KASMAUSKI

▲ **NEXT GENERATION** By the time this Bangladeshi child—here leaning against her pregnant mother—has children of her own, her offspring might number no more than two. The birth rate in Bangladesh, the most densely populated nation on Earth, had already declined from an average of 4.9 children per woman in 1990 to 3.3 less than a decade later—thanks in part to the efforts of the Bangladesh Rural Advancement Committee, a nationwide network of village clinics offering prenatal and postnatal care in a land of some 68,000 villages. It was while she was accompanying a health care volunteer in one of these clinics that photographer Karen Kasmauski encountered this child and her mother.

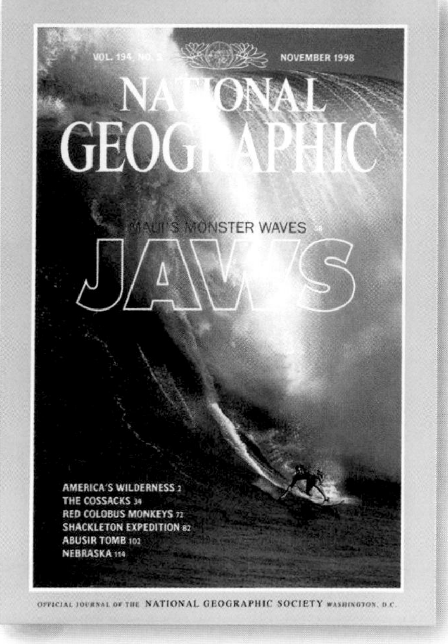

NOVEMBER | PATRICK MCFEELEY

▲ **SURF'S UP** Surfer Laird Hamilton merited not only the cover but also a triple gatefold within the article because he is skimming the edge of a 50-foot-high wall of water. About a dozen times a year, distant storms in the Pacific send monster waves thundering into Maui's northern shores—hence one spot's nickname, "Jaws." At times it is so dangerous that surfers need to be towed into position by Jet Skis, and the photographer makes most of his dramatic shots from a helicopter.

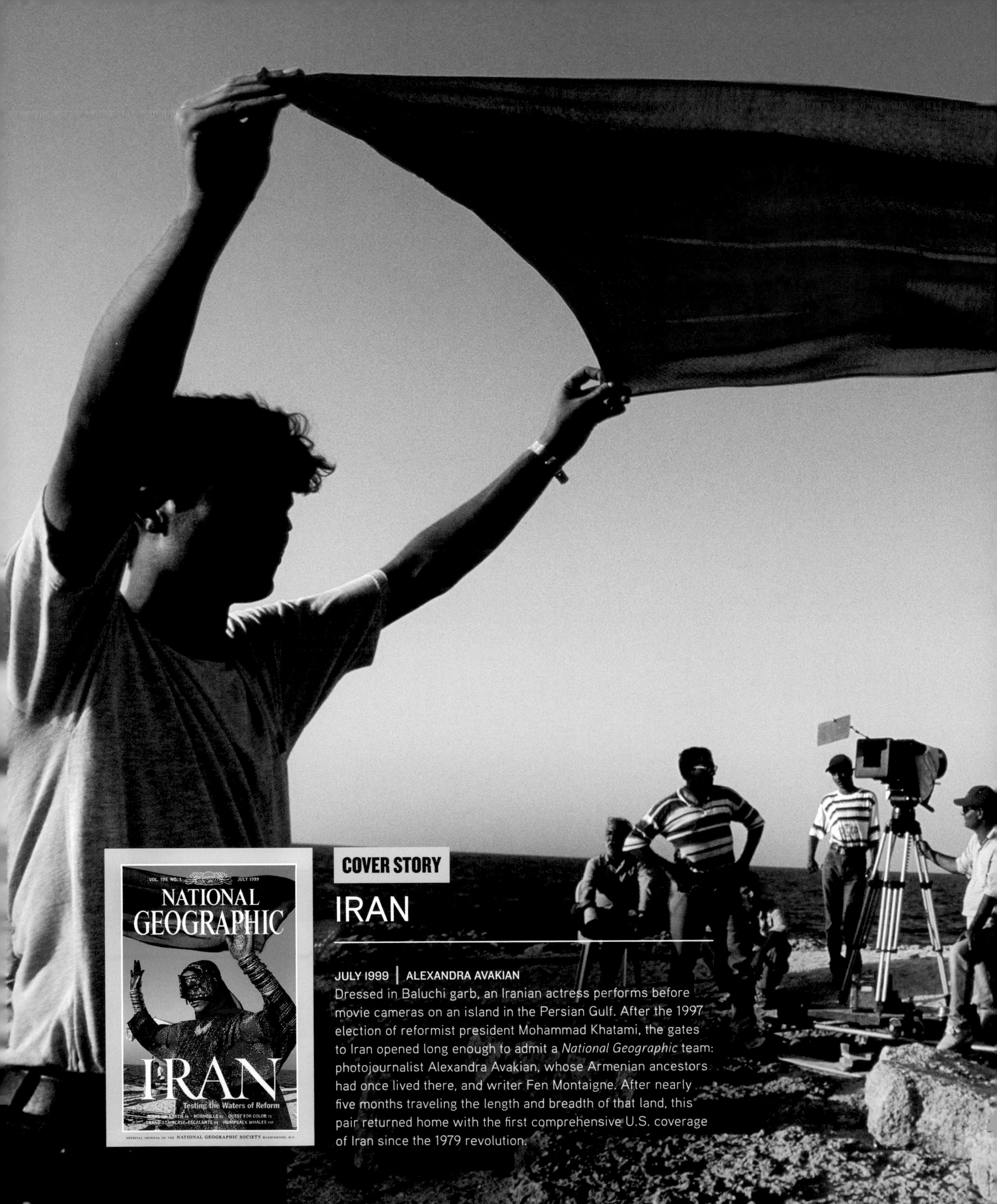

COVER STORY

IRAN

JULY 1999 | ALEXANDRA AVAKIAN

Dressed in Baluchi garb, an Iranian actress performs before movie cameras on an island in the Persian Gulf. After the 1997 election of reformist president Mohammad Khatami, the gates to Iran opened long enough to admit a *National Geographic* team: photojournalist Alexandra Avakian, whose Armenian ancestors had once lived there, and writer Fen Montaigne. After nearly five months traveling the length and breadth of that land, this pair returned home with the first comprehensive U.S. coverage of Iran since the 1979 revolution.

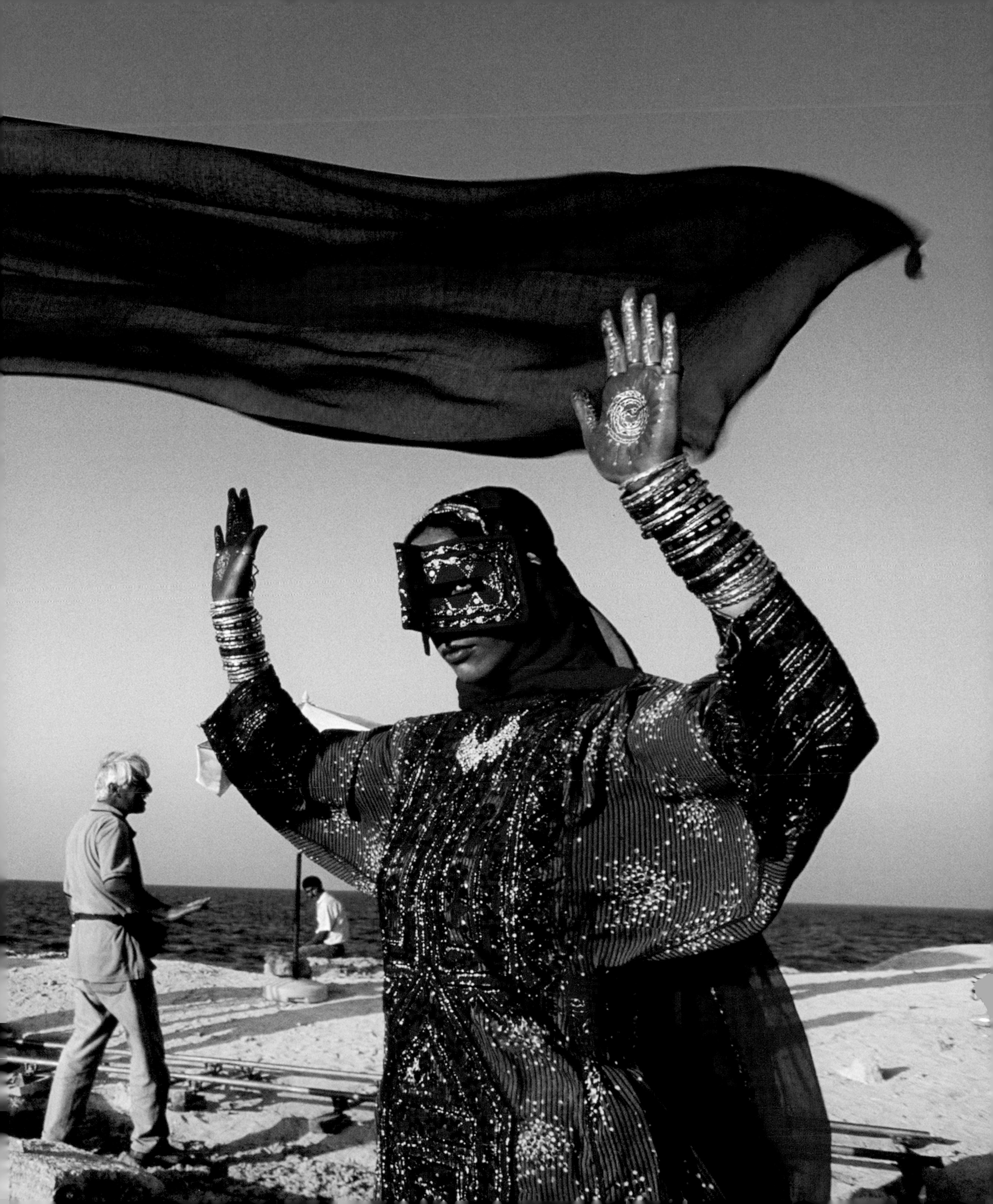

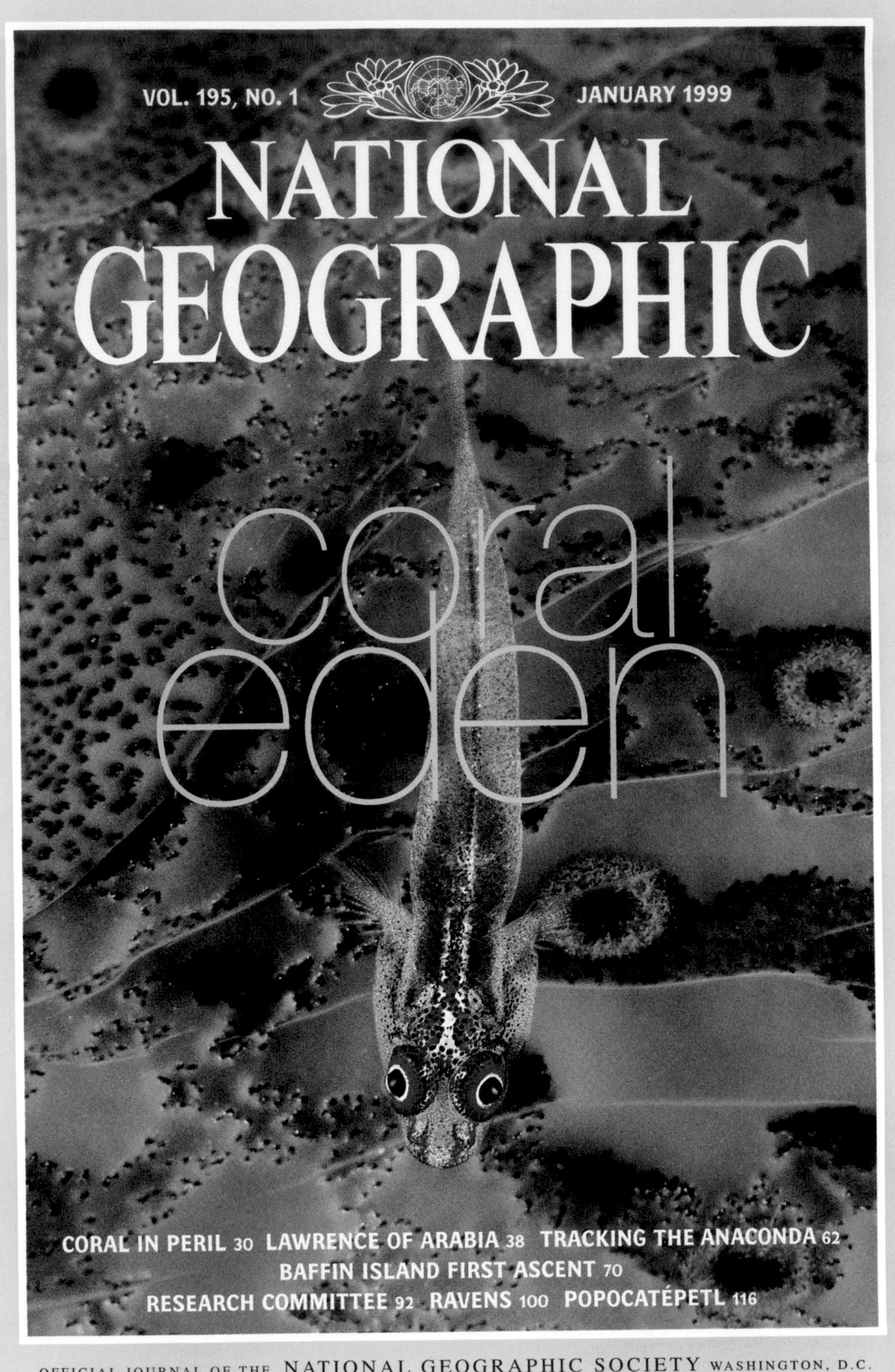

JANUARY | DAVID DOUBILET Off the coast of New Guinea, a goby finds shelter in a giant clam.

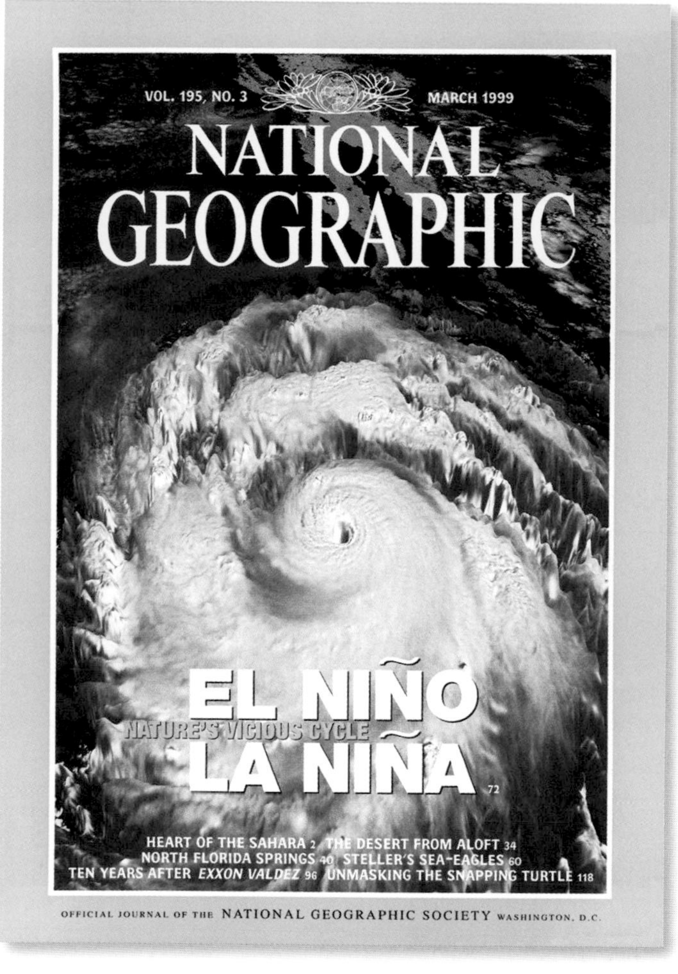

MARCH | NASA/NOAA

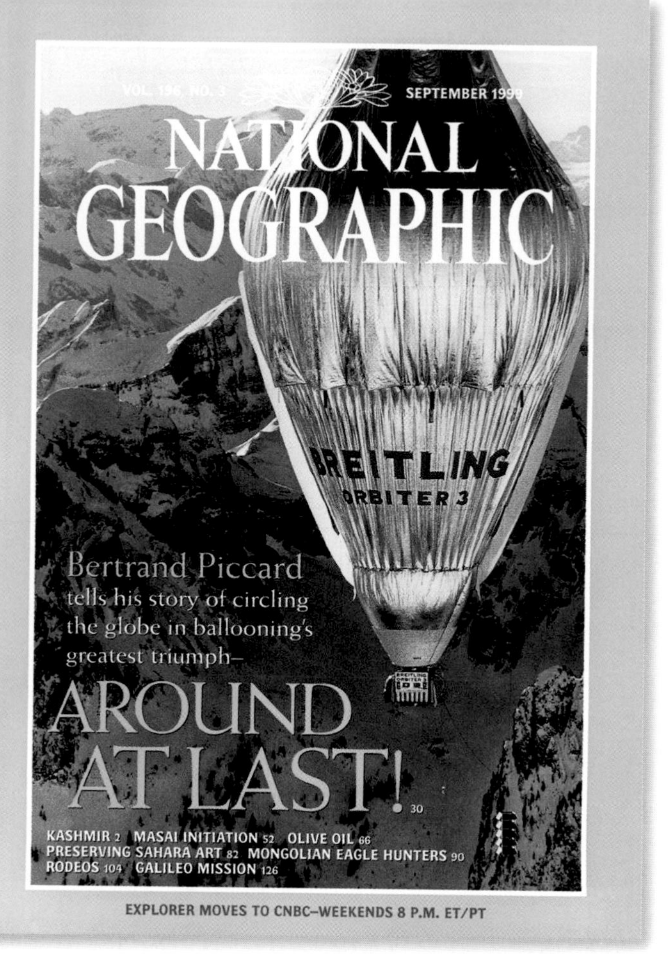

SEPTEMBER | BREITLING SA

▲ **MONSTER STORMS** Hurricane Linda brushes Mexico's Pacific coast before turning north to expend her fury in the open ocean. Linda, the largest hurricane ever recorded in the eastern Pacific, was only one of several cyclones that made the 1997 storm season so remarkable. Hurricane Pauline damaged parts of Mexico, while Hurricane Nora caused flooding in the U.S. Southwest. A record 11 typhoons ravaged settlements from Japan to the Marshall Islands. All were spawned in the Pacific's equatorial regions, especially those near South America, where midwinter perturbations in the climate pattern are termed El Niño—"The Boy"—a reference to the birth of Jesus at Christmas.

▲ **WORLD TOUR** The *Breitling Orbiter 3* soars over the Swiss Alps, embarking on the first nonstop balloon flight around the world.

"During the last night, I savor once more the intimate relationship we have established with our planet. Shivering in the pilot's seat, I have the feeling I have left the capsule to fly under the stars that have swallowed our balloon."

—Bertrand Piccard
from "Around at Last!"

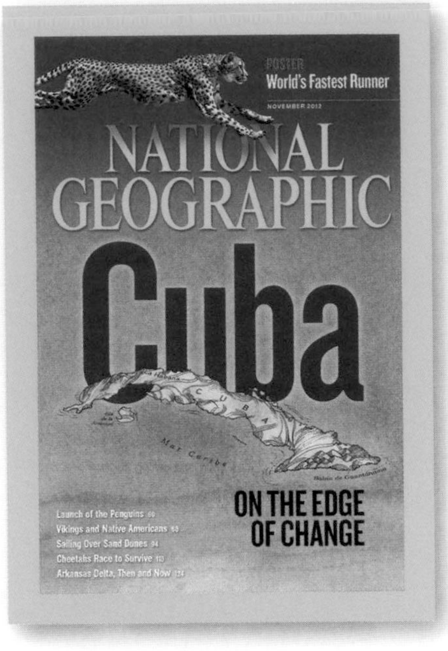

NOVEMBER 2012 | JEREMY COLLINS AND KEN GEIGER

CUBA THEN AND NOW ▶

THE FACE OF CUBA—young, eager, curious, open. And not at all bothered by cruising around in 1953 Chevrolets. Spare parts, not to mention new vehicles, had been hard to come by in the 40 years that had elapsed since Fidel Castro's 1959 Communist-inspired revolution. But though all the cars were old, most of the people were young, fully two-thirds of them being born in the years since Castro's ascendancy. This particular boy was photographed in Camaguey as he rode home from his ninth birthday party at a hotel swimming pool.

In 1997, after diplomatic maneuvering, *National Geographic* photographer David Alan Harvey was permitted to travel the island and saw a Cuba poised on the edge of change. Whether in crumbling cities, sugarcane fields, or cigar factories, he photographed much of the time-warp character of Old Cuba, but he also photographed the New Cuba, and those pictures captured a zest for *la vida* shining out of youthful eyes. Because he spoke fluent Spanish, Harvey could talk to anybody, and would often throw himself into spirited give-and-take repartee with strangers. He found them simpatico. That is the real story the pictures tell—and represents one of this celebrated photographer's finest and most enduring bodies of work.

2012 ▶▶▶▶ FAST FORWARD

THIRTEEN YEARS LATER Time for another cover story on Cuba. How had things changed? Despite Fidel Castro's retirement and some liberalizing reforms, author Cynthia Gorney found the island nation to be "young, energetic, and frustrated." Cubans were confronting even the possibility of change with a peculiar combination of "excitement, wariness, calculation, black humor, and anxiety."

> I wondered what the youth of Cuba thought about the future; it would belong to them. I ascended the great stairway leading to the University of Havana . . . I walked through the gate into a pleasant quadrangle: trees, paths, benches, law students taking a break. They gave varied answers to my question about the future. "About the same . . . more privatization . . . the government will take the private things back . . . much different . . . the same . . . we have to see who is coming after."
>
> —*From "Evolution in the Revolution," John J. Putnam*

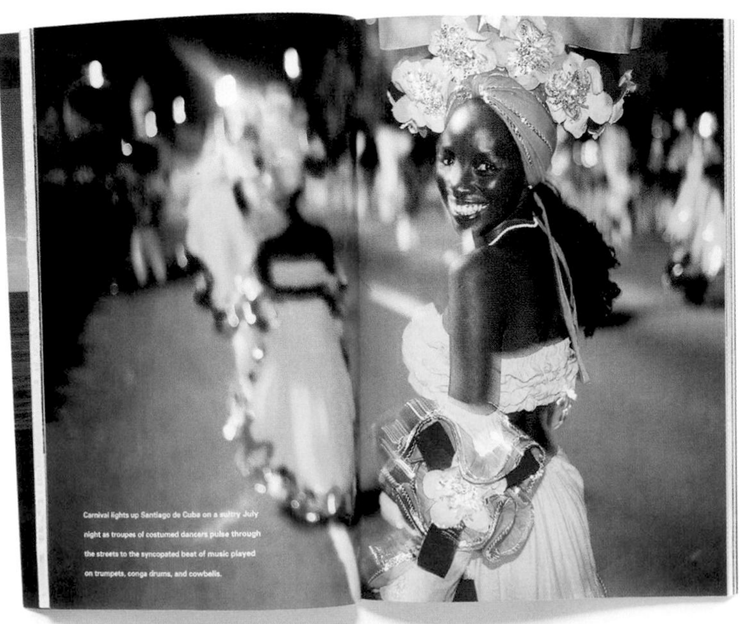

◀ JUNE 1999 | DAVID ALAN HARVEY It's Carnival time on the streets of Santiago de Cuba.

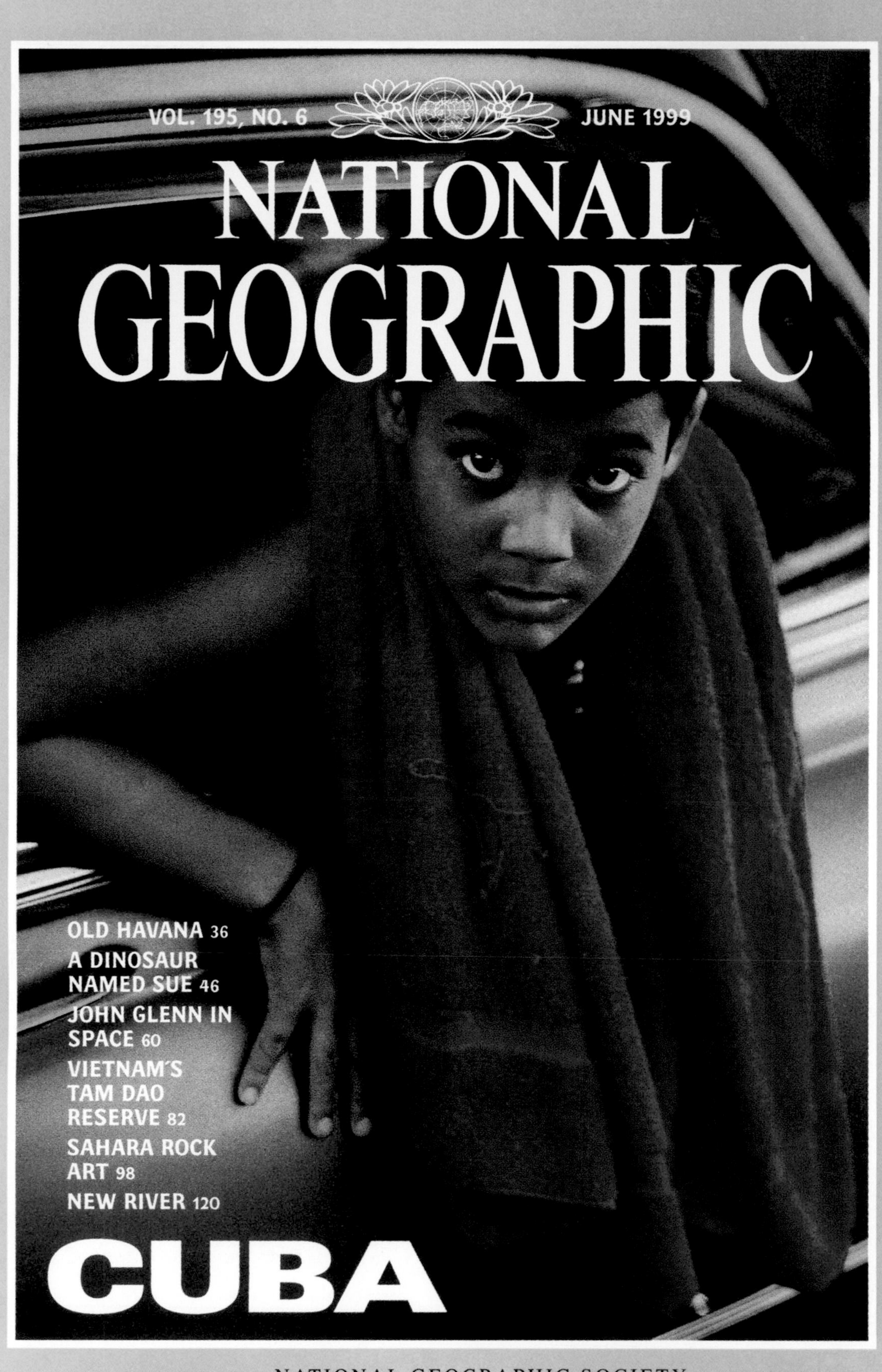

JUNE | DAVID ALAN HARVEY The photographer gets a last, lingering look from a boy he befriended.

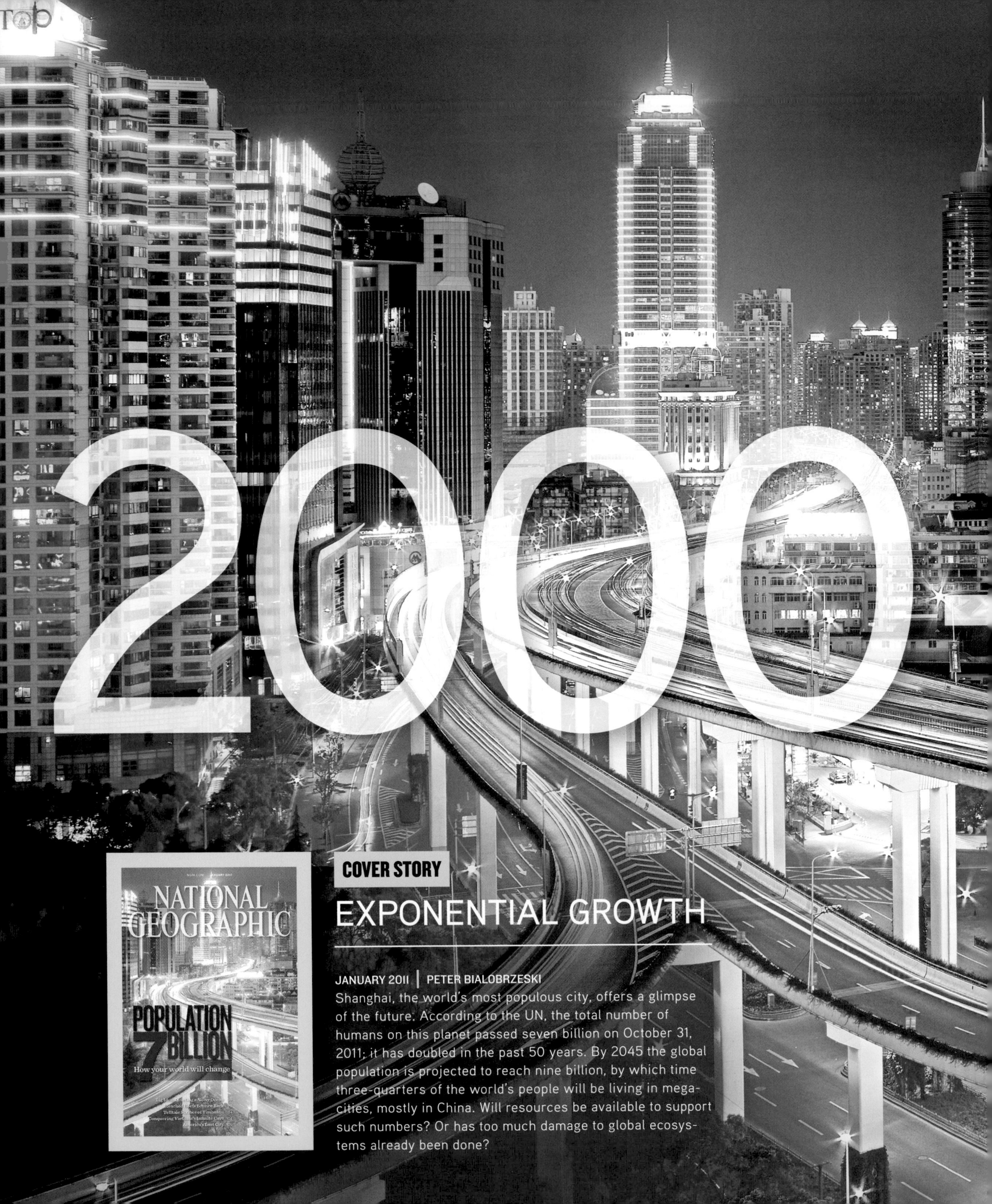

COVER STORY

EXPONENTIAL GROWTH

JANUARY 2011 | PETER BIALOBRZESKI

Shanghai, the world's most populous city, offers a glimpse of the future. According to the UN, the total number of humans on this planet passed seven billion on October 31, 2011; it has doubled in the past 50 years. By 2045 the global population is projected to reach nine billion, by which time three-quarters of the world's people will be living in megacities, mostly in China. Will resources be available to support such numbers? Or has too much damage to global ecosystems already been done?

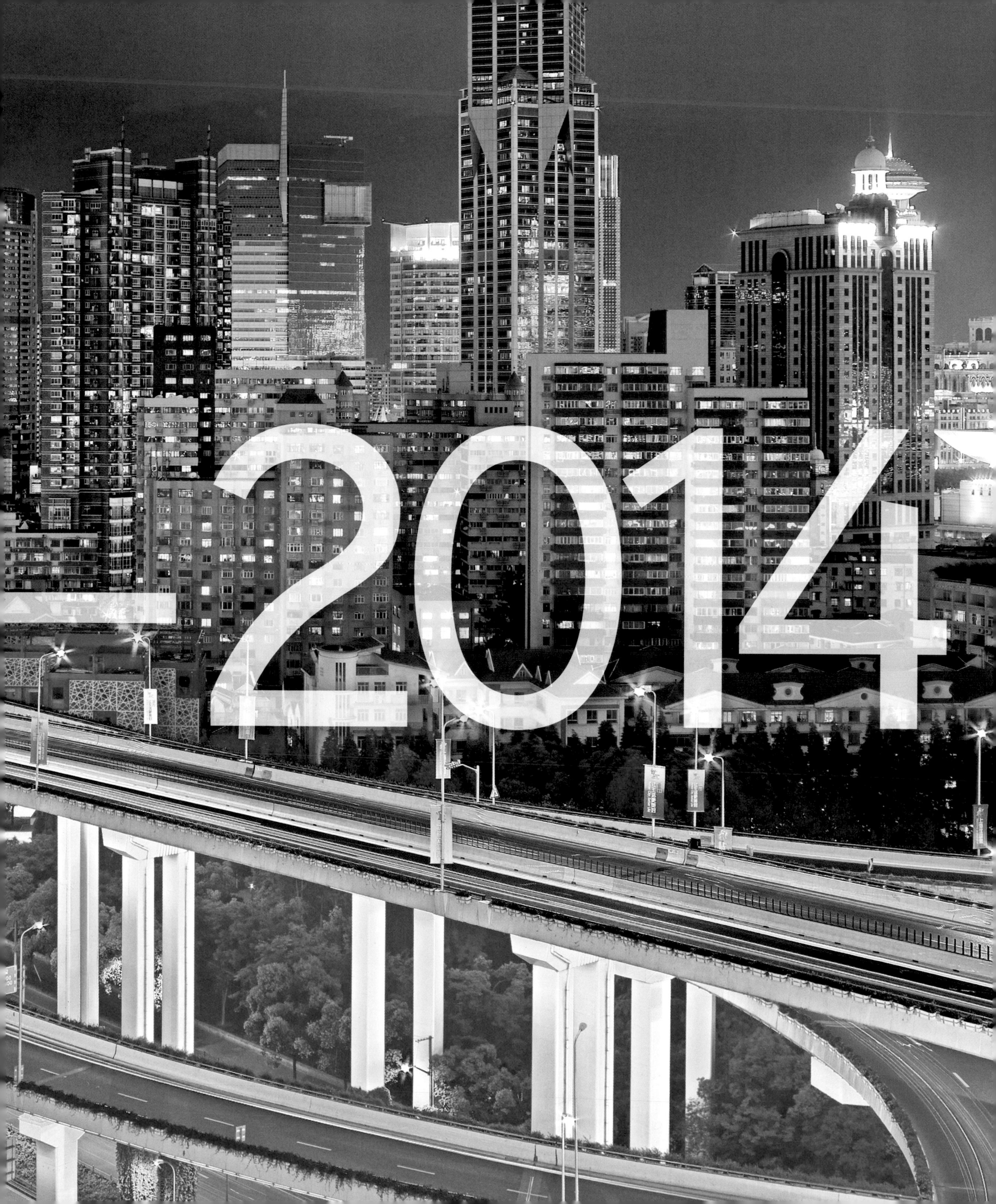
2014

NATIONALGEOGRAPHIC.COM/MAGAZINE SEPTEMBER 2004

NATIONAL GEOGRAPHIC

GLOBAL WARNING

BULLETINS FROM A WARMER WORLD

The New Face of the American Indian 76 Badgers With Attitude 96
Treasure From a Civil War Wreck 108 ZipUSA: Schooled in Tradition 128
PLUS Supplement Map: Indian Country

SEPTEMBER 2004 | PETER ESSICK A wildfire roars through a spruce forest north of Fairbanks, Alaska.

THE WORLD IN THE 2000S

"'The weather's going to change,' the cabbie tells me. 'It's fine now, but that's the end of it; it's turning rough tomorrow.'"

—Virginia Morell, from "Global Warning"

ALTHOUGH IT had been a rainy May, it had been a dry June in Alaska; and June was the month when lightning ignited many of the state's wildfires. By midsummer 2004, however, fires were raging out of control everywhere. The situation reminded photographer Peter Essick, in Fairbanks working on a global warming story, of a scientific paper he had read that predicted a statistical increase in boreal forest wildfires, possibly due to warmer and drier conditions. When he then heard that one conflagration was approaching the nearby trans-Alaska pipeline, Essick went immediately to the airport, found a Cessna and pilot, and within an hour was 500 feet above the inferno, snapping pictures as fast as he could.

When one of the frames appeared on the cover of the September issue—the "Global Warning" issue—it summed up pictorially what that headline states so graphically: Here is a world burning up.

Global warming was only one worrisome topic making headlines in the opening years of the third millennium. Many if not most people would mark September 11, 2001—when coordinated al Qaeda attacks on New York and Washington led to the fall of the twin towers and the deaths of nearly 3,000 people—as the most significant date in the past 15 years. That shocking event not only triggered wars in Afghanistan

FACTS & FIGURES THE 2000s

- **19** cover stories on environmental subjects or threatened species
- **15** cover stories on medical or physiological subjects
- **12** cover stories on ancient Egypt
- **11** cover stories on space
- **7** cover stories on the Muslim world

AROUND THE WORLD

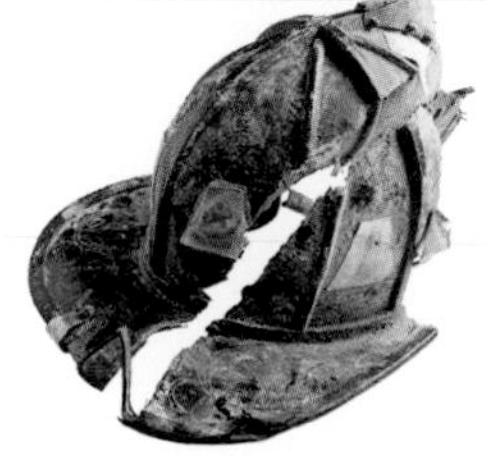

9/11 2001
Al Qaeda pilots planes into the World Trade Center towers and the Pentagon, killing nearly 3,000 people.

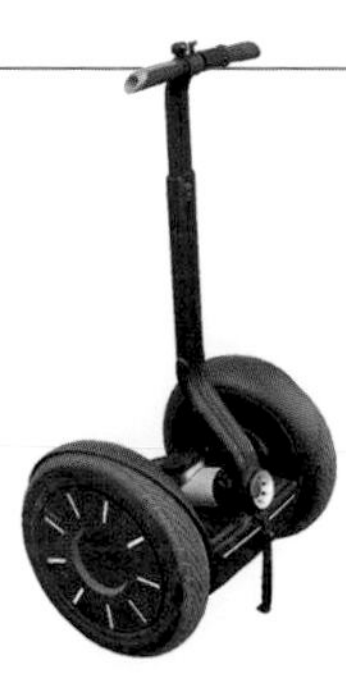

SEGWAY SCOOTER 2001
Humans on wheels will soon be claimed as representing "a new stage of evolution."

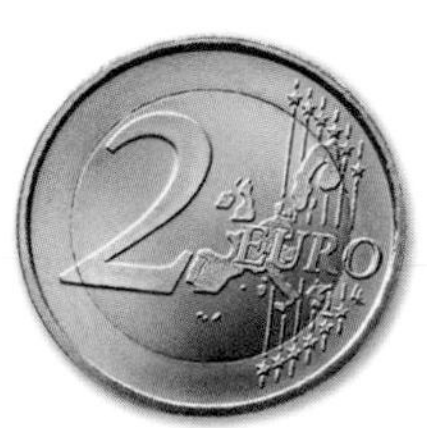

THE EURO 2002
Euro coins and banknotes—now the currency of 18 nations—enter circulation on January 1.

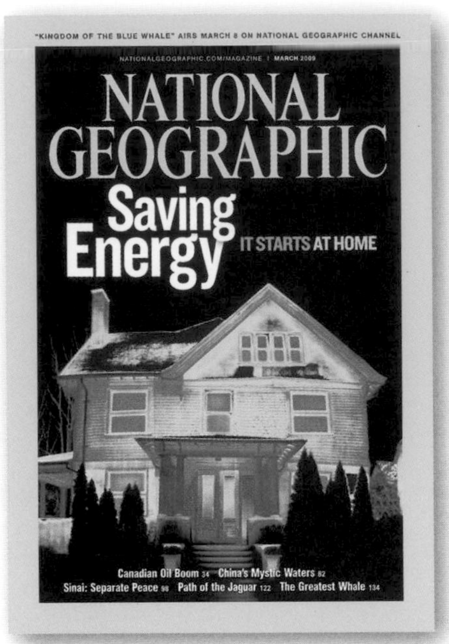

MARCH 2009 | TYRONE TURNER

▲ **HEAT LOSS** An infrared camera reveals that a 1910 Connecticut house is leaking heat through its old roof (the red and yellow areas) while retaining it where new double-pane windows have been installed (the blue areas).

and Iraq that soon turned into bloody stalemates but it also ignited widespread fears that terrorists or rogue nations might soon unleash weapons of mass destruction. Governments everywhere imposed security and surveillance measures—greatly facilitated by an explosion in information technology—that many people find alarming.

Widespread adoption of computers, cell phones, and the Internet, binding people everywhere closer together, can also be co-opted by criminal elements as well as by government snoops. The 2008 global financial crisis only further underscored how interconnected our world has become. Social media even played a crucial role in the mass demonstrations that sparked the "Arab Spring," which began so hopefully in 2010 but resulted in renewed repression in Egypt and an appalling civil war in Syria. Meanwhile, more people moving about in more places increases the risk of global pandemics.

In addition to such dismaying headlines, environmental problems continue to proliferate. Climate change, overpopulation, resource depletion, collapsing fisheries, and deforestation are only some of the concerns being voiced about the health of the global ecosystem. Indeed, strong environmental reporting has been a consistent feature in *National Geographic* over the first decade and a half of the 21st century—one reason its photojournalism has recently won numerous awards. A cover story on elephant poaching—in March 2007—even prompted the government of Chad to take steps to stem the slaughter around Zakouma National Park. Another cover story—October 2012's report on the illegal trafficking of elephant tusks—drew attention to the role an insatiable demand for carved ivory religious objects is playing in the ongoing tragedy.

Environmental coverage is only one of the *Geographic*'s strengths today. The scope of the Society's journal still remains refreshingly broad, with articles on archaeological discoveries vying for cover space with reports of faraway planets or other cosmic wonders. Scientists in this new age of exploration tease out of DNA more clues to evolution or map the genetic underpinnings of our bodies and minds. Such new trends also

AROUND THE WORLD

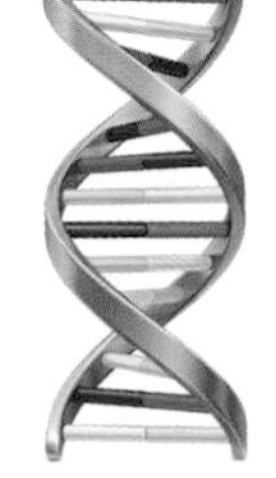

HUMAN GENOME 2003
The Human Genome Project finishes sequencing the approximately 20,500 genes in human beings.

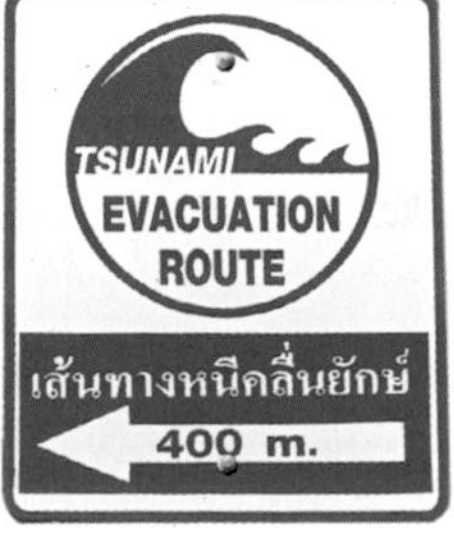

TSUNAMI 2004
A December tsunami kills more than 230,000 people in 14 Indian Ocean countries.

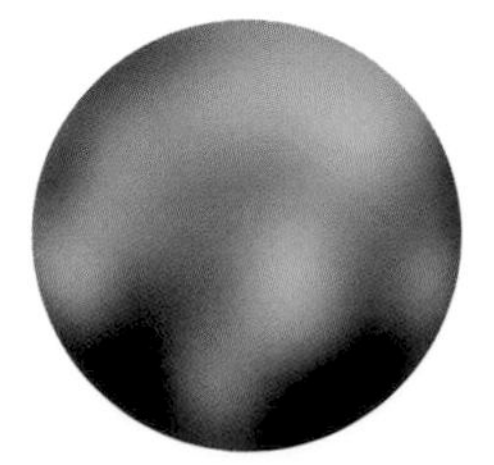

PLUTO 2006
The last solar system planet discovered becomes the first downgraded to "dwarf planet."

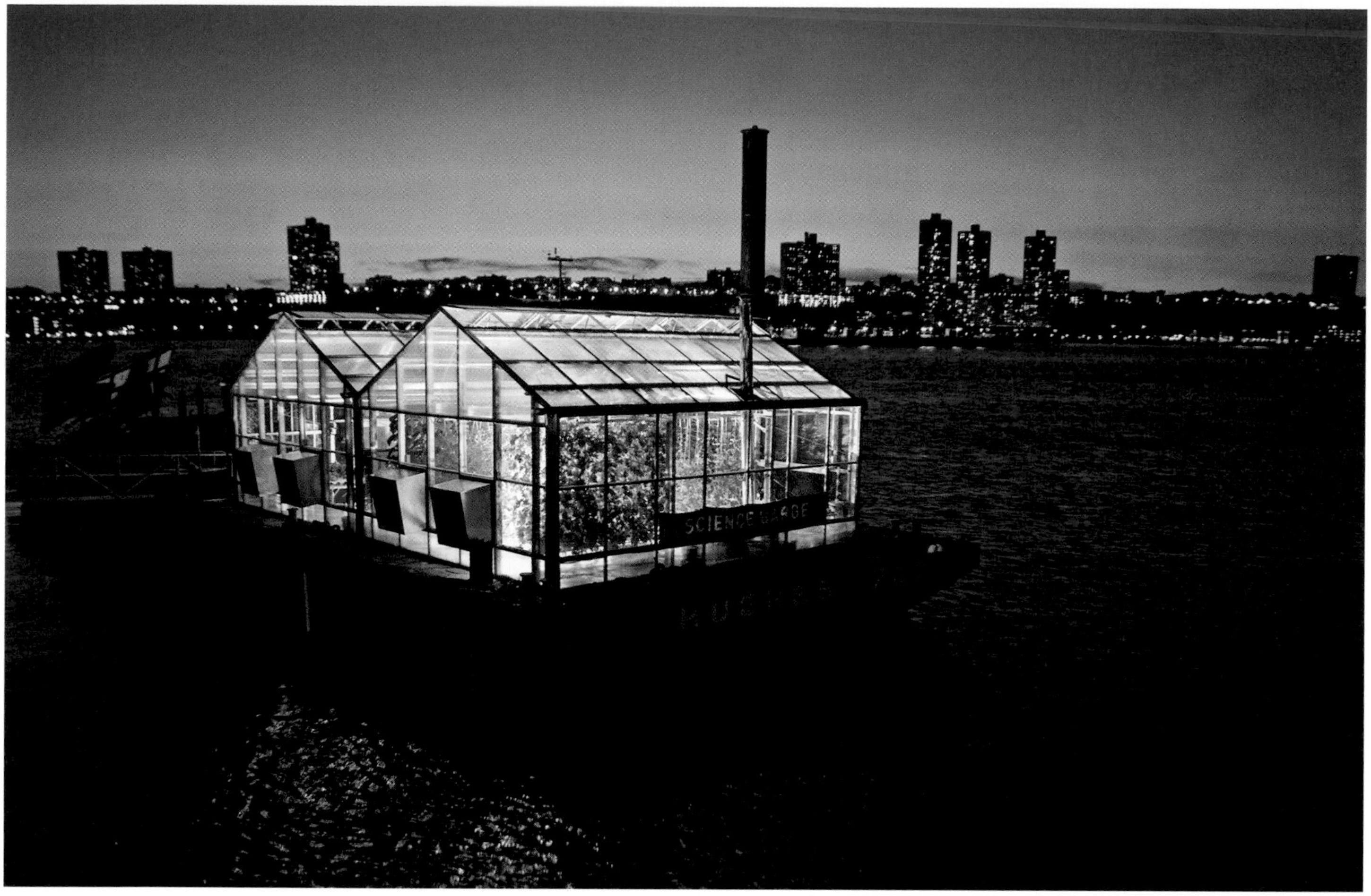

MARCH 2009 | TYRONE TURNER A carbon-neutral hydroponic farm floats down the Hudson River.

offer opportunities for new and more engaging covers. Long gone are the days when Kodachrome-illustrated travelogues were tucked safely behind that old oak-and-laurel-leaved border. Today's covers may reflect feats of digital wizardry—see the tree portraits on the October 2009 and December 2012 covers—and many involve considerable planning and forethought. But they also mirror the magazine's contents: The images are simple, stunning, and often provocative. Expect to see more of them in the future. ■

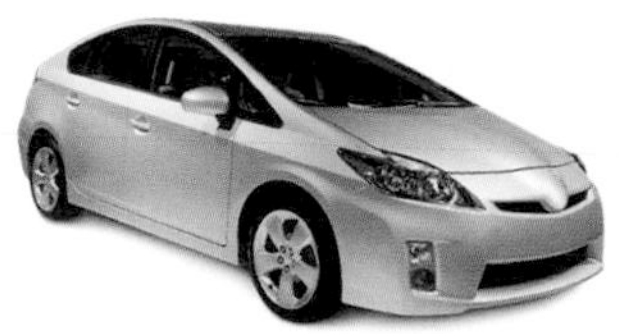

HYBRID CARS 2008
Worldwide sales of Toyota's Prius, the first mass-produced hybrid car, reach 1,000,000.

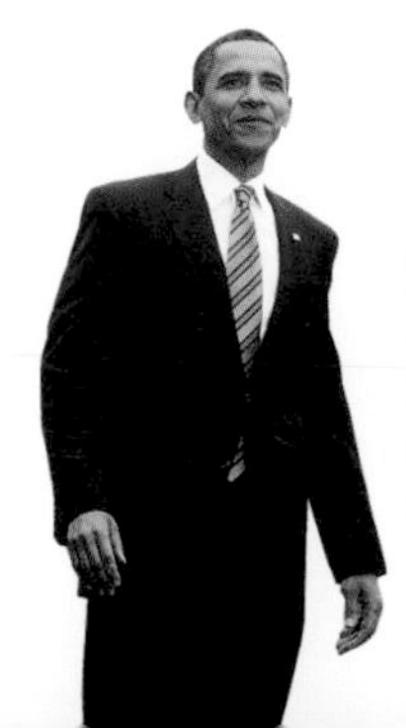

BARACK OBAMA 2009
Barack Obama becomes the first African American elected president of the United States.

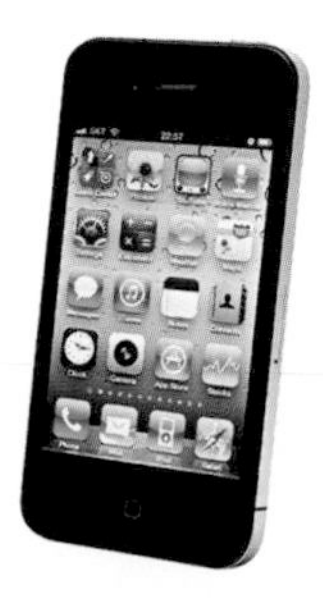

SMARTPHONES 2013
With over one billion in use, global smartphone sales surpass those for low-end phones.

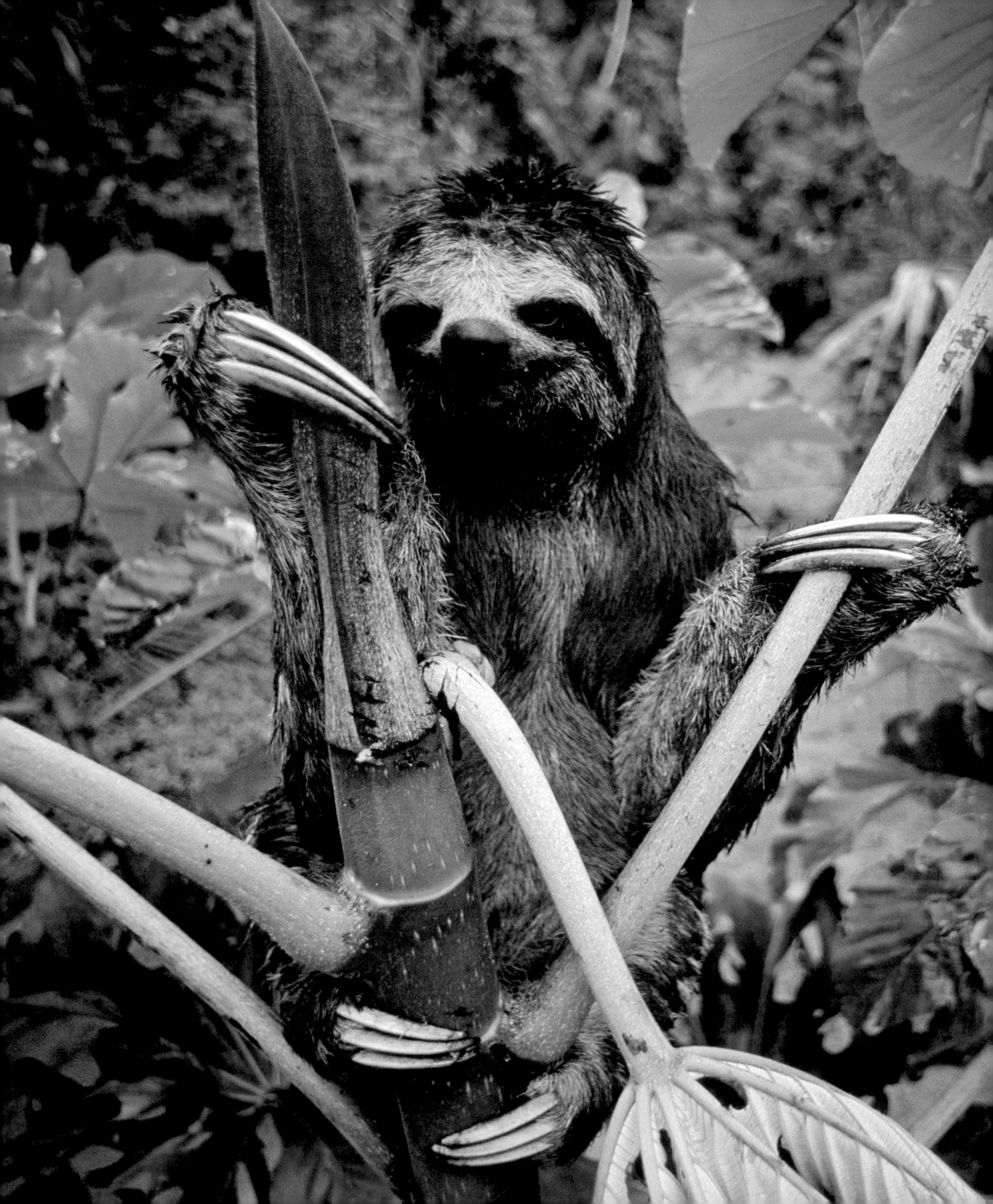

AMAZONIAN EDEN

At times it seemed like the worst kind of jungle nightmare. Botfly larvae burrowed into his skin. Bats urinated on him as he slept. Ants attacked his feet. Wasps stung his hands. Everything he touched was toxic.

But Bolivia's Madidi National Park, established in 1995, was also a wonderland, a lost world in the Amazon Basin that, with more than a thousand bird species alone, was among the most biologically diverse spots on the planet. Jaguars, spectacled bears, sloths, vicuñas, giant otters, peccaries, and macaws inhabited the forests.

Those macaws flashing above the treetops enchanted photographer Joel Sartore. Yet the only way to photograph them was to somehow get above them. That meant standing for ten days on the edge of a precipice overlooking the valley of the Río Tuichi, waiting for those "bursts of color" to rocket out from nests in the cliff wall and sail out over the green canopy to distant feeding areas. They were so fast he usually missed his shot. But finally he thought he got a sharp frame—and after the film was developed, that was the frame that made the cover.

Not long after the March 2000 issue reached the *Geographic*'s 40 million readers, drawing the world's attention to Madidi, plans to build a giant hydroelectric dam nearby were shelved. That made all the insect torments—as well as the leishmaniasis, a tropical disease Sartore contracted from a sand fly bite—worthwhile.

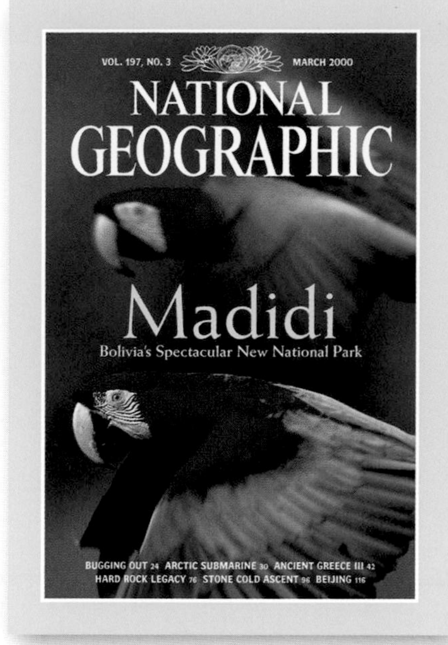

MARCH | JOEL SARTORE

▲ **TAKING FLIGHT** "Red-and-green macaws were among the most fascinating and endearing animals we encountered," recalled Joel Sartore. "These long-lived birds mate for life, and couples spend nearly every minute together. In the mornings we'd often see these birds grooming each other after feeding on fruit."

> Things scream here all night. Birds and bugs, I'm told. So many species that each has developed a specialized call. One bird sounds like water pouring out of a bottle. Another like a digital alarm clock. The locals say palm trees here grow legs and walk to find more sunlight.
>
> *—From "Into Madidi's Teeming Jungle," Joel Sartore*

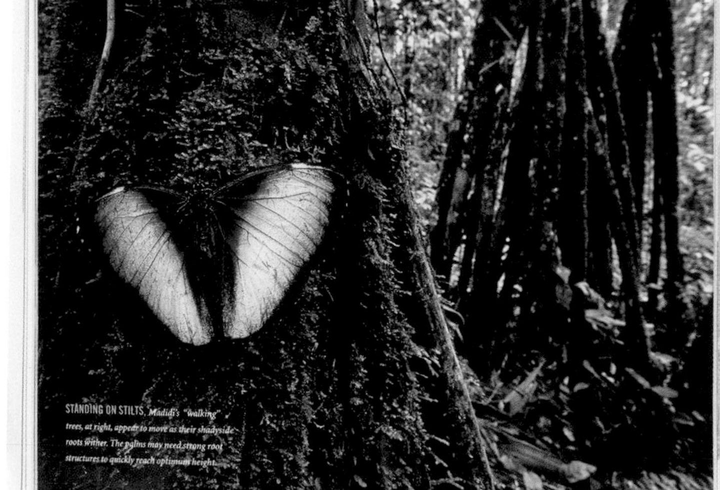

◀ MARCH 2000 | JOEL SARTORE A three-toed sloth fixes the photographer with a beady stare.

▶ MARCH 2000 | JOEL SARTORE "Walking trees" grow stiltlike roots to reach sunny openings.

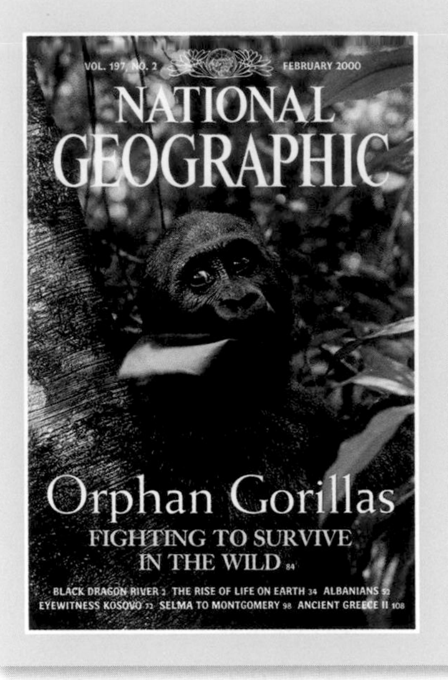

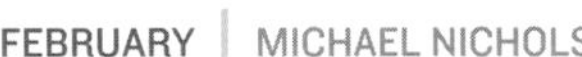

FEBRUARY | MICHAEL NICHOLS

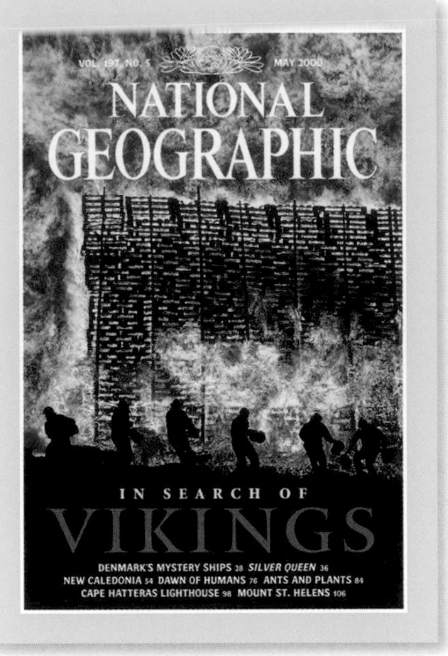

MAY | SISSE BRIMBERG

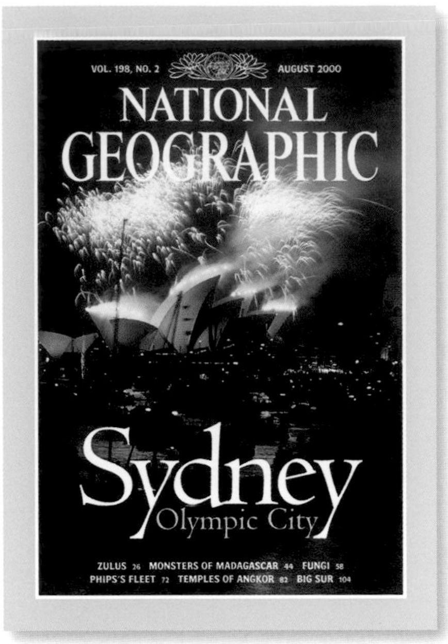

AUGUST | ANNIE GRIFFITHS

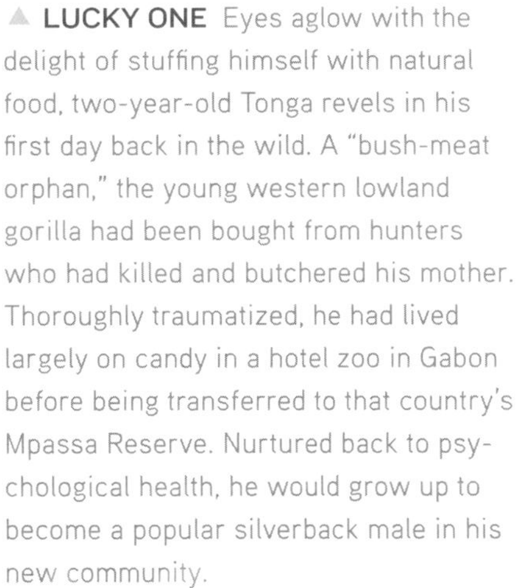

▲ **LUCKY ONE** Eyes aglow with the delight of stuffing himself with natural food, two-year-old Tonga revels in his first day back in the wild. A "bush-meat orphan," the young western lowland gorilla had been bought from hunters who had killed and butchered his mother. Thoroughly traumatized, he had lived largely on candy in a hotel zoo in Gabon before being transferred to that country's Mpassa Reserve. Nurtured back to psychological health, he would grow up to become a popular silverback male in his new community.

TOOTH AND MAW ▶

Twenty-five years after his *Jaws* terrified beachgoers, author Peter Benchley joined photographer David Doubilet off the coast of South Africa, where they watched as a dive-boat captain reached overboard, grabbed the snout of a breaching great white shark, where most of its nerves clustered, and thereby stunned it, putting it into a state of slack-jawed suspended animation that scientists call "tonic immobility."

> There, in an instant, was the mouth, the most notorious mouth in nature, the upper jaw dropping into view, extending its rank of serrated triangular daggers, the lower jaw falling open, studded with the needle-sharp grabbing teeth that, more than a century ago, gave the animal its scientific moniker: *Carcharodon carcharias,* "ragged-toothed" one . . . No one spoke. No one breathed. The only sound was the motor drive on David Doubilet's camera as it captured frame after frame after frame of man mesmerizing monster.
>
> *—From "Inside the Great White," Peter Benchley*

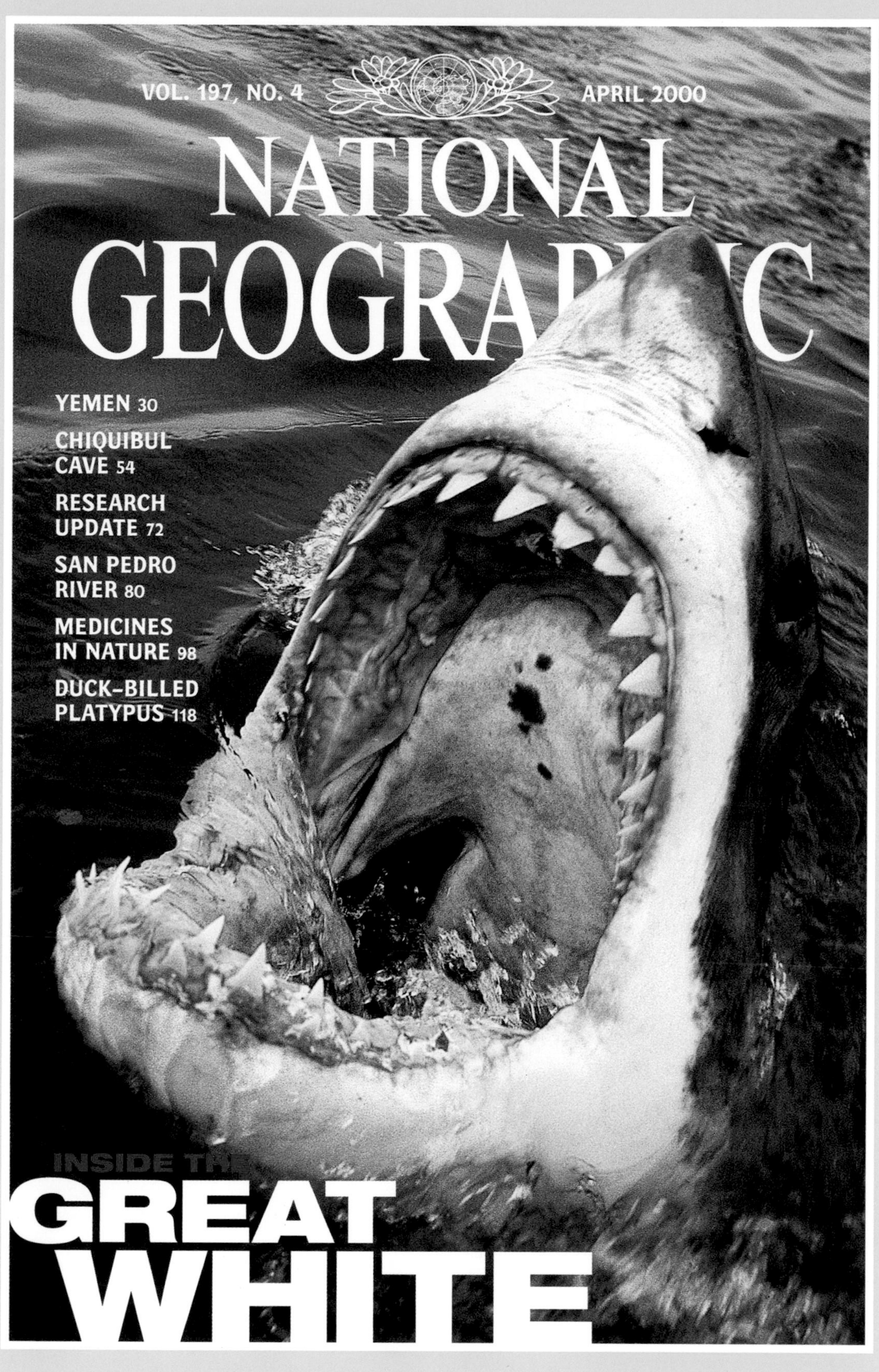

APRIL | **DAVID DOUBILET** A stunned great white shark sits slack-jawed in the sea.

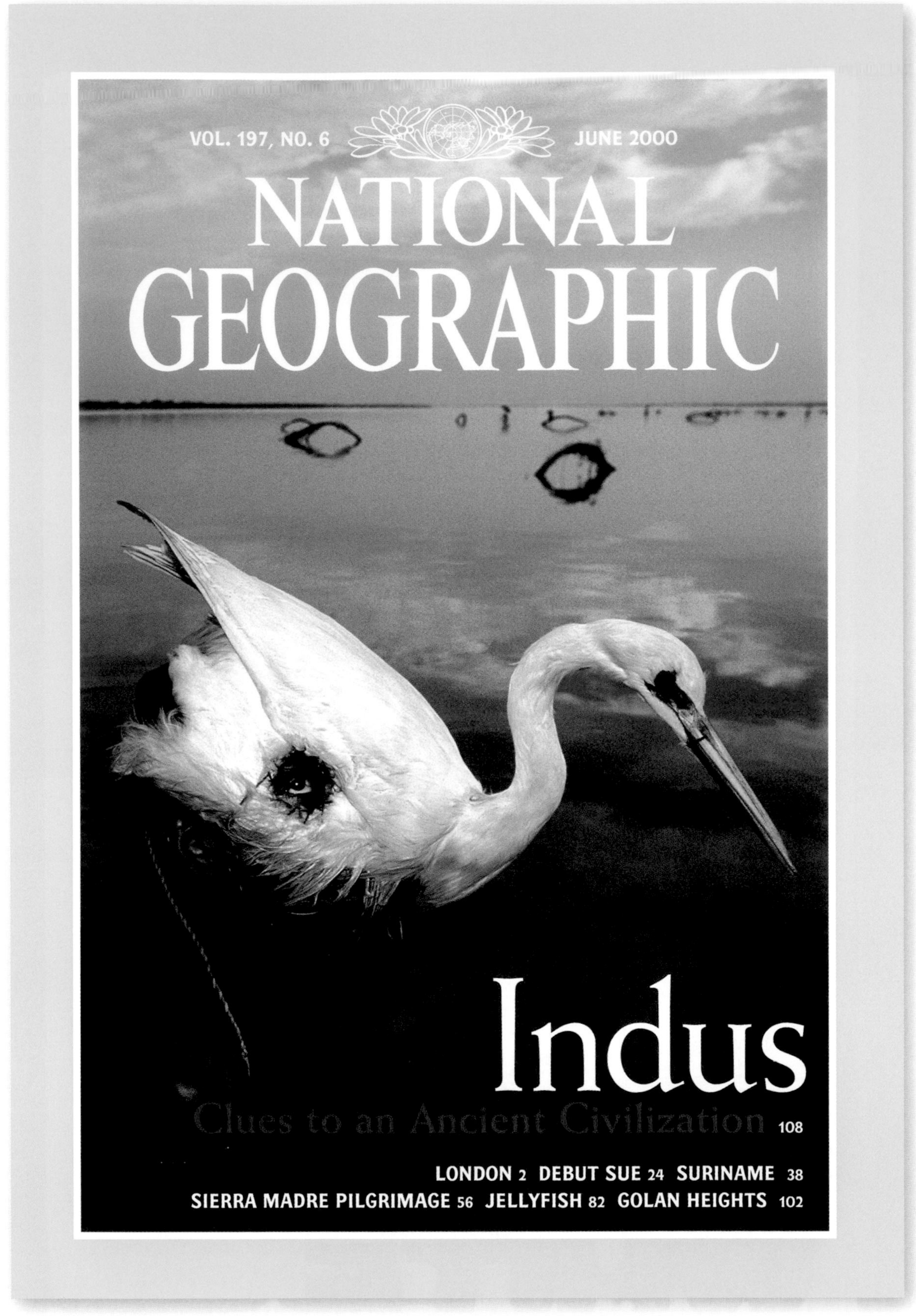

JUNE | RANDY OLSON

NEOLITHIC STYLE A hunter in Pakistan employs a technique thousands of years old. After tying live heron decoys to hoops in the Indus River, he wears an egret-skin headdress and mimics a swimming bird, grabbing anything he can lure within hand's reach—a practice depicted on artifacts found nearby that date back to 3300 B.C.

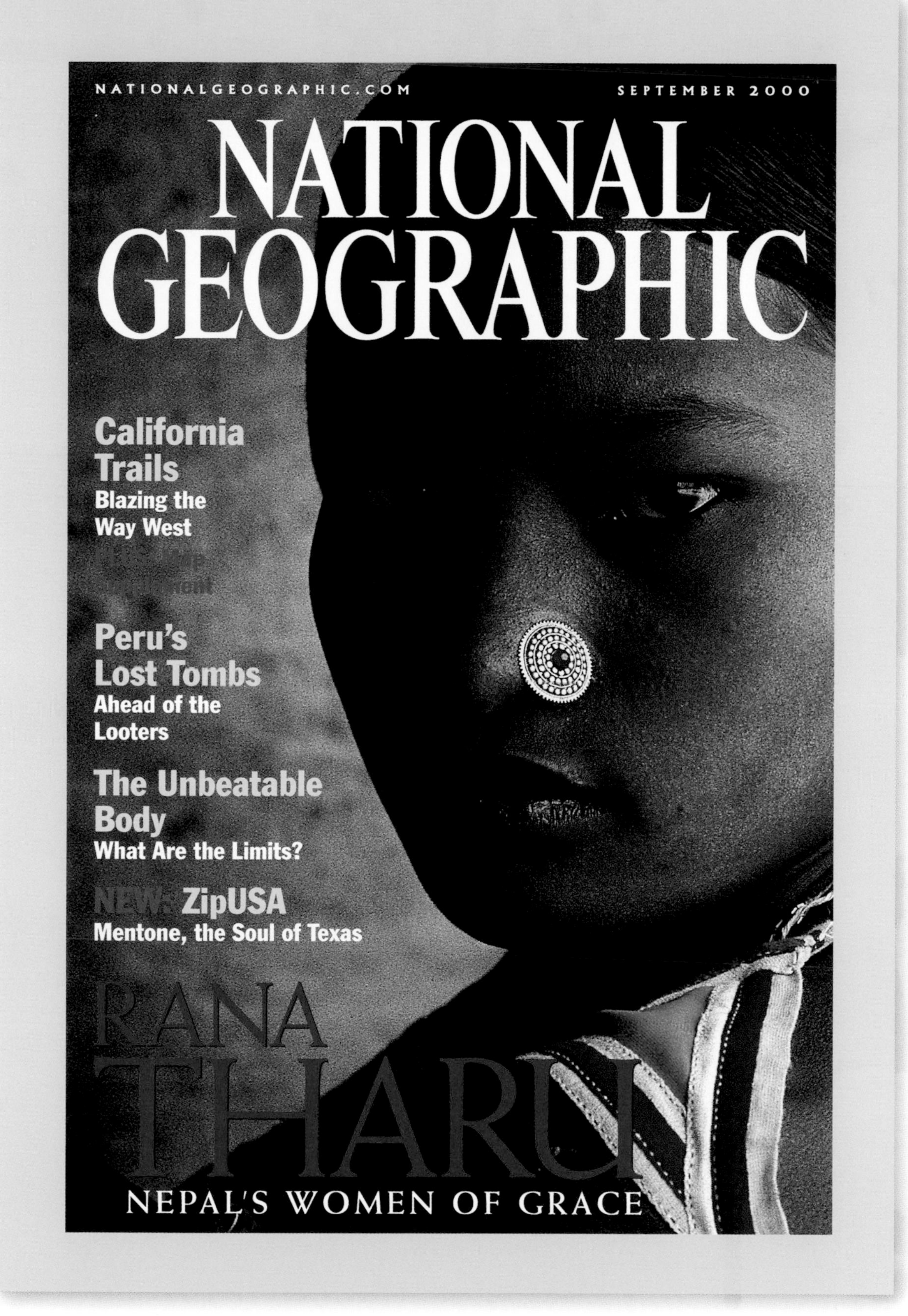

SEPTEMBER | ERIC VALLI AND DEBRA KELLNER

DIRECT ENGAGEMENT An unflinching gaze exemplifies the independent spirit of Rana Tharu women. Long isolated in the forested foothills of Himalayan Nepal, where malaria kept outsiders at bay, members of what perhaps was originally a matriarchal tribe developed their own colorful culture untainted—until recently—by those of its neighbors.

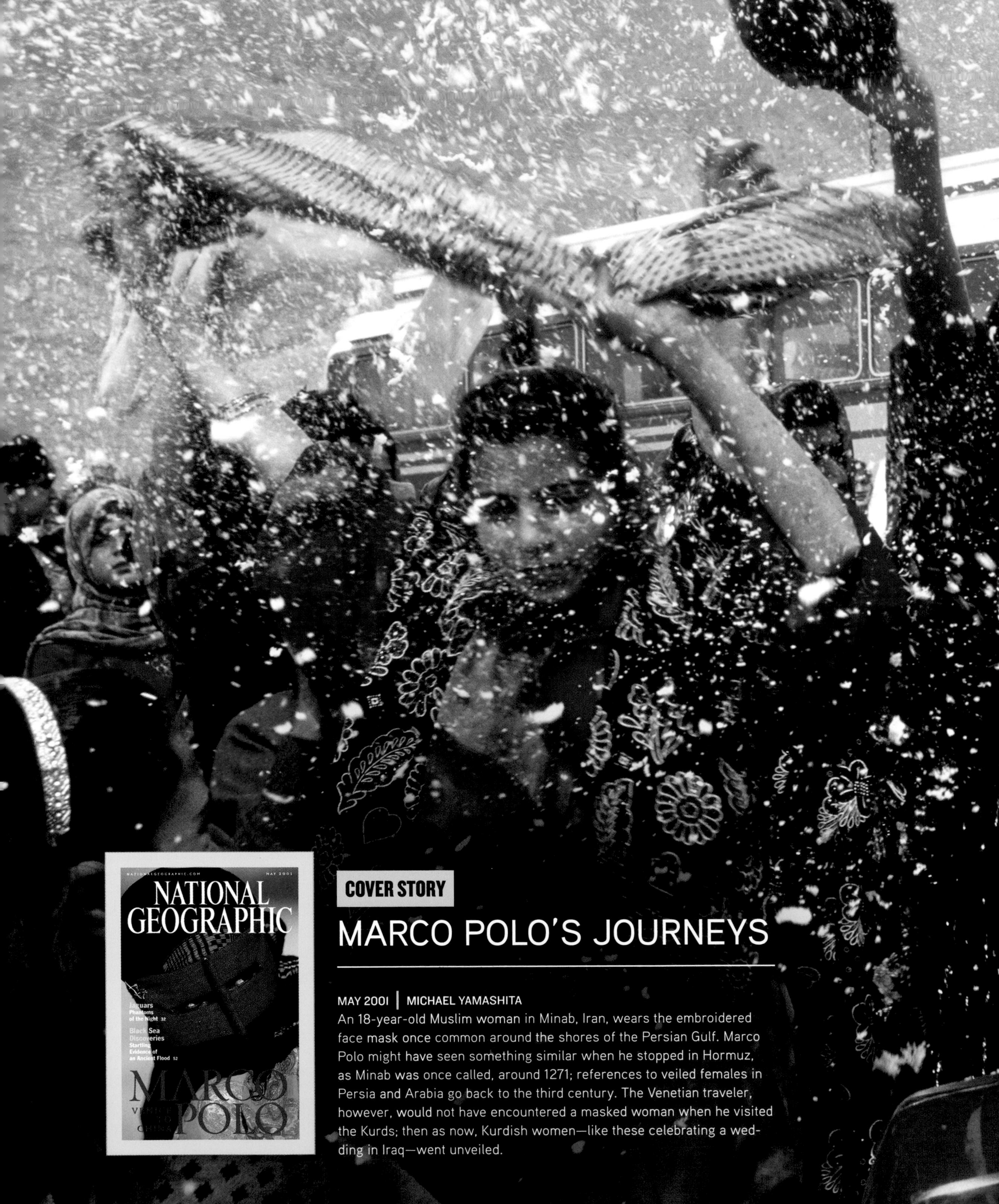

COVER STORY

MARCO POLO'S JOURNEYS

MAY 2001 | MICHAEL YAMASHITA

An 18-year-old Muslim woman in Minab, Iran, wears the embroidered face mask once common around the shores of the Persian Gulf. Marco Polo might have seen something similar when he stopped in Hormuz, as Minab was once called, around 1271; references to veiled females in Persia and Arabia go back to the third century. The Venetian traveler, however, would not have encountered a masked woman when he visited the Kurds; then as now, Kurdish women—like these celebrating a wedding in Iraq—went unveiled.

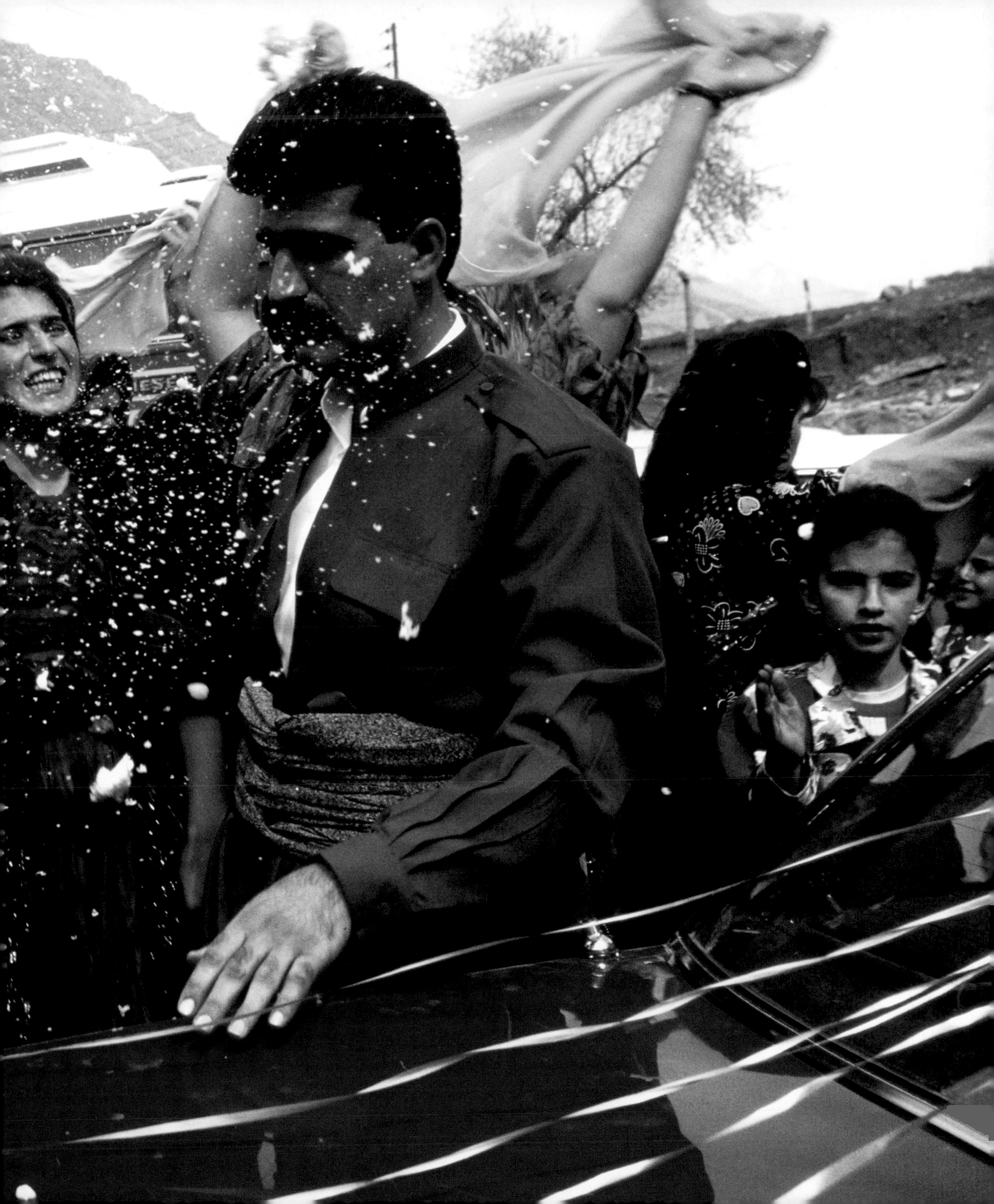

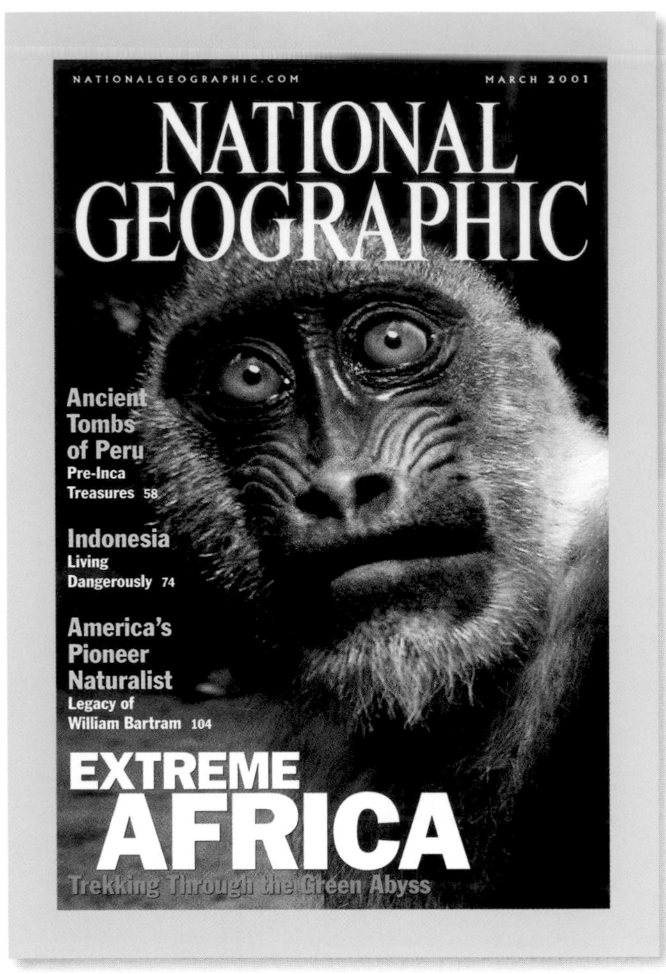

MARCH | MICHAEL NICHOLS

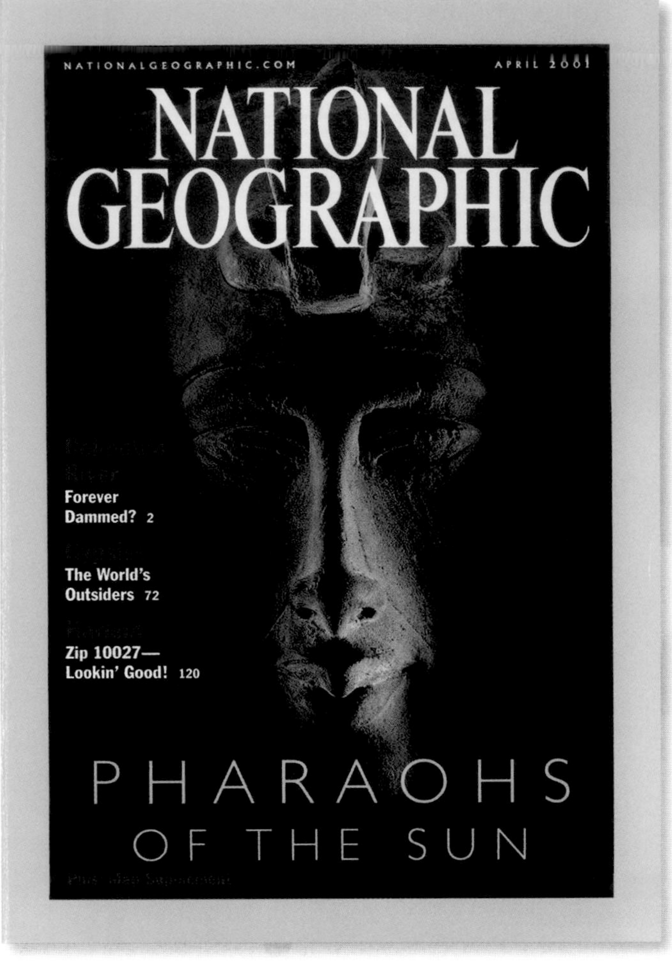

APRIL | KENNETH GARRETT

▲ **LOOK OF FEAR** Its red eyes looming out of the "Green Abyss," as the wilderness engulfing the Gabon-Congo border is called, a captive orphaned mandrill reaches out to block the photographer's lens. Tethered to a rope in a remote jungle camp, the monkey—member of a species found only in dense rain forests bordering Africa's Gulf of Guinea—will probably be eaten by the same bush-meat hunters who killed its mother.

▲ **ANDROGYNOUS AKHENATEN** "In the Egyptian Museum in Cairo are colossal statues—troubling and mesmerizing—of Akhenaten," wrote Rick Gore in the April issue. "His face is elongated and angular with a long chin. His eyes are mystical and brooding. His lips are huge and fleshy. Although he wears a pharaoh's headdress and holds the traditional symbols of kingship . . . the chest is spindly, and the torso flows into a voluptuous belly and enormous feminine hips." DNA analysis on Akhenaten's mummy, however, ruled out physical abnormalities. These traits were purely stylistic, so photographer Kenneth Garrett lit one statue so that it might loom out of darkness, embodying the essential mystery of this most enigmatic of Egyptian rulers.

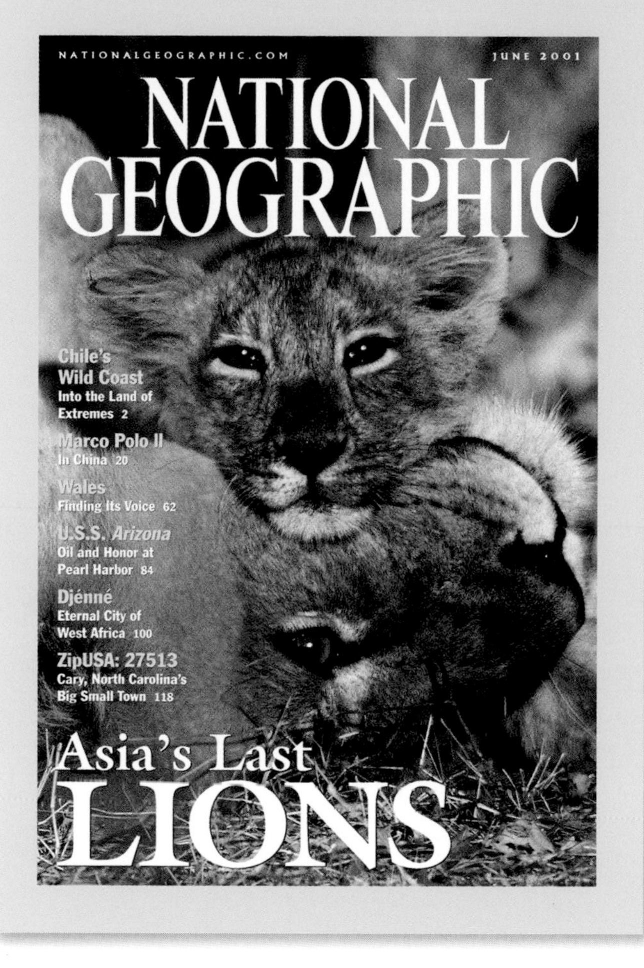

JUNE | MATTIAS KLUM

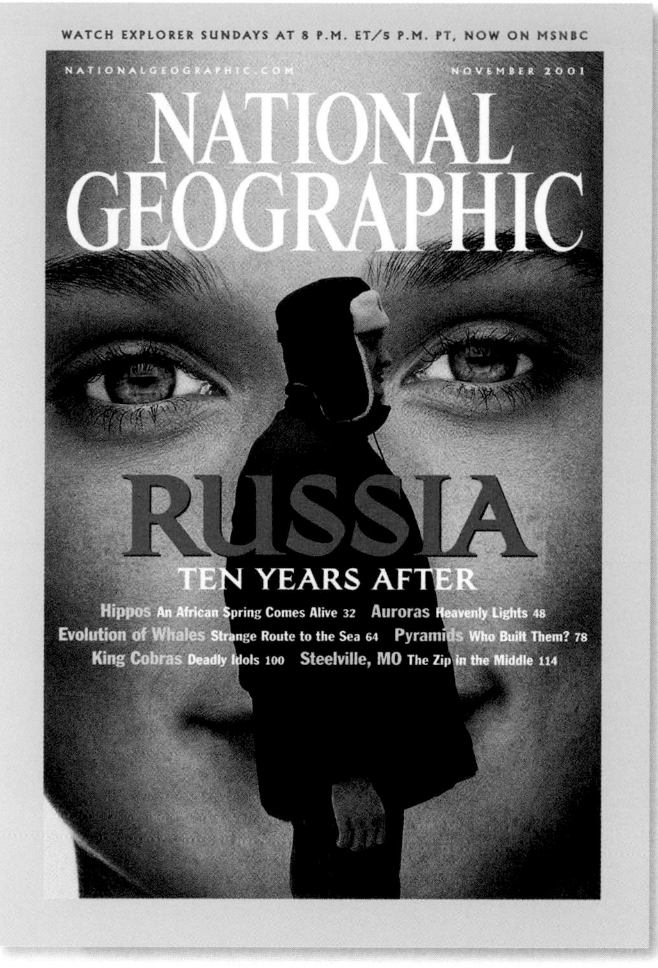

NOVEMBER | GERD LUDWIG

▲ **LAST LIONS** Asiatic lions—here a female and her cub—once roamed from Greece to the Ganges. Today they are confined to the dry scrubland of India's Gir Forest National Park.

> *"India is the proud steward of these 300 or so lions, which live primarily in a 560-square-mile sanctuary . . . In ancient India one of the greatest tests of leadership was to fight a lion. In modern India, where the Asiatic lion has become a national symbol, it may be to save one."*
>
> —Mattias Klum
> *from "Asia's Last Lions"*

▲ **MOSCOW CHIC** What you don't see, to the right of this cropped horizontal image, is the young man's companion as she shops for clothes in a Benetton megastore on Moscow's Pushkin Square, one of 19 that the Italian fashion emporium had then opened in Russia only ten years after the fall of the Soviet Union. What you do see, besides this fur-topped chap in fashionable cargo pants, are those eyes—eyes, staring out from a giant advertising billboard, which dominate even this 21,000-square-foot space, where once stood a shabby state-run department store.

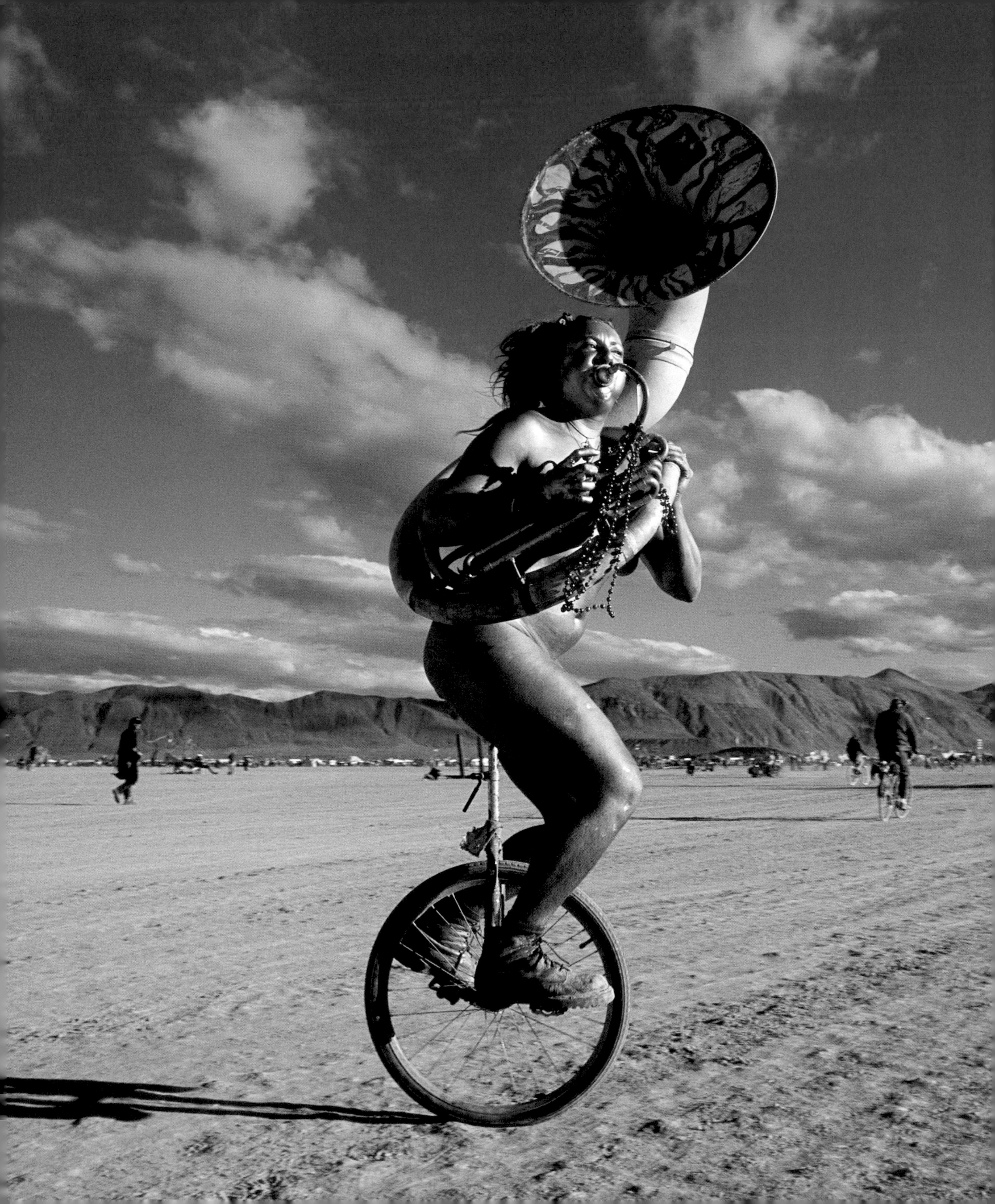

WILD WILD WEST

THE PUBLIC DOMAIN WAS once mostly terrain nobody wanted—a quarter billion acres of land the timber and mining industries had left behind, dry sagebrush country good only for grazing. Today, the Bureau of Land Management administers a public trust that has become a recreational paradise, a place to hunt, fish, camp, boat, bike, and party.

It was this contrast between the Old West and the New West that brought photographer Melissa Farlow to the dry lake bed of the Black Rock Playa Desert in Nevada. Here the weeklong Burning Man Festival is held, where each year that contrast is extravagantly displayed.

More than 25,000 people congregated in a makeshift city, each one dressed in the most outlandish costume imaginable (or in no costume whatsoever). They created temporary sculptures and indulged in performance art beneath the changing desert light.

"One afternoon I made my way across the salt flat hoping to see the effigy of the 'man' scheduled to be burned on the final night," she later recalled. "A storm blew through without warning and sand pelted my face. I closed my eyes and hunched over clumsily struggling to protect my camera. As the storm began to clear, dazed people slowly emerged. I was startled by a clownlike honk of a bicycle horn and turned to see an electric pink lady poised in the middle of the monochromatic desert—her face to the wind and her scarf blowing. It was a surreal scene. I stepped forward and shot a few frames, checked my camera settings, and when I looked up again she was gone."

A little later, a "fleeting mirage" came spinning by on a unicycle, wearing a sousaphone, a coat of silver paint, and little else. She was Erin "Red" Thompson, who told Farlow that at Burning Man, "there are no spectators, only participants."

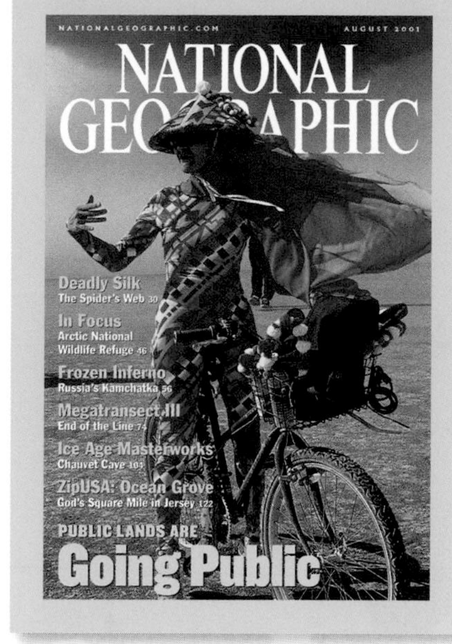

AUGUST | MELISSA FARLOW

▲ **DESERT WILDFLOWER** That "electric pink lady" was California costume designer Jeanne Lauren, one of many memorable characters Melissa Farlow met during her week at Burning Man. By day she rode a bicycle around the makeshift city, and after dark she slept in the back of her jeep.

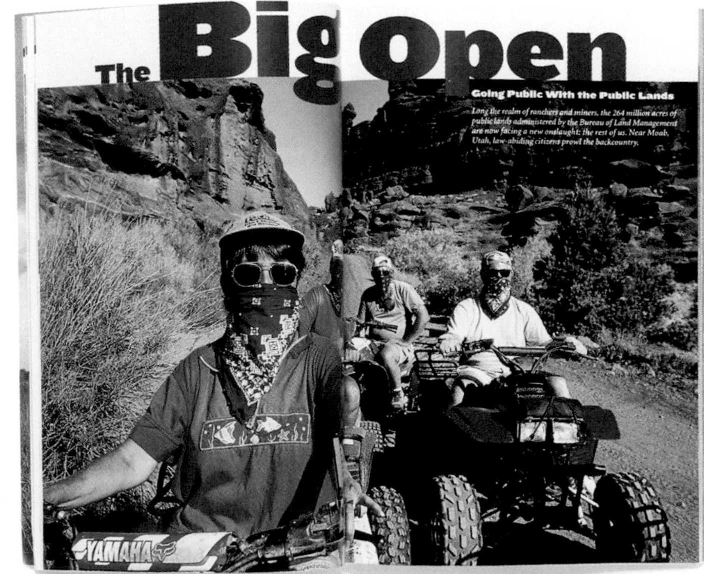

◀ AUGUST 2001 | MELISSA FARLOW Erin "Red" Thompson with her sousaphone and unicycle

▶ AUGUST 2001 | MELISSA FARLOW Off-road enthusiasts roll over public land in Utah.

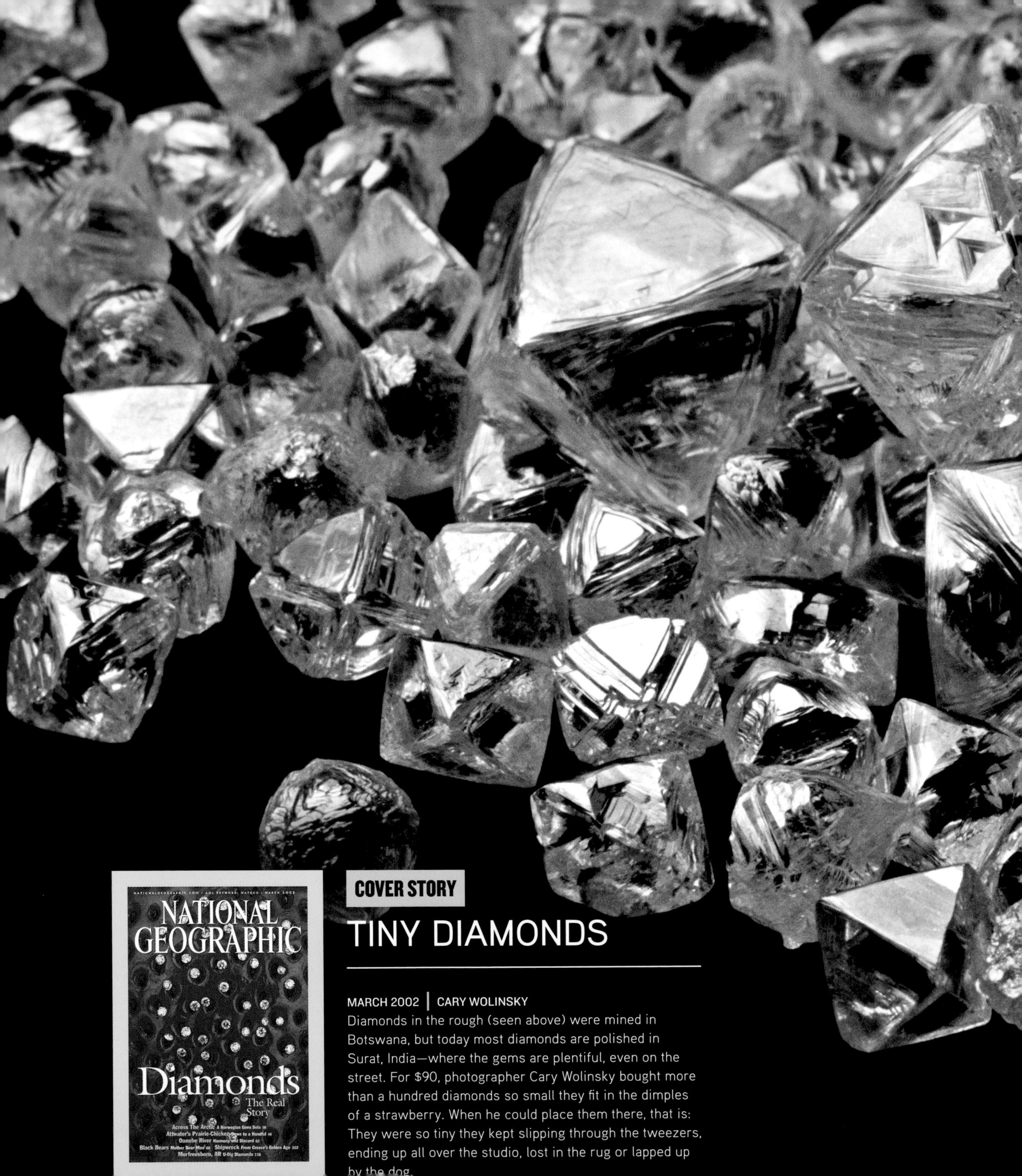

COVER STORY

TINY DIAMONDS

MARCH 2002 | CARY WOLINSKY

Diamonds in the rough (seen above) were mined in Botswana, but today most diamonds are polished in Surat, India—where the gems are plentiful, even on the street. For $90, photographer Cary Wolinsky bought more than a hundred diamonds so small they fit in the dimples of a strawberry. When he could place them there, that is: They were so tiny they kept slipping through the tweezers, ending up all over the studio, lost in the rug or lapped up by the dog.

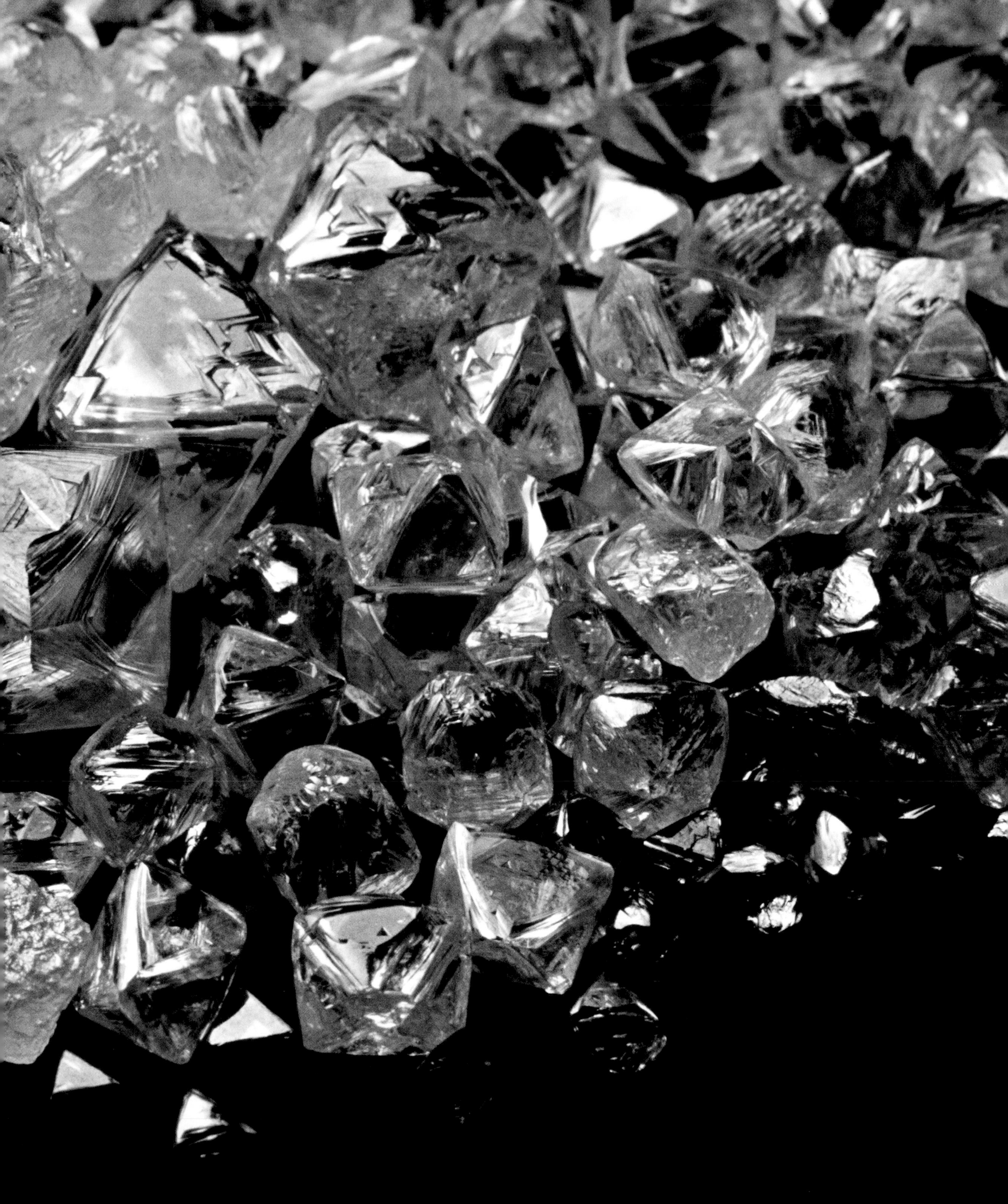

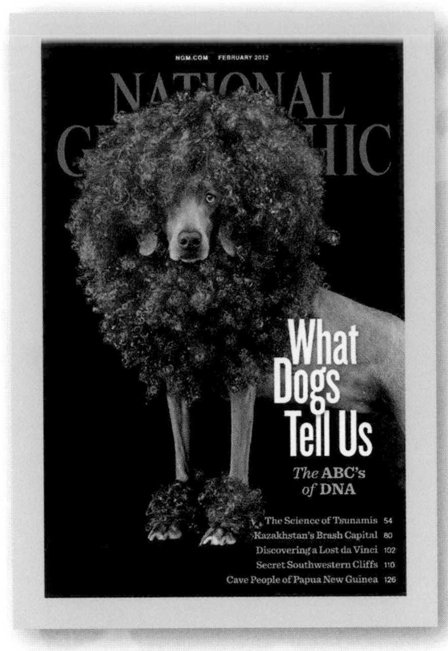

FEBRUARY 2012 | WILLIAM WEGMAN

2012 ▸▸▸▸ FAST FORWARD

TEN YEARS LATER It's not a Weimaraner you're likely to see in everyday life: Photographer William Wegman makes portraits of dogs dressed in surprising fashions. Yet a determined breeder might very well create something similar, for the great variety in dog's coats is due to deliberately manipulated mutations in only three genes. "For reasons both practical and whimsical," says author Evan Ratliff in the February 2012 issue, "man's best friend has been artificially evolved into the most diverse animal on the planet."

CANINE EVOLUTION ▸

"WHEN YOU'RE TRYING TO photograph a wolf in a garage," said Robert Clark, "a little planning goes a long way."

Planning. He needed an image that would sum up the offbeat title, "From Wolf to Woof: The Evolution of Dogs." So the New York–based photographer went to Utah, where he paid a visit to Doug Seus's Wasatch Rocky Mountain Wildlife.

Clark then transformed a garage into a studio and set up six strobe lights, the better for highlighting fur. Next he provided himself with raw meat and dog treats. And finally he welcomed Doug and his two companions, Simon the Maltese and Koda the Wolf.

The photo shoot took two days. And though he hoped all along to pose them as you see at right, his two stars proved initially uncooperative. Koda in particular—despite having starred in TV commercials and in an Imax movie—was skittish, at one point even giving voice to a low howl.

"Getting the wolf in the right position with the right expression was the hardest thing," Clark recalled. He coaxed his models to stand where they are with liberal offerings of that raw meat and those treats. But getting the right expression was trickier. He wanted their eyes to look directly into the 140mm lens on his Mamiya-RZ67 camera so that they might follow the reader "right off the page." It took 120 frames to do so.

There they stand, so different in appearance, so nearly identical in DNA. The divergence between wolf and dog began sometime between 14,000 and 100,000 years ago, whenever the first human tossed the first bone to a famished wolf hovering on the edge of a Paleolithic campfire. Subsequent breeders selected for those qualities of size and color and temperament that gave us the variety of dogs we cherish today. "But if we're so smart," asks author Angus Philips, "why do we work so hard while dogs loll around? Could it be that humans aren't the cleverest half of this ageless duet after all?"

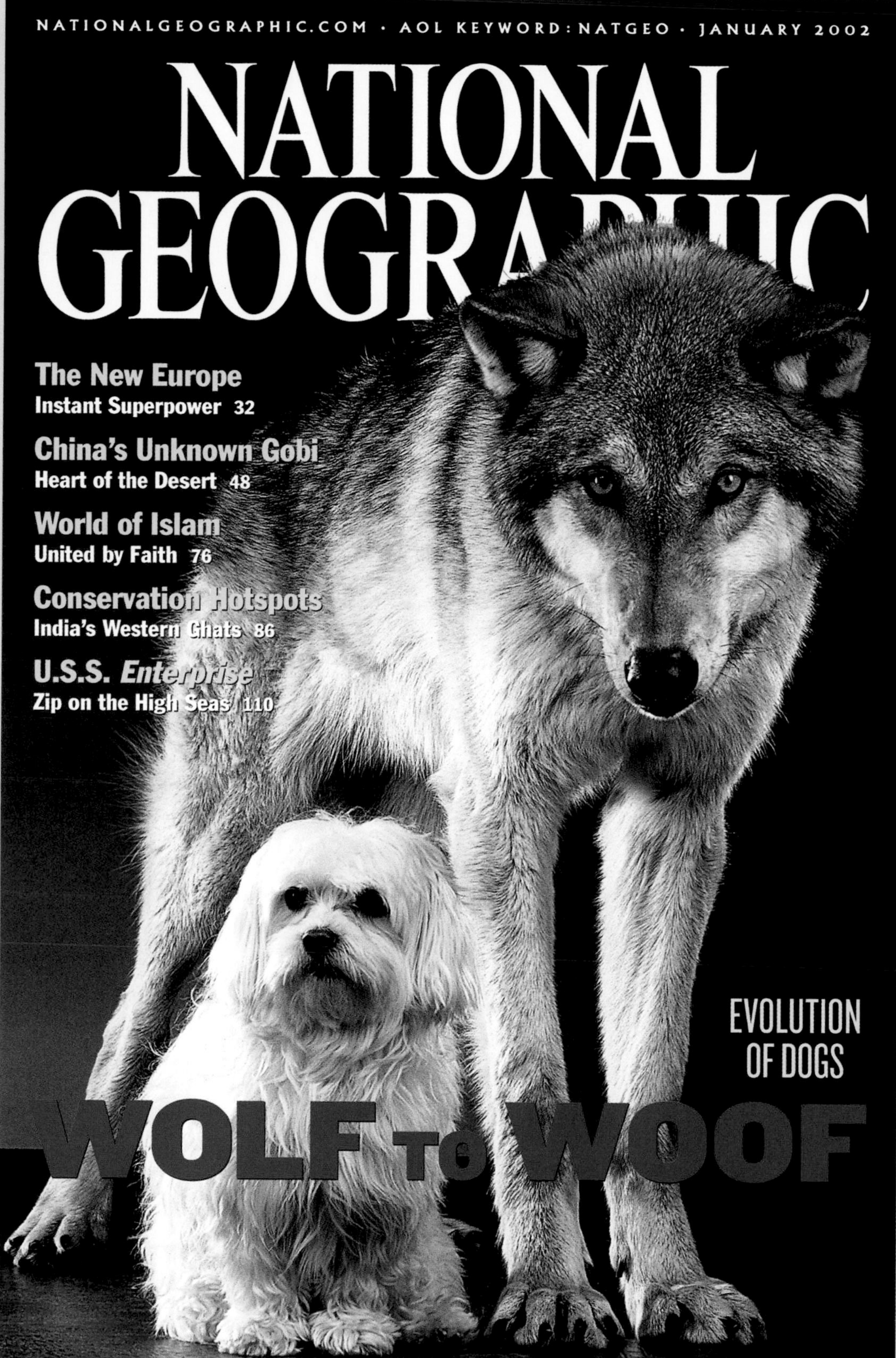

JANUARY | ROBERT CLARK Under the skin, Simon and Koda are practically identical.

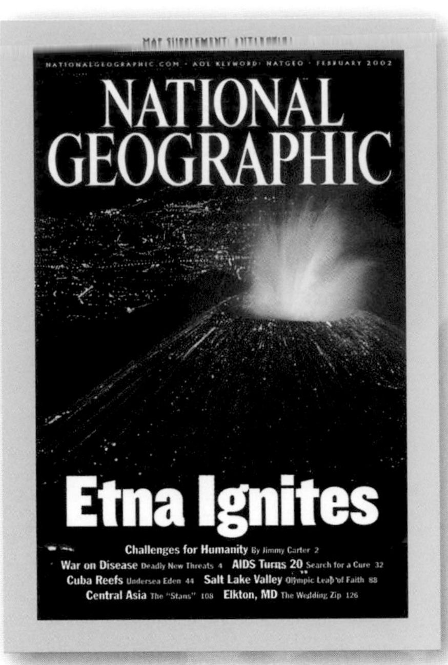

FEBRUARY | CARSTEN PETER

▲ **LAVA BOMBS** An aerial view of fiery Etna made the cover, but photographer Carsten Peter was usually within 20 feet of exploding lava during the Sicilian volcano's 2001 eruptions.

"You have to stand still, watch where the lava bombs are falling, and get out of the way . . . You must imagine, lava is quite heavy; after all, it's liquid stone flying around."

—Carsten Peter
from "Etna Ignites"

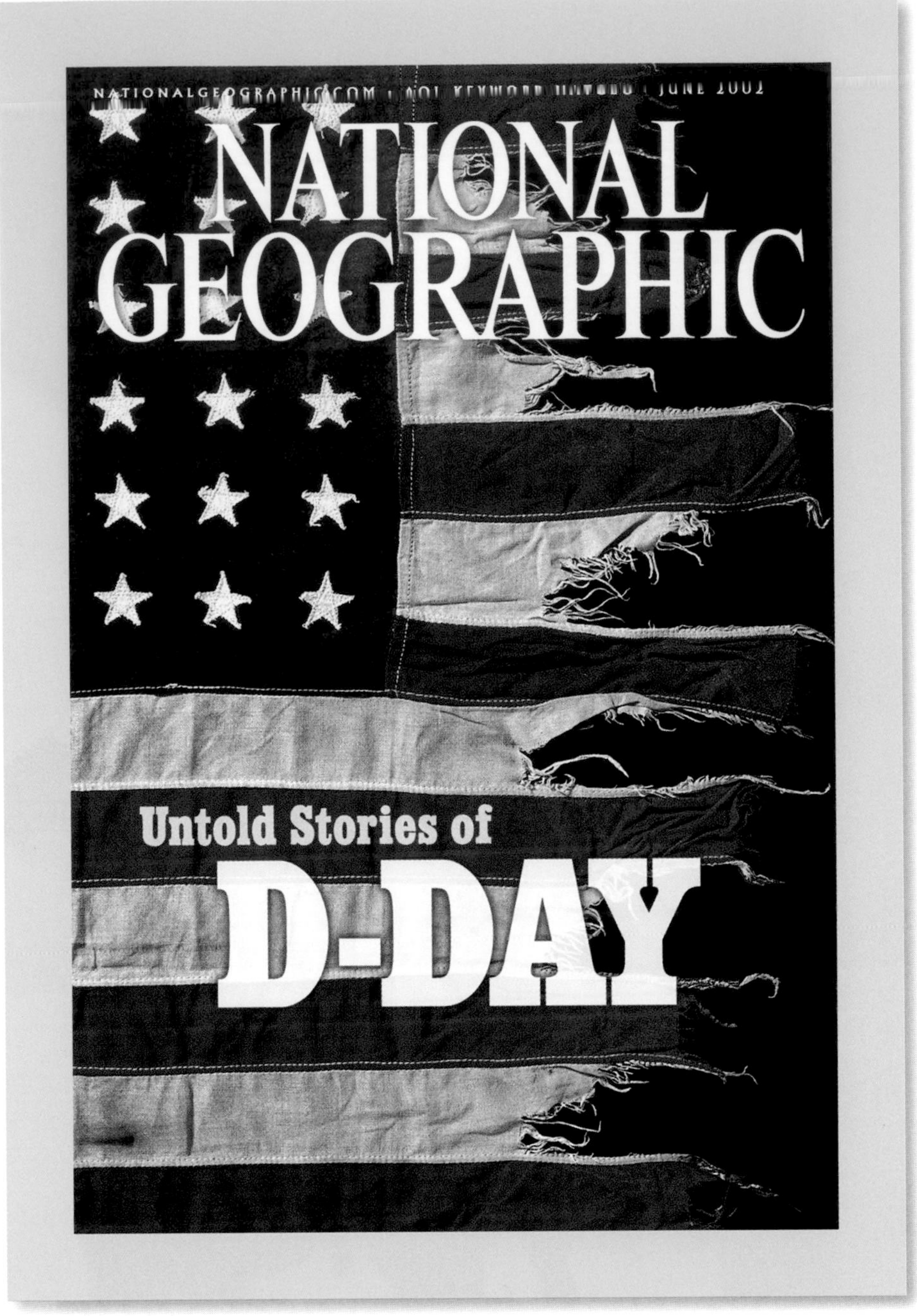

JUNE | MARK THIESSEN

▲ **OLD GLORY** It's the fourth American flag to appear on the cover, but it's the only one that certainly saw the rockets' red glare—having been snatched by Lt. Paul Garay from the mast of the U.S.S. *Corry* as it was sinking about 7 a.m. off Utah Beach. The destroyer had led the invasion fleet across the English Channel, but it hit a mine—or by some accounts, was hit by a salvo from German shore batteries—and foundered. Twenty-four men died, but 260 others, including Garay with the flag, were rescued from the 54-degree water.

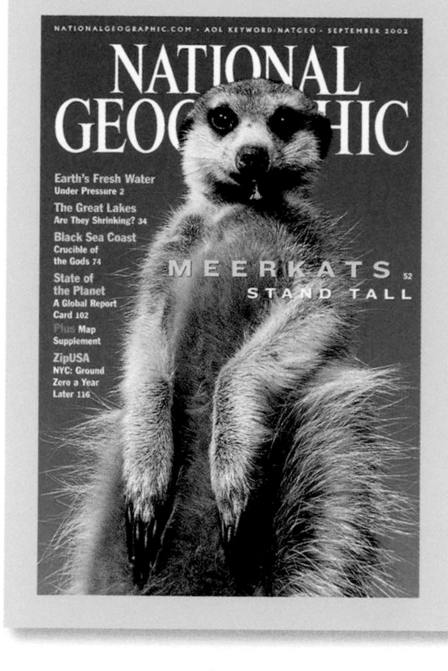

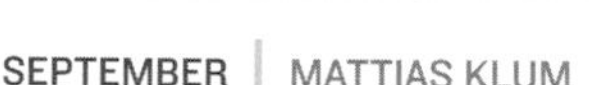
SEPTEMBER | MATTIAS KLUM

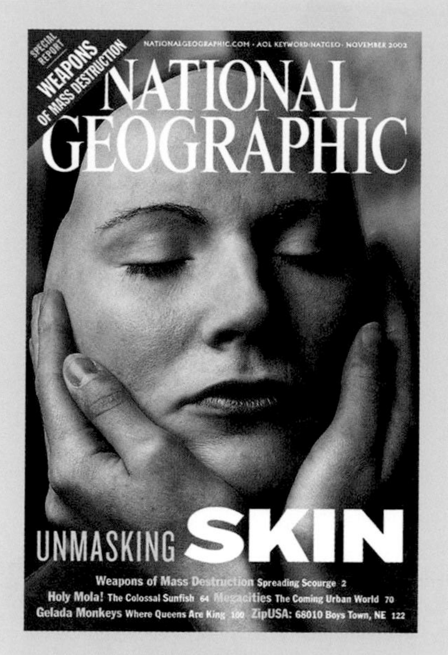

NOVEMBER | SARAH LEEN

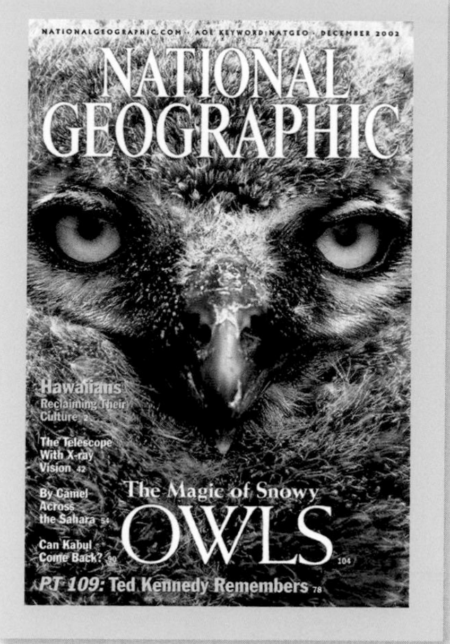

DECEMBER | DANIEL J. COX

▲ **TOUGH CHICK** Glaring out of its nest near Barrow, Alaska, an immature snowy owl defies the photographer. Caution rules, for both wildlife biologist and cameraman, when approaching a chick—its sharp-taloned mother is a fierce guardian, fully five pounds of fury whose powerful blow can knock a man down and whose rocketing dive has been known to drive off foxes, dogs, and even caribou wandering too close to the nest.

THE LONGEST DAY

PUBLISHED 58 YEARS AFTER D-Day, the June issue shed new light on an epic story, detailing secrets from newly declassified documents and revealing stories from surviving soldiers—one of whom, German Pfc. Heinz Severloh, who had only wanted "to get out of this hell," instead found himself manning a machine gun overlooking Omaha Beach.

> "My order," he recalls, "was to get them when they were still in one line, one after the other, before they started spreading. So I did not have to swing my gun sideways . . . Very soon the first bodies were drifting in the waves of the rising tide . . . In a short time, all GIs down there were shot." Severloh estimates that he fired 12,000 rounds from his machine gun and 400 from his carbine. But the Americans kept coming, and at the end of the day, Severloh surrendered, hoping the Americans would not know that he was the German who had fired what was probably the deadliest machine gun on Omaha Beach.
>
> —*From "Untold Stories of D-Day," Thomas B. Allen*

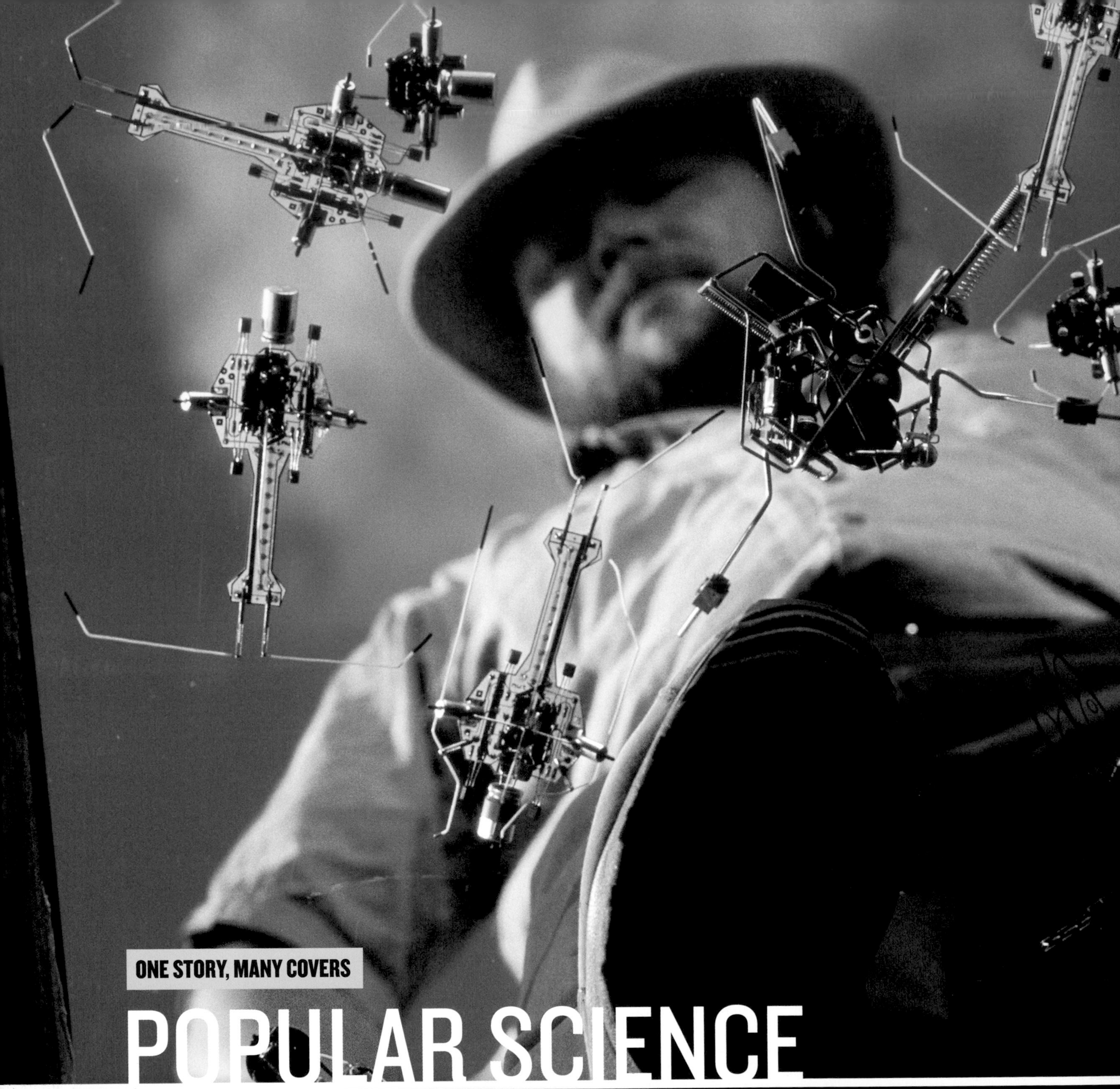

ONE STORY, MANY COVERS

POPULAR SCIENCE

▲ JULY 1997 | GEORGE STEINMETZ
Standing on bulletproof glass in Los Alamos, New Mexico, Mark Tilden studies his robot army.

ROBOTICIST MARK TILDEN'S OFFHAND comment that his "bots," originally designed to detect land mines, were better at cleaning up dust balls at home made George Steinmetz want to photograph him from a dust ball's perspective. So he placed Tilden on a sheet of glass atop some scaffolding and lay down beneath, shooting upward. Creative imagination has always been the hallmark of *Geographic* photographers who illustrate science and technology subjects—hundreds of them over the years—for the magazine

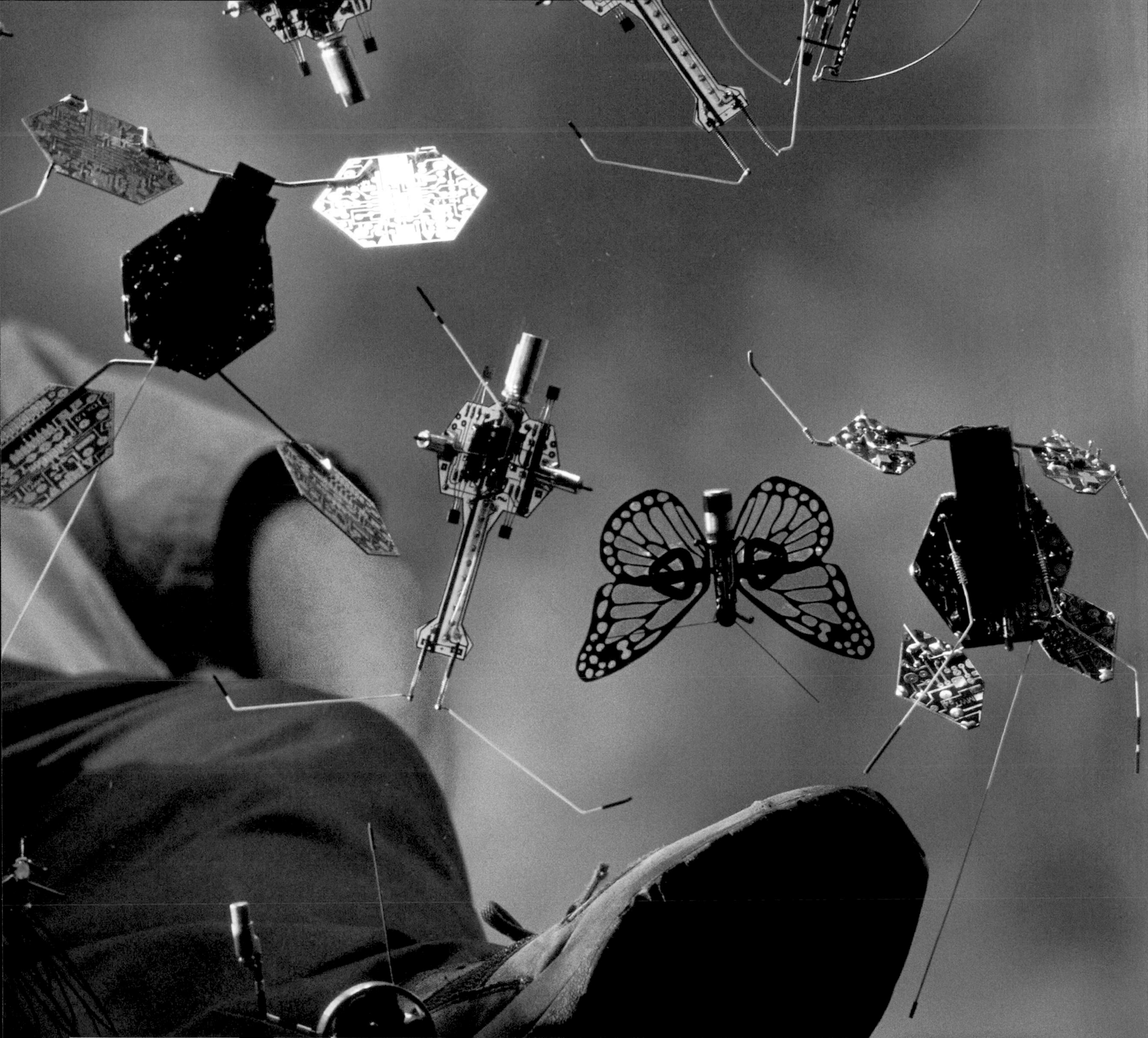

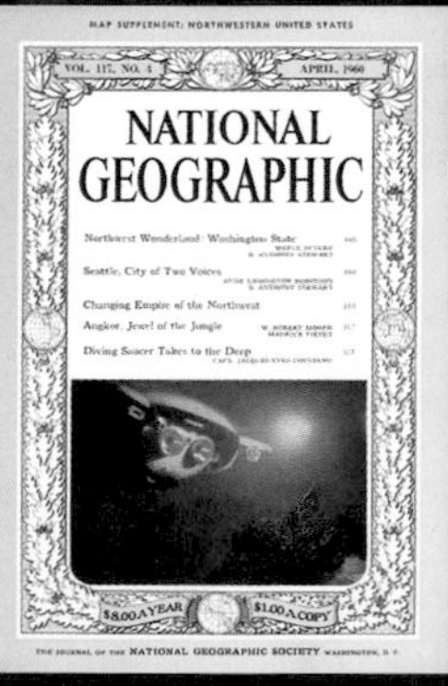

APRIL 1960

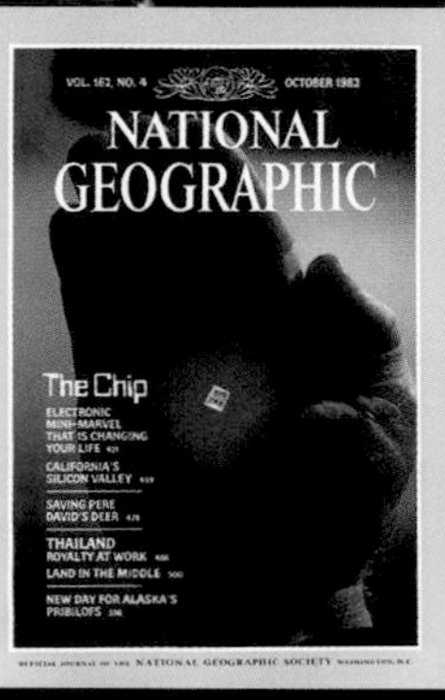

OCTOBER 1982

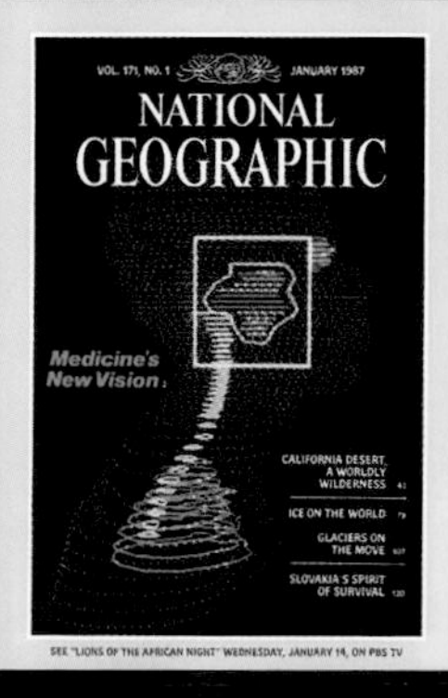

JANUARY 1987

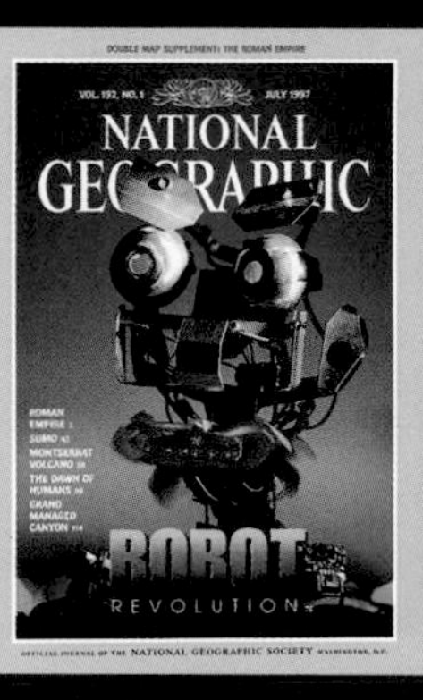

JULY 1997

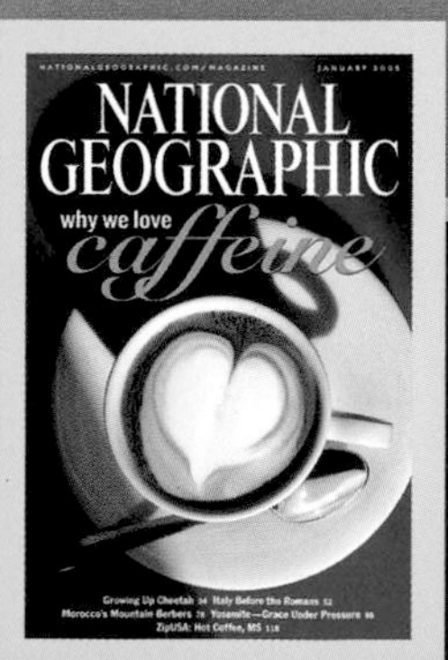

JANUARY 2005

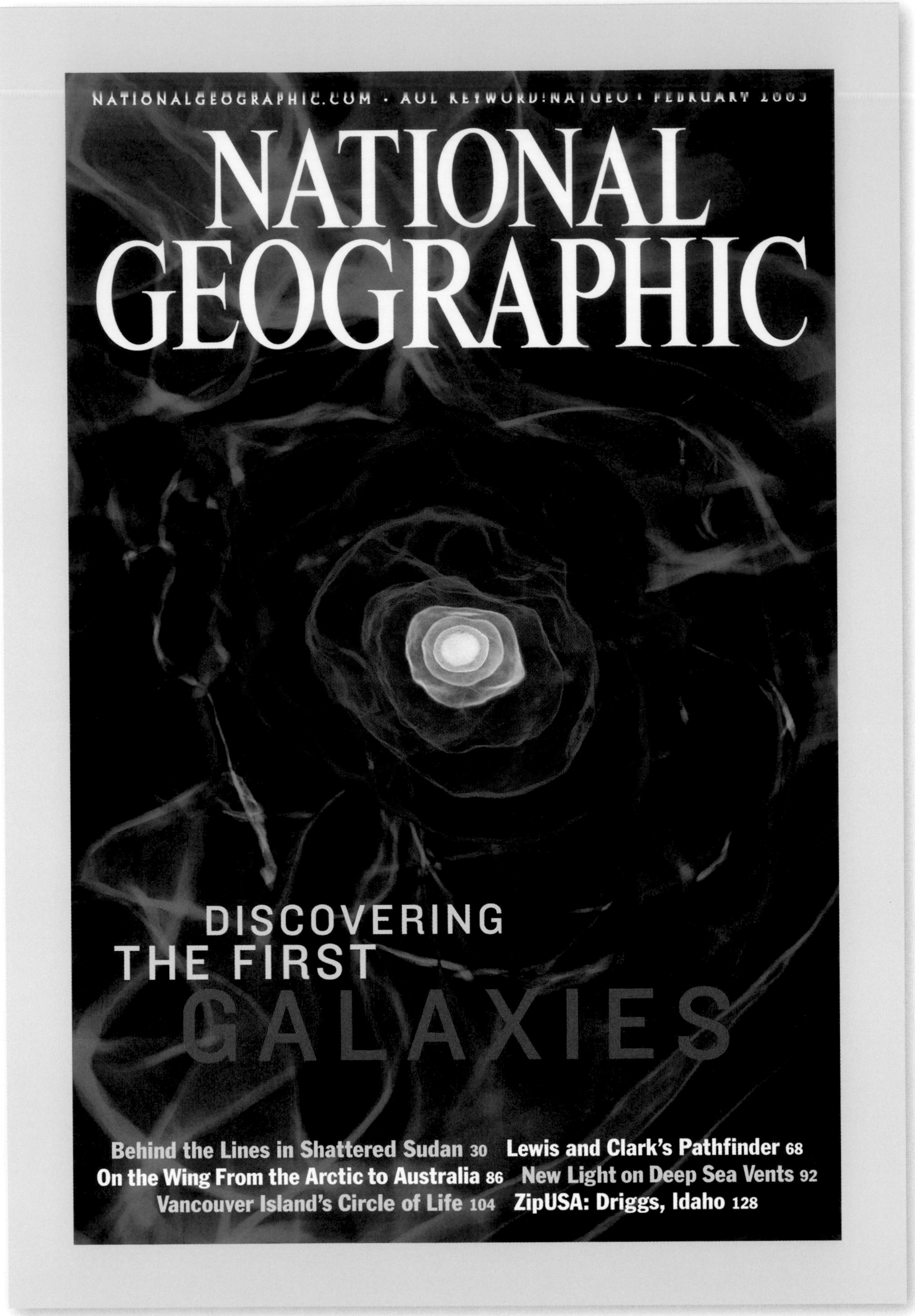

NATIONALGEOGRAPHIC.COM • AOL KEYWORD: NATGEO • FEBRUARY 2003

NATIONAL GEOGRAPHIC

DISCOVERING
THE FIRST
GALAXIES

Behind the Lines in Shattered Sudan 30
On the Wing From the Arctic to Australia 86
Vancouver Island's Circle of Life 104
Lewis and Clark's Pathfinder 68
New Light on Deep Sea Vents 92
ZipUSA: Driggs, Idaho 128

FEBRUARY | RALF KÄHLER AND TOM ABEL A stage in the birth of the first star

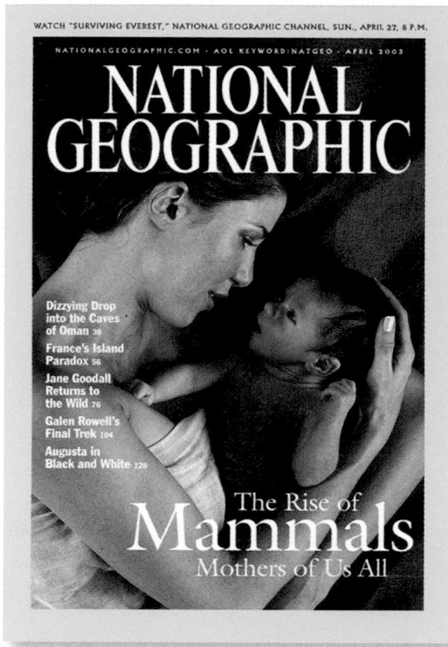

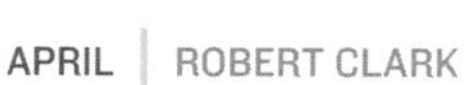

APRIL | ROBERT CLARK

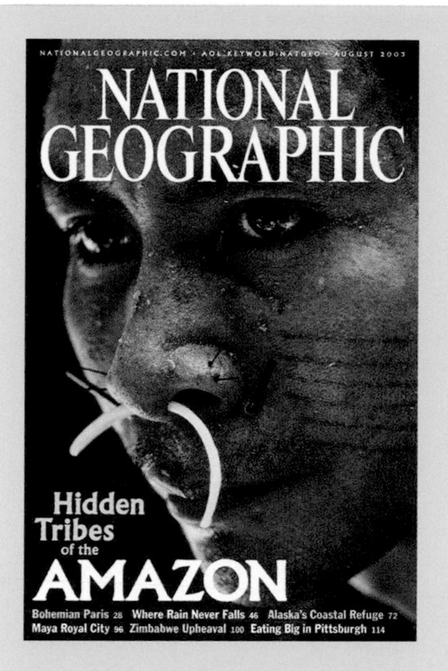

AUGUST | NICOLAS REYNARD

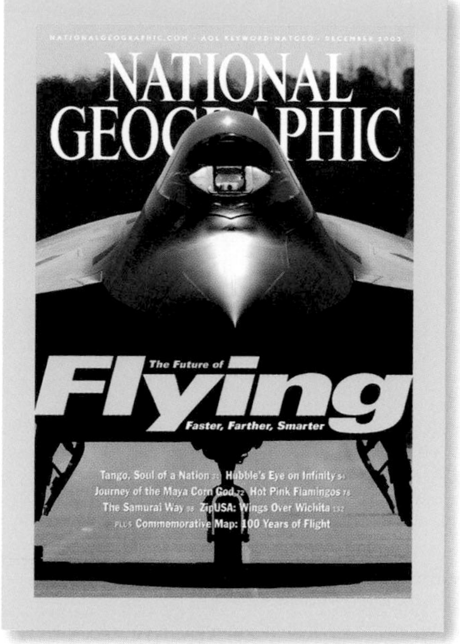

DECEMBER | JOE MCNALLY

COSMIC ROSE

IT WAS THE FIRST computer-generated image ever to appear on the cover, a tribute to the pioneering work of astrophysicist Tom Abel and his colleagues. Using supercomputers, they simulated how the first objects in the universe—stars and galaxies—coalesced out of undifferentiated darkness.

> The first step, according to the simulations, was when gravity gathered gases into diffuse clouds. As the gases cooled, they coalesced at the center of each cloud into a clump no larger than our sun. The clump collapsed further, while surrounding gas piled on top of it. In this way it grew into a behemoth about 100 times the mass of the sun. Finally, several million years after the entire process began, the intense compression forged a full-fledged star—and there was light.
>
> *—From "Discovering the First Galaxies," Ron Cowen*

▲ **THE FUTURE OF FLIGHT** Appropriately named the Raptor, the ominous-looking Lockheed Martin F/A-22 supersonic stealth fighter was the ne plus ultra of aircraft in the year that coincided with the 100th anniversary of the Wright brothers' first successful flight. Joe McNally's coverage was also suitably high-tech: It was planned from the get-go to be the first in *National Geographic* history entirely shot with digital cameras.

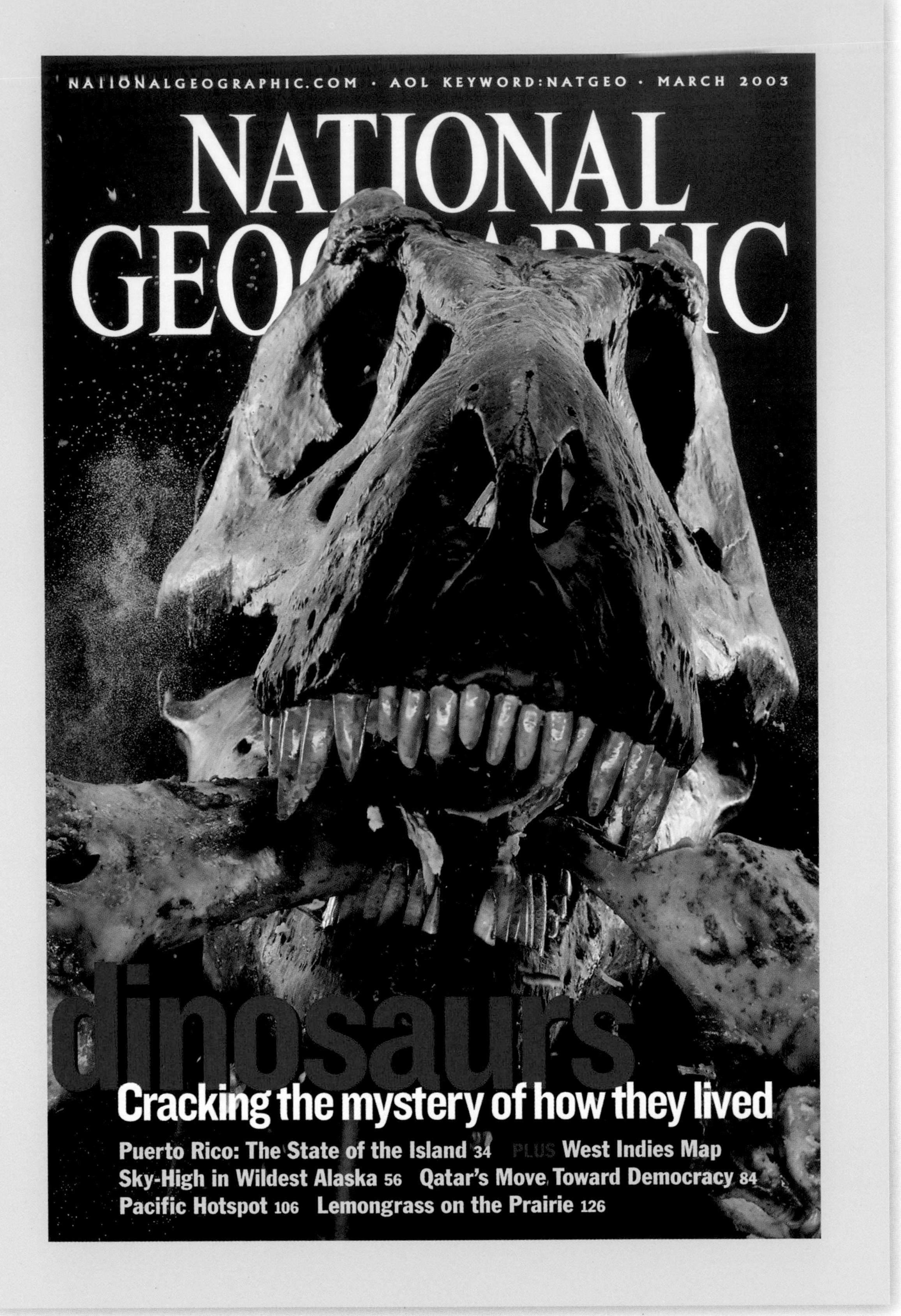

MARCH | ROBERT CLARK

CRUNCH To dramatize the force and power of *Tyrannosaurus rex*'s bite, photographer Robert Clark used a spring-loaded model of its skull to chomp ostrich bones. Only they arrived freshly butchered from ostrich farms, and those snapping jaws spattered his face with "gooey blobs of decaying bone marrow."

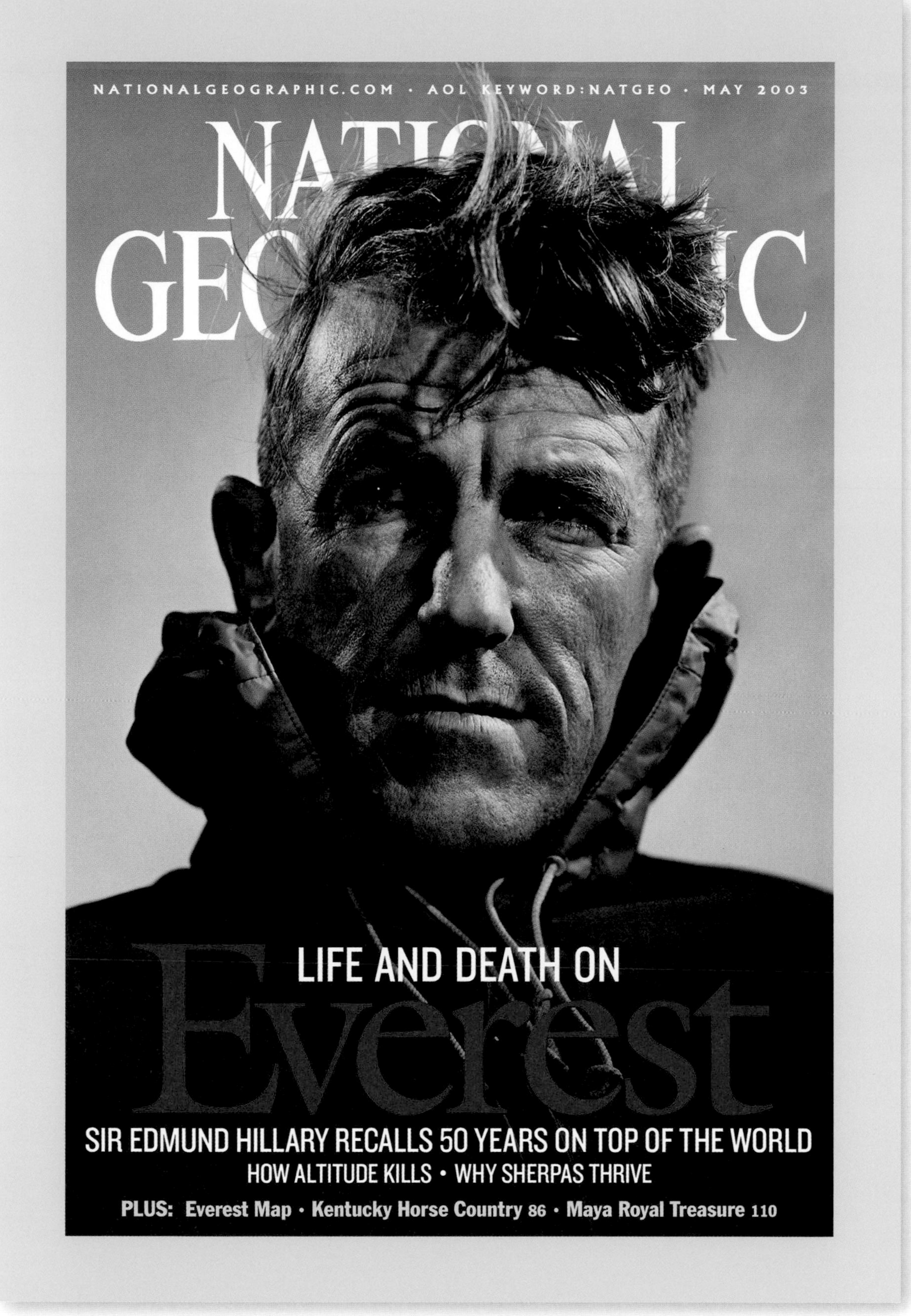

MAY | YOUSUF KARSH

INDOMITABLE With their craggy, weather-beaten aspect, Sir Edmund Hillary's features—seen in a 1960 portrait—reflect a steadfast invincibility. Yet 50 years after that day in May 1953 when he and Tenzing Norgay became the first men to summit Mount Everest, the New Zealand beekeeper still believed he was only "an ordinary bloke."

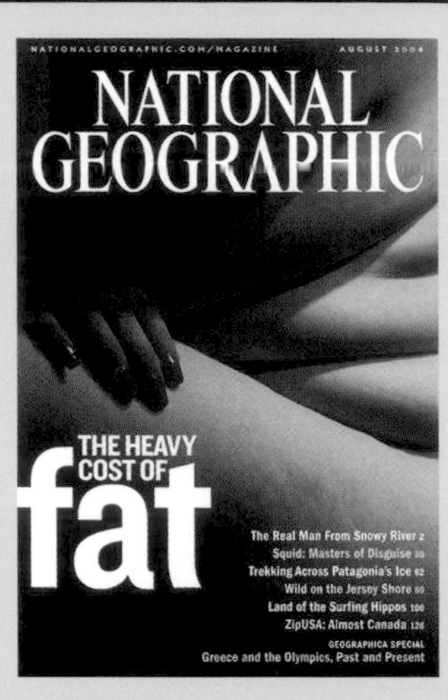

COVER STORY

BURDEN AND BEAUTY

AUGUST 2004 | KAREN KASMAUSKI

Too much of it can have health consequences, Karen Kasmauski acknowledged, but there are more facets to fat than its medical one. To illustrate different perceptions of both weight and beauty, she engaged a full-figured model who frequently posed for art students in Washington, D.C. In the studio she lit her subject with only one light, thereby illuminating the sensuality and voluptuousness of her flesh. The red nails, Kasmauski thought, were the finishing touch.

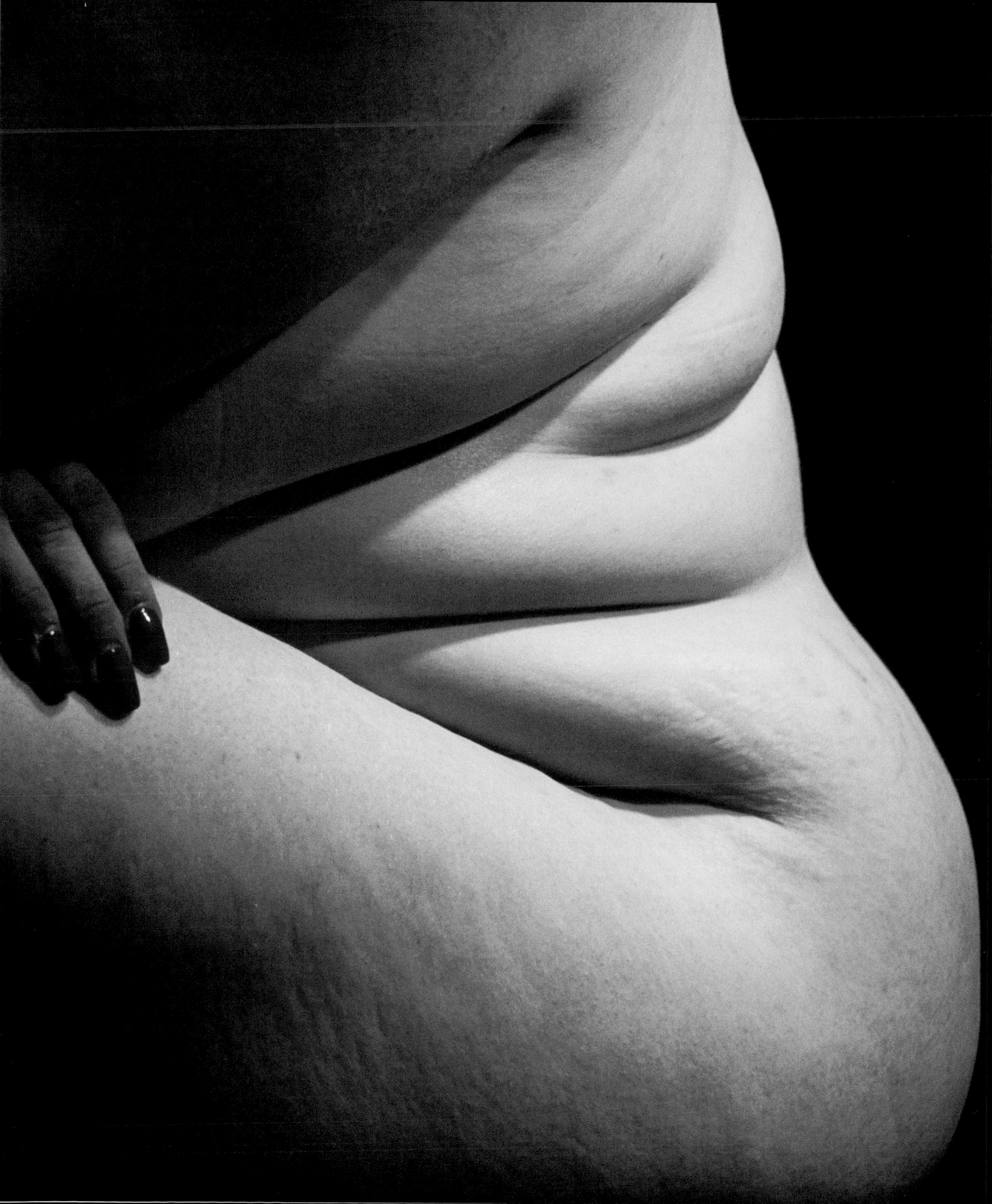

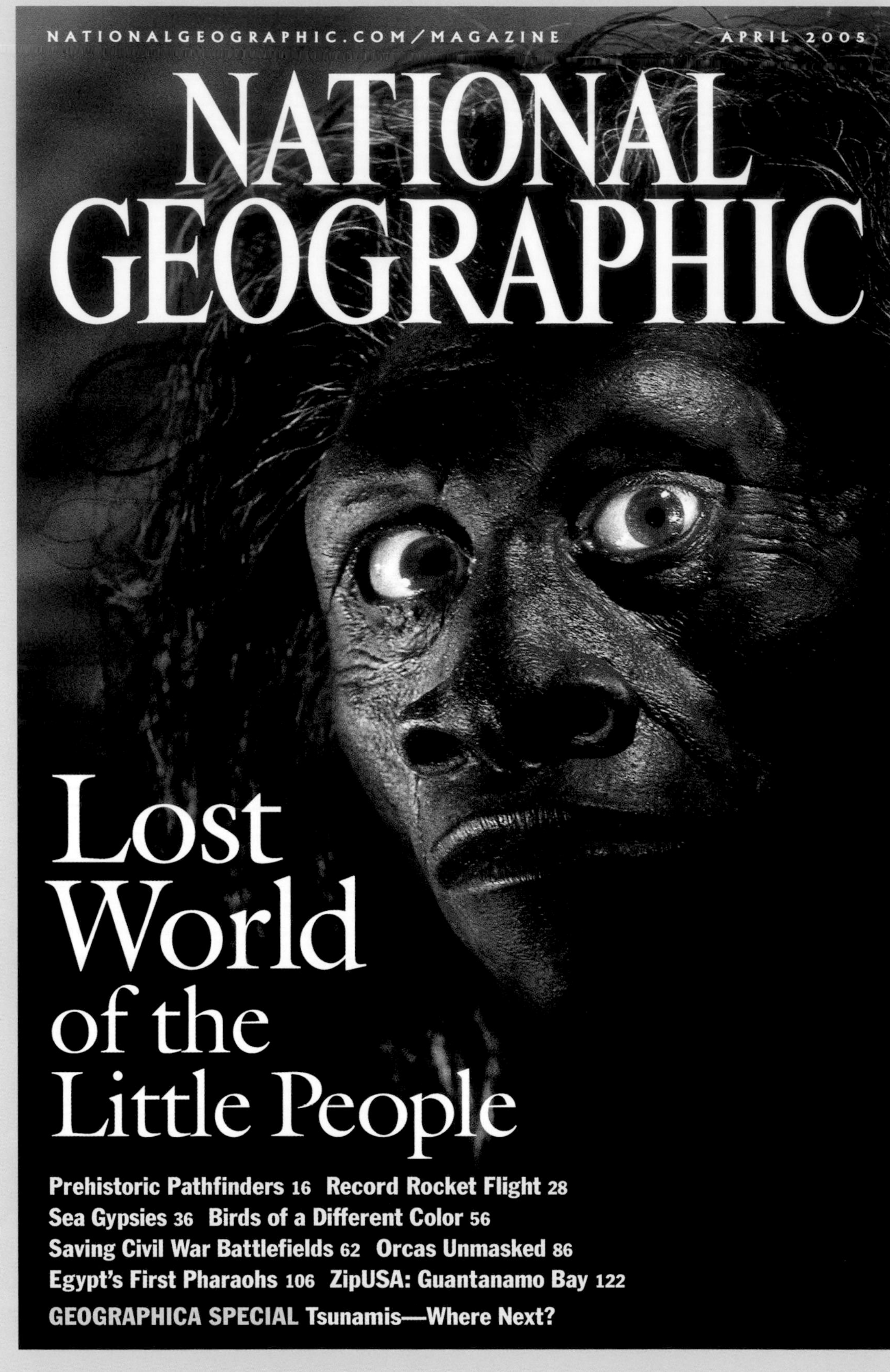

APRIL | KENNETH GARRETT, JOHN GURCHE The reconstructed face of *Homo floresiensis* stares back from the cover.

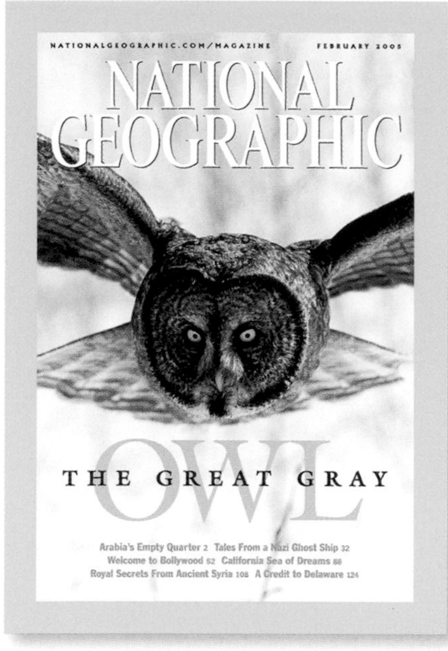

FEBRUARY | DANIEL J. COX

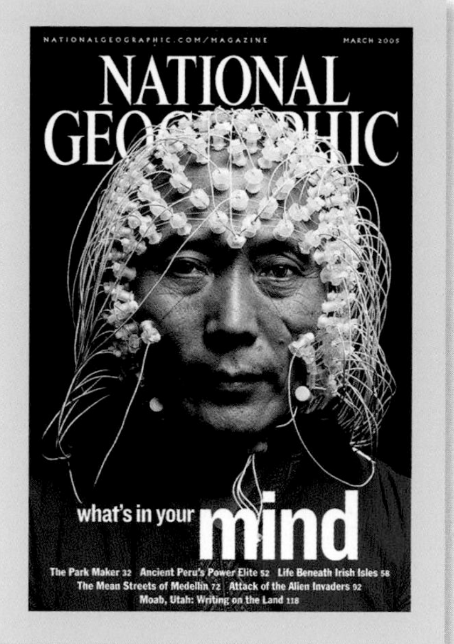

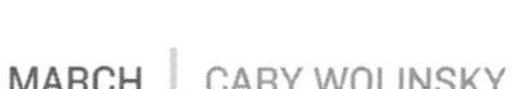
MARCH | CARY WOLINSKY

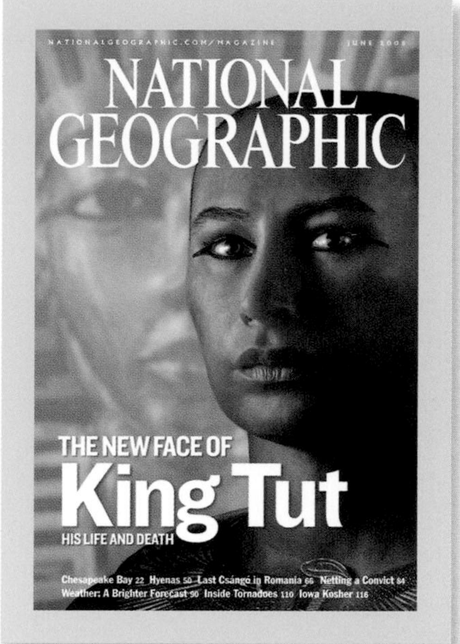

JUNE | KENNETH GARRETT, ELISABETH DAYNÈS

MEET THE "HOBBIT"

GAZING FEARFULLY BACK FROM the April 2005 cover is the life-size face of a hominid who stood no taller than a three-year-old child and possessed a grapefruit-size skull.

In 2003 archaeologist Mike Morwood had unearthed from the floor of Liang Bua cave on the Indonesian island of Flores the remains of a previously unknown species of elfin human beings he christened *Homo floresiensis*—but quickly nicknamed "hobbits"—that had been living in those remote jungles only 18,000 years ago.

While debate grew heated among paleoanthropologists—was this really a new species, perhaps an offshoot of long-extinct *Homo erectus?* Or was it instead a case of "island dwarfism" among a long-isolated population of modern humans?—artist John Gurche sculpted this reconstruction based on a female *floresiensis* skull. He molded facial muscles, covered them with silicone skin, and added synthetic hair. But the eyes brought her to life.

"What I wanted to get into the face was a sort of wariness," Gurche told one reporter, "as though the primitive little hominid is really encountering a human. What would we have seemed like to them?"

▲ **PHARAOH'S FACE?** King Tut did not die from a blow to the skull, as was formerly suspected. He might have been killed at age 19 in a chariot accident instead. Those were findings from the first full-body CT scan of his mummy, which also provided data for a forensic reconstruction of the youthful pharaoh's face. Using measurements taken from the scans, sculptor Elisabeth Daynès fleshed out his features in silicone; and after photographer Kenneth Garrett joined her in her Paris studio, they adorned Tut with jewelry modeled on pieces from his tomb. "Our cover image is a wonderful example of the power of science—and its limitations," wrote Chris Johns in the Editor's Page, meaning the skin tone was a guess. The coloring of modern Egyptians was chosen; but the cover still provoked criticism from Afrocentric scholars, who thought the reconstruction too Caucasian.

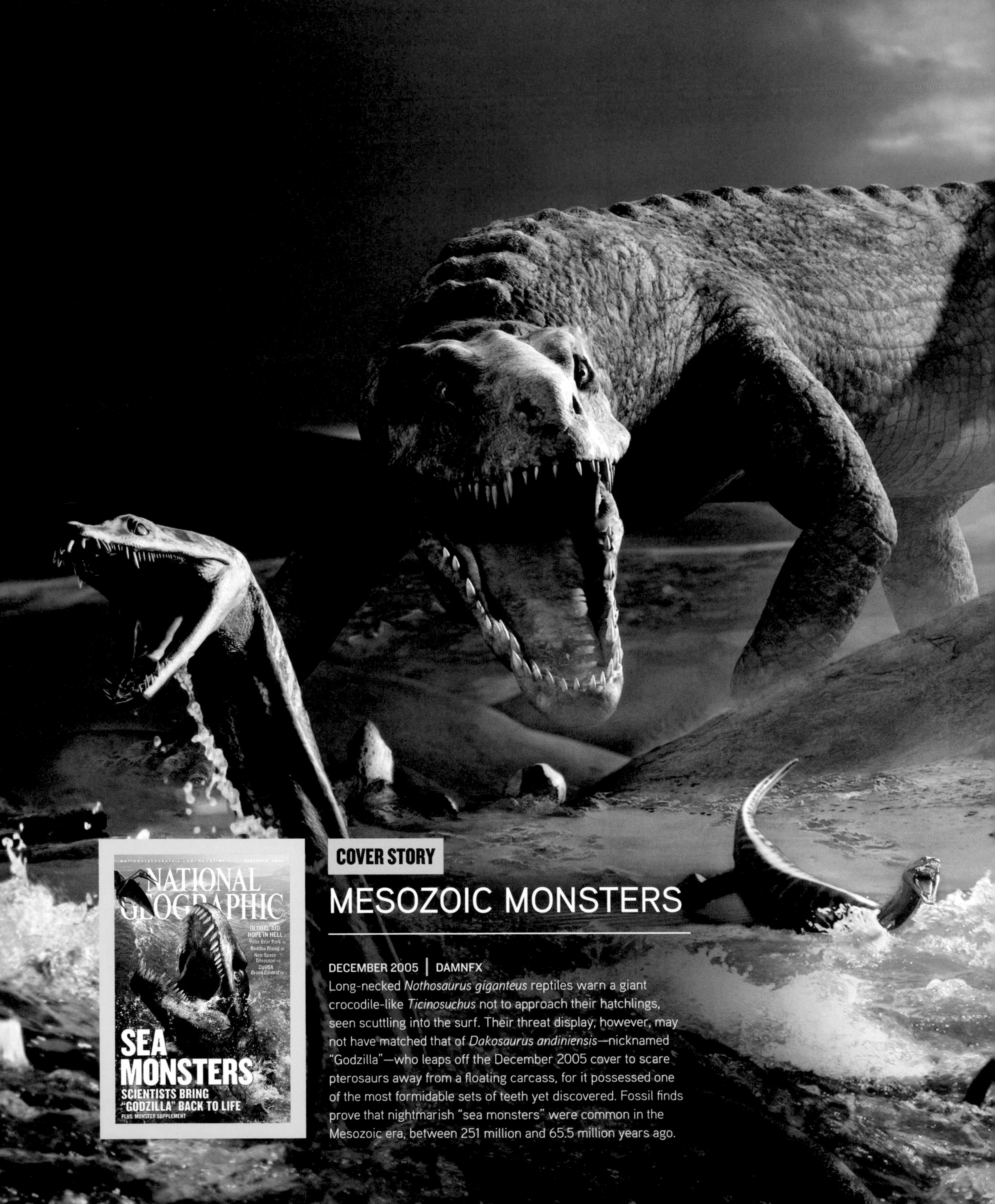

COVER STORY

MESOZOIC MONSTERS

DECEMBER 2005 | DAMNFX

Long-necked *Nothosaurus giganteus* reptiles warn a giant crocodile-like *Ticinosuchus* not to approach their hatchlings, seen scuttling into the surf. Their threat display, however, may not have matched that of *Dakosaurus andiniensis*—nicknamed "Godzilla"—who leaps off the December 2005 cover to scare pterosaurs away from a floating carcass, for it possessed one of the most formidable sets of teeth yet discovered. Fossil finds prove that nightmarish "sea monsters" were common in the Mesozoic era, between 251 million and 65.5 million years ago.

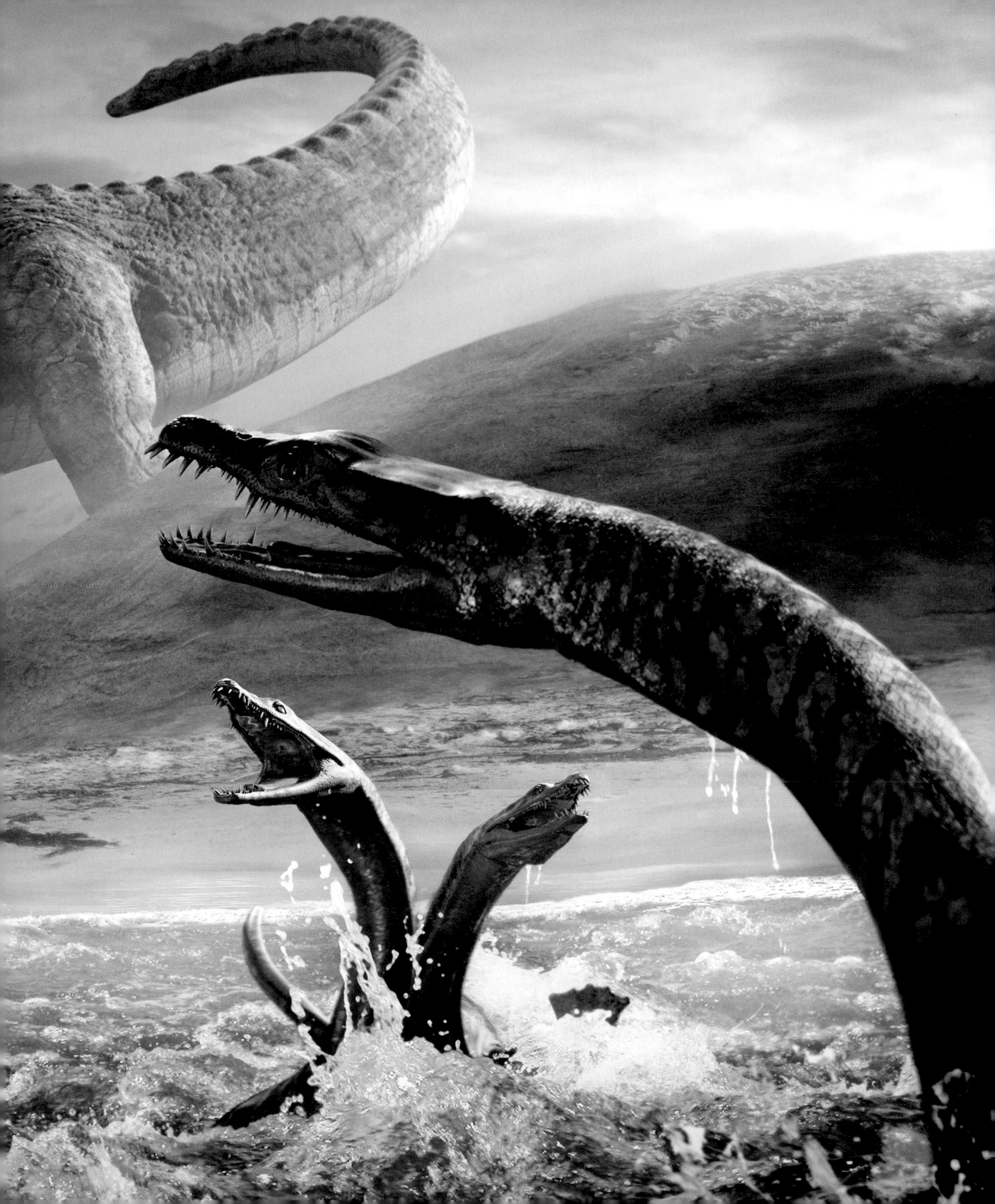

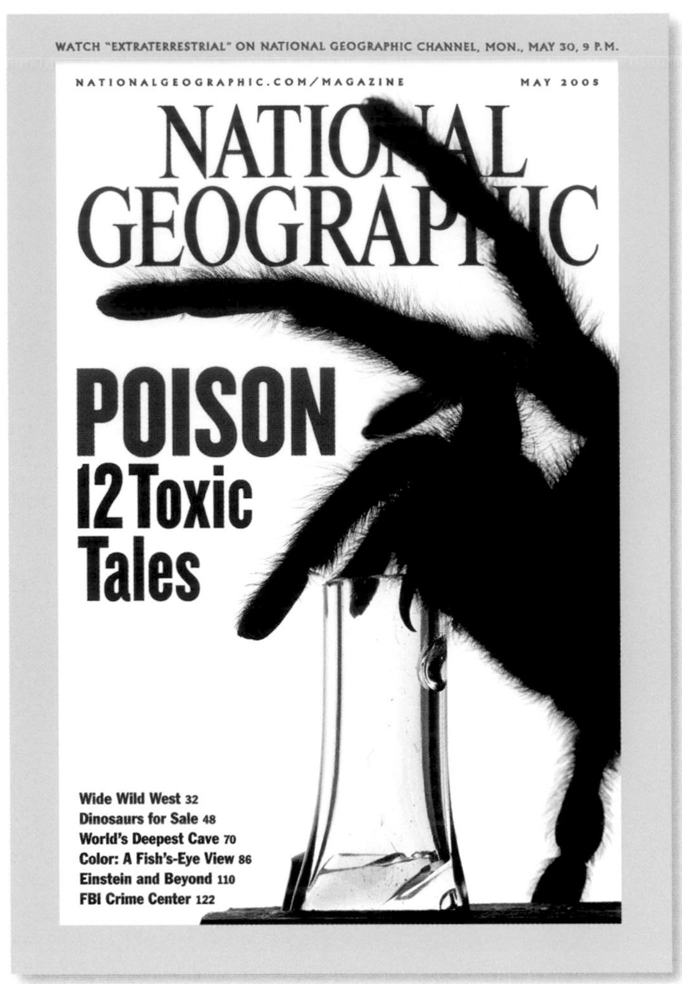

MAY | CARY WOLINSKY

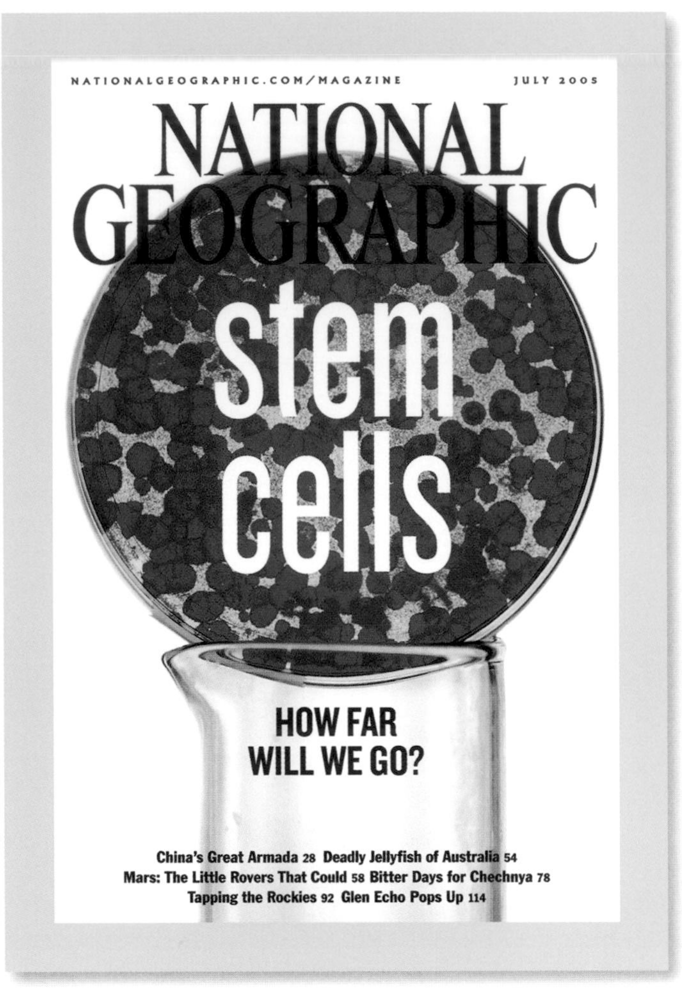

JULY | MAX AGUILERA-HELLWEG

▲ **COME INTO MY PARLOR** Venom from a tarantula is used to study neural and chemical pathways in humans.

> *"Poison is a stealth killer, effective in minuscule amounts, often undetectable. It's the treachery in the arsenic-tainted glass of wine. The fatal attraction: Snow White's poison apple, the death-defying art of the snake handler, the Japanese roulette practiced by those who eat fugu."*
>
> —Cathy Newman
> *from "Poison: Twelve Toxic Tales"*

▲ **PURPLE STEM CELLS** A sample of tissue from an eye biopsy is stained purple so that scientists can better see its abundance of cell colonies. That might indicate the presence of stem cells—ones that haven't yet differentiated into particular organ cells and so are still able to regenerate a variety of tissues. When Max Aguilera-Hellweg received the assignment to photograph this story, the photographer turned doctor had just started residency in a Boston hospital. He secured a leave of absence and spent the next month carrying a large-format view camera, which used 4 x 5 inch film, and 11 trunks of photographic gear to medical centers around the globe.

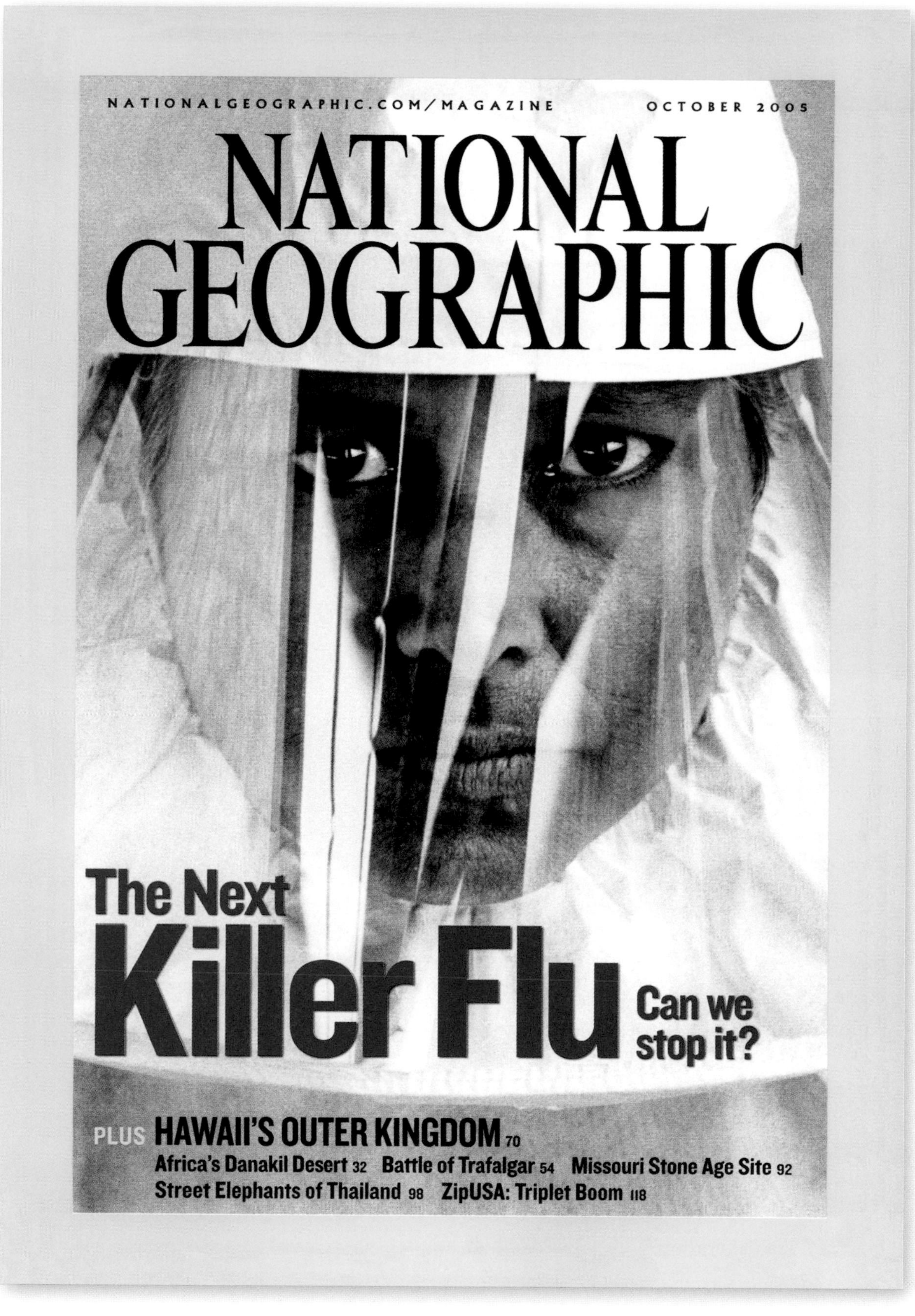
NATIONALGEOGRAPHIC.COM/MAGAZINE OCTOBER 2005

NATIONAL GEOGRAPHIC

The Next Killer Flu Can we stop it?

PLUS HAWAII'S OUTER KINGDOM 70

Africa's Danakil Desert 32 Battle of Trafalgar 54 Missouri Stone Age Site 92

Street Elephants of Thailand 98 ZipUSA: Triplet Boom 118

OCTOBER | LYNN JOHNSON

OUTBREAK Scientist Kanta Subbarao is developing a vaccine to stem influenza virus H5N1—the dreaded "bird flu." Mutating every season, the pathogens stay a step ahead of medical efforts to control them. A similar strain killed more than 50 million people in 1918. A pandemic tomorrow could be even worse.

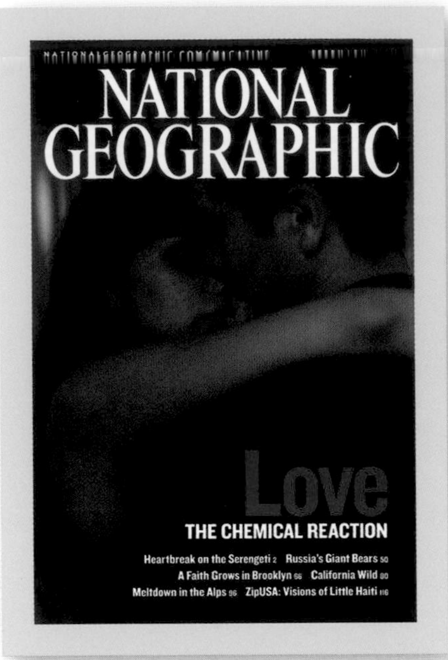

FEBRUARY | PABLO CORRAL VEGA

▲ **DANCE OF LOVE** It's courtship Argentine style as a couple sways to a slow tango in Buenos Aires.

> *"Scientists now believe that romance is panhuman, embedded in our brains since Pleistocene times . . . But though romantic love may be universal, its cultural expression is not."*
>
> —Lauren Slater
>
> *from "Love: The Chemical Reaction"*

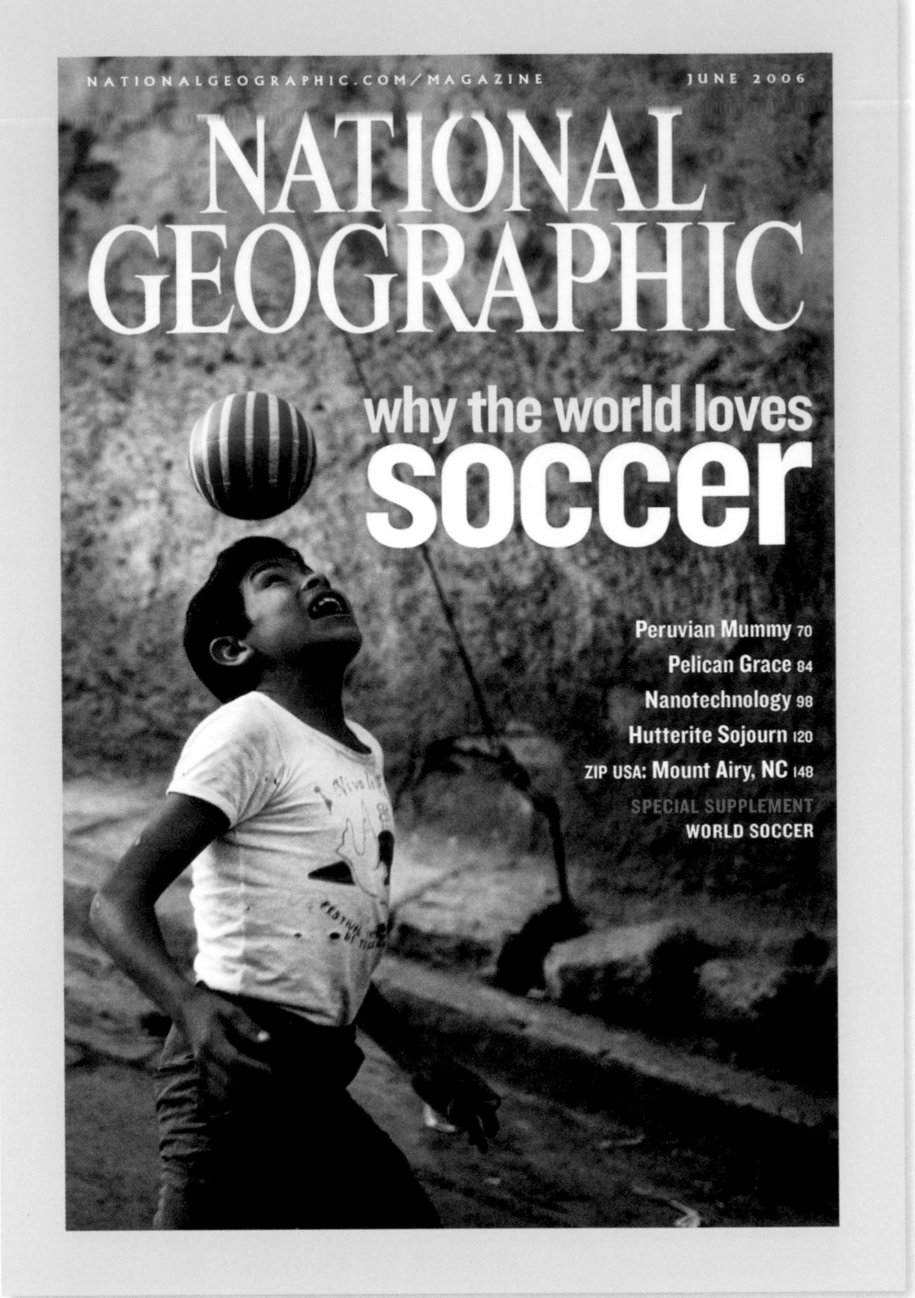

JUNE | DAVID ALAN HARVEY

▲ **PRACTICE MAKES PERFECT** A Honduran youngster practices his heading in Tegucigalpa. One reason that football (as most of the world calls it) is so universally popular is that it is so simple. All you need is a ball, two improvised goals, and a handful of fellow players and you have the makings of what might long be remembered as an epic match. That's only a step or two away from the quadrennial World Cup, when, as author Sean Wilsey put it in the June 2006 *Geographic,* "entire nations walk off the job or wake up at 3 a.m. to watch men kick a ball."

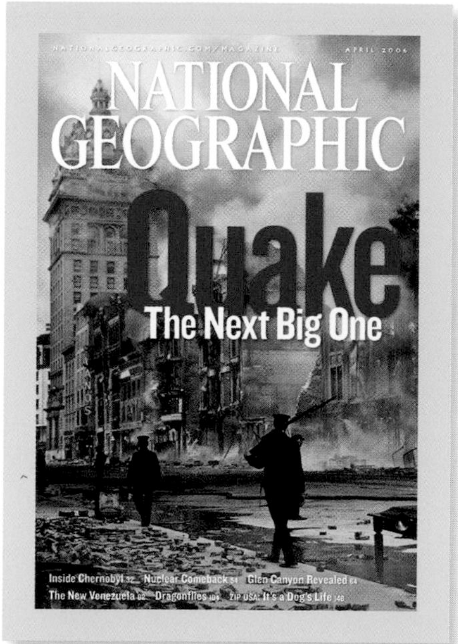

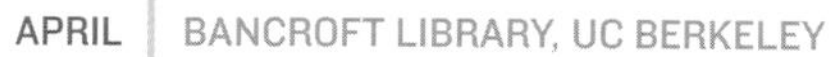

APRIL | BANCROFT LIBRARY, UC BERKELEY

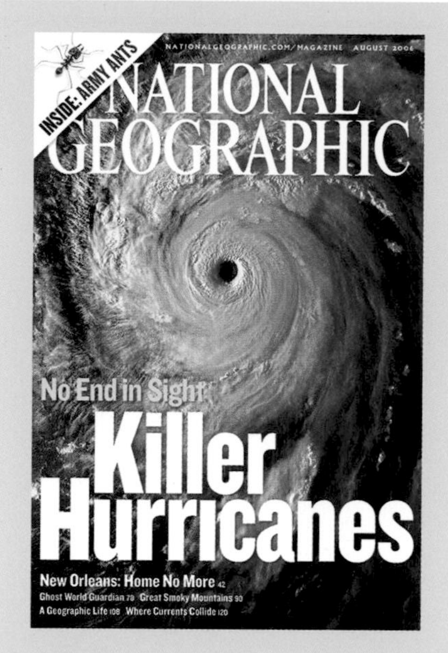

AUGUST | JOHNS HOPKINS UNIVERSITY AND NOAA

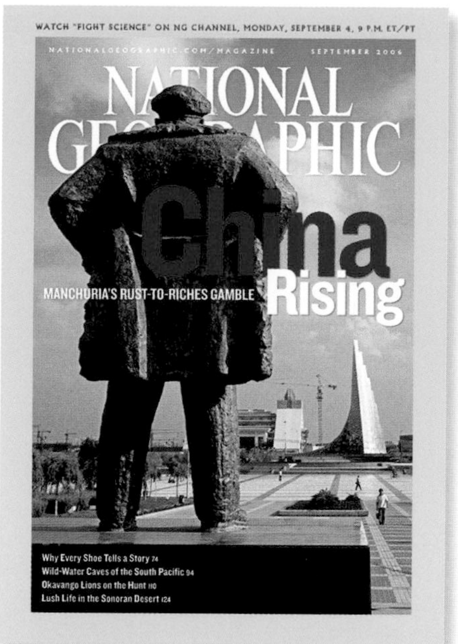

SEPTEMBER | FRITZ HOFFMANN

THE BEAUTIFUL GAME

SOCCER—IT'S A SPORT CHERISHED by millions of people around the globe. It is also a cause of frenzied animosities. These twin facets were explored in excerpts from a book entitled *The Thinking Fan's Guide to the World Cup* published in the June 2006 *Geographic.*

> There are, it sometimes seems, only two universal games: war and soccer. War is perhaps closer to the realm of fantasy, soccer to that of the real, but both share this ubiquity and centrality, as though arising from some collective libidinous source, primary and intuitive. Perhaps they are simply variations of the same game, modern industrial-era ritualizations of some common activity from the Dreamtime of the species, back when both used the same players and the same field—which is to say, all the men of the tribe and all of nature.
>
> —*From* The Thinking Fan's Guide to the World Cup, *Robert Coover*

▲ **ENGINE OF GROWTH** A statue of a "model workman" overlooks a square in Daqing, a former village in Manchuria transformed into a city by oil. American photographer Fritz Hoffmann moved to China in the mid-1990s at least partly because he saw it as a "chance to document an industrial revolution." While photographing factories in Manchuria, he found that the "settings formed grand epic scenes, heavy with steel and dated infrastructure. China is gearing up to turn its northeastern rust belt, once the centerpiece of Chairman Mao's planned economy, into the country's next engine of growth."

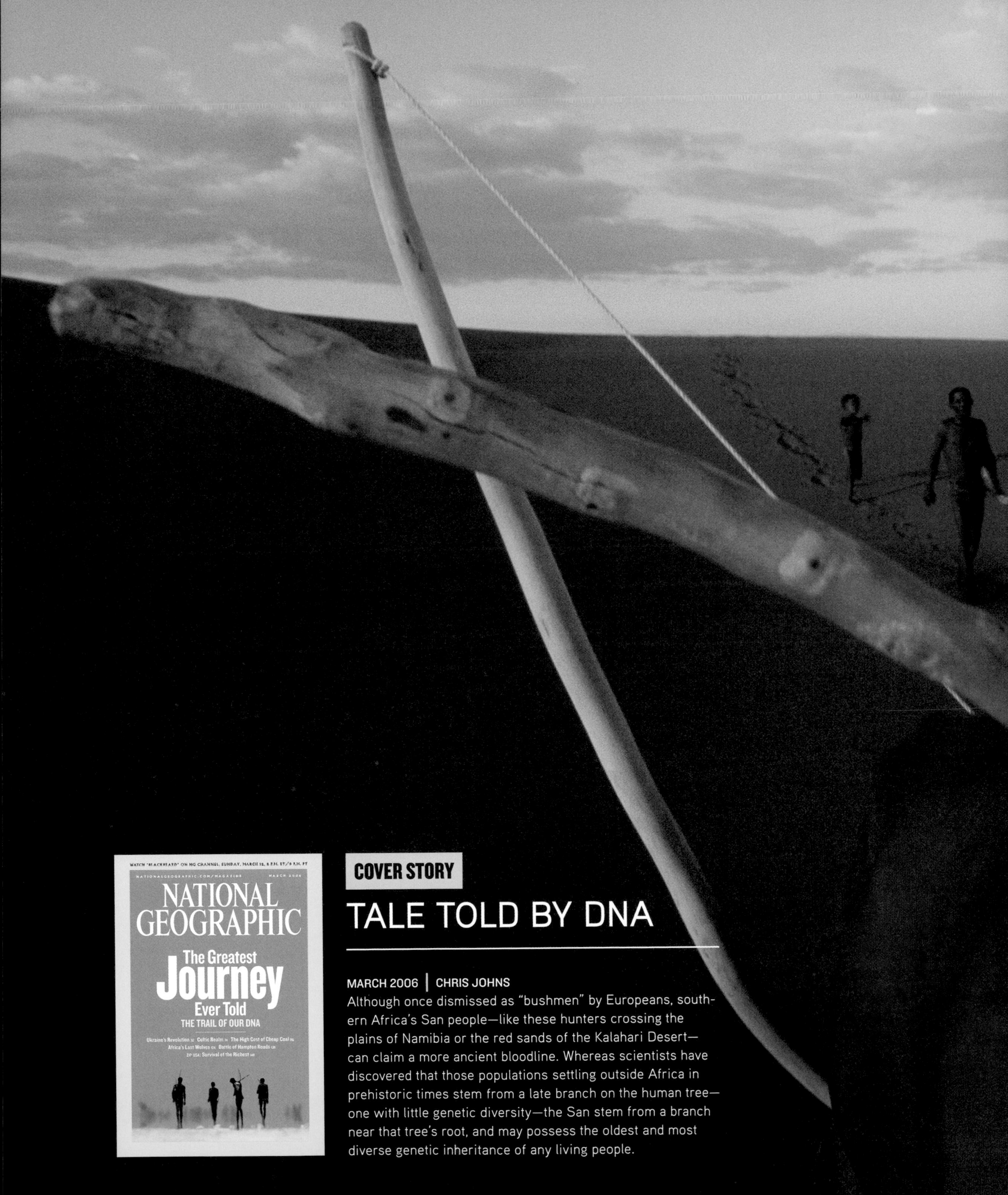

COVER STORY

TALE TOLD BY DNA

MARCH 2006 | CHRIS JOHNS

Although once dismissed as "bushmen" by Europeans, southern Africa's San people—like these hunters crossing the plains of Namibia or the red sands of the Kalahari Desert—can claim a more ancient bloodline. Whereas scientists have discovered that those populations settling outside Africa in prehistoric times stem from a late branch on the human tree—one with little genetic diversity—the San stem from a branch near that tree's root, and may possess the oldest and most diverse genetic inheritance of any living people.

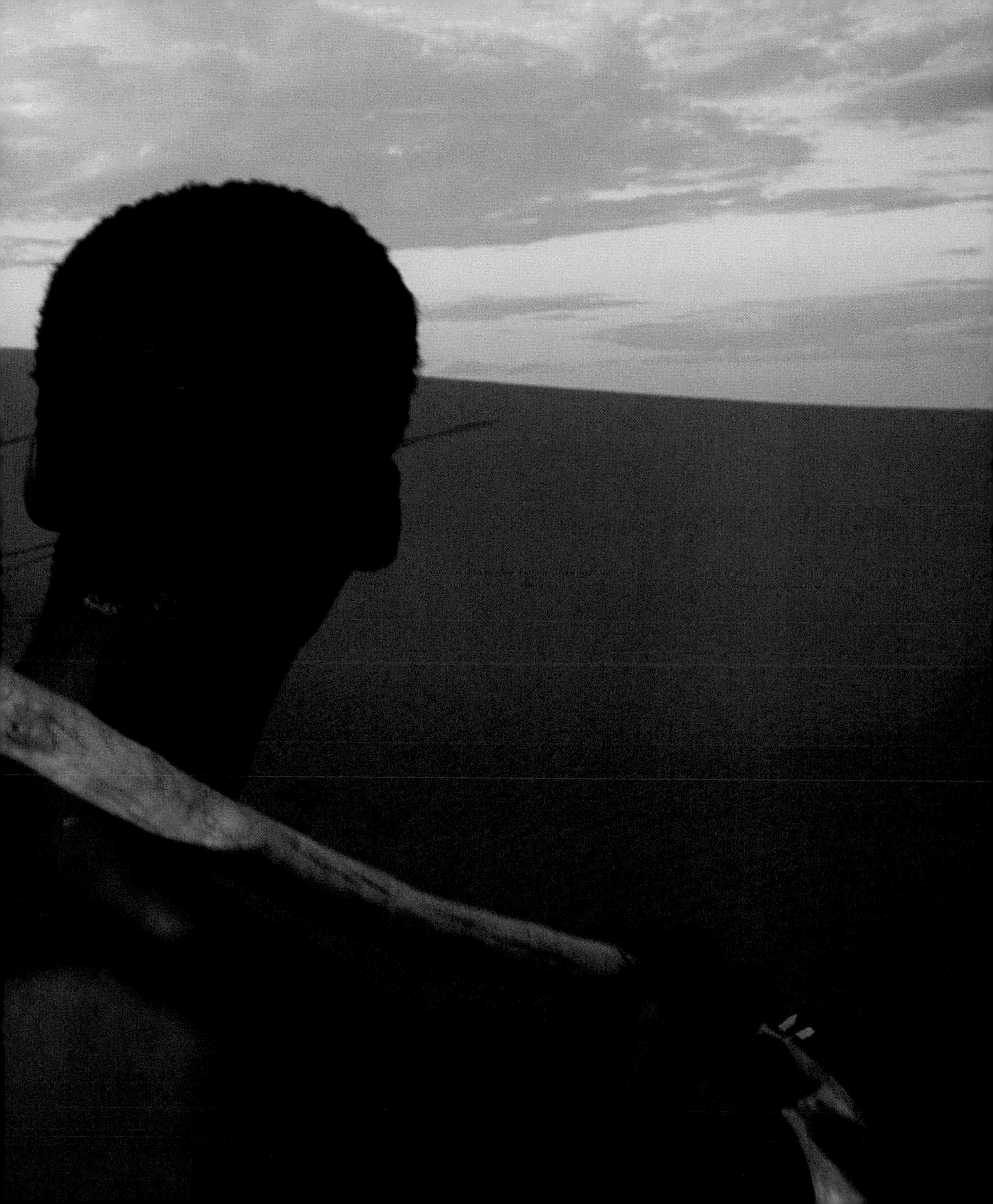

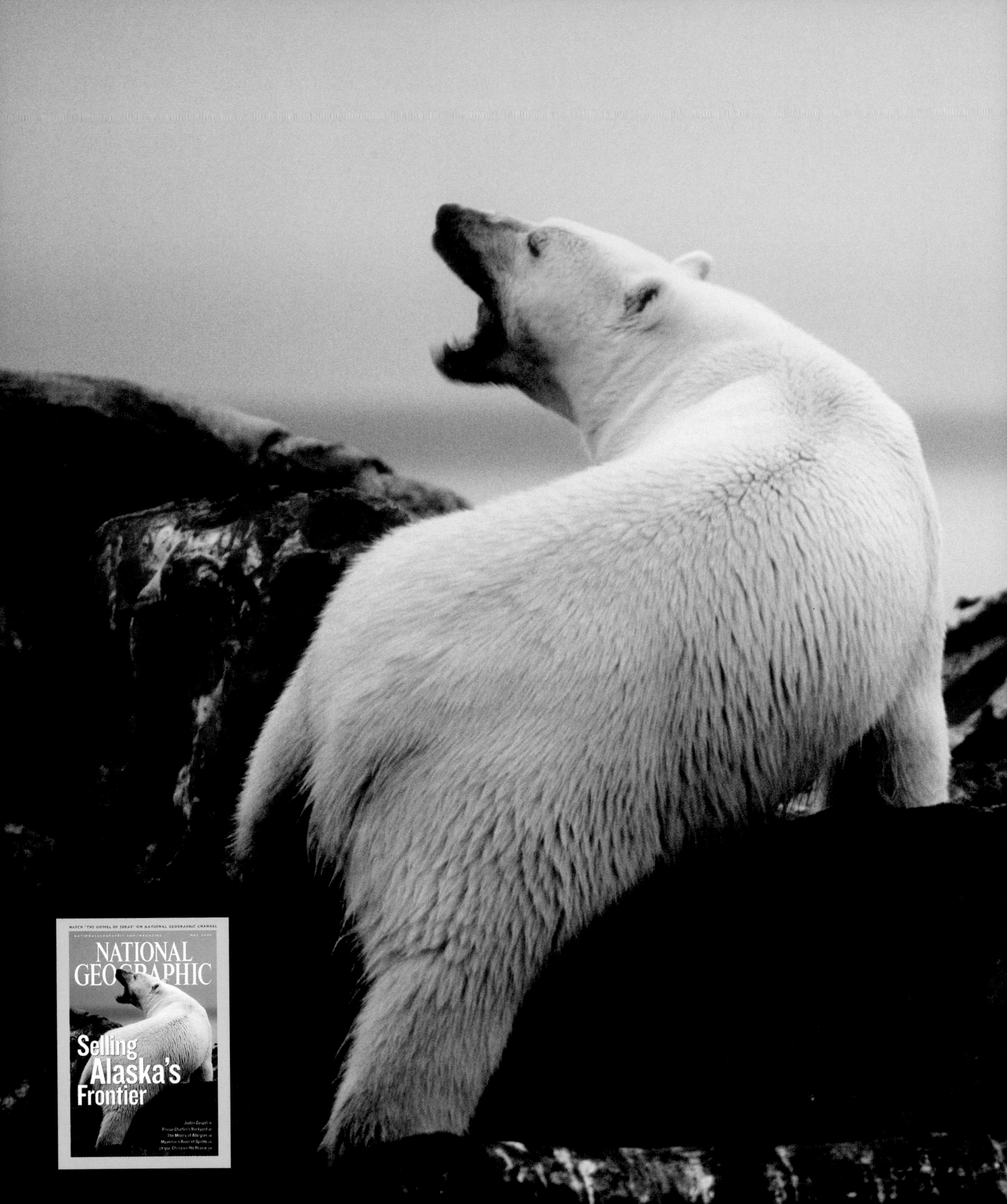
WATCH "THE GOSPEL OF JUDAS" ON NATIONAL GEOGRAPHIC CHANNEL
NATIONAL GEOGRAPHIC
Selling Alaska's Frontier
Judas Gospel
Prince Charles's Backyard
The Misery of Allergies
Myanmar's River of Spirits

ALASKA FOR SALE?

OUTSIDE THE INUPIAT VILLAGE of Kaktovik, Alaska, photographer Joel Sartore spent a week living in a rented van. There the remains of three bowhead whales taken in a subsistence hunt lay on the shores of the Beaufort Sea. As many as 40 polar bears might turn up to feed on them, presenting him with the opportunity to take a picture "just a little bit different"—instead of an immaculately white polar bear, a blood-smeared one made a guttier image of wild Alaska.

Sartore was in the Arctic National Wildlife Refuge (ANWR) to shoot a story on the continuing debate over oil exploitation on Alaska's North Slope, one of the last pristine ecosystems in North America. Herds of migrating caribou, packs of wolves, and numbers of grizzlies still roamed the tundra. Millions of birds nested in the mosses and sedges, while mosquitoes rose in clouds from the wetlands. Twice Sartore flew the entire length of the North Slope in a Piper Cub, and his photographs captured vast landscapes where few humans were found.

It was the largest intact wilderness left in the United States, but only the 19-million-acre ANWR and parts of the 23-million-acre National Petroleum Reserve were really protected. And 48 billion barrels of oil underlay it all. Oil companies around Prudhoe Bay were expanding operations, and drilling leases had jumped dramatically since 2001.

The energy versus wildlife debate was so important that to "sort matters out for ourselves," Editor Chris Johns noted in the May 2006 *National Geographic,* "we sent writer Joel Bourne and photographer Joel Sartore to the North Slope for an in-depth look. They spent months in remote locations. They listened to a broad range of voices. The result of their diligence is a compelling story that illuminates a landscape at risk."

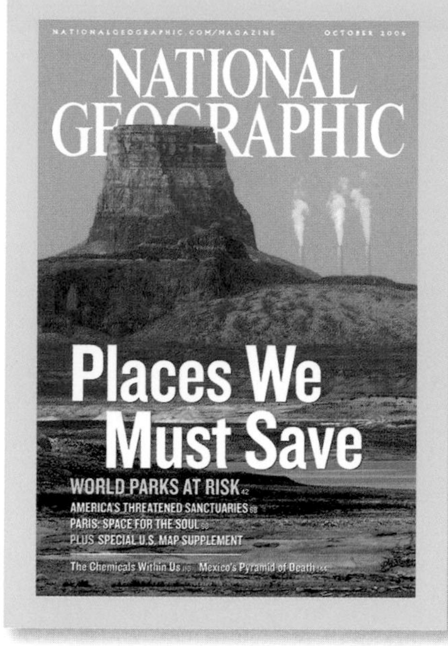

OCTOBER | MICHAEL MELFORD

▲ **PARKS AT RISK** A coal-burning power plant mars the scenic beauty of Glen Canyon National Recreation Area, one of many parks and sanctuaries imperiled worldwide. Writing in this issue, naturalist George Schaller urged every country to keep part of its natural heritage untouched, "as a record for the future, a baseline to measure change" and so that "people can see the splendor of their past, before the land was degraded."

◀ **MAY** | **JOEL SARTORE** A polar bear feeds on a bowhead whale carcass on Alaska's North Slope.

NATIONALGEOGRAPHIC.COM/MAGAZINE FEBRUARY 2007

NATIONAL GEOGRAPHIC

Healing the Heart

Beauty on the Border 66 **Curse of Nigerian Oil** 88
Hawaii's Unearthly Worms 118 **Forests of the Tide** 132

FEBRUARY | ROBERT CLARK This specimen of a human heart was photographed in a medical museum.

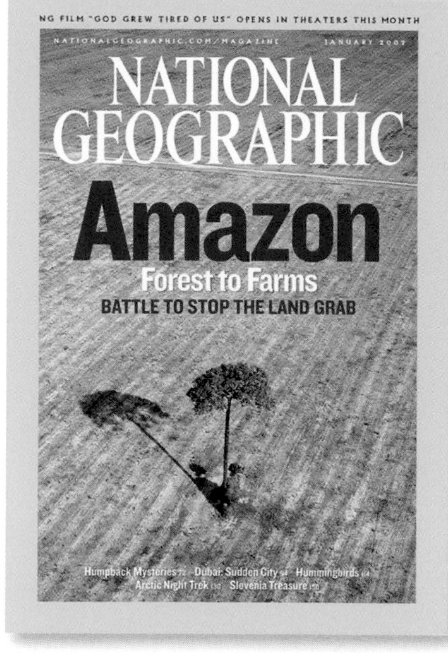

JANUARY | ALEX WEBB

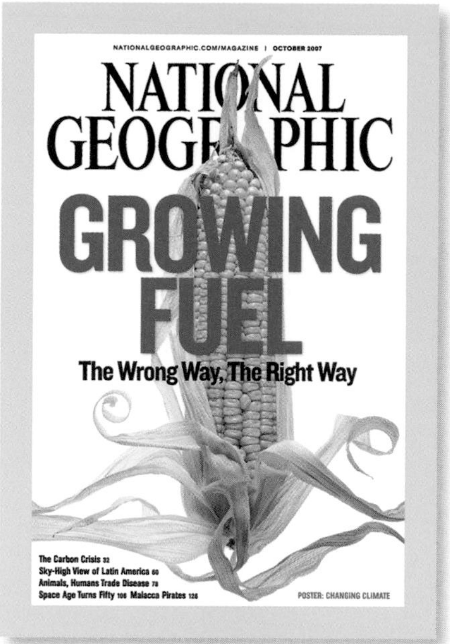

OCTOBER | ROBERT CLARK

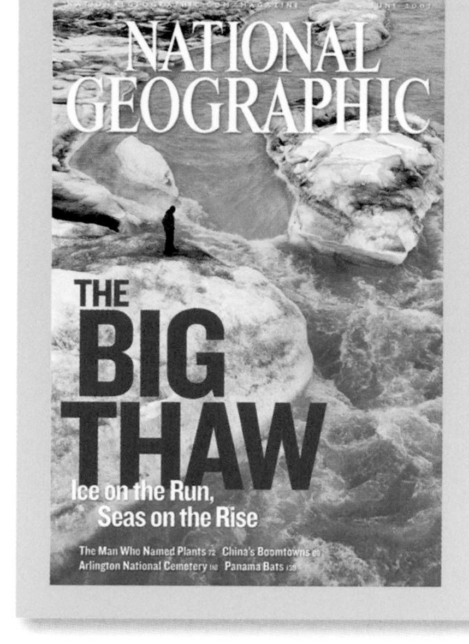

JUNE | JAMES BALOG

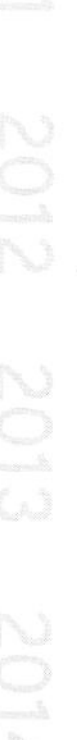

BROKEN HEARTS

Although his cover shot depicted a specimen in a medical museum, Robert Clark was given three minutes to photograph a live and beating human heart just before it was transplanted into a patient. "In that moment, I realized how lucky I am to have this job. Very few people would have had that kind of opportunity," he recalled. He then decided to lose some weight and start jogging.

> Contrary to the clogged pipes model, heart attacks generally occur in arteries that have minimal or moderate blockage, and their occurrence depends more on the kind of plaque than on the quantity . . . But understanding the root cause of the disease will require much more research. For one thing, human hearts, unlike plumbing fixtures, are not stamped from a mold. Like the rest of our body parts, they are products of our genes.
>
> *—From "Healing the Heart," Jennifer Kahn*

▲ **GOING . . .** Meltwater not only drains from a Greenland glacier but also undermines it, loosening ice from bedrock and speeding the glacier that much faster to the sea. Photographer James Balog's two-year coverage of melting ice, published in the June 2007 issue, spurred him to create the Extreme Ice Survey. This wide-ranging program has placed dozens of cameras—secured with anchors and guide wires—at selected glaciers around the world. Each camera makes thousands of time-lapse frames a year to provide an unprecedented photographic record of the rate of glacial retreat.

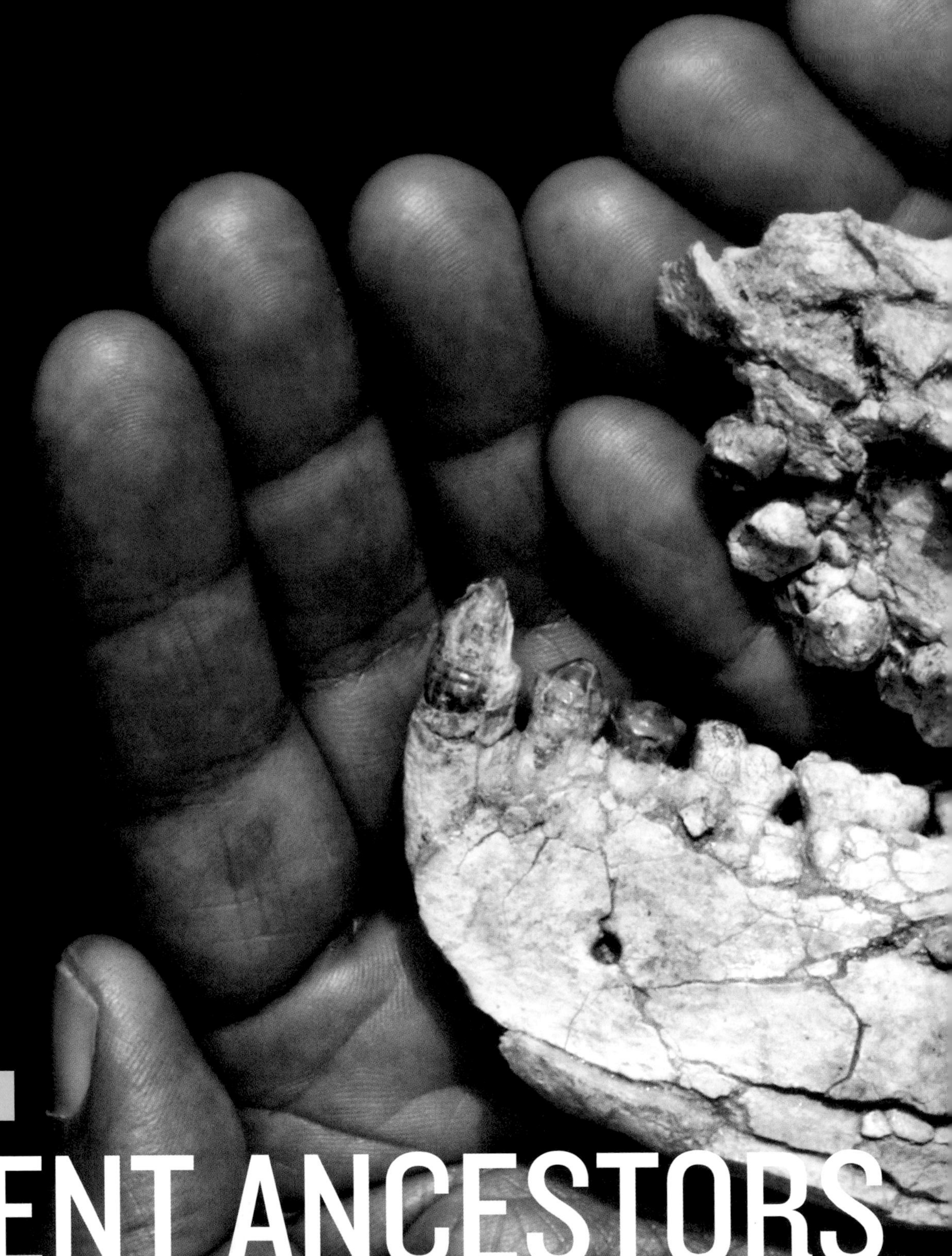

ONE STORY, MANY COVERS

ANCIENT ANCESTORS

▲ JULY 2010 | TIM D. WHITE
Teeth of *Ardipithecus ramidus* suggest an omnivorous diet less specialized than that of today's great apes.

PERHAPS THE EERIEST COVER ever to appear on *National Geographic* featured November 1985's hologram image of the 2.5-million-year-old Taung skull: It once held the large brain of a child who belonged to a species that might have given rise to humans. The Society began sponsoring paleoanthropologists in 1959, and its growing support of leading figures in the field—especially the Leakeys—has been neatly mirrored by the skulls and depictions of long-extinct hominids that have appeared on the cover.

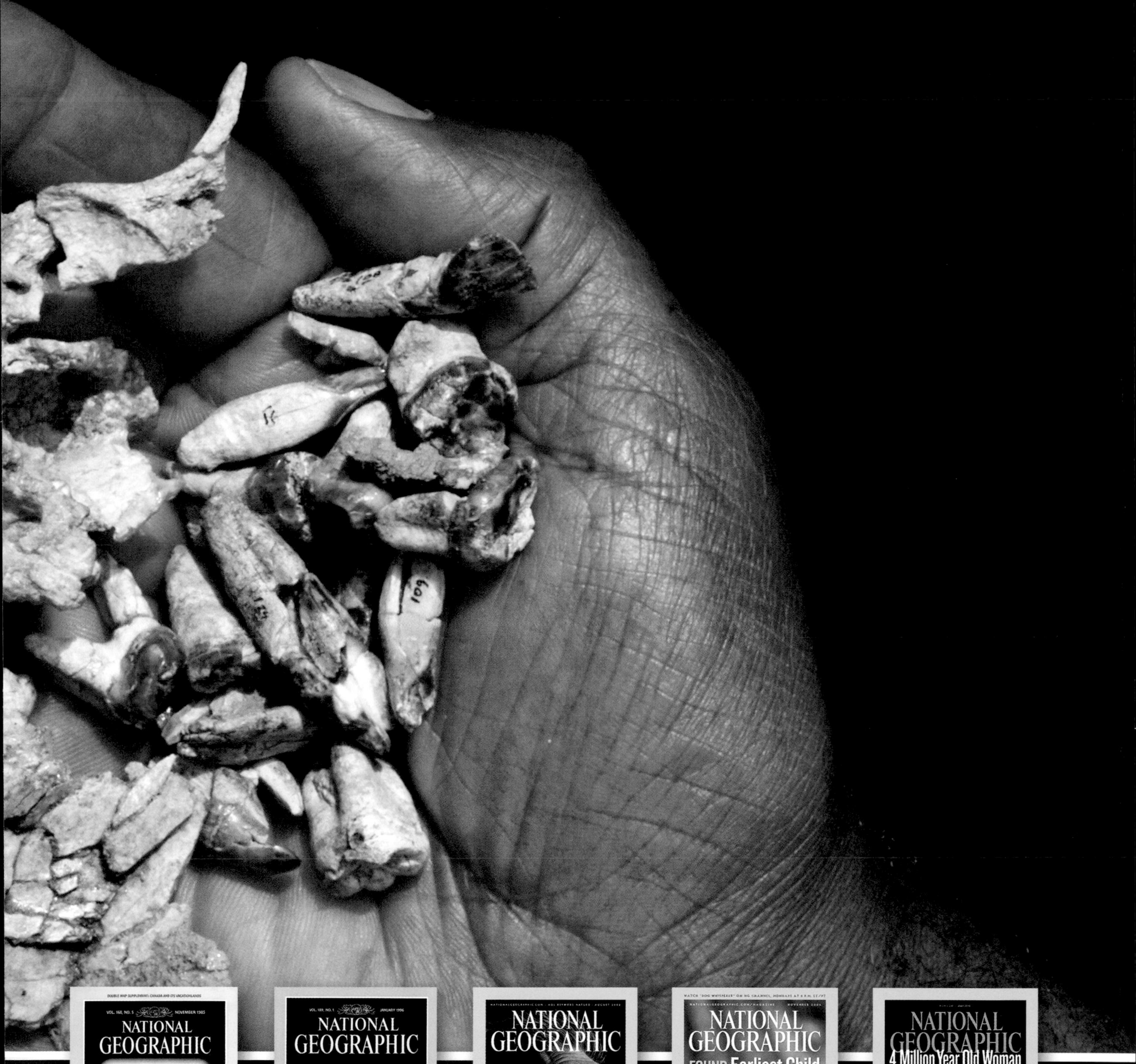

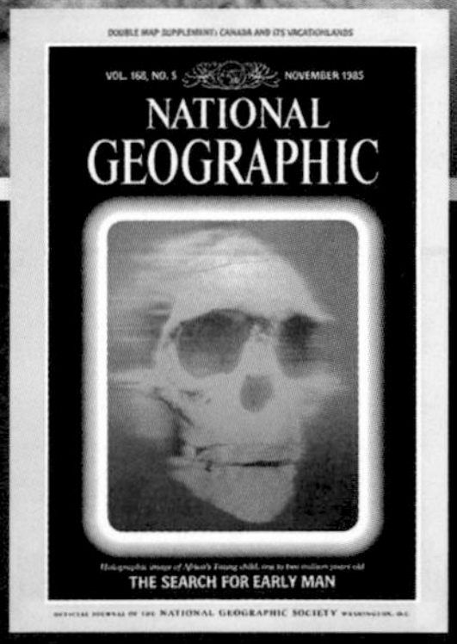

NOVEMBER1985

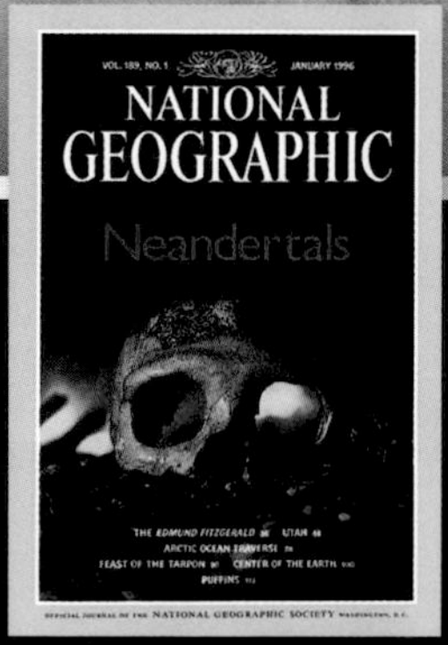

JANUARY1996

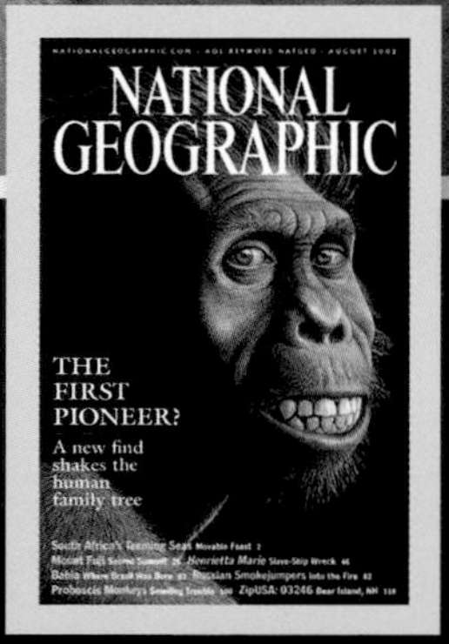

AUGUST2002

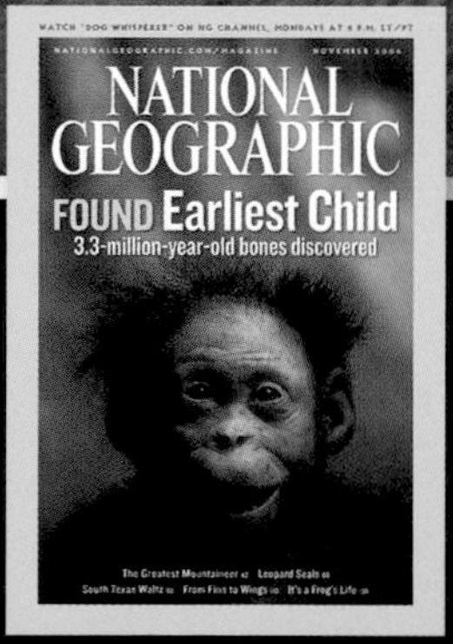

NOVEMBER2006

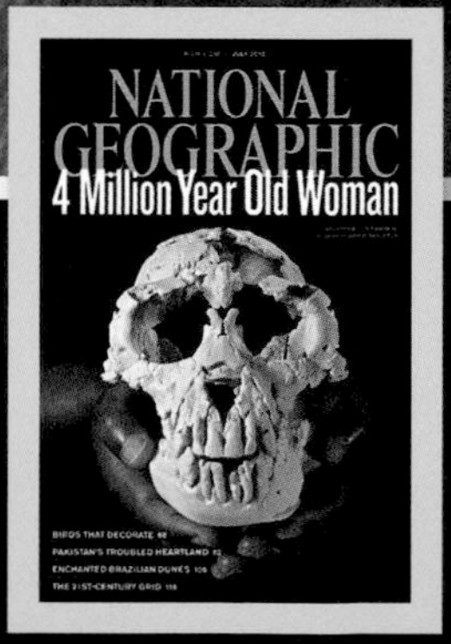

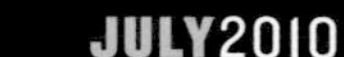

JULY2010

INSIDE ANIMAL MINDS ▶

THAT GLEAM OF INTELLIGENCE in Shanthi the elephant's eye may be a legacy bequeathed to her by generations of ancestors living in the jungles of Sri Lanka, but Vince Musi photographed her in Washington, D.C.'s National Zoo. Assigned to illustrate a story on animal intelligence, Musi opted to make portraits of individuals rather than photograph behavior in the wild.

Asian elephants like Shanthi have long memories and sometimes preen before mirrors. They are only one of the "superstars," as Musi put it, in the world of animal cognition. The photographer also met Uek, a New Caledonian crow and master toolmaker; Azy, an orangutan that communicates thoughts via abstract keyboard symbols; Alex, an African gray parrot that could speak, count, recognize colors, and grasp the concept of zero; Edward, a sheep that could recognize faces and recall them years later; Kanzi, a chimpanzee that understands thousands of spoken words and once played piano with rock musician Peter Gabriel; and Maya, a bottlenose dolphin that was not only a master mimic—imitating human postures—but also tried to drench Musi and his equipment.

Intelligence is more widespread among animals than some scientists had once imagined. "Indeed, Darwin went so far as to suggest that earthworms are cognitive beings," wrote Virginia Morell in the article. She also quoted Clive Wynne of the University of Florida, who has studied cognition in pigeons and marsupials. "We're glimpsing intelligence throughout the animal kingdom, which is what we should expect," he said. "It's a bush, not a single-trunk tree with a line leading only to us."

MARCH 2008 | VINCENT J. MUSI

▲ **GOOD DOG!** Betsy is a border collie living in Vienna, Austria. Not only does she understand 340 words, and counting, but she can also associate names with objects faster than a great ape can. Show her a photograph of a Frisbee, and she'll run off and retrieve the real thing. "She's a dog in a human [pack]," says her owner. "We're learning her language, and she's learning ours."

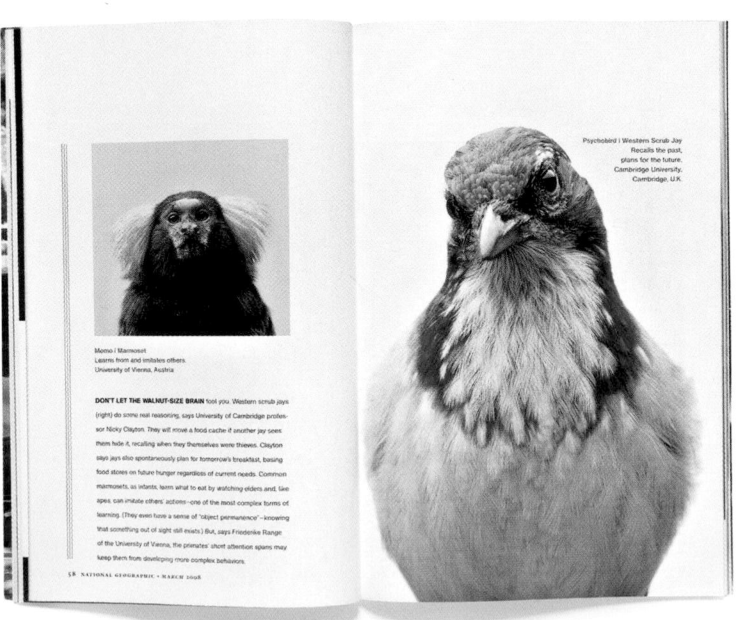

Momo | Marmoset
Learns from and imitates others.
University of Vienna, Austria

DON'T LET THE WALNUT-SIZE BRAIN fool you. Western scrub jays (right) do some real reasoning, says University of Cambridge professor Nicky Clayton. They will move a food cache if another jay sees them hide it, recalling when they themselves were thieves. Clayton says jays also spontaneously plan for tomorrow's breakfast, basing food stores on future hunger regardless of current needs. Common marmosets, as infants, learn what to eat by watching elders and, like apes, can imitate others' actions—one of the most complex forms of learning. (They even have a sense of "object permanence"—knowing that something out of sight still exists.) But, says Friederike Range of the University of Vienna, the primates' short attention spans may keep them from developing more complex behaviors.

58 NATIONAL GEOGRAPHIC • MARCH 2008

Psychobird | Western Scrub Jay
Recalls the past,
plans for the future.
Cambridge University,
Cambridge, U.K.

◀ MARCH 2008 | VINCENT J. MUSI Momo the marmoset and Psychobird the western scrub jay

▶ MARCH 2008 | VINCENT J. MUSI Shanthi, an Asian elephant, lives in the National Zoo in Washington, D.C.

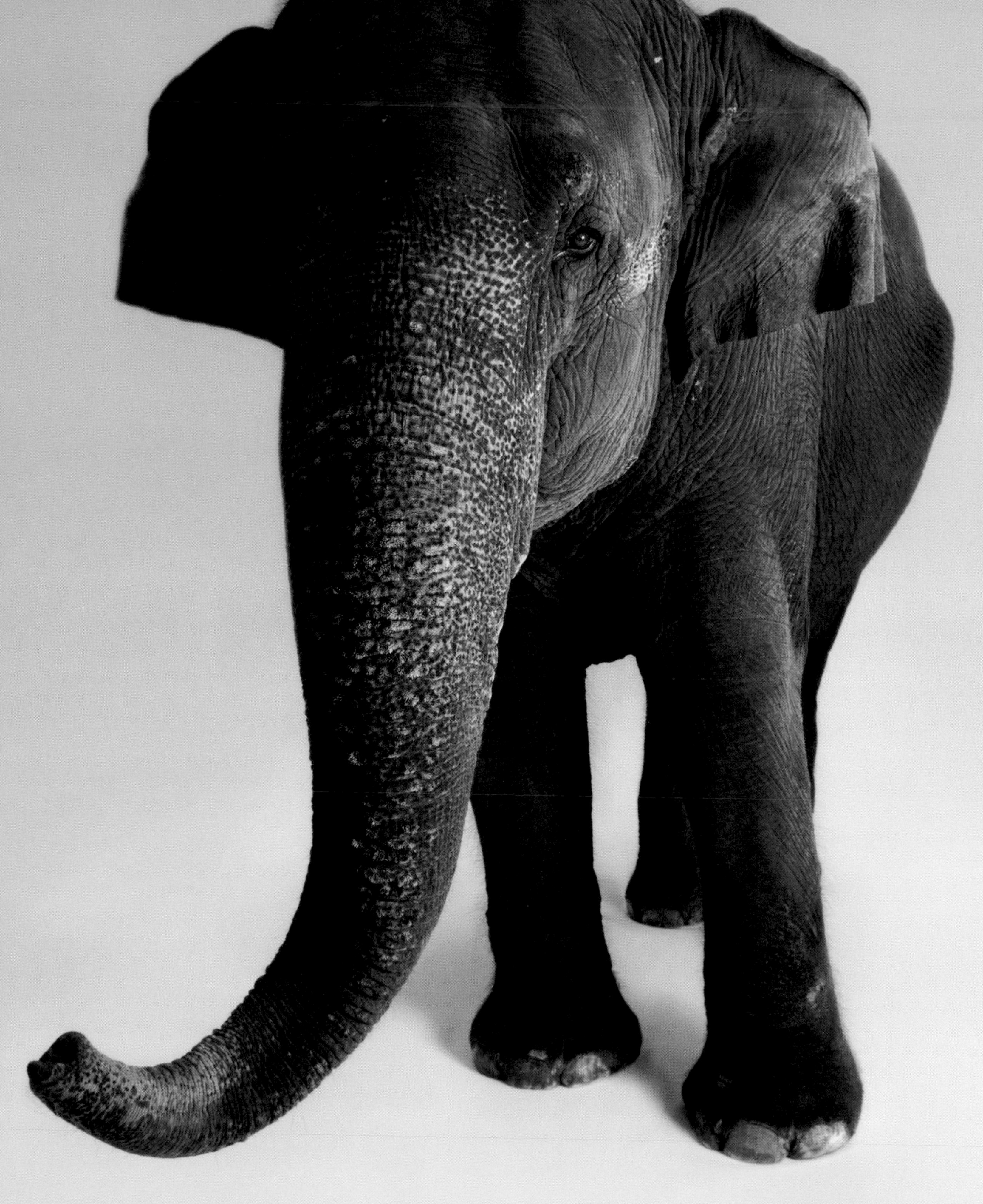

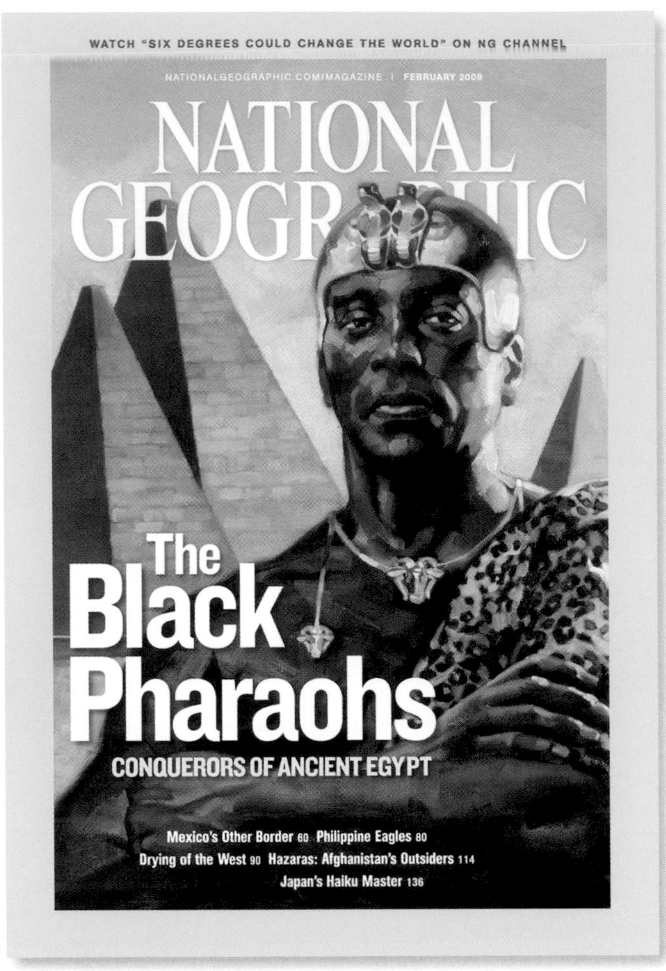

FEBRUARY | GREGORY MANCHESS

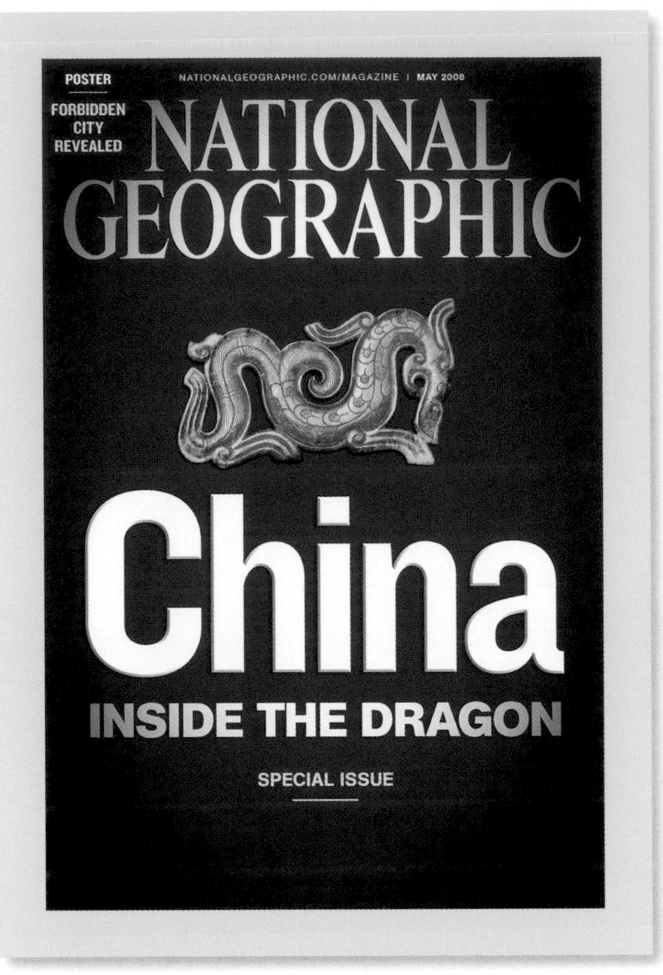

MAY | FREER GALLERY, SMITHSONIAN INSTITUTION

▲ **NUBIAN DYNASTY** Wearing the double *uraeus*—twin cobras of Upper and Lower Egypt—Taharqa, greatest of Egypt's Nubian pharaohs, stands serene and majestic before the kind of pyramids still seen in Meroe, Sudan. For more than a century—770–656 B.C.—this dynasty, hailing from those same regions on the upper Nile, ruled its northern neighbor, Taharqa's own reign lasting for 26 years. When this issue of *National Geographic* was published, much of northern Sudan's priceless archaeological heritage was about to be flooded by the new Meroe Dam.

▲ **DRAGON AGE** A Chinese jade dragon—depicted actual size on the cover—might be 2,500 years old. A new dragon, today's China, is now an economic superpower.

> *"The past decade has seen the rise of something Mao sought to stamp out forever: a Chinese middle class, now estimated to number between 100 million and 150 million people."*
>
> —Leslie T. Chang
> *from "Gilded Age, Gilded Cage"*

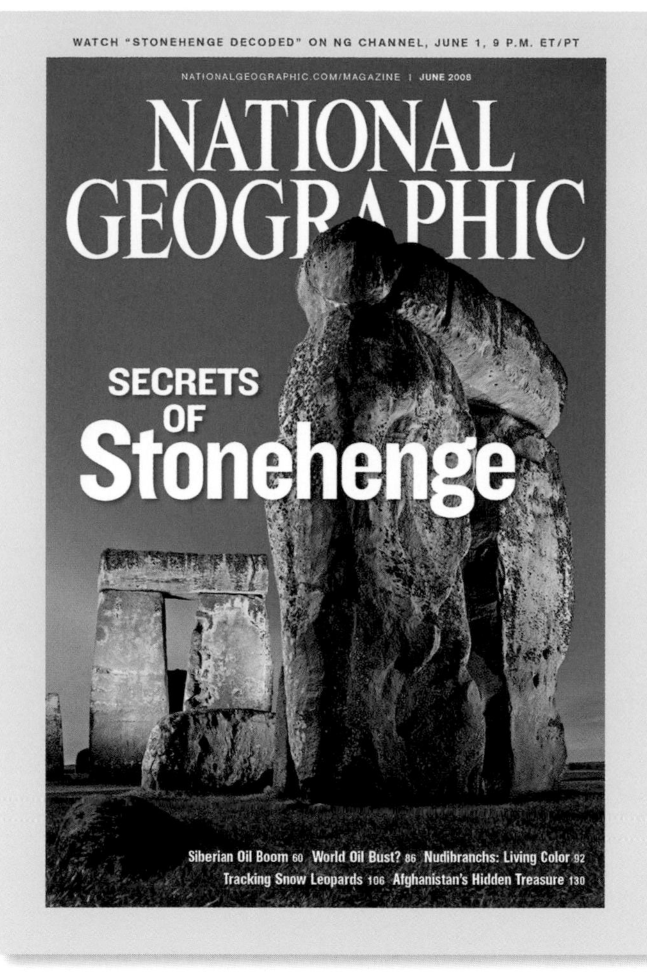

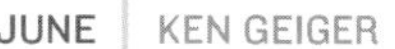

JUNE | KEN GEIGER

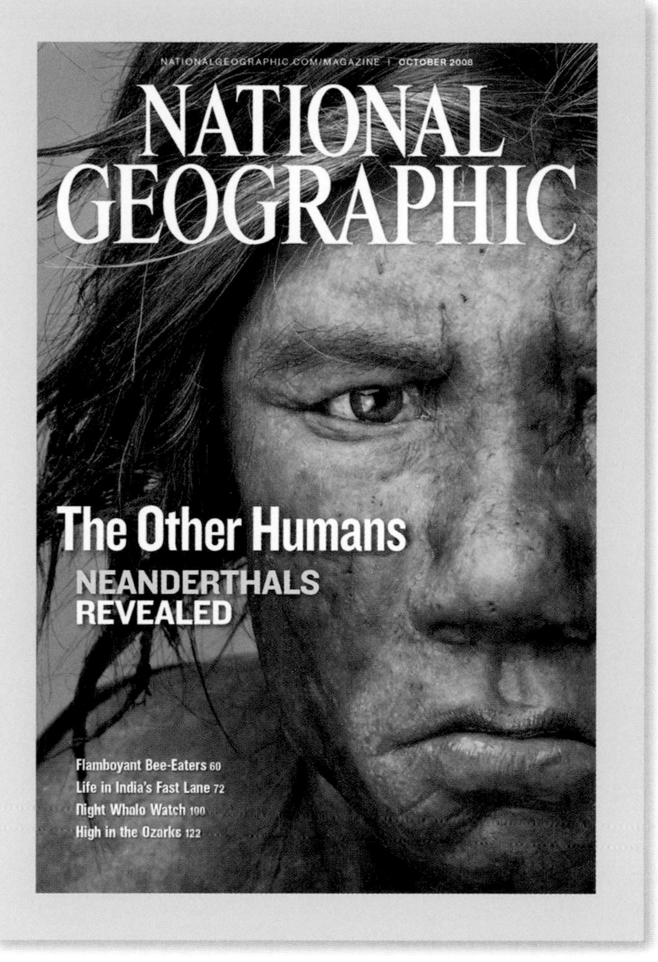

OCTOBER | JOE MCNALLY

▲ **LIGHT OF THE MOON** To illustrate an article on new archaeological finds at Stonehenge, *National Geographic* Deputy Director of Photography Ken Geiger obtained permission to photograph inside the famous English landmark on a night lit by the full moon. He mounted a camera on a tripod, opened its shutter for 15 minutes, and with up-and-down, back-and-forth sweeps "painted" the standing stones with the beam of a high-intensity flashlight.

▲ **ALL TOO HUMAN** She looks like someone who has led a hard life, but appears no less human for it. Only this Neanderthal woman is a reconstruction created by assembling casts of various *Homo neanderthalensis* bones, including some from males. Twin brothers Adrie and Alfons Kennis, both artists, then aspired to emulate a recognizable face. Genetic evidence proves that some Neanderthals had red hair and perhaps freckles. They were stocky and muscular and quite likely possessed language.

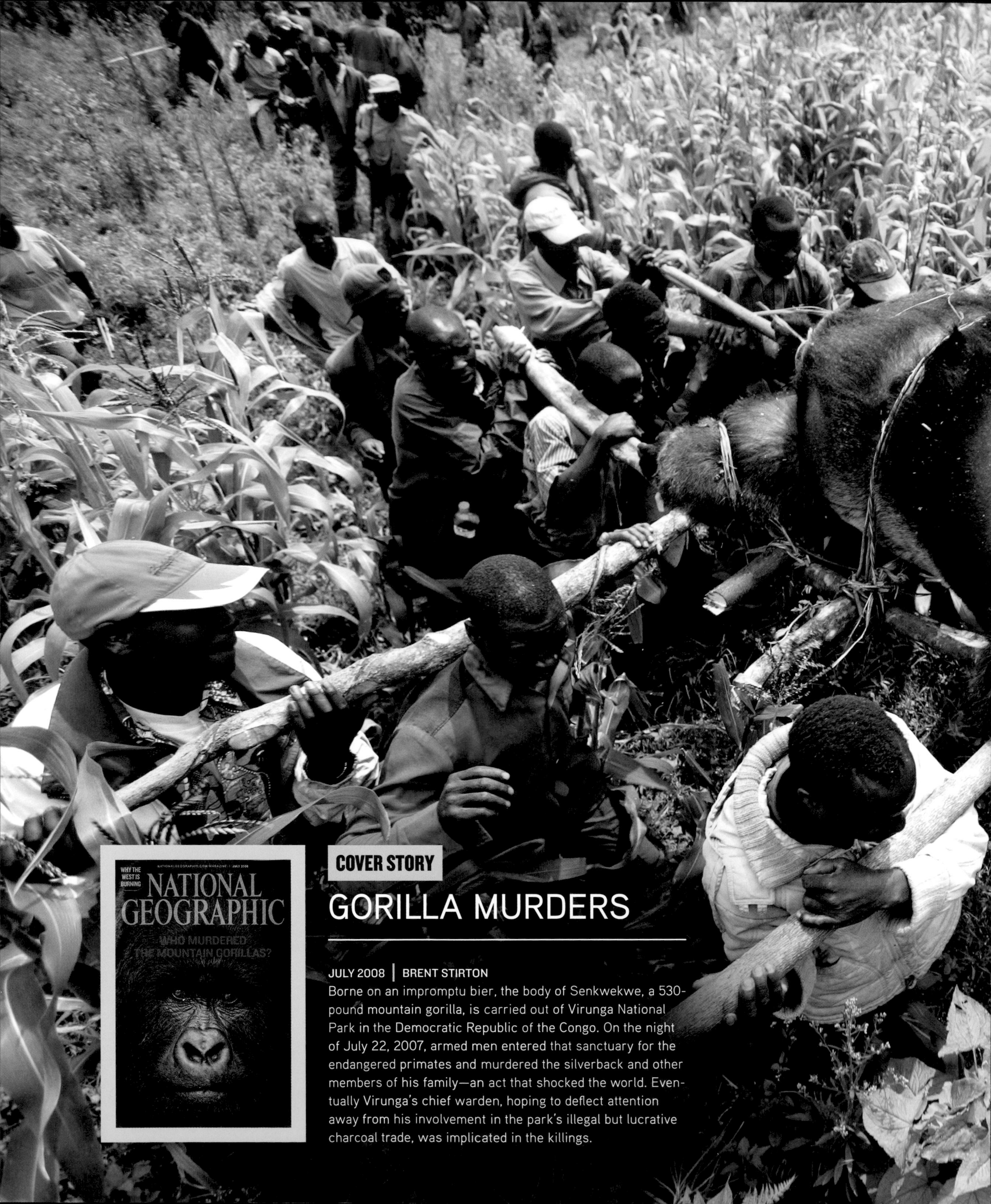

COVER STORY

GORILLA MURDERS

JULY 2008 | BRENT STIRTON

Borne on an impromptu bier, the body of Senkwekwe, a 530-pound mountain gorilla, is carried out of Virunga National Park in the Democratic Republic of the Congo. On the night of July 22, 2007, armed men entered that sanctuary for the endangered primates and murdered the silverback and other members of his family—an act that shocked the world. Eventually Virunga's chief warden, hoping to deflect attention away from his involvement in the park's illegal but lucrative charcoal trade, was implicated in the killings.

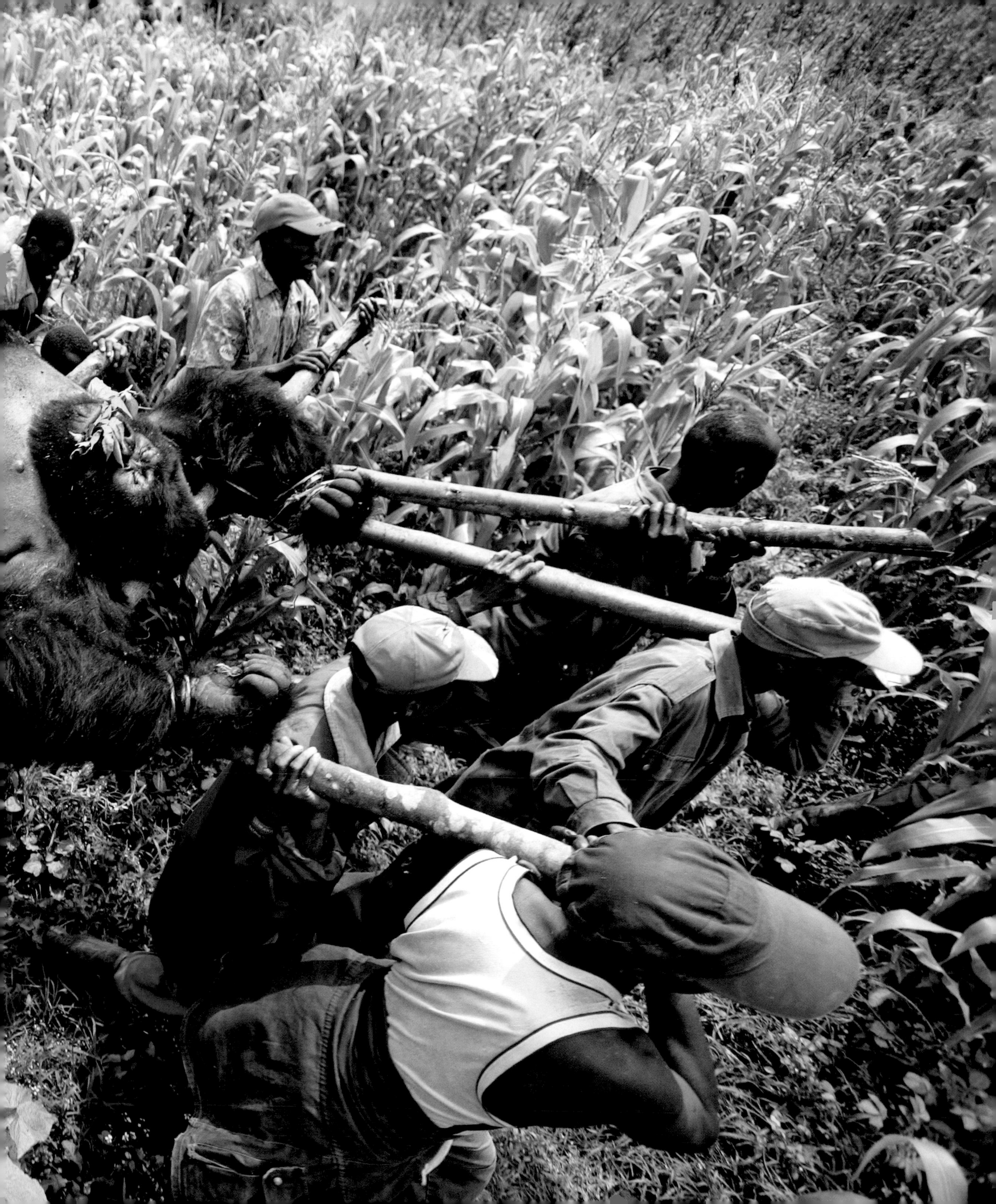

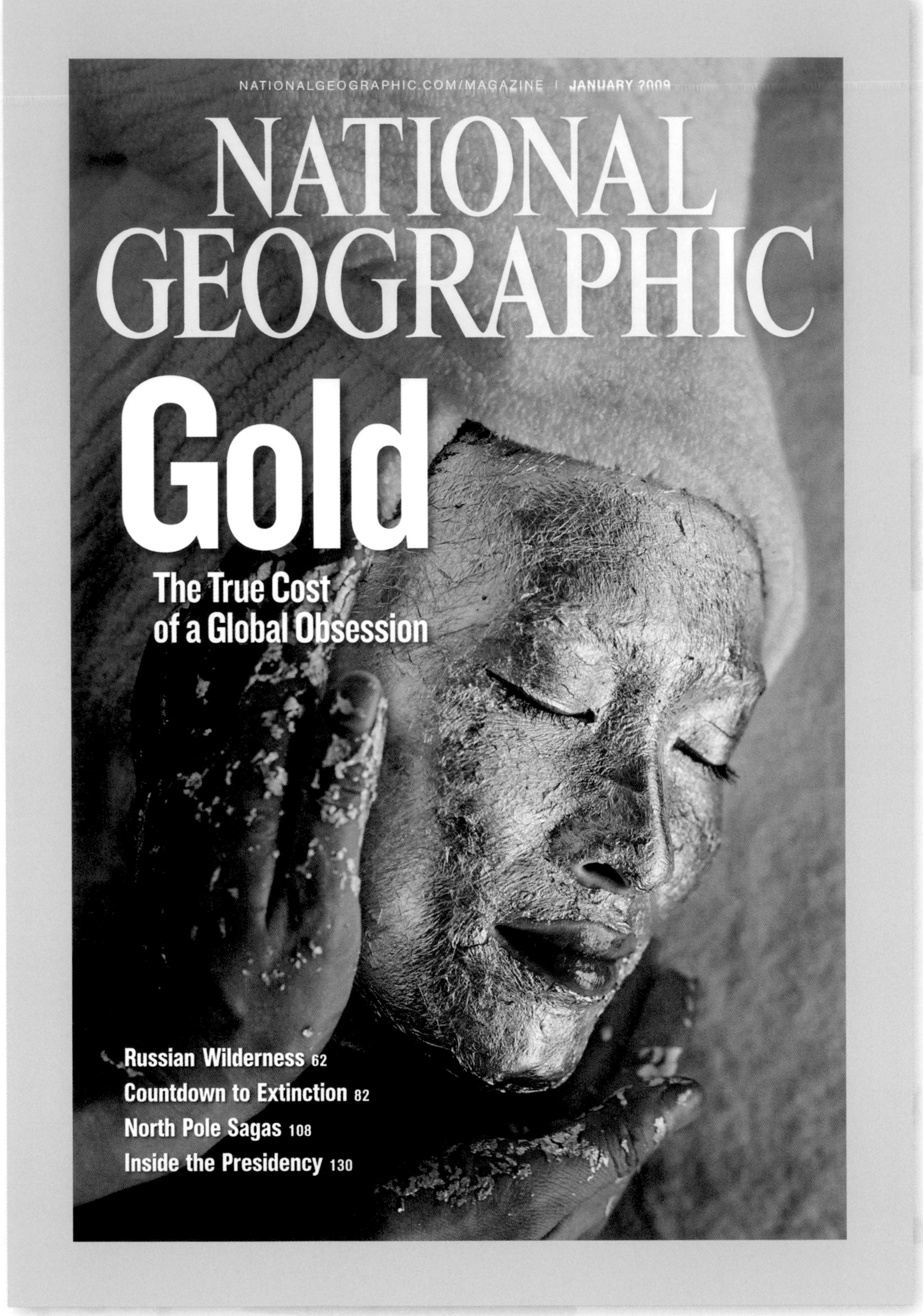

JANUARY | ROBERT CLARK

SOLID-GOLD SKIN CARE The $300 facial being applied to this model's face comes cheap when compared to the real costs being inflicted on desperate miners and their environment by the world's insatiable appetite for gold.

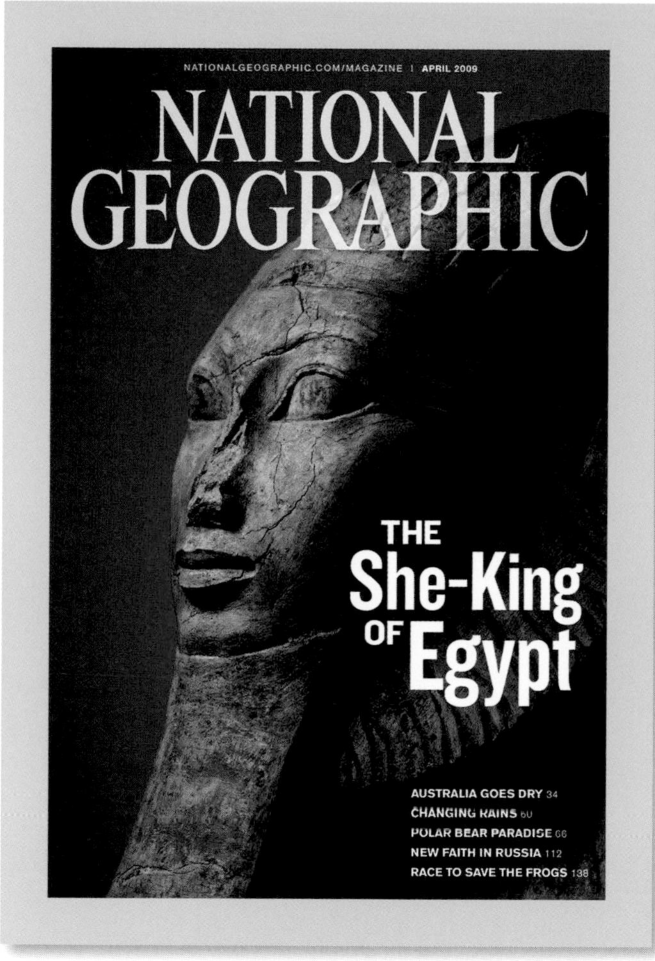

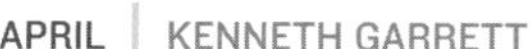
APRIL | KENNETH GARRETT

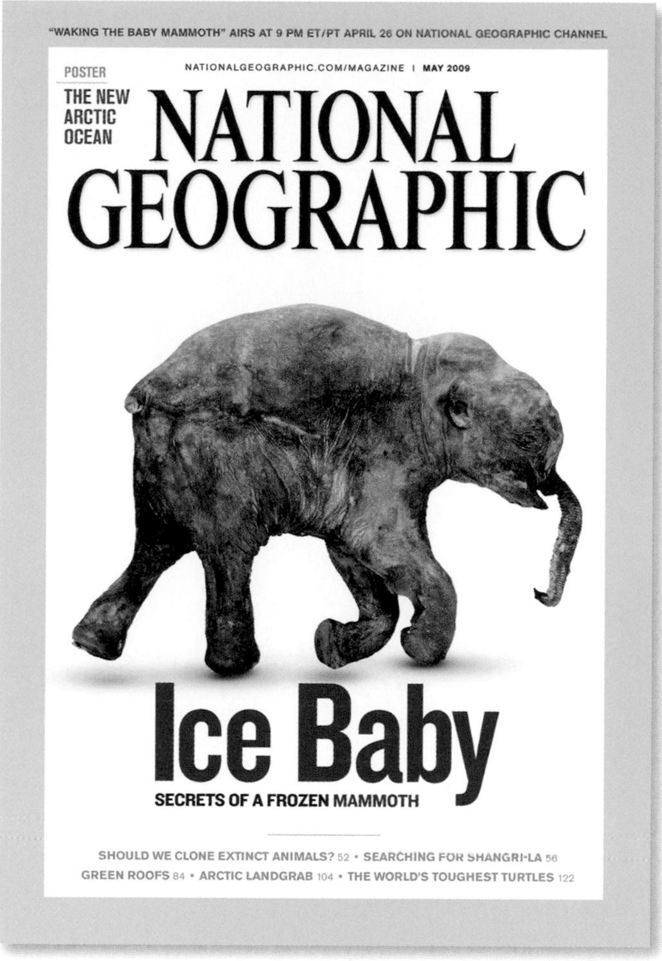

MAY | FRANCIS LATREILLE

▲ **FIT FOR A QUEEN** Crowning a limestone sphinx now in Cairo's Egyptian Museum, an effigy of Queen Hatshepsut wears the false beard and lion mane associated with male pharaohs. Reigning from 1479 to 1458 B.C., she was one of Egypt's most decisive rulers, a warrior and a monument builder who left so many statues of herself behind that they are now found in many of the world's major museums.

▲ **LYUBA'S STORY** Discovered by reindeer herders in Siberia, a one-month-old baby mammoth—frozen for 40,000 years—is the best preserved of the dozen or so mammoths that have been found in Arctic permafrost. Lyuba, as she was named, was missing only her toenails, part of her tail and one ear, and most of her hair, just traces of her undercoat remaining. She probably became mired in and was suffocated by mud.

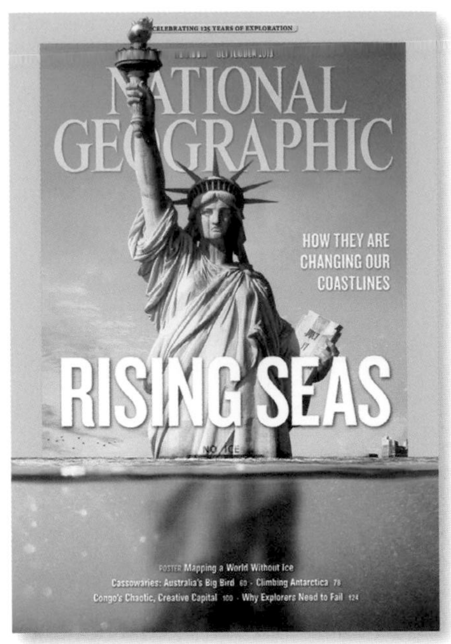

SEPTEMBER 2013 | NICK KALOTERAKIS

2013 ▸▸▸▸ FAST FORWARD

RISING TIDES Four years later, the *Geographic* reported on another impending natural disaster. Thanks to global warming, sea levels are certain to rise, perhaps three to five feet by the end of the century—putting 136 large coastal cities at increased risk of flooding. Should all the planet's ice sheets melt, seas might rise 216 feet, but that would take thousands of years.

WHAT LIES BENEATH ▸

George Steinmetz used a polarizing filter and practically sat on the helicopter's skid when he made this cover shot of Yellowstone's Grand Prismatic Spring. Yet trouble lies beneath the striking iridescence that draws admiring tourists. Since the 1870s geologists have known that Yellowstone lies on top of a massive volcano. It was assumed to be extinct, but new evidence indicates that it might be coming back to life.

So, the colossal question: Is it going to blow again? Some kind of eruption—perhaps a modest one like Mount Pinatubo's in the Philippines, which killed 800 people in 1991—is highly likely at some point. The odds of a full, caldera-forming eruption—a cataclysm that could kill untold thousands of people and plunge the Earth into a volcanic winter—are anyone's guess; it could happen in our lifetimes, or 100,000 years or more from now, or perhaps never. [Geologist] Bob Christiansen, now retired, suspects the supervolcano may be safely bottled up. For most of its history, the Yellowstone hot spot has formed calderas in the thin crust of the Basin and Range area of the American West. Now the hot spot is lodged beneath a much thicker crust at the crest of the Rockies. "I think that the system had more or less equilibrated itself," says Christiansen. Then he quickly adds, "But that's an interpretation that would not stand up in court."

—From "Yellowstone Supervolcano: What Lies Beneath the Park," Joel Achenbach

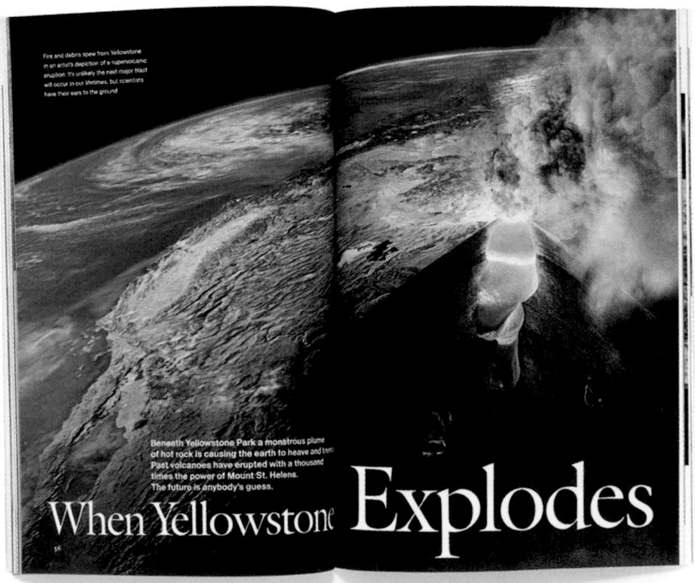

◂ **AUGUST 2009** | **HERNÁN CAÑELLAS** An artist's depiction of the Yellowstone supervolcano erupting

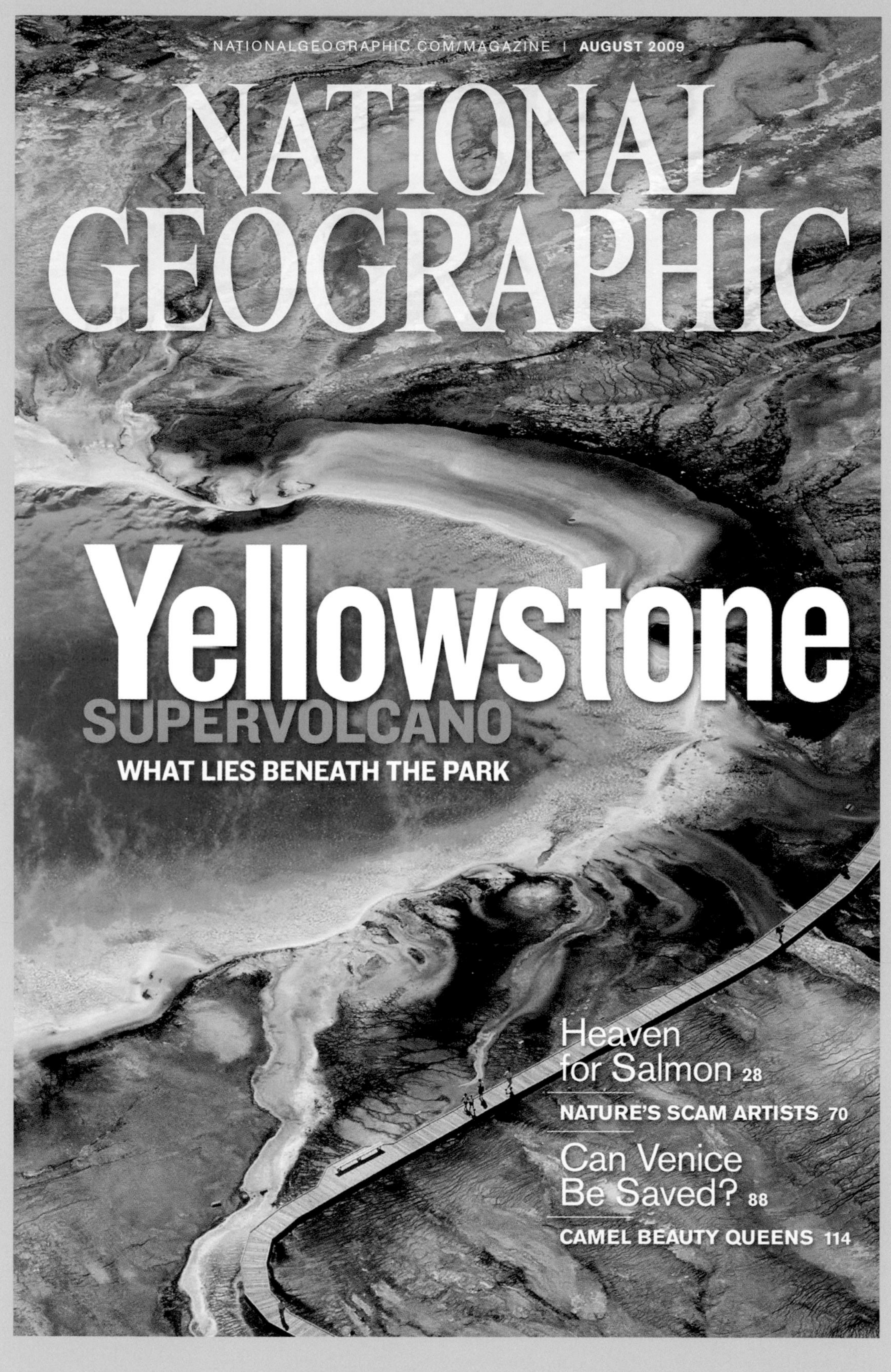

AUGUST | GEORGE STEINMETZ The popular Grand Prismatic Spring in Yellowstone

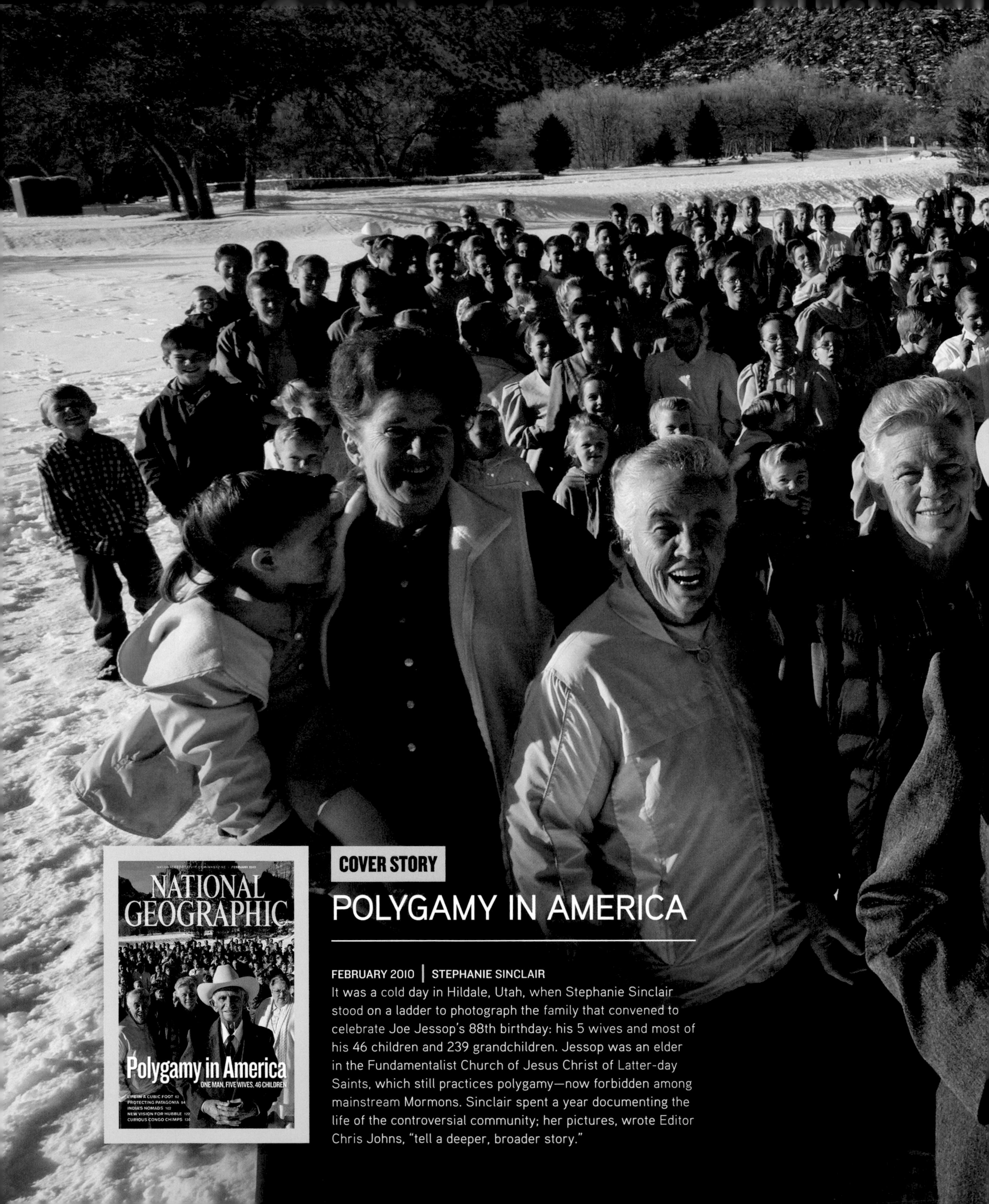

COVER STORY

POLYGAMY IN AMERICA

FEBRUARY 2010 | STEPHANIE SINCLAIR

It was a cold day in Hildale, Utah, when Stephanie Sinclair stood on a ladder to photograph the family that convened to celebrate Joe Jessop's 88th birthday: his 5 wives and most of his 46 children and 239 grandchildren. Jessop was an elder in the Fundamentalist Church of Jesus Christ of Latter-day Saints, which still practices polygamy—now forbidden among mainstream Mormons. Sinclair spent a year documenting the life of the controversial community; her pictures, wrote Editor Chris Johns, "tell a deeper, broader story."

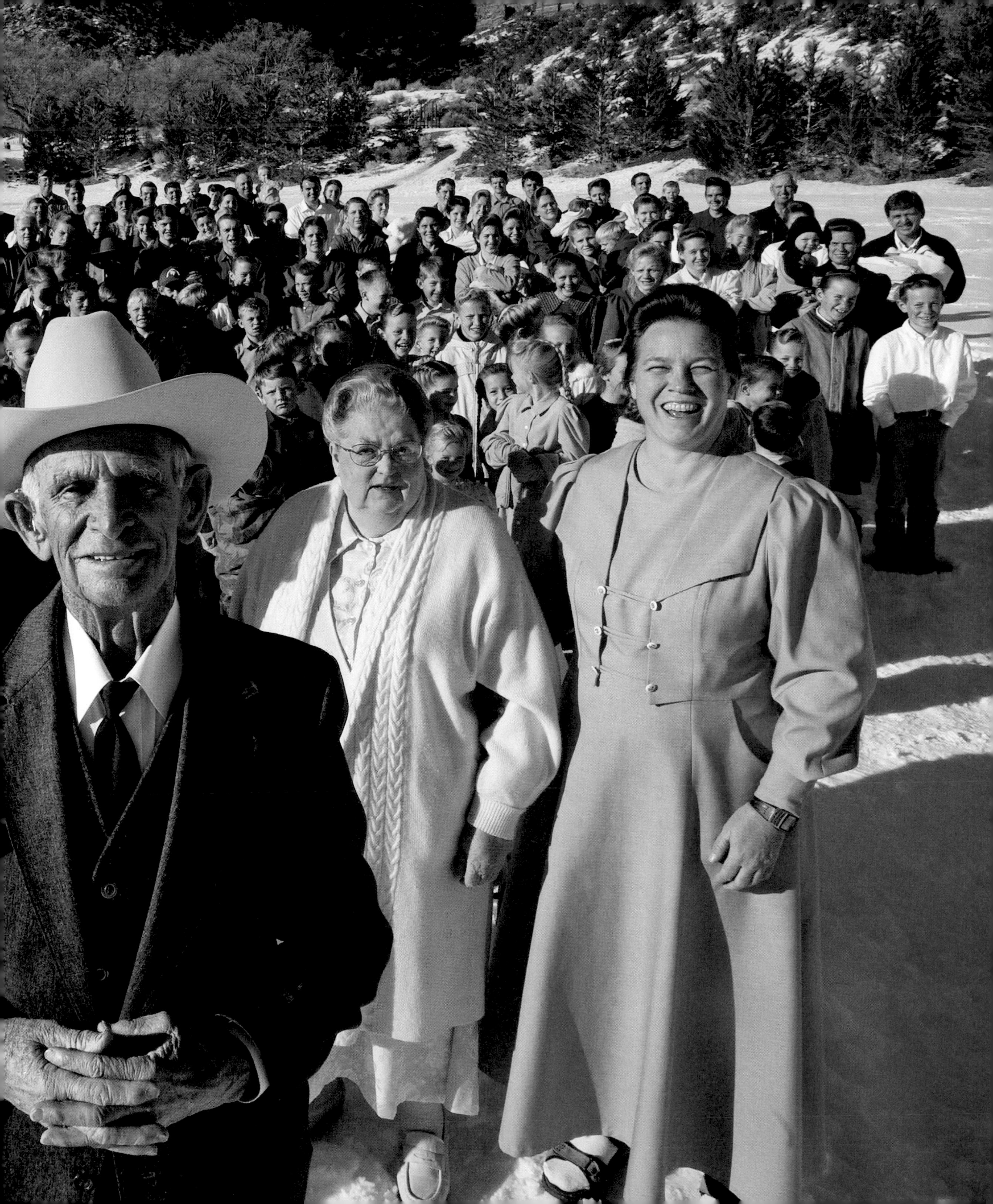

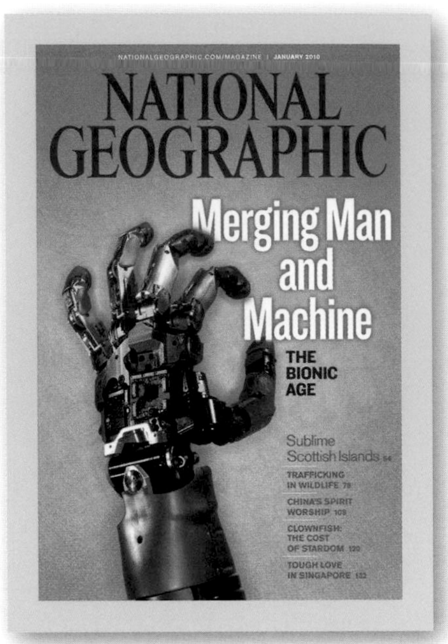

JANUARY | MARK THIESSEN

▲ **CYBORGS** So new that its paint was barely dry when this photograph was made, a prosthetic limb is nearly as dexterous as the real thing.

> *"[E]ven though the flesh and blood may be damaged or gone, the nerves and parts of the brain that once controlled it live on. In many patients, they sit there waiting to communicate—dangling telephone wires, severed from a handset."*
>
> —Josh Fischman
> *from "Merging Man and Machine"*

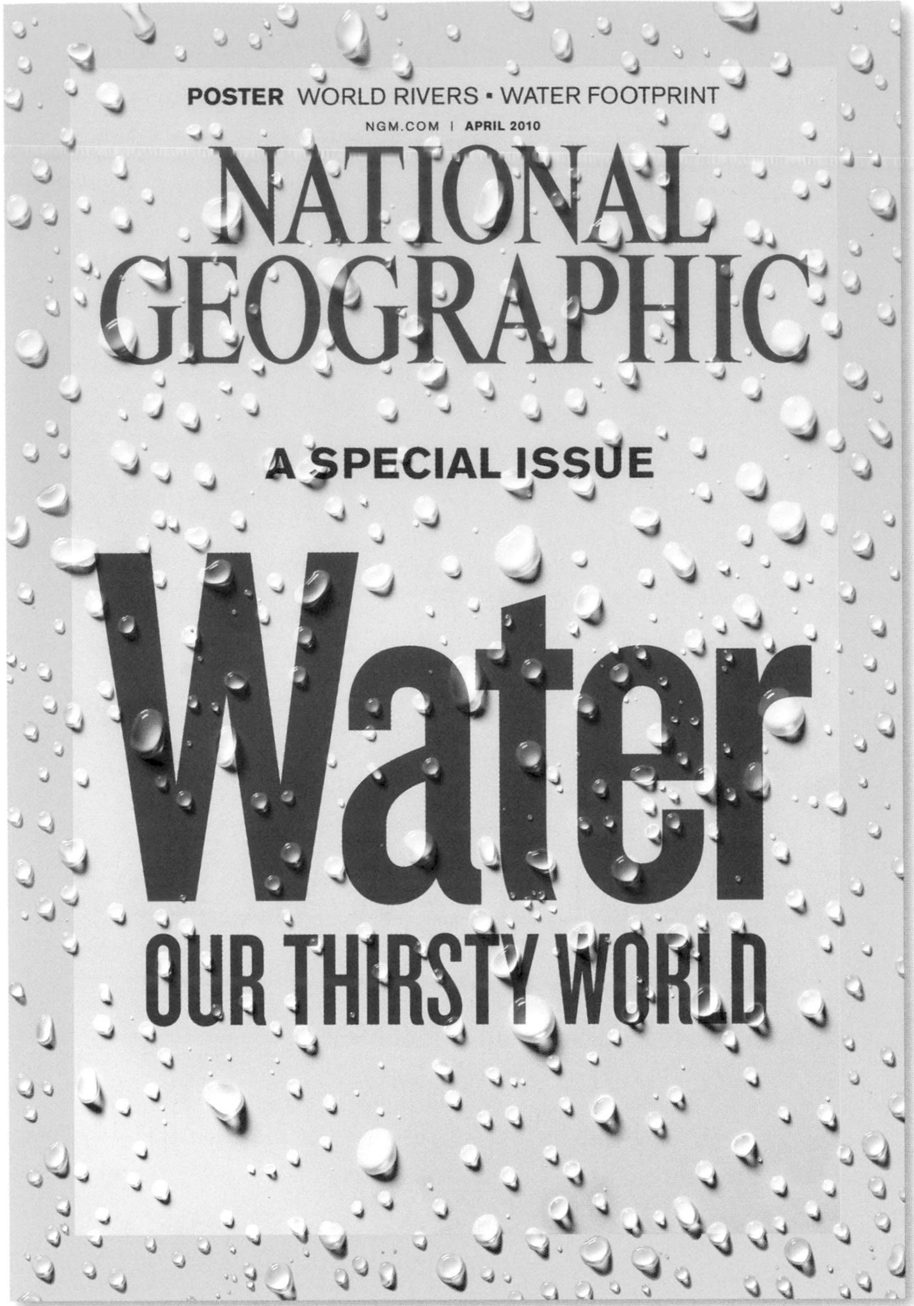

APRIL | MARK THIESSEN

▲ **NOR ANY DROP TO DRINK** Coleridge's Ancient Mariner understood how ironic it would be to die of thirst on a planet where the surface is about 71 percent covered by water—salt water. But as the April 2010 special issue reports, desalinization plants are increasing in numbers so rapidly that before long the equivalent of another Colorado River—13 billion gallons—will be entering the world's water supply every day. Good news, but not good enough when over 300 million Americans are each using about 100 gallons of water a day. You do the math.

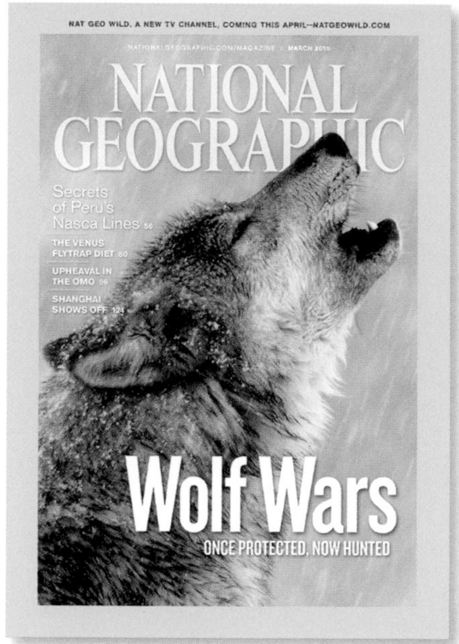

MARCH | JESS LEE

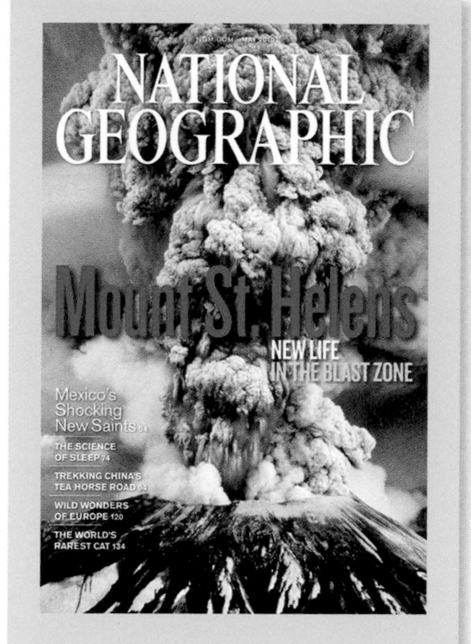

MAY | ROGER WERTH

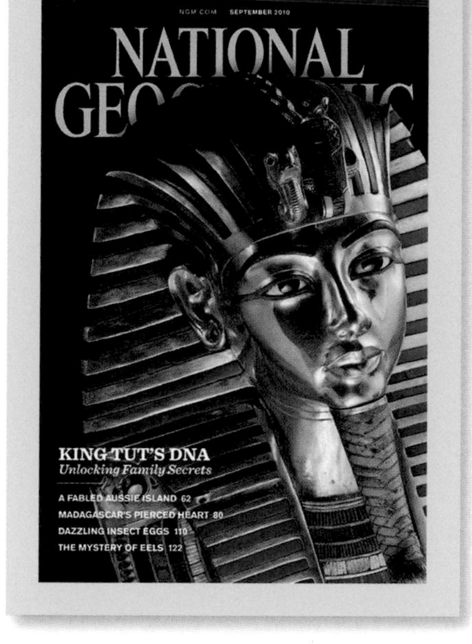

SEPTEMBER | KENNETH GARRETT

THE WORLD'S WATER

EIGHT MAJOR ARTICLES, SIX additional features, and a map supplement—the entire April 2010 *National Geographic* was a special issue devoted to examining the state of the world's water supply. Increasing numbers of people have too little of it; others take its presence for granted, forgetting how miraculous—and essential—it is.

> Water is life. It's the briny broth of our origins, the pounding circulatory system of the world, a precarious molecular edge on which we survive. It makes up two-thirds of our bodies, just like the map of the world; our vital fluids are saline, like the ocean . . . On my desk, a glass of water has caught the afternoon light . . . How can I call it mine when its fate is to run through rivers and living bodies . . . It is an ancient, dazzling relic, temporarily quarantined here in my glass, waiting to return to its kind, waiting to move a mountain.
>
> *—From "Water: Our Thirsty World," Barbara Kingsolver*

▲ **TRICK SHOT** Having persuaded officials at Cairo's Egyptian Museum to let him remove one of their iconic pieces from its glass case—King Tut's 24-pound gold burial mask—Kenneth Garrett tried to make the most of the 90 minutes they gave him to photograph it. But he couldn't adjust the lighting to his liking, missing the luminous sheen he hoped to capture with his medium-format camera. As his last seconds ticked by, he placed a small strobe light just beneath that golden beard. It worked—and the mask was soon back in its case.

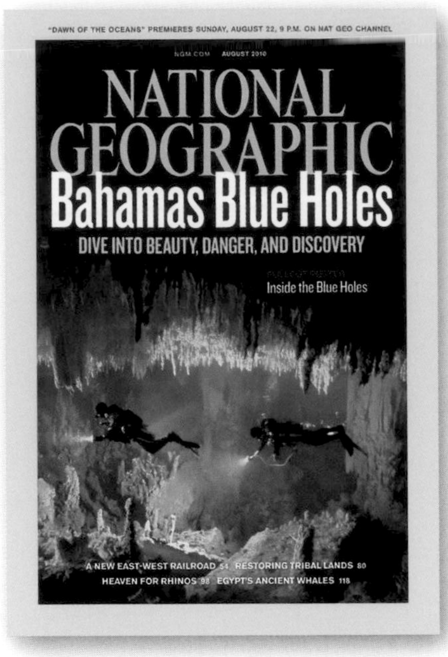

AUGUST 2010 | WES C. SKILES

▲ **UNDERWATER GROTTO** Framed by submarine stalactites and stalagmites, divers swim through the Cascade Room, a chamber found 80 feet beneath the surface of Dan's Cave on Abaco Island. Seven miles of its tunnels had been reconnoitered; no one knew how many more miles remained to be explored. The month this cover appeared, photographer Wes Skiles died while on an underwater assignment in Florida.

BAHAMAS BLUE HOLES ▶

Dean's Blue Hole on Long Island in the Bahamas is Earth's deepest known underwater cave, plunging more than 600 feet into darkness. It is only one of an estimated 1,000 blue holes that pockmark the limestone isles, 80 percent of them unexplored. In late summer 2009 the Bahamas Blue Hole Expedition, led by Kenny Broad, mounted a major effort to study their geology, water chemistry, biology, and archaeology. Its members well knew just how dangerous a task they were facing.

As living laboratories, inland blue holes are the scientific equivalent of Tut's tomb. From a diver's perspective, they're on par with Everest or K2, requiring highly specialized training, equipment, and experience. Even more than high-altitude mountaineers, cave divers work under tremendous time pressure. When something goes wrong, if they don't solve the problem and make it back to the cave entrance before their gas runs out, they're doomed . . .

As long as we follow the rule of thirds (one-third of your total gas going in, one-third coming out, and one-third in reserve for emergencies), we should always have enough to get home—even if one of our tanks or regulators fails. That's assuming we don't lose our guideline. In the labyrinth of passages, separation from the line can be fatal.

—From "Bahamas Blue Holes," Andrew Todhunter

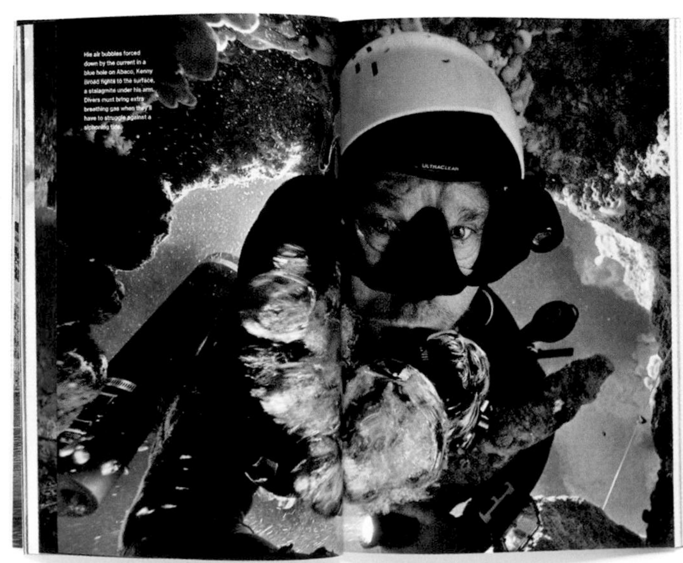

◀ AUGUST 2010 | WES C. SKILES Kenny Broad swims through a blue hole on Abaco Island.

▶ AUGUST 2010 | WES C. SKILES Dean's Blue Hole is the deepest known underwater cave.

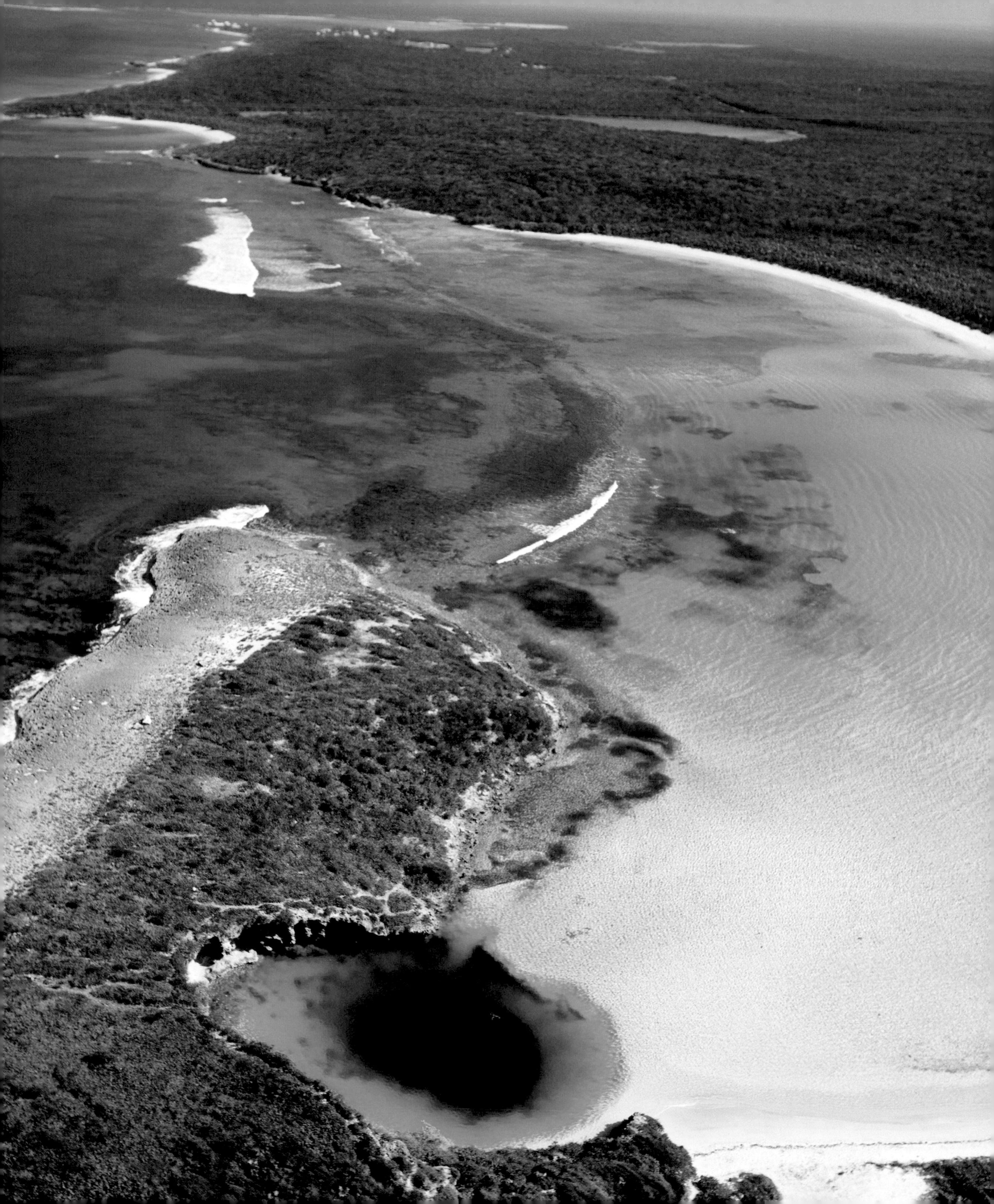

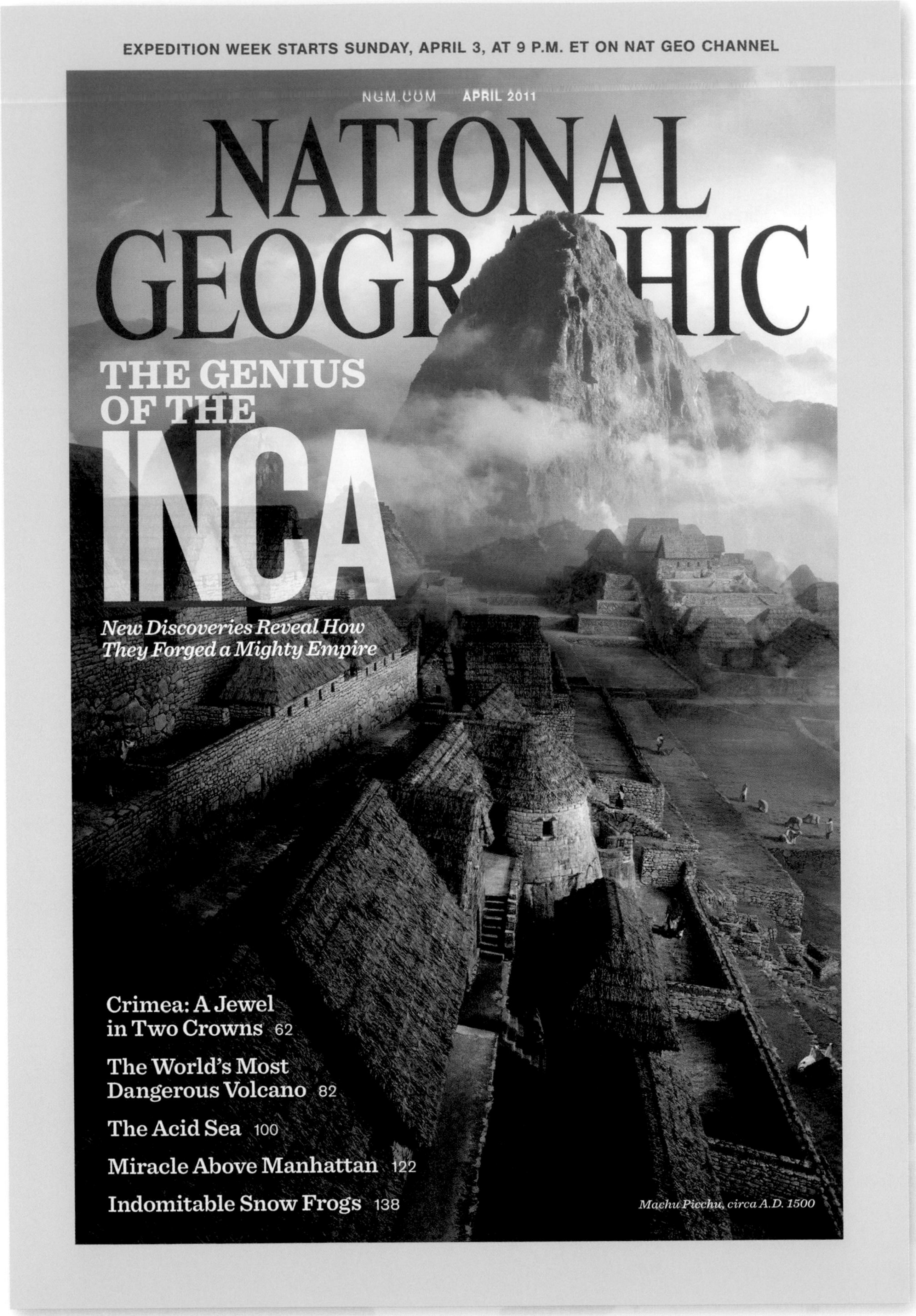

EXPEDITION WEEK STARTS SUNDAY, APRIL 3, AT 9 P.M. ET ON NAT GEO CHANNEL

NGM.COM APRIL 2011

NATIONAL GEOGRAPHIC

THE GENIUS OF THE INCA

New Discoveries Reveal How They Forged a Mighty Empire

Crimea: A Jewel in Two Crowns 62

The World's Most Dangerous Volcano 82

The Acid Sea 100

Miracle Above Manhattan 122

Indomitable Snow Frogs 138

Machu Picchu, circa A.D. 1500

APRIL | DYLAN COLE A digital reconstruction portrays Machu Picchu circa A.D. 1500.

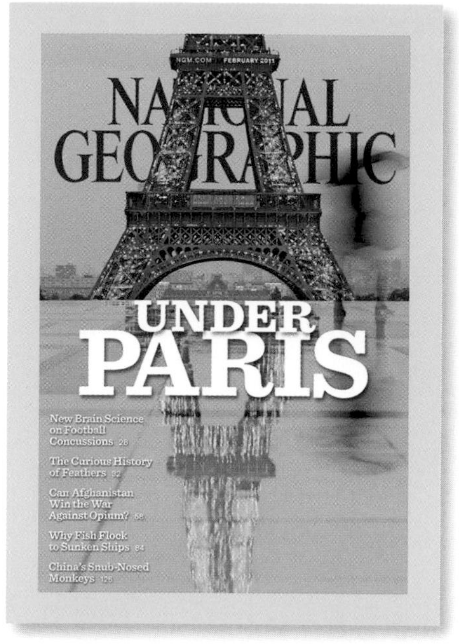

FEBRUARY | FERNAND IVALDI

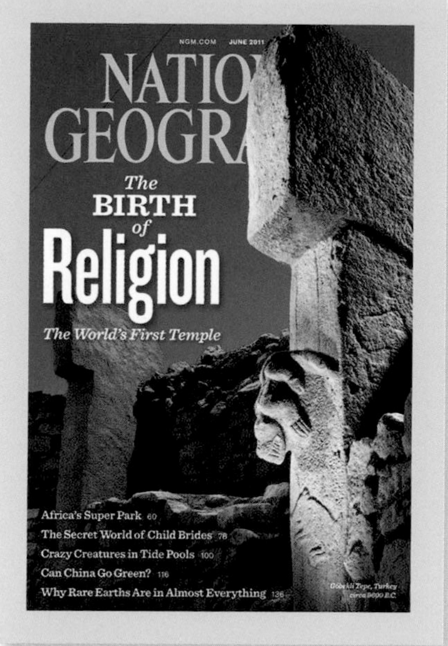

JUNE | VINCENT J. MUSI

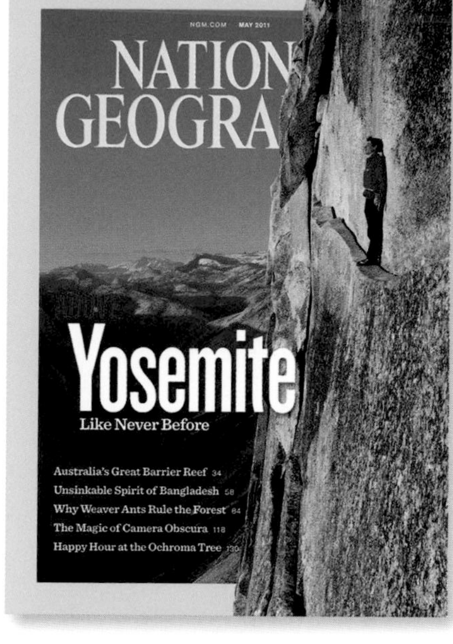

MAY | JIMMY CHIN

▲ **PRECARIOUS PERCH** Alex Honnold faces outward from Thank God Ledge on Yosemite's Half Dome—photographed by a cameraman hanging 3,000 feet in the air himself.

INCA GENIUS

THE DIGITAL RECONSTRUCTION OF Machu Picchu, the celebrated Inca ruins, owes its exceptional realism to the skill of artist Dylan Cole and to insights gleaned by a new generation of archaeologists. But the cover, which shows the site as it probably looked in its heyday, circa A.D. 1500, is also indebted to the efforts of University of Arkansas's Center for Advanced Spatial Technologies. Its researchers brought high-resolution laser scanning instruments to Machu Picchu and, operating largely at night when no tourists were around, created the first comprehensive 3-D data set for the site.

When he learned about that, *National Geographic*'s creative director, Bill Marr, dreamed up a cover illustration based on the 3-D data and put Cole to work. A related video for the iPad edition followed.

> Under Inca rule, Andean civilization flowered as never before. Inca engineers transformed fragmentary road networks into interconnected highways. Inca farmers mastered high-altitude agriculture, cultivating some 70 different native crops . . . And Inca masons raised timeless architectural masterpieces like Machu Picchu.
>
> *—From "The Genius of the Inca," Heather Pringle*

"In the sport of free soloing, which means climbing with only a powdery chalk bag and rock shoes—no rope, no gear, nothing to keep you stuck to the stone but your own belief and ability—doubt is dangerous."

—Mark Jenkins
from "Above Yosemite: Like Never Before"

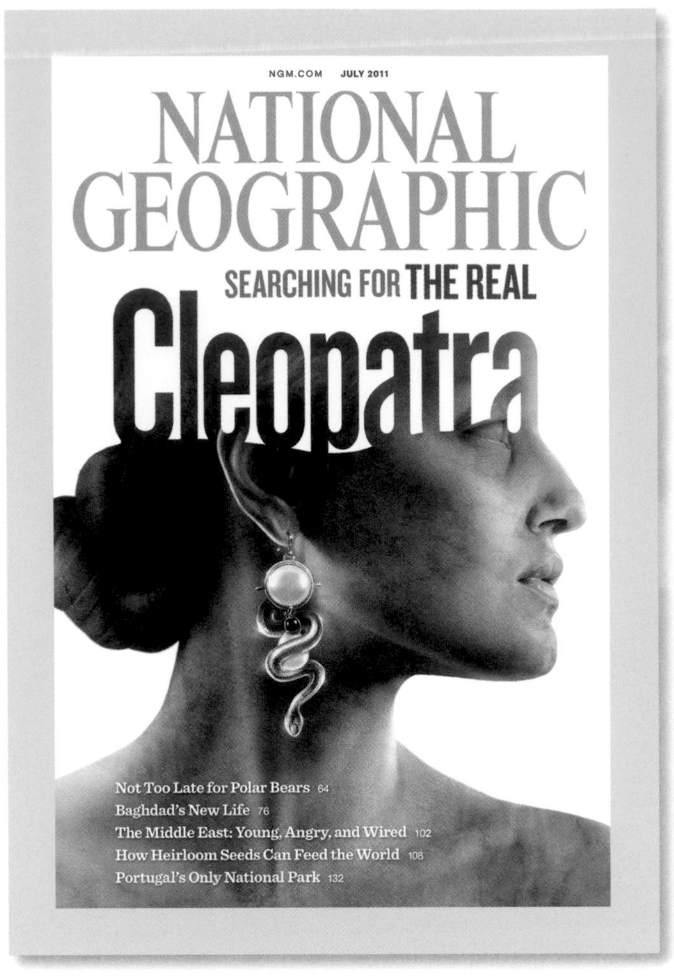

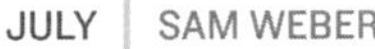
JULY | SAM WEBER

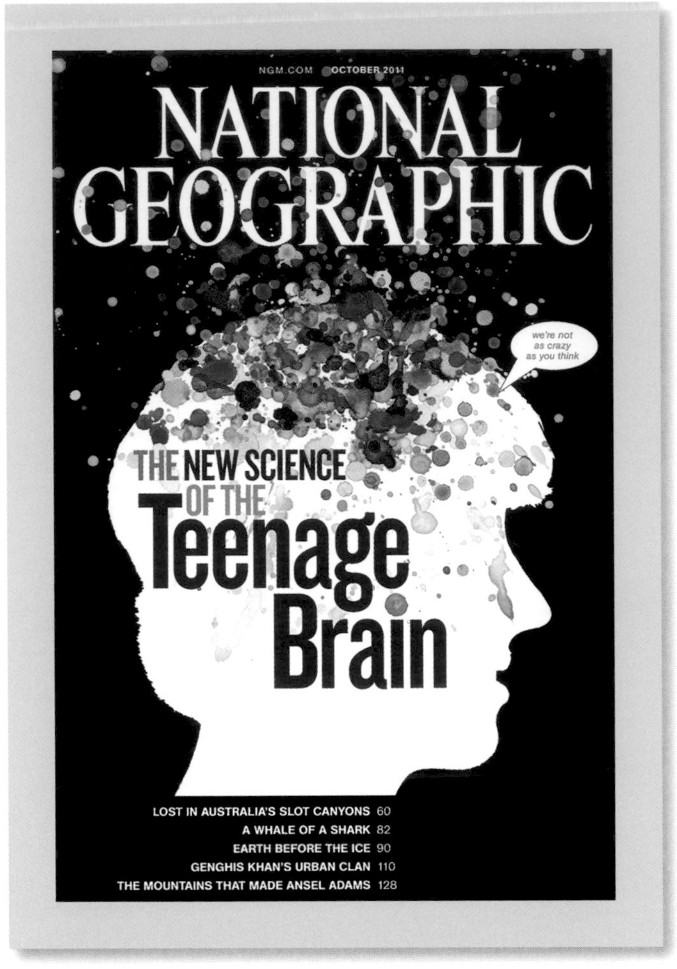

OCTOBER | SAM HUNDLEY

▲ **POWERFUL PERSONALITY** It was said she made her conquests not so much by beauty but rather by wit and charm. Nevertheless, since nobody knows what Cleopatra really looked like, artist Sam Weber used as a model a woman who shared the Egyptian ruler's Mediterranean heritage. The asp earring recalls the legend about her suicide: She applied the snake to her breast.

▲ **SCATTERBRAINED** Many parents would nod affirmatively at this paint-spattered depiction of the typical teenaged brain—one "vibrant and alive and messy," as the October 2011 *National Geographic* puts it. Others might worry more about risk-taking behavior—it peaks during the teen years—but science is showing it makes kids smarter, and in the long run better-adjusted adults.

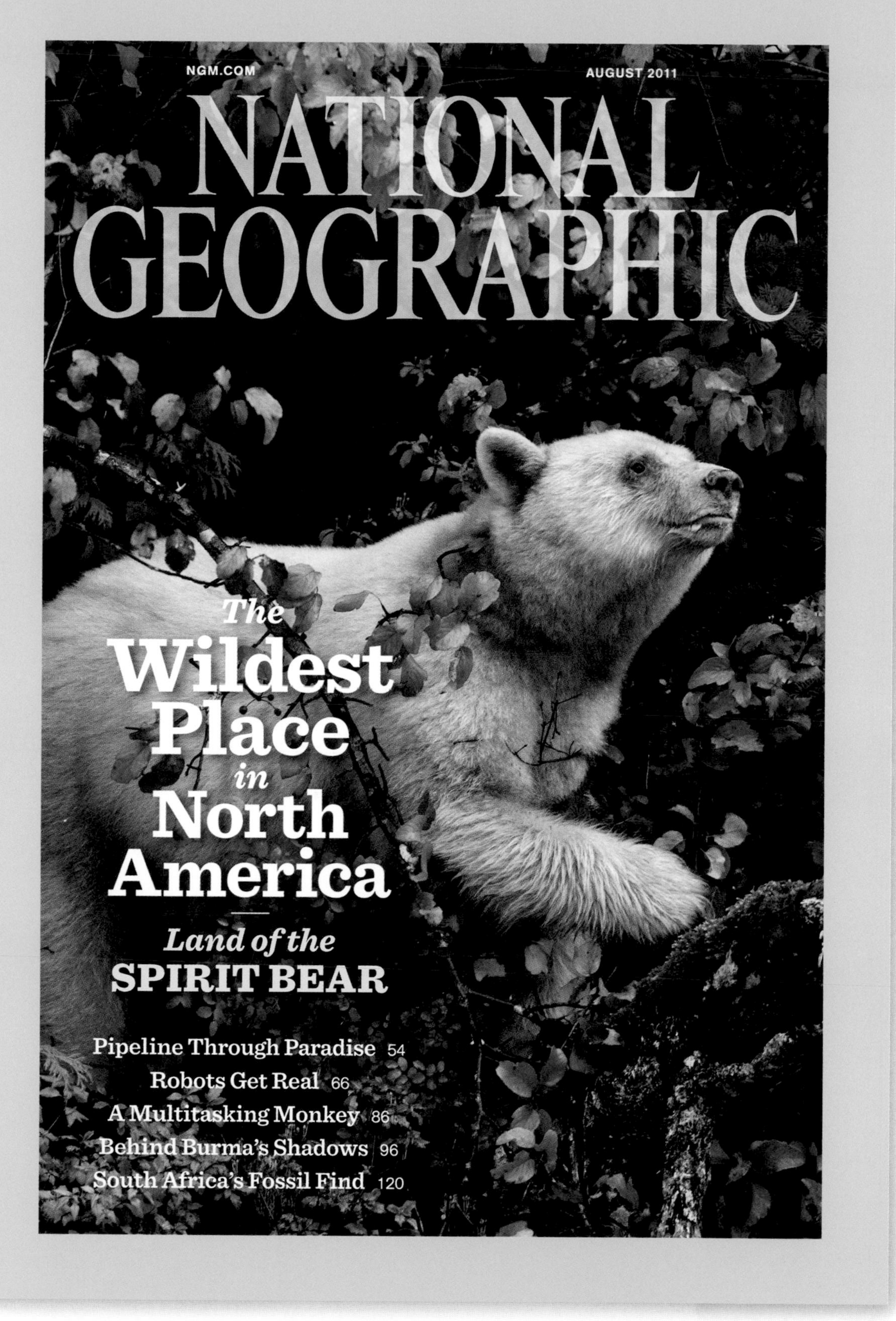

AUGUST | PAUL NICKLEN

SPIRIT BEAR Neither polar bear nor albino, the Kermode, or "spirit bear," is really a black bear with a recessive gene for light-colored coats. Living in the rain forests of British Columbia—where this female found crab apples so abundant she never bothered fishing for salmon—they tolerated photographer Paul Nicklen's proximity.

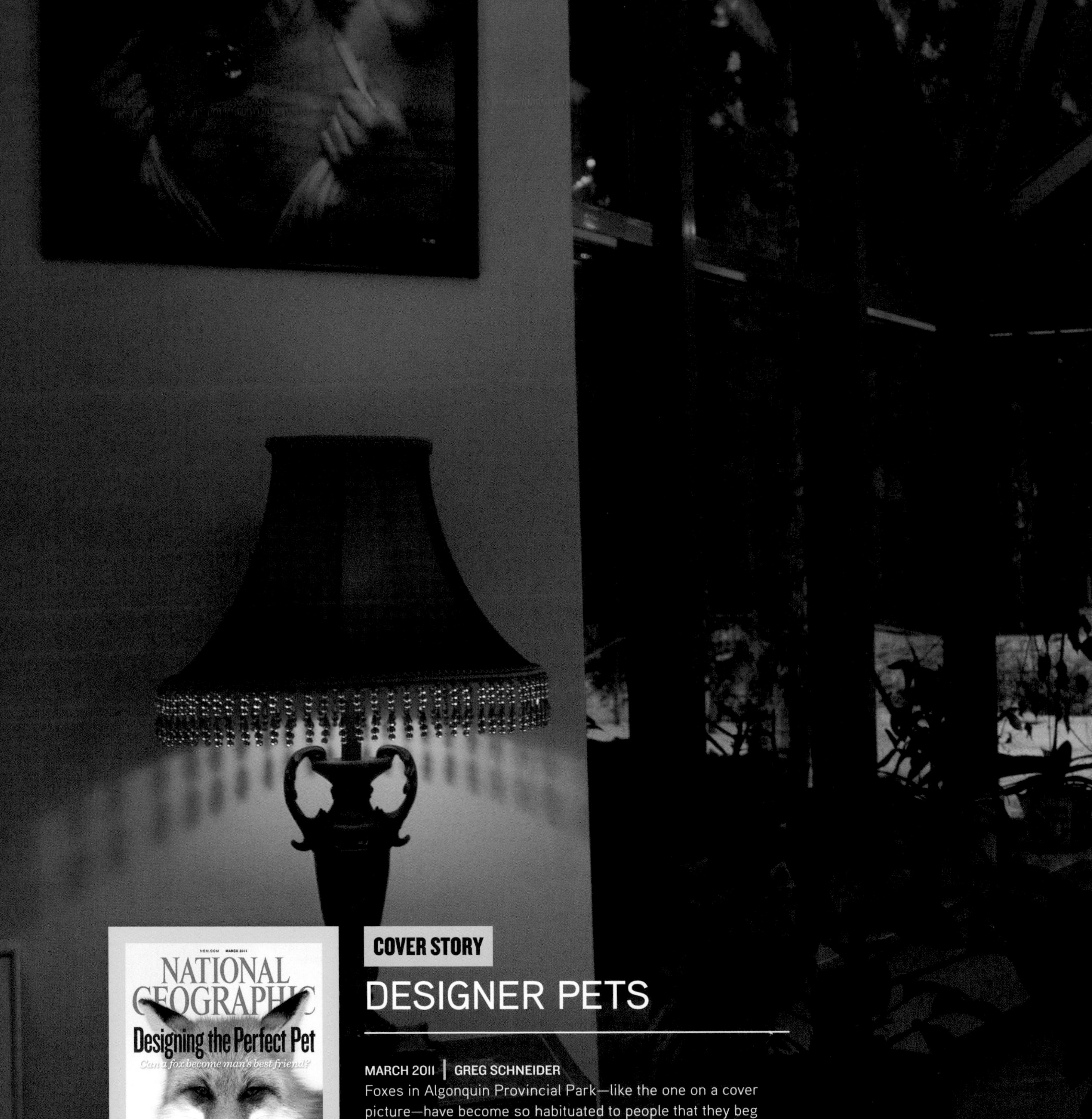

COVER STORY

DESIGNER PETS

MARCH 2011 | GREG SCHNEIDER

Foxes in Algonquin Provincial Park—like the one on a cover picture—have become so habituated to people that they beg shamelessly for food. Once upon a time, some wolves, too, grew tolerant of humans; their descendants became dogs. As scientists learn more about the genetic origins of animal domestication, people in Novosibirsk, Russia, are breeding the wildness out of foxes—turning them into pets such as Alisa (photographed by Vince Musi), who has the run of a wealthy household near St. Petersburg.

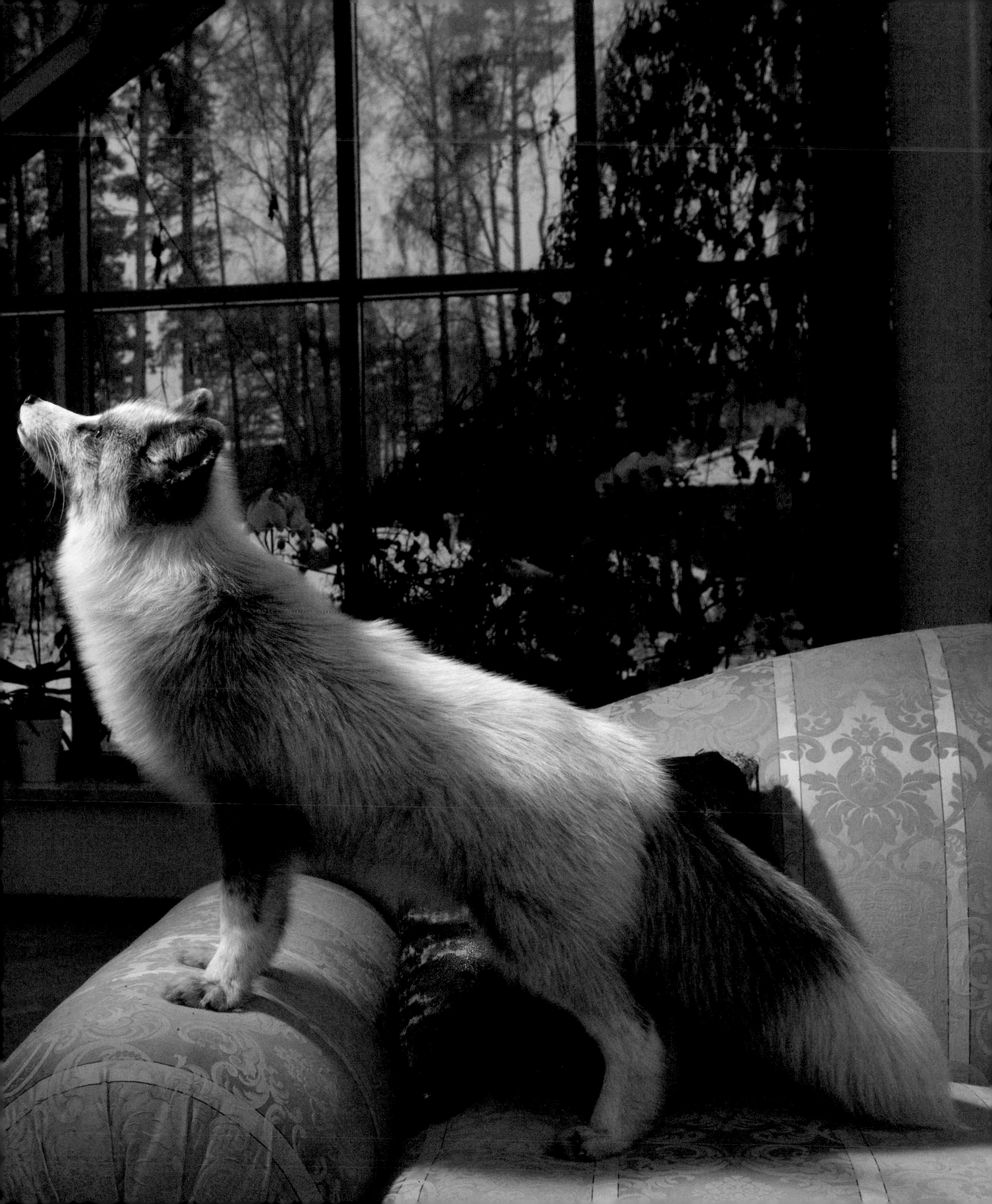

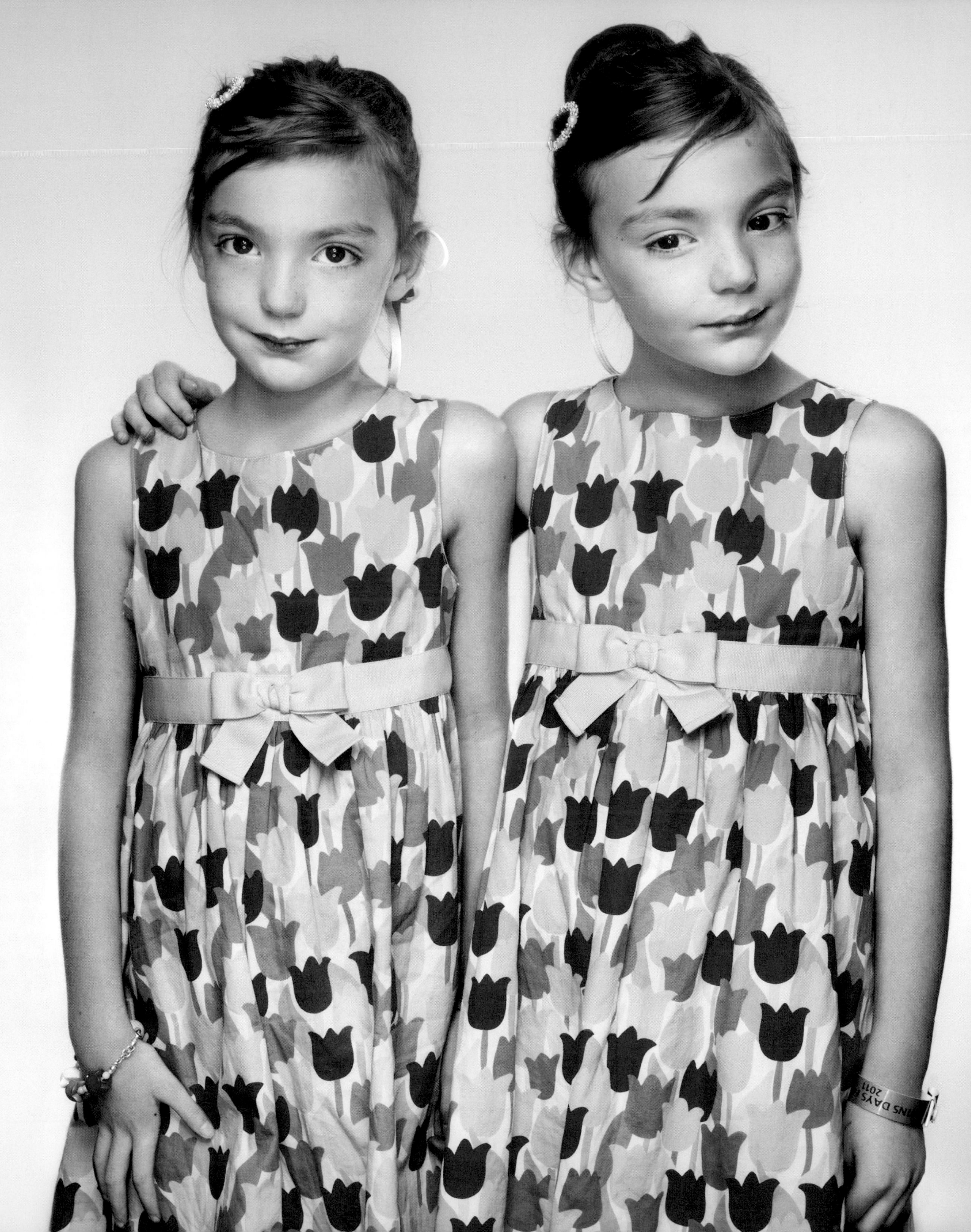

TWINS: EXACTLY ALIKE?

Modern science has been discovering some interesting things about twins. Unsurprisingly, much of their unique nature resides in their genes.

To these scientists, and to biomedical researchers all over the world, twins offer a precious opportunity to untangle the influence of genes and the environment—of nature and nurture. Because identical twins come from a single fertilized egg that splits in two, they share virtually the same genetic code. Any differences between them—one twin having younger looking skin, for example—must be due to environmental factors such as less time spent in the sun.

Alternatively, by comparing the experiences of identical twins with those of fraternal twins, who come from separate eggs and share on average half their DNA, researchers can quantify the extent to which our genes affect our lives. If identical twins are more similar to each other with respect to an ailment than fraternal twins are, then vulnerability to the disease must be rooted at least in part in heredity.

These two lines of research—studying the differences between identical twins to pinpoint the influence of environment, and comparing identical twins with fraternal ones to measure the role of inheritance—have been crucial to understanding the interplay of nature and nurture in determining our personalities, behavior, and vulnerability to disease.

—From "Twins: Alike but Not Alike," Peter Miller

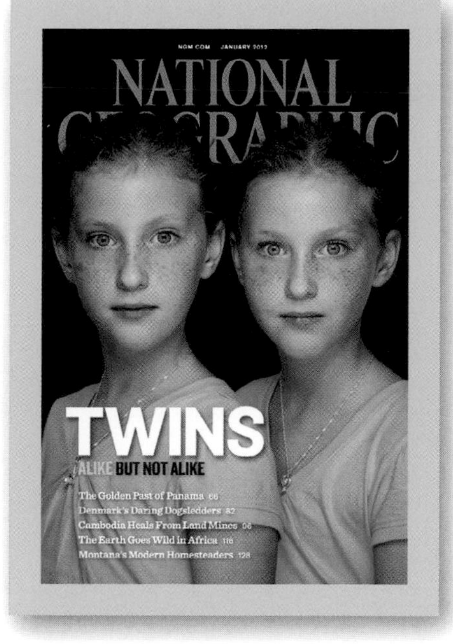

JANUARY | MARTIN SCHOELLER

IDENTICAL TWINS Katie (at left) and Sarah Parks, age ten, may look alike, but Katie is quiet while Sarah is talkative. Sarah also has diabetes, which Katie does not—perhaps an environmental rather than genetic trigger is involved. Photographer Martin Schoeller made numerous compelling portraits of twins to illustrate this article (as did Jodi Cobb, another photographer assigned to the story).

JANUARY 2012 | MARTIN SCHOELLER Six-year-old twins Johanna and Eva Gill both have mild autism.

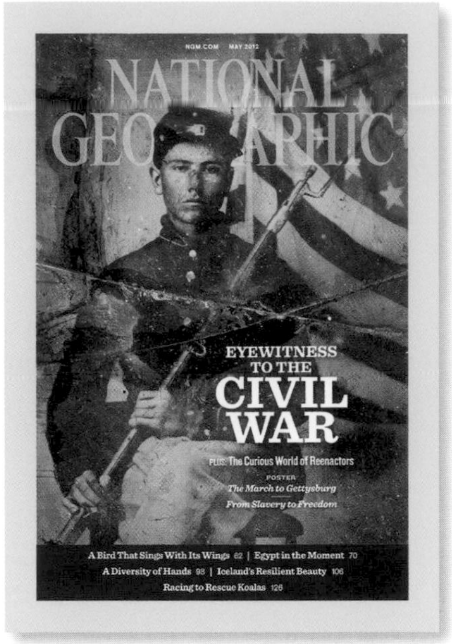

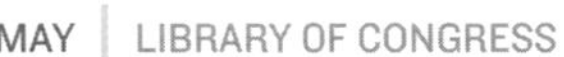

MAY | LIBRARY OF CONGRESS

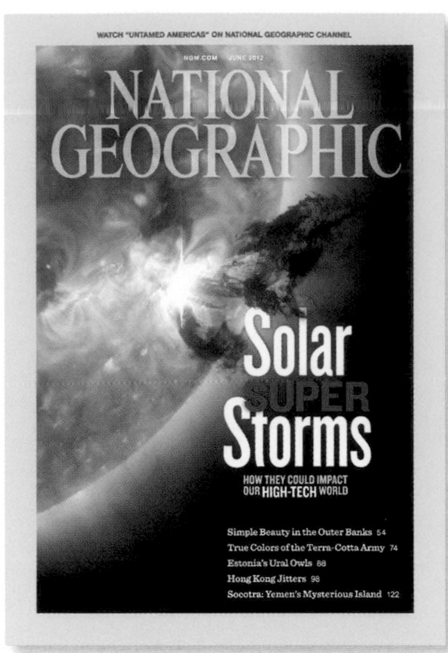

JUNE | NASA SOLAR DYNAMICS OBSERVATORY

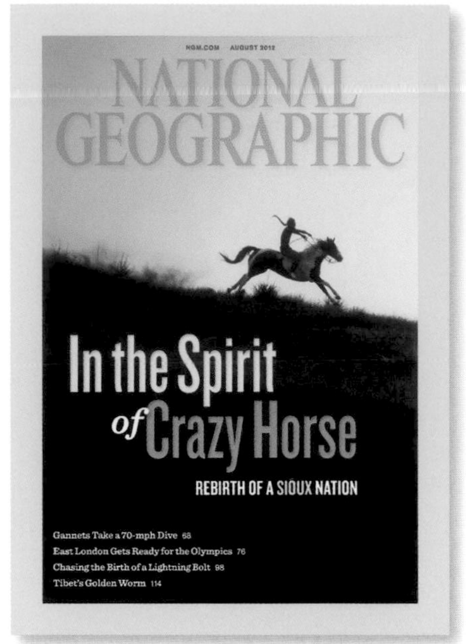

AUGUST | AARON HUEY

▲ **THE BLUE AND THE GRAY** Photographs—whether in the form of daguerreotypes, ambrotypes, or tintypes—of long-dead soldiers remain the most eloquent eyewitnesses of the American Civil War.

THE SINKING OF THE UNSINKABLE ▶

For the *Titanic*, this was the moment, having taken in so much water from its collision with the iceberg, when her bow begins to rip apart from her stern; which explains why the ship's two halves lie 1,900 feet apart on the ocean floor. At least that was the conclusion reached by a panel of nautical experts convened by Hollywood director James Cameron.

> What happened to the people still on board as she sank? Most of the 1,496 victims died of hypothermia at the surface, bobbing in a patch of cork life preservers. But hundreds of people may still have been alive inside, most of them immigrant families in steerage class, looking forward to a new life in America. How did they, during their last moments, experience these colossal wrenchings and shudderings of metal? What would they have heard and felt? It was, even a hundred years later, too awful to contemplate.
>
> *—From "Unseen* Titanic,*" Hampton Sides*

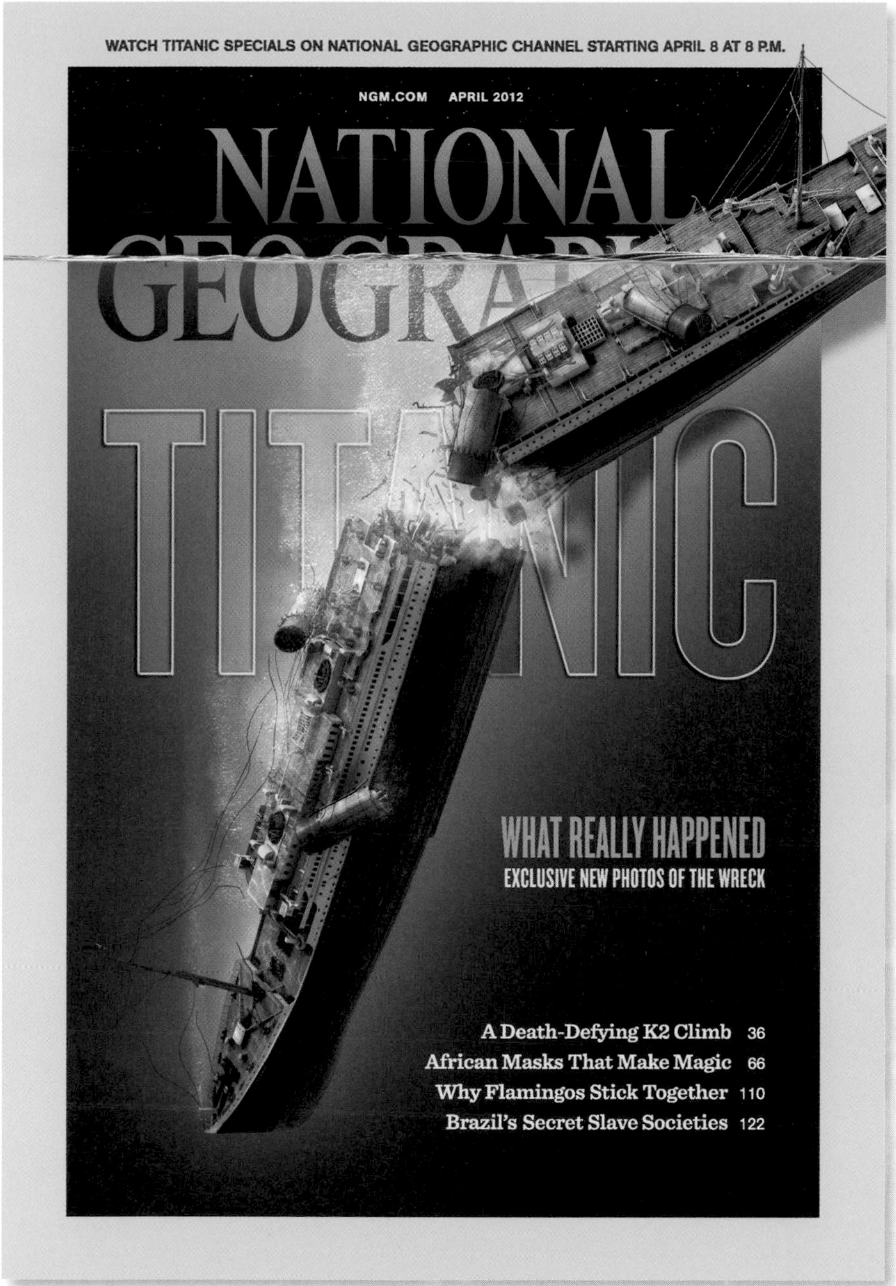

APRIL | NICK KALOTERAKIS

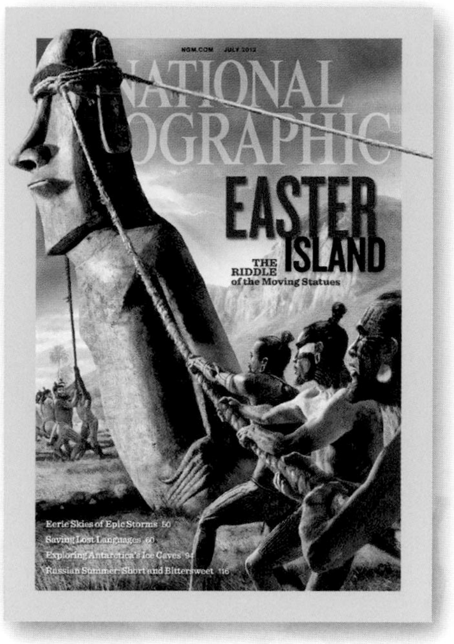

JULY | FERNANDO G. BAPTISTA

▲ **ROCKIN' RAPA NUI** How did they move those giant stone *moai* on Easter Island (or Rapa Nui, as the inhabitants call it)? One recent theory—and experiments with large stones have proved it possible—believes they were "walked," or rocked, from quarry to final destination, as illustrated on this cover. The artist, *National Geographic* graphics editor Fernando Baptista, also helped produce a stop-motion video illustrating the theory for the magazine's iPad edition.

> *"We didn't want the* Titanic *to have broken up like this. We wanted her to have gone down in some kind of ghostly perfection."*
>
> —James Cameron
>
> *from* "Titanic: *What Really Happened*"

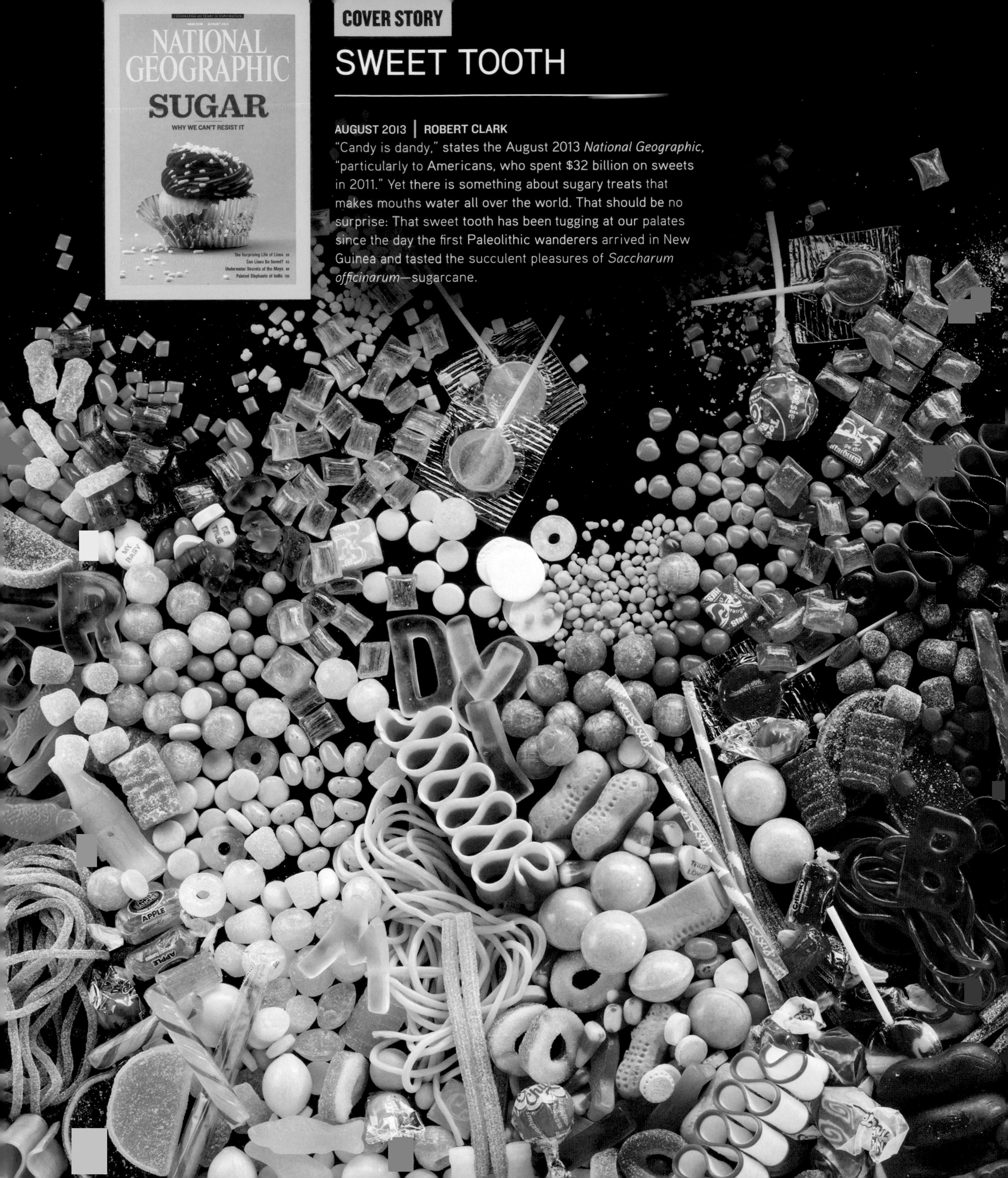

COVER STORY

SWEET TOOTH

AUGUST 2013 | ROBERT CLARK

“Candy is dandy,” states the August 2013 *National Geographic*, “particularly to Americans, who spent $32 billion on sweets in 2011.” Yet there is something about sugary treats that makes mouths water all over the world. That should be no surprise: That sweet tooth has been tugging at our palates since the day the first Paleolithic wanderers arrived in New Guinea and tasted the succulent pleasures of *Saccharum officinarum*—sugarcane.

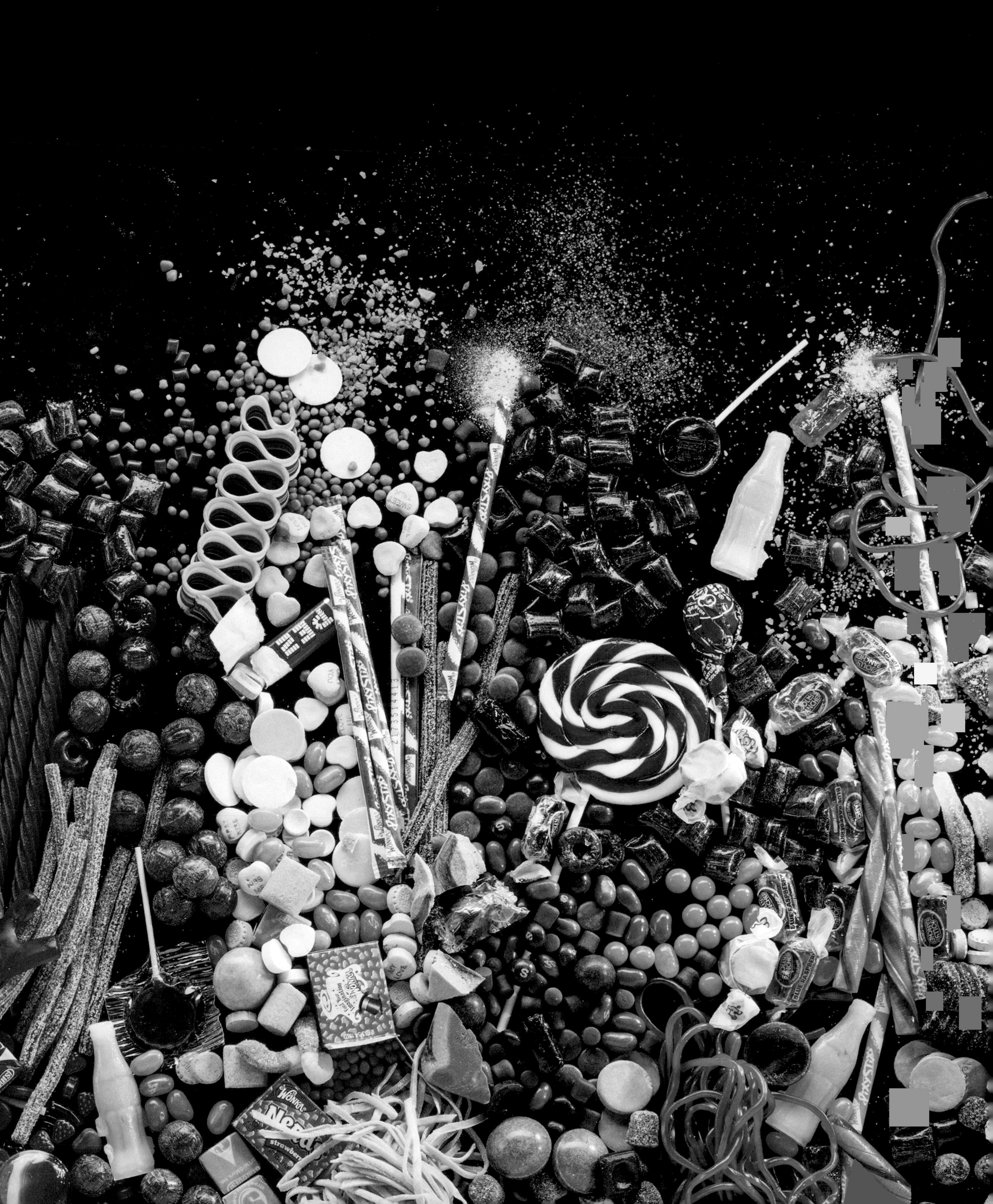

Wonka
Nerds
strawberry

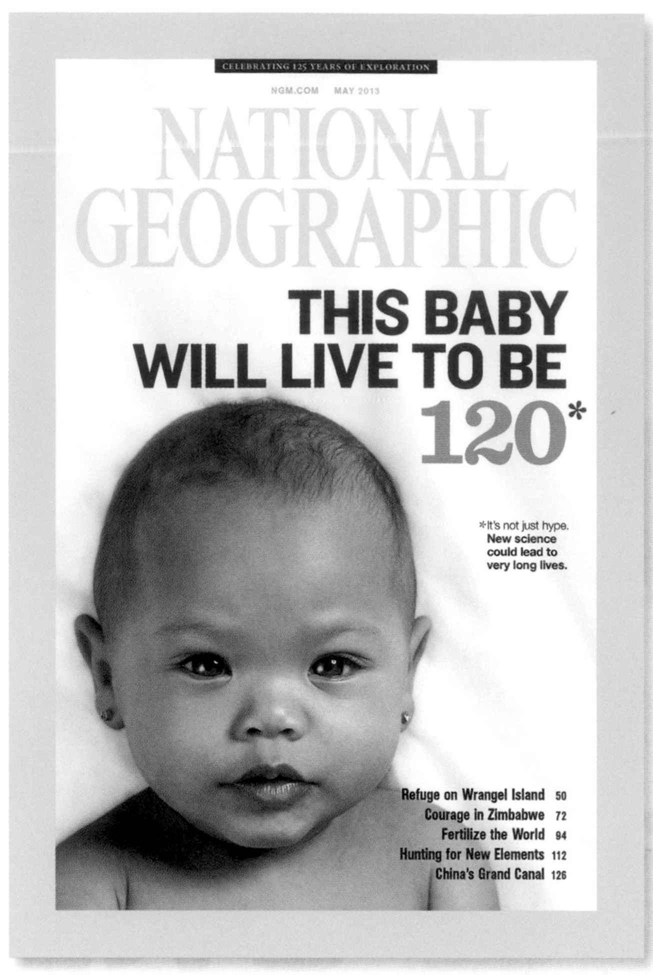

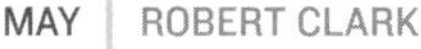
MAY | ROBERT CLARK

▲ **HI, MY NAME IS SOLEIL CHENNAULT.** I'm one of four babies who made the cover of this month's *National Geographic*. We're here because, thanks to advances in medical science, we might live to be 120 years old! But whether you see me, or whether you see one of my friends instead, is entirely a matter of chance. Each cover is being distributed randomly.

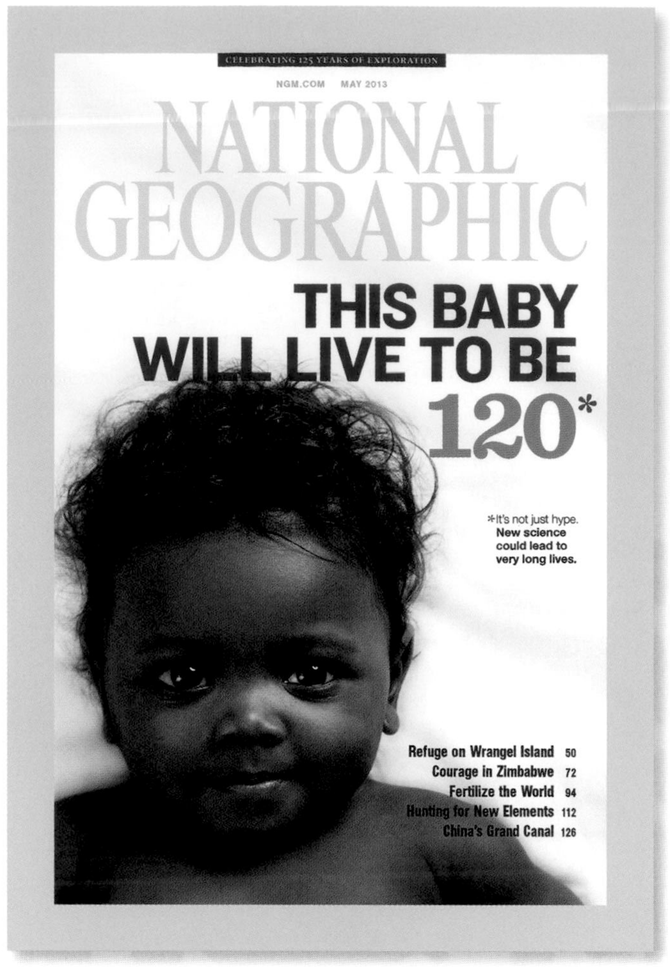

MAY | ROBERT CLARK

▲ **AND I'M ALIYA ALLEN.** There were more than 20 of us originally, all between the ages of 6 months and 18 months. We spent several days in a studio turned romper room, crawling, toddling, laughing, crying. Our parents were chasing us everywhere.

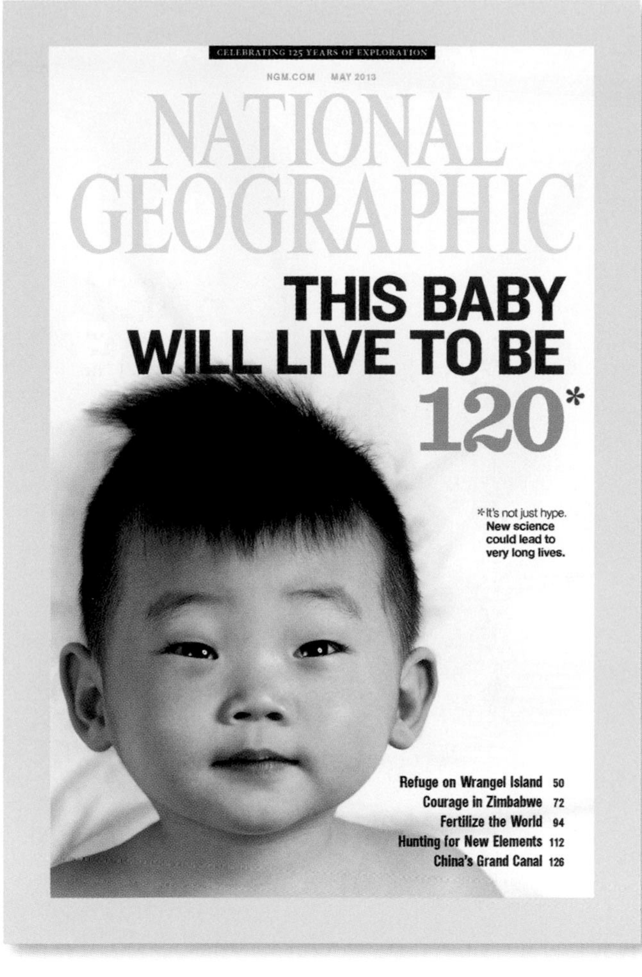

MAY | ROBERT CLARK

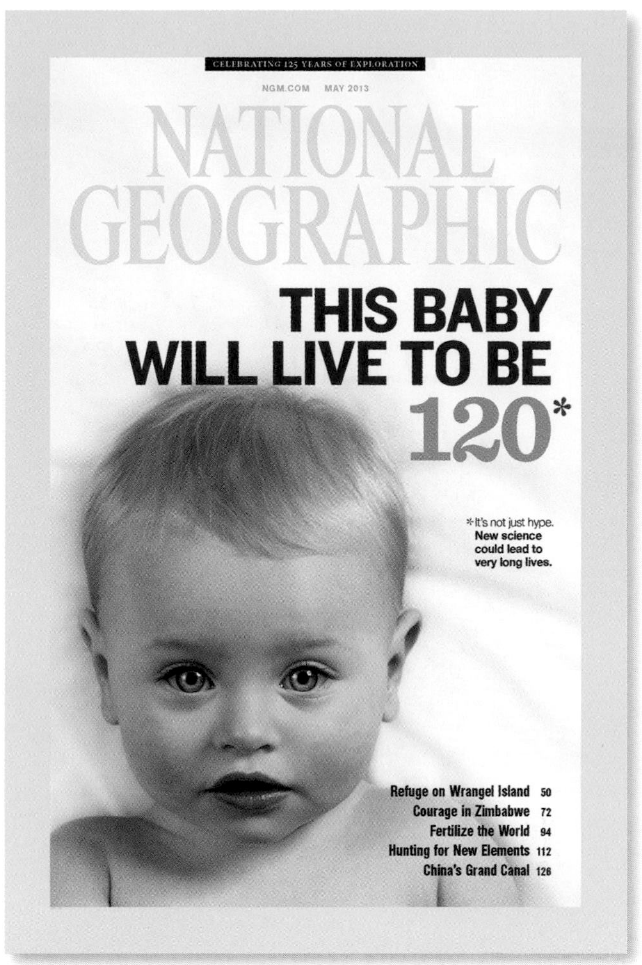

MAY | ROBERT CLARK

▲ **ME? I'M REMUS JEONG.** Rob had this cool camera, mounted to some scaffolding. And these big lights, which he never moved. That way, as he put it, the "only variable was the child in front of the lens." Some of us had to look at that lens for ten whole minutes. Boring.

▲ **MY NAME IS NORAH REEPS.** I liked Sophie, a little rubber giraffe Rob had. We all liked Sophie and wanted to play with her while the grown-ups talked about creating a Facebook app so that you, too, can put your own baby's pictures within that iconic yellow border. There should be lots of baby covers now.

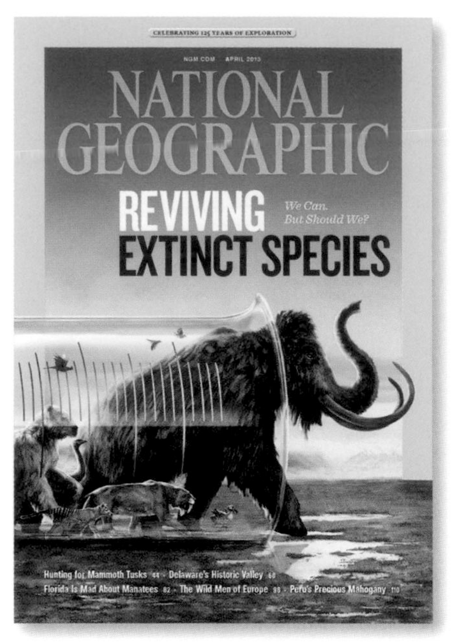

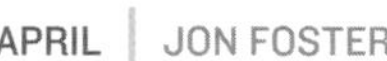

APRIL | JON FOSTER

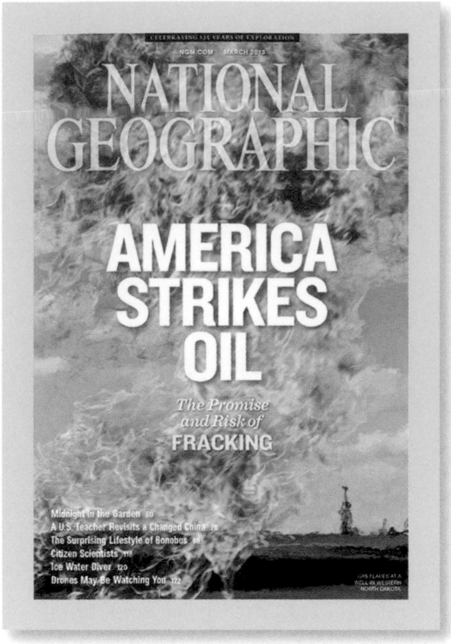

MARCH | EUGENE RICHARDS

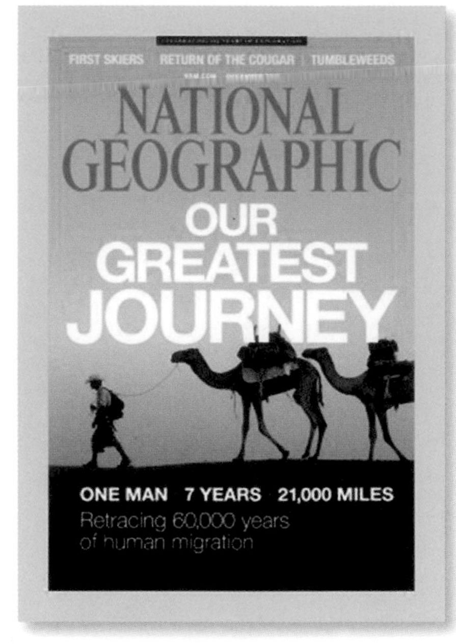

DECEMBER | JOHN STANMEYER

▲ **BACK FROM THE DEAD?** Whether stomping, slinking, or flying out of the test tube, there are a number of recently extinct species that humans might theoretically bring back to this world: giant sloths, Cuban red macaws, New Zealand giant moas, Tasmanian tigers, saber-toothed cats, passenger pigeons, dodos, and woolly mammoths. That depends, however, on our ability to recover ancient DNA, manipulate stem cells, reconstruct lost genomes, and clone the results. "Though the revival of a mammoth or a passenger pigeon is no longer mere fantasy," wrote Carl Zimmer in this issue, "the reality is still years away."

THE STORM CHASER ▶

JUNE 24, 2003, WAS the most memorable day of Tim Samaras's career as a researcher of severe storms. For weeks he had been racing up and down the Great Plains, hoping to deploy "turtle probes"—armored instruments that looked like flying saucers—in a tornado's path. On that day, turbulent weather conditions over South Dakota produced 67 tornadoes in that state. Samaras, with 82 seconds to spare, managed to place a device squarely in the path of the F4-category tornado that destroyed the hamlet of Manchester. When recovered, the probe had recorded an atmospheric pressure drop of 100 millibars in only seconds, the deepest and fastest such drop ever registered.

On May 31, 2013, Tim Samaras, his 24-year-old son, Paul, and fellow researcher Carl Young were in a subcompact Chevy Cobalt outside of El Reno, Oklahoma, when the hunted finally turned on the hunter. All three men were killed by a massive tornado that turned out to be the widest ever measured (2.6 miles) with the second strongest winds (296 miles an hour) ever clocked.

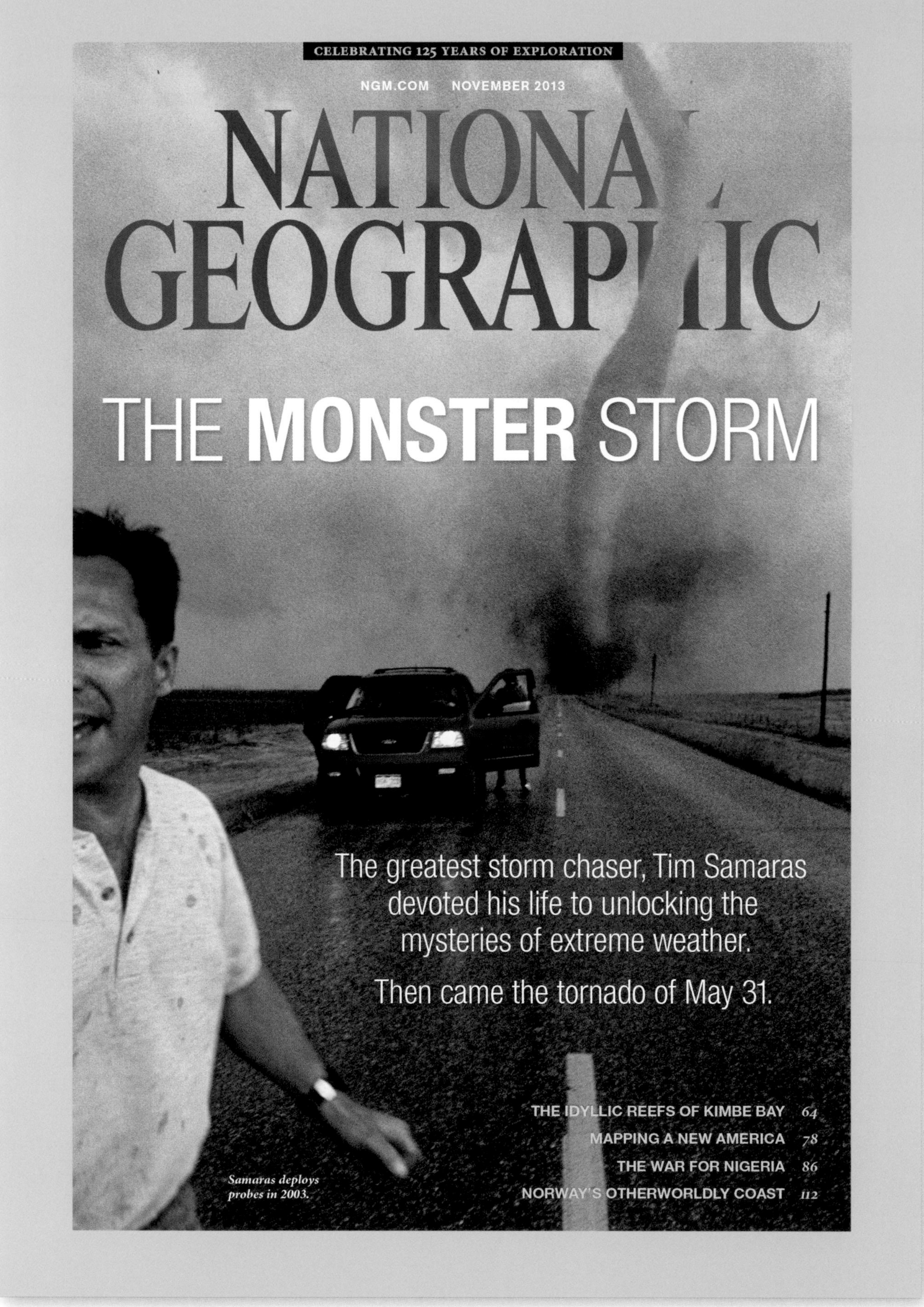

NOVEMBER | CARSTEN PETER Tim Samaras near Manchester, South Dakota, June 24, 2003

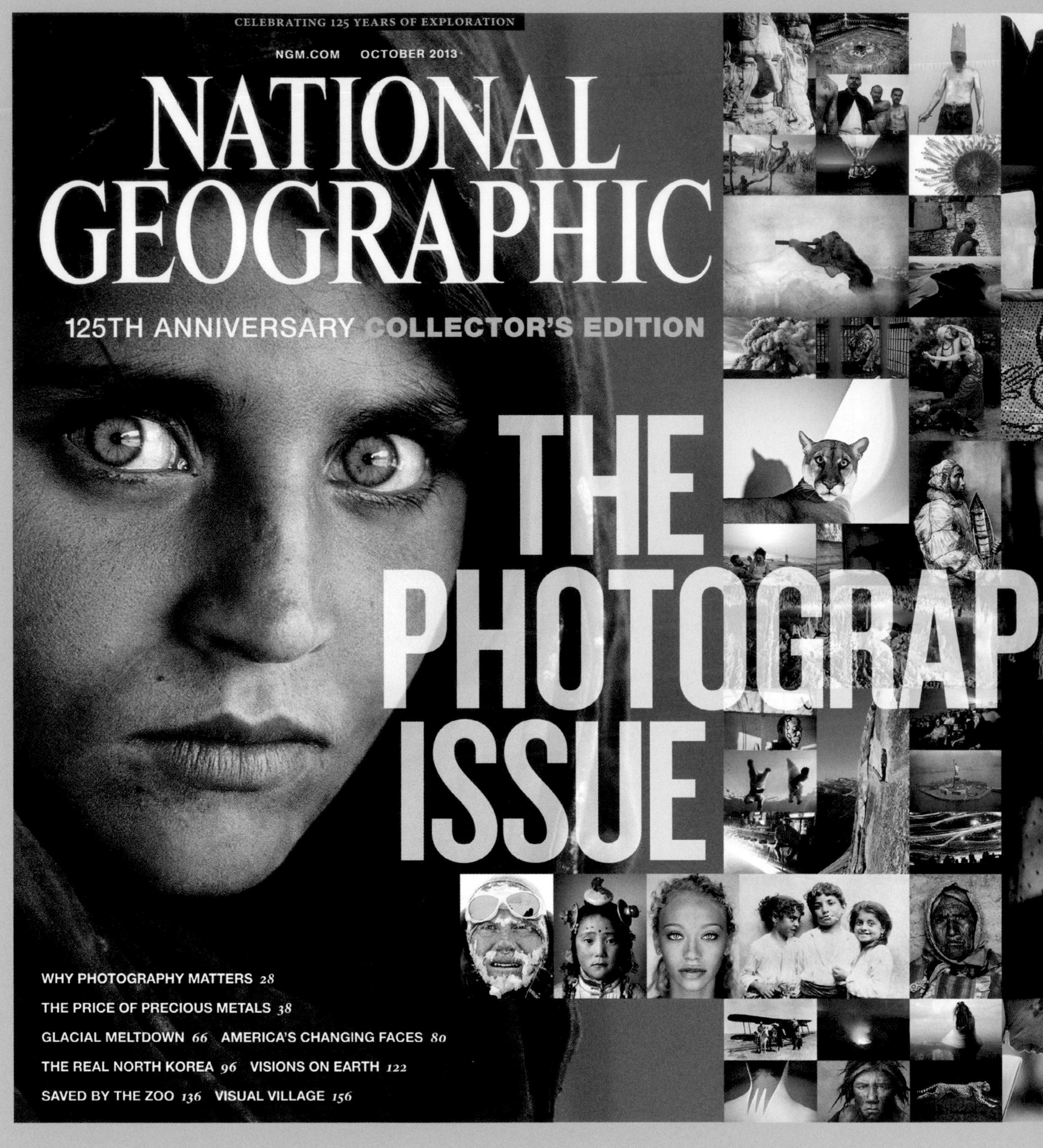
CELEBRATING 125 YEARS OF EXPLORATION
NGM.COM OCTOBER 2013
NATIONAL GEOGRAPHIC
125TH ANNIVERSARY COLLECTOR'S EDITION
THE
PHOTOGRAP
ISSUE
WHY PHOTOGRAPHY MATTERS 28
THE PRICE OF PRECIOUS METALS 38
GLACIAL MELTDOWN 66 AMERICA'S CHANGING FACES 80
THE REAL NORTH KOREA 96 VISIONS ON EARTH 122
SAVED BY THE ZOO 136 VISUAL VILLAGE 156

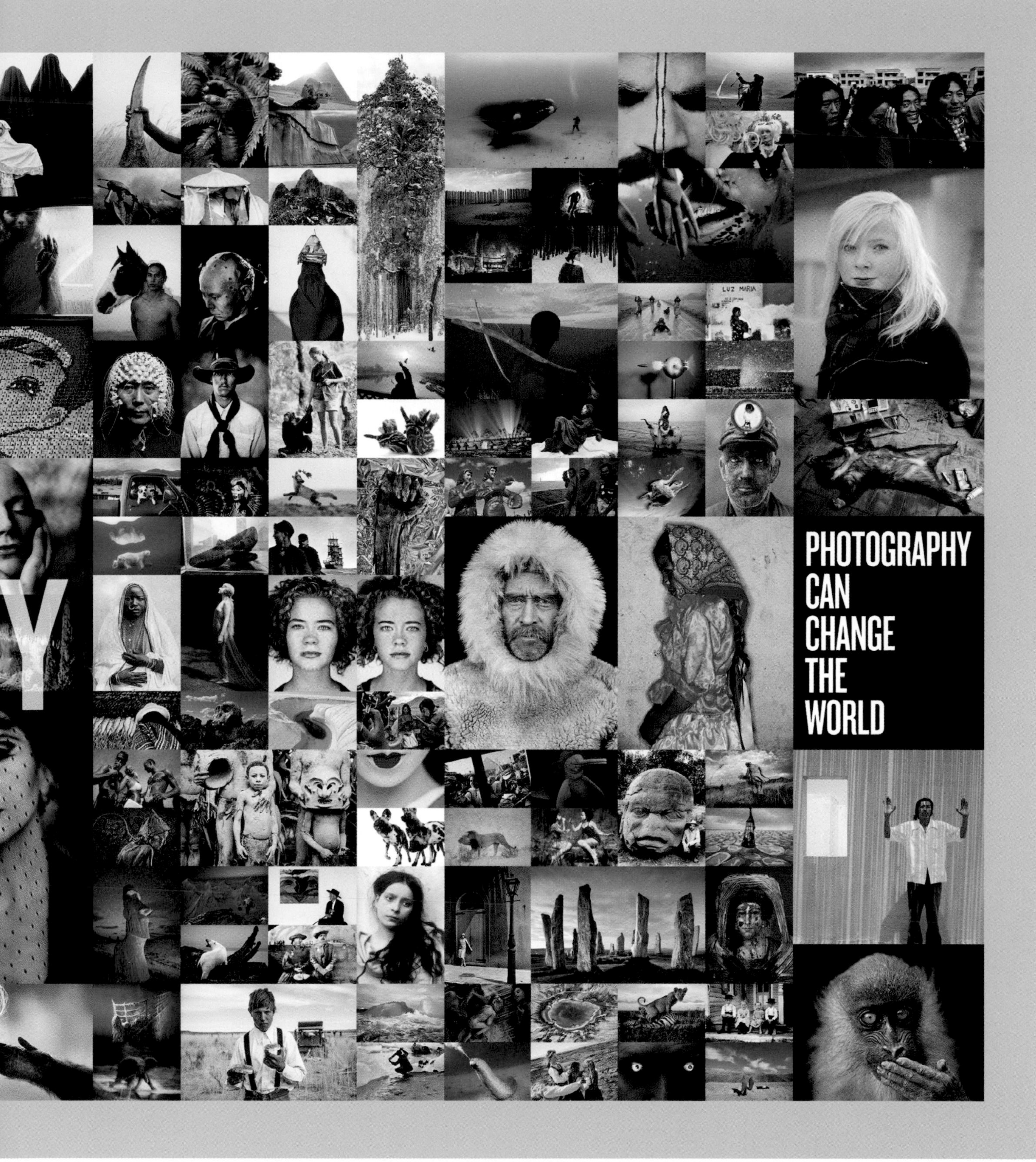

OCTOBER | MAIN PHOTO BY STEVE MCCURRY

125 YEARS OF PHOTOGRAPHY "Use pictures, and plenty of them," was Alexander Graham Bell's advice to young editor Gilbert Grosvenor in 1900; and that advice has kept the *National Geographic* at the forefront of magazine photojournalism. On its 125th birthday, in 2013, the *Geographic* celebrated that legacy with this special issue.

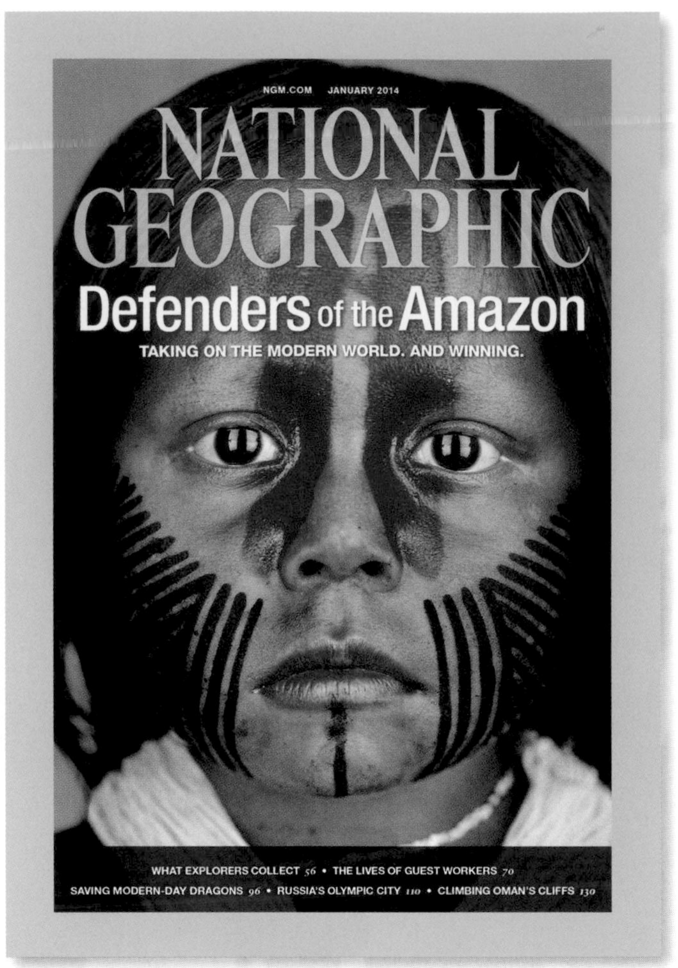

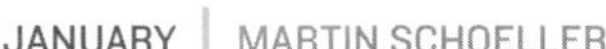

JANUARY | MARTIN SCHOELLER

▲ **THE KAYAPO** With shaved crown, oiled hair, plucked lashes, and newly applied facial paint, this girl of Brazil's Kayapo people is prepared to take part in a ceremony. The most resilient of that country's indigenous groups, the Kayapo have successfully repelled every attempt to seize parts of their Kentucky-size territory. "They know who they are," wrote Chris Johns on the Editor's Page. "This certitude also shines through in Martin Schoeller's remarkable portraits."

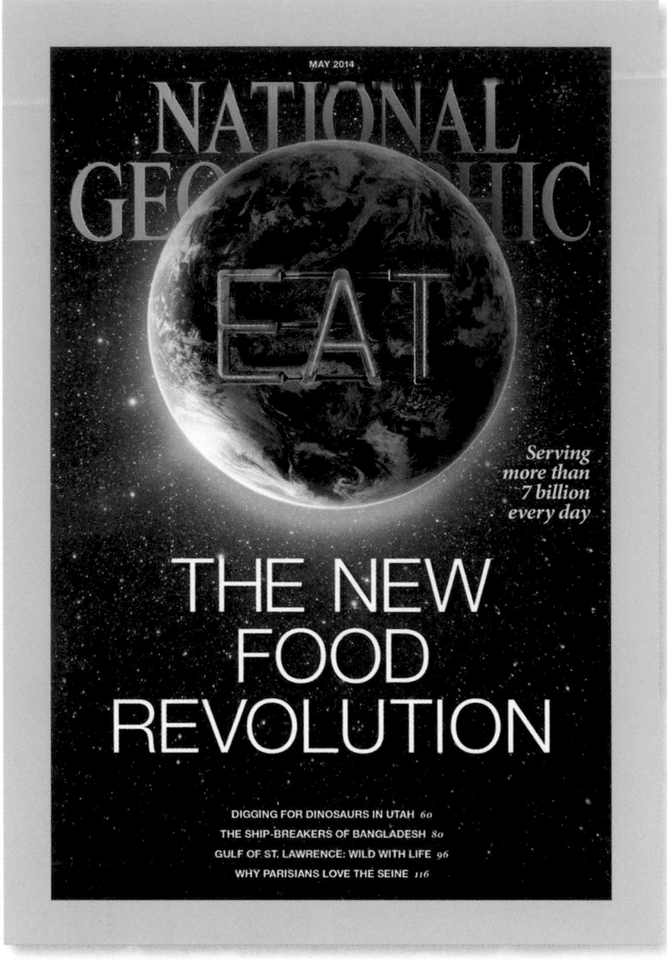

MAY | NICK KALOTERAKIS

▲ **FOOD REVOLUTION** There will be nine billion of us on this planet by 2050. We'll need to double crop production by then if everyone is going to be fed. How will we do that, considering that agriculture now occupies over a third of Earth's ice-free surface? By growing more food on less ground says author Jonathan Foley, who led a team investigating that question, and by eliminating waste while employing high-tech and organic farming practices.

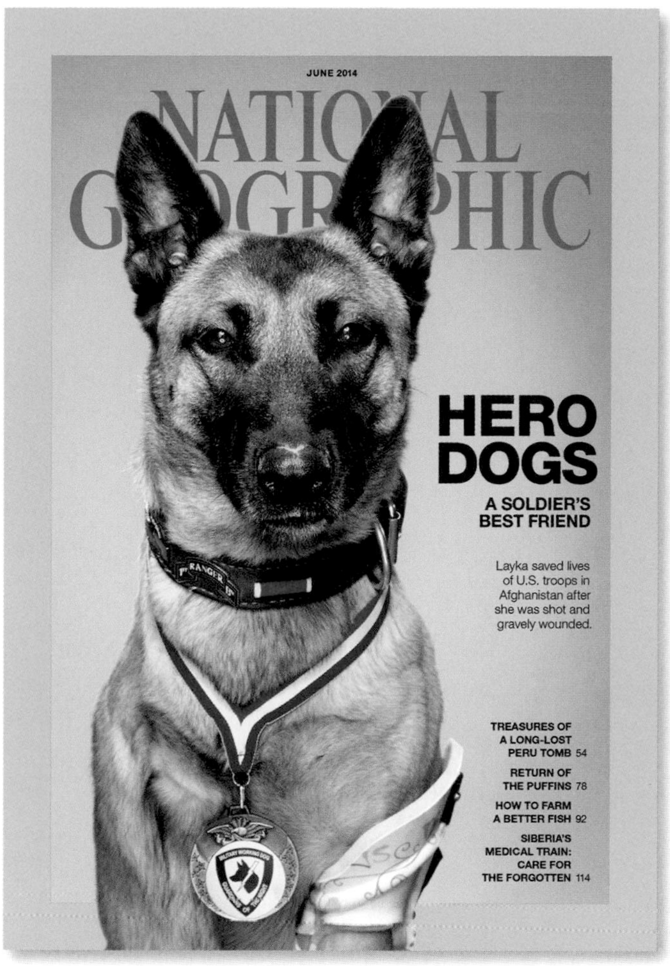

JUNE | MARTIN SCHOELLER

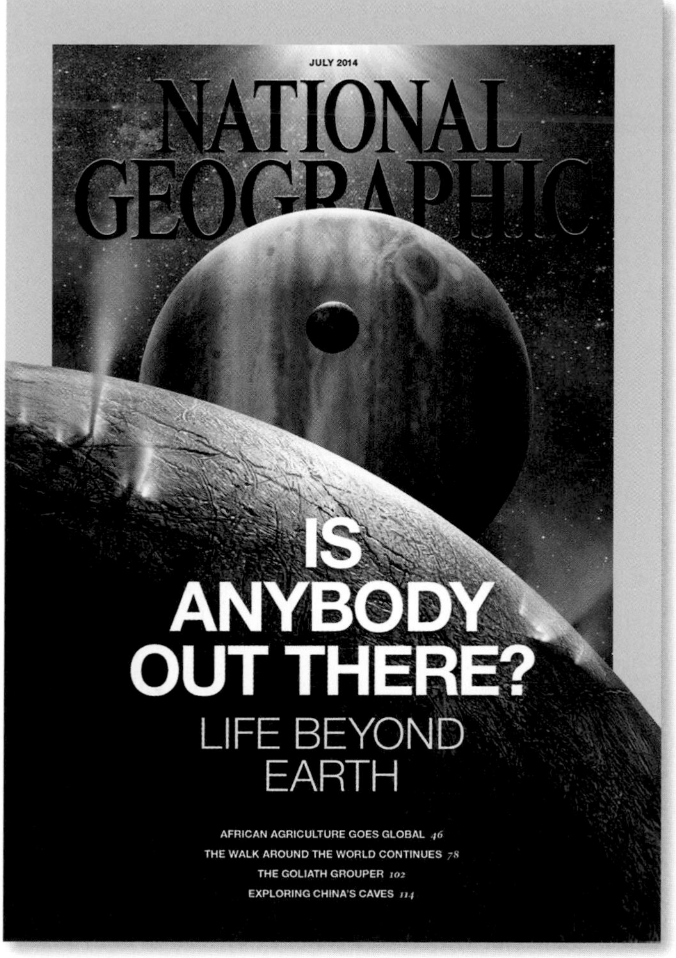

JULY | DANA BERRY

▲ **WAR HERO** Layka, a Belgian Malinois, was awarded an unofficial medal of heroism for her actions in Afghanistan. Although shot by a Taliban insurgent—four rounds from an AK-47 slamming into her and leading to the loss of a leg—she still managed to subdue her assailant and thereby save the lives of her human comrades. More than 500 trained canines accompany U.S. military patrols somewhere in the world, leading to close bonds between the people and dogs of war.

▲ **LIFE BEYOND EARTH** Jupiter's moon Europa (foreground) may harbor living organisms in the seas beneath its frozen surface. Astronomers have also identified thousands of planets in distant solar systems—increasing the chances that we might soon discover extraterrestrial life.

"No magazine has taken its readers more places—into the human past, into the minds of animals, into the deepest parts of the oceans and the ends of the known universe. Our photographers, writers, artists, and editors will keep telling those stories at the same time we investigate our global future."

—Susan Goldberg
Editor in Chief, National Geographic *magazine*

ACKNOWLEDGMENTS

Over half a century has passed since illustrations began appearing regularly on the *National Geographic* cover. Many of the photographers who made those early images are long gone. But the story behind the covers can still be teased out of a plethora of materials, including archival documents, oral histories, magazine articles, editorial notes, books, memoirs, websites, online video interviews, e-mails, and especially interviews and conversations with those artists and photographers who are still active today.

For providing any of the above—often over the course of years of friendship—the author wishes to especially thank Sam Abell, Tom Abercrombie, Bill Allard, Bill Allen, Dana Berry, Jim Blair, Jonathan Blair, Robert Clark, Jodi Cobb, Bruce Dale, David Doubilet, Peter Essick, Melissa Farlow, Bill Garrett, Ken Garrett, Gil Grosvenor, Melville Grosvenor, Dave Harvey, Chris Johns, Karen Kasmauski, Emory Kristof, Sarah Leen, Steve McCurry, George Mobley, Vince Musi, Nick Nichols, Randy Olson, Joel Sartore, Jim Stanfield, George Steinmetz, and Cary Wolinsky.

Renee Braden, Cathy Hunter, and the staff of the Society's Libraries and Information Services provided copies of old correspondence. Cathy Newman was generous with editorial suggestions and Susan Welchman with illustrations advice. The *Geographic*'s design wizard, Bill Marr, and its Editor in Chief, Chris Johns, reviewed the layout. To Chris a special thanks for also writing the foreword.

A word about a special class of unheralded contributors to this volume. Photographers and artists may get the credit lines, but a long line of photo editors heartened, encouraged, and inspired them—and often dreamed up the ideas for cover shots in the first place. Mary Smith, Tom Smith, Bob Patton, Jon Schneeberger, Elie Rogers, Al Royce, Dave Arnold, Susan Welchman, Bill Douthitt, Kurt Mutchler, and Kathy Moran are only a few names in the long line of talented photo editors who should be recognized for contributing so much to the making of the *National Geographic* cover.

And last, but not least, the talented and tireless editorial staff at National Geographic Books who made this publication possible, from Melina Bellows, Hector Sierra, and Janet Goldstein, whose excellent leadership of the Book Division has enabled the publication of titles such as this; to Lisa Thomas, whose creative vision for this book put us on our path; to editor and project manager Susan Straight, whose expert direction continuously moved us all forward; to art director Melissa Farris, whose gorgeous design brought the book to life; to Meredith Wilcox, who provided photo editing and rights clearance for the massive number of images in this book.

ILLUSTRATIONS CREDITS

FRONT COVER: (Main image) Steve McCurry; (Inside Animal Minds) Vincent J. Musi; (Ndoki) Michael Nichols; (Sicily) William Albert Allard; (China) Robb Harrell, Freer Gallery of Art/ Smithsonian Institution; (Lost World) model by John Gurche, photo by Kenneth Garrett; (Mexico) Tomasz Tomaszewski; (Stonehenge) Ken Geiger, NGS; (Titanic) Nick Kaloterakis; (Yellowstone) George Steinmetz; (Great White) David Doubilet; (African Gold) Carol Beckwith and Angela Fisher/photokunst; (Madidi) Joel Sartore/NG Creative; (Polar Bears) Norbert Rosing/NG Creative; (Vikings) Sisse Brimberg; (Minor League Baseball) William Albert Allard; (Jewel Scarabs) David Hawks; (Dinosaurs Take Wing) model by Brian Cooley, photo by O. Louis Mazzatenta

SPINE: Steve McCurry

BACK COVER: (L to R) Paul Zahl; Neil Armstrong/NASA; John G. Ross; Mitsuaki Iwago/Minden Pictures; Wes C. Skiles

NGM COVERS APPEARING IN THIS BOOK

1940s
July 1942: U.S. Government; July 1943: B. Anthony Stewart; July 1944: U.S. Treasury Department; June 1945: U.S. Government

1950s
1959: 7) B. Anthony Stewart; 9) W. E. Garrett; 10) Paul Zahl; 11) B. Anthony Stewart; 12) W. L. Newton.

1960s
1960: 1) Hannah Herz; 2) Kip Ross; 3) Robert B. Goodman/Black Star; 4) Thomas J. Abercrombie; 5) Gilbert M. Grosvenor; 6) Thomas Nebbia; 7) Paul Calle; 8) Frank and John Craighead; 9) George Rodger; 10) Helen and Frank Schreider; 11) Crawford H. Greenewalt; 12) John Launois **1961:** 1) B. Anthony Stewart; 2) E. Thomas Gilliard; 3) David Douglas Duncan; 4) wood engraving from the *Illustrated London News*, courtesy Library of Congress; 5) Helen and Frank Schreider; 6) Melville Bell Grosvenor; 7) L to R: Dean Conger, Dean Conger, B. Anthony Stewart, Volkmar Wentzel, B. Anthony Stewart; 8) W. E. Garrett; 9) B. Anthony Stewart and John E. Fletcher; 10) Kip Ross; 11) designed by William Palmstrom, painted by Joseph E. Barrett; 12) courtesy the Kress Foundation **1962:** 2) Frederick Kent Truslow; 3) Dean Conger; 4) Luis Marden; 5) John Scofield; 6) art—Robert C. Magis, photo—NASA; 7) Luis Marden; 8) John W. Lothers; 9) Winfield Parks; 10) Thomas Nebbia; 11) Dickey Chapelle; 12) B. Anthony Stewart **1963:** 1) Tom Lovell; 2) W. Robert Moore; 3) Margaret Durrance; 4) painting by Willem van de Velde the Younger/National Maritime Museum, Greenwich, London; 5) John Scofield; 6) Howell Walker; 7) Franc and Jean Shor (artifact), Phillip Harrington (Acropolis); 8) Thomas Nebbia; 9) Robert B. Goodman; 10) Barry Bishop (Everest), F. L. Kenett/George Rainbird Ltd. (Tut); 11) Albert Moldvay; 12) Tom Lovell **1964:** 1) George F. Mobley/U.S. Capitol Historical Society; 2) Bates Littlehales; 3) Davis Meltzer; 4) Robert B. Goodman; 5) B. Anthony Stewart; 6) David S. Boyer and Arlan R. Wiker; 7) George F. Mobley; 8) Peter R. Gimbel; 9) David S. Boyer; 10) Thomas J. Abercrombie; 11) Jørgen Bisch; 12) Brian Brake **1965:** 1) Howard Sochurek; 2) Winfield Parks; 3) Albert Moldvay; 4) James P. Blair; 5) Winfield Parks; 6) Treat Davidson; 7) Richard S. Durrance; 8) Harris & Ewing Collection, Library of Congress; 9) Albert Moldvay; 10) Michel Peissel; 11) Victor Englebert; 12) Hugo van Lawick **1966:** 1) Thomas J. Abercrombie; 3) Dean Conger; 4) Philippe Cousteau; 5) Jonathan Blair; 6) James P. Blair; 7) Emory Kristof; 8) photographed by special permission of the City of Bayeux by Milton A. Ford and Victor R. Boswell, Jr.; 9) Ted Spiegel; 10) Thomas Nebbia; 11) Dr. Walter A. Starck II; 12) Kenneth MacLeish **1967:** 1) Albert Moldvay; 2) Winfield Parks; 3) Jorge Sabater Pi; 4) Bruce Dale; 5) David S. Boyer; 6) Bruce Dale; 7) Walter Meayers Edwards; 8) Jonathan Blair; 9) Christopher Knight; 10) Albert Moldvay; 11) Jonathan Blair; 12) René Burri/Magnum **1968:** 1) Helen and Frank Schreider; 3) Winfield Parks; 4) Howard Sochurek; 5) Bob and Ira Spring; 6) Victor Englebert; 7) Joseph J. Scherschel; 8) W. E. Garrett; 9) Thomas J. Abercrombie; 10) Robin Lee Graham; 11) Winfield Parks; 12) W. E. Garrett **1969:** 1) Charles Moore/Black Star; 2) M. Philip Kahl; 3) Robert F. Sisson; 4) Robin Lee Graham; 5) Georg Gerster; 6) Robert W. Madden; 7) Bates Littlehales; 8) David Hiser; 9) James A. Sugar; 10) Arthur Bowland; 11) Gilbert M. Grosvenor; 12) Neil Armstrong/NASA

1970s
1970: 1) Robert I. M. Campbell; 2) M. Philip Kahl; 3) Thomas J. Abercrombie; 4) Donna K. Grosvenor; 5) Frederick Kent Truslow; 6) Winfield Parks; 7) William Albert Allard; 8) Ludek Pesek; 9) Naresh and Rajesh Bedi; 10) James P. Blair; 11) Emory Kristof; 12) Bruce Dale **1971:** 1) Carlo Mauri; 2) Guy Mary-Rousselliere; 3) W. E. Garrett; 4) Othmar Danesce; 5) Libby McGahan; 6) David Hiser; 7) NASA; 8) Robert W. Madden; 9) Alan Root; 10) © 2014 Succession Raghubir Singh; 11: Bill Curtsinger; 12) Audrey Topping **1972:** 1) Kal Muller; 2) Thomas Nebbia; 3) John J. Burns; 4) Roland Michaud; 5) Jonathan Blair; 6) Lowell Georgia; 7) Thomas J. Abercrombie; 8) John Launois; 9) David L. Arnold; 11) Declan Haun; 12) Donna K. Grosvenor **1973:** 1) John Launois; 2) Kay and Stanley Breeden; 3) Emory Kristof; 4) Paul Zahl; 5) Hans Silvester/ Gamma-Rapho; 6) Ron Taylor; 7) Emory Kristof; 8) Hope Alexander; 9) Malcolm S. Kirk; 10) George F. Mobley; 11) David Alan Harvey **1974:** 1) photo by James L. Stanfield, artifact from Walt Disney-Tishman African Art Collection, National Museum of African Art/Smithsonian Institution; 2) Farrell Grehan; 3) Colin Irwin; 5) William E. Schoening, Kitt Peak National Observatory; 6) Galen Rowell; 7) Linda Bartlett; 8) Winfield Parks; 9) Carl Johan Junge and Emil Lütken; 10) John Scofield; 11) Joseph J. Scherschel; 12) H. Edward Kim **1975:** 1) Alexander Marshack, courtesy the Peabody Museum of Archaeology and Ethnology, Harvard University; 2) W. Jesco von Puttkamer; 3) Robert W. Madden; 4) David Doubilet; 5) Timothy W. Ransom; 6) Joseph J. Scherschel; 7) painting by John Trumbull, Yale University Art Gallery, John Hill Morgan Fund; 8) Georg Gerster; 9) David Doubilet; 10) Rod Brindamour; 12) Otis Imboden **1976:** 1) Bill Curtsinger; 2) Dean Conger; 3) Des and Jen Bartlett; 4) Linda Bartlett; 5) Al Giddings; 6) George F. Mobley; 7) Jeff Foott; 8) Albert Moldvay; 9) Stanley Breeden; 10) James L. Stanfield; 11) Jonathan Blair; 12) Gilbert M. Grosvenor **1977:** 1) NASA; 2) Otis Imboden; 3) John G. Ross; 4) Joel F. Ziskin; 5) Bianca Lavies; 6) Joseph Bailey; 7) Ed Cooper; 8) Bruce Dale; 9) Erik Borg; 10) H. Edward Kim; 12) Nathan Benn **1978:** 1) Gordon Gahan; 2) Gordon Gahan; 3) Thomas J. Abercrombie; 4) Howard Nelson; 5) Rick Smolan; 6) Paul Zahl; 7) W. E. Garrett; 8) Roy H. Andersen; 9) Ira Block; 10) Koko; 11) Mehmet Biber; 12) Alain Dejean/Sygma/Corbis **1979:** 1) © 2014 Succession Raghubir Singh; 2) Des & Jen Bartlett; 3) Bates Littlehales; 4) Al Giddings; 5) John Roskelley; 6) James Tobin; 7) David Alan Harvey; 8) Skeeter Hagler; 9) David L. Arnold; 10) W. E. Garrett; 11) Georg Gerster

1980s
1980: 1) NASA; 2) Fred Ward; 3) Bruce Dale; 4) David Doubilet; 5) George and Lory Frame; 6) Rod Brindamour; 7) James L. Stanfield; 8) David Hiser; 9) Robert Azzi; 10) Jim Brandenburg; 11) James L. Stanfield; 12) David Hiser **1981:** 1) Douglas Miller Photography; 2) Steven C. Wilson/ENTHEOS; 3) Jon Schneeberger; 4) Cotton Coulson; 5) Ron Taylor; 6) Kevin Fleming; 7) NASA; 8) W. E. Garrett; 9) Steve Wall; 10) Jon Schneeberger; 11) Jim Brandenburg/ Minden Pictures; 12) George B. Schaller **1982:** 1) Cotton Coulson; 2) Gordon Gahan; 3) Robert Caputo; 4) Bruno Barbey; 5) David Alan Harvey; 6) Des and Jen Bartlett; 7) Richard Greenhill © Severin Archive; 8) David Robert Austen; 9) Bruce Dale; 10) Charles O'Rear; 11) Jerry D. Jacka; 12) Des and Jen Bartlett **1983:** 1) Carol and David Hughes; 2) David Alan Harvey; 3) Emory Kristof, courtesy City of Hamilton; 5) Donal F. Holway; 6) Royal Observatory, Edinburgh/Anglo-Australian Observatory/Science Source; 7) Emory Kristof; 8) Charles O'Rear; 9) NASA; 10) Carol Beckwith/photokunst; 11) O. Louis Mazzatenta; 12) James L. Stanfield **1984:** 1) Al Giddings; 2) Thomas Nebbia; 3) hologram produced by the American Bank Note Company; 4) Ivars Silis; 5) O. Louis Mazzatenta; 6) Steve McCurry; 7) Jerry Pinkney; 8) Stephanie Maze; 9) Fred Bavendam/Minden Pictures; 10) Martha Cooper; 11) James L. Stanfield; 12) Steve McCurry **1985:** 1) Ronald H. Cohn; 2) John Lee, National Museum, Copenhagen; 3) Fred Ward; 4) Roland Michaud; 6) Steve McCurry; 7) Bill Curtsinger; 8) David Robert Austen; 9) Cary Wolinsky; 10) Lynn Abercrombie; 11) hologram produced by the American Bank Note Company; 12) courtesy WHOI, IFREMER, and Robert D. Ballard **1986:** 1) The Mackay Collection, Montana Historical Society; 2) Peter Magubane; 3) George B. Schaller; 4) William Bond; 5) Mitsuaki Iwago/Minden Pictures; 6) Rodney Jackson; 7) Bob Sacha; 8) Denver Public Library, Western History Collection, X-11929 (detail); 9) Jim Brandenburg; 10) ITAR-TASS; 11) British Library; 12) Woods Hole Oceanographic Institution **1987:** 1) Howard Sochurek; 2) Bob Krist; 3) Annie Griffiths; 4) Marty Snyderman; 5) Jim Brandenburg; 6) Kenneth Garrett; 7) Chris Johns, NGS; 8) Steve McCurry; 9) Fred Ward; 10) Jodi Cobb; 11) James L. Stanfield; 12) Bill Curtsinger **1988:** 1) Fred Otnes; 2) Michael O'Brien; 3) Chris Johns, NGS; 4) David Doubilet; 5) Cary Wolinsky; 6) James Nachtwey; 7) Bruno Barbey; 8) Frans Lanting; 10) Alexander Marshack, courtesy the Peabody Museum of Archaeology and Ethnology, Harvard University [Peabody ID# 2005.16.214.32]; 11) Eric Valli; 12) Bruce Dale and American Bank Note Holographics, Inc. **1989:** 1) David Doubilet; 2) Stephen M. Dowell; 3) William Albert Allard; 4) Michael S. Quinton; 5) Cotton Coulson; 6) John Gurche; 7) James L. Stanfield; 8) Frans Lanting; 9) Peter Essick; 10) Kenneth Garrett; 11) David Alan Harvey

1990s
1990: 1) Natalie Fobes; 2) David Doubilet; 3) Steve Raymer; 4) James D. Balog/ Aurora Photos; 5) Joseph Rodriguez; 6) Michael O'Brien; 7) Farrell Grehan; 8) Steve McCurry; 9) Sisse Brimberg; 10) David Doubilet; 11) Larry C. Price; 12) Frans Lanting **1991:** 1) Sam Abell;

2) Jodi Cobb; 3) Michael Nichols; 4) William Albert Allard; 5) Frans Lanting; 6) James Nachtwey; 7) private collection, courtesy Brandywine River Museum; 8) Steve McCurry; 9) Jose Azel; 10) Jack Unruh; 11) Robert Caputo; 12) James L. Stanfield **1992:** 1) Robert Caputo; 2) Raymond Gehman; 3) Michael Nichols/NG Creative; 4) Annie Griffiths; 5) Raghu Rai; 6) Sarah Leen, NGS; 7) Jim Dutcher; 8) Ed Kashi; 9) Flip Nicklin; 10) Mark Wilson; 11) Joe McNally; 12) Roger Ressmeyer **1993:** 1) John Gurche; 2) Lu Zhi; 3) Gerd Ludwig; 4) Joel Sartore; 5) Ed Kashi; 6) Robert W. Madden; 7) Thomas H. Ives; 8) Robert Caputo; 9) Dilip Mehta; 10) Richard Olsenius; 11) David Doubilet/NG Creative; 12) James L. Amos **1994:** 1) Frans Lanting; 2) Bill Curtsinger; 3) Stuart Franklin; 4) Chris Johns, NGS; 5) REZA; 6) David Alan Harvey; 7) Jose Azel; 8) Beverly Joubert; 9) Sam Abell; 10) Kurt E. Smith; 11) Sarah Leen, NGS; 12) Mitsuaki Iwago/Minden Pictures **1995:** 1) Bill Curtsinger; 2) computer reconstruction by Doug Stern based on a photo by Enrico Ferorelli; 3) Joel Sartore; 4) Karen Kasmauski; 5) James L. Stanfield; 6) Joe McNally; 7) Michael Nichols; 8) William Albert Allard; 9) Chris Johns, NGS; 10) Michael Nichols; 11) Robb Kendrick; 12) Michael Nichols **1996:** 1) Kenneth Garrett; 2) Carsten Peter/NG Creative; 3) Frans Lanting; 4) Bill Hatcher/NG Creative; 5) Louie Psihoyos; 6) Sam Abell; 7) Chris Johns, NGS; 8) Tomasz Tomaszewski; 9) Adriel Heisey; 10) Carol Beckwith and Angela Fisher/photokunst; 11) digitized NASA image © 1996 Corbis; 12) James L. Stanfield **1997:** 1) David Doubilet; 2) Mark Moritsch/NG Creative; 3) Flip Nicklin; 4) Raghvendra Sahai and John Trauger (JPL), the WFPC2 science team, and NASA/ESA; 5) Steve McCurry; 6) David Doubilet; 7) George Steinmetz; 8) Mattias Klum; 9) Bob Sacha; 10) Chris Johns, NGS; 11) Jim Brandenburg/Minden Pictures; 12) Michael Nichols **1998:** 1) George Steinmetz; 2) Gordon Wiltsie; 3) Mark W. Moffett; 4) Raymond Gehman; 5) Joanna B. Pinneo; 6) Gerd Ludwig; 7) model by Brian Cooley, photo by O. Louis Mazzatenta; 8) image data by NASA/JPL, processing and color by Randolph Kirk, USGS; 9) Kenneth Garrett; 10) Karen Kasmauski; 11) Patrick McFeeley/NG Creative; 12) Annie Griffiths **1999:** 1) David Doubilet; 2) Frans Lanting; 3) image processed by NASA Goddard Laboratory for Atmospheres, with data from NOAA; 4) David Doubilet; 5) Chris Johns, NGS; 6) David Alan Harvey; 7) Alexandra Avakian; 8) Joe McNally; 9) courtesy Breitling SA; 10) Karen Kasmauski; 11) Maria Stenzel; 12) Chris Johns, NGS

2000s

2000: 1) Wolfgang Brandner (JPL/IPAC), Eva K. Grebel (Univ. Washington), You-Hua Chu (Univ. Illinois Urbana-Champaign), and NASA; 2) Michael Nichols; 3) Joel Sartore/NG Creative; 4) David Doubilet; 5) Sisse Brimberg; 6) Randy Olson; 7) REZA; 8) Annie Griffiths; 9) Eric Valli and Debra Kellner; 10) Tim Laman; 11) REZA; 12) Norbert Rosing/NG Creative **2001:** 1) Ira Bock; 2) David Hawks; 3) Michael Nichols; 4) Kenneth Garrett; 5) Michael Yamashita; 6) Mattias Klum/NG Creative; 8) Melissa Farlow; 9) Bill Ellzey; 10) Kim Wolhuter/NG Creative; 11) Gerd Ludwig; 12) Bridgeman-Giraudon/Art Resource, NY **2002:** 1) wolf and dog provided by Doug Seus's Wasatch Rocky Mountain Wildlife, Utah, photo by Robert Clark; 2) Carsten Peter/NG Creative; 3) Cary Wolinsky; 4) Steve McCurry; 5) Ira Block; 6) Mark Thiessen, NGS; 7) Norbert Rosing/NG Creative; 8) Mauricio Anton; 9) Mattias Klum; 10) Kenneth Garrett; 11) Sarah Leen, NGS; 12) Daniel J. Cox **2003:** 1) Kenneth Garrett; 2) Ralf Kähler (SLAC/Stanford) and Tom Abel (KIPAC/Stanford); 3) Robert Clark; 4) Robert Clark; 5) estate of Yousuf Karsh; 6) Sisse Brimberg; 7) Michael Yamashita; 8) Nicolas Reynard; 9) Anup Shah; 10) REZA; 11) Kenneth Garrett, courtesy Association Hypogées; 12) Joe McNally **2004:** 1) Kees Veenenbos; 2) Norbert Rosing/NG Creative; 3) Brian Skerry; 4) Carsten Peter; 5) Jim Richardson; 6) Sarah Leen, NGS; 7) SOHO/EIT, ESA/NASA; 8) Karen Kasmauski; 9) Peter Essick; 10) Frans Lanting; 11) Robert Clark; 12) Dana Berry **2005:** 1) Bob Sacha; 2) Daniel J. Cox; 3) Cary Wolinsky; 4) model by John Gurche, photo by Kenneth Garrett; 5) Cary Wolinsky; 6) model by Elisabeth Daynès, photo by Kenneth Garrett; 7) Max Aguilera-Hellweg, M.D.; 8) Sarah Leen, NGS; 9) WorldSat International, Inc.; 10) Lynn Johnson; 11) David McLain; 12) DAMNFX **2006:** 1) John Burcham; 2) Pablo Corral Vega; 3) Chris Johns, NGS; 4) courtesy the Bancroft Library, University of California, Berkeley; 5) Joel Sartore; 6) David Alan Harvey; 7) Michael Nichols; 8) Ray Sterner and Steve Babin/Johns Hopkins University Applied Physics Laboratory and NOAA; 9) Fritz Hoffmann; 10) Michael Melford/NG Creative; 11) model by Kennis & Kennis, photo by Sarah Leen, NGS, and Rebecca Hale, NGS; 12) NASA/JPL/Space Science Institute **2007:** 1) Alex Webb; 2) Robert Clark; 3) Michael Nichols; 4) Brian Skerry/NG Creative; 5) © The Trustees of the British Museum. All rights reserved; 6) James Balog; 7) David Scharf; 8) Simon Norfolk, with permission of the Ministry of Culture and Sport, Guatemala; 9) REZA; 10) Robert Clark; 11) Rebecca Hale, NGS; 12) DAMNFX **2008:** 1) John Stanmeyer; 2) Gregory Manchess; 3) Vincent J. Musi; 4) Pascal Maitre; 5) photo by Robb Harrell, Freer Gallery of Art/Smithsonian Institution; 6) Ken Geiger, NGS; 7) Brent Stirton/Getty Images; 8) Simon Norfolk; 9) Mark Thiessen, NGS; 10) model by Kennis & Kennis, photo by Joe McNally; 11) Jim Richardson; 12) Michael Melford **2009:** 1) Robert Clark; 2) Mattias Klum; 3) Tyrone Turner; 4) Kenneth Garrett; 5) Francis Latreille; 6) Ed Kashi; 7) Robert Clark; 8) George Steinmetz; 9) CGI by Markley Boyer, photo by Robert Clark; 10) Michael Nichols; 11) Richard Barnes; 12) Dana Berry **2010:** 1) Mark Thiessen, NGS; 2) Stephanie Sinclair; 3) Jess R. Lee; 4) Mark Thiessen, NGS; 5) Roger Werth, the Daily News; 6) Peter Essick; 7) Tim D. White; 8) Wes C. Skiles; 9) Kenneth Garrett; 10) Joel Sartore; 11) Chris Johns, NGS; 12) Norton Simon Foundation **2011:** 1) Peter Bialobrzeski, Laif/Redux; 2) Fernand Ivaldi/Getty Images; 3) Greg Schneider; 4) Dylan Cole; 5) Jimmy Chin; 6) Vincent J. Musi; 7) Sam Weber; 8) Paul Nicklen; 9) Alain Ernoult; 10) Sam Hundley; 11) Daniel Dociu; 12) Jim Richardson **2012:** 1) Martin Schoeller; 2) William Wegman; 3) Haltadefinizione Image Bank, Novara, Italy, courtesy Ministry of Culture, Superintendency of Milan; 4) Nick Kaloterakis; 5) Rebecca Hale, NGS, from Liljenquist Family Collection, Library of Congress Prints and Photographs Division; 6) NASA Solar Dynamics Observatory; 7) Fernando Baptista; 8) Aaron Huey/NG Creative; 9) Mike Hollingshead; 10) inset photos by Brent Stirton, background photo by Michael Nichols; 11) map by Jeremy Collins, photo by Ken Geiger, NGS; 12) Michael Nichols **2013:** 1) Dana Berry; 2) George Steinmetz; 3) Eugene Richards; 4) Jon Foster; 5) Robert Clark; 6) Marco Grob; 7) Dana Berry; 8) Robert Clark; 9) Nick Kaloterakis; 10) "Afghan Girl" photo by Steve McCurry; for information on other photos, go to ngm.com/photoissue; 11) Carsten Peter; 12) John Stanmeyer **2014:** 1) Martin Schoeller; 2) magnetic resonance image by Van Wedeen and L. L. Wald, Martinos Center for Biomedical Imaging, Human Connectome Project; 3) Mark A. Garlick; 4) Vincent J. Musi; 5) Nick Kaloterakis; 6) Martin Schoeller; 7) Dana Berry

▸ ADDITIONAL CREDITS

Front Matter: 2-3, Raul Touzon/NG Creative; 4-5, St. Cloud Normal School/NGS Archives; 6-7, Thomas Nebbia; 8-9, Dan Westergren/NG Creative; 10, Aaron Huey **Introduction:** 16, B. Anthony Stewart; 33 (spoofs uple), Kim Griffiths—MediAvengers; 33 (spoofs uprt), courtesy Harvard Lampoon; 33 (spoofs lole), created by Andrew Hearst for *Vanity Fair*, 2009; 33 (spoofs lort), courtesy the Portland Mercury **1960s:** 36-7, Georg Gerster; 39 (le), SSPL via Getty Images; 39 (ct), Ivan Bajic/iStockphoto; 39 (rt), Oliver Childs/iStockphoto; 40 (lole), Kostsov/Shutterstock; 40 (loct), ayzek/Shutterstock; 40 (lort), SSPL via Getty Images; 41 (up), James P. Blair; 41 (lole), MARKA/Alamy; 41 (loct), wolfman57/Shutterstock; 41 (lort), Andrey Lobachev/Shutterstock.com; 42, Thomas Nebbia; 44 (lo), W. D. Vaughn and Peter Turner; 46-7, Emory Kristof; 54-5, Dean Conger; 60, Tom Lovell; 61 (lo), Carlos Lacámara; 62-3, Robert B. Goodman; 68-9, Robert B. Goodman; 71 (lo), James P. Blair; 73, Hugo van Lawick; 74-5, Dickey Chapelle; 78 (lo), Dean Conger; 79, Dean Conger; 84-5, Winfield Parks; 88 (lo), W. E. Garrett; 90-91, Helen and Frank Schreider; 94 (lo), Otis Imboden **1970s:** 96-7, David Alan Harvey; 99 (le), NASA; 99 (ct), panchof/iStockphoto; 99 (rt), Eerik/iStockphoto; 100 (lole), Getty Images; 100 (loct), lenta/iStockphoto; 100 (lort), Iridiumphotographics/iStockphoto; 101 (up), Martin Rogers; 101 (lole) Nerus/iStockphoto; 101 (loct), thaagoon/Shutterstock; 101 (lort), scibak/iStockphoto; 102, Robert I. M. Campbell; 103 (lo), Dian Fossey; 108-109, Carlo Mauri; 112 (lo), John Launois; 113, John Launois; 114-15, Eliot Elisofon; 120-121, Mikey Schaefer; 126-7, John Scofield; 129 (lo), Colin Irwin; 132-3, Norbert Rosing/NG Creative; 134, Robert W. Madden; 138-9, Bruce Dale; 142 (lo), NASA; 144-5, Paul Zahl; 150-151, Mohamed Amin/Camerapix; 154, John Roskelley **1980s:** 156-7, James L. Stanfield; 159 (le), Raymond Kasprzak/Shutterstock; 159 (ct), chang/iStockphoto; 159 (rt), Stepan Bormotov/iStockphoto; 160 (lole), Eddie Adams/Corbis; 160 (loct), Paul Cowan/iStockphoto; 160 (lort), serts/iStockphoto; 161 (up), ©AnthonySuau.com; 161 (lole), dpmike/iStockphoto; 161 (loct), Sergeyussr/Dreamstime.com; 161 (lort), Michael Ochs Archives/Getty Images; 163 (lo), NASA; 166, Rod Brindamour; 168, Gary Rosenquist; 170-171, Emory Kristof; 178-9, Gordon Gahan; 184-5, Royal Observatory, Edinburgh/Anglo-Australian Observatory/Science Source; 189, Steve McCurry; 191 (lo), O. Louis Mazzatenta; 193, Steve McCurry; 196-7, Craig Fujii/the Seattle Times © 1989 Seattle Times Company. Used with permission; 202-203, Annie Griffiths; 208-209, Jim Brandenburg; 211 (lo), Fred Otnes; 214, Eric Valli; 215 (lo), Eric Valli; 220-221, Cotton Coulson **1990s:** 222-3, Stuart Franklin; 225 (le), NASA; 225 (ct), Urbano Delvalle/Time Life Pictures/Getty Images; 225 (rt), Chris Johns, NGS; 226 (lole), shingopix/iStockphoto; 226 (loct), Trevor Kelly/Shutterstock, 226 (lort), Tim Roney/Getty Images; 227 (up), Natalie Fobes; 227 (lole), Ben Molyneux/Alamy; 227 (loct), Getty Images; 227 (lort), jfmdesign/iStockphoto; 234-5, Frans Lanting; 242-3, Joe McNally; 248-9, James L. Stanfield; 250 (lo), Konrad Wothe/Minden Pictures and Jonathan Scott; 254-5, David Alan Harvey; 259, computer reconstruction by Doug Stern based on a photograph by Enrico Ferorelli; 262-3, Bill Curtsinger; 265 (lo), Stuart Franklin; 268-9, © 1993 Gurche; 274-5, Joanna B. Pinneo; 278, Mark W. Moffett; 279 (lo), Mark W. Moffett; 282-3, Alexandra Avakian; 286 (lo), David Alan Harvey **2000s:** 288-9, Peter Bialobrzeski, Laif/Redux; 291 (le), Ira Block; 291 (ct), pioneer111/iStockphoto; 291 (rt), Floortje/iStockphoto; 292 (lole), pagadesign/iStockphoto; 292 (loct), Roland Neveu/LightRocket/Getty Images; 292 (lort), NASA; 293 (up), Tyrone Turner; 293 (lole), Brian Sullivan/Dreamstime.com; 293 (loct), AP Photo/Haraz N. Ghanbari; 293 (lort), hanibaram/iStockphoto; 294, Joel Sartore; 295 (lo), Joel Sartore; 300-301, Michael Yamashita; 304, Melissa Farlow; 305 (lo), Melissa Farlow; 306-307, Cary Wolinsky; 312-13, George Steinmetz; 318-19, Karen Kasmauski; 322 (lo), Robert Clark; 323, Robert Clark; 326-7, DAMNFX; 332-3, Chris Johns, NGS; 334, Joel Sartore; 338-9, photo by and © T. White; 340 (lo), Vincent J. Musi; 341, Vincent J. Musi; 344-5, Brent Stirton/Getty Images; 348 (lo), Hernán Cañellas; 350-351, Stephanie Sinclair; 354 (lo), Wes C. Skiles; 355, Wes C. Skiles; 360-361, Vincent J. Musi; 366-7, Robert Clark

INDEX

Boldface indicates illustrations.

NATIONAL GEOGRAPHIC THE COVERS

MARK COLLINS JENKINS

Published by the National Geographic Society
Gary E. Knell, *President and Chief Executive Officer*
John M. Fahey, *Chairman of the Board*
Declan Moore, *Executive Vice President; President, Publishing and Travel*
Melina Gerosa Bellows, *Executive Vice President; Publisher and Chief Creative Officer, Books, Kids, and Family*

Prepared by the Book Division
Hector Sierra, *Senior Vice President and General Manager*
Janet Goldstein, *Senior Vice President and Editorial Director*
Jonathan Halling, *Creative Director*
Marianne R. Koszorus, *Design Director*
Lisa Thomas, *Senior Editor*
R. Gary Colbert, *Production Director*
Jennifer A. Thornton, *Director of Managing Editorial*
Susan S. Blair, *Director of Photography*

Staff for This Book
Susan Straight, *Editor*
Melissa Farris, *Art Director*
Meredith C. Wilcox, *Photo Editor*
Ruth Ann Thompson, *Production Designer*
Liesel Hamilton, *Researcher*
Carl Mehler, *Director of Maps*
Marshall Kiker, *Associate Managing Editor*
Judith Klein, Mike O'Connor, *Production Editors*
Mike Horenstein, *Production Manager*
Katie Olsen, *Production Design Assistant*
Anne Smyth, Andrea Wollitz, *Editorial Assistants*

Production Services
Phillip L. Schlosser, *Senior Vice President*
Chris Brown, *Vice President, NG Book Manufacturing*
Nicole Elliott, *Director of Production*
George Bounelis, *Senior Production Manager*
Darrick McRae, *Imaging Technician*

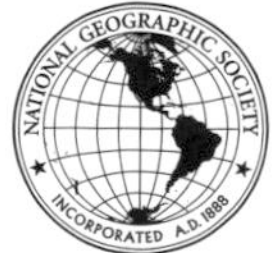

The National Geographic Society is one of the world's largest nonprofit scientific and educational organizations. Founded in 1888 to "increase and diffuse geographic knowledge," the member-supported Society works to inspire people to care about the planet. Through its online community, members can get closer to explorers and photographers, connect with other members around the world, and help make a difference. National Geographic reflects the world through its magazines, television programs, films, music and radio, books, DVDs, maps, exhibitions, live events, school publishing programs, interactive media, and merchandise. *National Geographic* magazine, the Society's official journal, published in English and 38 local-language editions, is read by more than 60 million people each month. The National Geographic Channel reaches 440 million households in 171 countries in 38 languages. National Geographic Digital Media receives more than 25 million visitors a month. National Geographic has funded more than 10,000 scientific research, conservation, and exploration projects and supports an education program promoting geography literacy. For more information, visit www.nationalgeographic.com.

For more information, please call 1-800-NGS LINE
(647-5463) or write to the following address:

National Geographic Society
1145 17th Street N.W.
Washington, D.C. 20036-4688 U.S.A.

For information about special discounts for bulk purchases, please contact National Geographic Books Special Sales: ngspecsales@ngs.org

For rights or permissions inquiries, please contact National Geographic Books Subsidiary Rights: ngbookrights@ngs.org

Library of Congress Cataloging-in-Publication Data

Jenkins, Mark Collins.
National geographic : the covers / Mark Collins Jenkins.
pages cm
Includes index.
ISBN 978-1-4262-1388-5 (hardcover : alk. paper)
1. Travel photography. 2. Documentary photography. 3. Photography. I. National Geographic Society (U.S.) II. Title.
TR790.J46 2014
770--dc23
2014018815

Printed in United States of America

14/CK-CML/1

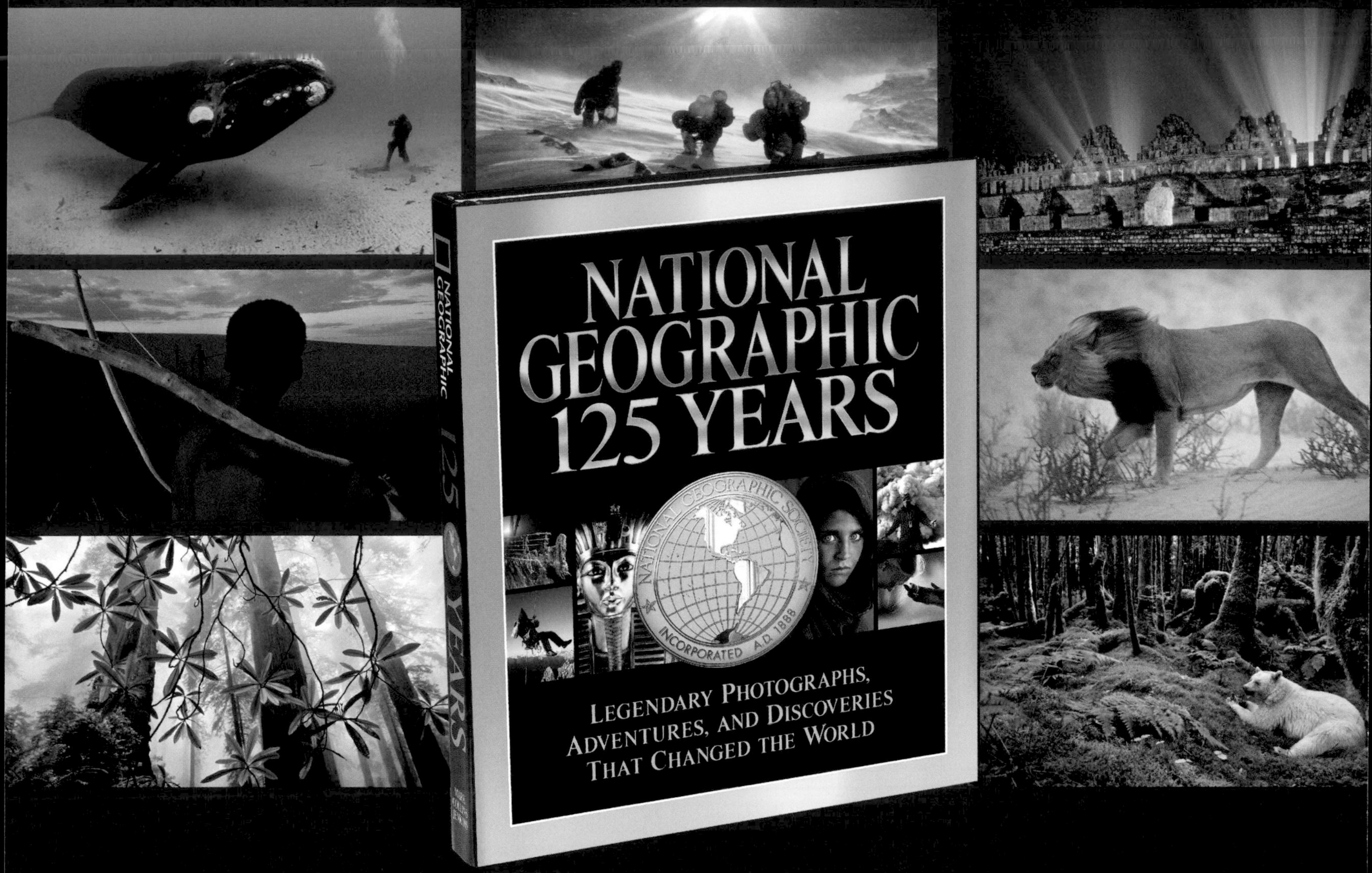